Bert Preiss

Conflict at the Interface

Für Karl
Herzlich,
Bert

Internationale Politik
International Politics

Band / Volume 34

LIT

Bert Preiss

Conflict at the Interface

Local Community Divisions and Hegemonic Forces
in Northern Ireland

LIT

Cover image: Virág Doczi

Editing: Ian Mansfield

Bibliographic information published by the Deutsche Nationalbibliothek
The Deutsche Nationalbibliothek lists this publication in the Deutsche
Nationalbibliografie; detailed bibliographic data are available on the Internet at
http://dnb.d-nb.de.

ISBN 978-3-643-91191-9 (pb)
ISBN 978-3-643-96191-4 (PDF)

A catalogue record for this book is available from the British Library.

© LIT VERLAG GmbH & Co. KG Wien,
Zweigniederlassung Zürich 2019
Klosbachstr. 107
CH-8032 Zürich
Tel. +41 (0) 44-251 75 05
E-Mail: zuerich@lit-verlag.ch   http://www.lit-verlag.ch
Distribution:
In the UK: Global Book Marketing, e-mail: mo@centralbooks.com
In North America: Independent Publishers Group, e-mail: orders@ipgbook.com
In Germany: LIT Verlag Fresnostr. 2, D-48159 Münster
Tel. +49 (0) 2 51-620 32 22, Fax +49 (0) 2 51-922 60 99, e-mail: vertrieb@lit-verlag.de

e-books are available at www.litwebshop.de

CONTENTS

LIST OF ILLUSTRATIONS AND TABLES

Figures

Plates

Tables

I have endeavoured to find all the owners of picture rights and obtain their consent to use their pictures in this study. However, should an infringement of copyright become evident, please inform me.

FOREWORD

Neil Jarman

The conflict in Northern Ireland has been a major subject of interest for some fifty years. For the first half of this period the focus was on the military, paramilitary and inter-communal violence, which was rare in Europe at that time. For the last twenty five years the focus has been on the work of peace-building and the processes of conflict transformation, and which have been cited by many as a model of good practice.

The peace process in Northern Ireland began at a time when the United Nations was becoming more aware of the challenges of building peace after a violent conflict, rather than simply focusing on the ending of political violence. It also began during a period when similar processes where underway in two other long running and high profile conflicts, in South Africa and between Israel and the Palestinians. The mid 1990s was a period of optimism with regards to international conflict transformation.

Twenty five year on the context appears somewhat less rosy. Although the peace has held in South Africa many believe there has been an insufficient focus on processes of social transformation. In the Middle East the peace process ushered in by the Oslo Accords is a distant memory. In Northern Ireland the fragility of the peace has been a major factor in negotiating the ways and means by which the United Kingdom can leave the European Union.

Bert Preiss's study of Northern Ireland some fourteen years into a peace process explores the history of the segregation and division, the context of transition and the challenges faced when trying to move on from a generation of violent and bloody conflict. It draws out some of the hopes and fears of those involved in the violence and those working to support the transition. Its value in large part is due to the focus it takes on looking from the bottom up, from what is happening in the working class communities in Belfast, a city that remains highly segregated, fragmented by walls and barriers, as well as by differentials of wealth, education and social mobility.

In taking an ethnographic approach Preiss's study provides insights into the complexity and sheer messiness of transforming a society through rebuilding relationships, developing trust, and exploring different perspectives on what happened and why, at the same time as new tensions surface and simmer between the two main ethno-national communities. This is all a long way from the comfort of an academic study and requires a degree of emersion in the society; listening to casual and more formal conversations; attending events and watching situations unfold in real time; thinking you understand what is going on and then realising that you do not understand as much as you thought.

The period that Preiss focuses on comes towards the end of what might be described as the second phase of the peacebuilding process. The first phase began with the declaration of ceasefire by the IRA on 31 August 1994 and continued to the signing of the Belfast/Good Friday Agreement in April 1998. This period was dominated by the political negotiations involving the British and Irish governments and the local political parties with support from American facilitators, but was also notable for two other key features: first the development of an extensive range of grass roots peacebuilding activities, which helped to build confidence in the process and gave hope for the future; and second, an annual cycle of protests against parades organised by the Orange Order and the Apprentice Boys of Derry, which undermined any sense of progress and frequently left Northern Ireland 'on the brink' of a return to full scale violence.

The second phase began following the signing of the Agreement with the referendum to approve the negotiated deal in May 1998 and elections to the new Assembly in June. The Agreement itself was largely focused on outlining the political and legal infrastructure for the new Northern Ireland, with a devolved government, a complex network of institutions linking Northern Ireland with other parts of the UK and Ireland, reform of policing and justice systems, and the introduction of legislation relating to human rights and equality. However, while the political parties agreed to the proposed political infrastructure, it proved more challenging to establish them as sustainable bodies. And while the suspension of the Northern Ireland Assembly in October 2002 might have acted to undermine the peace, the work being done on the ground by community networks and civil society groups helped to maintain momentum.

This was the most effective period of peacebuilding in Northern Ireland and Preiss's study provides some insights into the work being done on such things as promoting cross community dialogue, responding to tensions on the ground and in interface areas across Belfast, as well as the challenges faced by those involved. The result of this work was a big reduction in intercommunal tensions, fewer problems at parades, better relations between different communities and between community groups and bodies such as the police. The work that was being done by grass roots activists helped to provide the context in which the political parties returned to the institutions and the devolved government was re-established in May 2007.

But while it was possible to feel optimistic about the future trajectory of peacebuilding with the institutions up and running as had been anticipated in 1998, as well as the effective ending of paramilitary violence and the steady reduction of inter-communal tensions, the process also retained a number of challenges that have continued to create problems for attempts to consolidate a sustainable peace during subsequent phases.

One of the major challenges of the third phase that began in 2007 has been the failure of the political class to transcend their role as tribal leaders into statesmen and women. The newly restored devolved assembly arrived at an opportune time but has failed to build on the foundations it inherited and has struggled to develop effective policy or future road map for peacebuilding. Instead politics descended into little more than sectarian bickering and point scoring, and eventually imploded when the Assembly and Executive collapsed in January 2017.

Although Northern Ireland has remained largely peaceful, the paramilitary groups remain in place and while some republican groups continue to aspire to shoot and bomb their way to a united Ireland, the loyalist groups are largely content to line their pockets and in many cases have transformed into little more than organised crime groups. Thankfully the different groups on both sides have largely eschewed sectarian violence, but do exercise strong control in many working class communities, and continue to beat and shoot people who are accused of various crimes or who threaten their authority.

Furthermore, despite all the peacebuilding work, Northern Ireland remains a highly divided society. As Preiss clearly illustrates both through his words and his images, Belfast remains physically divided by a large number of walls, gates, fences and other physical barriers. And although some have been removed since the time of Preiss's main field research, most still remain. Only a small number of barriers have been removed over the past decade. The segregation of residential areas into single identity working class communities ensures a degree of suspicion, mistrust, fear and hostility remains on the ground. Furthermore, segregation also extends to the education system (up to university), religion and politics, as well as to much sporting activity and to people's social lives.

The question that Bert Preiss poses in the title of one chapter when he asks 'why can't they just all get along' therefore remains pertinent. But, in reality, most people can and do get along most of the time, but they do so because life largely functions in monochrome, amongst people of their own kind. What some have termed as a form of 'benign apartheid'.

Northern Ireland has obtained a certain stasis, in Johan Galtung's formulation it had achieved a form of 'negative peace', which was marked by an absence of violence and tentative ways of getting along, often through forms of avoidance, but has not yet addressed the structural factors of sectarianism and segregation that would enable a more positive peace to be worked towards.

And then came Brexit. By 2016 the border between Northern Ireland and the Republic of Ireland had become little more than an administrative boundary. It continued to exist in a virtual sense but had little impact on people's daily lives. It certainly did not encourage strong emotions among most people and only around 25% of those surveyed in Northern Ireland expressed a desire for an urgent re-unification. But Brexit changed that. The border became a live issue again. It mobilised support for a united Ireland among nationalists and among some neutrals. It raised the possibility of a visible border with security structures and customs posts and with it the reality of easy targets for residual armed members of the IRA. Three years on from the referendum, no clarity or certainty exists, just a lot of 'what ifs'.

Northern Ireland remains a good example of peacebuilding in the twenty first century. It highlights what can be achieved when people come together to debate and agree a political path out of a military conflict. It highlights what can be done by civil society groups in re-building relationships, developing mutual understanding, reducing tensions and working to achieve the dull normality of absence of violence.

It also highlights that such progress can only be achieved as a result of sustained and ongoing work over a long period of time; by developing an inclusive process which requires erstwhile enemies to discuss and debate; the need for political engagement, support and direction from national and international political leaders; the need for significant financial input, from national governments, but also from the USA and from the European Union. And it also highlights the challenges that emerge and those that remain when they are absent or when attention wanders. And the need to develop a level of resilience that enables the society to respond to the unexpected.

And yet after all that as Bert Preiss suggests 'the walls remain the same'. From some perspectives little has changed in Northern Ireland over the course of the past twenty five years. From others everything has changed, relationships have been built, trust has been developed and people have begun to live and work together, at least some of the time. The walls remain but the communities that live near them are not the same as they were a generation ago. "Plus ça change, plus c'est la même chose."

Neil Jarman
Director, Institute for Conflict Research
Belfast
24 September 2019.

ACKNOWLEDGMENTS

Many people have contributed to this research in various ways. They all had a share in keeping me on track on the arduous and winding road to finish my dissertation. They also encouraged me in my efforts to publish an updated, revised and expanded version as a book. In particular, I would like to express my sincere gratitude to Prof. Dieter Segert for his outstanding supervision throughout my dissertation and for his insightful comments and valuable suggestions for improvement of the book. Likewise, I am most grateful to Prof. Helmut Kramer for his profound advice and meticulous criticism and for the many inspiring discussions on both the dissertation and my book project.

I wish to express my cordial thanks to Gerald Mader, founding president of the Peace Centre Schlaining, for supporting and encouraging me throughout my endeavours and for providing me with insight into his 'realistic utopia for peace'. At this point I would also like to gratefully thank his colleague Hans Spiess and their *'Burgenländischer Verein zur Förderung von Friedensprojekten'* [Burgenland Association for the Promotion of Peace Projects] for the generous financial support of this publication. I would like to extend my deep gratitude to Neil Jarman for granting me access to the facilities of the Institute for Conflict Research (ICR) during my field research stay in Belfast. Moreover, he provided me with contacts to local actors and community experts, as well as with invaluable insights and research guidelines on Northern Ireland. Furthermore, he kept me up to date on the local situation and current political and social developments. I am likewise greatly indebted to Ian Mansfield for his linguistic advice and for inspiring conversations on Irish and British culture and politics. My heartful thanks go to Virág Doczi for drawing the cover image: *Köszönöm szépen*. I also wish to give my gratitude to Timna Holzer and the LIT publishing team for the courteous support.

There were many colleagues, academics and practitioners who gave me advice and feedback at various stages of this research and whom I would like to thank warmly for their intellectual camaraderie and overall support: Natalie Rougier, Gladys Ganiel, Andy Pollak, Patricia McCarron, Martin O'Neill, Michael Kennedy, Prof. Ulrich Brand, Prof. Rainer Bauböck, Prof. Luise Gubitzer, Prof. Wolfgang Gombócz, Prof. Rainer Gries, Prof. Karl Kaser, Prof. Anton Pelinka, Prof. Sieglinde Rosenberger, Prof. Josef Melchior, Thomas Schmidinger, Vanni D'Alessio, Wilfried Graf, Valdete Idrizi, Verena

Knaus, Vedran Džihić, Valerie Erwa, Christian Promitzer, Ronald Tuschl, Roman Pfefferle, Robert Pichler, Erwin Schweitzer, Thomas Griffiths, Kurt Gritsch, Leila Hadj-Abdou, Egin Ceka, Eli Krasniqi, Susanne Fröschl, Tahir Latifi, Anton Marku, Elisabeth Fandl and Flemming Bjerke.

The realisation of this book would certainly have been much more difficult without the assistance, encouragement and inspiration of numerous friends and local acquaintances. In particular, I am grateful to Tonie Walsh, Declan Martin, Brigid Loughran, Jimmy Costello, Eudes Brophy, Visar Hamza, Guri Shkodra, Armend Kabashi, Christine Petioky, Yvette Jeuken, Tanya du Toit, Iris Fasolt, Eugen Kment, Elisabeth Gmach, Caroline Maraszto, Andreas Pils, Til Ulbricht, Markus Siebert, Eva Letonja, Verena Kofler, Alexandra Prem, Rita Skultéty, Leo Bauer, Isabel Oswaldo Cruz Lehner, Anna Ambrosch, Susanne Leitner, Leo Tamul, Britta Kirchler-Mader and Gertrud Mader.

My dear mother, Christine Preiss, has also been highly supportive throughout this endeavour. I would like to express my sincere gratitude to her for always providing assistance when needed and for keeping the faith in me.

Finally, my deepest appreciation and thanks go to all the interviewees and informants in Northern Ireland. After all, this study would not have been possible without their openness and readiness to share their experiences and views with me. Listening to their stories has opened my heart and my mind to the incredible pain and loss that people had to endure during the armed conflict and to the difficulties and inner struggles that many of them still face on the path to peace and reconciliation. I was deeply moved to see that, despite all the adverse circumstances and setbacks they remained hopeful and committed to improve community relations and build peace.

After all, I wish to dedicate this book to three persons who played a significant role in my life: my dear father, Herbert Winter, my beloved grandmother, Walpurga Preiss, and Gerald Mader, a protagonist of peace and my paternal friend. Regrettably, they all passed away in the course of writing this book and can no longer witness its publication. I hope they have now found their eternal peace.

ABBREVIATIONS

AAI	Anglo-Irish Agreement
ACE	Action for Community Employment
ACP	Ardoyne Commemoration Project
APL	Anti-Partition-League
APNI	Alliance Party of Northern Ireland
BCE	Before the Common Era
BELB	Belfast Education and Library Board
BIC	British-Irish Council
BIIGC	British-Irish Intergovernmental Conference
BIP	Belfast Interface Project
CAIN	Conflict Archive on the Internet
CAJ	Committee on the Administration of Justice
CCRU	Central Community Relations Unit
CDC	Community Development Centre
CIRA	Continuity IRA
CLMC	Combined Loyalist Military Command
Co.	County
CPI	Communist Party of Ireland
CRC	Community Relations Council of Northern Ireland
CRJI	Community Restorative Justice Ireland
CRU	Community Relations Unit (OFMDFM)
CSI	Community, Sharing and Integration
CSJ	Campaign for Social Justice in Northern Ireland
CSO	Civil Society Organisation
CVSNI	Commission for Victims and Survivors in Northern Ireland
DCAC	Derry Citizen's Action Committee
DHAC	Derry Housing Action Committee
DOE	Department of the Environment
DRD	Department for Regional Planning
DSD	Department for Social Development
DUP	Democratic Unionist Party
EC	European Commission
ECNI	Equality Commission for Northern Ireland
ECtHR	European Court of Human Rights
ECUK	Electoral Commission of the UK

EEC	European Economic Community
ESF	European Social Fund
EU	European Union
FEA	Fair Employment Agency
FEC	Fair Employment Commission
GAA	Gaelic Athletic Association
GB	Great Britain
GCSE	General Certificate of Secondary Education
ICG	International Crisis Group
ICP	Independent Commission on Policing for Northern Ireland
ICR	Institute for Conflict Research
IHRC	Irish Human Rights Commission
IICD	Independent International Commission on Decommissioning
IFI	International Fund for Ireland
IMC	Independent Monitoring Commission
INLA	Irish National Liberation Army
IRSP	Irish Republican Socialist Party
IPP	Irish Parliamentary Party
IRA	Irish Republican Army
IRB	Irish Republican Brotherhood
IS	Islamic State
LC	Loyalist Commission
LCC	Loyalist Community Council
LCF	Lenadoon Community Forum
LINC	Local Initiative for Needy Communities
LOI	Loyal Orange Institution (Orange Order)
LVF	Loyalist Volunteer Force
MLA	Member of Local Assembly
MLK	Martin Luther King Jr.
MP	Member of Parliament
NBIN	North Belfast Interface Network
NBCDTG	North Belfast Community Development and Transition Group
NBIMG	North Belfast Interface Monitoring Group
NBIN	North Belfast Interface Network
NBP	North Belfast Partnership
NGO	Non-Governmental Organisation
NI	Northern Ireland
NIA	Northern Ireland Alternatives

NIA	Northern Ireland Assembly
NIAS	Northern Ireland Ambulance Service
NIC	Northern Ireland Committee
NICC	Northern Ireland Constitutional Convention
NICRA	Northern Irish Civil Rights Association
NIE	Northern Ireland Executive
NIFRS	Northern Ireland Fire and Rescue Service
NIHE	Northern Ireland Housing Executive
NIHRC	Northern Ireland Human Rights Commission
NILP	Northern Ireland Labour Party
NIMDM	Northern Ireland Multiple Deprivation Measure
NINIS	Northern Ireland Neighbourhood Information Service
NIO	Northern Ireland Office
NIPB	Northern Ireland Policing Board
NISRA	Northern Ireland Statistics and Research Agency
NIVC	Northern Ireland Victims Commission
NIWC	Northern Ireland Women's Coalition
NPNI	Nationalist Party of Northern Ireland
NSMC	North/South Ministerial Council
OFMDFM	Office of the First Minister and Deputy First Minister
OIRA	Official IRA
ÖVP	Österreichische Volkspartei [Austrian People's Party]
PAF	Protestant Action Force
PANI	Police Authority of Northern Ireland
PBP	People Before Profit
PCNI	Parades Commission for Northern Ireland
PD	People's Democracy
PIRA	Provisional IRA
PM	Prime Minister
PRG	Peace and Reconciliation Group
PSNI	Police Service of Northern Ireland
PUP	Progressive Unionist Party
QUB	Queen's University of Belfast
RAF	Republican Action Force
RDS	Regional Development Strategy
RHC	Red Hand Commando
RHD	Red Hand Defenders
RIC	Royal Irish Constabulary

RIRA	Real IRA
RTÉ	Radio Telefis Éireann
RUC	Royal Ulster Constabulary
RWG	Revolutionary Workers' Group
SCF	Suffolk Community Forum
SDAP	Sozialdemokratische Arbeiterpartei Österreichs [Social Democratic Workers' Party of Austria]
SDLP	Social Democratic and Labour Party
SEUPB	Special EU Programmes Body
SF	Sinn Féin
SLIG	Suffolk Lenadoon Interface Group
SRRP	Stewartstown Road Regeneration Project
T:BUC	Together: Building a United Community
TUV	Traditional Unionist Voice
UAC	Ulster Army Council
UDA	Ulster Defence Association
UDR	Ulster Defence Regiment
UDP	Ulster Democratic Party
UFF	Ulster Freedom Fighters
UK	United Kingdom
UKIP	United Kingdom Independence Party
UKUP	United Kingdom Unionist Party
ULC	Unionist Loyalist Council
ULDP	Ulster Loyalist Democratic Party
UN	United Nations
UNDP	United Nations Development Programme
UPA	Ulster Protestant Action
UPRG	Ulster Political Research Group
US/USA	United States of America
USC	Ulster Special Constabulary ('B-Specials')
USSR	Union of Soviet Socialist Republics (Soviet Union)
UUAC	United Unionist Action Council
UUC	Ulster Unionist Council
UUP	Ulster Unionist Party
UUUC	United Ulster Unionist Council
UVF	Ulster Volunteer Force
UWC	Unionist Workers Council
YCF	Young Citizen Volunteers

"The Interface is emblematic of contested origins."
"The Interface is the continual occlusion of the 'day after' question."
"The Interface is a published policy that specifies a government goal by 2023."[1]

---

[1] Selected quotes from O'Leary 2016.

1 INTRODUCTION
SETTING THE SCENE FOR THE RESEARCH

*"You cannot walk freely wherever you want to.
It is a deep-seated fear of being attacked."*[2]

*"If those 'peace walls' came down tomorrow –
all hell would break loose in these communities."*[3]

The above quotes derive from two interviews conducted in 'interface communities' in Northern Ireland, i.e. communities that are geographically located in close proximity to the other side. They indicate a specific problem this book aims to explore. In essence, the conundrum is: why do local flashpoints with intercommunal tensions and occasional violence still persist in Northern Ireland? After all, the society, though still deeply divided between two rivalling ethno-national communities, is generally regarded as being in a stage of conflict transformation and post-conflict reconstruction after a long period of armed strife. In these years of transition, the former parties to the conflict have made considerable efforts towards building shared governance and community relations in order to stabilise peace. Likewise, numerous civil society organisations and community activists have engaged in various efforts to transform and resolve conflict, and a substantial amount of academic studies and professional reports have been published, putting forward policy recommendations for conflict transformation and resolution.

However, even more than two decades after the cessation of protracted armed conflict and the signing of the peace agreement, community relations and social development in Northern Ireland are still clouded by tensions in certain locations, which can potentially erupt into violence. Thus, the purpose of this research is to gain understanding of why localised intergroup conflict in Northern Ireland continues to exist. It is believed that such an understanding will contribute to developing effective and sustainable strategies promoting progress towards reconciliation and peaceful coexistence between the communities. The gradual eradication of the sources of inter-community violence and discrimination based on ethno-national affiliation would, in turn, lead to more social cohesion and encourage politicians to forge more inclu-

---

[2] Morgan (interview).
[3] Poole (interview).

sive policies around commonly agreed objectives. This would contribute to stabilising and normalising the still fragile state of democracy and to reconciliation between the communities. Furthermore, by comparing and contrasting key research findings in several selected locations of Northern Ireland, it is intended to sketch a more general picture of the underlying reasons and factors in the persistence of local intergroup conflict and community divisions. This may provide insights and foundations for researchers, practitioners and policy-makers alike to develop effective ways of addressing conflict and divisions. Moreover, the results of this research might be informative for other cases of localised intergroup conflict in divided societies.

This book explores Northern Ireland during a period of profound social transition and political transformation from violent conflict to post-conflict peacebuilding and state reconstruction. This period began with the political peace process in 1985, when the Anglo-Irish Agreement was signed between the governments of the United Kingdom (UK) and the Republic of Ireland (cf. Hennessey 2001). It culminated in the signing of the Good Friday/Belfast Agreement on 10 April 1998. The intense period of transition lasted until 2010, when most of the major arrangements and architecture of the post-conflict political and social system were already in place. A decisive step was when justice and policing powers were devolved from the British Government to the Northern Ireland Executive (cf. Simpson 2010). This forms, therefore, the core of the empirical observation period for this research. Nevertheless, this study also includes more recent political and community developments when deemed necessary to ensure the accuracy, validity and clarity of the findings. In particular, the question of the potential impact of recent critical events on the fragile social and political situation on the ground will be addressed. These include the flag protests and, most notably, the collapse of Northern Ireland's power-sharing government and the dispute over the Irish border in the wake of the UK's Brexit process.

As the research focus is placed on local conflict, the strategy is thus 'to go local', i.e. to put a particular empirical emphasis on those communities in Northern Ireland which have been hotspots of armed conflict and which are still prone to intercommunal violence. Thus, the empirical study will focus in particular on certain deprived areas in North and West Belfast, but, for reasons of comparison, will also include other flashpoint areas in Belfast, Derry/Londonderry and Portadown. As will be shown, these areas, which are located in close proximity to the ethno-national group boundaries, are characterised by particularly high levels of group cohesion, segregation, socio-economic deprivation and class inequality. In fact, the division between the Protestant/Unionist/Loyalist and Catholic/Nationalist/Republican communities finds its most obvious, visual manifestation in interface barriers and so-called 'peace walls' separating the working-class areas of both sides in Belfast, Derry/Londonderry and other places. Moreover, evidence from reviewing relevant literature and studies undertaken indicates that the persistence of certain conflict hotspots might serve the interests and aspirations of the ethnonationally divided elites to achieve and maintain power and hegemony over the state. If so, they would thereby exert a considerable impact on local inter-community conflict.

A final remark at this point concerns the readability of this book. It has been written for a wider audience extending beyond the British Isles, who may not be so familiar with the details and particularities of the Northern Ireland conflict but interested nonetheless in gaining a better understanding of its background and causes. Therefore, more material and information has been included than readers in Northern Ireland, the Republic of Ireland and Great Britain might deem strictly necessary. A large part of these additional details have been moved to the footnotes and chronology. This is to improve the flow and not to distract from the main arguments and key findings of this study. Thus it is hoped that both informed and interested readers will enjoy the read.

THE CORE RATIONALE: WHAT IS THE PROBLEM?

Intergroup conflicts like the one in Northern Ireland are hardly a rare phenomenon. At any given time in modern history, a large number of conflicts has occurred, both between and within states. With regard to the latter, the quantity of armed intra-state conflicts has increased since the Second World War. Strikingly, an upsurge in such conflicts can be observed after the end of the Cold War, although many experts anticipated a 'peace dividend' (cf. Hewitt 2008). The International Crisis Group (ICG) think-tank has reported in its monthly Crisis Watch that in June 2019, for example, 87 countries were threatened by or were actually experiencing more or less violent strife within their territories (ICG 2019).[4] Many of

---

[4] In contrast, the Heidelberg Institute for International Conflict Research in its latest annual Conflict Barometer for 2018, which employs a different methodology, has counted a total

these conflicts take place in societies whose members are deeply divided by conflicting ethno-national identities and allegiances. As can be observed, the patterns of intergroup tensions and conflict often resemble one another: the antagonistic nationalist camps pursue irreconcilable political objectives, each claiming the legitimacy of their demands in the name of justice, freedom and equality. Demands for political self-determination and self-governance by one nationalist camp, representing a minority group in terms of overall population and/or power in the state, range from national autonomy to secession and independent statehood. These demands are often countered and repressed by the majority on the grounds of the democratic principle of majority rule and/or the 'sacred' duty to protect the sovereignty and territorial integrity of the state (cf. Archibugi 2003, Margalit & Raz 1990).[5]

Such minority-majority conflicts often have deeper roots and long traditions. Social scientists differ considerably in their approaches and in their interpretations of the reasons for such claims. Perceptions of belonging to a distinct national and/or ethnic group, exclusivist religious claims, deep resentment among minority groups due to socio-economic inequality and deprivation, discrimination, domination, imperialism and capitalist colonialism usually constitute the central and enduring themes of the differing approaches. Depending on the respective weight researchers attach to ethno-national divisions and to issues of class and socio-economic inequalities, analyses of the causes of conflict in divided societies can be classified into two broad categories: identity-based and materialist, i.e. socio-economic, resource-based, explanations (cf. Anderson 1991, Connor 1994, Gellner 1998, Horo-

---

of 52 conflict-affected and conflict-prone countries. Of these conflicts, 16 have been classified as full-scale wars, 25 as limited wars and 11 as inactive during the observation period (HIIK 2019: 10-13).

[5] These conflicting and seemingly incompatible claims are included in international law as fundamental principles, for example in the United Nations (UN) Declaration on the Granting of Independence to Colonial Countries and Peoples, which not only grants all peoples the right to self-determination, but at the same time also recognises the sovereignty and territorial integrity of existing states (cf. UN 1960). The unclear and contentious scope of the right to self-determination also becomes evident in several other UN documents, such as the UN Charter, Chapter 11 Declaration Regarding Non-Self-Governing Territories, the UN Resolution 36/103 Declaration on the Inadmissibility of Intervention and Interference in the Internal Affairs of States and the UN Resolution 57/337 Prevention of Armed Conflict (cf. UN 1945, UN 2003a, UN 2003b).

witz 2000, Tamir 1995; Bauer 2000, Beberoglu 2004, Nimni 1991, Peleg 2007, Sisk 1996).

However, despite the fact that a key characteristic of modern societies is indeed their diverse composition, this diversity, however, does not necessarily or systematically result in a conflict between rival ethno-national identities. This is demonstrated by the relatively stable and peaceful coexistence in several ethno-nationally divided societies, e.g. Switzerland, Canada or Belgium (cf. Keating 2001a, Kymlicka 1995, Taylor 1994, Tully 2001). Obviously, in these multi-national states the enterprise of creating "a model of social unity that can accommodate ethnic diversity" (Kymlicka 1996: 105) has so far been successful, at least to a considerable extent. Their governance structure is characterised by consociational and federal power-sharing arrangements, consisting at state level of a coalition government composed of the main ethno-national blocks, which at federal and local levels have been granted a considerable degree of autonomy and self-government (cf. Bauböck 2004, Elazar 1985, Lijphart 1977, 1984 & 2002). Notably, the implementation of governance arrangements with power-sharing and self-government mechanisms has been attempted as a means of peacebuilding and conflict transformation in a considerable number of deeply divided societies, such as Northern Ireland, Kosovo, North Macedonia, Bosnia and Herzegovina, the Basque Country, South Africa, East Timor, Cambodia and Lebanon. However, this has not resolved intergroup conflict on the ground, as displayed by ongoing intercommunal tensions and occasional outbreaks of violence in certain flashpoint areas (cf. Barma 2006, Byrne 2001, Díez Medrano 1995, Hepburn 2004, ICG 2005 & 2012, Jarman 2005b, Jarstad 2007, Keating 2001b, Kerr 2005, Mansvelt Beck 2008, McGarry & O'Leary 2004, Mitchell 2011, Norris 2008, Petroska-Beska & Najcevska 2004, Pinos 2016, Prelec 2017, Reka 2008, Strating 2015, Seaver 2000, Todosijević 2001). This leads to the conclusion that there must be specific elements and patterns that increase the likelihood that such local intergroup conflicts will emerge, or, if already existing, will persist in certain local hotspots, even in a general post-conflict setting.

As has been argued by many theorists focusing on material and socio-economic aspects of conflict, inequality in the distribution of resources and wealth between rival social groups are main factors provoking violent conflict. Yet, this inequality does not necessarily have to be based on facts, but is frequently rooted in a perception of deprivation and discrimination widespread among members of a subordinate group against the dominant one (cf. Cramer 2005; Gurr 1970). Indeed, it seems to be a striking feature of many

conflicts in divided societies that intergroup conflict is most intense and violent between those who are particularly deprived in terms of access to, and
possession of vital socio-economic resources, and who therefore belong to the
lower socio-economic classes. This also applies to the case under study. In
Northern Ireland the areas located in close proximity to the ethno-national
boundary saw the heaviest levels of violence during the armed conflict (cf.
Jarman 2004). Even more than two decades after the signing of the peace
agreement, the living conditions in these areas are still characterised by high
levels of (residential, personal, marital and educational) segregation, intergroup fear, prejudice and hostility. As a consequence, many of these so-called
'interface communities' in Northern Ireland, which in some cases also take
the form of enclaves, display particularly high levels of group cohesion (cf.
Duckitt 2003, Sidanius & Pratto 1999).

   To avoid confusion, a few remarks should be made on the definition and
use of the term 'interface communities' within the context of this research.
The term was specifically coined for Northern Ireland to describe residential
areas where segregated Protestant/Unionist/Loyalist and Catholic/Nationalist/
Republican communities share a physical boundary (cf. Heatley 2004, Jarman
2004). A more detailed discussion and conceptualisation of the term will follow in Chapter 2 in the section on 'The Locus of Conflict'. At this point, it
shall only be mentioned that, in reference to the definition by Neil Jarman,
'interface communities' "are those groups of people living at the intersection
of segregated, polarised and socio-economically deprived residential zones in
areas with a strong link between territory and ethno-national identity." (Jarman 2004: 5)

   The manifestations of ethno-national seclusion and group cohesion find
expression not only in the socio-economic domain, but also in the political
structure, especially in the system of governance, political representation and
ideological power relations organised around ethno-national blocks. In this
block-building and consolidating process, strong nationalist leaders play an
important role, for instance in acting as attachment figures or guardians of
security for their respective communities. Such a type of homogenisation of
ethno-national groups, however, does not sufficiently take into account the
variety of socio-economic class interests. Effectively, despite their shared
experience of deprivation, the lower social classes remain strongly divided
along ethno-national lines. The lack of class solidarity, joint class politics and
joint interest representation indicates that ethno-national divisions are likely
to dominate issues of class and socio-economic inequality. However, the par-

ticular concentration and persistence of intergroup tensions and conflict in most deprived areas, especially in those located adjacent to the ethno-national interfaces, highlight the inter-relatedness and interdependency between identity and inequality issues. With regard to the latter, the continuing high socio-economic deprivation in interface and enclave areas, especially in the urban areas of Northern Ireland, and the increasing gap between rich and poor also indicate marked resource inequalities within the communities (cf. Dignan 2003, Dignan & McLaughlin 2002, Hillyard et al 2003, Irwin 2002, McGregor & McKee 1995, NISRA 2010a).

To recap at this point, opposing ethno-national identities and socio-economic class inequalities seem not only to have a significant impact on the generation and maintenance of conflict in deeply divided societies, but are also likely to interact and potentially reinforce one another.

This is not all, however. There is another important element to be considered in this research. Political debates over identity and recognition frequently touch on issues of distribution and socio-economic inequality. According to some identity theorists, in societies bifurcated along ethno-national lines the politics of identity and difference have often been employed by the divided political elites as instruments of distributive inequalities (cf. Fraser 1997: 11-39 & 121-49, Fraser 2000, Young 1990). As is argued here, in deeply divided, conflict-ridden societies like Northern Ireland a related phenomenon can frequently be observed, which was not only present during the time of armed conflict, but also in the recent period of peacebuilding and post-conflict reconstruction. As the history of conflict suggests, there has been an ongoing struggle for political and socio-economic power between the rival ethno-national elites with the ultimate aim of achieving hegemony over the state. A particular logic seems to be inherent in it: depending on their actual position in the power struggle, the elites strive to create and maintain a hegemonic or counter-hegemonic system, in which divisive nationalist ideologies and political anxieties about being dominated by the 'other' side play an important role.

Even after the peace agreement, there are indications that the hegemonic interests of the rival ethnic-national elites continue to thrive. This seems to manifest itself in several ways, thereby perpetuating local intergroup conflict and impairing the potential for conflict transformation and resolution. It is frequently the case that partisan party politics aims to address exclusively members of one or other of the conflicting groups, thus reinforcing existing ethno-national divisions, especially among the disadvantaged socio-economic classes of both sides. Apparently, there is a greater tendency among people belonging to the deprived working classes to affiliate themselves with and vote for polarising nationalist parties. This also indicates that, despite the commonly shared level of socio-economic deprivation, they are more susceptible to such exclusivist ideologies. As far as this tendency is concerned, oppression, social control and community pressure, on the one hand, and feelings of insecurity and the perceived or actual sense of being threatened by the other ethno-national community, on the other, rank among the contributing factors. As history shows, the intensity of their support for nationalist ideologies is also contingent on the leaders' personalities and on certain events provoking intergroup tensions and violence. Frequently, the politics of nationalist exclusivism is also accompanied by a failure to deliver effective policies targeting community relations and reconciliation. Instead, in their power struggle the nationalist elites often engage in a blame game about who is to be held responsible for this policy failure. There is also another important way in which the hegemonic interests of the nationalist elites trigger off local conflict. To the extent that their ideologies are based on causing fear of and prejudice against the other ethno-national group, they reinforce intergroup hostility, intimidation, sectarianism and violence (cf. Gramsci 2000, Levy 2000, Peleg 2007, Robin 2004, Shklar 1998).

Thus, overall, the specific meaning and significance of power and hegemony in Northern Ireland, with deep community divisions based on rival ethno-national allegiances and socio-economic class inequalities, challenge the ability of traditional – i.e. identity-based and materialist – conflict studies to explore the causal processes at work. Moreover, as can be gathered from a literature review, the emphasis of the majority of research since the end of large-scale violence has been on the macro-level of conflict. The myopia of these approaches will therefore become most apparent when the lens of investigation is focused on those locations which have experienced particularly high levels of intergroup violence, i.e. on the interface and enclave communities of Northern Ireland. This is, broadly speaking, the rationale so far. However, whether this can conclusively explain local interface conflict between Protestant and Catholic working-class communities in Northern Ireland will be subject to the following analysis.

To sum up, the central research question of this study is: Why does local intergroup conflict still persist in Northern Ireland, although, at a general societal level, the country has moved beyond armed conflict to a stage of peacebuilding and post-conflict reconstruction? More specifically, what are the driving forces behind intergroup conflict in interface and enclave communities in Northern Ireland? In line with a thorough review of relevant literature, three factors are deemed crucial to understand intergroup conflict in Northern Ireland: conflicting ethno-national identities, socio-economic class inequalities and hegemonic relations of political power and governance (cf. Campbell 2008, Dixon 2000, McGarry & O'Leary 1995, Ruane & Todd 1996, Shirlow & Murtagh 2006). Consequently, this study will aim at exploring the impacts of these factors – and their interrelations – on intergroup conflict in interface and enclave communities in Northern Ireland. The specific objectives of this research are the following: firstly, to explore how issues of rival ethno-national identities and socio-economic class inequalities are manifested on the ground in selected interface and enclave communities; and, secondly, to investigate if, how and to what extent these issues are utilised by the divided ethno-national elites in their power struggles for political, cultural and socio-economic hegemony over the state. Due to the complexity of local conflict dynamics, case studies have been conducted in several locations in Northern Ireland, mainly in Belfast, but also in other places. The key findings of these case studies will then be placed in the broader context of socio-economic and political developments in Northern Ireland. Thereby, it is hoped to arrive at more general conclusions regarding the state, nature and dynamics of local intergroup conflict in Northern Ireland.

TERMINOLOGICAL CLARIFICATIONS: LABELS AND MARKERS USED IN NORTHERN IRELAND

Typically, not only in the field of peace and conflict studies, but also in political science and the broader social sciences, analysts and researchers draw on different terminologies, or even separate ones. At this point, some more general clarifications might be necessary on the key terms used in this study on the Northern Ireland conflict. This will afford the reader guidance on what, how and when labels and markers will be used, thus facilitating the readability and comprehensibility of this study.

The profound group divisions and the very narrow, politically and often also socially insignifant, neutral ground that still characterise the society of Northern Ireland are reflected in the diverse and complex terminology applied by the various analysts and actors involved. As a deeply divided society, Northern Ireland mirrors settings where names and places are signifiers of position and attitude and indicators of loyalty, attachment and affiliation. There are certain ciphers and codes that, if used, make an author appear biased in favour of one side or the other (Beresford 1994: 7). Therefore, finding the most appropriate, unambiguous and neutral labels and terms for analysing the issues at stake is a rather difficult and arduous, but an important task all the same. It is likewise expedient to engage in this endeavour, for identifying and making coherent use of the most uncontroversial terminology used in the Northern Ireland context will help minimise researcher bias.

Consequently, as John Whyte points out, in Northern Ireland "there is no consensus on the most appropriate labels to use for the two communities." (Whyte 1990: 245) Nevertheless, the most clear-cut demarcation between the conflicting groups can be drawn along religious and denominational lines, i.e. by distinguishing them into 'Roman Catholics' and 'Protestants'.[6] In Northern Ireland, religious difference serves an important function, i.e., as Richard Jenkins puts it, of "providing the main explicit boundary-maintaining mechanism" (Jenkins 1997: 93) between the two communities. The common use of these labels to describe and demarcate the main contending groups does not, however, indicate, as Paul Dixon remarks, that, "the conflict is ... to any great extent about religion or religious dogma." (Dixon 2001: 2) This is confirmed by Sally Belfrage. As she pointed out in her seminal anthropological study of the conflict in Belfast in the early 1980s,

> "It is not a religious war, nor is religious tolerance strictly an issue. Religion is more a badge of identification to distinguish two views of cultural superiority, two sets of mind about the border dividing Ireland, two kinds of fear." (Belfrage 1987: 406)

This is essentially in line with most researchers, who similarly regard religion as the key boundary marker between the two communities (cf. Brewer & Higgins 1998: 14, Mitchell 2006: 59-68, Shirlow & Murtagh 2006: 15, Spencer 2012: 1). So, following Will Kymlicka's argument, both groups, although religiously identified and distinguished, can be regarded as distinct ethnonational factions, which over time have developed a strong sense of nation-

---

[6] In line with most research on the Northern Ireland problem, 'Protestants' is used as a generic term, which encompasses the different denominations of Protestantism in Northern Ireland; i.e. the three main sects – Presbyterians, Episcopalians (Church of Ireland) and Methodists – and several smaller denominations like Brethren, Baptists and Congregationalists (cf. Ganiel 2008, Spencer 2012).

hood and community culture as a result of deep societal divisions. He describes this process of ethno-national identity formation as follows:

> "If racial and religious differences and discrimination within a given societal culture become so entrenched that a common life comes to be seen as impossible, a sense of separate nationhood may develop within a subgroup of the larger society. And, over time, this subgroup may develop its own distinct 'pervasive' or 'societal' cultures." (Kymlicka 1995: 217)

Speaking in political terms, a considerable majority of Northern Irish Catholics consider themselves either 'Nationalists' or 'Republicans', who both aspire to unification with the Republic of Ireland, the latter, however, supporting the idea of a united, socialist Irish republic. In order to achieve this goal, militant Republicans organised in paramilitary groups were prepared to employ violent means in the recent conflict. By contrast, a vast majority of Northern Irish Protestants regard themselves either as 'Unionists' or as 'Loyalists', who both strive to preserve the United Kingdom of Great Britain and Northern Ireland (UK). Loyalists, in addition, maintain allegiance to the British Crown. In order to defend the union with Great Britain, militant Loyalists, like their Republican counterparts, formed paramilitary groups who were ready to resort to violence during the conflict. Notably, there are class differences in political attitudes and voting behaviour. Whilst working-class Catholics tend to support the Republican political cause, their middle and upper-class counterparts are inclined to espouse Nationalist ideas and candidates. On the other side of the community divide, working-class Protestants regard themselves mainly as Loyalists and middle and upper-class Protestants consider themselves predominantly as Unionists (cf. Dixon 2001: 1-2, Duffy & Evans 1997, Evans & Tongue 2009, Garry 2016, Hayes & McAllister 1995). Thus, alternatively, the generic labels of 'Protestant/Unionist/Loyalist' and 'Catholic/Nationalist/Republican' are also quite frequently used to differentiate between the two conflicting communities. This applies in particular to the discussion of socio-political aspects.[7] Finally, an option, which is rather rarely applied, is to classify them in 'Ulster British' and 'Ulster Irish' (cf. Foster 1988: 410, Whyte 1990: 245).

Likewise, different terms are used for certain key events. The 'Troubles' is the popular euphemism for the recent violent intergroup conflict that lasted

---

[7] These labels are used mainly by public officials, government departments, local authorities, community practitioners and also by some conflict analysts and commentators.

from 1968 to 1998, and the 'Agreement Reached in the Multi-Party Negotiations', marking the official end to the Troubles, is commonly referred to by members of the Catholic/Nationalist/Republican community and by many international media correspondents as the 'Good Friday Agreement', whereas people belonging to the Protestant/Unionist/Loyalist community tend to call it the 'Belfast Agreement' or 'Stormont Agreement'. It is also common usage simply to call the peace accord 'the Agreement'. Furthermore, the issue of how to refer to Northern Ireland itself poses a specific problem, because as a political entity it is neither a country, nor a province, nor a state. Regarding the latter, Nationalists and Republicans sometimes call Northern Ireland contemptuously a 'statelet'. Furthermore, Nationalists, and Republicans especially, often refer to Northern Ireland as 'the Six Counties' or 'the North (of Ireland)', whereas they call the Republic of Ireland 'the Twenty-Six Counties' or 'the South (of Ireland)'. Unionists, Loyalists and the British media tend to use 'Ulster' synonymously for Nforthern Ireland, although, correctly speaking, it is the name of one of the four historical provinces on the isle of Ireland. As a province, Ulster consists of nine and not just the six counties of Northern Ireland.[8] As to place names, Derry (the name preferred by the Catholic/Nationalist/Republican community), Londonderry (the name used by the Protestant/Unionist/Loyalist community and the city's official, though disputed name) or L'Derry (as it is sometimes abbreviated and used in a neutral way) stands out.[9] [10]

Since a major goal of this thesis is to maintain an unbiased stance and achieve terminological clarity in the analysis of the Northern Ireland conflict, the following linguistic rules will be applied: When talking about the respective communities as a whole, the terms 'Catholics' and 'Protestants' will be used. As discussed above, regarding political and ideological issues, both 'Ulster Loyalism' and 'Irish Republicanism' can be regarded as being distinct from 'Ulster Unionism' and 'Irish Nationalism'. Therefore, in general, the

---

[8] For a map of the six counties of Northern Ireland and of the four historical provinces of the Irish island see Figure 8 and 9 in the Appendix, p. 405.

[9] The dispute between Nationalists and Unionists over the city's name climaxed recently, when the Derry City Council and Strabane District Council voted in favour of changing the official name of Londonderry to Derry. However, in order to implement this decision, the consent of the Northern Ireland Government is required, which is highly unlikely due to fierce Unionist opposition (cf. Ferguson 2015).

[10] For a comprehensive glossary of the terminology used in studies on the Northern Ireland conflict, see Dunn & Dawson 2000 and Melaugh & Lynn 2017.

encompassing terms 'Protestant/Unionist/Loyalist' and 'Catholic/Nationalist/ Republican' will be applied. The explicit use of the labels 'Unionists', 'Loyalists', 'Nationalists' and 'Republicans' will be restricted to highlight important differences within the two political camps and their communities and to point to specific circumstances and events. When referring to the 'Agreement Reached in the Multi-Party Negotiations', the terms 'Good Friday/ Belfast Agreement', 'Belfast/Good Friday Agreement' or simply 'the Agreement' will be used. Furthermore, attention will be paid not to use partisan place and country names. So, Derry/Londonderry will be used throughout the text. Terms like 'the North' and 'the South' will only be applied in a geographical sense. In line with common usage, Northern Ireland itself will alternatively be referred to as 'country', 'state' or 'province'. After all, and fortunately for this scientific endeavour, the conclusion of the Agreement has clarified at least one terminological issue concerning 'Northern Ireland'. Beforehand, the use of the term had a partisan connotation, since such an entity did not exist for many Irish Nationalists (Beresford 1994: 7). Finally, it should be noted that the partisan terms discussed above will appear in the text, yet only in the context of quotes taken from interviews and secondary sources.

THE STRUCTURE OF THE BOOK

"The very structure of a research paper is crucial to make the paper work. If you get things out of order, or if the order is not clear, it won't matter how much good information is there – the reader will see the paper as a failure." (Badke 2004: 160) This, of course, does not only hold for a research paper, but also, and even more so, to the comprehensive endeavour of writing a scientific book. Therefore, essentially, the structure has to be linked to the research questions, objectives and findings, and it has to present them in a logical, consistent and coherent manner (cf. Badke 2004: 160-162).

Bearing this in mind, the structure of this book on the study of local intergroup conflict in Northern Ireland is as follows. After the general introduction, which sets the scene for the study and provides clarifications of the terminology used, the overall research design will be outlined. This includes describing the research objectives, questions, preliminary assumptions guiding the study, methodology and focus of enquiry, and the potential research contribution.

Chapter 2 then sketches the theoretical framework for analysing and interpreting local intergroup conflict in Northern Ireland. This will be done by drawing on established approaches and identifying their relevance and weaknesses for addressing the specific set of problems of this research. Thus, after a brief genesis of conflicts in the world, some general reflections are made on approaches to the study of intercommunal conflicts in divided societies. Subsequently, the key dimensions and core components for this study are discussed. This includes, in particular, ethno-national identity divisions, socioeconomic class inequalities, hegemonic power and governance relations, and the geographical locus of conflict. At the end of this chapter, the results of the discussion will be synthesised and integrated into a theoretical-analytical framework providing general guidance for the empirical study of intercommunal conflict in Northern Ireland.

Subsequently, Chapters 3 and 4 put the spotlight on Northern Ireland. Initially, the dynamics of conflict and peacebuilding will be explored at the macro level, thus providing the ground for the analysis of the local situation and circumstances. In a first step, the history, dynamics and context of the Northern Ireland conflict will be investigated along the dimensions of ethno-national and socio-economic class divisions with a particular focus on power and hegemony. Special emphasis will be given to the role and impact of key events, parties and actors. Based on this overall analysis, the empirical field research study carried out in several conflict-prone and deprived Catholic and Protestant interface and enclave communities in Belfast and beyond will be explored. The focus is on the views and opinions of the local interview respondents. Thus, it is aimed to shed light on the underlying causes and mechanisms and the nature of inter-community divisions. This includes an account of some major incidents epitomising how these divisions materialise on the ground. In particular, the study will also explore how key issues and needs identified by local communities are addressed at local and state levels. To this end, strategies and activities of community groups and grassroots activists as well as key policies of community relations and development will be examined for their impact in specific local contexts and environments. In doing so, the question will also be addressed as to whether and how power interests and relations of Unionist and Nationalist actors play a role.

Finally, in conclusion, Chapter 5 wraps up the research findings on intercommunal conflict in Northern Ireland both from a local and a wider, more general perspective. Furthermore, it will provide an outlook on the potential local implications of current political developments around the tug-of-war over Brexit and the Irish border issue as well as the ongoing Northern Ireland government crisis. In the end, the attempt is also made to identify potential avenues for improving community relations and peacebuilding on the ground.

RESEARCH DESIGN

> *"The human mind is unable to grasp the full complexity of a social situation. We need an organizing principle, some thread to guide us through the intricacies." (John Whyte 1990)[11]*

> *"The best research in the world can be of no effect if those with power to influence the course of events show no interests in its findings." (John Whyte 1990)[12]*

The main aim of this section is to set out the overall methodological approach in light of certain guiding theoretical considerations and to position it within the broader context of studies on intergroup conflict in divided societies. As with all scientific research, this book likewise follows a particular cognitive process. Specifically, the aim is to make the research more accessible and comprehensible to readers and hopefully to convince them of its significance to the study of intergroup conflict in divided societies in general and in Northern Ireland in particular. It is therefore of salient importance to provide a detailed and concise account of the theoretical and methodological considerations guiding this study and, in particular, its field research. At this point, it should be noted that the overall research design is oriented towards what Sekaran calls "the hallmarks of scientific research": purposiveness, rigour, testability, replicability, precision and confidence, objectivity, generalisability, and parsimony (Sekaran, 1992: 10-14). Although being aware that these standards will not be fully achievable, it is nevertheless a worthwhile endeavour to aspire to come as close to them as possible.

RESEARCH OBJECTIVES AND QUESTIONS

The general research objective of this book is to explore the causes for the persistence of locally focused intergroup conflict in the divided society of Northern Ireland. To this end, the main emphasis of research is on those areas

---

[11] Whyte 1990: 249.
[12] Whyte 1990: 246.

where most of the violence and conflict has been concentrated, i.e. on inter-face and enclave communities, which are located in close proximity to the 'other' side of the divide. The fundamental issue to be addressed is if and to what extent local conflict is caused by ethno-national divisions and/or socio-economic class inequalities between the communities; or whether and to what degree the persistence of local conflict is in the interests of achieving and maintaining power and state hegemony by the divided political elites. In par-ticular, this book aims to explore the following questions:

1) What is the impact of ethno-national divisions and socio-economic class inequalities on local intergroup conflict in interface and enclave communities in Northern Ireland?

   More specifically: To what extent is local conflict between the com-munities caused by incompatible ethno-national identities and how far by inequalities and/or discrimination in socio-economic opportunities and class? What is the concrete impact of these factors on local com-munity relations and everyday life?

2) How do power and hegemonic interests of the ethno-nationally divid-ed political elites affect local intergroup conflict in interface and en-clave areas in Northern Ireland?

   More specifically: Do the political elites have vested interests in keep-ing local tensions and conflict between the communities alive? And if so, is this because it serves their aim for achieving and maintaining power and hegemony over the state? How do their strategies and poli-cies affect the interface and enclave communities?

TENTATIVE RESEARCH ASSUMPTIONS

From what has been said in the introduction some broad assumptions about the general conflict dynamics can be made. These assumptions, which are presented below, should, however, in no way affect or even predetermine the outcome of the research. Seen as preliminary, tentative and open to revisions as they are, they are deemed useful in providing some general guidance for this study on local intergroup conflict in Northern Ireland. In particular, the following assumptions are made:

1) The ethno-national dimension of conflict seems to be intertwined with important issues of socio-economic inequality and class division, and this correlation appears to be especially pronounced in deprived areas

located close to the ethno-national interface and enclave areas. In other words, it seems that the stronger the ethno-national identity and the higher the socio-economic deprivation, the higher is the potential for violent intergroup conflict.

2) The ethno-nationally divided political elites seem to have vested interests for power and hegemony over the state, which affect ethno-national and socio-economic class divisions in the communities. Apparently, this impact, which is expressed through divisive modes of governance, nationalist ideologies and exclusionary policies, is particularly strong in interface and enclave areas.

3) Areas geographically close to the ethno-national interfaces between the rival communities are evidently more susceptible to violence and conflict. In other words, there seems to be a general spatial pattern: the closer the ethno-national boundary, the higher is the likelihood of violent intergroup conflict.

4) There is arguably also a temporal pattern, since evidence shows that intergroup violence occurs most frequently and intensively at specific times commemorating and celebrating events important to the respective ethno-national identities of the rival communities.

RESEARCH METHODOLOGY AND ANALYTICAL FRAMEWORK

Finding the appropriate research strategies and methods to answer the research questions is a fundamental task for the successful completion of any research project. In general, as Miller and Dingwall point out, "the basic challenge that all methodological discussion must face is the question: how does all this help in the analysis of data and the production of explanation." (Miller & Dingwall 1997: 29) Thus, the main aim of this section is to provide a justification for and an accurate documentation of the methodology chosen for the purpose of research.

Research in the social sciences often draws a polar distinction between qualitative, also called interpretive, and quantitative research methods (Burnham et al 2004: 31). According to this view,

"Quantitative and qualitative methods are more than just differences between research strategies and data collection procedures. These approaches represent fundamentally different epistemological frameworks for conceptualising the nature of knowing, social reality, and procedures for comprehending these phenomena." (Filestead 1979: 45)

However, for some researchers this epistemological dichotomy between qualitative and quantitative research is false and fallacious; in their view, qualitative and quantitative methods are not to be regarded as mutually exclusive but rather have to be seen on a continuum, the actual position depending on the suitability for the research in question. Hence, they propose the integration of a mix of various modes of inquiry, which fundamentally depends on the type of research objectives, questions and hypotheses. Whereas "quantitative research can capture important statistical relationships" (Warren & Karner 2005: 2), qualitative research is more suitable for "interpretive or social constructionist understandings" (Warren & Karner 2005: 2), i.e. for interpreting these relationships as to their actual meanings and effects on the ground. Moreover, and against the widespread tendency to attribute scientific inference, generalisability and objectivity predominantly to the quantitative research tradition (cf. Brady et al 2004, King et al 1994), qualitative research methods can equally meet these methodological quality criteria (cf. Grix 2010: 122-125). As has also been emphasised, there is no difference between quantitative and qualitative research traditions in terms of their capability to meet the research quality criteria of validity and reliability (Bauer et al. 2000, Berg 2012, Ercikan & Roth 2006, Ridenour & Newman 2008: 1-14, Taylor 2005: 3-20).

Although taking the historical development of the conflict in Northern Ireland into account, this study focuses primarily on the period of profound social transition and political transformation from violent conflict to post-conflict peacebuilding and state reconstruction, i.e. Northern Ireland from 1986 to 2010.[13] Considering the variety of sources relevant to this research, a

---

[13] To recap what has been said in the introductory remarks: in Northern Ireland, this period started in 1986, which marked the beginning of the peace process, when the Anglo-Irish Agreement was signed between the governments of the UK and the Republic of Ireland (cf. Hennessey 2001). It came to an end in the early 2010s, when most of the key arrangements of the post-conflict political and social system had already been put in place. This was the case in 2010 with the devolution of justice and policing powers from the British Government to the Northern Ireland Executive (cf. Simpson 2010). However, as noted in the beginning of this book, recent politically and socially disruptive events will also be taken into account for the analysis of the present situation in Northern Ireland and intercommunity relations as well as for the assessment of potential future developments.

mixed methods approach will be adopted, drawing on background research and analyses of both quantitative statistical and survey data and (primary and secondary) qualitative research (Almond et al. 1996, King et al. 1994, Grix 2010: 135-136). Furthermore, the book will utilise a case study approach, since its main advantage is to "gain a better understanding of the whole by focusing on a key part." (Gerring 2007: 1, cf. Della Porta 2008: 206-207) To be more precise, the research will draw on a complementary case study approach.[14] The main focus will be on analysing intergroup conflict in selected hotspot areas in North and West Belfast – not least because of the complexity of local conflict dynamics, but also for reasons of feasibility. Likewise, selected key findings will be compared and contrasted with respect to their manifestations in other flashpoint areas in Belfast, Derry/Londonderry and Portadown. Such a methodological procedure provides the opportunity both to concentrate on an in-depth exploration of particular cases and, through complementary comparison and juxtaposition with other cases, enrich the findings of the overall research project. With regard to the latter aim, research results will also be placed in the wider context of socio-economic and political developments in Northern Ireland. So, it is hoped to shed light on more common patterns, causal mechanisms and broader implications for the study of conflict in Northern Ireland, in particular, and in divided societies, in general. As with all case studies, it is implicitly assumed that a micro-macro link exists in social behaviour, i.e. between the opinions and behaviour of individuals and the actions and strategies of decision and policy-makers (Burnham et al 2004: 53-55, Gerring 2007). An important focus will be placed on identifying the key issues mattering to the communities and the governance policies aiming at addressing the major local issues. This research also has a comparative dimension, since one of its aims is to foster our understanding of the conditions under which violent intergroup conflict occurs. As Mary Fitzduff aptly points out,

> "People who are in conflict often think there is nowhere else like them. They feel their problems are not replicated elsewhere, but there is enormous learning. Every

---

[14] The complementary case study approach has been applied, though rather infrequently to date, to research in various social science fields, such as comparative policy analysis, community studies, governance, international development and inequality studies as well as studies on conflict management and resolution (cf. Bakke & Wibbels 2006, Crush & Frayne 2010, Green 2007, Heclo 1972, Smismans 2008).

conflict is different, but every conflict has also usually got something to offer to different parts of the world." (Fitzduff 2003)

The empirical field research forms a major part of this work, as much of the information and insights needed to explore the nature, dynamics and underlying mechanisms of intergroup conflict at the interface as well as the impact of the divided political elites' policies and governance strategies on the communities can best be collected and traced 'first-hand' on the ground. Furthermore, the research aims at exploring intergroup conflict from a bottom-up perspective and at investigating the interrelations of the micro-, meso- and macro-levels of society. This requires an empirically driven approach, since the interests and concerns of the different actors involved cannot be sufficiently determined from quantitative data or from academic literature and research reports alone (cf. Byrne 2005: 65, May 2011: 40-42).

The analytical-theoretical framework for this research project will be developed and designed in such a way that it is both capable of providing interpretive guidelines for the empirical research and sufficiently open to potential revisions resulting from the empirical findings.[15] So, the theories stand in a dynamic, triangular relationship (cf. Novy 2002: 17). This is illustrated by the following figure, which was inspired by the so-called "research wheel model of the research process" (cf. Burnham et al 2004: 46).

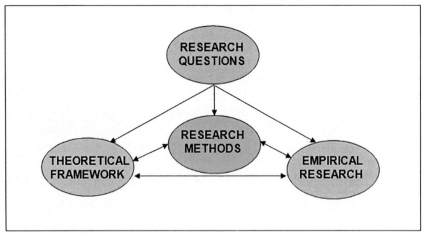

Figure 1. Triangular Research Model (figure created by the author)

---

[15] For this purpose, relevant concepts will be discussed in Chapter 2 on the theoretical-analytical framework.

Since the central research concern is to identify the impact of ethnonational divisions, of socio-economic class inequalities, and of hegemonic power interests of the divided political elites on local intergroup conflict in areas located at ethno-nationally defined interfaces in Northern Ireland, the analysis will proceed on three levels. Firstly, at the macro-social level, the power structure and power relations between the divided political elites will be at the centre of the analysis, which are reflected in the constitutional and institutional framework. Secondly, at the meso-social level, the focus will be on the relations between the elites and the interface and enclave communities under study. If and how these relations are affected by power-political interests will be assessed by examining contested policy areas that are deemed most relevant by the communities for their impact on the ground, i.e. whether and how far policy-making in these areas is effective or shaped by ideological content and partisan considerations. Thirdly, at the micro-social level, there will be an exploration of the living conditions of the interface and enclave communities on both sides of the ethno-national boundary, their attitudes and relations to the 'other' side. All three levels will be analysed from a developmental perspective by focusing on the dynamics of political and social change in the process from conflict to peace in Northern Ireland.

An initial literature review identified several theoretical approaches that potentially offer insightful explanations of how ethno-national, socio-economic and power-related aspects affect local intergroup conflict in Northern Ireland. What these approaches have in common is their comprehensive perspective, which is, nevertheless, also case-sensitive and takes the context, configuration and dynamics specific to particular conflicts in divided societies into account. This initial analytical-theoretical framework, as shown below, represents the starting point for further considerations. It will be revised in the subsequent chapter in order to provide the necessary guidance and interpretive frame for the local conflict analysis in Northern Ireland.

Analytical Level	Analytical Focus	Theoretical Approaches
Macro-Social	Power structure and power relations between the divided political elites	Power and Hegemony (Gramsci)
	Constitutional and institutional governance framework	Consociational Power-Sharing (e.g. Lijphart, McGarry, O'Leary)
Meso-Social	Relations between the elites and interface communities	Organic Intellectuals and Reactionary Forces (Gramsci)
	Governance policies addressing salient ethno-national identity and socio-economic issues (e.g. community relations, housing, education)	Policy-Making in Divided Societies (e.g. Guelke, Kevlihan, McEwen)
		Peacebuilding and Conflict Transformation approaches (e.g. Galtung)
Micro-Social	Interface community relations and living situation	Ethno-national Conflict (e.g. Horowitz)
		Relative Deprivation (Gurr)
		Conflict studies focusing on Territory, Borders, Segregation and Violence (e.g. Murtagh, Shirlow)
		Interface community studies (e.g. Jarman)

Table 1. Initial Analytical-Theoretical Framework for the Study of Local Intergroup Conflict in Northern Ireland (table created by the author)

The background information needed to prepare the ground for the field research and to contextualise the research topic is gathered through a comprehensive and systematic literature review of historical accounts and materialist and identity-based analyses of conflict in divided societies in general and of the particular case under study. The particular focus is placed on interface and enclave communities. For these purposes, quantitative statistical analyses will be conducted of survey and opinion poll data on Northern Ireland, and socio-economic and demographic statistics, community studies, policy documents, political pamphlets, speeches and other sources will also be consulted.

The objectives of the field research on interface and enclave communities in Northern Ireland are the following: firstly, to identify the key issues mattering to people living in these areas; secondly, to gain insights as to how these issues appear on the ground, especially with regard to their impact on community relations; thirdly, to explore the effects of socio-economic and ethnonational divisions on their living situation; fourthly, to gain insight into their interpretations of intergroup conflict and their views of the 'other' side: fifthly, to discover common patterns and dynamics of views, interpretations and interactions as well as of their causes; and sixthly, to gain a clearer picture of how these issues are addressed at the policy and governance levels, of both the intentions of the decision-makers and the perceptions of local community members, and thus in which way and to what extent the hegemonic power struggles of the divided political elites influence interface and enclave communities.

The field research in Northern Ireland was conducted in 2009, with several follow-up interviews until 2018. The main period was between beginning of June and end of July 2009. This was chosen due to the occurrence of significant divisive events potentially leading to intercommunal violence – i.e. the annual Orange Order parades and Loyalist bonfires celebrating the historic victory of the Protestant King William III over the Catholic King James II at the Battle of the Boyne. The field research was co-funded by a research grant from the University of Vienna and was hosted and supported by the Institute for Conflict Research (ICR) in Belfast.The generous support of the host organisation, which provided in-depth research guidance, expertise and office facilities, proved to be of immense benenefit to the field research. The field research included in-depth qualitative, semi-structured, narrative, personal interviews, informal talks, non-participant observation of community group meetings and events in working-class interface and enclave areas and other locations in Northern Ireland (cf. Hollander 2004, Manheim & Rich 1995, Ritchie et al 1994, Wengraf 2001). This mode of qualitative inquiry was selected because it will hopefully provide in-depth information about how people think about their ethno-national identity, class interests, socio-economic position, community situation and community relations and other important issues. The personal interviews were semi-structured along key topics and narrative in style, which gave the respondents the opportunity to tell their stories and express their views more openly and in greater depth. Besides, placing a particular focus on story-telling allows a better comprehension of what is going on within a certain section of society. Shadd Maruna, for instance, who has conducted extensive qualitative research into the reintegration of former prisoners, argues that

> "Self-narratives are explicitly contextual. Stories are cultural artefacts. One of the best ways to understand a particular subculture or group at a particular point in time is to analyze the stories that members of that group are telling." (Maruna 2002: 39)

Accordingly, the empirical analysis will present the most distinctive statements and illustrations of the interviewees in the original wording, thus depicting and accentuating their specific contexts and their subjective meanings. Hence, the presentation lays no claim to factual accuracy or truth of the opinions presented by the persons interviewed. No corrections have been applied to the interview responses, and additional contextual information has been added only where deemed necessary to improve understanding. The aim of this approach is to make the respondents' narratives more accessible to the reader and for the interpretation to ensure transparency and remain faithful to the original material. In addition, the presentation will be supplemented by informal talks with local residents and stakeholders to gain further insight into the in question. Their statements and opinions will be restated by the author in such a way that they preserve their original meanings.

An interview guideline was drafted that addressed the issues mentioned above, and, in addition, focused on individuals' perceptions of power, power relations and policy outcomes as well as on their personal experiences of intergroup conflict, assessment of the present political and socio-economic situation and future perspectives. In order to prepare for the field research, telephone interviews were held with experts on Northern Ireland and informal talks with Irish and British expatriates. The findings and impressions were incorporated into the revision of the field research interview guideline. Since the on-site field research dates back a considerable time, the objection might be raised that the empirical findings are outdated. Yet, in order to ensure the accurateness and validity of the results, there have been follow-ups to the field research, including telephone and Skype interviews, informal talks and conference visits. In addition, in-depth desk research has been done, focusing on recent developments in the communities under investigation. These updated findings will be included in the conclusions and outlook presented at the end of the main section of the book.

Specifically, the main empirical research focus in Northern Ireland is on conflict-prone and deprived interface and enclave communities and the wider working-class communities in which they are embedded. To this aim, two geographical areas were selected with local communities affected by inter-communal violence and socio-economic deprivation. One represents a rather negative example and one a quite positive example of recent developments in community relations and local living conditions. Thus, the localities chosen were: on the one hand, the working-class communities and interface areas of North Belfast with a specific focus on the Catholic/Nationalist/Republican community of Ardoyne and the nearby Protestant Loyalist community of the Shankill[16]; and, on the other, West Belfast with a specific focus on the interface area of the Protestant Loyalist enclave community of Suffolk and the adjacent Catholic/Nationalist/Republican community of Lenadoon. Ardoyne and the Shankill are both working-class communities with a long record of intercommunal violence and socio-economic deprivation, especially in the interface areas. By contrast, the situation in and between the communities of Suffolk and Lenadoon has improved over recent years.

In addition, the field research in Northern Ireland included several other locations that have also witnessed sustained and intensive violence and socio-economic deprivation. They included Protestant/Unionist/Loyalist and Catholic/Nationalist/Republican interface and enclave communities in other parts of North and West Belfast, in East Belfast, Derry/Londonderry and Portadown. This should allow identifying common patterns and differences, thus providing a more in-depth picture of the nature of local intergroup conflict. More specifically, the field research is expected to provide sufficient insight into the main issues, interests, needs and concerns of the divided communities. Moreover, light is to be shed on their views of and relations to the 'other' side – on sources of intergroup conflict, but also on opportunities for intergroup cooperation. In this respect, the field research in Northern Ireland is intended to reveal a clearer picture of the living conditions of Catholic and Protestant working-class interface communities in North and West Belfast and other urban locations. The major issues that matter to these communities should also be identified. Furthermore, the field research aims at pursuing the issue as to whether and how the power and hegemonic interests of the divided political elites affect the living conditions of the communities and community relations. A particular focus will be placed on examining the processes contributing to and instigating intergroup fear, prejudice and hostility, which in turn potentially lead to inter-community tensions and violence. On the macrolevel, the field research is to provide insights into current issues and dynamics of inter-community divisions in Northern Ireland. These results will inform the theoretical framework of the overall research project. Moreover, they are

---

[16] To be precise, as a local administrative unit, the city ward of Shankill is attached to West Belfast. However, the Shankill area subject to fieldwork for this research extends between North and West Belfast. The area, which is called the 'Greater Shankill' by many locals, encompasses the mostly Protestant/Unionist/Loyalist wards of Woodvale, Glencairn and Highfield.

intended to prepare the ground for drawing more general conclusions about the nature and dynamics of intergroup conflict and of the mechanisms at work in the divided society of Northern Ireland, in particular regarding the influence of ethno-national identity and socio-economic class aspects and of hegemonic forces and power relations on interface and enclave communities.

Here, an important methodological issue needs to be addressed. Apparently, there is a counter-argument advanced by Richard Rose that needs to be taken seriously. In his elaborate study on community relations and attitudes towards the state in Northern Ireland in the late 1960s, Rose states:

> "To enumerate all is not to quote all. Important as individual attitudes are, they cannot by themselves be used to explain how a regime manages to lack full legitimacy yet avoid repudiation, nor why some regimes survive while others fall. The attitudes of individuals are not translated automatically into policies of government." (Rose 1971: 201-202)

Yet Rose's arguments can be countered, since it is neither the aim nor the intention of this research to provide a complete picture of hegemonic power relations and their impact on intergroup conflict in interface and enclave communities in Northern Ireland. This research is also only indirectly concerned with the questions mentioned by Rose – however interesting they may be. The issues of legitimacy deficiency and regime survival will, however, be incorporated into the analyses of hegemonic structures of governance and power relations. Furthermore, it is an implicit research assumption that there is no automatic link between individual attitudes and governance policy outcomes. Regarding the conflict analysis, the important point here is that individual attitudes and views can impact governance policies and institutions, if they find expression in collective action through grassroots civil society organisations, local community groups and leaders. This may lead to a change in existing policies that affects the communities. On a larger scale, the expression of common attitudes through civil society and/or social movements may even trigger off a change in societal governance and hegemonic power relations (Gramsci 1971 & 2000, Lederach 1997: 40-44, Shapiro 2005). These various ways in which the divided communities and elites are interrelated are of major concern to this analysis of intergroup conflict in Northern Ireland.

The interview partners were selected on the basis of desk research and by drawing on the knowledge and recommendations of local informants and experts. The selection of the interviewees was made according to the three levels of analysis, aiming at a balanced number for each of the key groups involved in the conflict and at each analytical level. At the micro-social or local level, this included local residents from interface and enclave communities. At the meso-social or intermediary level, interviews were conducted with people who were said to be influential in shaping local opinion on key issues – such as community activists, representatives from local civil society organisations (CSOs) and non-governmental organisations (NGOs), former paramilitary combatants, local politicians, police officers, doctors, teachers and intellectuals. At the macro-social or state level, the interviewees consisted of officials of statutory agencies and government bodies as well as representatives of political parties. An important goal was to interview an equal number of people from both communities, which could almost be achieved with a distribution of 16 Catholics and 13 Protestants. In addition, several interviews were conducted with experts including policy advisors, conflict researchers and academics. In total, this book contains the voices of 37 respondents that were directly quoted and 15 more voices whose views were implicitly incorporated into the analysis and interpretation. Due to the sensitivity of the issues under investigation, such as the manifestation of power structures and community relations on the ground, it was deemed necessary in some cases to conceal the specific research aim to the respondents. The intention was to retrieve information on the motivation behind certain actions and the implementation of policies affecting people's lives (cf. Davies 2008: 92-93). Most of the interviews were recorded on audiotape and subsequently transcribed. In the rare instances where respondents did not grant permission for the interviews to be recorded, only notes were taken. Moreover, in the informal talks and meetings, the main points, core statements and informative quotes were documented in writing.

Conducting field research into sensitive conflict issues raises several ethical concerns. It is thus crucial to avoid regarding "people as objects without due regard to their subjectivity, needs and the impact of the research on their situation." (Smyth 2001: 5) The data collected needs to be properly contextualised, i.e. placed in a meaningful and real context of the respective case studies in Northern Ireland. So, the field research strategy is based on the strategy of 'going local', i.e. of becoming familiar with the culture, customs and traditions of the local population and engaging in local activities in order to gain trust but without losing critical distance to the research subject. The approach, which is commonly used in ethnographic research, "involves the study of groups and people as they go about their everyday lives." (Emerson et al. 2011: 1) It will guide especially the interviewing and documentation process of this research. As George Gaskell points out, "the understanding of the life worlds of respondents and specified social groupings is the *sine qua non* of qualitative interviewing." (Gaskell 2000: 39) Consequently, as the overall premise, every field research activity has to be considered as an acquisition of knowledge within the framework of everyday life (cf. Novy 2002: 9-10).[17]

Moreover, the sensitivity of the topic might involve a risk or even a threat to the interview partners and informants, particularly to those with vulnerable backgrounds and involvement in the conflict, which requires special awareness in the dissemination of the field research data. This inevitably raises privacy and data protection issues (cf. Brannen 1988, Dickson-Swift et al. 2007, Lee 1993: 179-182). So, as a general rule, the names of those who were interviewed in their private or professional capacities are disclosed only upon prior approval, i.e. upon verbal consent given at the interview. The names of interview partners have been anonymised upon request through the use of unique pseudonyms in the form of fictitious and unencumbered first names and surnames. The anonymisation of respondents is indicated in a footnote. Informants and persons who provided background information will not be mentioned by name.

Another important issue is reflexivity, which "broadly defined, means a turning back on oneself, a process of self-reference" (Davies 2008: 4). The fact that there is always a connection between researchers and the object of their research raises the question "as to whether the results of research are artefacts of the researcher's presence and inevitable influence on the research process" (Davies 2008: 3). In order to avoid this, it is necessary for a researcher to set herself/himself in relation to the object of research and to describe her/his personal background and history. To this end, and also to ensure at least partial reflexivity, a journal was kept during the field research stay in Northern Ireland, where anecdotes and reflections on personal experiences were written down. These field notes also serve as so-called 'ethnographic vignettes', i.e. as illustrations in the text to point to particular structural relations between the key issues under study and how these issues are manifested on the ground (cf. Willis & Trondman 2000).

The field research approach draws on interpretive social research methodology. In seeing the world as constructed from individuals' views and their

---

[17] This, however, should not be confused with the idea of 'going native', which was avoided as a field research strategy, since it bears the risk of becoming too involved and entangled as a member of the group under observation and thus of losing distance and objectivity (cf. Fontana & Frey 1994).

social and physical world, interpretive paradigms transcend the duality of objectivism and relativism. Instead, the world is seen as an interactive relationship between peoples' views and their respective social and physical reality. In interpretive social research, it is important to distinguish between subjective and objective meanings. The meaning is subjective in as far as individual actors attach significance to their actions and objective, if the actions are meaningful independently of individual awareness. Consequently, it is the task of the interpreting researcher to elaborate this more abstract and structured collective meaning and to place it in the wider social context (Novy 2002: 7-8; cf. Lueger 2001).

To ensure as much reliability as possible, the information obtained in the field and the interpretations developed were regularly cross-checked with experts on the topic and with the literature and statistical data already available (cf. Davies 2008: 97). The field research results were analysed following a two-stage process, which draws on qualitative content analysis methodology (cf. Bernard 2000: 456-458, Mayring 2000 & 2003, Schreier 2012). According to Peter Mayring, the qualitative content analysis can be defined "as an approach of empirical, methodological controlled analysis of texts within their context of communication, following content analytical rules and step by step models, without rash quantification." (Mayring 2000: 5) Hence, in the first stage of the field research analysis, the interviews were classified according to the respondents' group identity and affiliation and their position and function within the group to either the micro-social/local, meso-social/intermediary or macro-social/state levels. Following a mapping and clustering of the interviews into respondents holding strong, medium or weak oppositional views and positions, those with high levels of representativeness and expressiveness for each group were fully transcribed. The remainder of the interviews were analysed through meaning condensation, i.e. through identifying common units of meaning and transcribing and interpreting these relevant excerpts from the respective interviews (cf. Kvale 2007: 106-108). Subsequently, in the second phase, the textual content analysis of the interviews was carried out. The responses were grouped into topical categories, and the statements were quantified according to frequencies. Those statements that were deemed most relevant for explaining and illustrating a particular issue were selected and integrated into the analysis of the local interface and enclave communities. The interpretation was performed by means of the analytical-theoretical framework, which was open to revisions in case of explanatory shortcomings. Thus, this analytical procedure bears a resemblance to the qualitative content analysis' step model of deductive category application, as is shown by the following chart.

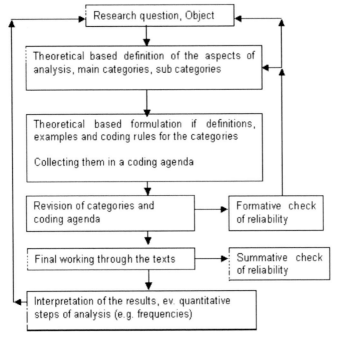

Figure 2. Method of Interview Data Analysis (based on Mayring 2000: 14)

RESEARCH CONTRIBUTION

As was mentioned earlier, it is assumed that three dimensions play a crucial role in improving understanding of local intergroup conflict in Northern Ireland: ethno-national divisions, socio-economic class inequalities and hegemonic power relations. Arguably, the study of these dimensions and their specific interrelations has so far not received sufficient attention in the field of conflict and peace studies. The present book seeks to address this deficiency. Specifically, by exploring the persistence of intergroup conflict in interface and enclave communities in Belfast and other locations from the perspective of these three dimensions, the study will make a contribution to the overall body of knowledge of the Northern Ireland conflict especially in two respects:

- It will contribute to the study of intercommunal conflict, particularly at local level, in the divided society of Northern Ireland.

- It will enhance our knowledge and understanding of the contentious issues and concerns of the people living in these community areas located close to the conflict interface in Northern Ireland.

- It will also shed light to shed light as to whether certain political actors have vested power interests in maintaining tensions and divisions between working-class interface communities.

Moreover, by providing an overview of the context and development of the Northern Ireland conflict and its aftermath and by analysing and interpreting the deeper and more general meaning of local conflict dynamics, the book also extends its contribution to the wider field of peace and conflict studies. In particular,

- it will demonstrate the relevance of an empirically-driven focus on particularly deprived communities for the study of local intergroup conflicts in divided societies.

Finally, there are two other general aspects to which this research will contribute. One is theoretical, in that

- it will facilitate theory-building and thus enable a better conceptual understanding of the impact and interdependence of ethnic-national divisions, socio-economic class inequalities and hegemonic power interests on the study of conflict between local communities.

The other one is practical, namely that

- it will provide insights into the effects of governance policies on local communities, which may be useful to practitioners and decision-makers in the fields of community development and community relations.

2 "WHY CAN'T THEY GET ALONG WITH EACH OTHER?"
TOWARDS A THEORETICAL FRAMEWORK FOR ANALYSING CONFLICT AT THE INTERFACE

"To tell the truth is revolutionary."
(Antonio Gramsci 1921)[18]

"The only thing that permits us to
acquiesce in an erroneous theory
is the lack of a better one."
(John Rawls 1971)[19]

The aim of the chapter is to elaborate the analytical-theoretical framework for this study of local intergroup conflict in the divided society of Northern Ireland. In particular, this framework will provide guidance for the analysis and interpretation of the empirical research on working-class interface communities in Belfast and other Northern Irish places. At this point, it should be noted that the theoretical concepts discussed will not be applied in a strict and comprehensive sense but only in a selective and eclectic manner; i.e. they are extracted and used with the aim of clarifying the context, information value and conclusiveness of the research results. In any case, particular care will be taken not to distort the original meaning of the concepts used. Starting with a brief account of the genesis and development of intergroup conflict and a general overview and discussion of the main branches of conflict studies, the chapter will proceed with an account and elaboration of the factors considered key to the study. At first, the issue of conflicting ethno-national identities is examined and then the issue of socio-economic class inequalities is considered. Besides conceptual discussions, conflict studies will be presented that are deemed relevant to exploring these issues. Building on that, the concepts of power and governance will be discussed, and particularly Gramsci's approach to hegemony and power relations and its explanatory value in the specific context of community divisions in Northern Ireland. Subsequently, the

---

[18] This quote by Ferdinand Lassalle, a Prussian-German writer, socialist and political activist appeared in 1921 in the first issue of 'L'Ordine Nuovo', a Communist newspaper edited by Antonio Gramsci.

[19] Rawls 1971: 4.

theoretical implications will be elaborated for the specific geographical locus of the study on interface and enclave communities. In conclusion, the theoretical considerations will be synthesised and integrated into a guiding framework for the empirical study of the ethno-national, socio-economic class and hegemonic power dimensions of local intergroup conflict in Northern Ireland.

THE PERENNIAL PROBLEM OF INTERGROUP CONFLICT

"Some things will never change. There is nothing that can be done about it." Is there anyone who has not heard this or a similar saying, or who has not thought that way him- or herself at some point? Such supposedly immutable circumstances are commonly referred to as, for example, the social system, the political power structure and relations, or the general nature of people – be it good or evil or any shade in-between. There are many people who hold a strong belief in the permanent character of certain socio-economic conditions, such as the market economy, capitalism and globalisation or the condition of intergroup antagonism that can lead to violent conflict within or between states. In such a way, these phenomena have become constructed realities, and all too often also self-fulfilling and self-perpetuating prophecies. However, there is also the reverse side of the coin. As Rose puts it,

> "In every political situation two equal and opposite assumptions compete for favour – the belief that everything will always continue as it has been, or that trends already immanent will make the future different from the past." (Rose 1971: 359)

In societies ridden by intergroup conflict, this belief in political and social change, which is ideally shared collectively, is one of the fundamental premises for finding common ground between the conflicting groups and for moving towards peaceful conflict resolution.

Intergroup conflict, which arises when two or more groups believe that their interests are incompatible or even irreconcilable with no agreement seemingly being possible, is a phenomenon inherent in the history of societal development. In fact, such conflicts extend to the early ages of humanity up to the present day. The origins of collective violence can be traced back to the first significant economic boom in world history, which occurred around 3000 BCE in Mesopotamian times due to favourable climate conditions. The growth in the production of tools, weapons, agricultural and other manufactured goods in the emerging urban centres and their exchange with the wider region for raw materials and labour created the need for the armed protection of these trade routes and for urban fortification and armament of the city-states. Political power became more and more centralised, institutionalised and vested in the hands of oligarchic elites. In order to expand their sphere of power, influence and control over resources, these elites frequently waged border wars with their contiguous adversaries. Subsequently, from the period of the Roman Empire onwards, the introduction of new materials, weapons and innovative warfare techniques spread these localised conflicts and wars over ever greater distances.

With the advent of the Industrial Revolution, the evolvement of modern capitalism and its progressive division of labour, and the formation of the nation-state in the early 19th century, more complex economic systems, social relations and political structures emerged. However, this has not diminished the tendency towards conflict. To the contrary, it significantly changed the way conflicts are conducted, which led to a greater number and intensity of conflicts and wars. The tribal character, based on feudal power relations and barter exchange, which had characterised conflicts in earlier days, was trans-formed into fierce and often violent struggles over socio-economic and cultural resources, fought with the use of technology. The root causes for these 'modern' conflicts can be found in national, ethnic, religious and class rivalries as well as elite struggles for political power.[20] In the industrialised, capitalist world, this tendency towards conflict was mitigated by the development of democratic institutions and the formation of modern political parties and interest groups. New conflicts arose from the continuously increasing competition between and diversification of interests within and between societies.

The leading role in shaping the global economic and political system that the European Great Powers, the UK, France, Russia, the Austrian Empire and Prussia, played until the eve of the First World War not only led to an increase in interstate warfare, but also nurtured conflicts within the boundaries of their empires. In order to maintain and expand their empires and, ultimate-

---

[20] A striking example of armed conflict between tribal and modern civilisations is the territorial war over land and resource control between the troops of the United States Federal Government and the native American population. The war lasted throughout the second half of the 19th century and ending with the final defeat of the plains Indians at the 'Battle of Wounded Knee' in 1890. This battle completed the Indian expulsion from the American West and marked the end of their traditional culture and values. From then on, they were assigned to legally designated territories called 'Indian reservations'. For an extensive and illuminating account of the history of the Native Americans and their fight against the U.S. Army and settlers in the late 19th century, see Brown 1970.

ly, to achieve hegemonic control over the global system, they waged great-power wars against one another, wars against weaker states, and, in the 18th and 19th centuries, colonial and imperial wars in Africa, the Americas and Asia. This period of European imperialism and colonialism and its concomitant expropriation and enslavement of large sections of the native populations caused many internal upheavals and civil wars, which destabilised the colonial empires, eventually leading to their demise. In this respect, two prominent European examples were the Easter Rising in Ireland in 1916 and the subsequent Irish Civil War, marking the end of the British empire in the southern part of Ireland, and the two Balkan Wars 1912/13, in which Serbia gained control of its entire ethnic territories, including Kosovo, from the declining Ottoman Empire (Bartlett 2010: 378-379, Hall 2002: 142).

The cataclysmic experience of the First World War led to the establishment of the League of Nations in 1919, which represented the first permanent international organisation whose principal mandate was to maintain global peace and security. However, the League failed in its mission, and in the course of the rise of Fascism and the global economic crisis of 1929 war clouds gathered over Europe once more. It should not take long and the Second World War broke out, which once again brought massive violence and destruction, and this on an even greater scale than the previous one. In its aftermath, the United Nations (UN) was established, building on and extending the League of Nations' peace-keeping aims and principles. The shift of inter-state warfare away from Europe to other parts of the world, the Cold War between the United States of America (USA) and the Soviet Union (USSR), and, following the latter's fall, the emergent new US imperialism, reshuffled inter- and intra-state relations between ethno-national groups, creating new sources for intergroup conflict. Moreover, the long-standing ethno-national divisions that existed within several states could not be resolved. In Europe, this is demonstrated by internecine intra-state conflicts that have erupted since the 1960s in Northern Ireland, the Basque Country, Corsica, Cyprus, Kosovo, Bosnia and Herzegovina and other parts of former Yugoslavia and beyond (Harff & Gurr 2004: 19-26, Jacoby 2008: 1-8 & 160-178, Kegley 2008: 525-532, Levy 2007, Spruyt 1994).

In the late 20th century, the evolution of information technology, the proliferation of the mass media and the growth of the communications and entertainment industries, which, according to Robert Putnam, "had become the very foundation of a new economic era" (Putnam 2000: 216), led to constantly more complex systems of governance and administration. However, this century-long period of transformation did not resolve ethno-national conflict and socio-economic strife, but nurtured new divisions and power struggles, also aggravating fragmentation within society. A further challenge is posed by the growing waves of migrants from poor to rich countries, mainly caused by increasingly uneven capitalist development, which in turn is driven by the hegemonic interests of powerful elites in the control and exploitation of global markets. Moreover, an unrestrained laissez-faire market capitalism poses a potential threat to social stability and peace.[21] Another persistent characteristic of many domestic conflicts is their bitter struggle over territorial claims. Unlike the globalisation discourse, which postulates a deterritorialised and borderless world with an increasingly seamless flow of goods, capital and people, territoriality, even in its most primordial form, is still a key cause of violent conflict (cf. Coakley 2003, Kahler & Walter 2006). Finally, and notably, the apparently accelerating pace of climate change and its potentially disastrous ecological, economic and social impacts on a global scale could be another major cause for internecine conflict (cf. O'Loughlin & Hendrix 2019, Ryan 2019, Werrell & Femia 2018).

So, essentially it can be said that even now, almost two decades after the turn of the millennium, in the age of postmodernism, globalisation, neoliberalism and sustained global economic, financial and ecological crisis, rival ethno-national identities, resource inequalities and conflicting power interests continue to be salient factors in ongoing intergroup tensions and occasional outbreaks of violence in many deeply divided societies (cf. Berberoglu 2004, Bieber 2006, Fisher 2001, Hartmann et al 2009, Horowitz 2000; Khazanov 2005, Kramer & Džihić 2006, Mansvelt Beck 2005, Peleg 2007, Preiss & Brunner 2013, Pullan & Baillie 2013, Richmond 1999, Verme 2004).

However, there is also more positive news. The fact that the general public today has much more access than ever before to information about the brutal realities of violent conflict has led to a significant rise in public awareness and global concern. Not least due to its increased civilian impact, as Mary Smyth points out, "violent conflict has a worse press now than ever before as a means of resolving disputes (Smyth 2001: 1)." Notwithstanding this negative publicity, however, violent intergroup conflicts continue to persist – be it at

---

[21] The detrimental consequences of laissez-faire market capitalism have already been indicated by Karl Polanyi in his seminal analysis of the economic and social changes brought about by the 'great transformation' of the Industrial Revolution (Polanyi [1944] 2001).

the international, domestic or, as in this study, the local level. Indeed, given more recent developments, such as the Arab Spring or the Islamic State's (IS) war in Syria and Iraq and Islamist terrorist attacks across the globe, there is palpable evidence that violent conflict is on the rise again (cf. IEP 2017). Yet, there is another encouraging sign. Throughout modern times, civil society activists and community groups have repeatedly engaged in ending large-scale violence and transforming intergroup conflicts by non-violent, peaceful means. In fact, as studies have shown, non-violent action and resistance have proven significantly more effective than violent measures in bringing about social and political change towards peace and democratisation (cf. Chenoweth & Stephan 2011, HIIK 2018, Pinckney 2018).[22]

GENERAL CONSIDERATIONS FOR THEORISING AND ANALYSING INTERGROUP CONFLICT IN DIVIDED SOCIETIES

So far, reference has been made to concepts like 'ethnic group', 'ethno-national identity', 'nationalism', 'socio-economic inequality', 'class', 'deprivation', 'power', 'hegemony', 'governance', 'sectarianism', 'interface communities' and 'enclaves', and 'conflict transformation' and 'conflict resolution'. As a review of the relevant literature has shown, these concepts are regarded as key to studies of local intergroup conflict in divided societies, such as Northern Ireland.

In a general sense, human conflict can be defined as "a social situation involving perceived incompatibilities in goals or values between two or more parties in a relationship, attempts by the parties to control each other, and antagonistic feelings by the parties toward each other." (Fisher 1990: 6) Conflict may occur in various spheres of life – both at inter-personal and inter-group levels. Considering the research focus of this work, the specific question here is: what are the potential causes for violent conflict between antagonistic groups within a divided society, particularly between those who are

---

[22] The study by Erica Chenoweth and Maria Stephan, for instance, examined 323 different violent and non-violent movements with more than 1,000 participants from 1900 to 2006, which aimed to achieve self-determination, remove a repressive regime or expel a foreign armed force. They concluded that non-violent movements are twice as likely to succeed as violent ones and that they often significantly increase the chances of transition to a more peaceful and democratic post-conflict government (Chenoweth & Stephan 2011: 192-231).

located close to a communal interface? This research will concentrate on the level of groups and not of individuals, because, generally speaking, group affiliations are in many ways formative for individual identity development. As Robert Fisher points out, "all individuals are members of social groups, either by birth or by choice, and the group identifications that one carries form the central element of one's social identity." (Fisher 2006: 182) Thus, people tend favourably to evaluate and describe commitment to their groups, which, as many social identity theorists believe, heightens their feelings of self-esteem. However, there is also the tendency among group members to conform to group norms and opinions and to demarcate themselves by devaluating and disrespecting other groups. This forms a potential source of violent intergroup conflict, especially in the case of antagonistic ethno-national groups within a divided society, where hostile images and threats have a crucial function in forging group bonds and in maintaining and reinforcing group boundaries (Fisher 2006: 182-183, Forsyth 2010: 430, Jenkins 2008: 112-113, Jesse & Williams 2005: 4-5).

At this point, an important argument needs to be addressed against the common usage of the concept of group as the main analytical unit for dealing with ethno-national conflict. Rogers Brubaker warns of imposing "over-ethnicized or overly groupist interpretations of (and interventions in) situations of conflict and violence" (Brubaker 2002: 176), since this would have several negative implications. First, it would lead to regarding ethno-national groups as homogeneous, thus turning a blind eye to the processes and dynamics of group formation, internal composition and stratification. Features considered as typical of the group, for instance, may be incorrectly attributed to members who do not in fact possess these characteristics as individuals. Secondly, viewing ethno-national conflict as being caused by ethno-national groups would neglect other interests (such as class, ideology and status) and the significance of ethno-political leaders and organisations. In Brubaker's view, these leaders and organisations are frequently the protagonists of conflict, claiming to act on behalf of their ethno-national community. Thirdly, regarding groups as given and high levels of groupness as the underlying cause of violent conflict would impede identification of the "processes through which groupness tends to develop and crystallize and those through which it may subside." (Brubaker 2001: 177) To put it in a nutshell: according to Brubaker, high levels of groupness are more likely to be the result of violent conflict than of voluntary group identification, and thus the formation of groups should be regarded as contingent events (cf. Brubaker 2002: 168-

177). Notwithstanding his arguments, an objection could be made when it is a question of intergroup conflicts in deeply divided societies such as Northern Ireland. For, as a consequence of the long-standing history and legacy of violent conflict, the groups became permanent phenomena, in which distinct ethno-national and cultural values were not only solidified, but group membership and boundary maintenance also became essential for personal security and protection (cf. Barth 1969: 9-38).

A vast number of studies have investigated the specific nature of intergroup conflicts in deeply divided societies. Yet, scholars profoundly disagree not only on how and why these conflicts have emerged, but also on whether they can be traced back to a singular, primordial cause or to a multiplicity of constituent factors. Identity-based approaches regard rival and often incompatible group identities as the fundamental reason for conflict. In this reading, the key to successful conflict resolution lies in the ability to find appropriate means to accommodate competing claims for the recognition of difference, which should be reflected in effective and inclusive identity politics and governance strategies and policies (cf. Fraser 2000, Kenny 2004, Young 1990 & 2000). For materialist and resource-based interpretations view intergroup conflicts as determined by class and socio-economic inequalities, discrimination and power imbalances. Given their focus on resources, they suggest that, in order to resolve violent conflict, these group disparities would need to be addressed through a reconfiguration and rearrangement of the social and political order in a way ensuring effective resource equality (cf. Katz 1965, Nimni 1994, Peleg 2007). Finally, there are also integrative approaches, which draw on elements from both conflict research traditions, thus aiming at offering a more comprehensive framework for conflict analysis and resolution (cf. Galtung 1990, Gurr 1970).

Moreover, conflict studies differ substantially in the methodology applied, depending on whether they regard the conflict causes as rigid or exposed to change. Walker Connor, for instance, uses a static model that describes intergroup conflicts as primarily caused by the rigidity of rival ethno-national group identities which are rooted in kinship and all its other elements as causally determined (cf. Connor 1994). Timothy Sisk, although agreeing with Connor that incompatible ethnicities and nationalities represent the main reason for identity conflicts, takes a more differentiated stance in that he distinguishes between the stable 'background conditions' and 'escalatory dynamics' of such conflicts (cf. Sisk 1996: 11-25). In his seminal theory of ethnic conflict, Donald Horowitz argues along similar lines, but also differs in that he regards the degree to which ethnicity is pervasive in deeply divided societies as variable, depending on a number of mainly group-based and psychological rather than economic factors. In his view, ethnic affiliations have a broad impact, not only on social, but also on family and organisational life (cf. Horowitz 2000: 3-54). Conversely, Brubaker develops a dynamic and inter-relational approach, focusing on the individual level rather than groups and regarding the relations, processes, and dynamics of multiple factors as constituent for conflicts of rival identities (cf. Brubaker 1996 & 2002).

A further important concept for studying the manifestations of local conflict is sectarianism. According to John Brewer, sectarianism can be defined as "the determination of actions, attitudes and practices by beliefs about religious difference, which results in them invoked as the boundary marker to represent social stratification and conflict." (Brewer 1992: 358-359) It thus consists of "a whole cluster of ideas, beliefs, myths and demonology about religious difference which are used to make religion a social marker, to assign different attributes to various religious groups and to make derogatory remarks about others." (Brewer 1992: 359) So, sectarianism is more than just a prejudice or attitude and includes behaviours, treatment and policies informed by religious difference. Since religion, as argued and specified before, is considered in this research as a constitutive element of ethno-national identity, the phenomenon of sectarianism is regarded as referring to ethno-national difference and ethno-national groups. In deeply divided societies, sectarianism can take on various forms, ranging from negative stereotypes, pejorative language and psychological harassment to physical intimidation and flagrant intergroup violence. Moreover, given its often deep-seated nature, sectarianism can also be manifested in different forms of direct and indirect discrimination at individual, group and institutional levels (Brewer 1992, Higgins & Brewer 2004).

Finally, there is another relevant conceptual issue, which concerns the question of how to define and assess the desired outcome of the process of transition from conflict to peace in a divided society like Northern Ireland. In this respect, 'conflict transformation' has often been employed as the generic term denoting this , because, as has been argued, this best acknowledges the fact that conflicts cannot necessarily be resolved, but should be viewed as being transformed into new peaceful dynamics instead (cf. Galtung 2007, Ramsbotham et al 2012). Conflict transformation is a quite recent concept within the broader field of peace and conflict studies. Since being coined in the early 1990s, there has been a debate on its conceptualisation and classification. Peace and conflict scholars disagree as to whether conflict transformation should be regarded as an integral part and, likewise, the most profound stage of peacebuilding and conflict resolution or as a separate, more comprehensive endeavour. Furthermore, the terms 'conflict transformation', 'conflict resolution' as well as sometimes also 'conflict settlement', 'conflict management', 'conflict engagement' and 'conflict regulation' have often been used interchangeably (Ramsbotham et al 2012: 8-14). Although there is no generally agreed definition of the term, it can be gathered from the substantial and growing body of research that in essence 'conflict transformation' refers to a holistic and consensual process of initiating and sustaining systemic change by addressing the underlying conflict causes, mechanisms and interests and transforming them into peaceful outcomes. In this regard, Johan Galtung's conceptual classification of peace has proven to be an eminently useful measure and instrument for assessing the effectiveness of peacebuilding and conflict transformation efforts. Thus, Galtung draws the distinction between 'negative peace' and 'positive peace'. In a nutshell, in the context of armed conflicts and civil wars, the state of 'negative peace' is achieved when large-scale direct physical violence has ceased. In contrast, the state of 'positive peace' requires moving beyond the mere absence of direct violence and eliminating sources of both structural and cultural violence. This means, on the one hand, systematically eliminating all forms of societal injustices that prevent certain categories of people from meeting their basic needs, such as those caused by mechanisms of discrimination, marginalisation, exclusion, intimidation, harassment and other forms of psychological harm. On the other hand, it requires addressing those symbolic aspects of culture that can be used to legitimise violence in its direct or structural form, such as flags, anthems, parades, inflammatory speeches and other public displays of supremacy. This then forms the foundation for building a culture of peace that promotes reconciliation and cooperation between all parties to create conditions of coexistence based on social, economic and political justice (Galtung 1969 & 1990, Galtung & Fischer 2013: 35-70). As increasingly recognised by researchers and practitioners, efforts for conflict transformation should focus not only on political institution-building and economic reconstruction, but equally on promoting civil society development and engagement. Therefore, ideally speaking, an approach to conflict transformation should be multi-level, multidimensional, multidisciplinary, multicultural, analytical, normative, theoretical, and with an applied empirical focus (cf. Berghof Foundation 2012: 22-27,

Darby 2001, Galtung 2007, Lederach 1997, Mac Ginty 2010, Ramsbotham et al 2012: 8 & 31).

CONFLICTING ETHNO-NATIONAL IDENTITIES

What is a nation? What creates and constitutes a person's national and/or ethnic identity, her/his sentiment of belonging to a particular nation? What are the main features of national identity? How does the concept of a nation differ from ethnicity? And what is (ethno-) nationalism? These are questions, which are very difficult – if not even impossible – to answer without relying on prior assumptions. Thus, it will be apparent that none of these terms can be defined objectively. There are no clear-cut definitions. The concepts intersect and overlap in many ways.

There is considerable ambiguity when it comes to the task of defining what constitutes a national or ethnic group, or, as the compound term combining them both runs, an ethno-national group (Fenton & May 2002: 6). Arguing in line with most traditional and contemporary theorists of national identity and ethnicity, the concepts of 'nation' and 'ethnicity' cannot be defined by objective criteria (cf. Anderson 1991, Gellner 2006, Hobsbawm 1992, Miller 1995, Smith 1986, Tamir 1995, Weber 1997). A national or ethnic group can thus be seen, following Benedict Anderson's diction, as an 'imagined community' of people with an affiliation to a particular territory, which share the belief in certain common cultural characteristics and heritage (cf. Anderson 1991: 6-7). Its members are tied together by their will to belong voluntarily – in an ideal sense, to use Ernest Renan's famous phrase, in 'a daily plebiscite' ('*un plébiscite de tous les jours*')[23] – to the same social, cultural, legal and political community (Gellner 1998: 3-4, Miller 1995: 19 & 22, Renan 1996: 52-54, Smith 1986: 136-137, Tamir 1995: 68, Weber 1997: 18-19). Notably, although the existence of these social collectivities is taken for granted by most theorists, the question of "how they exist – and how they came to exist – is much disputed." (Brubaker 1996: 13)

What now characterises the difference between a national and an ethnic community? A feasible way to distinguish between the two concepts is to regard ethnicity as one of the possible constitutive features of the nation, among others, including a common culture, language or religion. According

---

[23] This definition of a nation was given by the French historian Ernest Renan in his conference lecture, delivered at the Sorbonne on 11 March 1882 (cf. Renan 1992 & 1996).

to Max Weber, ethnic groups are those "human groups that entertain a subjective belief in their common descent because of similarities of physical type or customs or both, or because of memories of colonization and migration." (Weber 1997: 18-19) In David Miller's remarks, the relationship between nation and ethnicity arguably becomes clearer. Many nations have their origins in ethnic communities, and ethnicity, in turn, may nurture the formation of new national identities.[24] An ethnic group is likely to regard itself as a nation and develop nationalist sentiments when it perceives its identity to be threatened. This is frequently the case when an external group wields more power in the state (Miller 1995: 20). This results in an ethno-national group. In other words, members of groups unified by a common ethno-national identity define their national affiliation in ethnic terms. Frequently, such groups make demands for autonomy and self-determination for their ethnic nation. This is then called 'ethno-nationalism', a term that was coined by Connor, who regards it as a synonym for a specific, primordial form of nationalism. Accordingly, ethno-nationalism "connotes identification with and loyalty to one's nation", which ethnically defined is "a group of people who believe that they are ancestrally related." (Connor 1994: xi) Ethno-national identities are thus often defined through a common language, culture, religion and ancestral ideology (cf. Smith 2004). However, the opposite may also be true that "even nations that originally had an exclusive ethnic character may come, over time, to embrace a multitude of different ethnicities", such as the (US) American nation (Miller 1995: 20). To cut the story short, per definition there can be multi-ethnic nations, but there cannot be multi-national ethnicities (Miller 1995: 19-21). Taking the case of Northern Ireland into account, it can be said that, despite all recent constitutional and institutional efforts for rapprochement and reconciliation, the two distinct communities still predominantly consider themselves as belonging to separate ethno-national groups with homogeneous ethnic and national identities.

Furthermore, there are several 'multinational' states, i.e. states exercising their authority over citizens belonging to different nations. This brings us to the confusion of 'nation' and 'state', which are often employed as synonyms in colloquial usage and slipshod academic practice. However, clarifying the

---

[24] In the social sciences, identity is a rather slippery concept and hard to define precisely. Following Jenkins' general, minimal definition, identity "denotes the ways in which individuals and collectivities are distinguished in their relations with other individuals and collectivities." (Jenkins 2008: 18)

relationship between nations and states is important, especially in view of evaluating the right to national self-determination, which is often raised by competing national groups within a divided state. Following Weber's classical definition, "a state is a human community that (successfully) claims the monopoly of the legitimate use of physical force within a given territory." (Weber 1991b: 78) So, a nation is a community of people that aspires to political self-determination through control of the state apparatus (Miller 1995: 18-19). In a similar way, a distinction can be drawn between 'nationality' and 'citizenship'. Whereas 'nationality' "is in essence a cultural concept which binds people on the basis of shared identity, … citizenship is a political concept deriving from people's relationship to the state." (McCrone & Kiely 2000: 25) A further conceptual inaccuracy and confusion that needs to be remedied refers to the commonly employed equation of 'society', 'state' and 'nation'. However, in empirical terms there are several cases where the boundaries of society neither coincide with the territorial borders of the state nor with the nation (cf. McCrone & Kiely 2000: 22). This boundary overlap is especially pronounced in deeply divided societies, such as Northern Ireland, where societal bonds have usually been rather weak and the state as such is contested between two rival ethno-national groups. Both groups also maintain a strong identification with their respective parent nation-state. Therefore, the above-mentioned concepts of 'society', 'state' and 'nation' will be regarded as distinct terms in this work.

National, ethnic and ethno-national groups have another defining feature in common, which is their commitment to group demarcation and boundary creation and maintenance, achieved through (ethno-) nationalism (cf. Barth 1969: 11-14, Conversi 1995). There are two important characteristics that differentiate ethnic from national communities. One has been mentioned already, i.e. that ethnicity can be regarded as a constitutive element – among others – of the nation. The other differentiator is that national identity and nationalism, as the ideology in which it is embedded, inherently refer to the political realm, whereas ethnicity and ethnic identity do not necessarily have to include a political component. As Eric Hobsbawm aptly remarked,

> "Nationalism is a political programme, and in historic terms, a fairly recent one. It holds that groups defined as 'nations' have the right to, and therefore ought to, form territorial states of the kind that have become standard since the French Revolution." (Hobsbawm 2012: 256)

Yet, a problem is inherent in this state-building enterprise. Currently, there are 195 states, of which 193 are fully recognized members of the UN (Roeder

2007: 3, UN 2017, US DOS 2017). However, there are many nations without a state, their numbers running into several hundreds, if not thousands (cf. Buchanan 1991, Gellner 2006, Keating 2001a: 5, Minahan 2002). Many of these stateless national groups demand political self-determination and ultimately statehood for themselves. So, conflict is almost unavoidable within existing states. Ethnicity often becomes a principal identifying factor for nationalist ideologies in societies violently divided by incompatible claims to national self-determination, which frequently results in state contestation and secessionist claims. What makes ethnicity so attractive in these cases is, according to Hobsbawm, that it "is a readily definable way of expressing a real sense of group identity which links the members of 'us' because it emphasizes their differences from 'them'." (Hobsbawm 2012: 258) Likewise, modern nationalism and ethnicity become increasingly important matters of identity politics in the case of more than one national and ethnic group being present within one state. In such multi-national and multi-ethnic states, which most modern countries are de facto,[25] the phenomenon emerges of competing ethnonationalisms and nation-building projects, which may ultimately contest the legitimacy of the state (Kymlicka 2005: 45, Tierney 2000: 4; cf. Archibugi 2003, Kymlicka 1995, Margalit & Raz 1990).

Thus, a further question arises: what causes ethno-national divisions and opposing nationalisms, and in many cases, conflict between rival ethnonational groups? There is a plethora of literature addressing these issues (cf. Berberoglu 2004, Horowitz 2000, Miller 1995, Sisk 1996). It is not the aim of this section to provide an extensive overview of the various concepts of nationalism and related issues, but to draw on the most conclusive approaches with respect to their capability to explain intergroup conflict in divided societies. For this purpose, the starting point is to inquire as to the scope of a nation. In other words: what might be the defining characteristics of a nation? This question is best answered from the perspective of nationalism, which in its socio-cultural programme adopts different ideological meanings of the nation. Broadly speaking, theories of nationalism can be distinguished into two basic types, either emphasising the liberal, civic and cultural form of nationalism (cf. Gans 2003, Miller 1995, Smith 1991, Tamir 1995), or viewing

---

[25] Cases of mono-national states, i.e. of countries where "the boundaries of the state more or less correspond with those of the nation" (Kymlicka 2005: 45), are rather scarce. The most commonly cited examples are Iceland, Japan, Norway, Poland and Portugal (cf. Connor 1994: 77, Eller 1999: 19, Holton 1998: 137-138, Kymlicka 2005: 45).

it as a primarily ethnic, ethno-cultural and primordial phenomenon (cf. Connor 1994, Horowitz 2000, Sisk 1996). In other words, the main difference between the two forms is that

> "civic nationalism conceives of the nation as including all of its citizens – regardless of blood, creed or colour. Ethnocentric nationalism [or ethno-nationalism] believes, by contrast, that what holds a [national] community together is not common rights of citizenship (or humanity) but common ethnicity (or race)." (Kearney 1997: 57)

To conclude, in practical terms a specific pattern can be observed when looking at the evolutionary path of intergroup conflict in divided societies. In these societies, ethno-nationalist approaches often dominated the political arena during periods of intense violence, whereas civic nationalist ideas became important in phases of conflict resolution (cf. Horowitz 2000, Sisk 1996).

SOCIO-ECONOMIC CLASS INEQUALITIES AND DEPRIVATION

As for (ethno-) national identity, ethnicity and their related concepts, there is also a multitude of different conceptions when it comes to the definition of 'social class' (cf. Elster 1985: 318-397, Weber 1991a: 180-187, Wright 2005). What all these approaches have in common is their view of class as a hierarchically organised group determined by their relative power position within society. Generally speaking, class relationships are seen as being conditioned either by property relations and capitalist exploitation (the Marxist tradition), by market exchange (the Weberian approach), or by a variety of dimensions of social, economic and cultural capital (the Bourdieuan perspective). Furthermore, of these three theoretical traditions only Marxist thinkers view classes as real social phenomena. By contrast, in Weberian and Bourdieuan thought, class is mainly seen as an analytical category (cf. Anheier et al 1995: 860, Bourdieu 1984: 179-198, Howard & King 1985: 6-8, Parkin 2006: 139, Weber 1991: 181-183, Wright 2005: 3). For the purpose of this study, a middle position will be adopted that, while combining elements of all these approaches, seeks to remain 'ideologically unbiased'. Individuals' class positions are thus seen as being determined by their specific level of rights and powers over socio-economic resources (cf. Wright 2005: 10-12). In this sense, class and socio-economic position will be used interchangeably throughout this work. For the purpose of drawing specific intra- and inter-group comparisons, the compound term of 'socio-economic class' will be employed, comprising those people with a similar social, economic and educational status. Consequently, it is assumed that somebody belongs to the lowest or 'least advantaged class',[26] if she/he is most deprived in terms of access to and possession of vital socio-economic resources. These resources, such as nutrition, health care, education, housing, income, employment and occupation, are 'vital', in as far as they essentially determine the life chances of individuals and their status and positions in society (cf. Jackson 1979, Rawls 1971: 90-94).

In this respect, deprivation is not only a matter of objective measurement by looking at statistical figures such as unemployment rates, educational attainments, health conditions and poverty levels. It is also important to explore how individuals subjectively assess and experience their deprivation. They do so by comparing their socio-economic conditions with specific reference groups, i.e. those perceived as having similar class attributes and deserving similar socio-economic rewards (cf. Runciman 1966). Besides, there is another form of deprivation which affects individuals' attitudes and behaviour towards others and which is frequently of particular relevance in conflict-prone, divided societies. It is the sentiment of 'relative deprivation', which, according to Ted Gurr, is defined as "a perceived discrepancy between men's value expectations and value capabilities" (Gurr 1970:21), not only co-determines their class affiliation but, what is more, also influences the "potential for collective violence" (Gurr 1970: 21).

There are also other resources, which belong to the political, cultural and psychological sphere that impact on one's capability to make use of the socio-economic resources available. The liberal tradition focuses on political rights

---

[26] The term 'least advantaged class', which is used here in a more limited sense as equivalent to 'lowest social class', was coined by the liberal political philosopher John Rawls. Despite being a key element of his theory of social and political justice, Rawls concedes some unavoidable arbitrariness in defining what amounts precisely to being least advantaged. Broadly defined, however, the least advantaged class "includes persons whose family and class origins are more disadvantaged than others, whose natural endowments (as realized) permit them to fare less well, and whose fortune and luck in the course of life turn out to be less happy, all [...] within the relevant measures based on social primary goods." (Rawls 1971: 98) Without going into details here, it should be mentioned that there is some correlation between Rawls' idea of 'social primary goods' and the kind of 'vital resources' mentioned above (cf. Jackson 1979, Rawls 1971: 62 & 90-94, Rawls 1993: 76).

and liberties, which should be distributed equally among all members of society. Some egalitarian thinkers go further and also include in their concepts resources for psychological well-being. John Rawls, for instance, defines 'social primary goods' as "things that every rational man is presumed to want" (Rawls: 1971: 62) and which come directly under the control of the basic structure of society. Rawls' comprehensive idea, as advanced in his seminal works 'A Theory of Justice' and 'Political Liberalism', comprises rights, liberties, opportunities, income, wealth and self-respect (cf. Rawls 1971: 62 & 90-94; Rawls 1993: 76). John Baker, Kathleen Lynch, Sara Cantillon and Judy Walsh go beyond this in their comprehensive treatise on equality and propose five dimensions in which substantial equality between all members of society should be achieved and sustained: "respect and recognition; resources; love, care and solidarity; power; [and] working and learning." (Baker et al 2004: 24).

HEGEMONIC RELATIONS OF POWER AND GOVERNANCE

Closely related to the terms discussed so far, especially from an instrumental point of view, are some other important concepts for this research. Briefly speaking, what is meant by 'power', 'hegemony' and 'governance'? Based on a review of the relevant literature, some general statements can be made in advance concerning how power as a political phenomenon relates to intergroup conflicts in divided societies and to the possibilities of resolving and transforming them. Firstly, imbalances and misuse of power generate conflict and make it more difficult to resolve. Secondly, power differences shape the structure and dynamics of relationships. Thirdly, the way power is exerted is a predictor of constructive conflict transformation and resolution. Fourthly, power dynamics can determine the kinds of methods which will or will not be effective. Fifthly, the relative power of antagonists significantly influences the quality and nature of outcomes in terms of political decision-making and policy-making. Finally, equalising or rebalancing power relations is usually a *sine qua non* for reaching constructive and sustainable conflict solutions (cf. Hindess 1996, Lukes 2005, Rodgers 2003, Scott 2001, Stewart 2001) However, this overall picture is, of course, not revealing enough to offer concrete conclusions in specific conflict contexts. For this reason, a further theoretical discourse is required.

In Western political thought, power has been defined either in purely quantitative terms as the capacity to act, or also in qualitative terms as the capacity and right to act, with both being dependent on the consent of those subjected to those in power. For this research, which is interested in the deliberate nature of power and power relations in divided societies, the second, more comprehensive conception of 'power as legitimate capacity' will be used (cf. Hindess 1996: 1-13, Scott 2001: 1-5). However, in deeply divided societies, the legitimacy of those in power is often vehemently contested.

The idea of power as hegemony developed by Antonio Gramsci seems apt to the study of local intergroup conflict in divided societies like Northern Ireland, because it encompasses all spheres of social life, be they cultural, economic or political. In political terms, Gramsci's approach to hegemony describes a particular way how political elites gain and maintain legitimate power by winning popular consent. So, it is "a way of understanding the relations of domination and subordination between classes." (Davis 2004: 46) It is not confined to any special class, but involves the possibility of class ascendancy to hegemonic power. However, once gained, hegemonic power is constantly in flux and susceptible to opposition. There are always counter-hegemonic forces within society, which resist powerful elites. Therefore, in order to maintain and secure their hegemonic position, the ruling elite will have to broker compromises and take into account the needs and interests of subordinate classes. This need for compromise, which is materialised by seeking and forging cross-cutting class alliances, distinguishes hegemonic power from coercion (cf. Gramsci 1971: 12, Gramsci 2000: 194-195). However, in the case of societies bifurcated along ethno-national lines, which have experienced long-standing violent intergroup conflict, such as Northern Ireland, the power structure and relations are more complex. As their societies are deeply divided, so are also the elites, who engage in a peculiar form of power struggle in their quest for hegemony over the state.

Specifically, it is argued, it is Gramsci's idea of culture as a main stage of social and political struggle and his view on social relations as dynamic and interdependent that might facilitate better understanding of the issues and mechanisms shaping intergroup conflict on the ground. In this respect, his concern with creating a practice of social change offers particular insight. Such a social transformation can be initiated by progressive forces and elements within society, the so-called 'organic intellectuals', but can also be obstructed by dominant forces and by reactionary forces striving to maintain traditional hegemonic power structures and relations (Gramsci 1971: 3-14; cf.

Adamson 2002: 310, Crehan 2002: 71, Gill 2009: 102-103, Landy 1986: 59, Peleg 2007: 61).

Hegemony, as conceived by Gramsci, is the idea that the power of a ruling class is based less on their coercive, but more on their intellectual and moral capacity to gain the consent of the mass of the people. As Thomas Bates puts it, the concept of hegemony "means political leadership based on the consent of the led, a consent which is secured by the diffusion and popularization of the world view of the ruling class." (Bates 1975:352) This implies the permeation throughout society of an entire system of attitudes, beliefs, values and morality, i.e. of a comprehensive ideology that has the effect of maintaining the status quo in power relations.[27] In this meaning, hegemony can be defined as an 'organising principle' disseminated into everyday life and culture through 'organic intellectuals' by the process of socialisation.

The concept of 'organic intellectuals' is a key element in Gramsci's theory. As he argues,

> "Every social group, coming into existence … creates together with itself, organically, one or more strata of intellectuals which give it homogeneity and an awareness of its own function not only in the economic but also in the social and political fields." (Gramsci 1971: 5)

Consequently, if a particular social group wants to become hegemonic, it has to achieve intellectual and moral leadership by devising the necessary ideological conditions. To this aim, it has to win over the support of the 'organic intellectuals' of the so-called 'subaltern' groups in society, i.e. those social groups that are subordinated to the hegemony of the ruling class at the time (cf. Gramsci 2000: 351). The capability and readiness to engage in the improvement of the social complexities for a specific group or class distinguish the 'organic intellectuals' from the 'traditional intellectuals', the latter regarding themselves as not belonging to any group of society and thus as detached from engaging in such social endeavours. As Gramsci highlights the key functional distinction between the two groups,

> "The organic intellectuals are distinguished less by their profession, which may be any job characteristic of their class, than by their function in directing the ideas and aspirations of the class to which they organically belong." (Gramsci 1971: 3)

---

[27] Arguably, Gramsci's understanding of ideology is in line with the definition given by the British sociologist Anthony Giddens, who sees it as the "shared ideas or beliefs which serve to justify the interests of dominant groups." (Giddens 2009:1121)

Hence, the intellectual sphere is not to be conceived as limited to a specific elite, but as rooted in everyday life. In particular, the 'organic intellectuals' perform an important practical task that is essentially pedagogical and political. According to Gramsci, their specific task consists "in active participation in practical life, as constructor, organiser, "permanent persuader" and not just [as] a simple orator." (Gramsci 1971: 10) In this respect, the political party takes a unique position. It develops its own 'organic intellectuals', particularly in the political and philosophical fields, and has a specific responsibility in civil society to bring both the organic and traditional intellectuals together (Gramsci 1971: 5-14, Gramsci 2000: 189-221, Nimni 1991).

To recall: a ruling class is hegemonic, and not only dominant, if they manage, with the help of their 'organic intellectuals', to achieve approval to their rule also among members of other social classes. Thus, the more this rule is not only passively tolerated, but also actively supported, the more hegemony is secured. The scope of consent is usually dependent on the extent to which the ruling institutions match the specific interests of the subordinate groups. So, for a hegemonic elite or class to be successful and maintain their supreme position, and thus become what Gramsci calls a 'historical bloc', it is necessary to identify the views and concerns of large parts of their subaltern groups and make them their own. This will also lead to a transformation of the elite, as they then will not only attract some factions of society, but also develop an appeal to a much broader constituency. In other words, in order to maintain hegemony, the ruling class or elite has to be an active organ of civil society and engage in a continuous and evolving dialogue to ensure a broad base of popular support.

Gramsci views this complex process of cultural leadership as a dynamic interplay between the so-called 'superstructure' and 'structure' or 'base' of society – a distinction he adopts from Marx (cf. Marx 1977: 164-175). The superstructure consists of the 'political society' or 'the State', and the 'civil society', the former including the state institutions and the ruling political and intellectual classes, and the latter the non-state sphere, comprising the practices and institutions through which social life is organised and represented autonomously from the state. For Gramsci, civil society stands "between the economic structure and the state with its legislation and coercion" (Gramsci 1971: 208). It includes customs and traditions, representative institutions such as trade unions and employers' associations, political organisations, professional associations, educational, religious and cultural institutions and the private institution of the family (Gramsci 1971: 12 & 206-209, Gramsci 2000:

306, Jones 2006: 32). By contrast, the economic sphere itself, its functional institutions of firms and corporations responsible for organising production and exchange, constitute the base of society. The base-superstructure relationship is dialectical or reflexive, as both "impact upon each other with no level assumed to be the primary level of determinacy." (Jones 2006: 34).[28] On the one hand, the state and its institutions as well as civil society create the political and social regulatory framework for the economic sphere, whereas, on the other, changes in the modes of production and exchange reshape these general conditions.

In Gramsci's approach, political and cultural hegemony is manifested in the 'superstructure' of society. Although hegemonic rule is based more on consent than coercion, it is always a mixture of both. Whereas consent is achieved through civil society, the coercive task rests with political society (Gramsci 2000: 195-209; cf. Gramsci 1994). As already indicated earlier, hegemony denotes an established elite rule, which only has to resort to brute force in exceptional cases. The employment of such force becomes necessary in the event of groups being present in society that cannot be integrated in the cultural and political project of the hegemonic elite. According to Gramsci, "a social group dominates antagonistic groups, which it tends to "liquidate", or to subjugate perhaps even by armed force." (Gramsci 1971: 57) By contrast, "it leads kindred and allied groups" (Gramsci 1971: 57). The failure to eliminate resistance threatens the hegemonic position of the elite, leading to the emergence of counter-hegemonic forces and hegemonic power struggles.[29]

The concepts of power and hegemony stand in a specific relationship to the idea of governance that will be used for this research. In a nutshell, the rationale is as follows: power and hegemony both have ideological foundations

---

[28] This view of a dialectical or reflexive relationship is one of the fundamental differences to 'Orthodox Marxism', which postulates that the cultural and political superstructure is determined by the economic base (cf. Lukács 1972: 1-27; Mészáros & Bottomore 1971).

[29] Gramsci did not use the term 'counter-hegemony', but referred instead to the notions of 'war of manoeuvre' or 'war of position' – a struggle fought out either over a short or long period in the superstructure, where the working class and their allies would ultimately succeed in becoming the hegemonic force and challenging the fundamental principles of capitalism – capital accumulation based on exploitation and private property. However, in a broader Gramscian sense, the concept of 'counter-hegemony' as an oppositional, cultural force through which a formerly subordinate social and political group becomes sufficiently powerful to challenge the ruling ideology and eventually overthrow the hegemonic system is critical to Gramsci's theory (Gramsci 2000: 225-230; cf. Brand 2007, Cammaerts 2007, Cox 1983, Morton 2007).

and a conscious, interest-driven character. Governance, in turn, is the substrate of both and its performance can be assessed by efficiency and effectiveness criteria.

The term 'governance'[30] has come to prominence over the last three decades as a way of describing and explaining changes in the design and configuration of norm and regulation systems at various levels of authority. Typically, these changes are characterised by a shift from hierarchic bureaucratic rules towards a more market and network-oriented approach in the design and implementation of politics and policies. Despite the popularity of the term 'governance', however, no precise definition has been undertaken to date. Most of the approaches, nevertheless, share a common concern for the relationship between state intervention and societal autonomy (cf. Benz 2004, Jordan & Schout 2006, Rhodes 1996, Smismans 2008). Moreover, the different modes of governance can be classified according to the focus placed on the politics (actor constellations and power relations), polity (institutional properties) or policy (steering instruments) dimension of governance (Treib et al. 2007). For this research, which is interested in the impact of governance arrangements and policies on the ground in divided societies – and in the roles of the actors involved – a broad definition will be adopted encompassing all three dimensions. So, governance denotes the steering and coordination of society by both state and non-state actors at different levels of authority. Essentially, this involves all patterns of legitimate power – hierarchical as typically exerted by the state and non-hierarchical as in the case of governance networks, including civil society organisations and other non-state actors (cf. Bähr & Treib 2007: 3, Bevir 2007: 364-365, Torfing 2007: 3).

THE LOCUS OF CONFLICT: INTERFACE AND ENCLAVE COMMUNITIES

As was touched on in the introduction, many intergroup conflicts in divided societies are structured in such a way that the intensity of ethno-national divisions and socio-economic class inequalities coincide in specific geographical locations adjacent to the rival ethno-national groups. These so-called

---

[30] The origin of the term 'governance' dates back to the ancient Greek verb '$\kappa\upsilon\beta\varepsilon\rho\nu\acute{\alpha}\omega$ [kubernáo]', meaning 'to steer', which was first used in a metaphorical way by the Greek philosopher Plato (EC 2001, Fox 1957: 36).

interface and enclave communities are often the focal points for violent clashes with the 'other' side of the divide and with the authorities of the state. As far as the specific geographical focus of this study is concerned, the terms 'interface' and 'enclave' have been already mentioned on several occasions. In a general sense, an interface can be described as "a surface forming a common boundary between two regions" (Fowler et al. 1985: 523).

The term 'interface communities' was coined for the Northern Ireland conflict, especially to denote specific conflict-prone areas in the capital city of Belfast, but also in other urban locations such as Derry/Londonderry and Portadown. According to Jarman, interface communities are located "at the intersection of segregated and polarised working-class residential zones, in areas with a strong link between territory and ethno-political identity" (Jarman 2004: 5). Interfaces may consist of physical barriers or so-called 'peace walls' that separate and protect the antagonistic groups from each other. They are often marked with flags and symbols. They can, however, also be invisible to most people, except local residents. By contrast, an enclave, although by and large characterised by similar features to interface areas, is "an island community; one that is totally surrounded by the 'other' community." (Jarman & O'Halloran 2001: 4) More specifically, 'enclave areas', as understood in this work, denote locations with a large residential concentration of a particular ethno-national community that is completely encapsulated and surrounded by another ethno-national one (cf. Collins et al. 1996, Cox et al. 2008, Poulsen et al. 2001). A further common characteristic for both interface and enclave areas is that they both represent "intra-state territorial conflict points" (Kahler 2006: 6).[31] As such, interface and enclave areas are frequently exposed to intense intergroup violence, where ethno-national antagonism and sectarianism are considered to be among the main contributing factors. These interface communities have frequently been sites of sectarian tensions and violence due to intercommunal disputes over parades and other contentious events.

As stated earlier, interface and enclave communities display strong territorial attachments, which also epitomise a more general phenomenon. As Miles Kahler points out, "the world of the early twenty-first century displays both persistent attachments to territory and violent conflict over these territorial

---

[31] In his aim to explain territorial attachments, Kahler speaks of 'interstate territorial conflict points'. However, considering his emphasis also on the internal, intra-state dimensions of violent territorial disputes, there are certainly territorial conflict points that exist within states torn by intergroup conflict (cf. Kahler 2006: 6-15).

stakes. Even as interstate conflict has declined, many costly internal conflicts have taken on a territorial dimension." (Kahler 2006: 1) In essence, the salience of territoriality in ethno-national conflicts is manifested in at least three important ways.[32] Firstly, there is a considerable potential for the political mobilisation of specific territorial attachments in ways that reinforce intergroup conflict. This is particularly the case in areas located at the inter-community boundary or the intra-state border of the ethno-national divide, i.e. in interface and enclave areas, and in regions adjacent to another state. Regarding the former, an important aspect is mentioned by Hein Goemans: "Territorial specification of group membership – for example, "we" live "here" – has been and in many places still is a particularly powerful and attractive way to coordinate group members to provide a collective defense." (Goemans 2006: 26-27). The latter brings us to the second phenomenon. In conflicts in divided societies, territoriality may involve disputes over territorial stakes between the state and a neighbouring kin-state with whom the ethno-national minority has strong bonds of culture, language, history or/and religion (Goemans 2006).[33] If so, then intra-state conflict is exacerbated, due to external intervention in internal hegemonic struggles between the rival ethno-national elites (cf. Kahler & Walter 2006). Thirdly, another general pattern and driving force has been identified for localised intergroup conflict. If multiple ethno-national groups competing for power and resources are territorially concentrated, then the likelihood for violent conflict between them and the state will increase (Cunningham & Weidmann 2010). Thus, in sum, it can be said that ethno-national conflicts within the state frequently take on a territorial dimension, involving localised intergroup violence.

---

[32] It is plausible that territoriality also has other implications for ethno-national conflicts, especially regarding the increasing role of globalisation, which, on the one hand, may reduce the importance of state boundaries as sources of identification, but, on the other, may also create new transnational boundaries (cf. Cochrane et al 2003, Kahler & Walter 2006, Sassen 2005). However, taking the potential effects of globalisation also into consideration would exceed the scope of this work, whose focus is on the exploration of local intergroup conflict within the confines of the divided society of Northern Ireland.

[33] The term 'kin-state' refers to a state which has an ethno-national minority living in another country, called the host-state or home-state (cf. Cordell & Wolff 2009: 86, ECDL 2002: 16, McGarry et al 2006: 1, Wolff & Weller 2005: 8).

SKETCH OF THE THEORETICAL-ANALYTICAL FRAMEWORK

By adopting an integrative multidimensional perspective, the theoretical approach guiding this study of local intercommunal conflict in Northern Ireland will take several of the aspects discussed above into consideration. The analysis will be carried out at group level, since group affiliations exert significant normative and formative power on individuals' identities. It is argued that ethno-national divisions are most pronounced and visible in lower class areas with high levels of socio-economic deprivation and inequality and especially in those located close to the interface to the other ethno-national community. Therefore, special attention will be devoted to the salience of oppositional ethno-national identities and to their interrelatedness with socio-economic and class divisions.

As the common denominator, at least for this study, it can be said that national, ethnic and – as the compound term combining them both (Fenton & May 2002: 6) – ethno-national groups are constructed realities, i.e. characterised by a common will to belong to an imagined community that is rooted in commonly shared perceptions of its history (cf. Anderson 1991: 6-7). Both concepts will be regarded as real-world phenomena, considering the practical implications of class and socio-economic issues. However, they will also serve as analytical categories, especially with regard to intra- and intergroup comparisons between living conditions. Resources belonging to the political, cultural or psychological domain will be considered only for their impact on individuals' socio-economic class positions. Apart from the ethno-national and socio-economic class dimensions, there is also a third, political dimension. Essentially, this dimension is based on the idea of power as hegemony, which is driven by both interests and ideology. This is a crucial point to consider in the the analysis of local intercommunal conflict. As Ilan Peleg aptly points out,

> "Most conflicts are internal and most of them involve hegemonism. In the case of the hegemonic state, the state is not merely a reactive force to ethnic demands and violence. The polity's own behaviour – its aspiration to dominate other group(s) within its borders – could be a primary cause of conflict." (Peleg 2007: 23)

3 THE NORTHERN IRELAND CONFLICT
DIMENSIONS, DYNAMICS AND CONTEXT

*"Ireland is a small country where the greatest questions
of politics, morality and humanity are fought out."
(Gustave de Beaumont 1839)[34]*

*"Should an anthropologist or a sociologist be looking
for a bizarre society to study, I would suggest he comes to Ulster."
(Bernadette Devlin 1969)[35]*

The Northern Ireland conflict has become notorious for its protracted and embittered nature and is frequently ranked among the most intense intergroup conflicts in 20th century Western Europe. The recent violent conflict lasting from 1968 to 1998, infamously known as the 'Troubles', has caused over 3,600 deaths and left more than 47.000 injured, the vast majority of these casualties being civilians. On a comparative scale, the Northern Ireland conflict has been regarded as the most violent intra-state conflict that has occurred in the EU since its inception. As pointed out by Brendan O'Leary and John McGarry,

> "This small but deeply divided population has generated the most intense political violence of any part of the contemporary UK [and] the highest levels of internal political violence of any member-state of the European Community." (O'Leary & McGarry 1993: 8)

Moreover, in proportion to the population, ten times more people died in the Northern Ireland conflict than US Americans in the Vietnam War (O'Leary & McGarry 1993: 12). The Troubles have also had serious impacts on community relations between the Protestant/Unionist/Loyalist and the Catholic/Nationalist/Republican communities and on their socio-economic situation (Dixon 2001, Fay et al 1999, Sutton 1994 & 2002). Despite of the comprehensive peace accord reached between the main antagonists in 1998,

---

[34] This quote (cited in Rose 1971, title page) stems from Gustave de Beaumont, a French magistrate, prison reformer, friend and travel companion of the French diplomat, political scientist and historian Alexis de Tocqueville, who also was a connoisseur of Irish social and political life.

[35] This citation (Devlin 1969: 53) is from Josephine Bernadette McAliskey, better known under her maiden name Bernadette Devlin, who is a Northern Irish civil rights campaigner, former politician and member of the British Parliament from 1969 to 1974.

intercommunal violence still continues, albeit to a significantly lower extent. As indicated before, most of this violence occurs during certain divisive events and remains concentrated in particular locations.

The conflict in Northern Ireland has drawn enormous attention from social scientists, journalists, politicians and public officials, both at national and international level. Referring to the surfeit of research to which Northern Irish people have been exposed, David George Boyce remarks, not without a tinge of criticism and sarcasm:

> "Since the Northern Ireland troubles [sic!] first attracted media attention in the late 1960s, its people, and especially its politics, have been the subject of sociological, psychological, historical, politically scientific and legal scrutiny, so much so that they could be forgiven for thinking that they are condemned for ever to live like specimens in a jar, or like the fly in the fly-bottle, only with no hope (in their case) of ever escaping from the bottle." (Boyce 1991: 13)

To date, a plethora of books, articles in journals and newspapers as well as reports have been published about the conflict. What all these publications have in common are, as McGarry and O'Leary aptly put it, the "multiple disagreements over what conflict it is, and about whether it is 'one' or 'many'; in short there is a 'meta-conflict', a conflict about what the conflict is about." (McGarry & O'Leary 1995: 1) Furthermore, there is even less common ground among researchers when it comes to the themes of conflict transformation and conflict resolution. This considerable disagreement impairs the effectiveness of research on the Northern Ireland conflict. According to Whyte, several reasons could be advanced for this phenomenon: a lack of public interest; bias and prejudices of the recipients; insufficient evidence for sustaining 'objective' conclusions; difficulties to conduct research in particular, violence-torn areas; and the limited capacity of the human mind to comprehend the full complexity of the conflict (Whyte 1990: 246-249).

Generally speaking, the high diversity in the analysis of the causes for the community divisions in Northern Ireland can be grouped into two dominant positions: on the one hand, one-factor approaches, either static or dynamic, which regard these divisions as primarily caused by a singular conflict between two antagonistic nationalities (cf. Dixon 2000, McGarry & O'Leary 1995) or opposing religions (cf. Barnes 2005 Lambkin 1996); on the other hand, dynamic multiple-factor approaches, for which the community divisions either occur in many small conflicts, each reflecting a particular facet (cf. Darby 1995, Whyte 1990), or in one focused conflict determined by the overlap of various dimensions, such as nationality, ethnicity, religion, colonialism, class, economic, social, cultural inequalities, and imbalances in political power and representation (cf. Mac Ginty & Darby 2002, Ruane & Todd 1996). Despite these differences, there is, however, a common denominator insofar as all the studies seek to explain the Northern Ireland conflict within a historical continuum of strained relations between the Catholic and Protestant communities, between the Unionist/Loyalist and Nationalist/Republican traditions and between the British and Irish states (cf. McGarry & O'Leary 1995, Whyte 1990).

By adopting an integrative approach that explores and combines relevant historical, ethno-national, socio-economic class as well as the hegemonic governance and power relations dimensions this and the next chapter aim to shed light on the particular nature and dynamics of local intergroup conflict in Northern Ireland. The approach is based on the common view among researchers on the topic that both contextualisation and empirical material are essential for the study of local conflict (cf. McCratten 2010). Consequently, it consists of two analytical steps: at first, this chapter concentrates on the macro-level of the conflict, thus providing a general understanding for what is at stake. This sets the scene for the empirical analysis of local intergroup conflict conducted in the following chapter. The focus then will be on identifying the specific issues relevant to the selected cases of interface and enclave communities.

Before to start, it should be emphasised that what follows is not an attempt to provide a comprehensive overview of the conflict in Northern Ireland that covers all its aspects and facets. This is already due to the limitations of space but more so because this would go far beyond the scope and purpose of this book, thus risking losing focus of its particular objectives. Besides, there is already an abundance of comprehensive studies on the Northern Ireland conflict, which give an in-depth overview of its history (cf. Bew & Gillespie 1999, Hennessey 1997, McKittrick & McVea 2002) and of the different approaches to study the conflict (cf. McGarry & O'Leary 1995, Tonge 2006, Whyte 1990). Instead, the account will include more recent historical and contemporary developments with a particular focus on ethno-national, socio-economic class and power-related aspects of the conflict. In doing so, it will provide an overall picture and contextualisation of the evolvement and present situation of the communities and the political elites.

COMMUNITY AND POWER RELATIONS: A HISTORICAL PERSPECTIVE

In order to understand the conflict that happened – and in certain localities and around certain events it is still ongoing – in Northern Ireland, it is essential briefly to examine the historical development of the long-standing inter-group divisions and their manifestations in the political and socio-economic spheres. In a deeply divided society like Northern Ireland, which has a long history of violent inter-group conflict, it is hardly a surprise that there is often a wide gulf in views and attitudes between the Protestant and Catholic communities and between their respective Unionist/Loyalist and Nationalist/Republican political representations. This especially affects Northern Irish history, where the use of favourable interpretations of causes and effects has been widespread. Consequently, in describing the historical development of community and political power relations in Northern Ireland, an important aim is to strive for accuracy and validity and to avoid referring to biased scientific and journalistic sources and taking partisan information for face value. So there is the risk of falling into the trap of following a historical master narrative of perpetration and victimisation that favours one side over the other. To avoid this, this chapter will endeavour to provide a concise and unbiased historical overview starting from the origins of the conflict up to current developments in Northern Ireland's post-peace agreement era.[36]

THE EARLY ORIGINS OF THE CONFLICT

The early origins of the Northern Ireland conflict date back to medieval times, when the English invasion under Strongbow and his Norman troops occurred in 1170 (Cronin 2001: 14, Martin 2001: 101-102). Subsequently, Ireland witnessed the arrival of many English settlers, who were – like the native Irish – mostly of the Roman Catholic faith. English rule was established in Ireland, yet for the next almost five centuries all attempts failed to bring Ireland completely under English control. This was mainly because of the assimilation between the English colonisers and the native Irish, which led to the emergence of an Anglo-Irish elite, who considered themselves distinct

---

[36] Here, I refer to a revised, updated and expanded version of the historical account presented in my diploma thesis, because in essence it contains similar thoughts put in a nutshell (cf. Preiss 2003: 4-13).

from the English and favoured home rule for Ireland (Cronin 2001: 34; cf. Connolly 1998: 428-430). They were convinced that Ireland should have its own jurisdiction. To strengthen their position, they issued a declaration at the Irish Parliament in Drogheda, stating their judicial independence from England (cf. Connolly 1998: 428-430).[37]

In the second half of the 17th century, this period of relative autonomy came to an end, when Oliver Cromwell, Lord Protector of the Commonwealth of England, Scotland and Ireland, took Drogheda and attempted to reinforce the Protestant position in Ireland by means of so-called 'plantation'. This land reform meant that all the territory became reserved for English planters and only the western part of the island was left over for the Irish (Cronin 2001: 74). After the so-called 'The Flight of the Earls' in 1607, when the Earls of Tyrone and Tyrconnell, the last of the Gaelic chiefs to hold out against English Rule in their Ulster strongholds, fled to the sanctuary of Europe, their vast estates were confiscated. This encouraged plantation in Ulster, and particularly in its north-eastern part, where the scheme was different from the other parts of Ireland. Land allocations were tied to proven loyalty to the English Crown; so most of the country was given to civil servants or soldiers who were held responsible for maintaining order among the Irish. As a further condition, large sections of the territory were granted to those who promised to bring in further Protestant settlers from the British mainland. Ireland witnessed a sea change in land ownership from Catholics to Protestants. For example, while in 1641 Catholics still held 66% and Protestants 30% of the land in Ireland, by 1675 this ratio had reversed, with only 29% of the land belonging to Catholics and 67% to Protestants (McKenny 2008: 70-71). With plantation, the seeds of segregation in Ulster germinated and took root, as the native Irish Catholic population was concentrated and confined to rather small and defined areas. Thus, "a network of new, entirely Protestant communities could be created." (Clarke 2001: 153) So, this policy of English colonisation formed the basis for the heart of Irish Protestantism in Ulster. In the hope of regaining their lost property and social status, the Catholics in

---

[37] The first clearly documented Irish Parliament met in 1264. These medieval parliaments had a very different function from today's parliaments in democratic countries. Thus, the Irish Parliament served as a high court enacting Irish legislation and dealt with petitions from the lords. In the 15th century its role changed with the 'Declaration of Independence' at Drogheda in 1460, which was concerned with political and constitutional issues and above all proclaimed Ireland as a separate jurisdictional entity under the English Crown (Connolly 1998: 428-430, Johnson 2005: 27-28).

Ulster, continued resisting plantation and English rule. Their resistance culminated in the rebellion of 1641, when Protestant planters and their families living in isolated settlements were expelled or killed by the native Irish. The rebellion, which was violently quelled, intensified Protestant feelings of insecurity, paving the ground for what has since been termed their 'siege mentality' (Clarke 2001: 152-161, Foster 1989: 132-133). Eventually, in 1690, the Catholic James II, who had previously been deposed from the throne of England in the so-called 'Glorious Revolution', was defeated in the Battle of the Boyne by his successor, the Protestant King William of Orange.[38] [39] This "landmark battle in the history of Ireland" (Cronin 2001: 78) finally led to Protestant hegemony over Catholic Irish for the next two hundred years.

At the beginning of the 18th century, the British Parliament passed a series of anti-Catholic measures. These so-called 'Penal Laws' "barred Catholics from entering parliament, from holding any government office …, from entering the legal profession and from holding commissions in the army and navy." (Wall 2001: 177) The effectiveness of these laws relied on the prescription of qualifying oaths, which were aimed against the Catholic faith and thus unacceptable to them (Wall 2001: 177-178). In this period, the English administrative and legislative model was replicated in Ireland. Nationalist resistance against the colonial character of Irish governance formed with the foundation of the Society of United Irishmen in 1791, which consisted of both Protestants and Catholics.[40] The society, inspired by the American and French Revolutions, aimed at parliamentary reform, the revocation of the remaining Penal Laws, and ultimately at the establishment of an Irish Repub-

---

[38] The battle was preceded by the Siege of Derry, lasting from 18 April to 1 August 1689, in which Protestants loyal to King William III of Orange locked the city gates and successfully resisted the besieging forces of Irish Catholics fighting for King James II (cf. Armstrong 2014: 376-377, Bryan 2000: 32).

[39] The battle was fought on 1 July 1690 on the river Boyne near Drogheda. The decisive victory of William III of Orange over James II took place in the following year in the Battle of Aughrim, County Galway, on 12 July 1691. With 7,000 killed, it marked the bloodiest battle ever fought on the Irish island. Protestants in Northern Ireland celebrate these events every year as a victory for their cause, culminating on 12 July with Orange Order parades being held throughout the country (cf. Armstrong 2014: 386-387, Bryan 2000: 32-33).

[40] One of their leading members was Theobald Wolfe Tone, a young Protestant barrister and enthusiast for the French Revolution, who played a crucial role in the foundation of the Society of United Irishmen in Belfast and Dublin and in shaping their aims and philosophy (cf. McDowell 2001: 196-202).

lic, based on equality and peaceful coexistence between Protestants and Catholics. However, their demands were rejected by the British Government and, after the violent suppression of the rebellion in 1798, many United Irishmen were executed (McDowell 2001: 196-203).

In 1801, the United Kingdom of Great Britain and Ireland was established, the Irish Parliament was abolished and Ireland came under direct control from London (Barton 1996: 11). This period of British direct rule, which was to last until 1921, sowed the seeds for a new divide in Ulster; predominantly Catholic Nationalists and Republicans, who sought home rule for Ireland, opposed a majority of Protestant Unionists and Loyalists, who wanted to stay within the UK. Moreover, the split between the two rivalling historical factions was exacerbated by the growing economic crisis, which further deepened the already existing unequal distribution of resources and opportunities to the benefit of the Protestant community. The whole economy of Ireland finally collapsed with the advent of the 'Great Famine' in the second half of the 1840s. The Famine had devastating effects: within five years, the population of Ireland was reduced by over two million, with most of those affected being Catholics (Connolly 1998: 228-229, Green 2001: 226; cf. Kinealy 2002).[41] This tragic experience fuelled the Nationalist movement in their efforts to achieve Irish sovereignty, leading to several Nationalist rebellions and sectarian riots. A particularly severe incident of sectarian violence was the so-called 'Battle of Dolly's Brae', which occurred in 1849 in County Down, when a contested Orange Order procession went off its route into a Catholic residential area. The armed clashes between Protestant 'Orangemen' and Catholic 'Ribbonmen',[42] resulted in the deaths of an estimated 80 local Catholics (Bardon 1996, McKenna 2016a). Throughout the 19th century, there was also a more pragmatic faction of Irish Nationalists, who aimed at Irish home

---

[41] The Great Famine, which lasted from 1845 to 1849, had calamitous consequences for the Irish people. Over one million died from starvation and its accompanying diseases, whilst over another million people emigrated from Ireland – most of them to the United States – in order to find a better livlihood abroad (Connolly 228-229, Green 2001: 226; cf. Kinealy 2002).

[42] The supporters of the 'Ribbon Society', a secret society consisting mainly of poor, rural Irish Catholics in the 19th century, were called 'Ribbonmen'. They were active in preventing the mostly Protestant landlords and their agents from evicting Catholic peasant tenants. The 'Ribbonmen' strongly opposed the ideology of the Orange Order and engaged in fierce clashes with their supporters, the so-called 'Orangemen' (cf. Garvin 1982).

rule and land reform.[43] Although the land reform at the turn of the century, which transferred land ownership rights from landlords to the Irish people, improved the economic situation of the majority of the Irish, the bulk of wealth in Ireland remained in the hands of the Protestants in Ulster. Whilst the majority of Ireland continued to be agricultural in structure, Ulster prospered from its industry (Cronin 2001: 168-172, Jackson 1979: 50-52).

PARTITION – TWO IRELANDS ON ONE ISLAND

In the early 20th century, a change in the perception of the 'Irish Question' occurred within the British political establishment. A crucial point in this development was the introduction of the 'Home Rule for Ireland Bill' by the British Government led by Prime Minister Herbert Henry Asquith and the Chancellor of the Exchequer David Lloyd George in April 1912, which made it clear that "the 'Irish question' was in fact two questions: Nationalist Ireland's relationship with the rest of the United Kingdom, and Protestant Ulster's relationship with Catholic Ireland." (Hennessey 1997: 1-2) Ulster Unionists and Loyalists forcibly resisted the threat of Irish self-government. As an expression of their resistance to home rule, they drew up the 'Ulster Covenant',[44] which by 28 September 1912 was signed by nearly half a million people. Subsequently, they formed a Unionist militia called the Ulster Volunteer Force (UVF) and established a provisional Unionist government claiming jurisdiction over the nine counties of Ulster in Belfast. The Unionist government, spearheaded by Edward Carson, intended to partition Ulster off from the rest of Ireland and stay within the UK. Conversely, leading Irish Nationalists and Republicans such as James Connolly, Patrick Pearse, Tom Clarke and Arthur Griffith would not accept partition; they fought for freedom and liberation from British rule for the whole island of Ireland (Bell 1997: 30-36, Bowman 2007: 46-47, Coogan 2002: 17-22).

The 'Easter Rising' in Dublin in 1916, when Nationalist and Republican forces consisting of the Irish Citizens' Army, the Irish Republican Brother-

---

[43] Members of this faction were prominent Nationalist leaders such as Daniel O'Connell, MP, with his influential Catholic Association and the Repeal Association, and Charles Stewart Parnell, MP, leader of the Irish Parliamentary Party (IPP) and founder of the Irish National Land League (cf. Moody 2001, Whyte 2001).

[44] For the full text and more information on the Ulster Solemn League and Covenant, as is its official name, see Cable 2012.

hood (IRB) and the Irish Volunteers[45] proclaimed the Republic of Ireland,[46] marked "the beginning of a sustained campaign of violence against British rule in Ireland" (Cronin 2001: 195). However, the armed insurrection, which extended to skirmishes in southern and western counties, was suppressed and the rebels were forced to surrender within a week. The execution of Connolly, Pearse, Clark and thirteen other leaders by British firing squads fuelled Irish Nationalists/Republicans, North and South, to continue their struggle for Irish independence (Barton & Foy 1999, Bell 1997: 6-16, Coogan 2002: 22-23, McCartney 2001, McGarry 2010: 1-43, Ranelagh 1999: 177-192).

In the first General Elections to the UK Parliament after the First World War, held on 14 December 1918, the Irish Republican party of Sinn Féin led by Éamon de Valera gained a majority of 73 of Ireland's 105 seats. Subsequently, on 21 January 1919, they formed the first '*Dáil Éireann*' (Irish Parliament) and issued a manifesto, in which they refused to recognise the British Parliament and instead declared to establish an independent Irish legislature in Dublin. This implied that all of Sinn Féin's elected Members of Parliament (MPs) in the British House of Commons refused to take their seats (cf. Coleman 2014: 15-17). Moreover, the *Dáil* recognised the Irish Republican Army (IRA), which evolved from the Irish Volunteers and the IRB, as the legitimate army of Ireland. At the same day the IRA attacked and shot two Royal Irish Constabulary (RIC) officers. This incident is widely regarded as the beginning of the'Anglo-Irish War', also called the 'Irish War of Independence', in which Irish Republican and British forces engaged in a guerrilla warfare that lasted until 11 July 1921. On the Irish Catholic/Nationalist/Republican side, the IRA was the dominant armed force, which was countered on the British Protestant/Unionist/Loyalist side by the British Army, the Royal Irish Constabulary (RIC), the UVF and the Ulster Special Constabulary (USC). The latter, commonly known as the 'B-Specials', was a volunteer auxiliary police force organised along military lines and endowed with spe-

---

[45] After 1919, the IRB and the Irish Volunteers became increasingly known as the Irish Republican Army (IRA), but also retained their original names. The three organisations were part of the Fenian tradition – a predominantly cultural movement formed in 1858 to liberate all Irish people from British oppression – which, after the disbanding of the IRB and Irish Volunteers, is still kept alive in the form of the IRA (cf. Coogan 1993: 27-29).

[46] The 'Easter Proclamation', which was adopted and ratified as the 'Declaration of Independence' by the Irish Parliament on 21 January 1919. For the full text of the proclamation see Pearse [1916] 1975. For a detailed account of the Easter Rising, see McNally 2007.

cial powers in times of emergency (cf. Bowman 2007, Clark 2014: 57-60, Coleman 2014: 67-93, Kennedy-Pipe 1997: 15-17).[47]

The British response to the continuing unrest in Ulster was the 'Government of Ireland Act 1920', which became effective on 3 May 1921. Subsequently, Ireland was partitioned and two parliaments formed, "one in Belfast with jurisdiction over the six north-eastern counties ('Northern Ireland'), the second, in Dublin with authority over the other twenty-six counties ('southern Ireland')." (Barton 1996: 27) [48] The powers vested in both parliaments were limited and major areas of responsibility, such as foreign policy, defence, and almost all financial affairs, were excluded. Contrary to the hopes of leading British politicians "that the two new Irish states would, in due course, unite, whilst remaining closely bound to Britain" (Barton 1996: 28), violence spread pervasively between Northern Irish Protestants and Catholics. Thus, the birth of Northern Ireland was accompanied by many civilian casualties. The first Parliament of Northern Ireland, which was opened in Belfast at Stormont castle on 7 June 1921, had a large Unionist majority. It was composed of forty Unionist and twelve Nationalist members, with the Unionist James Craig becoming Northern Ireland's first Prime Minister (Hennessey 1997: 18).[49]

One of the most serious shortcomings of the 1920 Act was the application of the British system of simple majority rule to Northern Ireland, which then formed the basis for the absolute hegemonic power of the Unionist Party in the Belfast Parliament for the next fifty years (Barton 1996: 33).[50] [51] In addi-

---

[47] As a result of their ineffectiveness, the UVF were absorbed into the USC in 1922. The USC, who became infamous for their brutality towards Catholics, was disbanded and replaced by the Ulster Defence Regiment (UDR) in 1970 (Bowman 2007, Hennessey 1997)

[48] According to O'Leary, "a partition should be understood as an externally proposed and imposed *fresh* border cut through a least one community's national homeland, creating at least two separate units under different sovereigns and authorities (original emphasis)." (O'Leary 2001: 54) The 1921 partition led to the enduring division of Ireland, its 32 counties spread over four provinces, i.e. Munster in the south of the island, Leinster in the east, Connacht in the west, and Ulster in the north. The latter is composed of nine counties with six of them, e.g. Fermanagh, Tyrone, Derry/Londonderry, Armagh, Antrim, and Down, forming Northern Ireland, and three of them, e.g. Monaghan, Cavan, and Donegal being part of the Republic of Ireland. For a map of Northern Ireland and of Ireland, see Figure 8 and 9 in the Appendix, p. 405.

[49] At the first Northern Ireland general election, held in May 1921, the Unionist Party won 40 seats, whilst the Nationalist Party of Northern Ireland (NPNI) and Sinn Féin won 6 seats each (Hennessey 1997: 18).

[50] Remarkably, in the first Stormont period from 1921 to 1972 no Catholic Nationalist was ever a cabinet member (cf. Barton 1996; Hennessey 1997). Moreover, it only happened

tion, there was no bill of rights that could have protected the Catholic minority, so the establishment of a discriminatory sectarian state was encouraged. The provisional Irish government in Dublin, headed by Collins, refused to acknowledge the government of Northern Ireland and financially supported Northern Irish Nationalists. Collins' policy actually consolidated partition and the Unionist majority's siege mentality (Follis 1995: 189; cf. Coogan 1996). Collins equally played an essential role in the peace talks with the British Government (cf. Coogan 2001: 236-276). The outcome was the 'Anglo-Irish Treaty', signed in December 1921. The emergence of the 26-county 'Irish Free State' was accompanied by what became known as the 'Irish Civil War' between pro-Treaty forces, led by Collins and Griffith, and anti-Treaty forces, headed by de Valera and Cathal Brugha. The civil war lasted from 28 June 1922 to 24 May 1923 and cost the lives of approximately 4,000 people. In the end, those in favour of the Anglo-Irish Treaty emerged victorious, albeit having to endure the loss of Collins and Griffiths, who both died in August of the previous year (cf. Coogan & Morrison 1998, Kissane 2007).[52] The Irish Free State (*Saorstát Éireann*), which formally came into being on 6 December 1922, was endowed with substantially greater powers than the six counties in the North making up Northern Ireland. This aggravated the Unionists' feelings of threat and insecurity even further. Ultimately, the arrangement led to the secession of the Irish Free State from the UK (Barton 2003: 187, Hennessey 1997: 19-23).[53]

The Treaty also contained a provision relating to the formation of the Irish Boundary Commission. The Commission was concerned with revising the new inner-Irish border running 310 miles (499 km) between Northern Ireland and the Irish Free State. Its decision was supposed to take into account the

---

once that the Unionists agreed to an initiative of the Nationalist opposition. That occurred when the Wild Bird Act of 1932 got enacted into law (Darby 1996: 202).

[51] Unionist rule was based on the ideology of 'A Protestant Government for a Protestant People' – an expression stemming from James Craig (Melaugh 2016c). See also Footnote 199, p. 275.

[52] Griffith died on 12 August 1922, after collapsing in his government office in Dublin. Collins was killed 10 days later in an ambush in County Cork by anti-treaty forces (cf. Townshend 2013: 571-572).

[53] When the Irish Free State formally came into existence, Northern Ireland became part of it, thus terminating its membership of the UK. However, this remarkable constitutional episode lasted for only fewer than two days, when the Northern Irish government opted out of the Irish Free State (Barton 2003: 187).

wishes of the majority of the people living in these regions, but also economic and geographical conditions. The hopes of Northern Irish Catholics that their region would eventually come under the sovereignty of the Irish Free State proved to be completely forlorn. The governments of the Irish Free State and Northern Ireland agreed to conceal and thus not publish the Commission's report, which contained recommendations for rather significant adjustments of the border. So, by the end of 1925, when the Boundary Commission ceased its work, the border had remained unchanged (Ferriter 2019: 36-42, Hennessey 1997: 34-40).[54]

North-South relations deteriorated, not least because of the border issue, whereas sectarianism actually flourished in Northern Ireland. The regime governing Northern Ireland for the next three and a half decades was characterised by Unionist supremacy and Nationalist abstention. Throughout that period, the British Government treated Northern Ireland with benign neglect and did not interfere in Unionist rule (cf. Rose 1976: 20, Rose 2000: 178, Smith 2014: 20). With the establishment of a segregated education system for Catholics and Protestants and a mainly Protestant police force named the Royal Ulster Constabulary (RUC), the Unionist Government encouraged these developments. Moreover, it abolished proportional representation in local and in parliamentary elections. All these measures contributed to violence between the Protestant and Catholic communities and Nationalist and Republican non-participation in the process of political decision-making (cf. Barton 1996: 50-85). Besides, Northern Ireland's economic dependence on Britain grew from the early 1930s onwards, since there was insufficient local purchasing power and domestic products had to be sold on the markets of the British Empire. Furthermore, only matters of expenditure were left to autonomous decision-making by the Stormont administration. Britain, in turn, had authority over the bulk of taxation, and Northern Ireland only received a portion of the tax revenue back (Hennessey 1997: 56-59).

At that time, politics in the Irish Free State, led by de Valera, were dominated by Nationalist actions intended to provoke Unionists and strengthen the Catholic/Nationalist/Republican minority in Northern Ireland. In particular, it

---

[54] If the Commission's original proposal had been implemented, the inner-Irish border would have been shortened by 50 miles (82 km), amounting to about 17% of its total length. This would have transferred 50 square miles (742 km²) and 31,219 people to the Irish Free State and 77 square miles (199 km²) and 7,594 people to Northern Ireland (Ferriter 2019: 42, Hennessey 1997: 34-40).

was the wording of the first two articles of the new Irish constitution, official-ly known as '*Bunreacht na hÉireann*', in 1937 that caused outrage within the Protestant/Unionist/Loyalist community. Article 1 laid down the "inalienable, indefeasible and sovereign right [of the Irish nation] to choose its own form of government and to determine its relations with other nations", whereas Article 2 imposed an irredentist claim to Northern Ireland, declaring "that the national territory consisted of the whole island of Ireland" (Kennedy-Pipe 1997: 25). The neutrality of the Irish Free State during the Second World War sparked off further inter-community tensions in Northern Ireland and also clouded British-Irish relations. The Unionist affiliation to Britain became even stronger, when in 1949 the Irish Parliament declared full independence from the British Commonwealth and proclaimed the 'Republic of Ireland' ('*Poblacht na hÉireann*', or short: '*Éire*'). The Republic's complete secession encouraged Nationalists and Republicans in Northern Ireland and, for the first time since partition, galvanised their efforts to reunite Ireland into one organi-sation, i.e. the Anti-Partition-League (APL).[55] Yet, the APL was an ephemer-al organisation. When it was gradually disbanded in the 1950s, it left a vacu-um on the Nationalist and Republican side, which the IRA exploited to renew their paramilitary campaign. However, the IRA's 'Border Campaign' ('The Campaign of Resistance to British Occupation') launched in December 1956, found only marginal support within the Catholic community and was thus abandoned in February 1962 (Barton 1996: 93-95; Hennessey 1997: 87-107).

THE CIVIL RIGHTS MOVEMENT

"Faced with the impotence of their leaders, the imperviousness of their rul-ers and the indifference of the government which posed as the protector of their interests, northern Catholics turned on their own resources." (Staunton 2001: 310). This quote aptly describes the shift in attitudes on the part of Northern Irish Catholics in the 1960s, which represented a period of growing self-assurance in which they could articulate their rights more openly. On the Protestant side, a gradual shift in attitudes occurred towards more tolerance and intercommunal integration. Although the Northern Irish Government promised far-reaching institutional reforms and the eradication of Catholic discrimination, all attempts to reconcile the Catholic minority failed due to a

---

[55] For an extensive account of the APL and their links to the Northern Irish Nationalist Party (NPNI), see Lynn 1997.

paucity of support within the Unionist Party (Barton 1996: 110-117). Hence, Catholic grievances and impatience grew, resulting in the formation of civil rights pressure groups such as the Campaign for Social Justice in Northern Ireland (CSJ), established in 1964, and the Northern Irish Civil Rights Association (NICRA), founded in 1967 (cf. NICRA 1978).

Through their pamphlets, CSJ was pioneering in bringing the allegations of discrimination against Northern Irish Catholics to public attention (cf. CSJ 1969). The most prominent civil rights organisation, however, was NICRA, which initially also found considerable support among the Protestant population. To begin with, these pressure groups aspired to "raise awareness of inequality and pressurise ... [the Unionist Government] into conceding fundamental reforms." (Barton 1996: 126) NICRA decided to organise peaceful street protests in Northern Ireland. This posed a new threat to the Unionist Government, as they could not easily avail themselves of the RUC to suppress the demonstrations (Kennedy-Pipe 1997: 40-41, Purdie 1990: 82-135; cf. NICRA 1978).

Yet, in the end, NICRA's decision proved fateful, because, as it turned out, the protest marches developed a momentum of their own and frequently turned into violent clashes with the RUC and with Loyalists. The first civil rights march from Coalisland to Dungannon on 24 August 1968, which they held with CSJ and other groups, was directed against anti-Catholic discrimination in public housing. The march went without incident, despite being confronted with a Loyalist counterprotest and a ban by the RUC that prevented the protesters from entering Dungannon town centre. That changed with the second civil rights march on 5 October 1968 in Derry/Londonderry, Northern Ireland's second major city, which proved to be a key event triggering the 'Troubles' to come. Four days earlier the Apprentice Boys of Derry[56] announced their intention to simultaneously hold their annual march on the same route. However, this was only a pretext to ban the civil rights march through the RUC, which was a proven Protestant tactic to prevent Catholic nationalist marches and protests from taking place. As a consequence, the civil rights march, which was proposed to go from the Waterside to the Diamond, in city centre, was banned by the RUC. Notwithstanding the concerns

---

[56] The Apprentice Boys of Derry were founded in 1814 to commemorate the Siege of Derry from 1688 to 1689. The exclusively Protestant fraternal organisation is divided into eight 'Parent clubs', to which a number of branch clubs from Ireland, Scotland, England and beyond are affiliated (Bryan 2000: 114–115).

by some members of NICRA, the organisers of the Derry Housing Action Committee (DHAC) went ahead with the march. By the time the march began, however, it had already been stopped by the RUC, who attacked the protesters with batons and injured many of them. The incidents caused serious rioting between local Catholic residents and the RUC. There was also worldwide television coverage showing film footage of the events, which deeply affected many people, especially among the Catholic/Nationalist/ Republican community in Northern Ireland. It intensified their resistance to the Unionist regime and led to the formation of further civil rights and political organisations, such as the People's Democracy (PD), founded by Catholic students at Queen's University Belfast (QUB). PD supported the civil rights campaign, but its ultimate goal was to found a united socialist Irish republic by peaceful means. On New Year's Day 1969 they began a four-day march from Belfast to Derry/Londonderry, modelled on Martin Luther King's Selma to Montgomery marches.[57] They were attacked by Loyalists on several occasions. The most severe incident occurred on 4 January, when the march got into a Loyalist ambush at Burntollet Bridge, resulting in several injuries and serious riots (Dooley 1998: 49-58, Purdie 1990: 136-243).

By early 1969, NICRA's leadership had changed their strategy, and almost all of the liberal founding members were replaced by "young, militant, radical, Catholic working-class activists". (Barton 1996: 133) This confirmed Unionists' suspicions that NICRA's objective was to support the Republican struggle for Irish unification. As a consequence, the military campaigns by Loyalist paramilitary organisations like the Ulster Volunteer Force (UVF)[58]

---

[57] The three protest marches led by Martin Luther King Jr. (MLK) and other American black civil rights activists took place from 7 to 25 March 1965 from Selma, Alabama to the state capital of Montgomery. The marches, based on peaceful, non-violent resistance, were held in protest against the segregationist repression and racial injustice of the American Southern states against African American citizens. The unarmed marchers were, however, repeatedly attacked by state troopers and white supremacist vigilantes. In these attacks, a female black civil rights activist was beaten unconscious (what went down in history as the 'Bloody Sunday'), and a black pastor was murdered. In his speech in Montgomery at the conclusion of the marches, MLK praised the courage of the marchers and told an assembled crowd of thousands of non-violent demonstrators: "There never was a moment in American history more honorable and more inspiring than the pilgrimage of clergymen and laymen of every race and faith pouring into Selma to face danger at the side of its embattled Negroes." (King [1965] 2019) For an extensive account of the Selma to Montgomery marches, see Combs 2014.

[58] The UVF was originally established in 1913 to coordinate the paramilitary campaign of Ulster Unionists against Home Rule. It was revived in 1966 as a Loyalist paramilitary

found more ready acceptance among the Unionist community (Hachey 1996: 235-236). The UVF sought to destabilise the Unionist Government led by Terence O'Neill, whom they held responsible for pushing forward pro-Catholic reforms. Reverend Ian Paisley and his Protestant Ulster Party, which was renamed the Democratic Ulster Unionist Party (DUP) in 1971, were also fundamentally opposed to O'Neill's liberal policy of appeasement. Paisley had an exclusive view of evangelic Protestantism, which denied Northern Irish Catholics equal civil rights and also sympathised with Loyalist paramilitaries to combat Irish Catholicism (Arthur 1994: 93-95).[59] Facing resistance by the dominant conservative faction within his own party, O'Neill finally resigned in April 1969, leaving the Unionist Party in a state of weakness and dissension (Hennessey 1997: 160-161, McEvoy 2008: 34).

THE TROUBLES

By mid-1969, Derry/Londonderry had become the centre of violent clashes between armed Republican and Loyalist groups. The traditional annual parades, held by the Orange Order,[60] escalated sectarian riots further, with violence erupting throughout Northern Ireland (Connolly 1998: 415). In the city, a parade by the Apprentice Boys of Derry led to a large-scale communal riot, commonly referred to as the 'Battle of the Bogside', between Catholic/Nationalist/Republican residents of the Bogside area and local Protestants/

---

force. During the Troubles, the UVF's activities were primarily focused on sectarian assaults on the Catholic community in Northern Ireland. These attacks were often carried out under the *noms de guerre* 'Protestant Action Force' (PAF) and 'Ulster Protestant Action' (UPA) (Bruce 1992: 116, Connolly 1998: 563-564, McDonald & Cusack 2008: 89).

[59] Paisley also fervently campaigned against the civil rights movement. For instance, with his close associate Major Ronald Bunting, he led a Loyalist counter-protest against a NICRA march in Armagh on 30 November 1968. The march was stopped by the RUC, resulting in serious riots. As a consequence, Paisley and Bunting were imprisoned in January 1969 for unlawful assembly, but released two months later under a government amnesty (Heatley 1974: 10, Jordan 2013: 213-214, Purdie 1990: 212).

[60] The Orange Order, or Loyal Orange Institution (LOI) as it is officially known, is an exclusively Protestant fraternity and political society established in 1795 to celebrate the memory and victory of the Protestant King William of Orange at the Boyne in 1690. The Order's main aims are to further Protestantism and to maintain the Union with Great Britain. Despite several attempts at dissociation, the Order still remains closely linked to Ulster Unionism and its political leadership. By contrast, the Royal Black Institution, which separated from the Orange Order in the mid-19th century, has a less political but more religious orientation. For an extensive and insightful account of the history and development of the Orange Order, see Kaufmann 2007, and of the Orange parading tradition, see Bryan 2000.

Unionists/Loyalists alongside the RUC, which lasted over two days from 12 August to 14 August 1969. Hence, as the violence swept over Belfast and other Northern Irish towns, the Unionist Government saw no other way to restore law and order than call for the aid of the British Army. Finally, on 14 August 1969, British troops arrived in Northern Ireland (Hennessey 1997: 162-167). The British Army was initially welcomed by Catholics, as they hoped that the Army would protect them against the Loyalist street violence directed against them.

However, their aggressive behaviour and excessive use of physical force against Catholics soon turned the British Army into an occupying force, which, in turn, fostered the emergence of the Provisional IRA (English 2005: 81; Fay et al 1999: 11-14).[61] When their members, the so-called 'Provisionals', launched their military campaign, they aimed, by means of paramilitary force, to "drive the 'Brits out' and establish a thirty-two-county Irish Republic" (Barton 1996: 40). In addition, the Provisional IRA's short-term objective was to destabilise the Unionist Government and to persuade the Irish Republic to intervene in Northern Ireland. Although there was a growing feeling of solidarity with the Catholic minority in the North, the Irish Government did not want to become directly entangled in the conflict (Barton 1996: 46). The IRA had more success in provoking Loyalist paramilitaries into retaliatory violence. Most of these attacks were committed by the UVF and the Ulster Defence Association (UDA) (Connolly 1998: 560).[62] The large-scale intercommunal riots and paramilitary violence at the onset of the Troubles exceeded the capacities of the RUC and USC, which were the main security forces in Northern Ireland at the time. Following several incidents of undue force against Catholic civilians, the British Government decided to disband the USC and replace it with the Ulster Defence Regiment (UDR). Established in 1970, the UDR was an infantry regiment of the British Army, composed of local recruits and with the aim of protecting civilians against armed attack.

---

[61] The Provisional IRA was founded in 1970 as a splinter group by members of the IRA to express their dissatisfaction with the apathetic attitude and left-wing policy of the 'Official IRA'. Due to their armed campaign, the 'Provisionals' became much more significant than the 'Officials'. Yet, despite several clashes between the two factions, the 'Officials' remained (formally) the official voice of the entire Republican movement (English 2005: 81; Fay et al 1999: 11-14).

[62] The UDA evolved from Protestant vigilante groups in 1971 and started their assassination campaign in response to IRA sniping and bombing attacks. It soon became the largest Loyalist paramilitary unit (Connolly 1998: 560).

Despite the original intention of drawing recruits from both communities according to their population share, by and large the UDR failed to attract Catholics and soon became an almost purely Protestant military force (Potter 2001: 12-21 & 68-69). Moreover, throughout the 1970s both the UDR and the RUC "were given priority in security matters as part of the British government policy of 'Ulsterisation'." (Switzer & Graham 2009: 155)

Meanwhile, the British Government pressurised the Unionist leadership into introducing institutional reforms and implementing policies that would eventually eliminate Catholic discrimination. There was some hope for internal political settlement, when two new parties were founded: the Social Democratic and Labour Party (SDLP), who were committed to constitutional nationalism, and the non-sectarian, moderate unionist Alliance Party of Northern Ireland (APNI).[63] Nonetheless, all these developments did not produce the necessary effects to reconcile the Catholic community, since wide-ranging constitutional and political changes failed, largely due to the opposition of the majority of Unionist Party members (Hennessey 1997: 184-187). Thus, a growing number of Catholic Nationalists, particularly young working-class people from urban and suburban regions in Belfast and Derry/Londonderry, felt attracted to the IRA. The fateful decision of the Unionist administration in August 1971 to introduce the internment of terrorist suspects without prior trial as well as the aggressive conduct of the British Army in enforcing law and order fuelled paramilitary violence, estranging the Northern Irish Catholic community even more (Kennedy-Pipe 1997: 57).

The events of Bloody Sunday in Derry/Londonderry on 30 January 1972, when thirteen unarmed Catholic civilians were shot dead by British Army paratroopers during a NICRA march against internment,[64] caused further

---

[63] Initially, the two parties absorbed the bulk of the electorate of the Northern Ireland Labour Party (NILP), which eventually evaporated in 1987. For an in-depth account of the NILP, see Edwards 2009.

[64] The march was led by Ivan Cooper, a founding member of the SDLP and then member of the Northern Ireland Parliament. The first public investigation into the incidents of Bloody Sunday, the so-called 'Widgery Tribunal', was established two days later by UK parliamentary resolution. The report, which was completed within ten weeks, confirmed the official position held by the British Army that the soldiers had reacted to armed attacks by suspected IRA members (Widgery 1972; cf. BBC News 2000, Pringle & Jacobsen 2000). Following requests by the SDLP leader, John Hume, the British Prime Minister Tony Blair decided in January 1998 to commission a second inquiry, chaired by Lord Saville. After almost seven years of investigation, it took another more than five years until the final report was eventually published on 15 June 2010 (Bingham et al. 2010,

outrage and retaliation. The atmosphere in the city was already very tense, after the preceding anti-internment march held at Magilligan beach on 22 January had been violently suppressed by the British Army (Herron & Lynch 2007: 118-119).[65] In consequence, there was a mass influx into the local branch of the IRA. The vicious circle of violence span faster. As Marc Mulholland points out, "almost one third of the 320 killed in Derry during the Troubles died in street clashes and gun battles during this period." (Mulholland 2002: 98) Throughout Northern Ireland, violence proliferated and also spread south to the Irish Republic. Three days after Bloody Sunday, an enraged mob of demonstrators burnt the British embassy in Dublin to the ground. The failure of British and Unionist politics became more and more apparent. Eventually the Stormont Parliament was suspended and British direct rule was imposed on Northern Ireland. This put an end to fifty years of Unionist rule, and executive authority was handed over to the newly created minister called Secretary of State for Northern Ireland supported by the Northern Ireland Office (NIO) (Hennessey 1997: 206-208).

The most violent year of the conflict with 467 casualties heightened British efforts to solve the conflict (Sutton 1994: 206). In December 1973, the British Government, aided by its Irish counterpart, succeeded in their initiative to bring the Ulster Unionist Party (UUP), the Social Democratic and Labour Party (SDLP) and the Alliance Party of Northern Ireland (APNI) together to form a power-sharing executive. In the so-called 'Sunningdale Agreement',

---

Herron & Lynch 2007; cf. BBC News 2010e, Foy 2010). In its overall assessment, the report stated that "the firing by soldiers of 1 PARA on Bloody Sunday caused the deaths of 13 people and injury to a similar number, none of whom was posing a threat of causing death or serious injury." (Saville et al. 2010: 100)

[65] In August 1971, the meanwhile abandoned British Army camp at Magilligan in County Derry became one of the sites, including the Maze (see also Footnote 163, p. 174) and Crumlin Road prison, where suspected IRA members were interned, i.e. detained without trial, as part of the Army's so-called 'Operation Demetrius' (Gormally et al. 1993; see also Footnote 166, p. 178). On 22 January 1972, an anti-internment march took place at Magilligan beach, attended by several thousand people. As claimed by several witnesses, British Army paratroopers used excessive force to stop the marchers from approaching the internment camp. This involved the firing of rubber bullets and tear gas into the crowd and the severe beating of protesters (Herron & Lynch 2007: 118-119). The British Government remained unimpressed. Thus, in May 1972, Her Majesty's Prison Magilligan was opened. In 2012, the prison held more than 500 male prisoners serving sentences of fewer than seven years. It was officially announced that Magilligan would be closed down and replaced by 2018, mainly because of its low standard of accommodation and remote location from Belfast. More recently, however, the existence of such a plan has been officially denied (Bell 2017, Kearney 2012).

Unionists and Nationalists for the first time reached a compromise on the future status of Northern Ireland by making it dependent on the majority wish of the Northern Irish population whether they wanted to remain part of the UK or become part of a united Ireland. Moreover, the agreement contained a clause concerning the establishment of a Council of Ireland with a vaguely defined role of participation in decision-making for the Irish government (cf. McKenna 2016b). This 'Irish dimension' provoked Unionist opposition to the new constitution and only had few supportive effects for the Catholic minority (Boyce 1996: 119, Tonge 2000: 42). In addition, the Sunningdale Executive was vested with only limited legislative and executive powers. Security and certain economic powers remained with the British Government. Eventually, it was the general strike against the Sunningdale Agreement, announced by the Ulster Workers Council (UWC), a Loyalist workers' organisation set up in 1974 with the major involvement of the UDA, Paisley, William 'Bill' Craig and other Unionist party leaders, which delivered the final blow to this "first cross-community cabinet ever formed in Northern Ireland's history". (Barton 1996: 158) On 28 May 1974, two weeks after the strike began, Northern Ireland's Prime Minister Brian Faulkner and the other Unionist members of the Executive resigned - due to their perceived lack of support in the community. This marked the collapse of the power-sharing intermezzo. British direct rule from Westminster was reinstalled the following day, and for the ensuing ten years – despite several attempts at devolution – the conflict persisted at a high level of violence (Bruce 1994: 11-15, Hennessey 1997: 229-230, Tonge 2000: 42-46, Whyte 2001b: 294, Wood 2006: 34).

Some sporadic peacebuilding efforts at the grassroots community level were already underway, but remarkably they gained momentum after a tragic accidental incident. On 10 August 1976 the British Army fatally shot an IRA member while driving a car in West Belfast. The car then collided with a Catholic mother and her three children, who were walking on the pavement. Two children died on the spot and the third the next day. This provided the impetus for Mairead Corrigan Maguire, the children's aunt, Betty Williams and Ciaran McKeown to set up a grassroots movement campaigning against the violence in Northern Ireland. They called the movement the Peace People and organised a series of weekly peace marches and demonstrations in Belfast, across Northern Ireland, Dublin, Glasgow and Liverpool, which attracted over half a million people and considerable media attention. These rallies were the first since the beginning of the Troubles where a large number of Protestants and Catholics took to the streets and jointly called for peace.

However, as it turned out, they could not break the cycle of violence and the conflict raged on unabated (Bew & Gillespie 1999: 114, Gillespie 2017: 241, Maguire 2010: 3-9).[66]

On the Republican side, the party of Sinn Féin[67] (SF), as the political arm of the IRA, became increasingly popular among the Catholic minority, while the Provisional IRA prepared for a long armed struggle. The fatal hunger strikes of ten Republican inmates of Maze prison in 1981, which became known as the '1981 Irish Hunger Strike', led to a further rise in support for the Republican movement.[68] For their part, the Unionists sought to strengthen the union with Great Britain and aligned themselves more closely to the British Conservative Government, whereas the Loyalist paramilitaries continued their violent assaults on Catholics, Nationalists and Republicans. Meanwhile, the British Government took several steps to improve the economic and social situation in Northern Ireland, albeit with only mediocre success (Barton 1996: 176, Dixon 2001: 159-183).[69]

THE PEACE PROCESS

In the mid-1980s, a significant shift in British – and to some degree also in Irish – government policy towards Northern Ireland occurred, which paved the way for what has become known as the Northern Irish peace process. When the 'Anglo-Irish Agreement' was signed on 15 November 1985 by the

---

[66] In 1977, both Maguire and Williams were awarded the 1976 Nobel Peace Prize for their efforts. Whilst Williams resigned from the Peace People in 1980, Maguire has remained involved in the organisation and currently serves as their honaray president (Gillespie 2017: 68 & 331, Peace People 2019). McKeown, the other driving force behind the Peace People, died recently on 1 September 2019 (BBC News 2019a).

[67] The name 'Sinn Féin' is an Irish-language phrase literally meaning 'We Ourselves' (cf. Adshead & Tonge 2009: xv).

[68] The main protagonist and spokesperson of the hunger-strikers, Bobby Sands, who became a legend of the Republican movement, was elected as a member of the British Parliament (MP). He died on 5 May 1981. Sands' compelling resistance to the British regime earned him considerable international support. His stalwart attitude can be seen in statements like "They have nothing in their whole imperial arsenal that can break the spirit of one Irishman who doesn't want to be broken", or "Our revenge will be the laughter of our children." (McEvoy 2014: 62) The hunger strikes finally ended on 3 October 1981 with the deaths of ten Republican inmates. For an in-depth analysis of the '1981 Irish Hunger Strike', see Beresford 1994 and O'Malley 1990.

[69] The unemployment rate in the early 1980s, for instance, especially among male Catholic adults, was consistently higher in Northern Ireland and the regional growth rate remained at a substantially lower level than in Britain (Barton 1996: 176).

British Prime Minister Margret Thatcher and the *Taoiseach* (Prime Minister) of the Republic of Ireland Garret FitzGerald, Unionists were filled with dismay, since they had neither been consulted nor was their acquiescence or participation needed to render the agreement effective (Barton 1996: 179). The treaty granted the Republic substantial rights of codetermination over Northern Irish affairs, as it provided for the formation of an "Inter-Governmental Conference dealing with political matters, security and related matters, legal questions, and the promotion of cross-border co-operation." (Hennessey 1997: 273) In addition, in Article 1 both governments acknowledged the status of Northern Ireland as part of the UK and affirmed that a prospective united Ireland could only become reality by majority consent of the Northern Irish people (cf. NIO 1985).

Nationalists, both North and South, perceived the agreement as a victory, whereas Unionists saw themselves betrayed by Britain and were committed to opposing the treaty by any means. As a corollary, Unionists became involved in serious riots incited by militant Loyalists of the UDA and UVF. These attacks were even directed at British security forces with the aim of pressurising Westminster not to withdraw British troops from Northern Ireland. On the 'other' side, the Provisional IRA intensified their campaign finally to oust the British from Ireland (Kennedy-Pipe 1997: 123-126). However, despite the persistent violence throughout the period between 1985 and 1993, the Anglo-Irish Agreement remained on the political agenda as the prevailing framework for the settlement of the Northern Ireland conflict.

In the early 1990s, Britain and the Irish Republic increased their efforts to break the stalemate into which the talks between the Northern Irish parties had deteriorated (cf. Boyce 1996: 132-147; Dixon 2001: 235-238).[70] In parallel, community-based peacebuilding efforts took place, which, however, were

---

[70] This was preceded by secret political talks within the Nationalist camp between the SDLP and Sinn Féin as well as between the British Government and Sinn Féin. In the 'Hume-Adams talks' of 1988, John Hume, the then leader of the SDLP, and his Sinn Féin counterpart, Gerry Adams, finally reached agreement over Nationalist aspirations for Northern Ireland. By contrast, the talks between Sinn Féin and the British Government produced no substantial results. However, they demonstrated the British efforts to include Sinn Féin in the peace process. Consequently, Unionists felt alienated and politically isolated. Nevertheless, they decided, albeit reluctantly, to take part in the so-called 'Brooke-Mayhew' talks (April 1991 – November 1992, initiated by the British and Irish governments and chaired by the Northern Ireland Secretary of State Peter Brooke and his successor Patrick Mayhew – hence the name. In part as a concession to Unionists, Sinn Féin was excluded from the talks (cf. Boyce 1996: 132-147; Dixon 2001: 235-238, Gillespie 2017).

largely detached from the political process. An important impetus in this respect was the so-called Initiative '92, also known as the Opsahl Commission after its chair the Norwegian human rights professor Torkel Opsahl. The result of this independent citizen inquiry was the Opsahl report, published in 1993. It presented the views of around 3,000 Northern Irish people about the Troubles and their expectations and concerns about the peace process, which were collected in focus groups and public hearings (Opsahl et al 1993). The report also contained proposals for consideration in the political peace negotiations, one of the most essential being the strong involvement of civil society groups in the peace process. Many of the proposals proved however too controversial at the time and thus were not taken up by the political actors. Nevertheless, some of the recommendations were later included in the broader political agenda (Aughey 2005: 152-153, Elliott 2013, Opsahl et al 1993).

On 25 November 1993, the British and Irish governments issued the 'Downing Street Declaration', which sought to get the political antagonists back to the negotiating table. In this officially denoted 'Joint Declaration on Peace', the British Government pursued the objective "of removing the main republican justification for violence, namely British imperialism in Ireland" (Hennessey 1997: 286) and recognised Irish unity by majority consent. Moreover, Britain denied having any "selfish strategic or economic interest in Northern Ireland." (Mullan 2016) The Irish Government, on the other hand, fully accepted that a united Ireland could only come about through the free will of the majority of the Northern Irish people. In addition, the Republic of Ireland guaranteed the Unionist community that it would examine any elements in the Republic that might possibly threaten them. Both sides agreed that only those parties should be entitled to participate in decision-making that completely committed themselves to the exclusive use of democratic and peaceful means. Nevertheless, the two governments argued over the relevant entity to determine Northern Ireland's state affiliation. Whereas for Britain the entity of pertinence was Northern Ireland, the Irish Republic regarded the whole island of Ireland as the area in question (Hennessey 1997: 287-288).

The Declaration marked the onset of the multi-party political peace process that endeavoured to include all relevant parties involved in the conflict. Its first significant outcome was the ceasefire declared first by the Republican and then by the Loyalist paramilitaries (Hennessey 1997: 288-294).[71] The relative absence of paramilitary violence and the growing focus on the issue of disarmament in the peace talks, chaired by US Senator George Mitchell, accelerated the speed on this path to peace (Dixon 2001: 259-267).[72]

THE BELFAST/GOOD FRIDAY AGREEMENT

The inter-governmental and cross-communal efforts for peace culminated in the 'Agreement Reached in the Multi-Party Negotiations'. This officially put an end to thirty years of armed conflict that had claimed the lives of some 3,400, if not more, people (cf. Dixon 2001, Fay et al 1999, Sutton 2016). To illustrate the conflict's extent and intensity, the following figure shows the distribution of the Troubles' death toll.

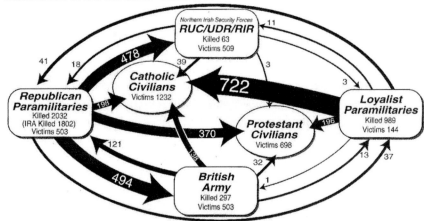

Figure 3. Distribution of Deaths among the Conflicting Groups: "Who killed whom during the 'Troubles' 1969 – 2000" (Dixon 2001: 24)

[71] The IRA declared their ceasefire on 31 August 1994, whereas the UDA and the UVF followed suit on 13 October 1996. Nevertheless, the IRA revived their paramilitary campaign in early 1996, but finally restored their ceasefire on 20 May 1997 (cf. Dixon: 2001: 267; Hennessey 1997: 288-294).

[72] Eventually, elections were held in May 1996 to the so-called Northern Ireland Forum for Political Dialogue, which was established as part of the peace negotiations. According to the election results, ten parties were granted seats in the Forum and were admitted to the multi-party peace talks running in parallel. They were: On the Unionist side the UUP, the DUP, the United Kingdom Unionist Party (UKUP), the Ulster Democratic Party (UDP) and the PUP, on the Nationalist side the SDLP and Sinn Féin and as representatives of the political centre the Alliance Party of Northern Ireland (APNI), the Northern Ireland Women's Coalition (NIWC) and Labour (Whyte 1998).

The peace accord was signed at Stormont Castle in Belfast on Good Friday, 10 April 1998, by the governments of the Republic of Ireland and the UK as well as by most of the major Unionist/Loyalist and all the Nationalist/Republican parties in Northern Ireland. The only main party who did not sign the Agreement was the Democratic Unionist Party (DUP) led by Paisley (Ruane & Todd 1999: 9-13).[73] Subsequently, in order to give legal validity to the Agrements' provisions, the British Government passed the Northern Ireland Constitution Act in 1998. The 'Belfast/Good Friday Agreement' proved by far the most wide-reaching compromise and consensus ever reached between the two rivalling communities.[74] This was not least due to considerable pressure by the British and Irish governments, a substantial intervention from the US and a limited facilitating role of the EU.

The Agreement allowed all the main Northern Irish parties adhering to democratic principles and rejecting violence to participate in devolved institutions, based on consociational power-sharing and the equal representation of both communities. Because of the unique history and circumstances of conflict, both Unionists and Nationalists must join together in a power-sharing Northern Ireland Executive in order to lead the Northern Ireland Assembly (NIA). In particular, the Executive is to be jointly headed by a First Minister and a Deputy First Minister, appointed by either side according to their respective electoral strength. The two roles are practically identical: they share equal power in a joint Executive Office, referred as the Office of the First Minister and the Deputy First Minister (OFMDFM), and can only exist with the full support of the other. Moreover, the Agreement contains a formula, aiming to resolve the intercommunal constitutional dispute, which recognises the right of self-determination of the people of the island of Ireland and stipulates the need for majority consent – North and South – to any change in the constitutional status of Northern Ireland. In particular, the Secretary of State should call a referendum, or so-called 'border poll',

---

[73] The Nationalist signatory parties to the Agreement were the SDLP and SF, whereas their Unionist counterparts were the UUP, PUP, and UDP, and, in addition, there were three middle-ground parties, the APNI, NIWC and Labour. Two Unionist parties, the DUP and the UKUP, representing nearly 43% of the Unionist electorate, had already left the multi-party peace talks earlies and refused to participate in any further talks with SF without prior disarmament of the IRA (Ruane & Todd 1999: 9-13, Wolff 2004: 18).

[74] For the full text of the Belfast/Good Friday Agreement, see NIO 1998.

"If at any time it appears likely to him that a majority of those voting would express a wish that Northern Ireland should cease to be part of the United Kingdom and form part of a united Ireland." (NIO 1998: 5)

Notably, the Agreement was also aimed at preserving and improving the balance of relationships throughout the British Isles. Thus, it provided for a North/South Ministerial Council (NSMC), a British-Irish Intergovernmental Conference (BIIGC) and a British-Irish Council (BIC) to improve both North-South and Anglo-Irish relations (Horowitz 2002, O'Leary 1999, Ruane & Todd 1999). The NSMC, consisting of ministers from both jurisdictions, was vested with special powers to deal with designated cross-border issues agreed as being of common interest. However, the existence of the NSMC and the NIA has been made mutually interdependent and indispensable: i.e. if one body is not operational, the other cannot exist either. By contrast, the BIIGC, which is concerned with promoting bilateral cooperation between the British and Irish governments, has no immediate executive responsibility. Yet, in the event of suspension of the Northern Irish institutions, devolved matters fall within the remit of the BIIGC. This means that the Government of the Republic of Ireland, through its involvement in the NSMC and BIIGC, may exercise joint authority in certain policy areas of Northern Ireland. Finally, the BIC, composed of all admistrations on the British Isles, was established as a primarily consultative intergovernmental forum aiming to improve the development and relationships on the Anglo-Irish islands. This institutional framework for promoting all-Ireland and British-Irish relations has also been embedded in a wider European context. In particular, the NSMC was granted special authority to deal with EU issues of an all-Ireland importance. Moreover, the Special EU Programmes Body (SEUPB), one of the 'implementation bodies' created to promote North-South cooperation, was given exclusive responsibility for administering EU cross-border initiatives (Lynch & Hopkins 2001, McLoughlin 2009: 612, Meehan 2000, Pollak 2001).

A core concept of the Agreement is 'parity of esteem', which gives equal recognition to the cultural, social and political identities of both the Protestant/Unionist/Loyalist and the Catholic/Nationalist/Republican communities. This means that the political aspirations of Nationalists/Republicans for a united Ireland are equally legitimate as those of Unionists/Loyalists for the maintenance of the UK. Moreover, all people born in Northern Ireland can choose to be British citizens or Irish citizens, or both.[75] The principle of 'parity of esteem' is also an essential element of a comprehensive equality agenda enshrined in the Agreement. In particular, equal civil, cultural, social and political rights and freedom from discrimination, and equality of opportunity are granted to all Northern Irish citizens. All government and public authorities are obliged to uphold these guarantees. In addition, under Section 75 of the Northern Ireland Act 1998, they are required to make equal opportunities and good relations a central part of policy-making and service delivery (McCrudden 1999, Thompson 2002, ECNI 2019).

Two referenda followed: one in Northern Ireland on the Agreement's provisions, and the second in the Republic of Ireland on the abandonment of its constitutional claim to jurisdiction over Northern Ireland. They both elicited a substantial majority of supporters of the Agreement, amounting to 71.1% in Northern Ireland and as much as 94.4% in the Irish Republic. Notably, even though the referendum in Northern Ireland yielded a resounding yes vote, it also revealed the deep communal divisions. While practically all Catholics voted for the Agreement (99%), there was only a relatively slim majority of 57% Protestants who did so (Hayes & McAllister 2001: 79-80). Elections to the Assembly were held in June 1998 and produced the following results: on the Nationalist side, the SDLP achieved 22% of the vote and Sinn Féin 17%, whereas the UUP gained 21%, thus, together with the votes for the APNI and the Progressive Unionist Party (PUP) and the Ulster Democratic Party (UDP),[76] securing the Unionist parties endorsing the Agreement a majority of the Unionist electorate. Subsequently, David Trimble, the leader of the UUP, and the SDLP candidate, Seamus Mallon, were elected as First and Deputy First Minister and were to preside over a 10-member 'Executive Committee' (Mac Ginty & Darby 2002: 42-44).

---

[75] In Article 1 (vi) of the Agreement, the British and Irish governments and the other signatory parties committed themselves to "recognise the birthright of all the people of Northern Ireland to identify themselves and be accepted as Irish or British, or both, as they may so choose, and accordingly confirm that their right to hold both British and Irish citizenship is accepted by both Governments and would not be affected by any future change in the status of Northern Ireland." (NIO 1998: 3)

[76] The UDP was established in 1989 as the successor to the Ulster Loyalist Democratic Party (ULDP) that had been founded by the UDA in 1981. The party was dissolved in 2001 as a result of ongoing disputes between the pro- and anti-Agreement factions of its leadership. Its role within Loyalism has been largely taken over by the Ulster Political Research Group (UPRG), which was founded in 2002 as a political advisory body with close links to the UDA (Melaugh 2016a, Wood 2006).

In addition to the political institutions, several independent statutory bodies aiming at rectifying the legacies of the conflict were established in the course of the implementation of the Agreement. These bodies included the Equality Commission for Northern Ireland (ECNI), the Independent Commission on Policing for Northern Ireland (ICP), the International Independent Commission on Decommissioning (IICD), the Northern Ireland Human Rights Commission (NIHRC) and the Parades Commission (PCNI) (Hennessey 2000: 196, O'Leary 2019: 175-229, Ruane & Todd 1999: 24, Tonge 2006: 201). Notably, the Agreement also provided for the establishment of a consultative Civic Forum, consisting of representatives from the main sectors of Northern Irish society.[77] The Forum, which was already a late bloomer, had, however, only a short-lived existence of two years, and was finally dissolved in October 2002, due to persistent political controversy over its viability (Melaugh & Lynn 2019, McCaffrey 2013, Nolan & Wilson 2015).

POST-CONFLICT RECONSTRUCTION IN THE AFTERMATH OF THE AGREEMENT

The conclusion of the Agreement and the endorsement by its signatories of their "total and absolute commitment to exclusively democratic and peaceful means of resolving differences" (NIO 1998)[78] raised hopes that violence had been eschewed in Northern Ireland. Soon afterwards, however, these hopes were dashed. In August 1998, one of the worst atrocities of the whole conflict, the so-called 'Omagh bombing', which killed 30 people, was perpetrated by the Real IRA, a dissident faction of the IRA that emerged in 1997 (Smyth 2006: 18). Nevertheless, negotiations on the implementation of the provisions of the Agreement continued, in particular concerning the composition of the ministries, the North-South Council, the police reform, and the decommissioning of the paramilitary organisations (Tonge 2006: 189-190). Finally, on 2 December 1999, power was devolved from the British Government to the Northern Ireland Assembly and Executive (Dixon 2001: 276-

---

[77] Following the Assembly's approval in February 1999, the Civic Forum was to be composed of a chairman and 60 members from the voluntary and community sector, business, trade unions, churches, arts and sports, culture, agriculture and fisheries, community relations, education and victims organisations, as well as personal nominations from the First Minister and Deputy First Minister (Melaugh & Lynn 2019).

[78] See 'Declaration of Support', Section 4 in the Agreement (NIO 1998: 1).

277). Yet, the implementation of the terms of the Agreement remained under the permanent threat of whether the pro-Agreement Unionist party UUP would succeed in securing the necessary support from their party members. For the UUP, another major challenge developed from the persistent electoral gains of the anti-Agreement DUP (Whyte 2005).[79]

Notwithstanding some modestly positive results of the UUP-SDLP-led power-sharing government in Northern Ireland on topics such as integrated education, fair employment and policing, the crucial issue of decommissioning the IRA remained unsolved. It was this impasse and the ongoing failure of Sinn Féin to persuade the IRA to surrender their arms that made Unionists demand the party's exclusion from the devolved government (Aughey 2005, Smith 2002). The British Government did not accept the Unionist demand and decreed the fourth suspension of the Assembly in October 2002, which led to its dissolution in April 2003 due to persistent political stalemate. Thus, Northern Ireland was placed once more under the *ancien régime* of British direct rule (Tempest 2002, Tonge 2006: 200). Yet, the governance crisis could be resolved, and devolution was restored with the elections to a new Assembly in November 2003. The election resulted in a shift in power relations with the middle-ground parties losing ground and the more radical parties of DUP and Sinn Féin becoming the largest parties (Whyte 2004).[80] Due to a lack of agreement between the Republican/Nationalist and Unionist/Loyalist blocks, however, power was not transferred to the Assembly and Executive. After the major dispute over the decommissioning of weapons of the Provisional IRA was finally settled in 2005,[81] further major obstacles

---

[79] At the Local Government Elections in 2001, the DUP increased their share to 21%, whereas the UUP's share fell to 23%. For an overview of Northern Irish election results, see Whyte 2013.

[80] In the Assembly elections on 26 November 2003, the DUP got almost 26%, SF almost 24%, leaving behind the former largest parties UUP (23%) and SDLP (17%). Moreover, the middle-ground parties of APNI and NIWC saw a decline in votes, the latter even losing their two seats in the Assembly (Whyte 2004).

[81] On 28 July 2005, the Provisional IRA issued a statement ending their armed campaign and destroying all their weaponry (Melaugh 2005). Subsequently, on 26 September 2005, the Independent International Commission on Decommissioning (IICD) confirmed that "the IRA has met their commitment to put all their arms beyond use in a manner called for by the legislation." (IICD 2005: 2) It took four more years for the Loyalist paramilitary organisations of the UVF, UDA and Red Hand Commando (RHC) to follow suit. The completion of their decommissioning process was subsequently confirmed by the IICD (BBC News 2009b, IICD 2009, 2010c & 2011, Melaugh 2009). Shortly afterwards, in February 2010, the Republican paramilitary organisations of the Irish National Liberation

emerged preventing the restoration of power-sharing institutions. Whilst Sinn Féin had great difficulties in supporting the Police Service of Northern Ireland (PSNI), the major issues for the DUP were the acceptance of power-sharing with Republicans and the devolution of judicial powers to the Assembly.

In order to overcome the political impasse over these contentious issues, the British and Irish governments under Prime Minister Tony Blair and *Taoiseach* Bertie Ahern in October 2006 agreed on the so-called 'St Andrews Agreement',[82] which set out a timetable for the restoration of devolution and power-sharing in Northern Ireland. The fulfilment of this timetable was made contingent on the major parties' acceptance of the terms of the Good Friday/Belfast Agreement and on their consensus on the topics of policing, power-sharing, institutional changes, human rights and finance. Following the parties' agreement, a transitional assembly to prepare the way for devolved government was formed in November 2006 and remained in existence until the end of January 2007 (Wilford 2008: 67-68). The subsequent Northern Ireland Assembly elections of 7 March 2007 confirmed the electoral trend that had already commenced four years earlier. Whereas the DUP (30% of the votes) and Sinn Féin (26%) consolidated their positions as the two largest Northern Irish parties, the SDLP (15%) and the UUP (15%) lost further ground (Melaugh 2007). Two months later, on 8 May 2007, a remarkable moment in Northern Ireland's troubled history occurred, when the former archenemies during the Troubles, Ian Paisley (DUP) and Martin McGuinness (Sinn Féin), were inaugurated as Northern Ireland's First Minister and Deputy First Minister (cf. Ruxton 2017). One year later, Paisley stepped down both as First Minister and also as DUP leader, a position he held for 36 years. He died on 12 September 2014 at the age of 88 years after a prolonged severe illness (McCreary 2014). His party colleague Peter Robinson succeeded him in both positions. During the first three years in power, the relations in public between the DUP and Sinn Féin were characterised more or less by demonstrative harmony.[83] In terms of *realpolitik*, however, the achievements of the

---

Army (INLA) and the Official IRA verifiably decommissioned their arms (IICD 2010a & 2010b).

[82] For the full text of the Agreement at St. Andrews, see NIO 2006.

[83] This demonstrative harmony in public was most evident with Ian Paisley and Martin McGuinness. They even went so far as to be described in the media as "The Chuckle Brothers" after a famous English comedy double act on children's television (cf. BBC

power-sharing government were limited. Many tough decisions were by-passed on contentious issues such as community relations, education reform, housing and parades (Bartlett 2010: 575-586).

In the first two months of 2010, there was a serious dispute between the DUP and Sinn Féin about the devolution of policing and justice and about the issue of contentious parades, which threatened the continuation of the power-sharing institutions (BBC News 2010b, Belfast Telegraph 2010c). Eventually, with the intervention of the British and Irish governments, the parties managed to resolve their differences and reach an agreement. The so-called 'Agreement at Hillsborough Castle' set out a roadmap for the devolution of policing and justice and for the constitution of an Assembly working group dealing with parades (Belfast Telegraph 2010a).[84] On 12 April, after policing and justice powers had been transferred to the Assembly, APNI leader David Ford was appointed Justice Minister of Northern Ireland – the first one after 38 years (BBC News 2010a, Belfast Telegraph 2010b, McDonald 2010).

BREXIT, THE IRISH BORDER ISSUE AND THE WIDER IMPASSE IN POLITICAL AND COMMUNITY RELATIONS

In recent years, post-conflict reconstruction in Northern Ireland has been hampered by continuing disruptions in community and political relations. Promoting good relations between the Protestant and Catholic communities forms an integral part of the Good Friday/Belfast Agreement[85] and thus had to be made a priority of the post-conflict political agenda. Consequently, several governmental attempts have been made to develop and implement a community relations strategy. All these attempts failed, however, because the Unionist and Nationalist political camps could not agree on the principles and priorities for a common policy framework. First, in 2005, during suspension of devolved government, the direct rule administration published the strategic document 'A Shared Future: Policy and Strategic Framework for Good Relations in Northern Ireland' (cf. OFMDFM 2005). Yet the document lacked the

---

News 2007, Belfast Telegraph 2017a). Their good working relationship even developed into a friendship after Paisley's retirement, and McGuinness visited Paisley in his private home and later at his sickbed (BBC News 2014).

[84] For the full text of the Agreement at Hillsborough Castle, see NIO 2010.

[85] For instance, in its 'Code of Conduct', the Agreement obliges all Ministers of the Northern Ireland Executive to "operate in a way conducive to promoting good community relations and equality of treatment." (NIO 1998: 13)

sense of ownership and thus the support of the subsequent governing parties DUP and Sinn Fein, who eventually replaced it with their own community strategy, the so-called 'Programme for Cohesion, Sharing and Integration' (CSI), published in 2010 (cf. OFMDFM 2010). The two parties in power were, however, unable to agree on a concrete implementation plan, and so a new strategic document called 'Together: Building a United Community' (T:BUC) was launched in 2013.[86] In particular, both parties paid special attention to the situation of interface communities and declared their commitment to removing all 'peace walls' by 2023 (OFMDFM 2013: 6; cf. Devenport 2013). Moreover, the most recent governance arrangement entitled 'A Fresh Start: The Stormont Agreement and Implementation Plan' of 17 November 2015 also included the pledge by the UK Government to provide substantial financial support for measures aimed at dismantling the 'peace walls' (NIE 2015: 8 & 29). However, as with previous community relations strategies, there seems to be no real commitment from the parties, since only some minor steps have been taken so far to put it into practice. To date, neither a significant number of interface barriers have been removed, nor has their community relations strategy been effectively implemented (cf. Campbell 2017, NIE 2019).

As regards community relations on the ground, there have been some worrisome developments. The term of office of the DUP-Sinn Féin power-sharing government has been fraught with inter-community tensions and violent incidents in hotspot locations, especially during the annual Orange Order parade season.[87] The intensity of sectarianism peaked with the Belfast City

---

[86] In the document, the DUP and Sinn Féin acknowledged that it was time "to move from policy development to implementation and action, by means of promoting cross-community initiatives around education, housing, youth volunteering, interface barriers and sports." (OFMDFM 2013: 1)

[87] In general, the aftermath of the Agreement has been characterised by many violent inter-communal attacks, one of the most infamous happening in 2001 and 2002 the escalating dispute at Holy Cross Roman Catholic Girls' Primary School between the pupils and parents and the residents of a neighbouring Loyalist area (BBC News 2001c & 2002). Severe sectarian riots had already occurred repeatedly during the peace process. An infamous example is the long-standing dispute over the annual Orange Order march to the Drumcree Church in Portadown between the Order and local Catholic residents, which had intensified since the beginning of the Troubles. From 1995 to 1998, the march led to intense violent clashes that spread throughout Northern Ireland. Since then, the violence has decreased significantly, however, as the march has been banned from most of the Nationalist areas (Bryan 2000: 1-10, McKenna & Melaugh 2016).

Hall flag protests in early December 2012. Loyalists and Unionists protested against the City Council's decision by SF, SDLP and APNI councillors to limit the waving of the Union flag from the City Hall from year-round to 18 days, which was in line with British government guidelines for official buildings in the UK. (Melaugh 2013; cf. UK DCMS 2013). This was seen as part of a wider cultural assault on the Britishness of Northern Ireland (McDonald 2013b). Consequently, the protests continued and sparked severe sectarian rioting over other contentious issues throughout 2013, such as restrictions on traditional Orange Order marches. They persisted with less intensity and became locally concentrated in a few interface areas in subsequent years, before eventually fading in 2016 (Jarman 2019, Nolan et al 2014, Williamson 2016). The paramilitary violence and intimidation in the communities, mainly caused by Loyalist feuds and dissident Republican factions, has been another destabilising element for the fragile post-Agreement peace process (Canning 2009, McDonald 2005, Rowan 2000 & 2009, Morrison & Horgan 2016).[88] According to a recent study by Paul Nolan, the paramilitaries have committed most of the 158 'security-related' killings since the Agreement up to 2018, with members of their own community being the main target group (Nolan 2018). Dissident Republicans, however, have also repeatedly targeted and killed security forces (Morrison & Horgan 2016: 590, Tonge 2014: 15).[89] Recently, dissident violence claimed another tragic victim, when on Good Friday, 19 April 2019, investigative journalist Lyra McKee was fatally shot by members of the so-called 'New IRA' during riots in Derry/Londonderry (Bell 2019, Weaver & Rawlinson 2019).

At the political level, Northern Ireland has been marked over recent years by two events of particular significance, both of which could have a disruptive impact on community and power relations as well as on the overall peace process. These are, on the one hand, the UK's withdrawal from the EU, commonly known as 'Brexit' (British exit from the EU), and the inextricably

---

[88] Between 2000 and 2010 at least six feuds between the Loyalist paramilitary organisations occurred causing several paramilitary and civilian casualties. Republican dissidents of the Real IRA and Continuity IRA have become increasingly active in stirring up tensions at Orange parades – mainly in North Belfast – and in targeting security and military forces (cf. BBC News 2009, 2010c & 2010d, The Independent 2010).

[89] According to Jonathan Tonge, from 2006 to 2014, "republicans have been responsible for more than 600 shooting and bombing incidents and killed British Army soldiers, Police Service of Northern Ireland officers and a Prison Officer, along with several civilians." (Tonge 2014: 15).

linked Irish border issue, and, on the other, the collapse of the Northern Ireland power-sharing government.

The Brexit process started on 23 June 2016, when a narrow majority of the people in the UK (51.9%) voted in a referendum in favour of leaving the EU. Consequently, on 29 March 2017, the UK invoked Article 50 of the Treaty on European Union (EU 2012:43-44) This triggered a two-year process for the UK's withdrawal from the EU, which is due, after an agreed extended transition period, on 31 October 2019 (cf. EU 2019). However, the referendum results varied widely across the UK, with a significant majority in Northern Ireland (55.8%), Scotland (62%) and the City of London (59.9%) voting to remain in the EU (ECUK 2016). In Northern Ireland there were stark differences in voting behaviour between the two communities. While, according to an analysis of the Northern Ireland Assembly's election study in 2016, about 85% of Catholics voted to stay in the EU, the proportion among Protestants amounted to only around 40% (Garry, O'Leary & Coakley 2017).[90]

This communal cleavage is reflected in the political chasm between the Unionist and Nationalist camps. In particular, the DUP and Sinn Féin take diametrically opposed positions on Brexit, based on arguments about identity, sovereignty, economic issues and implications for the peace process (cf. Doyle & Connolly 2019: 84-85). The DUP is strongly in favour of the UK leaving the EU and demands that Northern Ireland must exit the EU on the same terms as the rest of the UK (cf. Belfast Telegraph 2017b, Wilson 2017). Sinn Féin, by contrast, takes a resolutely pro-EU stance and strives to reverse the withdrawal process through a second referendum or, if that cannot be achieved, to secure a special designated status within the EU (cf. Sinn Féin 2019). In general, the smaller parties on both sides, the UUP and SDLP, have adopted similar positions, albeit to a more moderate degree. Thus, the UUP endorses Brexit after abandoning its support for the Remain referendum campaign (cf. O'Driscoll 2017, UUP 2016), while the SDLP is strongly in favour of staying in the EU (cf. Eastwood 2016, Walker 2019). Likewise, as a declared pro-European party, the centrist APNI wants Northern Ireland to remain and calls for a second referendum on the UK's EU membership (cf. APNI 2019, Carroll 2019).

---

[90] Moreover, given the territorial distribution of the Catholic and Protestant communities, 11 out of the 18 Northern Irish constituencies voted in favour of Remain, with them being located close to the border with the Irish Republic and in Belfast North, West and South (BBC News 2016b).

Notably, the Brexit negotiations between the UK Government and the EU are beset by a continuing tug-of-war over the specific terms of a withdrawal agreement, particularly over the Irish border issue, which has become the most vexing bone of contention. In fact, the border between Northern Ireland and the Republic of Ireland, which was heavily militarised during the Troubles, has become virtually invisible as a consequence of the Good Friday/ Belfast Agreement, allowing people and goods to move freely back and forth. The essential question is now whether the Irish border can remain open after Brexit or whether it will as an external border between the EU and UK have to be fortified with customs and immigration checks between Northern Ireland and the Irish Republic. Moreover, such a customs regime would also extend to Irish ports and airports, thus creating a de facto border in the Irish Sea. Both the EU and UK negotiators have repeatedly stated their commitment to avoid such a hard border, not least to protect the Northern Irish peace process. The proposed solution to maintain a soft, frictionless border, both on the island of Ireland and in the Irish Sea, is the so-called 'Irish backstop'. As a position of last resort, it provides a fallback option of keeping Northern Ireland aligned to some regulations of the EU single market in the event that the UK leaves the EU without securing an all-encompassing trade deal. In November 2018 the UK and EU published a draft Withdrawal Agreement that included a backstop, which would provide for additional controls on some goods arriving in Northern Ireland from Great Britain and maintain a customs union between the EU and the whole of the UK (EC 2018).

Subsequently, however, the negotiations reached a dead end (cf. Campbell 2019). While the EU insisted on the backstop in its existing form, the strong faction of hardline Brexiteers within the ruling UK Conservative Party (also known as the Tories), along with the parliamentary opposition UK Independence Party (UKIP), rejected it altogether. Moreover, the latter are strongly in favour of a no-deal withdrawal, which would most likely make a hard Irish border inevitable. As a result of the ongoing dispute between hardliners and moderates, Prime Minister Theresa May failed to reach an agreement with the EU. Ultimately, after several unsuccessful attempts to win a parliamentary majority for her proposals, she was forced to resign first as Conservative Party leader and subsequently, on 24 July 2019, also as Prime Minister (cf. Allen 2019, Sparrow 2019a, Thomas & Noble 2019). Her successor Boris Johnson has been a staunch Brexit hardliner from the very beginning. Nevertheless, Johnson has affirmed that he will continue to seek a compromise with the EU, but only if they agree to remove the backstop. At the same time, however, the

British Government intensified preparations for a hard Brexit scenario. According to a recent official government document, a no-deal withdrawal would have serious economic and social consequences for Northern Ireland. In particular, a hard border would lead, inter alia, to severe trade disruptions, job losses and road blockages (Armstrong & Holton 2019). In its attempt to avoid the negative economic impact of a hard Brexit on the UK, the British Government has already attempted to forge closer ties with the US and to conclude a trade agreement with the US government (BBC News 2019c, Payne 2019; cf. Blanchard 2019).

However, there cross-party resistance to Johnson's hardline Brexit strategy has been formed in the British Parliament, including moderate Tories and MPs from the opposition Labour Party, Scottish National Party (SNP), Liberal Democrats, The Indendent Group for Political Change, Plaid Cymru and the Green Party. The group intends to stop a 'hard Brexit' either by legislative means or by bringing down Johnson's government through a no-confidence vote (Mason & Elgot 2019). Johnson's response was not long in coming. In an surprising move that the opposition described as scandalous and outrageous and as a breach of the constitution, he got the Queen's approval to suspend parliament from the week starting 9 September to14 October. This would have left the MPs only a few days to stop a hard Brexit or Brexit at all. In addition to fierce political reactions, the prorogation of parliament led to a public outcry with thousands of protesters taking to the streets across Britain (cf. Castle 2019, Mohdin et al 2019). Yet subsequently, another unexpected turn has occurred, deepening political turmoil over Brexit.The so-called 'Benn Bill' was passed by both chambers, preventing the UK from leaving the EU on 31 October 2019 and giving the British Parliament the right to decide on the exit arrangements. This means that the ultimate power of decision rests with Parliament, i.e. it has the choice of approving a withdrawal agreement or voting for a no-deal outcome or even for a second Brexit referendum. In the absence of an agreement by 19 October, the Prime Minister is obliged to ask the EU to extend the UK's membership until 31 January 2020, and, if the EU agrees, he has to follow suit (Murray 2019; cf. Peers 2019). Johnson, however, has expressed his refusal to ask the EU for an extension, stating he would even consider breaking the law in order to maintain the planned Brexit date (Stewart & Carrell 2019). Meanwhile, further strain has been added to the tense political climate when on 24 September the UK Supreme Court, on appeal by a political campaigner, has ruled Johnson's Parliament suspension unlawful, void and of no effect. Consequently, Parliament has resumed its work the day after the court decision (BBC News 2019b). Most recently, another initiative has been taken to break the deadlock in the Brexit negotiations. Johnson has proposed a so-called 'pared down' free trade agreement, which has already been approved by the Irish *Taoiseach* Leo Varadkar and subsequently by EU negotiators. In essence, the proposal provides for the relocation of the heavier customs checks between the UK and the EU to Irish ports and airports, thus effectively creating a border in the Irish Sea and ensuring an open Irish land border. Although this would keep Northern Ireland in the UK's customs union, it would also remain in regulatory alignment with the EU. This alignment arrangement would initially run for four years and its extension would then depend on majority decision of the Northern Ireland Assembly. Ultimately, however, Johnson's proposal still requires the approval of the UK Parliament. In an extraordinary sitting on 19 October, a slim majority of MPs voted in favour of the so-called 'Letwin amendment', which states that Parliament will withhold approval until the withdrawal bill implementing Brexit has been adopted. It also requires Johnson by law to ask the EU for a further extension. He has already followed suit, albeit reluctantly, by sending the request to the EU without signature along with two follow-up letters confirming the UK government's commitment to leave the EU by 31 October (Proctor 2019, Siddique & Phipps 2019).

In Northern Ireland the Irish border dispute has aggravated already existing political tensions over Brexit and other issues. In fact, as early as January 2017, the power-sharing Executive collapsed mainly because of a dispute over the mismanagement of a renewable energy programme signed by First Minister and DUP leader Arlene Foster. She rejected Sinn Féin's call for an independent inquiry into the alleged scandal. Consequently, Martin McGuinness resigned as Deputy First Minister. Under the terms of the Good Friday/ Belfast Agreement Foster was thus forced to follow suit and step down from her office as First Minister. Sinn Féin had also other reasons for ending power-sharing with the DUP, complaining in particular about their unequal treatment of the Irish language and their persistent refusal to allow same-sex marriages (Doyle & Connolly 2019: 83, Fenton 2018: 170-171, Kelly 2018). In an effort to restore power-sharing, snap elections for the Assembly were held at the beginning of March. It confirmed the DUP and Sinn Féin as the largest parties, but the gap between them had narrowed dramatically to only 1,000 votes. The DUP fell by 10 seats to 28, with Sinn Féin only one seat behind on 27. Moreover, for the first time since the formation of Northern Ireland, the Unionist parties lost their parliamentary majority (Clarke et al 2017, Whyte

2017).[91] Shortly after the elections, on 21 March 2017, Martin McGuinness died of ill health at the age of 66 (McHardy 2017). The following month, the two leading parties held talks to restore power-sharing government. However, the talks soon came to a standstill, because the parties could not agree on key issues, such as the adoption of an Irish language act and dealing with the legacies of the Troubles. To date, their impasse still continues, despite repeated extensions of the deadline on power-sharing talks by the Northern Ireland Secretary of State and various interventions by the British and Irish governments (cf. Mohdin 2019, Sparrow 2019b).[92] In fact, direct rule has not been imposed so far, and Northern Irland is practically run by civil servants. Yet, the UK government has already signalled that this could change in the event of a hard Brexit and that they consider taking over the government affairs of Northern Ireland (cf. Parker & Boland 2019).

The gulf between the DUP and Sinn Féin has only grown since the collapse of power-sharing talks, mainly due to both parties' intransigence on the Irish border issue. The DUP has been in close alliance with the Tories, in a so-called 'Confidence & Supply Agreement', since June 2017, otherwise Prime Minister May would not have had a parliamentary majority for her government. With this decision, however, May also caused considerable resentment in her own party and in the general public (cf. Savage & McDonald 2017). Likewise, Sinn Féin was upset. They argued that this impedes the resumption of talks, as under the Good Friday/Belfast Agreement the UK government, like their Irish counterpart, must be an impartial intermediary between the two sides. In their overriding concern to safeguard the union with Great Britain, the DUP adamantly rejects the Irish backstop and any other proposal that would set Northern Ireland apart from the rest of the UK (cf. McCormack 2019). At the same time, however, the party has repeatedly affirmed their opposition to both a hard border on the island of Ireland and in the Irish Sea, albeit without specifying how this could be prevented if there is

---

[91] The election resulted in the following distribution of the 90 Assembly seats (and of the 1st preference votes): DUP 28 (28.1%), Sinn Féin 27 (27.9%), SDLP 12 (11.9%) UUP 10 (12.9%), APNI 8 (9.1%), Green Party 2 (2.3%), TUV 1 (2.6%), People Before Profit Alliance 1 (1.8%), Independent 1 (0.6%) (Whyte 2017). For a detailed election report see also Russell 2017.

[92] Northern Ireland thus holds the unofficial world record for the country with the longest period without a fully functioning, elected government in peacetime. Actually, the previous record of Belgium, which had been 588 days without a government, was surpassed already on 28 August 2018 (cf. Maza 2018).

no backstop (cf. Geoghegan 2017). For Sinn Féin, the seamless character of the Irish border and its environment must be preserved by all means after Brexit, thus leaving no room to change any aspect of the current backstop draft agreement. In February 2018, there was a change in leadership in the party when Gerry Adams retired after 34 years as Sinn Féin president (cf. BBC News 2018b). Thus, after Paisley and McGuinness the last of the main protagonists, who shaped both the conflict and peace process, left the stage. His successor Mary Lou McDonald and new vice-president Michelle O'Neill continue to drive Sinn Fein's Irish unity campaign forward. Like Adams, they have repeatedly called for a border poll on Northern Ireland's constitutional status, initially in the event that there is no backstop agreement, but lately even regardless of the UK's withdrawal from the EU (cf. Moriarty 2019, Ó Scannáil 2019, Walker & Elgot 2019). The Irish Government has, however, rejected such demands. *Taoiseach* Varadkar expressed already his concern that a border poll in the immediate aftermath of a hard Brexit would pose a threat to community relations and the peace process in Northern Ireland. Furthermore, it would also add to the existing strain in Anglo-Irish relations (Breen 2019b; cf. O'Carroll 2019a). The reluctance seems to be shared by the UK Government. According to the DUP, they were told by Prime Minister Johnson during recent talks in Stormont that under current circumstances he sees no reason to arrange a border poll. Moreover, in the midst of mounting tensions, they accused Sinn Féin of violating the Belfast/Good Friday Agreement, because the conditions for a border poll, i.e. a likely majority vote for a united Ireland, are not met (Madden 2019). Soon afterwards, the two parties clashed again when Johnson claimed that the Irish backstop posed a threat to the peace process (Young 2019). Both are also dicordant on Johnson's recently proposed 'pared down' free trade agreement. The DUP firmly rejects the proposal, because it would set Northern Ireland apart from the rest of the UK and thus threaten the union. By contrast, Sinn Féin is basically in favour, as this would preserve economic and political relations with the Irish Republic (Belfast Telegraph 2019c, Lehane 2019). Recently, Loyalist paramilitaries have also announced to resort to civil disobedience if the status of Northern Ireland within the UK is diluted after Brexit. This threat of violence has been condemned by leading Unionist politicians (McGovern 2019).

Apparently, the political turmoil over Brexit and the Irish border issue and the fact that there is still no power-sharing government in sight have created a lot of economic and social insecurity among people in Northern Ireland. This also seems to have led to significant changes in public attitudes towards the

Brexit process and Northern Ireland's political stalemate. In particular, four broad tendencies can be identified from the various survey research and opinion polls that have been conducted since the UK's EU referendum.

Firstly, there is evidence for growing support for the UK staying in the EU. For instance, a face-to-face survey conducted for Queen's University Belfast (QUB) in March 2018 found that since the referendum overall support for the EU had risen by 13% to 69%.[93] Nevertheless, a decreasing majority of Protestants (56%) would still vote to leave the EU in the event of a second referendum (Garry et al 2018: 33). A majority of the Northern Irish people (56%) would also support the holding of such a referendum, according to the online LucidTalk (LT) Tracker Poll of Winter 2018. However, there was a wide gap in opinion between adherents of the two political camps, with Nationalists/Republicans overwhelmingly supporting a second referendum (83%) and Unionists predominantly opposing it (71%) (LT 2018: 4).

Secondly, on the assumption that Brexit will happen, there seems to be significant cross-communal support for the softest possible withdrawal based on a UK-wide arrangement with the EU. According to the QUB survey, a clear majority in both communities – 61% of Catholics and 62% of Protestants – would be against a no-deal Brexit and a hard Irish border and in favour of Northern Ireland to remain in a customs union and single market with the EU. Preferably, such a 'soft Brexit' should extend to the UK as a whole.[94] Both sides mentioned concern about the economic impact of any border controls as reason for their choice. They were firmly opposed to a different customs regime for Northern Ireland from the rest of the UK. In addition, Protestants were also worried that this could pose a threat to the union with the UK. Therefore, the vast majority of Protestants resolutely rejected any form of special status for Northern Ireland after Brexit, whilst a third of Catholics would actually prefer such an arrangement. Still, for a sizeable minority of Protestants (24%) a hard Brexit would remain the preferred option.[95]

---

[93] This is confirmed by a Belfast Telegraph online survey in December 2018, with 65% of Northern Irish people stating they would vote in favour of Remain if a second referendum was held (Belfast Telegraph 2018).

[94] Likewise, a more recent Irish Times poll, conducted face-to-face by Ipsos MRBI in March 2019, found that a similarly large majority of Northern Irish voters (67%) would prefer this option (Leahy 2019).

[95] The LT online poll of Winter 2018 found a more sizable minority of 44% of Unionists that would prefer a no-deal exit. Otherwise, the results were similar. For instance, the poll showed that 62% would be in favour of the UK remaining in the EU (LT 2018: 7).

Yet, both sides shared a strong concern that protests against customs checks at the Irish border or in the Irish Sea would rapidly deteriorate into violence (Garry et al 2018: 32-38). A new hard border could also very likely become a target for dissident Republicans opposed to the peace agreement, as senior PSNI officials have repeatedly warned (cf. Maguire 2017, Marsh 2019). The New IRA has confirmed their intention to capitalise on a hard border, while claiming that Brexit would already attract new supporters to their campaign (Belfast Telegraph 2019a). Furthermore, since the EU referendum there has apparently been a growing interest among people in Northern Ireland in preserving the privileges of European citizenship, as indicated by the rapid surge in demand for Irish citizenship. Thus, until the end of June 2019, more than 150,000 Irish passport applications had been submitted (O'Carroll 2019b).[96] Notably, although no official figures are available, it seems that there was also a considerable number of Protestant among the applicants (cf. Dickson 2018, Ferguson 2017).

This leads to the third and most controversial point. There are actually indications that overall popular support for a reunification of Ireland has increased, particularly in light of the realistic possibility of a no-deal Brexit. To what extent, however, remains unclear. Survey results vary widely. In any case, the Catholic/Nationalist/Republican and Protestant/Unionist/Loyalist communities are deeply divided over the issue. Regarding public sentiment about a border poll, some opinion polls indicate that the number of supporters and opponents of a united Ireland could be fairly evenly divided in the event of a hard Brexit. According to the LT NI online poll of winter 2018, for example, 55% of respondents stated they would 'probably' or 'certainly' vote for a united Ireland if the UK left the EU without a deal. By contrast, the corresponding figure for proponents of the union with the UK was only 42%. There was, however, an enormous gap in constitutional preference between Nationalists/Republicans and Unionists, the former supporting Irish unity almost unanimously with 98% and the latter the union with an overwhelming majority of 86%. Yet, the overall support for Irish reunification dropped to 48% if the UK leaves on the terms of the draft Withdrawal Agreement, and to

---

[96] In the first six months of this year alone, the number of first-time passport applications from Northern Ireland amounted to 47,645, comparing to 20,325 in 2015, the year before the referendum. A similar upward trend can be observed for applications from Britain, which have exceeded 100,000 since the Brexit referendum and amounted to 31,099 in the first half of 2019, as compared to 6,011 in 2015 (O'Carroll 2019b).

just 29% in the event of the UK staying in the EU. Notably, the desire for a border referendum seems rather limited, with only 44% saying they would welcome it within the next five years. Again, Nationalists/Republicans were overwhelmingly in favour (89%) and Unionists against it (92%). A sizable overall minority of 29% and even 60% of Unionists would want such a referendum never to happen (LT 2018: 14-17).[97] Other surveys, however, have yielded contrary results, showing a clear lead for the pro-UK camp. For instance, the QUB survey suggested that in any case 50% would favour staying within the UK, whilst only 21% would back a united Ireland. By community background, 79% of Protestants stated they would vote for remaining in the UK, compared with 20% of Catholics. Contrariwise, 42% of Catholics and only 4% of Protestants were in favour of Irish unity (Garry et al 2018: 46).[98] Remarkably, it appears that public sentiment in Great Britain is rather negative towards the continuation of the union with Northern Ireland. According to an online poll in February 2019 for King's College London, just over a third (36%) of British people would prefer Northern Ireland to vote to remain part of the UK if given the choice; another third (36%) would be indifferent and almost one fifth (18%) would like Northern Ireland to choose to leave and form part of a united Ireland (Mortimore 2019). In contrast, public opinion in the Irish Republic seems to be considerably more positive on this issue. As a Sky News online poll in February 2019 showed, almost two-thirds (64%) of the Irish respondents said they would support a united Ireland, with only 16% opposing the proposition (Carr 2019).

Fourthly and lastly, it is hardly surprising in the circumstances that apparently people in Northern Ireland are deeply dissatisfied with the way the British Government handles the Brexit process and also with the role of the Unionist and Nationalist parties in it. Moreover, an overall majority seems to be

---

[97] The Deltapoll survey of August 2018, commissioned by the pro-European youth movement 'Our Future Our Choice', painted a similar picture: In the event of a hard Brexit, 56% favoured a united Ireland, with 40% choosing to stay in the UK (Deltapoll 2018). An earlier LT online poll in May 2018, commissioned by the BBC, showed slightly lower support for a united Ireland (42%) than for Northern Ireland remaining in the UK (45%) – yet without any Brexit conditionality (Devenport 2018).

[98] Likewise, the Northern Ireland Life and Times (NILT) 2017 survey, which included a question on a border referendum, showed 55% support for maintaining the union and just 22% for Irish unity (ARK NILT 2018). The Irish Times poll of March 2019 found a narrower gap, but still a significantly higher proportion of respondents in favour of the union with Great Britain (45%) than those backing a united Ireland (32%) (Leahy 2019).

in favour of restoring power-sharing in Northern Ireland, albeit in a reformed way. At the same time, people have little confidence that the Executive and Assembly will actually be reinstated in the near future. There also appears to be a significant minority preferring other governance options, namely British direct rule, wanted mainly by Protestants/Unionists/Loyalists, and British-Irish joint authority, favoured mostly by Catholics/Nationalists/Republicans. The QUB survey, for instance, showed that the respondents' satisfaction levels with the representation of the interests of the Northern Irish people in the Brexit negotiations was very low for all main actors involved. Sinn Féin attracted the least positive evaluation, with only 10% stating that the party did a very good or fairly good job. However, with around 14% positive rating, the DUP and the British Government did not perform much better. Even the highest-rated actors, the Irish Government and the EU, were positively evaluated by less than a fifth of respondents: 19% and 18% respectively. Again, variations emerged between the two communities. 24% of Protestants believed that the DUP and the British Government were doing a good job, whereas 28% of Catholics thought so about the Irish Government and the EU (Garry et al 2018: 39-40).[99] Regarding power-sharing, a face-to-face poll by Ipsos MRBI for the Irish Times in March 2019 indicated a vast majority of almost 80% want the Assembly to be reinstated (Leahy 2019). In addition, according to the LT Post Elections Poll of June 2017, there is overall support of almost 60% in the Northern Irish electorate for the reform of the Executive.[100] This received the least backing (45%), however, from DUP voters. Among them, and also among voters of Sinn Féin, were many who expressed other governance preferences: More than one in three Sinn Féin voters favoured joint authority between the British and Irish governments and even slightly over half of DUP voters preferred British direct rule, either for a tem-

---

[99] The Irish Times poll of March 2019 arrived at very similar results, but showed the lowest satisfaction rate of 12% for the UK Government. Two thirds of the respondents said the DUP was doing a bad job of representing Northern Ireland at Westminster parliament. Moreover, 60% wanted Sinn Féin to give up their refusal and take their parliamentary seats (Leahy 2019) Yet over half of Sinn Féin voters stated that they would not like such a policy change of their party, according to an earlier LT online poll of June 2017 (LT 2017: 4).

[100] For example, the QUB survey questioned people in Northern Ireland about the idea of replacing the current need for support of the Executive by the largest Unionist and Nationalist parties with 60% support from all MLAs. As a result, a majority in both communities, although more so on the Catholic (62%) than on the Protestant (53%) side, would be in favour of the proposition (Garry et al 2018: 41).

porary period or permanently (LT 2017: 8-10). In any case, only a small minority seems to expect that the power-sharing institutions will soon be restored (cf. LT 2019: 16).[101]

In sum, the UK's Brexit process has caused a lot of confusion and controversy between the Protestant/Unionist/Loyalist and Catholic/Nationalist/Republican communities. In particular, the two sides are divided about whether and how Brexit should happen, and if so, how the Irish border issue should be resolved. The possibility of a hard Brexit has increased public concern about the economic and social consequences and about the constitutional future of Northern Ireland. In fact, the latter has become a major bone of contention – as to whether Northern Ireland should remain within the UK or join a united Ireland. In addition, the ongoing row between the DUP and Sinn Féin and the absence of a power-sharing government has exacerbated the communal rift. In light of these developments, it seems that not only has the progress in community relations and peacebuilding made in the aftermath of the Agreement stalled now, but there may even be a danger that the overall peace process will be jeopardised.

COMMUNITY INEQUALITIES, CLASS AND ETHNO-NATIONAL DIVISIONS IN THE MIRROR OF TIME

> "Inequality between Protestants and Catholics in Ireland originates from the policy of English and Scottish settlement carried through by the British Government in the sixteenth and seventeenth centuries to consolidate its earlier military conquest of the Gaelic and Catholic population. Over most of the period of four centuries since that 'plantation' began, inequality between planter and Gael was created and sustained by deliberate acts of policy." (Smith & Chambers 1991:1)

This view that systemic inequalities and discrimination against Catholics were deliberately established and perpetuated by the British Government and the ruling Protestant Unionist political elite since the Protestant plantation of Ulster is shared by many scholars (cf. Brewer & Higgins 1998: 115, Jenkins

---

[101] In the online LT European Election 'Tracker' Poll, for instance, respondents were asked about their confidence that the Stormont all-party talks convened by the British and Irish governments in May 2019 would lead to a restoration of Northern Ireland's power-sharing institutions. Less than a fifth said they were absolutely certain or partly confident that this would happen. As it turned out, this has not been the case and the institutions remain suspended (LT 2019: 16; cf. Sparrow 2019b).

1984: 260, McGarry & O'Leary 1995: 334, Melaugh 1995: 131, Rowthorn & Wayne 1988: 21, Ruane & Todd 1996: 201). In the following discussion, the socio-economic disparities between the Catholic and Protestant communities represent one side of the coin, and the other is the issue of class divisions within both communities, and, consequently, the lack of cross-community class politics. The latter is exemplified in a telling quote by David Ervine, the then leader of the Progressive Unionist Party (PUP). In setting out his political vision for Loyalism and, concurrently, for the peace process in Northern Ireland, he called for the introduction of bread-and-butter class politics cutting across ethno-national community divides.

> "The politics of division has seen thousands of people dead, most of them working class, and headstones on the graves of young men. We have been fools; let's not be fools any longer. All elements must be comfortable within Northern Ireland. We have got to extend the hand of friendship, we have to take the peace lines down brick by brick, and somehow or other we have got to introduce class politics. You can't eat a flag." (David Ervine 1994)[102]

Let us cast a look back. In 1969, when the Troubles broke out in Northern Ireland, resources were unequally distributed between the two communities. Although there is considerable disagreement about the actual extent of disadvantage and discrimination, it can be said that, overall, Protestants were in a more advantageous economic, social and political position than Catholics. They lived in better housing and received better education. They were more likely to be found in the higher social classes and less likely to be unemployed. They had higher incomes, their cultural and national identities received greater public recognition, and their community interests were far better represented in and protected by the political system, both at the local and state levels (cf. Barritt & Carter 1972, Bew et al. 1979, CSJ 1969, Cormack & Osborne 1983, Eversley 1989, Gallagher 1989b & 1991, Rowthorn & Wayne 1988, Rose 1971, Smith & Chambers 1991, Whyte 1983).[103] Despite im-

---

[102] Cited in McKittrick 1996: 40.

[103] However, there are a few analysts who qualify or disagree that Catholics were systematically discriminated. David Eversley, for instance, points out that there were also other important factors, such as demographic characteristics (e.g. higher birth rates) and geographic concentrations that contributed to the Catholic community's disadvantaged position on the labour market – expressed by higher rates of unemployment and inequalities of opportunity (cf. Eversley, 1989). Graham Gudgin holds the view that a higher proportion of Catholics received public housing and, like Eversley, attributes this and the higher Catholic unemployment rate to their growing share in the population. As regards the civil

provements in the Catholic position during the Troubles, especially in the areas of employment, education and housing, the pattern of relative Protestant advantage persisted (cf. Breen 2000, Gallagher 1989a, Cormack & Osborne 1995, Melaugh 1994, Sheehan & Tomlinson 1999). In his longitudinal analysis of socio-economic class inequality between the two communities, Richard Breen, for instance, concludes that "the class structures of Protestant and Catholic men have become more similar over the 1973-1996 period." (Breen 2000: 392) Furthermore, "there has also been a decline in the importance of ascriptive features (e.g. class origins and ethnic group membership) in determining class position." (Breen 2000: 392) In his view, these developments were largely due to a convergence between the communities in educational performance and employment opportunities.

Thus, social class, which is defined here in terms of socio-economic position and status,[104] is a salient factor, because it plays an important role in determining people's life chances, be they in educational attainment, employment prospects, potential earnings, health and life expectancy, or in the likelihood of becoming the victim of a violent attack (Coulter 1999: 96, Kilbane 1995).[105] This is not to dismiss the impact of ethno-national affiliation, which in the case of the Catholic/Nationalist/Republican working class has been reflected in their considerable, some even call it systematic, discrimination by Unionist regimes since the foundation of Northern Ireland in 1921. Yet, there is evidence that the working-class of both communities are similarly deprived in terms of their life chances, and that their opportunities are considerably fewer than those of the middle and upper classes (Borooah et al 1995). The gap in life chances between the Catholic/Nationalist/Republican and Protestant/Unionist/Loyalist working-class communities and their middle and upper-class counterparts has continued to widen in the post-industrial environment of Northern Ireland. In particular, the industrial decline, and especially the collapse of the manufacturing sector, has led to a significant in-

---

service, he concedes Unionist ministers' preferential appointments of Protestants because they viewed them as loyal (cf. Gudgin, 1991).

[104] See also the conceptual discussion in Chapter 2 on 'Socio-Economic Class Inequalities and Deprivation', pp. 47-48.

[105] Regarding poorer health among the deprived working-class communities in Northern Ireland, Paula Kilbane points out that "here is a clear relationship between death rates and social deprivation. Amongst under-75s, differences in deprivation between areas account for 60 per cent of the variation in deaths. Amongst the 30-65s, the deprived have a death rate twice that of the affluent." (Kilbane 1995: 65)

crease in unemployment among the working class on both sides of the communal divide. The worst affected from this decline have been men from the Protestant/Unionist/Loyalist working class because of their traditionally privileged position within the industrial labour force. Many of those who lost their jobs, Protestants and Catholics alike, have become long-term unemployed, which is due to a lack of skills and to less numerous employment opportunities being created in trade and services and other sectors (cf. Coulter 1999: 61-100, Gallaher 2007: 56-59, Teague 1993: 60-62).

However, despite the shared experience of deprivation, so far it has only happened once in the history of Northern Ireland that the Protestant and Catholic working-class communities have joined hands and gone on strike for a common cause. This unique case, in which class unity managed to sideline sectarian loyalties, occurred in 1932 when, at the so-called 'Outdoor Relief Workers' Strike', ten thousands of Catholic and Protestant workers jointly protested for an increase in unemployment benefits. Months of complaints about conditions for the unemployed preceded the strike. All over Ireland and Great Britain, poor people were protesting against their situation, in work and out-of-work. In Northern Ireland, Jack Beattie, the only Labour MP in Northern Ireland at that time, Harry Midgley, Belfast City Councillor of the Northern Ireland Labour Party (NILP), Tommy Geehan, a local leader of the Communist Party of Ireland (CPI), and Betty Sinclair,[106] a local Irish communist activist from Ardoyne, set up the Revolutionary Workers' Group (RWG). The RWG organised rallies and spoke up for the unemployed, thus becoming the driving force behind the 'Outdoor Relief Workers' Strike'. Considering the deeply entrenched sectarian divisions, which were by then already engrained in the very fabric of community relations, it was certainly a huge achievement on the part of the RWG to make the Protestant/Unionist/ Loyalist and Catholic/Nationalist/Republican working class stand up for a common cause. The strike, which began in Belfast on 3 October 1932, lasting for twelve days, led to severe riots, in which two men, a Protestant and a Catholic, were killed by the police. Eventually, on 14 October 1932, the strike came to an end, when, on the request of Belfast City Councillors, the Unionist Government agreed to raise relief rates – yet for married couples only and still

---

[106] Sinclair also became a leading figure of the Civil Rights Movement in the 1960s and was appointed as the first chairperson of the Northern Ireland Civil Rights Association. (NICRA). See also the section on 'The Civil Rights Movement', pp. 71-74 and NICRA 1978.

to a lower level than equivalent rates in England. Notably, single men still remained excluded from receiving outdoor relief (Bardon 2001: 528-529, Bew & Norton 1979, Brewer & Higgins 1998: 97, Devlin 1981, Mitchell 2017: 89-111).

During the 1970s and 1980s, anti-discrimination legislation and policies took root in Northern Ireland. In response to mass violence during the early Troubles and to appease the Catholic community, the British Government took legislative steps to tackle religious discrimination in Northern Ireland. The Fair Employment Act 1976 banned discrimination in the workplace on religious grounds and provided for the creation of a Fair Employment Agency (FEA) (Cormack & Osborne 1987). In 1989, a new Fair Employment Act was enacted, which reinforced the existing law and introduced an obligation for employers to monitor the religious composition of their workforce. Moreover, it established the Fair Employment Commission (FEC) that replaced the FEA. The Good Friday/Belfast Agreement promised a further amelioration of Catholics' conditions in that it formally and constitutionally recognised the principles of equal opportunity, parity of esteem and power-sharing between the Protestant and Catholic communities. Section 75 of the Northern Ireland Act 1998 is a key provision for implementing both a comprehensive equality agenda and a community relations policy. Its aim is "to change the practices of government and public authorities so that equality of opportunity and good relations are central to policy making and service delivery." (ECNI 2019) The other important piece of legislation is the Fair Employment and Treatment (Northern Ireland) Order 1998, which extended the existing anti-discrimination law to cover the provision of goods, facilities and services. Subsequently, in 1999, the FEC was merged with the Equal Opportunities Commission, the Commission for Racial Equality and the Northern Ireland Disability Council to become part of the Equality Commission for Northern Ireland (ECNI) (cf. McCrudden 1999, McGarry & O'Leary 2004).

However, despite improved access to and distribution of resources for Catholics, a considerable degree of socio-economic class inequality between the two communities has persisted in the aftermath of the Agreement. For instance, a study by Christine Bell and Robbie McVeigh in 2014 for the Northern Ireland Equality Coalition shows that although significant progress in intercommunal equality has been made in terms of employment,[107] profound inequalities have still remained in other areas, notably housing, health and poverty. In particular, the poverty gap between the two communities has widened, with one in three Catholics and just less than one in five Protestants living below the poverty threshold in 2012. In addition, 38 of the 50 most deprived areas in Northern Ireland were located in areas with at least 90% Catholic population. However, inequality has also become increasingly an issue for the Protestant community, especially for the working-class (Bell & McVeigh 2014: 5 & 35). A major source of concern is the educational under-achievement of young Protestant males in socially deprived areas, which makes them most vulnerable to being unemployed. Moreover, there is consistent evidence that youth unemployment has become as acute a problem for the Protestant community in recent years as for the Catholic one (Nolan 2014: 13, NIE 2017: 34; Grey et al 2019: 13-14).[108] Overall, the persistent, widespread economic and social deprivation among both the Catholic and Protestant working classes and the increasing gap between rich and poor also point to pronounced resource inequalities within the communities (cf. Beatty 2004, Dignan 2003, Hillyard et al. 2003, NISRA 2005a & 2010a).

The divisions between the Protestant and Catholic working classes also find expression in different perceptions of community relations and political issues, particularly in relation to the importance attached to certain key issues of the peace agreement and views of its benefits. The following table presents a selection of relevant findings from the Northern Ireland Life and Time (NILT) survey series, illustrating the marked differences in the social and political attitudes of the unskilled working class of both communities.

---

[107] Thus, the economic activity gap between working age Protestants and Catholics almost closed between 1992 and 2014, and the ratio of unemployed Catholics to Protestants fell considerably from 2 (2.4 for men and 1.3 for women) to 1.3 (1.2 for men and 1.6 for women). Catholics, however, remain more vulnerable to long-term unemployment, accounting for 59% of those unemployed for 12 months or more in 2014 (Bell & McVeigh 2014: 29-30). According to the Northern Ireland Labour Force Survey, overall unemployment rates for Protestants and Catholics have converged further in the following years, even reaching the same level of 4% in 2017. As pointed out, this was "the lowest shared unemployment rate recorded since 1992" (NIE 2019: 37).

[108] For instance, the Northern Ireland Labour Force Survey showed that, contrary to usual trends, youth unemployment in 2016 was much higher for Protestants than for Catholics, at 24% compared to 18% for Protestants (NIE 2017: 34).

NILT Survey (year)	1998				2003				2008			
Community Background of Respondent*	Catholic		Protestant		Catholic		Protestant		Catholic		Protestant	
Occupational Class[+]	Un-skilled	All	Un-skilled	All	Un-skilled	All	Un-skilled	All	Un-skilled	All	Un-skilled	All
Actually live in mixed religion neighbourhood	29%	31%	22%	31%	n/a[1]	n/a[1]	n/a[1]	n/a[1]	n/a[1]	n/a[1]	n/a[1]	n/a[1]
Prefer to live in mixed religion neighbourhood	74%	73%	38%	66%	82%	77%	57%	66%	84%	81%	77%	79%
Spouse/partner is of the same religion	90%	89%	88%	86%	95%	93%	90%	88%	94%	92%	83%	89%
Children ever attend mixed religion school	6%	13%	7%	14%	7%	12%	7%	12%	16%	14%	16%	14%
Prefer to send children to mixed religion school	48%	53%	26%	53%	54%	57%	56%	52%	78%	66%	81%	67%
Protestants and Catholics not treated equally	33%	33%	34%	21%	18%	24%	34%	25%	n/a[1]	n/a[1]	n/a[1]	n/a[1]
Relations between Protestants and Catholics better than 5 years ago	56%	60%	41%	44%	48%	48%	36%	41%	53%	67%	68%	62%
Unionists and Nationalists benefited equally from the Agreement	n/a[1]	n/a[1]	n/a[1]	n/a[1]	44%	49%	15%	18%	59%[2]	62%[2]	52%[2]	40%[2]
Northern Ireland Assembly has achieved only a little/nothing at all	n/a[1]	n/a[1]	n/a[1]	n/a[1]	71%	71%	89%	86%	63%	65%	74%	76%
National Identity – British	5%	8%	75%	68%	6%	8%	75%	66%	9%	8%	71%	58%
National Identity – Irish	68%	64%	3%	3%	66%	63%	2%	3%	63%	62%	3%	4%
National Identity - Northern Irish	15%	25%	7%	17%	20%	25%	13%	20%	16%	23%	19%	30%
Long-term policy for Northern Ireland: remain part of UK	27%	21%	89%	84%	25%	21%	87%	82%	79%	85%	22%	34%
Long-term policy for Northern Ireland: united Ireland	56%	48%	3%	3%	43%	48%	3%	5%	56%	40%	0%	4%
Would again vote yes in the Agreement	n/a[1]	n/a[1]	n/a[1]	n/a[1]	64%	73%	15%	28%	n/a[1]	n/a[1]	n/a[1]	n/a[1]

* Religious background categorised

[+] The classification by social class (categorised) has not been included in the NILT surveys since 2010.

[1] Not available: question not asked in the survey.

[2] Different wording: Protestants and Catholics benefited equally from NI's political changes since 1998.

Table 2. Social and Political Attitudes of the Unskilled Catholic and Protestant Working Classes, 1998 – 2008 (calculated by the author from Northern Ireland Life and Time (NILT) survey data: ARK NILT 1998, 2003, 2008)

As indicated in the table above, stronger oppositional ethno-national identities exist between the working classes of the two communities than between their middle- and upper class counterparts.[109] Nevertheless, as it appears, there is also the readiness to mix with the other side. For instance, according to the table's figures for 2008, around 80% of the Protestants and Catholics of the unskilled occupational class stated that they would prefer to live in a mixed religion neighbourhood and also send their children to a mixed religion school. Yet, apparently, the vast majority of them live under conditions that run counter to these intentions.

In the first ten years after the agreement there has been some rapprochement and reconciliation, albeit mostly between the middle and upper classes. After all, there is still a large communal divide between the Catholic and Protestant working classes, which is reflected in a persistently high level of residential and educational segregation, and recurring sectarian violence. This can be seen as one of the regrettable legacies of the Troubles (cf. Anderson & Shuttleworth 1998, Boal 1981, McCann 1995, Murray 1985, Murtagh 1996 & 2002).[110] It was the unskilled manual working class, the most disadvantaged and poorest section of the population within both communities, who experienced and evinced the highest levels of violence (cf. Hillyard et al. 2005). These people rank among the most vulnerable segment of Northern Irish society and, as such, have been more susceptible to both intra- and inter-community intimidation, violence and control (cf. Burton, 1978, Darby 1985, 1986 & 1997, Lennon 2004). The aftermath of the Agreement witnessed recurring episodes of Loyalist turmoil, which took place mainly in Protestant

---

[109] This is also shown in a study by Brian Graham and Peter Shirlow, which examined the national attitudes of working-class Protestants and Catholics in Belfast, Derry/ Londonderry and Newry in 1996. Thus, with regard to constitutional preferences, they found a significantly lower level of support among the Catholic working-class than among the managerial/professional class: in Belfast 9% vs. 50%, in Derry/Londonderry 5% vs. 39% and in Newry 4% vs. 29%. By contrast, Protestants overall were overwhelmingly in favour of retaining the union with Great Britain, with approval rates exceeding 80% across all classes and locations (Graham & Shirlow 1998: 248-249).

[110] According to Frederick Boal, residential segregation caused by ethnic divisions as resources serve four functions: defence, avoidance, preservation and attack (cf. Boal 1981). In line with Boal, Murtagh points out that "residential segregation between two ethnic groups is likely to indicate some significant degree of difference between them ... [which may] contribute and reinforce division" (Murtagh 1996: 31). For levels of residential segregation and violence in specific areas of Belfast, see Table 4 and Table 5 in the section on 'The Local Communities' of Chapter 4, p. 133 and p. 152.

interface communities in North and West Belfast and were directed in part against state institutions. The resurgence of such riots also suggests a growing sense of alienation and discontent among Protestant working-class people with regard to the course of the peace process. At the same time, there has also been a rise in dissident Republican activity in Catholic working-class communities, aiming to stir up tensions and to destabilise the peace process. Thus, all this indicates that there is still a considerable potential for communal violence and that sectarianism continues to run high in Northern Ireland. (cf. Campbell 2000, Finlay 2001, Frampton 2012, Hayes 2005, Lynn 2016, McAleese 2005, Monaghan & Shirlow 2011, Morrow 2000).

At the political level, the dominance of ethno-national identity issues over socio-economic class issues has been obvious throughout the conflict. After the Agreement, this development has obviously continued up to now, as indicated by the ongoing turmoil and polarisation over Brexit and the power-sharing stalemate in Northern Ireland. The main political parties on both sides of the communal divide still appeal almost exclusively to either Catholics or Protestants and usually gain the vast majority of their votes.[111] Apparently, they still consider issues of class and socio-economic inequality to be of subordinate importance to nationalist politics and, especially, to the national question of Northern Ireland's constitutional status (cf. Breen & Hayes 1997, Coulter 2019, Duffy & Evans 1996). This is particularly evident in the lack of an effective social policy. For example, the latest report on peace monitoring in Northern Ireland for 2017/18 concludes that "the lack of progress in day-to-day social policy issues permeates every aspect of life and disproportionately affects the most vulnerable in society." (Gray et al 2018: 12)

Except for a short-lived period in the 1950s and 1960s, when the Northern Ireand Labour Party (NILP) attracted considerable support among both the Protestant and the Catholic working-class communities,[112] the impact of

---

[111] This is illustrated by the results of the first elections to the Northern Ireland Assembly after the 2003 agreement, where about 52% of voters voted for the Unionist bloc and about 41% for the Nationalist camp, with the more moderate ruling parties UUP and SDLP for the first time gaining less votes than the more radical parties DUP and Sinn Féin: (DUP 26% vs. UUP 23% and SF 24% vs. SDLP 17%. Just 5% voted for non-sectarian middle-ground parties (APNI 4%, NIWC 1%). From then on, the process of gradual erosion of the middle ground and shift to the more extreme parties has continued, as evidenced by all election results since 2005 (Whyte 2013 & 2017).

[112] Traditionally, the major stronghold of the NILP was in industrial Belfast, especially in Protestant working-class areas in North and East Belfast. Before the outbreak of the Troubles the party also attracted considerable support among the Catholic working-class. There

cross-community class politics has always been very limited. Even that marginal impact of joint working-class representation has disappeared since the demise of the NILP in 1987 (cf. Edwards 2009, Hadden 1994). In the current political landscape of Northern Ireland, however, there are actually political parties aiming to represent the interests of both working classes. One of these is the PUP, founded in 1979 and closely linked to the Ulster Volunteer Force (UVF). They seek to empower the Protestant/Loyalist working class, but also to reach out to the Catholic working class. The other is the People Before Profit (PBP) alliance, which was founded in 2005 and which is also active in the Republic of Ireland. They aim to create a new 32 county united Ireland based on socialist ideas and principles. However, the electoral base of both parties has so far been almost exclusively in their community and they have achieved only very modest electoral success. The PUP achieved its greatest political strength in the elections to the first post-Agreement Assembly, gaining 2.5% of the vote and two parliamentary seats (cf. Whyte 2002). Since then, their support has declined. In the last elections in 2017, they garnered only 0.7% of the vote, which left them without a seat in the Assembly. The PBP currently holds two Assembly seats, amounting to 2% of the votes (cf. Whyte 2017). So, in other words, both parties fail to galvanise any sizable support from their community, let alone from the other side. Apparently, this is because of their rather radical outlook and their partisan and divisive position on Northern Ireland's constitutional status and on other controversial ethno-national issues. Thus, the PUP is strongly committed to the union with Great Britain, whereas the PBP wants Northern Ireland to become part of a united Ireland (cf. Edwards 2010, McCann 2016, PBP 2019, PUP 2019).

The labour and trade union movement, by contrast, has a relatively better record in representing Protestant and Catholic working-class interests. Its strategy to adopt a politically neutral position, to avoid sectarianism, and to concentrate on the improvement of employment conditions helped the Northern Ireland Committee (NIC) to maintain a considerable trade union membership in both working-class communities. However, because of its approach of non-interference in nationalist politics and its lack of connection with and support from a labour party, labour and trade unionism has had a fairly lim-

---

were fewer Catholic supporters, however, as the party had officially declared itself in favour of Northern Ireland's union with Great Britain.The NILP reached its electoral peak in 1962 when it garnered over 25% of the votes and four seats in the Stormont Parliament, making it the second largest party in Northern Ireland. (Edwards 2009: 85-86).

ited impact on Northern Irish politics (cf. Helle 1998, Norton 1998, O'Dowd et al 1980, O'Connor 2014: 63-64). So, when seen from the perspective sketched above, it seems rather superfluous to ask whether Catholic and Protestant working-class interests have been truly and effectively represented in the political arena of Northern Ireland.

4 LOCAL CONFLICT IN INTERFACE AND ENCLAVE COMMUNITIES
EMPIRICAL CASE STUDIES IN BELFAST AND BEYOND

"We have got to extend the hand of friendship,
we have got to take the peacelines down brick by brick."
(David Ervine 1994)[113]

"It is senseless to speak of optimism or pessimism.
The only important thing to remember is that
if one works well in a potato field, the potatoes will grow.
If one works well among people, they will grow.
That's reality. The rest is smoke."
(Danilo Dolci 1972)[114]

The aim of the previous chapter was to elaborate on the causes, dimensions and dynamics of conflict in Northern Ireland from a general perspective. Equipped with this knowledge, the focus of the enquiry will now be placed on the local level in order to investigate how intergroup conflict manifests itself on the ground. Thus, the aim of this section is to explore the selected conflict-prone interface and enclave communities in Northern Ireland, specifically in Belfast, and the wider local communities in which they are embedded. The intention behind this is to develop a vivid picture of how and why inter-community tensions and violence occur in these localities. This is done first by presenting personal experiences, observations and reflections on my most recent and previous field research stays in Northern Ireland. The personal story will then feed into the account of the local communities, which draws on the interviews and informal conversations with residents and stakeholders. This will be supplemented by demographical and statistical data in order to

---

[113] This is a quote (cited in McKittrick 1996: 40) from David Ervine, who was a Loyalist politician, leader of the Progressive Unionist Party (PUP) and member of the Northern Ireland Assembly from 1998 to 2007.

[114] This quote (cited in Mangione 1972: xiv) is from Danilo Dolci, an Italian social activist, sociologist, architect and popular educator. He became known as the 'Gandhi of Sicily' for employing an innovative form of non-violent struggle against the Sicilan mafia to improve the living conditions of the local peasantry and working class, particularly of children and youth (cf. Dolci 1970).

provide a comprehensive picture of the circumstances and environment in which the people live. Contemporary and historical studies dealing with local community issues will also be consulted to explore local community development and to further elucidate local views and attitudes to the other side of the ethno-national divide. Moreover, combining these various sources will enable to identify and comprehend the key issues affecting local living conditions, community relations and relations to politics, political power and hegemony.

APPROACHING AND REFLECTING ON THE FIELD

The field research in Northern Ireland was conducted from 7 June to 2 August, 2009. This period was chosen mainly because June and July have traditionally been the months with the highest level of intergroup tensions and violence in Northern Ireland, particularly in interface areas. It is the period when the Orange Order 'marching season' reaches its peak and most of the contentious parades occur that pass by or sometimes even through Catholic interface areas. The rationale behind this is that the differences and divisions between the communities are usually more pronounced and visible in times of heightened intergroup tensions. There are also more cross-communal and political activities targeted at maintaining and, in the case of riots, restoring local peace and security.

As a researcher from Austria, a Central European country where no noticeable social conflict has occurred since the Second World War,[115] I was aware that my own background was very different from that of the people in North-

---

[115] As a side remark, it should be noted that in the interwar period Austria experienced a brief "civil war" in February 1934, which lasted for four days. The so-called '*Februaraufstand*' [February uprising] was an armed conflict between the militia of the Social Democratic Workers' Party of Austria (SDAP) and the government forces and militia of the Austrian People's Party (ÖVP). It marked a culmination of the political and social disturbances that plagued the country throughout the interwar period (Brook-Shepherd 2002: 259 & 281-283). According to a study by Otto Bauer, between 350 and 360 people were killed in the conflict with civilian casualties amounting to almost 38% (Bauer 2015: 12). After the suppression of the uprising, the SDAP was banned and an authoritarian, one-party regime was installed under the leadership of the '*Vaterländische Front*' [Fatherland Front]. The regime, however, soon came under increasing pressure from Nazi Germany and was eventually overthrown on 12 March 1938. On the following day, the so-called '*Anschluss*' [annexation] of Austria by Germany was proclaimed (cf. Bischof et al. 2003, Brook-Shepherd 2002: 282-325).

ern Ireland, who had a long legacy of armed conflict. However, not least because of my experience in previous research visits I felt well prepared to conduct the fieldwork. During my research stay for my diploma thesis on the Northern Ireland conflict in spring 1998 I was in Belfast to conduct interviews around the time that the peace agreement, the so-called 'Belfast Agreement' or 'Good Friday Agreement', was signed (cf. Preiss 2003). Back then, I already received a vivid impression of the wide gulf in attitudes, opinions and views on the peace agreement between the Catholic and Protestant communities, especially in working-class areas. Just after the Agreement had been signed, I visited a local pub in Ballymacarrett, a deprived Protestant/ Unionist/Loyalist working-class area in Inner East Belfast, and the mood there was dejected. To my question why, a local replied that there was nothing to celebrate, since Republicans and Nationalists had won and Loyalists and Unionists had lost out in the Agreement. In another Protestant pub in Belfast city centre, the atmosphere was equally gloomy. Feelings of bitterness and deep resentment were expressed about the Unionist and British political leadership who, they said, had abandoned Loyalism and given in to the Irish Nationalist agenda. Their tenor was that the "Irish terrorists" had won. When I moved to a pub in a deprived Catholic/Nationalist/Republican working-class area of the Falls in West Belfast, the situation there was completely different. People were in an optimistic mood, celebrating the Agreement as a victory and expressing their belief that this would mark a first decisive step towards ending Catholic discrimination and Unionist domination. Many shared the opinion that British state rule would soon be over and a united Ireland would be in the making. In more affluent areas, the differences between the communities were less pronounced. A feeling of hope and relief was more common among them that the armed conflict had finally come to an end and that community relations would begin to normalise.

On my walks around the city, I could see the striking inequality in living standards that existed between the working-class areas of North, West and Inner East Belfast and the middle and upper classes areas mostly to be found in South and outer East Belfast and in the outskirts of the city. There was also another noticeable difference. Whereas the working-class communities lived in highly segregated areas with the overwhelming majority of the local population belonging to either the Protestant or the Catholic community, more mixed housing estates could be seen in middle-class areas.

Upon my return visits to Belfast in 2005, again to conduct fieldwork in preparation for a research project on perspectives of social justice and equality in Northern Ireland, I noticed that the situation was quite similar to seven years earlier. The socio-economic conditions for Protestant and Catholic working-class communities remained poor, the level of segregation remained high, and their views on the Agreement still differed widely. Yet, in my talks with Catholic working-class people in North and West Belfast I noticed a sense of disillusionment, when they complained that the heralded 'peace dividend' of an improvement in living conditions had not materialised for them. When talking to their Protestant counterparts in North and East Belfast, I gained the impression that they held similar views on their socio-economic situation and that their mentality of siege and betrayal had even intensified.

As described earlier in the section on the research design, one of the main aims of my field trip for the research at the time was to 'go local' and explore the way people lived and related to their local environments and communities. This approach proved to be successful in many respects, as will be shown. Many people – researchers, practitioners and local residents alike – assisted me in my endeavours. They referred me to interesting new contacts for the field research. I was invited to join them to attend community meetings, cultural events and practices, such as Orange Order marches, Loyalist bonfires and a Gaelic football match. I was given guided tours through local community areas and shown important 'peace walls', Republican and Loyalist murals and memorials and other conflict-related places in Belfast, Derry/Londonderry and Portadown. Moreover, my attention was drawn to many other interesting sites to visit and events to attend for my research. What follows is the personal story of my experiences, impressions and encounters during my fieldwork stay in Northern Ireland, which cannot be complete, but merely aims at providing initial insight into the issues at stake due to the constraints of space.

During my field research, I stayed in a comfortable private house in the Rosetta ward in South Belfast, which is a mixed area composed of mainly middle-class Catholics and Protestants. Upon my arrival at the small Belfast City Airport late in the evening, I was welcomed and driven there by Neil Jarman[116], who, in his capacity as director of the Institute for Conflict Research (ICR), had kindly agreed to be the host organisation for my field re-

---

[116] As explained in the section on "Research Design" of Chapter 1, due to privacy and data protection issues the names of interview partners and informants have been anonymised upon request. The identity of respondents or informants has only been disclosed upon their consent (see also p. 28).

search. With my hospitable landlady, Brenda Miller, from a mixed Catholic-Protestant middle-class family, and her partner Tony Farrell, a former Republican community activist who was unemployed at that time, I had many interesting and numerous conversations. They provided me with valuable background information on the place, sites to visit and people to contact for my research. Moreover, in our sometimes intensive discussions they gave me valuable insights into their views on and experiences of the Northern Ireland conflict and on the current situation and issues. From what they told me, I got an idea of the magnitude of differences still present in the interpretation of the reasons for the conflict and its impact on present-day life. Whereas Brenda, for instance, condemned the use of violence by both sides involved in the conflict, describing the perpetrators as barbarians, Tony justified Republican violence during the armed conflict as a legitimate means to defend the Northern Irish Catholic community and to liberate Northern Ireland from British rule. However, he denounced the violence in the post-Agreement period, caused by Loyalist and Republican paramilitaries alike. Another example of the discrepancies in their views concerned the socio-economic situation of working-class people in Belfast. Brenda held the Catholic and Protestant working classes primarily responsible for their deprived situation, because they supported nationalist parties which pursued their self-interest in staying in power rather than enacting policies to ameliorate the living conditions of the poor. Tony saw the Catholic working class as victims of a dysfunctional power-sharing government and regarded Sinn Féin as a corrupt party, lacking leadership and selling out the Republican goal of a united socialist Irish republic. There was a sense of bitterness in the way he talked, which might have been due to – what Brenda later told me – the killing of his nephew (among eleven other Catholics) in West Belfast by the Loyalist Volunteer Force (LVF) in retaliation for the death of their leader Billy Wright.[117]

---

[117] Billy Wright, who was nicknamed 'King Rat', was one of the most notorious militant Loyalists. During the Troubles, he joined the UVF in the mid-1970s and became one of their leading commanders. He is alleged to have been responsible for at least twenty, blatantly sectarian killings. Wright was a fervent opponent of the peace process and became increasingly out of line with the UVF leadership's approach of entering into ceasefire negotiations. Eventually, after he had tried to stir up sectarian tensions around the dispute over the Orange Order parade at Drumcree in 1996, which led to the murder of a Catholic taxi driver, he was expelled from the UVF and was told by the Combined Loyalist Military Command (CLMC) to leave Northern Ireland within 72 hours. Subsequently, Wright set up his own paramilitary group, the LVF, but was arrested soon afterwards and jailed for eight years in connection with the killing of a Catholic in Portadown. On 27 December

I also got an impression of what it is like living in a very wealthy neighbourhood of Northern Ireland, when Brenda took me out to Helen's Bay, a beautiful sleepy little village by the sea in the north-eastern environs of Belfast with sandy beaches surrounded by lightly wooded areas. As she told me, this was probably one of the richest areas in the country, where mostly Protestants resided in their large English-style houses with spacious gardens, and which remained almost completely unaffected by the conflict. My landlady was also very helpful with her advice that cycling would be the best way to get around Belfast and the environment. She introduced me to a bicycle cooperative in South Belfast, which was run by former Republican prisoners and where I got a good and affordable bicycle. The bicycle served me well on my regular rides from my place to ICR and back and on all my other field trips in Belfast and other locations of Northern Ireland. It should be noted at this point that cycling was not only an inexpensive, healthy and environmentally friendly option to get around in Belfast, but also it proved to be the fastest means of transport. Due to safety concerns and less demand, there are usually no direct public transport links between adjacent Catholic and Protestant working-class areas. Moreover, cabdrivers are also often reluctant to drive directly through these areas. Ironically, at the end of my field research stay I sold the bicycle cheaply to a Loyalist paramilitary ex-prisoner, who was one of my interviewees and who was very thankful because it made it much easier for him to get to his workplace in a community centre in the Greater Shankill area of North-West Belfast. When I told him that I had got the bicycle from a shop run by former Republican prisoners, he was not astonished, but remarked that Republicans were always very smart in engaging in any kind of business.

The ICR, the host institution for my field research, is located in a fringe area of the Duncairn ward in North Belfast, with a Protestant majority population, mostly from the lower middle class. It is an interface area between the Catholic ward of New Lodge and the Protestant Tigers Bay area, which became a major flashpoint of intercommunal violence in the course of the Troubles. On the way to the institute, crossing the city from south to north, I cycled along the River Lagan, Belfast's main river, before passing the edge of

---

1997, he was shot dead in Maze prisons at the age of 37 by three members of the Irish National Liberation Army (INLA) (Anderson 2004, Bruce 2004: 509-512, McKittrick 1996).

the city centre and going through a rather run-down industrial area close to Belfast Harbour. This gave me an initial visual impression not only of the diverse places and recreational spaces but also of the territorial manifestation of communal divisions, both along ethno-national as well as socio-economic lines. Regarding the latter, from a central European perspective I was astounded by the enclosed spaces of the working-class communities located close to the Lagan cycle and pedestrian path. Many of the neighbourhoods, schools and playgrounds, in particular, were fenced off and marked by para-military symbols. What was also striking were the stark, visible differences in the living conditions between these areas and the wealthier neighbourhoods just a stone's throw away to the south of the city. Whilst the working-class areas were full of tight-knit housing estates with shabby grey facades and tiny front gardens, the more affluent neighbourhoods had much more appealing houses and spacious gardens, similar to my landlady's home. Moreover, the area there was much tidier, with public litter bins on almost every corner. Offensive symbols were rare except for the Ulster, Orange Order and Loyalist flags that were put up for the 'marching season' in some Protestant neighbourhoods.

The picture changed on passing through Belfast City Centre with its contrast of Victorian houses, construction sites and modern architecture, such as the so-called 'Beacon of Hope', a recently built, almost twenty metre-high modern art metal sculpture. When I moved into the core of the city centre to have a coffee, I could see the tidy city squares and parks and the neat pedestrian precincts full of stylish shops, modern office buildings and a rash of appealing restaurants and cafes. Moreover, I came across St. George's market, a charming marketplace in a refurbished Victorian building offering a wide range of delicious groceries from the area, which became my favourite spot for buying local organic food. So, all in all, from seeing only the city centre I guess one could easily get the impression that Belfast is just another modern European city worth visiting and not a place that had to endure thirty years of fierce intercommunal conflict.

Heading further north involved a drastic change in scenery, as it brought me to the city's old dock area with many disused warehouses bearing testimony to the industrial decline that occurred some fifty years ago. After crossing a main conjunction road, I finally arrived at the ICR, which is located in the backyard of a small office complex. The estate is surrounded by high opaque fences, which is due to security concerns, as it is situated in a tense area between Catholic/Nationalist/Republican and Protestant/Unionist/Loya-

list working-class communities. So, it turned out that the location of the institute was an ideal gateway for approaching the interface community areas of
North Belfast, where I intended to conduct a major part of my fieldwork.

Staying at ICR, which is a renowned organisation with a long-standing
record of applied research, particularly on issues related to local conflict in
Northern Ireland, was an excellent experience and highly conducive to my
research. Neil Jarman and his team provided me with expertise, background
information, ideas, contacts for interviews and advice on how to conduct my
field research. I was also provided with a workspace with a personal comput-
er, access to the internet, printing, copying and telephone facilities, which was
an excellent setting for conducting desk research and for establishing contact
to potential interview partners. Just two days after my arrival, I already had
the first of my regular meetings with Neil, when he familiarised me with the
local circumstances and issues of interface communities, especially in North
Belfast, and pointed out to me how to avoid risks and dangerous situations.
Moreover, he referred me to a number of relevant contacts for interviews,
including local community workers, activists, ex-combatants, clerics, local
politicians, public officials, academics and other experts in Belfast, Derry/
Londonderry and Portadown. Neil also invited me to join him on research-
relevant events such as the so-called 'Tour of the North' parade through
North Belfast and the launch of a book called 'Beyond the Banners: The Story of the Orange Order' in Carrickfergus, a prosperous lport town north of
Belfast in the Protestant-dominated County of Antrim. Both events organised
by the Orange Order provided me with a glimpse into the organisation's
views and practices, which by many, especially from the Catholic community, are considered sectarian and divisive. In our many fruitful discussions,
Neil always appeared unbiased, neither siding with the Nationalist/
Republican nor with the Unionist/Loyalist cause. Although he was a
Protestant from England, his own background had no impact on his views
and interpretations of issues related to the conflict. I was kindly invited to his
house and he familiarised me with the surroundings – a mixed middle-class
area in upper North Belfast with Catholics and Protestants living side by side
separately, but peacefully.

Researchers from ICR also provided me with valuable background information on the customs and practices of the Orange Order. They informed me
that in general 95% of the almost 3,000 annual parades pass off peacefully
and that the 'Tour of the North' is regularly considered to be the first major
contentious Orange Order parade of the year, which happens in North Belfast,

usually in mid-June. They told me about the tensions that usually build up before the parade, which frequently erupt in intercommunal riots during and after the event, particularly around the interfaces between Loyalist and Republican working-class communities. Moreover, they also informed me about the various local community activities aimed at involving all stakeholders to prevent violence and suggested me certain events to attend. According to them, there three more contentious Orange Order parades subsequently take place in Belfast's working-class areas, which frequently lead to the outbreak of sectarian violence: the Whiterock parade in the Falls area of West Belfast (usually taking place close to the end of June), the Battle of the Somme anniversary parade (1 July) in Ballymacarrett in East Belfast and the Trevor King parade (first week of July) in the Shankill area in North-West Belfast. Around all these parades, the local crisis management was similar, though with less intensity compared with that for the 'Tour of the North' parade. Furthermore, I was given an account of the tensions and violence in certain interface areas surrounding the so-called 'bonfire night' or '11th night' on 11 July and of the 12th of July parades of the Orange Order, which are the two main events with which Protestants celebrate the 'Glorious Revolution' and the victory of King William of Orange's forces at the Battle of the Boyne.

Dennis Nolan, to whom I was referred by a fellow colleague from the University of Manchester, was very helpful in my research. We had several pleasant encounters, when he introduced me to new social and cultural aspects of life in Belfast. He gave me a guided tour through the city, in which he showed me a personal selection of sites of the conflict and of other places that mattered to him. I became aware that what he showed and told me reflected his own particular perspective, which was heavily influenced by his socialization in an urban Catholic working-class environment. At certain sites like the Bobby Sands mural in West Belfast or the 'peace line' along Cupar Way, separating the Catholic/Republican Falls from the Protestant/Loyalist Shankill area, he became passionate in sharing his personal views and insights. He told me about the specific significance of the murals and the conflict memorials for Republicans and about the symbolic power that bound his community together in times of the Troubles. I was introduced to some of the derogatory expressions that were commonly used by Republican and Loyalist militants as paramilitary slogans in their armed struggle. KAT, for instance, is the acronym used by Loyalist paramilitary groups for 'Kill all Tags', where 'Tags' is a pejorative expression for 'Catholics'. The equivalent on the part of Republican paramilitaries is KAH, which stands for 'Kill all Huns', with

'Huns' being a slur term for 'Protestants'. As I observed, these slogans were still daubed on several walls in working-class areas in Belfast, and to a lesser extent also in Derry/Londonderry and Portadown. On my visit to Derry/Londonderry, a local resident of the Catholic/Nationalist/Republican Bogside area drew my attention to graffiti on the wall with another revealing slogan reading 'UTH – Up the Hoods'. As I was told, the slogan was originally used during the Troubles, mainly in Republican working-class communities, to express an act of defiance against the authority of the IRA and similarly against the forces of the state. Since then, its meaning has changed radically and the expression is now commonly used by young people engaging in joyriding, rioting and other anti-social behaviour. According to Dennis, the slogan can be found on many walls in West and North Belfast. On an exploratory walk through Lenadoon, I myself could see it sprayed over a mural depicting an armed female Republican volunteer surrounded by portraits of local women.

It was also very interesting to visit the small Amish community, where Dennis used to work as a social worker, and to see the poor conditions in which this tiny religious minority lived in the western outskirts of Belfast. As a particular highlight, he took me to a Gaelic football match at Casement Park in Andersonstown, West Belfast, which is the principal Gaelic Athletic Association (GAA) stadium in Northern Ireland, to see the 'Ulster Semi Final' between '*Tír Eòghain*' (Gaelic name of Tyrone) and '*Doire*' (Gaelic name for Derry). The game was well-attended with around 30,000 visitors and ended with the score of 15 - 7 for Tyrone. The national anthem of the Republic of Ireland, which was played by a traditional Irish band and sung by many of the audience before the game started, the striking presence of the Irish 'Tricolour' flag and many (even kids) wearing Irish dresses and other national symbols made me feel that this place was not in Northern Ireland, but rather in the Irish Republic. When I told this to Dennis, he confirmed my impression. He pointed out that Gaelic football matches were a perfect way of expressing and celebrating his Irishness together with fellows – just like on St. Patrick's Day. Most Protestants did not attend such games, as they either preferred Rugby or, mainly the middle and upper classes, cricket and hurling.

I had intensive talks with Dennis about the conflict and ongoing community divisions. As a man in his early thirties, growing up in a Catholic working-class community in West Belfast, he had his own particular experiences and views of Republicans, Loyalists, the Protestant community, the Northern Ireland authorities and the British state. He told me about the tight-knit community structure and the social cohesion that existed in his area during the Troubles. On the one hand, this was to provide protection against violent attacks from Loyalist paramilitaries, Northern Ireland security forces and the British Army. On the other, it served the purpose of a local socio-economic structure covering the basic needs of the community in view of the lack of state provision. According to Dennis, the flip side of this was that within the community there was a lot of social control exercised by the IRA and other militant Republicans, with severe punishments for dissenters not being uncommon. He also told me of two occasions when his family was more or less forced to hide IRA members in their home. Since the living conditions in his community did not really improve after the Agreement, he decided to leave and look for a better place to live somewhere else in the city. Eventually he and his girlfriend found a new home in a mixed middle-class area in Inner East Belfast. When they invited me to their neat, modest house in a tidy living area, it confirmed my impression that there was a considerable gap in living standards between the working and the middle classes.

To prepare for the interviews in the communities, I gathered relevant background information and cycled and walked around the area to get my own impression of the living situation. Without anticipating the account of the local communities that follows, some illustrative observations will be mentioned briefly at this point. There were striking similarities not only within the Catholic working-class areas in North and West Belfast and the Protestant working-class areas in North and East Belfast, but also between them. In all the areas, nationalist symbols could be seen quite frequently, such as murals and slogans on walls and hoisted flags. The residential zones were mainly composed of small, simple brick houses, many of them single-storey with narrow front gardens and built in a row. Several of the houses on the main streets and of those closer to the community boundary were in a deplorable condition. As regards local business, there were many closed shops and several abandoned industrial sites. To my astonishment, however, I could see quite a number of smaller retail and grocery stores on the main streets and also in the neighbourhoods. Regarding more substantial shopping facilities, there were only some big supermarkets and shopping malls on the outskirts of the areas. This seemed to confirm what ICR researchers had told me that many people living in interface communities preferred shopping in their area simply because they were used to staying within their community and not least also because they did not feel comfortable or safe in areas on the other side of the ethno-national boundary.

Within the communities, local pubs and fast food outlets were also quite numerous, yet restaurants were rather rare. There was obviously a shortage of leisure facilities such as public parks, sports fields and playgrounds. To some extent, this seemed to be compensated for by the considerable number of community centres, which, according to their signs, offered various social activities and facilities as well as advisory services. What also struck me was that there were only few local police stations. Those that I saw were heavily barricaded and surrounded by high brick walls topped with metal fences and razor-blade wire, which left a rather grim impression on me. In general, high fences, metal bars and walls were frequent phenomena in the interface areas of North and central West Belfast. This also applied to the two small Protestant enclave communities I visited: Suffolk in Outer West Belfast and Cluan Place in Inner East Belfast, which were both fenced off against their Catholic neighbours in Lenadoon and Short Strand respectively. The presence of high fences heightened the atmosphere of seclusion, which more or less pervaded all the community areas I visited for my research. Regarding the community situation in North Belfast, there was a pronounced difference in that there was much more empty space available in the Protestant working-class communities than in the Catholic ones.

THE LOCAL COMMUNITIES: MOVING THROUGH TURBULENT TIMES

The following will shed light on the investigated interface and enclave communities and the areas in which they are embedded. The particular empirical focus is on four local communities and their surroundings in Belfast: the Catholic/Nationalist/Republican community of Ardoyne in North Belfast and the adjacent Protestant/Unionist/Loyalist community of Shankill located in the north-western part of the city and the interface communities of Protestant/Unionist/Loyalist Suffolk and Catholic/Nationalist/Republican Lenadoon situated in the outer Western part. All the selected locations have several features in common: they are situated in urban working-class areas with long-standing communal cleavages that are characterised by politicised and territorialised spaces, residential segregation, socio-economic deprivation and reoccurring intercommunal violence. Beside of the common pattern of development there are also context-specific differences in terms of the present community situation, state of community relations and manifestation of intergroup tensions and violence. Therefore, bearing in mind the legacy and enduring memory of intergroup conflict, the description will start with a brief overview of the more recent historical development of the Protestant and Catholic working-class communities in Belfast. Specific attention will be given to spatial distribution, community relations, violence and socio-economic conditions. Following this contextualisation the present situation of the selected communities will be explored. To provide a broader picture of the living conditions and of community relations and divisions reference will also be made to other interface and enclave areas in North, West and Inner East Belfast and outside Belfast in Derry/Londonderry and in Portadown.

THE EVOLUTION OF WORKING-CLASS INTERFACE COMMUNITIES IN BELFAST AND BEYOND

Intergroup divisions and tensions between the Protestant/Unionist/Loyalist and the Catholic/Nationalist/Republican communities are most pronounced in Belfast, which is the capital and largest city of Northern Ireland. According to the 2011 Census, the city has a population of 281,000, of which 48.8% are of Catholic and 42.5% are of Protestant background (NISRA 2012: 8 & 19). Belfast has been in the centre of the communities' struggle for territory, power and resources throughout the history of the conflict. The first indications of segregation were reported in the western and southern parts of the city by the early 19th century. Sectarianism began to take its roots in the working-class areas that existed back then, such as the Catholic Pound in West Belfast and the Protestant Sandy Row in South Belfast. As Hirst points out, "The sectarianism of these districts was initially due to the importation of conflict from the Ulster countryside, which was reflected in the establishment and growth of the Orange and Ribbon societies in Belfast." (Hirst 2005: 62) The supporters of these secret sectarian societies, commonly called 'Orangemen' and 'Ribbonmen',[118] as well as their local leaders came mainly from within the Protestant and Catholic working-class communities. Consequently, in the 1820s, intercommunal tension in the city mounted, resulting in recurring disturbances at the 12th of July Orange Order parades. In 1829, particular severe riots erupted over the banning of parades, which spread to the counties Armagh and Tyrone and claimed at least the lives of at least 20 people (Hirst

---

[118] For further information, see 'The Early Origins of the Conflict' the section on 'Community and Power Relations: A Historical Perspective' of Chapter 3, Footnote 42, p. 65.

2005: 62-64). The influx of Catholics in the course of the Great Famine fuelled the growing frictions between the Protestant majority and the increasing Catholic minority, which erupted in severe sectarian violence. Subsequently, in 1857, in the wake of the 12th of July parades, further large-scale sectarian rioting broke out in Belfast, lasting for ten days (cf. Doyle 2010: 76-107). Since then intercommunal rioting remains a recurring phenomenon that has often led to serious casualties.[119]

By 1861, the proportion of Catholics amounted to the-then historic height of 34% of the city's population. At that time the city experienced an industrial boom due to the expansion of the linen, engineering and shipbuilding trades, which lasted until the partition of Ireland and led to the emergence of a larger urban working class on both sides of the communal divide (Lynch 1998: 7-8).[120] The Catholic and Protestant working-class communities were concentrated around the industrial areas of the city, though mostly in separate locations. Catholics had more difficulties to find employment in these industries, which was seen due to prejudice from the Protestant employers against them but also because many Catholics lacked the necessary occupational skills. For many of those who were employed the work situation was difficult and likewise perilous because of frequent intimidation and periodic expulsions. Both the workplace expulsions and residential segregation intensified in the course of fierce intercommunal strife during the Irish Civil War of the early 1920s. The civil war erupted in so-called anti-Catholic 'pogroms' that were initiated in July 1920 by the Unionist leadership not only in Belfast but also in Derry/Londonderry and other places across Northern Ireland. Thus, thousands of Catholic workers were sacked from many shipyards and industries in the city if they refused to curse the pope or to take an oath to the king. As a further consequence, many Catholic families were evicted from mixed working-class residential areas (Cunningham 2013, Hepburn 1996, Parkinson 2004).

When Northern Ireland came into being, the Catholic working-class lived mainly in two wards in West Belfast, Smithfield and St. George, which cov-

---

[119] For example, the so-called '1886 Belfast Riots' were a series of violent clashes between the Catholic and Protestant communities, mainly because of the defeat of the first Irish Home Rule Bill in the British Parliament. During these riots, which took place between June and September 1886, 31 people were killed and hundreds were injured (cf. Bardon 2001: 381-382, Doyle 2010: 241-249).

[120] The industrial boom also led to a massive increase of Belfast's population reaching almost 387,000 by 1901 (Lynch 1998: 7).

ered large parts of the later Falls ward, in North Belfast in the then suburban villages of Ardoyne and the New Lodge, and in the area immediately south-east of the centre, including what was later called 'Short Strand'. The generally poor and overcrowded living conditions of Catholics in these areas corresponded with their disadvantaged socio-economic position in terms of lower occupational status and higher unemployment rates. In part their deprivation was because of discrimination by the Unionist regime against the Catholic Nationalist minority, especially in employment and housing (Darby 1976: 77-78; Whyte 1983: 8-20).[121] Another reason was Northern Ireland's segregated education system. Catholic children who went to schools maintained by the Catholic Church had lower outcomes than their Protestant counterparts attending schools controlled by the state (cf. Murray 1985, Osborne & Murray 1978). By contrast, the majority of the Protestant working-class were to be found in relatively less crowded and deprived areas in Inner East Belfast and around the Shankill Road, Woodvale and the Crumlin Road in North-West and North Belfast. Both the Protestant and Catholic working-class communities, however, were suffering from the acute shortage in housing and the poor state of many dwellings in their areas (cf. Darby & Morris 1974).[122] By and large, the spatial pattern of residential segregation along ethno-national boundaries remained the same until the 1960s (cf. Hepburn 1990, Jones 1956 & 1960). This is illustrated in the following map drawn and calculated by Emrys Jones, which shows the density in 1951 of the Catholic and upon reversion also of the Protestant population of Belfast.

---

[121] As Whyte points out, the extent to which Catholics were discriminated against under the Unionist regime from 1921-1968 remains unclear. Aside from public and private employment and public housing there were also other areas where discriminatory practices were reported, i.e. electoral practices, policing and regional policy (cf. Whyte 1983).

[122] According to the study by John Darby & Geoffrey Morris, it was estimated by the Northern Ireland Housing Trust in 1945 that 44% of the dwellings in the county borough of Belfast were in need of substantial repairs and that 23,000 new dwellings were required to meet the housing needs for the city's growing population. However, in their view, that was a conservative calculation to meet the requirement of providing decent living standards for all its inhabitants. As they pointed out, "Belfast had the greatest average number of people per acre of open space and the most crowded living conditions of any major industrial city in the UK. Sixty per cent of the population lived in wards which were so overcrowded that in order to meet health standards only one-third of the residents would have been allowed to remain 'in situ'." (Darby & Morris 1974: 33)

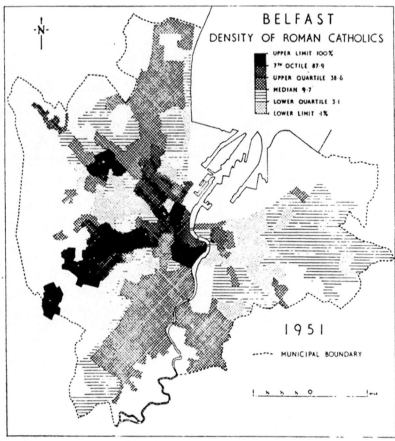

Figure 4. Density of Roman Catholics in Belfast, 1951 (Jones 1956: 177)

The advent of the Troubles led to large enforced population movements, due to increasing intimidation and political violence. There is no exact figure on internally displaced persons, but it is estimated that from August 1969 to February 1973 between 8,000 and 15,000 families in the Belfast area were forced to leave their homes. Those most affected were Catholics from mainly Protestant working-class areas in the north of the city, who fled to the already overcrowded Catholic areas of West Belfast and Short Strand in the eastern inner city area (Darby 1986, Poole 1969).[123] Moreover, thousands of Catholics flocked in from other areas in Northern Ireland, most of which coming to West Belfast (Hillyard et al 2005: 113). Thus, due to the increasing lack of space, many of these new settlers were crammed into the jerry-built houses which still characterise the area today. By contrast, most of the Protestants who abandoned their homes came from isolated minority communities in West and North Belfast and moved to safer places on the outskirts of the city and to other parts of Northern Ireland (cf. Boal & Murray 1977).

In effect, this exodus of Protestants and influx of Catholics led to a significant demographic change in the working-class areas of North and West Belfast with shrinking Protestant and growing Catholic communities. The higher Catholic birth rate was also a contributing factor to this development. As Elliott notes, the Protestant population in the 'Greater Shankill'[124] area in West Belfast had dropped from 76,000 to 27,000 and in North Belfast from 112,000 to 56,000 between the early 1970s and early 1990s (Elliott 2007: 178-179; cf. O'Malley 1994: 29). By contrast, Catholic West Belfast experienced a considerable expansion. North Belfast saw a consolidation of its patchwork geography of Catholic and Protestant working-class areas lined up close together. These areas became ever more segregated and the rather few relatively mixed housing spaces that existed before the Troubles almost disappeared (Darby 1986: 58-59 & 88; cf. Calame & Charlesworth 2009: 61-81, Hayes & McAllister 2005: 614, O'Malley 1994).[125]

The increasing residential segregation of Catholics and Protestants, especially in Belfast's working-class areas, reinforced other types of segregation that existed throughout the history of community relations in the city. These included personal, marital, educational, work, leisure and sports segregation

---

[123] In drawing on Michael Poole's analysis (Poole 1969), Darby points out that alone in August and September 1969, which were the first two months of the Troubles "about five per cent of Belfast's Catholic households vacated their homes […], some of them personally intimidated, many fleeing to the security of Catholic areas (Darby 1986: 58)." Moreover, as Robert White emphasises by drawing on official figures, of the "more than 1,800 families [that] were burned or intimidated out of their homes in July, August, and September 1963, 83 percent of them were Catholic (White 1993: 78)."

[124] The 'Greater Shankill', as the area is called by locals, includes the wards of Woodvale, Glencairn and Highfield. See also Footnote 16, p. 25.

[125] Notably, as Padraig O'Malley points out, in the early 1990s there were only two residential areas in Belfast with "substantial religious integration" – one in the northern and one in the southern part of the city." (O'Malley 1994: 29) For a map showing the distribution of Catholics and Protestants in Belfast in 1991 see Figure 11 in the Appendix, p. 406.

(cf. Doherty & Poole 1995, Gallagher 1989, Hayes et al 2007, Morgan et al 1996, Niens et al 2003, Osborne & Cormack 1986). After the peace agreement, the great majority of Belfast's Catholic and Protestant communities continued to live in highly segregated areas. As a Census-based calculation by Peter Shirlow and Brendan Murtagh shows, in 2001 over two thirds of Catholics and nearly three quarters of Protestants lived in places with a share of at least 81% Catholic or Protestant residents.[126] Most of these places are in the working-class areas in the north, west and inner east of the city (Shirlow & Murtagh 2006: 59-60).[127] This situation has remained unchanged in recent years. Notwithstanding initiatives to develop shared neighbourhood schemes, housing policy in working-class areas is still fraught with community segregation and territorial division and housing is allocated according to ethno-national criteria (cf. Capener 2017, McCord et al 2017). Yet, apparently, there is a contradiction between the high level of residential segregation, on the one hand, and the statistical preference for mixed neighbourhoods. This is illustrated by the findings from the 2010 report by the Independent Commission on the Future for Housing in Northern Ireland, which states:

> "But while 80% of people have said they would prefer to live in a mixed-religion neighbourhood, the reality is that public housing estates became more segregated through 30 years of conflict. Over 90% of public housing is segregated on religious

---

[126] There is, remarkably, no common standard for defining what constitutes residential segregation in Northern Ireland, since different authors have often used different percentage thresholds for the majority and minority communities in their calculations. The minimum proportions of Protestants or Catholic residents specified to define an area as (highly) segregated vary between 61 and 90% (Byrne et al 2006: 15, Shirlow et al 2005: 27). Mike Morrissey and Frank Gaffikin, for instance, have calculated that in 2005 55% of Belfast's population living in severely segregated wards of 90% or more either Protestant or Catholic (Morrissey & Gaffikin 2006: 881).

Thus, considering the subjective nature in defining segregation, the following thresholds, which are based on the classification scheme by Shirlow and Murtagh, are used for the purpose of this research: at least 81% of Protestant or Catholic residents for classifying an area a highly segregated area, at least 71% for regarding it as a segregated area, and less than 71% for considering it a mixed area (cf. Shirlow & Murtagh 2006).

[127] As a study conducted by Shirlow et al shows, a similar spatial pattern of segregation can be observed in Derry/Londonderry, where in 2001 77% of Catholics lived in places that were at least 81% Catholic. By contrast, the proportion of Protestants living in highly segregated areas was much lower, at 17%. This was due to their considerably smaller share of around one fifth of the city's population, which by then amounted to 105,066. Yet, 53% of Protestants lived in areas which were at least 61% Protestant, and which according to the classification by Shirlow et al were thus considered as segregated areas (Shirlow et al 2005: 23-25).

grounds, with the most polarised estates having more than 80% of one community." (Madden 2010)[128]

The demographic change has remained a factor in the social geography of Belfast. Between 2001 and 2011 there has been an increase of Catholics in all parts of the city, except for West Belfast, where in its outer wards a slightly growing number of Protestants is recorded. In all other parts the proportion of Protestants has fallen significantly with East Belfast showing the sharpest decline of almost 12%. As a result, for the first time Catholics have outnumbered Protestants in the city. In terms of the overall population, the slight population loss in North and West Belfast has been more than compensated by higher gains in the east and south of the city (NINIS 2001, NISRA 2013a). These developments are illustrated in the following table, which shows the population figures for 2001 and 2011 and the change in the proportions of Catholics and Protestants in Belfast and in Northern Ireland as a whole.[129]

Community Background[1]	All residents			Catholic			Protestant		
Geographical Area: LGD[2]	2001	2011	Change	2001	2011	Change	2001	2011	Change
Belfast North	104208	102531	-1.6%	44.0%	46.9%	2.9%	52.7%	45.7%	-7.0%
Belfast West	94431	93986	-0.5%	82.8%	80.1%	-2.7%	16.0%	16.7%	0.7%
Belfast East	89929	92221	2.5%	7.5%	12.7%	5.2%	87.0%	75.4%	-11.6%
Belfast South	106534	111402	4.6%	41.0%	44.0%	3.0%	52.6%	43.7%	-8.9%
Belfast	395102	400140	1.3%	44.2%	46.0%	1.8%	51.7%	45.1%	-6.6%
Northern Ireland	1685267	1810863	7.5%	43.8%	45.1%	1.3%	53.1%	48.4%	-4.7%

[1] The remainder of residents belongs to the other categories: a few to 'Other religions' and most to 'None'.
[2] Local Government District Belfast - Assembly Area: N = Belfast North, W = Belfast West (electoral classification)

Table 3. Community Background of Resident Population of Belfast by Geographical Area, Census 2001 and 2011 (calculated by the author from NINIS 2001, 2013a)

When looking at the population development of the working-class communities of North and West Belfast, more pronounced changes in the spatial distribution of Protestants and Catholics can be detected. In all the wards there has been a proportionate increase of the minority community and, corre-

---

[128] As also shown in the report, the figures were similar for both communities. Whilst 80% of Catholics stated that they would prefer to live in a mixed neighbourhood, the corresponding percentage for Protestants was 77%. (Independent Commission on the Future for Housing in Northern Ireland 2010: 30; cf. Morris 2016).

[129] These figures have been calculated from the Northern Ireland Census data of 2001 and the most recent one of 2011. The census collects information about people and households in Northern Ireland every 10 years. The next will take place in 2021 (cf. NISRA 2019).

spondingly, a proportionate decrease of the majority community. Most working-class communities, however, have remained highly segregated. The only exceptions are the formerly highly segregated Protestant areas of Glencairn and Duncairn that have become more mixed. Overall, the local population gains in North and West Belfast have been greater for Catholics than for Protestants. This is because more Catholics have settled in Protestant areas than Protestants in Catholic areas and because more Protestants have moved out of their areas than Catholics. In this regard, the increase in upward social mobility has also played a role. However, there have been some occasions of Catholics being forced to move out of predominantly Protestant or mixed neighbourhoods (cf. Jarman 2004). The demographic change occurring in the working-class areas of North and West Belfast between 2001 and 2011 is presented in the table below. It reflects a general trend, which, as Jarman notes, "in Belfast and many other towns has involved a shift of communal identity from 'Orange' [Protestant/Unionist/Loyalist] to 'Green' [Catholic/Nationalist/Republican] (Jarman 2004: 10)."[130]

---

[130] Regarding Belfast, this general trend is demonstrated in the revised data from the 2011 Northern Ireland Census. The figures not only show that Catholics, amounting to almost 49% of the city's population, have for the first time outnumbered Protestants, with a proportion that dropped to just over 42%, but also Belfast's entrenched spatial divisions between the largely Protestant eastern part and the solidly Catholic western part. In North and South Belfast the size of the two communities is more even, although Catholics have also become a slim majority there. Moreover, there is a difference in age structure with the Catholic population being on average considerably younger than the Protestant one (NISRA 2012: 8 & 19, Purdy 2014, Russell 2013: 14-15).

Community Background[1]	All residents			Catholic			Protestant		
Geographical Area: Ward[2] (LGD[3])	2001	2011	*Change*	2001	2011	*Change*	2001	2011	*Change*
Ardoyne (N)	6601	5987	*-9.3%*	96.4%	92.8%	*-3.6%*	3.2%	5.1%	*1.9%*
Crumlin (N)	4376	4582	*4.7%*	3.6%	11.3%	*7.7%*	93.9%	82.3%	*-11.6%*
Duncairn (N)	4007	4901	*22.3%*	5.6%	23.6%	*18.0%*	90.2%	63.9%	*-26.3%*
New Lodge (N)	5225	4950	*-5.3%*	97.3%	89.2%	*-8.1%*	2.2%	7.6%	*5.4%*
Woodvale (N)	4594	4088	*-11.0%*	2.6%	6.0%	*3.4%*	95.1%	87.0%	*-8.1%*
Glencairn (W)	4026	3749	*-6.9%*	12.3%	17.5%	*5.2%*	85.2%	75.5%	*-9.7%*
Highfield (W)	5308	5651	*6.5%*	4.2%	9.5%	*5.3%*	94.0%	82.6%	*-11.4%*
Shankill (W)	3784	3816	*0.8%*	3.2%	7.9%	*4.7%*	94.3%	84.5%	*-9.8%*
Falls (W)	5046	5184	*2.7%*	96.3%	87.6%	*-8.7%*	2.7%	7.5%	*4.8%*
Whiterock (W)	5424	5694	*5.0%*	99.0%	93.1%	*-5.9%*	0.7%	4.7%	*4.0%*

[1] The remainder of residents belongs to the other categories: a few to 'Other religions' and most to 'None'.
[2] Electoral district of Belfast
[3] Local Government District Belfast - Assembly Area: N = Belfast North, W = Belfast West (electoral classification)

Table 4. Community Background of Resident Population in Selected Wards of North and West Belfast, Census 2001 and 2011 (calculated by the author from NINIS 2001, 2013a)

The massive increase in residential segregation at the beginning of the Troubles found its physical manifestation in the so-called euphemisms of 'peace lines' or 'peace walls'. These physical barriers were installed at inter-face locations, mainly between Catholic and Protestant working-class areas, with the official intention – as claimed by government – to contain and pre-vent inter-community tensions and violence. The first wall, which is still the biggest and probably the most famous one in Northern Ireland, was built by the British Army in September 1969 in West Belfast to separate the Catholic Falls from the Protestant Shankill area (for pictures, see below).[131] Subse-quently, barriers were constructed in the interface areas of Catholic Ardoyne and Protestant Glenbryn in North Belfast and around the Catholic Short Strand in the inner east of the city. Yet, they have become permanent phe-nomena of segregation and security that demarcate the still existing fractured space and reinforce the divisions between the working-class communities, especially of those living in interface areas (Boal 2002: 692-693, CRC 2008:

---

[131] Interestingly, Seán Brennan, community development officer at Intercomm in North Belfast, pointed out in a personal interview with the author that actually the first 'peace wall' – although not called that back then – was built already in 1945. It was installed down York Street in the Belfast docks area as a late consequence of the Outdoor Relief riots to separate the Catholic from the Protestant working class (Brennan 2009, interview; see also the section in Chapter 3 on 'Community Inequalities, Class and Ethno-National Divisions', pp. 105-106).

3, Gormley-Heenan et al 2013: 357, Jarman 2004: 10; cf. Boal 1969).[132] As Shirlow and Murtagh point out, "the immediate impact of interface walls is to create social, political and cultural distance between communities." (Shirlow & Murtagh 2006: 9). According to a later report by the Belfast Interface Project (BIP), as of 2011 there has been a staggering number of "99 different security barriers and forms of defensive architecture across the city associated with residential areas." (BIP 2011: 11)[133] This means an enormous increase since 1994, the first year of the paramilitary ceasefires, where there were only 16 of such physical interfaces (Shirlow & Coulter 2007: 213).[134] The great majority of these interface barriers are located in North and West Belfast with 44 in the northern part and 30 in the western part of the city (BIP 2011: 11). Thus, notably, the majority of the 'peace walls' have been built at a time when most of the conflict-related deaths had already occurred (Cunningham & Gregory 2014: 67).[135] Indeed, as previous research has indicated, a substantial majority living in interface areas want the barriers to be there, mainly for security reasons. According to a survey of 2012, commissioned by the OFMDFM, for instance, 69% of local residents believe that the "'peace walls' are still required because of the potential of violence." (Byrne et al

---

[132] Most of the 'peace walls' are located in Belfast. Yet, interface barriers have also been constructed in other flashpoint areas of Northern Ireland – amounting to five in Derry/Londonderry, five in Portadown and one in Lurgan (cf. BBC News 2009, Heatley 2004, Jarman 2005). Moreover, certain forms of defensive architecture have also been put in place in other towns like Antrim, Ballymena and Larne, which, over recent years, have become affected by, as Jarman puts it, "more formalised segregation and associated violence" (Jarman 2004: 6).

[133] Many of those barriers are walls made of stone, concrete or steel which can be over six metres high. Moreover, there are several roads where gates have been installed. The gates are locked during the night with trustworthy community members appointed as gatekeepers, thus preventing access to people from the 'other' side (cf. BIP 2011, Jarman 2005).

[134] A study by the Community Relations Council (CRC), which confirms the massive increase of interface barriers in Belfast, comes up with slightly different figures, probably due to the differences in the time frame. Accordingly, there were 18 barriers in the early 1990s and 88 in 2008 (CRC 2008: 3).

[135] In fact, as evidenced, for instance, by the study of Niall Cunningham & Ian Gregory, over 90% of conflict-related fatalities occurred before 1994. Moreover, "deaths were ... heavily skewed to the early period of conflict, with almost one in five occurring within a single year of the Troubles, 1972." (Cunningham & Gregory 2014: 67) As they argue, "this is important because the temporal spread of fatalities effectively represents the inverse pattern to that of peaceline construction during the conflict, which intensified much later on from the 1990s, well after fatalities had peaked." (Cunningham & Gregory 2014: 67)

2012: 13) Remarkably, Protestant interface residents had a higher proportion than their Catholic counterparts (76% vs. 67%).[136] Nevertheless, the DUP-Sinn Féin-led power-sharing government has repeatedly expressed its intention to remove the walls. This is also reflected in its latest community relations strategy, 'Together: Building a United Community', dating back to 2013, where the Northern Ireland Executive set itself the ambitious objective to "Create a 10-year Programme to reduce, and remove by 2023, all interface barriers." (OFMDFM 2013: 6; cf. Devenport 2013) To date, however, little concrete action has followed this commitment, apparently because of the ongoing row over Brexit and the Irish border and also because of local resistance (cf. Black 2018, Campbell 2017). As recently reported, there seems to be growing resentment and frustration among Protestant and Catholic interface residents that their concerns about the future of the 'peace walls' and community relations on the ground are neglected by high-level politicians in the Brexit debate (Savage 2018). Yet in the meantime, at least two notorious 'peace walls' situated in highly dangerous sectarian faultlines in North Belfast did come down after 30 years, one along Crumlin Road in Ardoyne near Holy Cross and the other on Springfield Avenue (BBC News 2016a, McDonald 2017) Otherwise, the number of interface barriers in Belfast has remained virtually the same. BIP's latest study on interfaces in 2017, for instance, identified 97 such barriers in Belfast, only two less than in 2011 (BIP 2017: 4).[137]

---

[136] A more recent survey, conducted in 2015, shows similar results. Therein 36% of interface residents stated that they want the 'peace wall' in their community removed, but only 18% believed that this represented most people in their community. Notably, again, there was a significantly higher proportion of Catholics than Protestants that want their 'peace wall' down, i.e. 57% vs. 18% (Byrne et al 2015: 20-21)

[137] In particular, the report points out that, apart from some minor count discrepancies from the previous report, since 2012 only six barriers in Belfast have been removed, two have been partially dismantled, another three have lost their interface function due to redevelopment, and even a new barrier has been erected. The study also examined the other interface barriers in Northern Ireland, with 11 barriers recorded in Derry/Londonderry, 1 in Lurgan and 7 in Portadown, corresponding to a total of 116 barriers (BIP 2017: 4).

Plate 1. 'Peace Wall' along Cupar Way, West Belfast, seen from the Falls
(Photos taken by the author, 15/07/2009)

As mentioned before, the relations between the Catholic and Protestant communities particularly in West and North Belfast were already clouded by tensions and recurring violent clashes long before the Troubles started. With the outbreak of armed conflict in August 1969 the situation deteriorated dramatically. Throughout the Troubles Belfast was the focal point of intergroup conflict. The city experienced a much greater intensity of violence than other hotspot areas in Derry/Londonderry, Portadown, Armagh and Newry and Mourne. Almost half of the about 3,600 deaths from the 30 years of conflict happened in Belfast, of which most were local residents.[138] The working-class communities of North and West Belfast were most affected with around 80% of the fatal incidents occurring in their areas. Moreover, there is a huge gender gap in the death rates, for around nine out of ten victims were male (Fay et al 1999: 142-161, Shirlow & Murtagh 2006: 72-73, Sutton 2016a).[139] The

---

[138] According to the study by Therese Fay, Mike Morrissey and Marie Smyth, almost one third of the conflict-related deaths occurring between 1969 and 1998 were children and young people under the age of 24 (Fay et al 1999: 181). In addition, it is estimated that as a consequence of the Troubles around 43,000 people were injured, of which more than two thirds were civilians (Fay et al 1999: 160, Heenan & Birrell 2010: 37).

[139] Various analyses have been conducted on those who have been killed by the Troubles. These analyses, however, have come up with different figures due to different timeframes and definitions used regarding which deaths to be included (cf. Melaugh 2016f). The study by Fay et al, for instance, shows that between 1969 and 1991 1,352 of the total of 2,902 fatal incidents occurred in the city. In North Belfast 463 people were killed and 678 in West Belfast – yet this calculation is for the years 1969 to 1998 (Fay et al 1999: 142 – 149). According to Sutton's database on the deaths from the Northern Ireland conflict, which covers the period from 1969 to 2001, the corresponding figures show that 1,541 of the total of 3,532 deaths happened in Belfast, of which 577 (519 men and 58 women) were

Catholic communities were worst hit with nearly two thirds of all civilians who were killed in North and West Belfast having a Catholic background (Sutton 2016b).[140] This was mainly due to the intense campaign by the Loyalist paramilitaries that primarily targeted Catholics and the massive presence of the security forces mounting a counter-insurgency campaign in Catholic working-class areas (Fay et al 153; cf. O'Duffy & O'Leary 1990: 324-325).[141] Notably, as the study by Shirlow and Murtagh shows, there is a correlation between conflict-related deaths and interface areas and residential segregation (as illustrated in the figure below). According to their calculation, nearly half of all conflict-related deaths within the Belfast urban area between 1969 and 2004 occurred within 300 metres distance of an interface between segregated Catholic and Protestant neighbourhoods, and around two thirds less than 500 metres away from the 'peace lines' (Shirlow & Murtagh 2006: 72-73).

---

in the northern part and 623 (579 men and 44 women) in the western part of the city (Sutton 2016b). By contrast, Shirlow & Murtagh covering the period from 1968 to 2005 come up with lower figures of conflict-related deaths in North Belfast 511 and West Belfast 597 – both taken together amounting to 78.3% of the total of 1,417 conflict-related deaths that occurred in the Belfast urban area (Shirlow & Murtagh 2006: 72-73).

[140] As calculated by the author from the figures provided in Malcolm Sutton's database, 311 of the 577 people killed in North Belfast were Catholics. In West Belfast Catholics amounted to 353 of the 623 conflict-related deaths (Sutton 2016, "Crosstabulations": First Variable "Religion Summary", Second Variable "Location").

[141] According to the calculation by Fay et al of the perpetrators of the conflict-related resident deaths 1969-1998 in a part of North Belfast, more than 60% of the Catholic civilians were killed by loyalist paramilitaries and almost 25% by the security forces (Fay et al 1999: 153). In contrast, the calculation by Brendan O'Duffy & Brendan O'Leary of the perpetrators of conflict-related deaths 1969-1989 in Northern Ireland as a whole shows lower figures: loyalist paramilitaries were responsible for 56% of all Catholic civilian deaths and the security forces for less than 17% (O'Duffy & O'Leary 1990: 325).

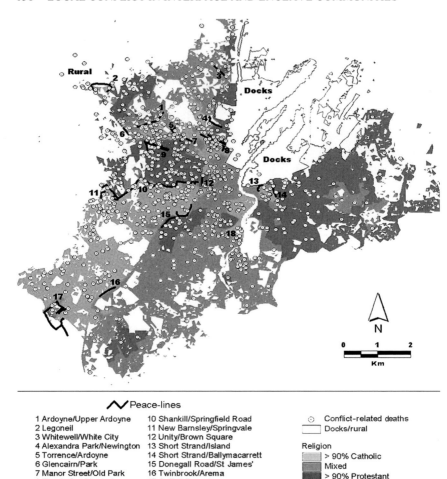

Figure 5. Prominent Interfaces, Segregation and Politically Motivated Deaths in Belfast 1969 – October 2005 (Shirlow & Murtagh 2006: 61)

Aside from segregation and its concomitant processes of separation and seclusion there were other factors that contributed to the monolithic, homogeneous character of the communities and that deepened the divisions between them. The fierce violence that occurred especially during the early years of the Troubles led to an upsurge of militant nationalism. While the Catholic

working-class areas of North and West Belfast came increasingly under control of militant Republicans of the Provisional IRA,[142] the Protestant working-
class areas in the north-west, north and inner east of the city became strongholds of the Loyalist paramilitary groups either of the UDA or the UVF (cf.
Bruce 1994, Coogan 1993, White 1993, Wood 2006). Several factors contributed to the unprecedented support for the Provisional IRA in Catholic
working-class areas: fear and the need for protection against sectarian assaults
and excessive force by state security forces, tradition, and spectacular actions
by the IRA themselves, such as the hunger strikes by Bobby Sands and other
Republican inmates. There were also several key events, where the British
and Unionist governments played a leading role, and British policy decisions
that caused an outrage among Catholics and thus boosted the IRA's popularity. According to Coogan these included "the growth of the Civil Rights
movement, the Falls Road curfew of July 1970 [and] the unilateral introduction of internment in August 1971, when no Protestants were interned
(Coogan 1993: 434)." During that time more – especially young – Catholics
from Belfast's working-class areas joined the IRA, yet their number remained
relatively small. The support to the militant Republican movement was traditionally more passive through providing resources such as shelter, food or
money (Coogan 1993: 472-473). By contrast, the Loyalist paramilitary
groups of the UVF and UDA attracted considerably less support among the
Protestant working-class communities. This is partly attributed to the fact that
their role as 'defenders' of the Protestant/Loyalist community put them into
direct competition with the state. For Protestants could generally rely on the
state security forces for protection. Moreover, they could join the security
forces of the police (RUC) or the army (UDR), and in Protestant working-
class areas there were quite some who took this opportunity – partly also because of the aggravated employment situation. As Steve Bruce points out,
there was another reason why militant Loyalism lacked popularity among
Protestants. The Loyalist paramilitaries were heavily involved in racketeering,
not least due to a lack of funding; this was unlike their Republican counter-

---

[142] The Irish National Liberation Army (INLA), an Irish Republican Socialist paramilitary
group that split off from the Official IRA, was also active in the Catholic working-class
areas. INLA had their base in the Divis Flats buildings in inner West Belfast; yet beyond
the immediate surroundings, the group's influence was rather insignificant (Coogan 1993:
568, Hanley & Millar 2009: 283-292, McDonald & Holland 2010).

parts, who could draw on substantial financial support from Irish-American and other external sources (Bruce 1992: 280-286).

The UVF and UDA employed forceful means to gain control in Protestant working-class areas, which their counterparts from the IRA equally did in the Catholic working-class areas. This led to the establishment of informal justice systems, where the paramilitaries assumed a policing role in the communities which frequently involved punishment beatings and shootings of petty criminals and dissenters (Knox & Monaghan 2002: 31-50, Monaghan 2004, Silke 2000).[143] The fierce paramilitary violence within the two communities is demonstrated by the fact that during the Troubles one out of four Catholic civilians was killed by Republican paramilitaries and one fifth of the Protestant civilian casualties were committed by Loyalist paramilitaries (Smyth 2006; cf. O'Duffy & O'Leary 1990).[144]

The Northern Ireland peace process, in which the aim to find a political solution to the armed conflict became the focus of attention, brought about both a lessening of violence and a shift in its nature. At the intra-community level, the situation of paramilitary violence, intimidation, vigilantism and informal social control gradually eased. The community restorative justice schemes that have evolved in several Republican and Loyalist working-class areas in North, West and Inner East Belfast and also in Derry/Londonderry have made an important contribution in this respect. In some communities, however, remnants of the informal justice systems continue to exist (Knox 2013, Monaghan 2002, Topping & Byrne 2012).145 In the aftermath of the peace agreement, the working-class areas became the scene of internal struggles between factions of the Republican and Loyalist paramilitary organisations, which caused several local casualties. Between 2000 and 2010 at least six

---

[143] According to official figures presented by Fay et al, between 1973 and 1996 2,096 people were shot for punishment and a further 1,283 people were victims of punishment beatings including kneecappings and broken limbs. Among the victims there were almost 500 young people less than 20 years old. Republican paramilitaries were more heavily involved than their Loyalist counterparts and accounted for nearly 60% of all the cases (Fay et al 1999: 195).

[144] According to Mary Smyth's calculations, between 1969 and 1998, Republican paramilitaries killed 381 of total 1,543 Catholic civilians while their Loyalist counterparts were responsible for 207 of the total of 1,064 deaths (Smyth 2006: 13).

[145] Although the number of punishment attacks has dropped significantly as compared to the time of the Troubles, it has still remained considerably high. Shirlow & Murtagh, for instance, recorded 1,129 of such incidents occurring between 1994 and 2004 (Shirlow & Murtagh 2006: 52).

feuds occurred within militant Loyalism, involving the UDA and UVF and the dissident groups of the Loyalist Volunteer Force (LVF) and Red Hand Defenders (RHD) (Gallaher 2007: 129-157, Monaghan & Shirlow 2011, McDonald 2005, Southern 2011). Republican dissidents of the Real IRA and the Continuity IRA have also become increasingly active in recent years in stirring up tensions and violence around Orange parades and other contentious events, mainly in interface areas in North Belfast (Canning 2009, Frampton 2012, Horgan & Morrison 2011, McDonald 2009, Lynn 2016).

As regards the conflict between the communities, violence on a large scale came to an end after the Republican and Loyalist paramilitary ceasefires of 1994. The tensions in the working-class areas, however, persisted, and frequently turned into sectarian clashes around contentious parades, protests and other events. An indicative example was the Orange Order's marching season of 1996, which led to intercommunal violence throughout Northern Ireland. The riots and disturbances were particularly severe in North Belfast with its many interface areas. The 'Tour of the North' in June marked the beginning of the street violence that broke out at several flashpoints between Catholic/Republican and Protestant/Loyalist working-class communities with heavy involvement of the RUC police force (McLaughlin et al 1997: 13-25). Major civil unrest surrounded the Orange Order parade at Drumcree Church in Portadown in early July – first by Protestant Loyalist supporters because of the RUC decision to ban the marchers from passing through the Catholic Garvaghy Road residential area, and then by Catholic Nationalists due to the RUC's reversal of the ban.[146] This decision and the massive operation by the police and the British Army heightened intercommunal tension in North Belfast and led to serious clashes in several interface areas. As a consequence of the violence, many families were forced to leave their home. According to Jarman, "Throughout Drumcree week there were also numerous cases of more personalised threats and intimidation, which resulted in one hundred and ten officially recognised displaced households in North Belfast alone." (Jarman 1999: 8) Moreover, the sectarian violence spread to other interface

---

[146] To illustrate, the RUC decision to re-route the Orange Order's Drumcree march from the Garvaghy Road led to a four day stand-off between the police with the support of the British Army and Orangemen and Loyalist supporters. The results of the stand-off were: the "death of ... a Catholic taxi driver, over 100 incidents of intimidation, 90 civilian injuries, 50 RUC injuries, 758 attacks on the police, 662 plastic baton rounds fired by police, 156 arrests made." (McKenna & Melaugh 2016) For an outline map of the Drumcree parade and Garvaghy Road area see Figure 13 in the Appendix, p. 407.

areas such as Suffolk and Lenadoon in Outer West Belfast and the Short Strand in the inner east of the city. During the next two marching seasons the severe disturbances were repeated with Drumcee and North Belfast remaining particular flashpoints (BIP 1999, Jarman 1999, McKenna & Melaugh 2016; cf. Garvaghy Residents 1999, Kaufmann 2007: 149-201). Such spill-over effects of violence point to a more general issue, for, according to Eithne McLaughlin et al, "Disputes in one part of Northern Ireland can result in riots in other places, particularly at interfaces between Catholic and Protestant communities." (McLaughlin et al 1997: 9)

In the post-Agreement period this cyclical pattern of local violence and counter-violence continued despite the decline in overall conflict intensity. A significant number of parades still remain a source of contention that leads to recurring violent protests and disturbances. Belfast and Portadown have borne the brunt of these events. For instance, as Jarman et al have calculated, between 2005 and 2008 almost half of the in total 977 contentious parades in Northern Ireland took place in the two cities – amounting to 226 in Belfast and 224 in Portadown (Jarman et al 2009: 68-69).[147] Apart from the parading issue, there have been numerous sectarian attacks directed at sites of specific symbolic importance to the communities, such as Protestant and Catholic churches, GAA clubs and Orange halls (Jarman 2005b: 14-16, Shirlow & Murtagh 2006: 51). Sectarian disorder including criminal damage, assaults, riots and disturbances has been intense in Belfast's working-class communities, especially in the interface areas of North Belfast. As can be seen from the figures presented by Jarman, between 1999 and 2004 a staggering number of almost 5,000 sectarian attacks occurred in these areas (Jarman 2005b: 20).

An infamous example is the dispute at Holy Cross Catholic Girls' Primary School that occurred in 2001 and 2002 in the Ardoyne area.[148] The harassment of Catholic school girls and their parents by local protesters from the adjacent Protestant Loyalist Glenbryn estate that was on the route to the front entrance of the school led to recurrent intercommunal violence with involve-

---

[147] It should be noted that compared to the overall number of parades the proportion of contentious parades is relatively small. For instance, according to official figures a total of 3,801 parades were reported for the parading season 2008/09, of which less than 6% were classified as "contentious" (PCNI 2010: 10). However, the fact that these parades take place in commemoration of significant "key events in Portadown, Derry Londonderry and parts of Belfast, and the annual cycles of celebration and commemoration, have ensured that tensions have recurred each year." (Bell 2007: 13)

[148] For an outline map of the area see Figure 12 in the Appendix, p. 407.

ment of the police, the British Army and paramilitaries on both sides. Remarkably, as Heatley points out, there was never any protest by Loyalist residents outside Holy Cross before, even during the worst times of the Troubles (Heatley 2004). On 19 June 2001 Loyalists began to blockade the school and riot police were deployed to escort the pupils and their parents through the picket line. On the subsequent day the Loyalist protesters blocked the front gates of the school thus forcing it to close and preventing the school children from accessing the school. The protest, which was orchestrated by Loyalist paramilitaries, continued for the next ten days until the end of school term. Upon the initiative of a Catholic priest, Father Aidan Troy, who was appointed as new superior of Holy Cross monastery and school, there were talks over the summer between residents from Ardoyne and Glenbryn. Yet, no agreement could be reached. On 1 September, the first day after the summer break, the protest resumed and the pupils and parents were escorted daily to and from school by Fr Troy. The situation escalated soon afterwards. For the following three nights sectarian rioting erupted with Loyalists wreaking havoc in the area around Holy Cross. The violence was orchestrated by Loyalist paramilitaries. Parents from Ardoyne received death threats by the RHC and on the fifth day of the school term UDA members threw a blast bomb into the crowd of school girls and parents in front of Holy Cross. The assault which injured four police officers caused an outrage even among some leading Loyalists like Billy Hutchinson, Northern Ireland Assembly member of the Progressive Unionist Party (PUP) for North Belfast, who said: "I am totally ashamed to be a Loyalist today after seeing these people attack young Catholic girls." (BBC News 2001c) By the end of September sectarian violence spread across many interface areas of North Belfast, such as the Protestant Loyalist Tigers Bay and the Catholic Republican New Lodge. Attacks on Catholic and Protestant pupils increased dramatically, including an assault with a concrete block that was thrown on a school bus and injured seven children on their way to Hazelwood Integrated College[149] (BBC News 2001a, Campbell 2013: 52). The blockade at Holy Cross was called off on 23 No-

---

[149] Hazelwood Integrated College is a mixed comprehensive primary and secondary school attended by pupils from Protestant and Catholic and other religious and community backgrounds. Founded in 1985, the college is one of the first integrated schools in Northern Ireland. It is located along the Whitewell Road, which is an interface area in the outskirts of North Belfast stretching to the suburb of Newtownabbey that has become a site of sectarian tensions and violence since the Drumcree disturbances of 1996 (Campbell 2013, McLaughlin et al 1997: 58-78, O'Connor 2002).

vember when the Office of the First Minister and Deputy First Minister (OFMDFM) finally got involved and local residents from Glenbryn accepted a regeneration and security package for their estate. However, violent confrontations at Holy Cross broke out again on 9 January 2002, but after a short upsurge of widespread rioting across North Belfast the situation eventually calmed down a few days later. As a consequence of the Holy Cross dispute, the significance of the interface between Ardoyne and Glenbryn as a territorial demarcation line was reinforced, which found its visual manifestation in nationalist flags and emblems being festooned by both communities at either side. Moreover, the incidents contributed to heightened sectarian tensions and interface violence during the ensuing two parade seasons (Campbell 2008: 145-159, Cowan 2002, Heatley 2004; cf. Hall 2003: 3).

The reasons for the Loyalist protest at Holy Cross are disputed. As Kauffmann points out, the initial spark was caused by a parading dispute, when a contentious Orange Order parade was re-routed from the Ardoyne area (Kauffmann 2007: 291). According to Colm Heatley, there were allegations made by Loyalist residents from Glenbryn that the IRA would use the school children to gather intelligence about their community (Heatley 2004). Beatrix Campbell, by contrast, argues that the recurring Loyalist paramilitary feuds in the area was also a contributing factor, but the main trigger for the protest was the threat perceived by Glenbryn residents that Catholics would encroach on and take over what was regarded as their territory. In support of this view, she quotes Jim Potts, a spokesman of the Glenbryn residents' group, who pointed out: "Catholics have to accept that there are lines and boundaries, you can't just keep claiming protestant homes because you are over-populating. That was what the protest was about." (Campbell 2008: 151) The conduct of the police and public authorities during the blockade at Holy Cross is criticised by Campbell. In particular, her main critique is that the rights of the parents and children and the rights of the protesters were regarded as equally legitimate. Policing was driven by the overriding concern to contain the protest and thus severely restricted the children's freedom of walking to school. Likewise, public authorities were reluctant to intervene and protect the Catholic pupils from sectarian harassment (Campbell 2008: 146-149).

A more recent incident is the so-called 'flag dispute', which was caused by a majority vote of the Belfast City Council on 3 December 2012 to restrict the days of the flying of the UK's union jack at the City Hall to 18 designated days each year. The decision was brought about by the Republican, Nationalist and middle-ground councillors against the opposition by their Unionist counterparts. It caused an outrage among wider sections of the Protestant Loyalist/Unionist community and, in consequence, led to weeks of riots and street protests involving attacks on the police, on Catholic Republican/ Nationalist communities and on Republican, Nationalist and middle-ground politicians. Moreover, throughout 2013 the flag dispute precipitated further Loyalist and Unionist unrest about related issues such as restrictions on contentious Orange Order parades. The flag protests came to an end only three years later, yet the issues of contention remain unresolved to this day (Clubb 2013, Jarman 2019, McDonald 2012, Nolan et al 2014, Williamson 2016). Since then, however, sectarian tension in the city has not reached levels seen in the past. By and large, the recent marching seasons have passed peacefully without major incidents, except for the sporadic violence around Loyalist 11th night bonfires[150] and the 12th of July parades in 2018 (cf. RTÉ 2017 & 2019, The Guardian 2018).

One issue that has become a bigger concern in the years after the peace agreement is the increasing involvement of young people in sectarian violence and anti-social behaviour around interfaces in deprived working-class areas of Belfast (Hansson 2005, Jarman & O'Halloran 2001, Leonard 2010). This rather recent phenomenon of youth-led violence finds its particular expression in what has been coined locally as 'recreational rioting', which according to Neil Jarman and Chris O'Halloran describes "the low-level but persistent trouble caused by children and youths at interface areas across the city." (Jarman & O'Halloran 2001: 2)

The communal strife of the Troubles greatly exacerbated the already dire socio-economic situation of the Catholic and Protestant working-class communities. Unemployment was already on the rise with the industrial decline that occurred in Belfast since the 1950s, and until 1979 half of the jobs in the main industries were lost (Kennedy-Pipe 1997: 32-33). In general, the Catholic population suffered from much higher unemployment levels, with Catholics being consistently more than twice as likely as Protestants to be unemployed (Bradley 1996: 50, Osborne & Cormack 1986: 218, Smith & Chambers 1991: 1995). Comparing the unemployment rates for men, which were significantly higher than for women, shows that in 1981 nearly one-third of

---

[150] The so-called '11th Night' or 'Eleventh Night', on which large towering bonfires are lit in many Protestant/Loyalist neighbourhoods, marks the beginning of the annual Protestant Orange Order's 12th of July, also called 'The Twelve' celebrations. For an in-depth account of the bonfire tradition in Northern Ireland, see Gailey & Adams (1977).

Catholic men were unemployed, as compared to just one out of eight Protestant men. The figures for 1991 reveal a similar picture (Fay et al 1999: 97, FEC 1995: 38-45, Osborne & Cormack 1986: 215).[151] The situation was particularly severe in the predominantly Catholic working-class areas of West Belfast, such as Whiterock with over 56% and the Falls with nearly 53% male unemployment in 1981. It was also severe, though to a slightly lesser extent in the Catholic working-class areas of North Belfast, such as the New Lodge with corresponding figures for male unemployment of almost 46% and Ardoyne of nearly 41%. By contrast, unemployment in Protestant working-class areas was markedly lower, with the Shankill experiencing the highest male unemployment level of almost 28% (Rowthorn & Wayne 1988: 117). According to Bob Rowthorn and Naomi Wayne, Protestants were in a relatively better off situation, not least because many jobs were provided for them in the security forces and other security-related occupations. This kept Protestant unemployment, especially of men, artificially low during the Troubles. Those Catholics who were in employment had a disadvantaged position, for they were "crowded into low-paid, insecure forms of employment." (Rowthorn & Wayne 1988: 119)

The recovery of Northern Ireland's economy set in with the political peace process gaining momentum in the early 1990s. This led to an increase in employment due to public sector expansion and increase in foreign private investments. In effect, the unemployment rate in Northern Ireland dropped and in 1994 amounted to 11% (Gudgin 1999). The unemployment differential between the two communities, however, remained high with Catholic unemployment rates being around twice that of Protestants, and more than twice for Catholic males (NISRA 2001a: 7). The unemployment and poverty situation was much more severe for people living in interface areas. As shown in a study by Brendan Murtagh of the interface areas of Ardoyne, Suffolk and Short Strand, 31% of them were unemployed in 1994 – nearly three times as high as the overall unemployment rate – and almost 70% were below the

---

[151] Between 1971 and 1981 Catholic male unemployment increased from 17.3% to 30.2% and in 1991 slightly decreased to 28.4%; by contrast, the figures for Protestant males increased from 6.6% in 1971 to 12.4% in 1981 and with 12.7% in 1991 remained at that level. The female unemployment rate for Catholics amounted to 7.0% in 1971, 17.1% in 1981 and 14.5% in 1991. The respective unemployment rates for Protestant women were 3.6% in 1971, 9.6% in 1981 and 8.0% in 1991 (Fay et al 1999: 97, Osborne & Cormack 1986: 215).

poverty threshold – as compared to 45% in Northern Ireland as a whole (Murtagh 2002: 49-50).

In the post-Agreement period unemployment has fallen and remained relatively low. In 2011 the overall unemployment rate has been 7.5%. Catholics, however, still have been 1.5 times more likely to be unemployed than Protestants (NISRA 2013b: 3). Poverty has continued to be a significant issue for both communities; yet, as shown in the study by Paddy Hillyard et al, Catholics have been more affected. According to their surveys in 2002 and 2003, 36% of Catholic households as compared to 25% of Protestant households have been in poverty (Hillyard et al 2003). In recent years, the situation has generally improved. Thus, the Northern Ireland Labour Force Survey shows that the overall unemployment rates for Protestants and Catholics have converged, reaching an all-time low of 4% in 2017 (NI Executive 2019: 37). Catholics are, however, still more likely to be long-term unemployed. In 2014, for instance, they amounted to 59% of those without a job for 12 months or more (Bell & McVeigh 2014: 29-30). Both unemployment and poverty have remained widespread among Catholic and Protestant working-class communities in North and West Belfast, particularly among those living close to an interface. These communities still record the highest unemployment and poverty rates in Northern Ireland, which can be attributed to the low level of economic activity due to the lack of industries, businesses and commercial premises in the areas (cf. NIA 2012a, NIA 2012b).[152] Beyond that, the communities face other forms of deprivation in terms of income, employment, health and disability, education, training and qualifications, proximity to statutory welfare and other services, level of mobility, living environment and crime and disorder (Jarman 2002: 24-25). According to the Northern Ireland Multiple Deprivation Measure (NIMDM) developed by the Northern Ireland Statistical Research Agency (NISRA), the deprivation levels in all these domains are persistently the highest in Catholic and Protestant working-class areas in North and West Belfast. Although the gap between them has narrowed significantly, Catholic communities still tend to be more

---

[152] In 2011, for instance, almost 9% of the working age population in West Belfast and almost 8% of those in North Belfast claimed unemployment-related benefits – as compared to the Northern Ireland average of slightly more than 5% (NIA 2012a/NIA 2012b: 24). As at April 2012, in West Belfast more than half (almost 53%) and in North Belfast half (50%) of the population aged 16 and over claimed low income benefits – as compared to the Northern Ireland average of just 40% (NIA 2012a/NIA 2012b: 27).

deprived than Protestant ones. There is, however, one notable exception: In recent years, Protestant working-class communities have become most affected by poor education. According to the NIMDM 2010, Protestant working-class areas accounted for seven of the ten areas with the lowest levels of educational attainment in Northern Ireland (cf. NISRA 2001b, 2005a & 2010a, Nolan 2013: 105-106).[153] In general, as a more recent study on education inequalities revealed,

> "The persistent and overarching trend in terms of educational attainment of schools leavers is that a greater proportion of Catholics achieved the education targets than Protestants and 'Other' groups across all three categories (A Levels; GCSEs; GCSEs incl. English and Maths) and the gap between Catholics and the other groups widened between 2007/08 and 2011/12 in all three categories." (Burns et al 2015: 10)[154] [155]

Notably, the period after the peace agreement saw an increase in socio-economic class inequalities in the city that cut across ethno-national lines. This finds its spatial expression in the fact that people belonging to different socio-economic classes tend to live in different parts of the city which are moving at very different paces. Murtagh, for example, has referred to Belfast as a "twin speed city ... in which those with education and skills are doing well in key growth sectors whilst those without resources are increasingly corralled in 'sink' estates, stratified by poverty, segregation and fear." (Murtagh 2008: 4)

---

[153] According to the NIMDM 2010 list of areas with the lowest level of educational attainment, the three most deprived areas are all Protestant. The list is headed by the Shankill, followed by Crumlin and Woodvale. On the Catholic side, the most deprived area in terms of education is the Falls, which ranks fourth in the NIMDM score (NISRA 2010a, Nolan 2013: 105).

[154] 'Other' groups refer to all school leavers who do not identify as Catholic or Protestant, i.e. those of other or no religious faith (Burns et al 2015: 10, Fn. 4).

[155] 'A Level' means 'General Certificate of Education Advanced Level' and 'GCSE' stands for 'General Certificate of Secondary Education'. Both are school leaving certificates awarded by schools in the UK to pupils at the end of compulsory secondary education, i.e. at completion of their eleventh year in school.

OVERVIEW OF THE CURRENT SITUATION IN AND AROUND INTERFACE AREAS

In sum, as could be seen from this account of the Catholic/Nationalist/ Republican and Protestant/Unionist/Loyalist working-class interface communities of Belfast and their wider living environment, there are certain salient factors shaping the development of the situation and the relations between the communities. Although some change has occurred in the course of the peace process and the period subsequent to the Agreement these factors continue to affect the local dynamics of intercommunal tensions and conflict. In particular, three central and enduring dimensions have become apparent:

- *Segregation*: Despite the evidence of increased residential mixing in some areas in Belfast, most of the working-class communities in the north, west and inner east of the city are still highly segregated along ethno-national lines. Thus, residential segregation occurs along class lines, with deprived Catholic/Nationalist/Republican and Protestant/ Unionist/Loyalist working-class areas experiencing much higher levels than affluent middle-class areas. Moreover, the demographic change that occurred in Belfast during the Troubles has continued, thus leading to a growing Catholic and a shrinking Protestant population in most parts of the city. A particularly striking feature in North and West Belfast is the frequent presence of various types of interface barriers that demarcate and separate the segregated neighbourhoods from each other. Remarkably, the number of these euphemistically called 'peace lines' or 'peace walls' has increased during the peace process and has remained stagnant in the post-Agreement period. Despite the declared commitment of the two leading Unionist and Nationalist parties to remove the interface barriers, almost none has been dismantled so far. The segregation of the communities has not been limited, however, to residential space and housing but has permeated many other areas of life including the personal sphere (e.g. friendships and marriage), education, employment and workplace, as well as sports, cultural and leisure activities.

- *Violence*: A lessening of and shift in violence both within and between the Protestant/Unionist/Loyalist and Catholic/Nationalist/Republican working-class communities has occurred since the cessation of the Troubles. At the intra-community level, the violence committed by Republican and Loyalist paramilitaries has decreased. Their informal justice systems have been superseded in several working-class areas of Belfast and also in Derry/Londonderry by community restorative justice schemes. Yet in some areas these systems are still partly in place. On both sides militant splinter groups have emerged and replaced the traditional paramilitary organisations as prime perpetrators of violence within the communities. Inter-community tensions and violence persist in working-class areas in North, West and Inner East Belfast, specifically in those areas located close to an interface. Unlike during the Troubles when local conflict between the communities was a daily reality, it became in the aftermath of the Good Friday/Belfast Agreement a recurring cyclical phenomenon: Every year on the occasion of contentious parades during the Orange Order marching season local tensions in interface areas have mounted and frequently turned into violent clashes involving paramilitary groups and the security forces. There have also been incidents when sectarian unrest in other sites of contentious parades swept to working-class areas in Belfast, thus causing riots and disturbances particularly in the numerous interface zones. Inter-communal violence, however, has not been restricted to the parading issue but has also occurred on several other occasions such as the Loyalist protest at Holy Cross primary school or the flags dispute. Moreover, there have been numerous incidents of sectarian disorder, especially in the interface areas of North Belfast. This has included criminal damage, riots, disturbances and assaults as well as attacks on sites of symbolic value for the communities. However, no major sectarian incidents have yet occurred since the end of the flag protests in 2016.

- *Deprivation*: Despite the overall improvement of the socio-economic situation in Northern Ireland and in Belfast, the working-class communities in North, West and Inner East Belfast continue to experience profound deprivation in multiple ways. Catholics and Protestants living in these areas, especially those in interface residential zones, still face higher levels of unemployment and poverty, lower educational attainments, poorer health conditions, higher crime rates, poorer housing conditions, lower levels of mobility and less geographical access to statutory welfare and other services. A particular problem in interface areas is the lack of industries, businesses and commercial premises. Although the gap between the communities has narrowed considerably,

Catholic working-class communities continue to be in a more disadvantaged socio-economic position than their Protestant counterparts. The exception is education, where Protestant working-class communities are in a worse position now. Furthermore, there is an increasing class divide, as socio-economic inequality between the working class and the middle and upper classes within both communities has widened significantly in the post-Agreement period.

How the dimensions of segregation, deprivation and violence affect selected working-class areas of North and West Belfast is illustrated in the following table. From what can be seen, most of the areas show considerably high levels of residential segregation, multiple deprivation, unemployment and school leavers with no or low qualifications, and conflict-related deaths. Yet, by and large, by all three dimensions the Catholic/Nationalist/Republican communities have been more affected than the Protestant/Unionist/Loyalist communities: They tend to be more segregated and more deprived with higher unemployment rates, and a significantly greater number of at least twice as many residents have been killed there in the course of the Troubles. The only field where the Protestant communities are generally more disadvantaged is education, which is indicated by higher proportions of school leavers with low or no formal qualifications for mainly Protestant areas than for Catholic ones.

Community	Segregation		Deprivation				Violence
Ward[1] (LGD[2])	Community Background		Northern Ireland Multiple Deprivation Measure (NIMDM) Score			Unemployment	Education: No or Low Qualifications	Conflict-related Deaths
	2011[3]		2010[4]	2005[5]	2001[6]	2011[3]	2011[3]	1968-1991
			Rank			All Persons aged 16-74 (Rank[8])	All Persons aged 16 & older (Rank[8])	Residents (Rank[8])
	Catholic	Protestant	NI (Belfast)[7]					
Ardoyne (N)	92.8%	5.1%	9 (7)	7 (6)	12 (11)	10.0% (1)	63.8 % (6)	67 (1)
Crumlin (N)	11.3%	82.3%	6 (5)	4 (4)	1 (1)	7.2% (15)	70.4% (1)	22 (24)
Duncairn (N)	23.6%	63.9%	14 (8)	12 (9)	19 (14)	7.4% (14)	54.3% (12)	24 (19)
New Lodge (N)	89.2%	7.6%	3 (3)	5 (5)	8 (7)	8.3% (7)	64.2% (5)	62 (2)
Woodvale (N)	6.0%	87.0%	19 (12)	13 (10)	7 (6)	8.1% (10)	65.9% (3)	23 (22)
Glencairn (W)	17.5%	75.5%	31 (15)	24 (14)	35 (19)	7.0% (17)	61.1% (9)	24 (19)
Highfield (W)	9.5%	82.6%	78 (22)	73 (21)	76 (23)	5.5% (33)	52.0% (15)	30 (12)
Shankill (W)	7.9%	84.5%	4 (4)	1 (1)	9 (10)	8.5% (5)	67.4% (2)	24 (19)
Falls (W)	87.6%	7.5%	2 (2)	2 (2)	2 (2)	9.1% (2)	63.5% (7)	57 (3)
Whiterock (W)	93.1%	4.7%	1 (1)	3 (3)	3 (3)	8.4% (6)	65.3% (4)	55 (5)
					Belfast	5.7%	41.4%	1216
					Northern Ireland	5.0%	40.6%	2678

[1] Catholic (lighter grey) or Protestant (darker grey) wards: fully coloured cells = highly segregated (81% or more Catholic or Protestant); strongly hatched cells = segregated (between 71 and 81% either Catholic or Protestant); lighter hatched cells = mixed (less than 71% of either community)

[2] Local Government District Belfast - Assembly Area: N = Belfast North, W = Belfast West (electoral classification)

[3] Northern Ireland Census 2011

[4] NIMDM Score 2010, composed of 52 indicators in seven types/'Domains' of Deprivation: Income; Employment; Health and Disability; Education, Skills and Training; Proximity to Services; Living Environment; Crime and Disorder.

[5] NIMDM Score 2005, comprising 43 indicators in seven dimensions/'Domains' of Deprivation: Income; Employment; Health; Education; Proximity to Services; Living Environment; Crime and Disorder.

[6] NIMDM Score 2001, consisting of 45 indicators in seven dimensions/'Domains' of Deprivation: Income, Employment; Health Deprivation and Disability; Education; Skills and Training; Geographical Access to Services; Social Environment; Housing Stress.

[7] Rank of all 582 wards in Northern Ireland (rank of all 51 Belfast wards) where 1 is most deprived.

[8] Rank of all 51 Belfast wards where 1 shows the highest value.

Table 5. Community Profiles of Selected Areas in North and West Belfast: Segregation, Deprivation and Violence (calculated by the author from Fay et al 1999: 144-145; NINIS 2013a, 2013b, 2013c; NISRA 2001c, 2005b, 2010b)

As regards the local communities that have been at the centre of the empirical field research, it should be noted that two of the four locations are missing in the table above. The residential areas of the Protestant/Unionist/ Loyalist working-class community of Suffolk and the Catholic/Nationalist/ Republican working-class community of Lenadoon in Outer West Belfast cut across ward boundaries and therefore could not be included, because wards are the smallest administrative units for which the corresponding data is available. There is, however, evidence that both communities face similar conditions as shown in the table for the other communities of North and West Belfast. For instance, according to the Suffolk Lenadoon Interface Group (SLIG), both communities have been and still are affected by multiple deprivation. Likewise, they have been hit by high levels of violence during the Troubles (SLIG 2008; cf. Hall 2007a).

Regarding the other two locations of central empirical interest, both Ardoyne and Shankill stand out as particularly vulnerable and disadvantaged communities. Ardoyne is a highly segregated area with almost 93% of Catholic residents. It is among the most multiply deprived areas in Northern Ireland and records the highest unemployment rate of all wards in Belfast, which is almost twice as high as the overall unemployment rate in the city. The educational achievements are low in Ardoyne with almost 64% of people leaving school with low or no qualification, thus exceeding the overall figure for Belfast by more than 20%. In terms of violence, Ardoyne has experienced the highest number of conflict-related deaths that occurred in the city. In comparison, Shankill is equally an area with high residential segregation with over 84% of Protestants. It ranks highest on the multiple deprivation measure among all mainly Protestant wards in Belfast and is the fourth most deprived ward in Northern Ireland. It has the highest Protestant unemployment rate, which is 1.5 times higher than the overall unemployment rate in Belfast. The educational attainments in Shankill are the second lowest of all Belfast wards with over two thirds of the local population leaving school with low or no qualifications. Shankill has also been considerably affected by violence during the Troubles, although to a much lesser extent than Ardoyne and the other predominantly Catholic wards where almost three times as many local residents were killed.

SELECTED COMMUNITY PROFILES

At this point, mainly for reasons of clarification, some summarising and additional remarks will be made on the local circumstances and particularities of the communities of Ardoyne, Shankill, Suffolk and Lenadoon, and their surroundings. This should improve understanding of the local situation and key issues of the Catholic and Protestant working-class interface communities, which will be discussed in more depth in the empirical analysis that follows in the next two sections. The remarks particularly refer to specific area names used by locals, to the location and significance of interfaces and to the spatial boundaries of the communities in question. Notably, the boundaries of

communities often do not coincide with the borders drawn on maps for administrative purposes, but they differ sometimes even considerably in terms
of geographical scope and extent. This is because community boundaries are
defined primarily by "the way people live their lives and with whom they
share their experiences and identify themselves." (ACP 2002: 7) In this process of community identification and demarcation, as pointed out by experts
in the field, there are several factors that play a role, such as the political divisions, ideological competition, sectarian geography and the history of local
conflict (ACP 2002: 7-8, Shirlow & Murtagh 2006: 58).

Ardoyne

Plate 2. Aerial Photograph of Ardoyne and   *Plate 3. Interface along Alliance Avenue,*
Surrounding Areas, late 1980s   view on Glenbryn, seen from Ardoyne
(Ardoyne Commemoration Project 2002: xvi) (Photo taken by the author, 10/06/2009)

Ardoyne is a mainly Catholic/Nationalist/Republican working-class area
and ward in North Belfast, which evolved from a suburban village that was
founded in 1815 by a Protestant linen mill owner. On Census day 2011, the
Ardoyne ward had a population of 5,987 residents, with 92.8% belonging to
the Catholic community (NINIS 2013a). Since the early 1970s the resident
population has almost doubled (Shirlow & Murtagh 2004: 59). The wider
community of Ardoyne extends beyond the ward boundaries and is estimated
to amount to a total of around 11,000 people (ACP 2002: 8). The 'Greater
Ardoyne' area, as it is named by Catholic locals, includes the adjoining mostly Catholic/Nationalist/Republican areas of the Bone estate in the mixed Cliftonville ward, the Mountainview area in the Protestant Woodvale ward and
parts of the mixed Legoniel and the mostly Catholic Water Works wards
(ACP 2002: 8, Jarman 2005a: 12). Ardoyne is surrounded on three sides by
Protestant/Unionist/Loyalist areas: in the south by the Greater Shankill area
consisting of the Glencairn, Woodvale, Highfield and Shankill wards as well
as of the Crumlin ward; in the north-west by Protestant/Unionist/Loyalist

neighbourhoods of the Legoniel and Ballysillan wards and in the north by the Glenbryn estate (NINIS 2016a).

There are several interface barriers that have been installed at contentious locations in Ardoyne and immediate surroundings. As of 2011, 13 such 'peace lines' have been identified (BIP 2013). For instance, Glenbryn or 'Upper Ardoyne', as the small Protestant Loyalist enclave is frequently referred to by its residents, is separated from Ardoyne by an up to nine metres high sheet metal fence running along the northern edge of Alliance Avenue (see Plate 2 above). The area around the interface barrier, which is one of the oldest 'peace lines' erected by the British Army in 1971, was and is still a particular flashpoint of intercommunal violence (BIP 2011: 96, Shirlow 2003: 81-82, Jarman 2002: 23). According to Shirlow, "a quarter of all murders during the contemporary conflict in Northern Ireland, occurred within a mile radius of Alliance Avenue." (Shirlow 2003: 81) As mentioned already, in the aftermath of the Agreement, the Ardoyne/Glenbryn interface in Alliance Avenue was the focal point of fierce intercommunal rioting during the Holy Cross school dispute. Moreover, there have been recurring incidents of sectarian violence during contentious Orange parades, such as the 'Tour of the North', that hit the interfaces around Ardoyne, especially along the southern edges of the area (cf. Blake 2019: 47-48, Jarman 2005b, McAleese 2011, McLaughlin et al 1997). Nevertheless, more recently there has also been a positive development: As previously noted, in 2016, on official initiative, a security barrier was removed at a notorious interface near the Catholic Church Holy Cross (BBC News 2016a).

Shankill

Figure 6. Shankill Ward and Greater Shankill, Outline Map (extracted and edited by the author from the Map of Greater Belfast Area Electoral Ward Boundaries, produced by CAIN ARK 2011)

Plate 4. Interface between Greater Shankill and Ardoyne at the Roundabout Twaddell Avenue, Crumlin Road and Woodvale Road, seen from Crumlin Road (Photo taken by the author, 19/06/2009 - before the passage of the 'Tour of the North' parade)

Shankill is a predominantly Protestant/Unionist/Loyalist working-class area and a ward at the northern fringe of West Belfast. It historically dates back to a medieval settlement around the main arterial route of the area, which since 1835 is named the Shankill Road (cf. CCRU 1995). According to the Census 2011, the population of the Shankill ward amounts to 3,816 residents with 84.5% having a Protestant background (NINIS 2013a). As with Ardoyne, the wider Shankill community, which is locally known as the 'Greater Shankill', spreads over a larger area than the ward itself. Thus, the 'Greater Shankill' area stretches between West and North Belfast and comprises the adjacent, mainly Protestant wards of Woodvale, Glencairn and Highfield and adjoining Protestant neighbourhoods. Its population is estimated at slightly less than 20,000 people, which means a decrease of about three-quarters since the early 1970s (Elliott 2007: 178-179, Heatley 2004). Geographically, the 'Greater Shankill' area together with the Crumlin ward forms a continuous belt of Protestant/Unionist/Loyalist residential zones that is squeezed between mostly Catholic/Nationalist/Republican neighbourhoods of the Falls, Clonard, Whiterock and Upper Springfield wards in West Belfast, and of the New Lodge, Water Works, Ardoyne and Legoniel wards in North Belfast (NINIS 2016a & 2016b).

Interface barriers have been constructed at numerous locations prone to intercommunal violence, particularly close to the community's boundaries in the south to Catholic West Belfast and in the north to the Catholic working-class areas of North Belfast. By 2011, 25 such barriers have been reported in and around the Greater Shankill area (BIP 2013). As aforementioned and illustrated, the first 'peace wall' built in 1969 runs along Cupar Way separating Shankill from Falls in West Belfast (cf. Geoghan 2014). It is a multi-level corrugated iron barrier that stretches for over 800 metres in length. A more recent example is an interface between the Greater Shankill and Ardoyne, which occurs at the roundabout area where the Crumlim Road is joined by Woodvale Road and Twaddell Avenue (see Plate 4 above; cf. Jarman 2002: 40). The interface area, which is surrounded by metal fences built in the 1990s, has recently become a central focus of enduring contentions and sectarian violence around Orange Order parades. In July 2013 a protest camp at Twaddell Avenue was set up by Protestants/Unionists/Loyalists who vented their anger against the official ban on a parade that was supposed to take place in the Shankill/Ardoyne interface area. The protests led to a standoff that lasted for over three years and recurrently erupted into fierce sectarian violence when the ban on marching past Catholic Ardoyne was maintained.

They eventually ended in September 2016, following an agreement between local Orange Order lodges and a Catholic residents group (BBC News 2016c, Blake 2019: 47-48, Curran 2014, Moriarity & McGarry 2015).

Suffolk and Lenadoon

Figure 7. Suffolk and Lenadoon , Outline Map (edited and redrawn by the author based on maps and geographical information from DfC 2016; NINIS 2016a; SRPP 2001)

Plate 5. (above). *Suffolk Estate*, seen from SLIG office (Photo taken by the author, 02/07/2009)
Plate 6. (below). *Gated Interface Area between Suffolk and Lenadoon*, close to Stewartstown Road (Photo taken by the author, 20/07/2009)

Suffolk is a small, almost exclusively Protestant/Unionist/Loyalist working-class housing estate situated in Outer West Belfast, which is administratively split between the mainly Catholic wards of Ladybrook and Poleglass. The population of the Suffolk community, which has recently been estimated to be around 800 residents, has steadily declined over the years (BIP 1999: 11, SLIG 2008a; cf. Shuttleworth & Lloyd 2008: 37). By contrast, the adjoining, predominantly Catholic/Nationalist/Republican working-class community of Lenadoon is considerably more populous. According to a recent estimate, Lenadoon has a population of around 10,000 residents (SLIG 2008a). The community covers a much larger residential area that stretches between the mostly Catholic wards of Glencolin and Ladybrook and borders in the east to the Catholic ward of Andersonstown and in the west to the Poleglass ward. Originally, both communities emerged during the 1950s, when "the greater estate, now known as Suffolk and Lenadoon, was built by the Northern Ireland Housing Trust .... mainly for families from inner city redevelopment areas." (Murtagh 2002: 66) Back then, the area was mixed with Catholics and Protestants living alongside each other, although both preferring different locations: Catholics the northern and Protestants the southern part of the area. As with Ardoyne, Shankill and other working-class areas in Belfast, the current state of residential segregation and divisions between the communities dates back to the population movements and displacements during the early 1970s that were caused by the sectarian intimidation and violence of the Troubles. In consequence of the influx of Catholics and the outward migration of Protestants, the Protestant community of Suffolk has shrunk to a small area on the southern side of Stewartstown Road, which has become an enclave completely surrounded by much larger Catholic/Nationalist/Republican communities. The Catholic community of Lenadoon, on the contrary, which is located north of Stewartstown Road, has simultaneously experienced a rapid expansion both in terms of geographical area and population size (BIP 1999: 11-12, Hall 2007a: 3-6, Hall 2008: 3, Murtagh: 66-67, SLIG 2008b: 5-6).

A number of interface barriers have been installed in and around Suffolk and the immediate neighbourhood of Lenadoon with the first 'peace line' along the southern edge of Stewartstown Road constructed in 1983 (Jarman 2002: 23; see also Plate 5 and 6 above). As of 2011, 7 such barriers have been counted (BIP 2011). Throughout the Troubles, the interface area of Suffolk and Lenadoon "was characterised by high levels of inter-community violence, fear, mistrust and division, which included shootings, bombings and large-scale rioting." (SLIG 2008a) In response, community initiatives on both sides were formed in the early 1990s by committed community workers, most of them women, which eventually, with the aid of public funding, joined under the umbrella of the Suffolk Lenadoon Interface Group (SLIG) and their economic arm, the Stewartstown Road Regeneration Project (SRRP). Since then, considerable progress could be made in terms of community development and economic regeneration of the interface area and also regarding the reduction of intercommunal violence (Hancock 2013: 240, LCF 2003, SLIG 2008b). However, tensions between the communities continue to flare. This is evidenced by recurring incidents of sectarian violence in the Suffolk and Lenadoon interface area, such as the flag protests by local Loyalists or the repeated attacks by Nationalist youth from Lenadoon on the Suffolk estate (McDonald 2013a, O'Hara 2013).

COMMUNITY ISSUES AND RELATIONS: WHAT IS AT STAKE?

"Both the Catholic and Protestant working-class share the same problems though in different degree." (Thompson 1973: TC 02:19-02:24) This assessment from the documentary film 'A Place Called Ardoyne', which was made in the heights of the Troubles, still appears to be valid, when considering the presentation above of the current living situation of Catholic/Nationalist/Republican and Protestant/Unionist/Loyalist working-class communities in Belfast. As has been shown, both communities have been, and still are, affected by high levels of socio-economic deprivation, which is particularly severe in interface areas. In general, Catholics have been in a more disadvantaged position than Protestants, although the gap between them has narrowed considerably in recent years. Despite similar experiences of deprivation, however, the Catholic and Protestant working-class communities remain deeply divided. Most of them continue to live segregated lives: they reside in segregated areas, get married to someone from the same community, send their children to segregated schools, work in segregated environments and engage in segregated leisure activities. Even after the cessation of the armed conflict the relations between the communities remain clouded by recurrent sectarian tensions with violent confrontations occurring with regularity over contentious issues such as parades and flags. The interface areas continue to be the flashpoints of intercommunal antagonism and violence. Apparently, however, there are also spatial differences between the working-class communities, especially of North and West Belfast, regarding the manifestation and experience of deprivation, segregation and violence.

In view of this overall situation, the question now is what exactly are the key issues that matter to the Catholic and Protestant working-class communities in the areas under investigation? Moreover, how do these issues impact on community relations and on local intergroup conflict? What are the divisive forces in this regard? Are there signs of local accommodation between the communities? A particular question is how locals from both communities and from different locations experience and perceive these issues, and what similarities and differences exist between their experiences and perceptions. This section therefore focuses on those issues that have been identified as most relevant by local people living in Catholic and Protestant working-class communities and by practitioners and researchers in the field alike.

For clarification some remarks should be made on the methodical and analytical approach that also applies in its essential aspects to the subsequent section on community and power relations.[156] The analysis draws largely on field research on selected interface locations and surroundings in North and West Belfast and other urban places in Northern Ireland, which consists mainly of personal interviews with local residents, practitioners, academic experts, officials and politicians. In addition, the fieldwork included telephone interviews, informal talks and attendance of (cross-)community meetings.[157] Excerpts of selected respondents' narratives highlighting significant experiences and views are presented in their original wording. This will reveal their specific context and subjective meaning and ensure a faithful interpretation of the statements and illustrations, which will both enable a better understanding of the key issues at stake (cf. Maruna 2002: 39). Significant statements and opinions expressed by local residents and stakeholders in informal talks are restated in the author's own words without distorting their original meaning. This is supplemented with empirical studies by experts in the field, dealing with local community issues and their relevance for community relations. These sources, together with relevant theoretical approaches discussed in Chapter 2, will provide the reference frame for interpreting the empirical findings.

With a view to the current state of local intergroup conflict and its potential causes, the issue of community relations is at the core of the analysis, because it arguably is the overarching theme that pervades all other relevant aspects, such as memory of the Troubles, violence, and ethno-national identity as well as living conditions and socio-economic class inequalities in areas like education, employment, housing, health, security and justice. Moreover, this approach will provide more insight into how the material and psychological

---

[156] For a detailed presentation of the overall analytical approach see the section on 'Research Design' in the Introduction.

[157] In the post-Agreement period cross-community meetings have become institutionalised at the local level, especially in North Belfast, as a means to address tensions in interface areas and prevent violence between the communities. In particular, these meetings, which in many cases have developed into cross-community partnerships, are concerned with contentious parading issues faced by those living close to an interface. They operate on an all-inclusive basis seeking to include all relevant stakeholders including local Catholic and Protestant residents, community workers and local representatives from the churches and statutory agencies such as the Police Service of Northern Ireland (PSNI), the Northern Ireland Fire and Rescue Service (NIFRS) and the Northern Ireland Ambulance Service (NIAS).

mechanisms operate and interact on the ground and how they shape local conflict dynamics (cf. Byrne & Carter 2002: 742).

MEMORIES OF THE TROUBLES

History provides a good starting point for the analysis. As indicated already, the Troubles have left a profound legacy on the Protestant and Catholic working-class communities in affecting both their living conditions and the relationships between them (cf. Coulter 2000, Fay et al 1999). Apart from the real situation based on facts and figures, the question arises as to what extent the conflict has shaped the mindsets of local people. More precisely, the question is how the impact of the conflict is perceived by local people from both communities and how it has influenced their views of and attitudes to the 'other' side. When asked about the Troubles, several interview respondents reported quite extensively on the living conditions and particular events before and during the armed conflict. These recollections were based on personal experiences or drawn from stories from their family and friends, which shows that memories of the conflict still figured prominently in their minds.

Maria Bannon, operation manager of SLIG who grew up in the Catholic/ Nationalist/ Republican working-class community of Lenadoon, remembered the local situation during her childhood years:

> "In the late 1970s and early 1980s the living situation in West Belfast, Lenadoon could be described as 'abnormally normal'. The police and army presence and raids on houses were perceived as the usual. The area was rather segregated, although there were a few Protestants living there at that time and up to now." (Bannon, interview)

Her Protestant colleague and chairwoman of Suffolk Community Forum (SCF), Jean Brown, who has a long-standing record of more than three decades of cross-community work,[158] recalled the forced evictions of the early 1970s that led to the current segregation of the communities. At that time she was also forced to leave her home in a relatively mixed neighbourhood of Lenadoon, where she lived from when it was built in the 1950s. As a result,

---

[158] In 2009 Jean Brown and her colleague from Lenadoon, Renee Crawford, were honoured for their long-standing commitment and efforts in local peacebuilding and improving community relations with the Northern Ireland Community Relations Award for Exceptional Achievement (CRC 2009: 8, LaMarche 2012: 314).

she moved to the Protestant Loyalist/Unionist working-class estate of Suffolk. According to Brown,

> "Hundreds of families, both Protestants and Catholics, were been forced to move out from their house. The areas became very polarised ... and for Catholic families who were burnt out of their homes in other parts of Belfast this was a natural sort of migration to come here. And they in turn forced Protestant families out of their homes." (Brown, interview)

However, in Brown's assessment, the expulsion of local Protestants over the following years occurred systematically and led to increased feelings of insecurity and threat within the community. As a consequence, after the first 'peace line' was built, "the people in Suffolk were actually quite happy to live behind that gate, because that was a security barrier to them." (Brown, interview)

The emergence of the interface area between the communities had spatially different effects on the living conditions within Lenadoon. Referring to the upper part of the community that is located further away from the interface area, Bannon pointed out that there was a sense of self-sufficiency and insularity:

> "Upper Lenadoon was like a self-sufficient community at that time. Because it was not an interface ... you could operate within the community almost without having to go outside it, because you could go to [Catholic] Andersonstown without having to go anywhere else. There were shops. There was a cinema, there was a leisure centre. It was almost as you could be insular if you wanted and never really leave the community, and the transport network would have supported that." (Bannon, interview)

In contrast, the area of Lower Lenadoon was more exposed to intercommunal conflict. In an informal talk with the author a local Catholic resident recalled the time when she was a teenager in the early 1980s. She stressed that among the residents of her neighbourhood there was a profound sense of insecurity due to the violence happening in the interface zone. This was because it was feared that the interface violence could easily spill over to her neighbourhood which was located very close nearby. In addition, the socio-economic situation in the area was tense, exacerbated by a serious lack of employment opportunities. This was confirmed by Bannon, who, referring to the wider Suffolk/Lenadoon interface area, noted:

> "There was high unemployment at that time and a lot of people were on benefits. If you were young there was nothing that helped you getting access to the labour market. Many people had to rely on their families and relatives." (Bannon, interview)

Likewise, as a consequence of the events of the Troubles, the Catholic/Nationalist/Republican working-class community of Ardoyne became an insular community, which had to rely on their own socio-economic structure. The situation there, however, was more severe. Unlike Upper Lenadoon, Ardoyne was less capable of being self-sustainable. This was because of the more limited availability of resources within the community. In particular, there were only few jobs available, not least because, as stressed by local residents in an informal discussion with the author, Protestants had a considerable bias against Catholic work ethics.[159] Lee Morgan,[160] for instance, a Catholic Republican working-class resident of Ardoyne working in the crane industry near Belfast Docks, recalled the sectarian prejudices of his Protestant colleagues:

> "I remember as a young person being told by Protestants that I work with that they were told that Catholics do not wash or … that they did not want to work – that was another favourite one – and that was why we were more likely to be unemployed." (Morgan, interview)

Moreover, due to the fact that Ardoyne was more secluded with numerous interface barriers separating it from the surrounding Protestant/Unionist/Loyalist neighbourhoods and the British Army controlling the area, its opportunity to use the services and infrastructure from adjacent Catholic communities was very limited. As Morgan described his experience as a young man living in the community during the Troubles of the early 1980s:

> "For a community of 7.000 people living in the Ardoyne area at that time we had about five or six working men's clubs or bars or social places where you could gather. There were small shops, but there were not many. All that was done out of necessity: we could not go to the centre of the town. We could not go anywhere where we felt not close to our own area; and this place had barriers around and the British Army was patrolling it." (Morgan, interview)

According to him, the presence of the British Army was pervasive and extended even to the local bus stop and the flax mill being under their control. This had a grave impact on community life and created a feeling of being "under occupation" (Morgan, interview).

---

[159] This view was expressed by three local residents and community workers in an informal talk with the author in the context of a multi-agency meeting on local parading issues at Ardoyne Community Centre on 12 June 2009.

[160] The name of the interview respondent has been anonymised upon request.

The living conditions at that time were similar in the nearby Catholic/Nationalist/Republican working-class community of the New Lodge. The area was likewise surrounded and controlled by the British Army, along with the police and other state security forces. The insecurity and threat that were felt in the community was illustrated by a local Catholic Republican working-class resident. In an informal talk with the author he emphasised that it was highly unsafe to walk around in the area at night. This was because of the constant presence of the Army and of Loyalist paramilitaries from the UDA and the UVF, which he deprecatingly called 'thugs'. In a similar vein, Morgan's remark shows the sense of insecurity that was widespread in the area: "You could not just get … any taxi you want; you had to get a taxi from your own community." (Morgan, interview) This view was also echoed by John Loughran, a community development worker at Intercomm Belfast based in Duncairn Gardens who grew up in a family with a strong Republican background in North Belfast. He recalled the fear caused by the upsurge of sectarianism around the time of the Anglo-Irish Agreement in the mid-1980s, when he was in his early teenage years:

> "There was a real sense of fear in the community in which I lived. I remember my father saying: 'If a car slows down and you're going home, you better run for your life.' That's how children were brought up here." (Loughran, interview)

Hence, there was a need for protection and defence against state violence and sectarian attacks, which, as pointed out by several respondents, was common to Catholic working-class communities not only of North Belfast but also of West and Inner East Belfast and in other urban areas in Northern Ireland such as in Derry/Londonderry and Portadown. In all these places Republican paramilitaries, mainly from the IRA, took care of these needs and assumed the role of local community policing. This situation was mirrored in Protestant working-class areas, where Loyalist paramilitaries, mostly from the UVF or UDA, acted as a local police force to protect and defend the community against Republican paramilitary attacks. In the view of Winston Irvine, a Protestant Loyalist working-class resident of the Shankill and interface worker in North and West Belfast, there was considerable acceptance within the local community, "for these armed Loyalist groups … performed their role and duty the police and the British Army could not perform, and that was the defence and protection of the people." (Irvine, interview) However, according to some respondents, the policing role of the paramilitary groups did not remain uncontested among local residents from both communities. There were incidents reported where paramilitaries intimidated and threatened people to comply with their rules of informal community policing. In particular, it was the paramilitaries' practice of punishment beatings of alleged criminals that was criticised for the excessive and arbitrary use of force and for the ineffectiveness in preventing and stopping criminal activity. Moreover, this would have had detrimental consequences to their image and level of support, especially among young people in the community. For instance, as Morgan, in referring to the punishment practice of the IRA in the Ardoyne area, pointed out:

"It was basically if somebody broke into somebody's house A, B, C or D would be done: You would be brought somewhere, you would be questioned, and maybe you would be beaten. It would be almost like a court martial, and that was prevalent. But I know for fact, as I remember speaking to several people all over the years and they were adamant that it did not work. Because there were many people who were on punishment shootings brought upon them on several occasions. They may have robbed the house this year and two years later they were seen joyriding in cars, stealing cars, and then maybe they were getting another punishment attack, and … it did not make any difference. So people that I spoke to have often said to me it was counterproductive. It just made certain elements of young people within the community hate the 'Provos' [Provisional IRA] as they call them." (Morgan, interview)

Like in Ardoyne, the socio-economic situation in the New Lodge was described as equally grave and characterised by widespread unemployment and poverty. Margaret Valente, a local resident and community and youth worker at Star Neighbourhood Centre who, due to the enforced population shifts in 1969, moved from a Catholic area in West Belfast to the New Lodge, enumerated the most pressing issues afflicting the community during the conflict in the early 1980s:

"There was an urgent need for affordable housing, leisure centres, community zones, learning zones, retail shops, small businesses, education and training for young people, and for jobs, which was the most important thing." (Valente, interview)

Housing was already perceived as an urgent issue in Catholic working-class areas in North Belfast in the 1960s before the Troubles. Dympna McGlade, programme director for community policy and development at the Community Relations Council (CRC), grew up in the small Catholic/Nationalist/Republican working-class community of the Bone, which is adjacent to Ardoyne and otherwise surrounded by Protestant/Unionist/Loyalist areas. As she pointed out, "Housing was the big issue at that time. Large Catholic families and young single women with children were desperately in need of decent accommodation." (McGlade, interview) Furthermore, she described the poor housing conditions in the Bone, which differed significantly from those of the adjacent Protestant working-class neighbourhood of the Ballybone:

> "Ours were houses that were tied to the linen industry. So there were outside toilets, no gardens, just terraced houses and in a very poor state of repair. When you went over into the Ballybone, there were houses that had a small garden in the front, an inside bathroom and a toilet." (McGlade, interview)

In her opinion, the Bone was nearly bursting at the seams in the early days of the Troubles, due to an influx of Catholics who had been evicted from the then mixed Rathcoole estate and other places. Yet, the community's residential space soon expanded, when Protestants moved out of the Ballybone and other adjoining estates. As a result, the area became almost completely segregated into Catholic and Protestant neighbourhoods. Drawing to her own experience McGlade pointed out that residential mixing was already uncommon before, and "where there was mixing … it tended to be mixed marriages." (McGlade, interview)

Her childhood reflections are also informative in other ways, as they provide insight into how community relations in the 1960s in working-class areas were affected at an early age already by ethno-national differences and sectarian predispositions. Her upbringing was in a traditional Irish family with her father coming from a Republican and Socialist background. Notably, however, her parents also taught her to adopt an anti-sectarian and inclusive attitude of tolerance and respect for the beliefs and views of the Protestant community, which was unusual at that time. Thus, it was quite common that Protestant children from neighbouring areas came to her house and that she visited them in their home. However, as she emphasised, these encounters proved to be problematic due to divisive national and religious symbols on display in their homes:

> "I had friends from the Protestant community. Protestant children came to our house and they looked around and saw the sacred heart picture with the red light below. And the Irish proclamation was hanging on the wall, because we were a Republican family. … And I knew that they would come into the house and would have known that this is different. This is intimidating. And when I went to their house I saw pictures of the Queen and maybe pictures of their parents or grandparents in British Army uniform. And I would have known that this is different, at a very young age." (McGlade, interview)

What she referred to here was the deep-seated nature of sectarianism that had been embedded in the social fabric since what she called the anti-Catholic "pogroms of the 1920s". (McGlade, interview)

The outbreak of the Troubles not only had a grave impact on the already dire living conditions within Catholic working-class communities but it also caused profound disruption in people's lives. Séan Brennan, like Loughran a community development worker at Intercomm Belfast, vividly remembered the events of that time. After having spent his early childhood until the mid-1960s in a Catholic housing estate at the bottom of the Shankill Road, he moved to Turf Lodge located in what was then considered the outskirts of West Belfast. It was a poor and deprived Catholic working-class residential area which because of Catholic evictions from other places became heavily overcrowded. As Brennan described it,

> "that was where all the refugees were brought, when the conflict broke out in 1969, and a lot of children were brought to school in Turf Lodge, because that was considered the safest place [for Catholics] to be in Belfast." (Brennan, interview)

He also emphasised that the eruption of the Troubles hit many of the younger generation in the community by surprise, including him and his parents, because they felt ill-informed about the emergence of the conflict. Thus, their sense of cautious optimism that evolved in the 1960s during the time of the Civil Rights Movement were destroyed and what Brennan characterised as "the age of innocence for young people" (Brennan, interview) came to a sudden end.

On the Protestant/Unionist/Loyalist side of the communal divide, Jackie Redpath, executive director of the Greater Shankill Partnership and local community worker since the early 1970s, offered deeper insight into how it was to live in Greater Shankill at the time of the outbreak of the Troubles. Redpath, who grew up in a working-class family in the Woodvale area of the Upper Shankill Road where he still lives, pointed out that by then there were a series of highly disruptive developments which the community had to endure.

> "The Shankill was going through massive upheaval on three fronts: one was the Troubles; a second was the whole process of redevelopment and urban renewal; and a third was … the collapse of Belfast's industrial base, which was happening there in shipbuilding, engineering and linen that were all disappearing. Those three things … were a triple assault on the life of the community here in Shankill." (Redpath, interview)

In consequence, as he went on, "there were dreadful levels of deprivation and disadvantage." (Redpath, interview) The events also had a strong personal impact on him. They caused him to renounce his very strong Baptist religious beliefs with which he was brought up and to adopt socialist ideas and become involved in working-class issues and local community work. Furthermore, he stressed the dearth of knowledge and understanding and the prevalence of prejudices towards the 'other' side that shaped community relations and thus exacerbated tensions and divisions. In his view, a major contributing factor was the "sectarian geography of Belfast" (Redpath, interview), with large parts of the city being split into homogenous Catholic/Nationalist/Republican and Protestant/Unionist/Loyalist community areas. As he explained further,

> "When all you know about the other side is either at the end of a rock or the end of a gun barrel. Or all you know of the other side are myths that have been built up over the years. Or all that you know or think of the other side is that they are out to get you, or take your job, or do away with where you live. That lack of knowledge, that myth building leads quite easily to demonising and not hearing the other side, and therefore that leads you directly into confrontation." (Redpath, interview)

Likewise, Tom Winstone, the director of Northern Ireland Alternatives (NIA), a community-based restorative justice scheme in Loyalist areas with headquarter in Woodvale, got personally affected by the developments in Shankill at that time. In recollecting his childhood, Winstone shared his personal experience of forced relocation:

> "I lived in the Shankill from the time I was born in 1955 until 1968, just prior to the Troubles. There was a large redevelopment of the Shankill and many people were moved out of the area to rebuild new homes. My family was moved to New Barnsley in West Belfast, which was at that time a mixed area. But when the Troubles started we were actually put out of our home by Republicans, because they wanted the houses for people who were put out of their homes. We were lucky that we heard about a Catholic family who wanted to move out of their neighbourhood. So we exchanged houses and moved to a predominantly Loyalist area in Upper Shankill called Springmartin. That sure had quite an effect on my life, having to move all the time." (Winstone, interview)

Like in the Catholic/Nationalist/Republican working-class areas of North and West Belfast, a deep sense of insecurity and threat during the early Troubles was also present among Protestant/Unionist/Loyalist working-class people in the Shankill. However, as mentioned before, the threat did not emanate from the state security forces but from Republican paramilitaries, primarily from the Provisional IRA. Billy Hutchinson, a local resident and community development worker at Mount Vernon Community Development Forum, who grew up under poor circumstances in the Shankill area, recalled his impression of the perilous local situation:

> "In 1971 there were many bombs and killings already in the city and the IRA were planting bombs and just killing people all over the place … So this was a terrible time, for young people in particular. We lived under constant threat of attacks. It was very difficult to move around safe in your own area." (Hutchinson, interview)

This experience left a profound impact on his life, which he described as follows: "I suppose I have been marked by history in terms of what happened. I grew up as a teenager who felt under siege by Republicans." (Hutchinson, interview)

The last statement indicates not only the level of division between the Protestant and Catholic communities but also the intensity of intercommunal hostility that existed during the strife of the Troubles. In general, there was a resentful and embittered undertone in several remarks that were made by local respondents on both sides when referring to their experience of encountering the 'other' side at that time. This leads us to the issue of how the violence of the conflict has impacted on the life trajectories of local working-class people and on their perception of and attitudes toward the 'other' community. Therefore, the questions arise as to what the respondents from both communities remembered of the Troubles and, more specifically, what were key biographical experiences in the course of the conflict that prompted them to make life-changing decisions?

Among the memories shared there were many stories of personal exposure to violence and of personal loss due to the conflict. There were several incidents reported where close relatives and friends were killed or injured by Republican or Loyalist paramilitary groups. A striking example is given by Margaret Valente, who had a profoundly tragic experience of personal bereavement and grief in New Lodge at that time. As she recounted,

> "My husband was killed in 1980 by the IRA in a Republican feud. They said he was an informant, which just is not true. I think it was collusion and that he was killed because of hiring people as informants. But before that, in 1975, my sister's husband was also killed by the IRA in a Republican feud. My sister died four years later because she could not cope with the loss. And I was the first on the scene when my daughter's boyfriend was killed in the house by Loyalists in a sectarian attack. So it had been pretty tough to live through this time." (Valente, interview)

Despite all that happened to her, she nonetheless did not become embittered but decided to engage in community work aimed at improving local living conditions in the New Lodge and adjacent Catholic residential areas. In the course of the peace process of the early 1990s she expanded her field of activity and became involved in community relations work, where she has been active ever since (Valente, interview).

In a similar manner, Derek Poole, who grew up in a Protestant family in a segregated neighbourhood of Portadown, had to face a personal loss caused by the Troubles. As he pointed out, this experience marked a watershed in his life, which led him to commit himself to work for a peaceful solution to the armed conflict:

> "I was seventeen years of age and within a year of the Troubles my best friend was killed. It was a murder that was in retaliation for the killing of a young Catholic boy that occurred a few nights earlier. And that was a crossroads for me and the small group of friends that I belonged to. We were kind of in rage and anger at the killing of our friend. Some of those young men joined the Protestant paramilitaries and some of us didn't. And I was one of those who didn't. Some of them took the route of actually going on to ... kill other people and to become paramilitary activists. Some of us, including me, took the route of asking the question 'What is wrong with us as a society and how did we get here and how do we get out of this?' So that was the choice I made, and it was a choice basically to, in a sense, respond to my friend's death by seeing what we could do for life in this society in terms of addressing the divisions, addressing the sectarianism, addressing the history and asking the hard questions." (Poole, interview)

Since then he has been involved in peace and reconciliation work in various roles. In the early 1970s he started to engage in conflict mediation between the two sides, including working with Loyalist and Republican prisoners to facilitate dialogue about the conditions for peacemaking. Subsequently he began working with politicians and community leaders to foster their understanding of the historical, cultural and political background of the conflict. During the peace process he has become involved in working closely with church and community groups to support them in capacity-building for local community development and peacebuilding activities. The latter field of activity has become central to his current work as director of LINC (Local Initiative for Needy Communities) Resource Centre in Tigers Bay, which focuses mainly on aiding communities in North Belfast to find ways for local conflict transformation (Poole, interview).

Michael Doherty, who was brought up in a Catholic Nationalist family in Derry/Londonderry, had a different but equally divisive experience of the Troubles, which made him embark on a similar path in life as Poole. As he recalled, he was taken out of school without any formal educational qualification in the late 1950s to start working full-time at the barbershop that his father ran for a Protestant family. This was also the time of his first encounter with Protestants. The shop was situated in the then mainly Protestant Waterside area of the city, which meant that from then on he met people from the 'other' community on a daily basis. He stressed that there were three decisive experiences related to the conflict that led him toward becoming a community activist for peace and reconciliation. The first was when his father introduced him to the peaceful protests of the Civil Rights Campaign in the mid-1960s. This left a big impression on him and he thus became a supporter of the campaign. At the dawn of the Troubles tensions in the city mounted and the barbershop was increasingly at the centre of events. From there he witnessed RUC police officers beating people who took part in the civil rights march of 5 October 1968. As he pointed out, the shop was actually used as a provisional first aid station to dress the wounds of injured protesters. This was his second decisive experience. As a consequence, he became involved in several protest rallies and marches against state violence. He participated in the Bloody Sunday march, where, as he noted, the person marching behind him was shot at an army barricade. It was this first-hand experience of the magnitude of the event that shaped his mindset about the ferocity and futility of state repression at that time. In his view, this only provoked an influx of new recruits to the IRA and thus accelerated the spiral of violence – a development to which he was strongly opposed. His fiercely critical stance towards the role and attitude of the British Army and the British Government is expressed in the following statement:

"My view is that mass murder was committed on our streets, and that was sanctioned by the British Government, who sent the paratroopers in … to teach us a lesson that backfired on them in a big way. And how that manifested itself was that a number of people then joined the Provisional IRA, and then this led to the escalation of the conflict – to a higher degree than people had ever imagined it would ever get to. I decided that that was not the route I wanted to go down, that there was another story to be told." (Doherty, interview)

He went on to elaborate on his third decisive experience of the Troubles, which was when the IRA planted a bomb and blew up the barbershop in retaliation for what they perceived as collaboration with the enemy. This incident provided the final impetus for his decision to become involved in conflict prevention and peacebuilding activities.

"In 1974, the IRA in their wisdom blew up the barbershop that we owned on the Waterside, because we were seen as collaborating with the enemy. And that was we were cutting the hair of off-duty British soldiers and off-duty RUC men at that time. And who would discriminate against any customers coming into their open shop? But because we were seen as fraternising with the enemy in their view we were classified as legitimate targets. So they put a bomb into our shop while we were still in it. And on the Sunday after that … I was sitting and reflecting with the buzzing of the bomb still in my head, saying to myself that I was actually now more determined to do something about this conflict than ever." (Doherty, interview)

However, as he remarked, it took him another three years to start putting his plan into action. Eventually, in 1986, after completing his studies of social administration, public administration and law, he was offered a government-funded post as a project officer to develop community relations work. Since then, he has been involved in various projects focussing on youth, cross-community development and interface issues in Derry/Londonderry. Furthermore, he has played a key mediating role in resolving the parading dispute between the Apprentice Boys and the local residents from the Catholic/ Nationalist/ Republican Bogside area. In his present position as director of the Peace and Reconciliation Group (PRG) he has kept the focus of his work on the grassroots level, especially on facilitating dialogue between polarised Protestant and Catholic communities. When asked about his motivation to keep working in this field, he was unequivocal in his response: "I am still as passionate and committed to stop my community from killing one another as I was in 1986." (Doherty, interview)

By contrast, the life trajectory of Mervyn Gibson, who grew up in the 1960s in a Loyalist area of East Belfast, was affected in a different way by the Troubles. He was raised in a Protestant family with a strong evangelical Unionist background and affiliation to the Orange Order. In view of the armed conflict, he felt the need to defend his country against Republican paramilitary groups and hence joined the RUC police force at the age of 18. For the first two years he was a uniformed police officer in North Belfast. Then he moved to the RUC special branch dealing with terrorism, in which he served for the next sixteen years. He recounted the threats from Republican paramilitaries to which he and his family were exposed during the height of the Troubles:

"When you were in duty the IRA could have attacked anywhere. You were in a vehicle or in shelter or fired in the area. You were constantly on your guard. Equally at home, you were constantly on your guard. I had to move house on one occasion with my family overnight, because of a threat coming at that time from Republicans. So you were constantly aware of the threat. You had to adjust your lifestyle accordingly. My children learned to check under the car for bombs since they were at an early age. They learned not to say what their father did at school, or anywhere else, for fear of attacks. But that was what it was. It was part of the living at that time. It might seem strange now and oppressive, but it was just part of what you did in those days." (Gibson, interview)

During his time in the RUC he took a firm stance against Republicanism. Thus, although being generally in favour of the peace process, he was opposed to the Belfast/Good Friday Agreement and actively campaigned against it. As he pointed out, this was for two reasons: firstly, he "believed that the RUC was going to be sacrificed with no guarantees … and secondly, there was an opportunity for IRA men to be in the government of the country with no guarantees about decommissioning or no guarantees that the IRA had gone away." (Gibson, interview) In the mid-1990s, after his time in police service, he became a local Presbyterian Church minister in East Belfast. In 2001, he also assumed the chair of the Loyalist Commission (LC).[161] In this capacity he was involved in mediating several feuds between Loyalist paramilitary groups in Loyalist working-class communities in Belfast. He had to resign, however, in 2006 due to concerns among LC members about his alleged involvement in a cross-community initiative that would have included the Loyal Orders[162] and Catholic/Nationalist/Republican residents' groups. Nevertheless, as a senior member of the Orange Order he has maintained his liaison role with Loyalist paramilitaries and kept engaging in discussions on parading with Republicans (Gibson, interview; cf. BBC News 2006, Kilpatrick 2014 & 2015).

Among the respondents there were many whose lives took a different turn and who resorted to violent means in consequence of the Troubles. Billy Hutchinson was one of them. Unlike Valente and Poole, he did not experience the loss of close relatives or friends due to the conflict. Instead, he en-

---

[161] The Loyalist Commission (LC) has been an umbrella group consisting of members of the UDA, UVF and RHC as well as of Protestant clergymen and community representatives and members of the Unionist and Loyalist political parties. The Commission, which superseded the Combined Loyalist Military Command (CLMC), was formed upon the initiative of Unionist politicians in 2001 in response to parading controversies and the Holy Cross dispute in Ardoyne and to recurring Loyalist feuds (Kaufmann 2007: 291, Melaugh 2016). Yet, just like the CLMC, the Loyalist Commission eventually also failed to create unity among the different sections of Loyalism. Meanwhile, another initiative has been launched and a new umbrella group called the Loyalist Community Council (LCC) has been established in 2015. It is composed of representatives of almost all factions of the UDA, UVF and RHC (Morris 2015b).

[162] The Loyal Orders is an umbrella term that comprises the range of Protestant fraternal societies active in Northern Ireland: the Orange Order, the Royal Black Institution, the Apprentice Boys of Derry, the Royal Arch Purple, the Independent Orange Institution, the Junior Orange Institution and the Association of Loyal Orange Women (Bryan 2000: 97).

countered the violence at the onset of the conflict when facing an IRA death threat at his first workplace in the Greater Shankill area. As he recalled,

> "When I left school I went to work in a local engineering firm, which would be called the technical college here, to learn practical technical skills, and the IRA was aware of it. I was about 16 at the time. And then I was in work one day and the police and the British Army came in and told me that I would have to leave work because the IRA would try to murder me. Just for what I worked. So at a very young age I got into it and I sort of did not do anything. But I suppose I was not really different… Any young person who had anything to do with being pro-British became target to the IRA." (Hutchinson, interview)

This incident reinforced his perception that the Protestant/Unionist/Loyalist community was under siege and that their British heritage and the union with Great Britain itself were threatened by Republicans. In consequence, he joined the UVF's youth wing called Young Citizens Volunteers (YCF) and got involved in the armed struggle on the Loyalist side. In 1974 he was charged with murder for killing two Catholics at the Shankill/Falls interface and imprisoned for the next sixteen years. While being in the Maze Prison[163] he went through a personal change that altered his views on violence. He also commenced studies in community planning, which, upon release, led him to engage in local community work in the Greater Shankill area with a special focus on reducing and preventing violence in interface areas. Moreover, his interest in Loyalist working-class politics made him become active in the Progressive Unionist Party (PUP), where he assumed a leading role in promoting the benefits of the peace process within militant Loyalism and establishing contact to Republicans. Throughout the post-Agreement period he has maintained close ties with the UVF, which is exemplified in his involvement

---

[163] Her Majesty's Prison Maze, as is its official name, which is also known as 'Long Kesh' or, due to the distinctive shape of its buildings, as 'H-Blocks', was the main top-security prison in Northern Ireland for in total around 15,000 paramilitary prisoners on the Republican side and around the same on the Loyalist side during the Troubles. The prison, which was located at the former Royal Airforce base at Long Kesh, on the outskirts of Lisburn close to Belfast, was in operation from 1971 to 2000 (cf. Dillon 2016: 231, Foster 2000, Ryder 2000). Some of its buildings were demolished afterwards, but, according to an official announcement in 2013 by the Northern Ireland Executive, the remainder would "be transformed into a peace centre and an agricultural show arena." (McDonald 2013c). So far, however, if and how the Maze will be redeveloped remains unclear. More recently, private investors have shown interest in turning large parts of the historic site into a shopping mall (Legg 2016). In November 2016 the First Minister Arlene Foster and Deputy First Minister Martin McGuinness announced that the site will become the new host to Northern Ireland's first air ambulance. This was then also realised and the service finally went live in the following year (McCurry 2016).

in their feud with the UDA (Hutchinson, interview; cf. Taylor 2014: 137-138).

Likewise, Tom Winstone's teenage years in the Upper Shankill area of Springmartin were characterised by the violence of the early Troubles. He explained how this experience shaped his decision to become involved in militant Loyalism and join the UVF:

> "In my earlier days living there it was a violent place to live. There were lots of bombings and shootings. Growing up in that type of environment obviously had an effect on many people living around the communities. Therefore people either chose to fight or actually sit back and watch. I chose to take the path of fighting the enemy." (Winstone, interview)

At the age of 19 he was jointly convicted with Hutchinson of killing two Catholics and sentenced to the Maze where he spent fifteen years. Like his then comrade, he used the time in prison for reflection and discussions with fellow inmates on social and political affairs, which induced him to focus on preventing young people from the Loyalist community from getting involved in the violent conflict. Thus, after his release in 1989, he began to engage in local community work where he became mainly concerned with the issue of punishment attacks by Loyalist paramilitaries. He also got involved in the peace talks as a PUP delegate, in which he contributed to the development of community-based restorative justice schemes (Winstone, interview; cf. Taylor 2014: 137).

Violence also figured prominently in Syd Trotter's story of his experience of the Troubles during his childhood and youth. Coming from a Protestant background, he grew up in the 1960s and 1970s in Enniskillen, a town in the western, mainly Catholic part of Northern Ireland. He made his first encounter with the conflict when two of his father's friends, both policemen, were shot dead by local Republicans. Throughout his childhood he lived in a mixed working-class housing estate, with the majority of residents being Catholics. This was a dreadful experience for him because he was constantly harassed and intimidated. In consequence, he just wanted to leave Northern Ireland and moved to London at the age of 17. On his return, three years later, he settled in East Belfast in the Protestant Loyalist Clarawood estate. As he pointed out, it was a tragic incident that made him eventually become involved in the armed conflict on the side of the UDA:

> "I had a friend who I was very fond of. He was in the security forces. I was out with him one night and two men came up and shot him dead in front of me. So my decision was: I will sort this problem out myself. And once I decided to join, I

committed myself really to the organisation, and whatever that might entail." (Trotter, interview)

In 1987 he was convicted of racketeering on the evidence of the Cook Report[164] and imprisoned for seven years. In prison he also went through a change. Although being offered by his brother who served a life sentence to come over to the Loyalist wings he decided to sever his ties with the UDA but instead to improve his education via distance learning at Open University. Upon release in 1994 he started getting involved in local community development work and in his current position at LINC Resource Centre his main focus is on the improvement of community relations in Tigers Bay and other interface areas of North Belfast (Trotter, interview).

The experience shared by Norman Burgess[165] of his growing up in a Loyalist working-class environment in the eastern outskirts of Belfast was different at first but eventually took a similar turn. Although neither he nor his family were physically exposed to the violence of the Troubles, he, like Hutchinson and Winstone, became a member of the UVF. In his case, a major impetus was given by Ian Paisley's radical anti-Catholic evangelism, which attracted him already in his youth.

"In 1968 my family moved from Inner East Belfast to Ballybeen, a large working-class housing estate, in Dundonald, which would have been six miles from the city centre on the east side. And that was important, because when the Troubles started we were not that badly affected ... In about 1970 the UDA, who were emerging as the largest Loyalist paramilitary group, were putting out in one or two nights all the Roman Catholics that were living in the Ballybeen estate. So it was a hundred percent Loyalist housing estate after that. We had no real contact with Roman Catholics there. By then I was very much influenced by Ian Paisley. I used to go to his church as a young lad, and I went to his rallies. When I was 16 or 17 I joined the YCF, which was the junior wing of the UVF. In fact I felt it was my duty to join the UVF. I did not get heavily involved until I got married at 21 and moved back to Inner East Belfast. And I was transferred from a moderate UVF wing to a quite cutting-edge UVF platoon, the battalion for East Belfast. So I became a UVF

---

[164] The Cook Report was a series of current affairs programmes on British television lasting from 1987 to 1999 that featured investigative journalist Roger Cook conducting undercover sting operations into serious criminal activity around the world. In August 1987, Northern Ireland became the scene of Cook's covert investigative techniques, in the course of which several UDA members were convicted of racketeering and extortion. This also gave a serious blow to the image and credibility of the UDA within Loyalist communities and led to the ousting of some of their senior staff members (Dingley 2009, Wood 2006: 126-128).

[165] The interview respondents name has been anonymised upon request.

gunman around the middle of 1981, and for about the next eighteen months I became one of the UVF's most active gunmen." (Burgess, interview)

Thus, the fact that he was socialised in a radical Loyalist environment certainly played a formative role in his decision to join the UVF in their armed campaign, which he saw as a matter of duty. In 1982 he was charged with serious offenses and in 1985 sentenced to four life sentences for his involvement in several murders, robberies and armed attacks. He was sent to the Maze and was released on licence under the conditions of the Good Friday/ Belfast Agreement in 1998. In the mid-1990s, while still in prison, he got involved in the peace process as part of the UVF leadership. Due to this experience and encouraged by a fellow UVF member he started to engage in community development work after his release. Since then he works for Interaction Belfast, a cross-community project engaging in local conflict transformation work at Northern Ireland's longest interface along Springfield Road in West Belfast (Burgess, interview).

On the Republican side, Malachy Mulgrew provided insight into how the advent of the Troubles in North Belfast impacted on him and explained his rationale for joining the Provisional IRA and the reasons why he subsequently renounced violence and became engaged in local community work after his time in prison.

> "I grew up in the countryside and I came to North Belfast in 1965 when I was 14 years old. So it was really a bad time to come at that age, because as I started to find my feet in the city that was when the Troubles really started. We had really bad violence in North Belfast and by the time 1969 came I was 18 years of age. There was no avoiding it, the conflict was there, you either got involved in it or you didn't get involved in it. I got involved and joined the IRA. I was in jail until 1972. When I got back out of jail, I worked in my community… I helped in the community and I have always tried to do that ever since. I have seen the whole Troubles here in Belfast. I was involved in the Troubles, but I think my learning curve always was: I believe in people helping each other. I did not have any bitterness towards the people on the other side. Yes, I thought they were a problem, because they were stopping us from getting what we wanted, but there was never bitterness." (Mulgrew, interview)

What he alluded to was the inescapability of violence at the outbreak of the Troubles, which at a young age made him feel that he had to become involved and join the IRA. However, the time in custody changed his views and he subsequently committed himself to work for the benefit of his community in the Catholic/Nationalist/Republican Cliftonville area. Although militant Loyalists made three attempts on his life and killed his brother and his brother-in-law, he did not reengage in violence but remained committed to local community work. As he emphasised, his background as an ex-Republican prisoner proved to be very helpful in his work, because it earned him a lot of respect in the Catholic/Nationalist/Republican community. In the course of the peace process he became involved in cross-community interface work. In his current position at the North Belfast Interface Network (NBIN) he deals with issues of interface communities in the area of the Cliftonville and Water Works wards (Mulgrew, interview).

There were more personal stories of local respondents from both Republican and Loyalist working-class backgrounds that took a similar course from paramilitary involvement, imprisonment to subsequent engagement in community work. Jim Auld is an ex-Republican prisoner and director of Community Restorative Justice Ireland (CRJI), which, as a counterpart to the Loyalist NIA, is a community-based restorative justice scheme in Republican areas based in Andersonstown in West Belfast. As he pointed out, he was 20 years old when he became "the first internee in the North in 1971 [and] … was one of twelve people that were taken away by the British Government and tortured." (Auld, interview) He was suspected of being a high ranking officer in the Provisional IRA who was involved in serious crime including murder, shooting and bombing attacks, but was never convicted.[166] Charged with these offenses he spent two terms for a total of six years in prison. After being released he qualified as a youth worker and began working with young people from Catholic/Nationalist/Republican communities in West Belfast who were subjected to physical punishment by the IRA. He strongly opposed the punishments, because, as he emphasised,

---

[166] The case of Jim Auld and his fellow detainees became known as the 'hooded men' case. In August 1971 the twelve men were taken by the British security forces to a secret place in a rural area in County Derry/Londonderry. This was part of a British Army operation in Northern Ireland termed 'Operation Demetrius', which involved the mass arrest and internment, i.e. imprisonment without trial, of 342 people who were suspected of being members of the IRA. The 'hooded men' were subjected by the British Army and the RUC to horrific interrogation methods called the 'five techniques', which included hooding, wall-standing, continuous exposure to white noise, sleep deprivation and deprivation of drink and food. In 1976, the Irish Government on behalf of the 'hooded men' took the case to the European Commission of Human Rights, which, however, turned it down in 1978. In 2014, the Irish Government took up the case again and referred it to the European Court of Human Rights (ECtHR), which took over the Comission's mandate in 1998, asking the Court to revise the Commission's earlier judgment. Finally, in September 2018, the ECtHR rejected the appeal, thus confirming the judgment that the British and Northern Irish forces had not tortured the 'hooded men'. (BBC News 2018a, Coogan 2002: 149-150, Fields 1980: 76-79, Gallagher 2015, McCleery 2015, Newberry 2009, Page 2011).

"They were getting more and more severe, more and more brutal. They also were without any human dignity, without any real evidence against people. It was hearsay, word to mouth, there was no proportionality, and there were no human rights involved in it." (Auld 2009)

Like Auld, Umberto Scappaticci is an ex-Republican prisoner involved in community work in the outer West Belfast area. He likewise reported of having been subjected to state violence in his youth. He grew up in Newry, a mostly Catholic town around 50 km south of Belfast close to the Irish border. As a young person he witnessed a lot of harassment and violence by state security forces against local Catholics at the time of the outbreak of the Troubles. At the age of 16, the RUC and B-Specials raided his home. He got arrested and taken to an army barrack where he was beaten up. This was a decisive experience for him that made him determined to join the IRA. As he put it, "I realised then that for young people in the community the only way that we could hit back was to get involved in Republicanism. I wanted to fight the Brits and hit them back for what they had done to me and my family." (Scappaticci, interview) In 1975 he was sentenced for, in his words, "political offense" (Scappaticci, interview), and while imprisoned for almost 15 years, he renounced violence yet without abandoning his firm Republican beliefs. Thus, he became an advocate of the peace process and of Sinn Féin's active participation in it. Since his release he has been involved in community work, and in his current position at the Colin Neighbourhood Partnership he focuses on youth, education and health issues Catholic/Nationalist/Republican neighbourhoods in the outskirts of West Belfast (Scappaticci, interview).

Turning to Derry/Londonderry, Donncha MacNiallais, another former Republican prisoner, shared his experience of the Troubles in the city during his growing-up years, in which he revealed a similar motivation for becoming involved in the IRA's armed struggle. Born in 1958 in the Catholic/Nationalist/Republican working-class area of the Bogside his childhood was shaped by his father's involvement in the Civil Rights Movement. This brought him in touch with issues of Catholic discrimination and civil rights demands for equality, jobs and housing. He recalled the violence that swept across the city during the early days of the Troubles and the impact it had on him:

"In August 1969 when the Battle of the Bogside occurred there was a lot of fear and tension. The British Army came on the streets of Derry shortly after that, and within a few short years the British Government had started the internment of Republicans, Nationalists and Catholics. There was major conflict on the streets, including armed conflict between the IRA and the British Army. In my teenage years

I witnessed the events of Bloody Sunday and I witnessed people being shot in the streets and maimed with … rubber bullets. And I made a courageous decision at a quite young age that I would be part of that struggle against the British occupation." (MacNiallais, interview)

He was captured in 1976, as he called it, "on an IRA operation in possession of arms" (MacNiallais, interview) and sentenced to the Maze, where he took part in the so-called 'blanket protest'[167] by Republican prisoners. Like Scappaticci, he relinquished his militant attitude while in prison and after his release got involved in Sinn Féin's political Republicanism. He also played an active role in the peace process on the issue of contentious parades. In particular, he was concerned with establishing dialogue and negotiation with the Apprentice Boys of Derry – a process in which he is still involved. Since then he has also engaged in local community activism in the Bogside. In his current work at the local Irish language cultural centre of 'An Gaeláras' he aims to promote and encourage the widespread use of Irish in everyday life within not only the Catholic community but also reaching out to the Protestant side (MacNiallais, interview).

By contrast, Nigel Gardiner, a local resident of Derry/Londonderry with a Loyalist working-class background, experienced the events at the outbreak of the conflict from the other side of the communal divide. He was born and raised in a mixed housing estate in the then mainly Protestant area of the Waterside, where Catholics are now in the majority. His childhood was characterised by sectarianism. As he pointed out, "there was an 'ethnic cleansing' of Protestants from the Cityside who were forced to move to the Waterside and to other places in Northern Ireland and abroad." (Gardiner, interview) He told how he was beaten up by Republicans on the way to college just because he was a Protestant. At the age of 15 he saw how Protestants were attacked dur-

---

[167] The 'blanket protest', which began in the Maze in September 1976 and lasted for five years, was a protest by Republican prisoners of the Provisional IRA and INLA against the removal of their status as political prisoners. In particular, the prisoners refused to wear ordinary prison uniforms, which was one of the consequences of losing the so-called 'special category' status. As a consequence of their persistent refusal, they were left with just blankets and mattresses in their cells. As the terms of detention were more and more tightened, the prisoners resorted to more drastic measures of protest. This led to the so-called 'no-wash protest' or 'dirty protest' and culminated in the '1981 Irish Hunger Strike'. The protests petered out in October 1981 after the fatal end of the hunger strikes and the subsequent announcement of the British Government to improve prison conditions, which included the permission for paramilitary prisoners to wear ordinary cloths (Coogan 1993: 502-503 & 614-619, English 2005: 190-193; cf. Beresford 1994, O'Malley 1990).

ing the civil rights march of October 1968 and also at the Apprentice Boys parade of August 1969. Subsequently he got involved in the intercommunal riots in response to British Army deployment by throwing stones at Catholic Nationalists. These experiences left a lasting mark on him, which in 1971 made him decide to join the UDR, in which he served until 1990 as a part-time member in the counties of Derry and Tyrone. His objective, as he put it, was "to deter the Irish [Republican] terrorists from their atrocious activity by keeping the two communities separate." (Gardiner, interview) According to him, the fatal incidents on Bloody Sunday occurred because people were participating in an illegal march that got banned and thus they had to bear the consequences. During his time in the UDR he encountered numerous incidents of Republican violence. As he emphasised, he lost 34 of his colleagues who were killed by the IRA and INLA. As a consequence of these events, his strong Protestant Loyalist beliefs were strengthened and after the end of his service he decided to work for the benefit of his community in the Waterside area. At present he works for EPIC – Ex-Prisoners Interpretative Centre, where he deals with the reintegration of ex-combatants from the Loyalist community (Gardiner 2009).

As can be seen from these personal recollections of Republican and Loyalist ex-combatants, there are many striking parallels in their experiences during their childhood and youth that shaped the course of their lives in a similar way. Most of them grew up in areas with high levels of residential segregation and socio-economic deprivation. Due to the segregated nature of their living environment they lacked contact with age-mates from the 'other' community, and the rare occasions of intercommunal encounters were characterised by hostilities such as shouting verbal abuse and throwing stones at each other. Those few, all from the Loyalist side, who grew up in a mixed neighbourhood reported of having experienced sectarian harassment and intimidation. The Troubles loomed large in all their stories. As a common feature they were all exposed to the violence of the conflict at a young age – either by observing, witnessing or being subjected to violence themselves. Adding to this was the general climate of sectarianism and political radicalisation that was prevalent in their living areas. Thus, the experience of growing up under such conditions had a decisive and formative impact on their lives, which made them determined to get involved in the armed conflict on either side. Many joined paramilitary groups or the state's security forces already in their late teenage or early adulthood years. As to the reasons given for their decision, they described numerous circumstantial factors that drew them towards violence. There was however considerable difference between the two sides. Loyalist respondents expressed a perception of being under siege by Republicans and feelings of threat to their British national identity and to the union with Great Britain. In contrast, their Republican counterparts emphasised a sense of being under British occupation and feelings of domination, oppression and discrimination by the Unionist regime. As a common denominator, both regarded it as a necessity and, as some stressed, also their duty to protect and defend their community against attacks from the 'other' side. The time of imprisonment marked another watershed in their lives, which made them reflect on their paramilitary role in the Troubles. In consequence, they renounced violence and became supporters of the peace process. They kept, however, their political beliefs and affiliations and those who got involved in the peace negotiations did so as representatives of the political arms of their paramilitary groups. Moreover, upon release they all have become engaged in local community development work. Some have also committed themselves to peacebuilding in interface areas by working on reducing intercommunal tension and violence and promoting cross-community understanding.

Notably, although in their narratives all the Loyalist and Republican ex-combatants talked openly about their personal experience of violent events of the Troubles they remained reticent about stating the reasons for their sentences. Furthermore, there was a general reluctance to show remorse for their deeds. Instead the emphasis was placed on explaining their personal change and on highlighting their positive role in society.

There was another important aspect that became apparent from the ex-combatants' responses. This refers to the already mentioned general lack of positive inter-community contact, which ran through all the respondents' memories of their childhood and youth before or during the Troubles. Actually, as some of those who were imprisoned pointed out, it was the environment in prison that provided them with their first opportunity to establish contact to members of the 'other' community and to engage in dialogue with their adversaries. These discussions resulted in growing tolerance and respect for the views and beliefs of the 'other' side and also a mutual understanding of common working-class issues. For instance, as Syd Trotter recalled his encounter with Republican inmates:

> "My first introduction to Nationalists or, if you like, to Republicans was with some of those guys who came off the Republican wing. They were at the same wing as I was. It was a mixed wing. And we did speak with each other in relation to their

backgrounds, where they were coming from, from an ideological point of view. And where I was then, and where I was coming from. And I found very little difference between us other than the very small, central and core piece that divided us – and that was the 'Green' and 'Orange' issue. Certainly, socially and economically within working-class communities there was little or no difference." (Trotter, interview)

The perception that Catholic and Protestant working-class areas were facing similar socio-economic issues and levels of deprivation was also expressed by other respondents such as Dympna McGlade, who described the local situation of working-class communities in North Belfast in the 1960s as follows: "We had equally nothing. We were equally dependent on the linen mills, which all closed down in the area we lived, both the Catholic community and the Protestant community." (McGlade, interview) Therefore, as she argued, it would have been obvious that in the Civil Rights Movement working-class people joined forces for the common cause of improving their living conditions. That was, however, not the case, as their socio-economic class concerns were overshadowed by deep sectarian and ethno-national divisions. In fact, the civil rights campaign divided the working-class communities even further (McGlade, interview).

Likewise, George Ramsey became aware of the many similarities that existed between the two communities. He grew up during the 1960s in a Protestant/Unionist/Loyalist working-class neighbourhood of Woodvale located at the interface with the mainly Catholic/Nationalist/Republican area of Springfield Road in West Belfast. In recalling his first encounters with members of the Catholic working-class community, he described it as "a very quick learning process, coming to realise that they are exactly the same as us and that we all have the same issues." (Ramsey, interview) This happened when he was already working at his first job in a local engineering company. Notably, it was not until then that he came into contact with people from the 'other' community. The reason for this was that he spent his childhood and youth in a closed living environment, which was typical for many Protestant and Catholic working-class communities at that time. He pointed to two more characteristic features that also figured prominently in the personal recollections of other respondents: firstly, the strong cohesion that existed within the community and, secondly, the deep sense of belonging and pride to be a part of the community. As he stressed:

"I was very proud to come from that area. There was a very close community identity. I felt very much a part of the community. It was a close-knit community with close ties. The difficulty with it, looking back, was that it was an insular community. It was really all Protestant Loyalist Unionist … and there was no real engagement in those days with people from any other community." (Ramsey, interview)

His childhood was also typical in other respects. Like many people growing up in working-class areas of Belfast in the 1960s, he left school without formal qualifications. In fact, he later realised from the conversations with his Catholic and Protestant work colleagues that many of them had the same low educational level like him. He also recalled the violence at the onset of the Troubles which raised his awareness of the sense of insecurity and threat that surrounded the interface area where he lived. However, although he grew up under similar conditions as those who chose to become involved in armed conflict, he did not follow the path toward violence. Instead, he made a different life-changing decision and joined the Northern Ireland Fire and Rescue Service (NIFRS), in which he has served for more than thirty years and is now retired. This position gave him the opportunity to establish positive relationships with people from both the Protestant and Catholic communities and thus to see and experience the intercommunal conflict in a different light. He emphasised the good work relations and cooperative spirit that existed between him and his Catholic and Protestant colleagues:

> "What I found, when I actually joined the service, was that there were Protestants and Catholics working together. And there was never a difficulty, because that was one of those environments where we had a job to do, and we did that job together. Certainly, during my time, there were not any religious or sectarian issues within the Fire and Rescue Service." (Ramsey, interview)

As he pointed out, there was also never an incident of sectarian violence against the NIFRS during the Troubles and he never felt threatened or intimidated in any of the areas of North and West Belfast that he was responsible for. Moreover, he had many discussions with local residents from both communities in which they openly shared their views and experiences of the Troubles. According to him, all this was only possible because in his capacity as an NIFRS officer he provided a service that was seen as uncontroversial and that had a good level of acceptability in all communities. In expressing his gratitude for having had this work experience, he added: "I think it has been a real privilege working in a job or an occupation where you would have both sections of the community working together. I think that is fantastic." (Ramsey, interview)

EARLY GRASSROOTS ACTIVISM AND CROSS-COMMUNITY INTERFACE WORK

Thus, it can be seen that, despite the violence of the Troubles, there was space for positive contact and dialogue between the Protestant/Unionist/Loyalist and Catholic/Nationalist/Republican working-class communities. In many cases, this space was created and mutual understanding was facilitated by local community groups and individuals who engaged in peace and reconciliation work. Michael Hall is one of those who became active in the field already in the early 1970s. He is also the project coordinator and editor of the so-called 'Island Pamphlets', a publication series of booklets that was launched on his initiative in 1993 and that offers a forum for various community sections to discuss and explore important issues of concern at grassroots level.[168] As Hall noted in one of the booklets, he had a secular and non-sectarian upbringing during the 1960s, which, however, did not spare him from being subjected to Catholic and Protestant sectarianism. Moreover, for his early cross-community endeavours he received personal threats from both Republicans and Loyalists (Hall 2007b: 4). In an interview with the author he provided an insider's perspective on the emergence and development of local community work and of inter-community engagement in peace and reconciliation during the Troubles. According to his assessment, this process already began with the onset of the conflict: "When the Troubles started, the peace process also started. Because right from the very beginning, right from when the very first stone was thrown, there were individuals in both communities trying to put a stop to it." (Hall, interview) Within a very short time more people became engaged and local community groups were formed. Initially, their primary concern was protecting the well-being of their own communi-

---

[168] So far, 111 booklets have been published within the Island Pamphlets series, tackling various "historical, cultural, socio-economic, political and other matters pertinent to Northern Irish society." (Hall 2016) Each pamphlet presents the summarised outcome of a series of small group discussions on a particular issue between representatives of various sections of the community, including senior residents, young people, community activists, ex-prisoners, conflict victims and others (Hall 2016). According to Hall, the pamphlets, aided by funding, were widely distributed free of charge among both communities and by the time of the interview he had already delivered 180,000 copies. Their grassroots think-tank character received acceptance by all sections across the communal divide, because, as he pointed out, "In fact, the series was seen as standing separate from the conflict, and that separateness was tempting to create dialogue, debate and encourage more extensive discussions." (Hall, interview)

ties. However, this proved a tremendous task, as the violence at the onset of the Troubles was pervasive and the state became increasingly incapable of providing essential services in working-class areas. As Hall described the precarious local conditions at that time:

> "They soon realised that by getting involved in their communities they were confronted with all the complexity of problems like the housing problems, the youth alienation and interface violence … So a lot of different activities started to mushroom. A lot of community groups started to form, basically out of necessity. They had to, because at the beginning of the Troubles a lot of the normal institutions of the state collapsed. The police could not go into certain areas. Even the refuse collection, they would not go in. Ambulances could not get into the barricades until those routes were secured, and people died of heart attacks because ambulances could not get in and find them." (Hall, interview)

Consequently, as he pointed out, the necessity to rely on self-help generated a spirit of grassroots activism within the communities. Eventually that turned into joint activism, in which local volunteers and community groups from Catholic and Protestant working-class areas began to cooperate on certain innocuous issues of mutual concern.

> "People tentatively made the first steps towards the other community, saying 'look, these are the problems that we are confronting. We know that you are confronting the same problems. Should we not work together?' And sometimes when they worked together they did not discuss national or political issues. They knew that those were too divisive. But they were able to work together on socio-economic and youth issues, things like that … They knew that what they were doing was building contacts. And also try to maintain a hope of peace." (Hall, interview)

Like Hall, Derek Poole became involved in peace and reconciliation work in the early days of the Troubles. He stressed that local peace activists and cross-community workers had to take great risks, for they were regarded as traitors, thus being exposed to retaliation and ostracism from their community. As he explained,

> "In the midst of a complete all out and intractable conflict the worst thing that any side can have are traitors, people who are breaking ranks with their side wanting to talk with the others. Like for instance, in the Protestant tradition we have many slogans, and one of the great slogans is 'United we stand, divided we fall', the implication being if anyone breaks solidarity with the unity of the whole, you are worse than the enemy because you've become the enemy within. You become a fifth columnist: you're the one that can't be trusted. So yes, there were many good peace workers and people involved in community and reconciliation work who had to take that risk." (Poole, interview)

During the 1980s, grassroots cross-community work moved into a phase of consolidation. There was a considerable increase in the number of community groups, projects and initiatives with many new links being forged and activities spreading across more working-class areas. The government provided substantial funding for community development,[169] which, according to Hall, was certainly helpful but also caused problems. On the one hand, it created opportunities for paid employment that attracted more people to become engaged in community work. However, on the other hand, this led to divisions between volunteers and those now getting paid for doing the same work. Moreover, community groups had to conform to agendas and regulations set down by the funding institutions that involved the channelling of some of the funds through intermediary agencies such as the churches. This not only posed an administrative burden but also required them to adapt and streamline their activities accordingly (Hall, interview). In any case, throughout that time inter-community cooperation remained, by and large, confined to dealing with common bread-and-butter issues of everyday life. This was because, against the background of the ongoing violence of the Troubles, the gulf between the working-class communities was too deep to address contentious issues revolving around national identity or political aspirations and affiliations.

There were, nevertheless, a few initiatives already back then that made tentative steps towards peace and reconciliation. Occasionally, attempts were also made to address interface problems. Chris O'Halloran, the director of the Belfast Interface Project (BIP) who grew up in a mixed neighbourhood in North Belfast, was involved in cross-community work in interface areas in the mid-1980s. In recalling his experiences he pointed to the great risks and dangers for local people participating in such activities:

> "I worked in some interface areas … and there were cross-community meetings, but in those days the fear of retribution accompanied those meetings. That was fear of retribution that would be brought by people from within your own community. They were saying you were meeting with people from the other community. The fear of retribution was so strong that those cross-community meetings would have generally happened in secret." (O'Halloran, interview)

---

[169] Government funding was primarily provided under the so-called Action for Community Employment (ACE) scheme. The primary aim of the scheme, which was introduced in the early 1980s with financial aid from the European Social Fund (ESF), was to provide training and employment opportunities for the long-term unemployed. As Arthur Aughey & Duncan Morrow in referring to official figures point out, "By 1990, nearly 11,000 people … were employed in over 300 different community schemes." (Aughey & Morrow 2014: 183) See also the discussion on funding in the section on 'Policies on Community Relations and Development', pp. 294-297).

The changing structural context of the conflict in the wake of the peace process of the early 1990s expanded the scope of inter-community cooperation and created opportunities for joint peace and reconciliation activities. As the responses suggest, this can be attributed mainly to the following contributing factors: Firstly, the violence of the Republican and Loyalist paramilitary groups lessened and, driven by their political factions, they eventually abandoned their armed struggle and got involved in the peace talks. Likewise, as described above, many former paramilitary prisoners changed their attitudes towards violence and played an active role in the peace process. Secondly, a mood for peace emerged in Protestant and Catholic working-class communities, as people were getting tired of the Troubles and became more receptive to local peacebuilding initiatives. Finally, there was an increase of funding and a push by the government for engagement in community relations work.

Many of the local respondents have become involved in activities aiming to improve the living conditions in working-class areas. While some have been mainly concerned with working for the benefit of their community, others have concentrated their efforts on addressing common problems and promoting better relations between the communities. In this regard, the ongoing tensions and disorder in deprived working-class interface areas have become a common focus of activity. The following will present two telling examples out of the many that featured in the respondents' stories that illustrate the achievements, challenges and difficulties involved in cross-community interface work. These are, on the one hand, the development of the Suffolk-Lenadoon Interface Group (SLIG) in Outer West Belfast and, on the other hand, the emergence and expansion of interface networks in North Belfast.

THE SUFFOLK-LENADOON INTERFACE GROUP

The first example concerns the experience made by the working-class communities of Protestant/Unionist/Loyalist Suffolk and Catholic/Nationalist/Republican Lenadoon in their long journey from establishing contact to eventually working together on common interface issues. As has already become apparent, the Troubles had a profound impact on the two communities both in terms of their living conditions and the relations between them. Due to the forced resettlements that occurred in the early days of the conflict the area became segregated with a large Catholic community living in Lenadoon and a small Protestant community living in the Suffolk estate. Throughout the 1970s and early 1980s intercommunal violence spread pervasively through the area and, in consequence, a permanent 'peace line' emerged along Stewartstown Road. Moreover, socio-economic deprivation reached an unprecedented scale. The people living in the interface area bore the brunt of the violence and deprivation. At the height of the conflict the interface was the focal point of violent attacks by the UDA and IRA who both asserted their territorial claims on the area. This was illustrated by Jean Brown, who in an interview with the author presented a photo showing the Suffolk side of the interface in the early 1980s:

> "As you can see the front of the building has IRA slogans, and the back has UDA and UFF. So that was very much a good snapshot of what the interface was like through all the years of the Troubles here." (Brown, interview)[170]

Thus, in view of these adverse developments, the communities became deeply polarised, antagonistic and alienated from each other (cf. Hall 2007). There were, however, activists on both sides who set aside their personal antagonism and strove to work together on improving the dire living conditions at the interface. The process, which started in the mid-1980s, was facilitated by Chris O'Halloran. As part of a community development project targeting the most deprived and disadvantaged housing estates of Northern Ireland he was in charge of forming a local residents' group in Suffolk to identify and address the issues arising from the environment of the interface. In this role

---

[170] The acronym UFF stands for Ulster Freedom Fighters. The UFF was founded in 1973 as a militant special operations group within the UDA and served as a cover and *nom de guerre* to claim responsibility for the killings of Catholic Nationalists and Republicans. The purpose behind this was to avoid an official ban of the UDA as a terrorist group (Crawford 2003: 25-26, Wood 2006: 21-23).

he also established contact between the community groups from Suffolk and Lower Lenadoon. For precautionary reasons, some of the early meetings were held secretly. In these talks the two groups managed to overcome their initial resentments and mistrust and eventually came to realise that the situation was similarly difficult on both sides of the 'peace line'. This made them decide to cooperate on dealing with common everyday issues affecting the interface area, such as the lack of traffic lights, leisure facilities and a children's playground. As Hall, who organised a series of reflection discussions with those involved at that time, explained their particular motivation for cooperation:

> "The emphasis from those two community groups was: we have to get together for practical survival reasons. Now, obviously through that relationships had been built up, and, as they hoped, these would spread, and there would be a form of conflict reconciliation taking place. But the important thing is that was not their focus. Their focus was a real change in the area. And in fact, whenever the two groups started to get together, they had the focus on actual things. For example, they could not say let's have a talk about politics ... So what they did was they focussed on, for example, the need for a pedestrian crossing on the main road. This was something the two communities could say: yes, there is value in this. When they succeeded in that, they were saying: yes, joint work can achieve benefits." (Hall, interview)

In a similar vein, O'Halloran emphasised the beneficial effects of cross-community cooperation for the Suffolk community that led to a considerable improvement of local living conditions:

> "First of all, it was a good, successful project. The group was formed. They did survey the local area and identify the issues. They did set up a whole bunch of different ways of making contact with other agencies. And they were fruitful. So a lot of the things they identified they needed they got. They got the playground. They got the housing improvements. They got the pedestrian crossing." (O'Halloran, interview)

However, the cooperation, which gradually increased with more joint activities being organised, was met with attacks from paramilitary groups. This was especially the case in Suffolk, where Loyalist paramilitaries of the UDA were highly active during the Troubles. On several occasions, local UDA members threatened Catholic community workers employed at Suffolk community group and launched assaults on the group's office. As Jean Brown, who was a leading member of the Suffolk community group at that time, recalled the UDA campaign:

> "Throughout the years of the Troubles when we were trying to get this project up and going, they were one of our biggest detractors. They gave us a lot of aggrava-

tion. They petrol-bombed our buildings, they threatened us, they did a lot to try and stop our work." (Brown, interview)

Moreover, as she pointed out, she was personally subjected to a smear campaign by the UDA:

"The UDA put my pictures up on posters all around South Belfast as a threat to Loyalists ... because of my engagement as a cross-community worker. And they painted all of the Suffolk estate ... and all around the shops – all those with black slogans and black paint: 'Jean Brown is a tout! Jean Brown is a traitor!'" (Brown, interview)

As a consequence of these ongoing attacks, cross-community cooperation came to a standstill in the early 1990s. Yet, on both sides community development efforts continued and more comprehensive community groups were formed: the Lenadoon Community Forum (LCF) on the Catholic side and the Suffolk Community Forum (SCF) on the Protestant side. Eventually, in 1997, cooperation was resumed. This was, however, preceded by a year-long period of talks between LCF and SCF. These talks were again facilitated by O'Halloran who returned with a new project that targeted deprived interface communities. Against the background of severe interface violence spilling over from the civil unrest at the Orange Order Drumcree parade it proved to be arduous and cumbersome to rebuild trust between the two sides. Moreover, the Suffolk side faced a precarious situation, as SCF was threatened with eviction due to plans by the Northern Ireland Housing Executive (NIHE) to demolish the derelict buildings along Stewartstown Road on the Protestant side of the interface. As Maria Bannon described the difficult circumstances under which this process of rapprochement between the community groups took place:

"It started off in one of the worst years of the violence. Because of what was happening at Drumcree at that stage obviously had a ripple effect here. So it rippled out into all interfaces. It was very bad. They started basically talking, because the Housing Executive had said to Suffolk Community Forum, 'Look we are giving you notice of five years to get out of the building', which were these old shops, 'because we are going to knock them down, unless you can come up with an alternative, but for us to rebuild these would not be viable for such a small community.' ... That initiated conversations ... but to be able to work together it took over a year to sell that back to the communities. Because Jean [Brown] from Suffolk Forum would often say that the Protestant community would have said, 'We spent years and years trying to keep them out and now you want us to go and work with them?' So it was quite a long process until the dialogue started. I suppose what they would always call a success was building honesty, openness and acceptance." (Bannon, Interview)

This indicates the feelings of being threatened and besieged that were widespread in the Suffolk community. Moreover, as Bannon also mentioned, there was a strong sense of national identity and community belonging present within both communities. However, it was nevertheless possible for them to accept their differences and to reach agreement on certain common issues to work on:

> "Somebody would have said, 'Yes I am a Nationalist, I am Catholic and I am proud of it.' And somebody else would have said, 'I am Protestant, I am Loyalist and I am proud of it.' That was upfront …There are things that we are not going to agree on here, but let us look on what we can work on together. So it was always taken from that ethos, as long as we are honest with each other." (Bannon, Interview)

In order to prevent the violence in the interface area from reoccurring, both community forums decided to make joint preparations for the 1997 Drumcree parade. Working together with local residents' groups, they issued joint statements calling upon all sides involved to refrain from violent protests at the parade. Additionally, the community activists organised a basic mobile phone network that served as an early warning system to monitor the interfaces and defuse riotous situations. As their endeavours were successful and the interface area remained relatively peaceful throughout the summer, confidence grew and they eventually decided to institutionalise their cooperation. In consequence, the Suffolk-Lenadoon Interface Group (SLIG) was formed by LCF and SFC. As the main principle it was agreed that SLIG had to be run as an equal partnership. In the following statement, Bannon explains the modus operandi of the group:

> "They did agree that regardless of the size – Suffolk is only 750 people and Lenadoon is 12,000 – everything had to be on equal partnership. So the services and outcomes would be equal: what one got both got. And there would be no right of veto. All had to be through consensus. So our management committee of SLIG is made up of half coming from Suffolk Community Forum, which is representing Protestant Suffolk, and half coming from Lenadoon Community Forum, which represents Catholic Lenadoon. And they then go back out to all of the parties from each of the areas and filter back things and come back to us." (Bannon, interview)

This fundamental arrangement that irrespective of the large difference in the population size between Lenadoon and Suffolk both community forums had an equal say in the management and operations of SLIG facilitated their efforts to achieve accountability and obtain support from their communities. In particular, this meant that the board was to be composed of equal numbers of representatives from LCF and SCF, all decisions had to be unanimous, and all services and outcomes were to be shared equally between the two communities. There was also consensus that creating a participatory process that includes all sections of the communities and thus would allow them to develop a sense of ownership was crucial for the successful operation of SLIG. Moreover, it was agreed that at first both community groups would develop their individual plans on how to deal with particular issues and then discuss how these could be solved. Those issues that they could not agree on would be set aside and classified as contentious.

As the first major challenge the members of SLIG were confronted with NIHE's decision to knock down several buildings along the Suffolk side of the 'peace line', including the office premises of SCF. In response, they started a joint initiative and in 2000 founded a social community enterprise called the Stewartstown Road Regeneration Project (SRRP), which was likewise based on the principles of parity and equality. In order to secure the company's operability it was agreed that LCF and SCF would each receive one-third of the profits to fund projects in their communities and the remaining third would be retained by SRRP to continue their development and implementation plans. The main task of the company would be to replace some of the derelict buildings on the interface corridor along Stewartstown Road with a newly constructed two-storey block of shops and offices. It took them considerable effort to bring the communities on board and to secure sufficient funding, yet they succeeded in both. In the planning process particular consideration was made on the selection of the facilities and tenants to be included on the premises. According to Bannon, the guiding principle was to exclude "anything that encourages gambling, drinking, running a taxi depot, anything at night, where it is likely to attract young people, and therefore attract attention to the interface which would increase the likelihood of violence then." (Bannon, interview) The SRRP proved to be a success, and when in 2008 the final phase of the building complex was completed it contained several shops, offices, a youth centre and a children's day care centre that turned out to be well received by local residents from Suffolk and from Lenadoon. The redevelopment of the interface area, which could be achieved over a period of less than ten years, is illustrated in the following two photographs.

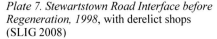

Plate 7. Stewartstown Road Interface before Regeneration, 1998, with derelict shops (SLIG 2008)

Plate 8. Stewartstown Road Interface after Regeneration, 2008, with the newly built office and commercial complex (SLIG 2008)

SLIG was also successful in other ways. The fact that the group's coopera-tion yielded tangible and beneficial results for both communities made it pos-sible to start addressing the contentious issues, such as shared housing, land use and policing, which were previously put on hold. To this purpose, a series of residential meetings on these issues has been initiated in 2008, aiming to build comprehensive involvement and trust from both communities. This includes especially efforts to get the hard-liners from both sides on board. Local paramilitary members were invited to the first meeting and they attend-ed. According to Bannon, they turned out to be supportive and confirmed their readiness to engage in further talks. The meeting was generally well received and even those residents who were most resistant said that they were willing to meet again and continue discussions (Bannon, interview). Encour-aged by this sign of growing confidence among the communities the mem-bers of SLIG decided to expand their scope of operations. While until then the joint activities were confined to the interface corridor, they now started to look in areas located within Suffolk and Lenadoon for regenerating derelict sites and creating shared community space. In another recent initiative they try to tackle the issue of Loyalist bonfires[171] in Suffolk and turn them into

---

[171] In many Protestant/Unionist/Loyalist neighbourhoods across Northern Ireland large towering bonfires are set up and lit on the night before the annual Twelfth of July celebra-tions that mark the culmination of the Orange Order's marching season. The bonfire tradi-tion is met with opposition from the Catholic/Nationalist/Republican community who considers it a demonstration of Protestant/Unionist/Loyalist sectarianism and supremacy. The main source of their contention is the fact that on many bonfires Catholic/Nationalist/ Republican flags, symbols and effigies are burnt. Moreover, the bonfires, which are usual-

safer and more family-oriented events. As a consequence of all these efforts and achievements, the group has received considerable recognition from public authorities and community organisations involved in interface work. Meanwhile, SLIG has become a role model for setting up corresponding processes of cross-community cooperation, peacebuilding and reconciliation in other interface areas in Belfast. Notably, as Hall pointed out, the group's work has also attracted the attention of individual paramilitary leaders from other parts of the city who came to see if they could replicate parts of it in their areas (Hall, interview).

Notwithstanding the accomplishments of SLIG so far, there are still several outstanding issues to be resolved. The violence between the communities could be greatly reduced with no significant riots occurring anymore since the major disturbances following the events at the Drumcree parade of 1996. However, tensions remain in the interface area and sectarian violence continues to flare up at contentious events such as parades, bonfires and the more recent flags dispute. Moreover, residents from Suffolk are still subjected to attacks by people from Lenadoon, resulting in damage to their homes, cars and other property. The fact that young people are heavily involved in perpetrating these violent acts has become a major issue of concern. According to Bannon, there has been an increase in anti-social behaviour, under-age drinking and recreational rioting along the 'peace line'. To counteract these developments, SLIG has put several measures and strategies in place, which have already yielded positive results. Upon the group's initiative the management of the supermarket that is located close to the interface area tightened the security measures to prevent under-age alcohol sales and consumption on its premises. On parading, there has been cooperation for some time now between the community groups, the local Orange Order band in Suffolk, the Parades Commission and the police, which contributed considerably to the decrease in intercommunal violence. The mobile phone network, which was set up in 1997 and which has been upgraded and extended since then, has

---

ly constructed of wooden pallets and tires, have been criticised for causing environmental damage and pollution. A further point of criticism is levelled at some bonfire celebrations for being a magnet for anti-social and violent behaviour of young people. In recent years, public authorities and community groups have made attempts to address these issues and to make the event more family-friendly and environmentally safe. Therefore, the use of 'beacon' type fires is promoted, which, however, so far has found only limited acceptance in Protestant/Unionist/Loyalist communities (Maguire 2013, Simpson 2009, Smithey 2011: 93-97).

proven to be an effective tool in reducing tensions and dealing with violent incidents occurring at the interface and its adjacent neighbourhoods. This was illustrated by Dennis McKendrick,[172] a local resident of Suffolk who works for SLIG as a community capacity builder on the Suffolk side of the interface. On a guided tour through the interface area he reported of an incident that occurred just the night before when the house of a 60 years old Protestant lady from Suffolk was attacked by young people from Lenadoon.

> "Four years ago there was cross-community contact at a higher level, but not at a lower level, where basically the paramilitaries would be dealing with situations. Suffolk was always being attacked. The attacks came from the Nationalist side and had to be stopped by the Nationalists. I worked on that, trying to make contact between the two sides to try and stop incidents. … We have now a working relationship on the mobile phone network where we have exchanged our personal mobile numbers. So Nationalists would respond to incidents. For instance, last night an incident happened at the interface. First, Nationalists were throwing stones over to Suffolk, and half an hour later there was a petrol-bombing incident. And the PSNI responded and we responded. It is a coordinated process sending out the message that both communities know that the two sides and the PSNI are working together now trying to prevent the attacks. Before it was always perceived that it is one side against the other. … So it is sending out a stronger message to them that they are getting nowhere with that. They were kids who did it. The youngest was 13 and the oldest was about 16. And I am going to the Glen Parent Youth Club [in Lenadoon] tonight to speak with their kids and say that this was a 60 year old lady that had her house attacked. So I think this shows how far we have come that I would go over and talk with them, because that would have never ever happened four years ago." (McKendrick, interview)

As McKendrick pointed out, during his several years of working at SLIG there has been considerable progress in cross-community cooperation, not only concerning the prevention and management of violence but also in dealing with contentious cultural practices and traditions. He commended the Lenadoon community for their supportive role in the recent parade in Suffolk which went off without incident. In particular, due to the fact that Suffolk is surrounded by Catholic/Nationalist/Republican communities, the parade would not have been possible without the support coming from Lenadoon to get the bus with the bands into the estate. Moreover, the bonfire issue has also been addressed and efforts are on the way to make the local bonfire festival in Suffolk more acceptable to the Lenadoon community. However, as McKendrick stressed, these efforts towards accommodation would have a

---

[172] The name of the interview respondent has been anonymised upon request.

limit, as "the Nationalists have to understand that this is what we celebrate. We should be allowed to do this, and, in turn, we need to respect what the Nationalists do." (McKendrick, interview) According to Bannon, significant advances have also been made on the contentious issue of Loyalist flags in the Suffolk estate, especially those with UDA signs. Many of these flags – at that time amounting to over hundred – have been removed and will be set up again only temporarily around the annual 12th of July celebrations (Bannon, interview).

SLIG had to face a major setback to their cross-community development work when in 2009 the primary school for Protestant children and the nursery that offered mixed places to both communities were closed. The causes and circumstances that led to the closure will be discussed in more detail in the next section. Nevertheless, what should be mentioned here is that all interview respondents involved in the activities of SLIG, i.e. Bannon, Brown, Hall, McKinley and O'Halloran, expressed their criticism and concerns about the closure of the only educational facilities in Suffolk.[173] In their view, this could cause parents to leave Suffolk and thus lead to a further shrinking of the local population, which could eventually put the community's very existence at risk. However, SLIG has already taken successful steps to prevent these developments from occurring. Thus, the continuous provision of early childhood services on the school's premises could be secured. The group has also entered into discussions with statutory agencies on possible ways of reconstructing the former school building and creating a shared space on the site with facilities that can be used by both communities. According to Bannon, SLIG's ability to respond to this crisis situation swiftly and effectively demonstrates that cooperation based on strong ties and mutual trust has been developed between the two communities. All in all, the following assessment by Hall sums up in a nutshell SLIG's recipe for success:

> "The important lesson was that if it's a process that is seen to be non-threatening and … as bringing some sort of advantage to their living conditions, then people will move towards it. If they are brought on board they will also give their blessing. So to me the Suffolk-Lenadoon experience is one of the most important of the Troubles." (Hall, interview)

---

[173] See also the discussion in 'Policies on Community Relations and Development' in the next section on 'Communities, Politics and Power Relations', pp. 303-305.

NORTH BELFAST INTERFACE NETWORKS

Turning to the situation in North Belfast, cross-community initiatives have likewise been set up in the wake of the peace process, aiming to address common interface issues. In particular, the declared focus is on reducing intercommunal tensions and sectarian violence, promoting good community relations and on improving the socio-economic conditions of people living in interface areas. However, there are specific problems arising from the spatial geography of North Belfast. As outlined in the previous section, the divided and fragmented nature of space is characterised by a mosaic of segregated Protestant/Unionist/Loyalist and Catholic/Nationalist/Republican working-class communities. The communities are located in very close proximity to each other, such that it would be possible to pass from one territory to another in a matter of blocks or sometimes even by just crossing the street. At numerous places, though, such border-crossing is prevented by interface barriers that have been installed between Catholic and Protestant neighbourhoods at various stages of the Troubles and the subsequent post-conflict period. These 'peace walls' serve as protection against attacks from the 'other' community. Moreover, the barriers also fulfil the purpose of demarcating the territories of the communities, which, according to Séan Brennan, has become increasingly important since the cessation of the armed conflict. As he explained:

> "What the walls actually do is they mark out territory. This can be seen most clearly in North Belfast, where interestingly enough from the ceasefires in 1994 more 'peace lines' have gone up than there were during the conflict. More interface violence has occurred since the ceasefires than during the conflict. This is because interfaces were areas of extreme danger during the conflict where people did not want to be seen. But in the absence of conflict people then started moving around and started walking down those interfaces. People felt challenged: 'She is walking down my street, she must be a Catholic. He must be a Protestant.' This brought out tensions and then a lot of interface violence erupted. ... And that is all down to territoriality and insecurity." (Brennan, interview)

Brennan also pointed to the opportunities for collaboration between the communities that were created by the peace process. At the beginning, however, these cross-community initiatives were confronted with major challenges arising from the upsurge of sectarian violence that occurred in the interface areas of North Belfast during the Orange Order marching season of 1996. Neil Jarman, an expert in research on interfaces, parades and related issues was involved at that time in a research project with community groups on the events. He described the local situation as follows:

"In 1996 there was a lot of rioting in North Belfast, which was sparked by parades. There was a high level of violence but also very limited cross-community contacts – not non-existent, but very limited – and a very limited understanding of each side's position. So the Nationalists did not really know anything about why people paraded, or anything like that. It was like the armed conflict had come to an end and people were starting to become aware of issues, which had been very much submerged by the armed conflict, like segregation and the impact that segregation had on accessing resources and fragmenting communities. You know, as people started to put their heads up and started entering into dialogue with each other. But there was a huge lack of understanding of each other, a lot of mistrust, a lot of suspicion, a lot of fear – both between the communities but also within the communities." (Jarman, interview 1)

Thus, the violence was exacerbated by a profound lack of understanding, mistrust, suspicion and fear that existed both between and within the Protestant/Unionist/Loyalist and Catholic/Nationalist/Republican working-class communities. In addition, inter-community contacts were very limited. The situation was further deteriorated by the frequent breakdowns of communication lines occurring during the time of the disturbances. As Jarman noted in his report on responses of the communities to the violence in North Belfast,

"The problems in maintaining a good network of communication within communities, between communities, with the police and with the statutory agencies was [sic] seen as an important contributory factor in the scale of the trouble that was experienced during 1996." (Jarman 1999: 10)

This awareness led to a joint initiative by the Community Development Centre (CDC)[174] and community groups from both sides to establish a local mobile phone network for responding more effectively to potential and actual civil unrest in the interface areas of North Belfast. Eventually funding was secured, and, as there were still funds available, it was decided to provide mobile phones also to other interface areas in the city, including Suffolk and Lenadoon, the Short Strand and the Shankill/Springfield Road interface. The mobile phone network in North Belfast went into operation in early July

---

[174] The Community Development Centre (CDC) was established as an independent NGO in 1974 and ceased its operations in 2001. The work of CDC focussed on supporting and collaborating with community groups, projects and partnerships, providing information and advice to local communities, developing educational and training schemes, and promoting festivals and other cultural activities across North Belfast. In particular, CDC played a major role in setting up a conflict management initiative for building cross-community capacity to respond to the high level of violence that occurred in North Belfast during the summers of 1996 to 1998 (CDC 2000, Jarman 1999: 11-14).

1997. Two interface groups were formed, which were composed of community activists from most of the contentious interface areas. The groups were provided with mobile phones including a list of all the participants' numbers and other relevant contacts such as ambulance services, emergency social services, NIHE and local councillors. The activists operating at street level had to keep their phones turned on 24 hours a day throughout the marching season with the aim of calming tensions at the interfaces, deterring people from violent acts, defusing rumours and dispelling fears. The level of violence during the summer of 1997 was significantly lower than in the previous year. Hence, it was generally recognised that the mobile phone network played a significant role in reducing interface tensions and violence. The success of the network could be repeated in the parades season of 1998 which saw a further drop in intercommunal violence (Jarman, interview 1; Jarman 1999).

In the post-Agreement period the mobile phone networks have expanded and many of them have become integrative parts of more comprehensive interface networks, in which various channels of communication were established to support and facilitate interface work. Thus, numerous cross-community networks have been formed aiming to develop a strategic response to violence and to improve community relations in interface areas across Belfast (Jarman 2006: 13-15). According to interview respondents engaged in community work on North Belfast's interfaces, the Holy Cross dispute[175] provided the impetus for increased networking activities of community groups on both sides of the communal divide. In response to the spate of interface violence, the North Belfast Interface Network (NBIN) was formed in 2002 by community organisations from the mainly Catholic/Nationalist/Republican areas of Ardoyne, Cliftonville and the New Lodge. In the same year, the Protestant Interface Network (PIN) was established covering several Protestant/Unionist/Loyalist interface areas in North Belfast and the Greater Shankill. Yet, in view of the heightened tensions, there was a lack of communication links between the two communities. According to Malachy Mulgrew, a Republican ex-combatant working for NBIN, this was particularly the case on the Loyalist side. He elaborated on the difficulties of

---

[175] For a detailed account of the Holy Cross dispute, see the previous section on 'The Local Communities', pp. 142-144. For an outline map of the area see Figure 12 in the Appendix, p. 407.

establishing contacts and initiating talks with representatives from Loyalist communities involved in the Holy Cross dispute:

> "The Holy Cross School dispute ended in September 2003, and the relationships in North Belfast were at a very low ebb. They were really, really bad, because not only were the two communities very angry at each other about what was going on in the school, but there were also three internal feuds among the Loyalist community that year. So they were not even getting on with each other, which made it even more complicated. We were trying to see if we could build some relationships that would improve the situation. But for almost a year there was very little we could do. It was very difficult to get even contacts. But we worked hard at it, and we eventually got some contacts when we met with people from PIN, which was a Protestant Interface Network who were trying to do some work on their side. The first thing we tried to do was to agree on some baselines. We told them that these people in interface areas were living on their nerves. We tried to get an agreement from them that the pipe bombs and the blast bombs were wrong and we got a basic agreement." (Mulgrew, interview)

However, once the initial communication difficulties had been overcome and the tensions around Holy Cross had subsided, community activists from both sides of the interfaces began to meet more frequently. These meetings eventually resulted in the formation of the North Belfast Interface Monitoring Group (NBIMG). The initiative developed by NBIN acts as a platform for exchange of information and experience on dealing with violent incidents across North Belfast's interfaces. In the following statement, Mulgrew describes how this has facilitated cross-community interface work:

> "And from those meetings back in 2002 and 2003 we now meet across the interface every second Monday morning. We meet and we talk about what has been happening, and how we should deal with the incidents. Before that it was just a mobile phone network and if something happened we would ring each other, but we never met. So we changed that and we started to meet … and discuss what the problems were and the things that we didn't get sorted out over the phone, to make sure we didn't repeat the same mistakes." (Mulgrew, interview)

Community activists from NBIN also took the initiative to promote understanding among Catholic residents in the Holy Cross area for the positions of their Protestant neighbours. There was, however, local resistance to such efforts. Thus, Rab McCallum, the coordinator of NBIN and a former Republican paramilitary who grew up in Ardoyne, was met with resentment among when he invited a leading member of the Protestant residents' group in Glenbryn to talk to Catholic residents in Ardoyne. As he remarked:

> "I asked him to speak about Holy Cross and about the parades, and lots of people didn't like it. Lots of people were angry about that, but we felt that these people are next door to us, in the next community. They are neighbours. They can influence

our future. Therefore, we need to understand where they are coming from and begin to deal with that. And that was a risk, because many people were not happy about them coming in. There was a negative response from some people to us. They thought that it was not right to go there." (McCallum, interview)

Yet, as McCallum stressed, the continuous efforts to engage with representatives of Loyalist and Unionist communities proved fruitful in that they resulted in return invitations and thus promoted dialogue and mutual understanding.

"There have been many occasions where we've asked people from a Loyalist or Unionist perspective to come in and talk about things. We are already due to get that invite back: Come in and let us know what Republicans think, come in and let us know what Nationalists think. Let's discuss. We already get the opportunity to do that within the Protestant Loyalist side." (McCallum, interview)

This view was confirmed by Winston Irvine, a Loyalist ex-combatant and community worker in the Shankill and also a leading member of the North/West Parades Forum, who likewise emphasised the progress made in terms of community relations:

"It would have been unthinkable for Republicans to be invited onto the Shankill Road, and vice versa for that matter. We do now have regular face-to-face meetings around a whole host of different issues, and I think that in some ways community activists in particular have been much more progressive in terms of the peacebuilding aspect to the conflict." (Irvine, interview)

Furthermore, the aftermath of the Holy Cross dispute saw increasing interaction between local residents' groups that were set up in Catholic and Protestant working-class areas to deal with tensions around parading and other interface issues. As a member of the Ardoyne Parades Dialogue Group, Lee Morgan became involved at that time in cross-community talks with members of the North/West Parades Forum. He pointed out that the initial meetings were overshadowed by mutual prejudices and recriminations. Moreover, the national cleavages between the representatives of the Republican and Loyalist residents' groups presented a further obstacle to establishing dialogue.

"For about six or seven years I have been in a group here called the Ardoyne Parades Dialogue Group, and it is basically a residents' group. To put it in very simple terms: we oppose parades coming along this part of the road. Over the years I had to go to meetings with another group called North/West Parades Forum. That parades forum is made up of people from the Loyal Orders, people from a UVF and UDA background, people from the Apprentice Boys, people from the Orange Order, and in particular people from Ballysillan and the Shankill. But at the start I found it very difficult to talk to them, because there was just such a national distance between us and there was a sense of 'you have done this to us and we cannot forget that'." (Morgan, interview)

Yet, as the meetings proceeded, the participants from both groups eventually managed to put aside their divisive sectarian attitudes. This made it possible to identify shared concerns and issues regarding parades and to discuss possibilities for working together and for finding a compromise.

"But after the first four or five meetings of trashing out the sectarian part and we got that all behind us, I started talking particularly with one of them who is a guy regarded as an ex-paramilitary. There was almost a bond there, because some of the things we were talking about that were problematic for us on the day of the parade were the exact same mirror image of the problems that they had, like anti-social elements and drinking. And that's why we used to say to them: 'If you could do your cultural thing and parading in the mornings, we could facilitate it better.' And it would mean we would not have to deal with people that have alcohol on board at night time. And they had the exact same issue. They had to contain people who had alcohol on them and they wanted to address it." (Morgan, interview)

As Morgan went on to remark, there was the belief among Loyalist participants that his group would be totally opposed to Orange Order parades in the vicinity of Ardoyne. It turned out, though, that his working-class affiliation and socialist background was very helpful for clarifying this misperception and for finding some common ground on the parading issue between the two sides.

"One day at one of our meetings – it was about parading – there was a terminology or a slogan that was brought about during Drumcree, and it was by the residents down there, basically saying 'no Orange feet on Garvaghy Road'. So one of them said to me at that meeting, 'We're of the opinion that Ardoyne Parades Dialogue Group is basically just saying you don't want Orange feet on the Crumlin Road'. And at that stage I felt comfortable enough to say that this is not the case and that I believe that they did have a tradition of coming down the Crumlin Road and that I thought that that should be preserved in some form. Just I did not like it in the form that it was at the moment, which is 'we come when we want on any evening'. So we found a commonality there, and afterwards the guy said to me, 'I am glad that you are at the meeting, because you got this socialist background. I think that we can draw on that, because we are committed doing the right thing for our own communities.'" (Morgan, interview)

According to the respondents involved in cross-community work in North Belfast, the various initiatives and projects addressing issues of contention for interface communities have been increasingly integrated into a comprehensive, coordinated approach. A particular focus has been placed on easing sectarian tensions and interface violence at contentious parades. To this purpose, preparatory meetings have been held beforehand with all stakeholders involved, including local community groups, youth organisations, residents' groups, the police, fire service, ambulance service, statutory agencies and local politicians. Among other activities, a poster campaign to address interface violence during the summer parades season has been launched in 2007 upon the initiative of NBIMG. Due to the growing concern about youth involvement in sectarian rioting and anti-social behaviour, NBIMG members initiated collaboration with local youth organisations to engage young people in the campaign development process. Meanwhile, young people living in interface areas have designed several campaign posters and leaflets in which they urge their peers to steer clear of interface trouble. The campaign has been regularly promoted through extensive outreach activities. These include distributing the posters and leaflets widely across North Belfast to local schools, youth clubs, community centres, businesses and on the main local bus routes. Moreover, the campaign has been presented at official receptions hosted by OFMDFM, in the local media and at various community events. As members of NBIMG and local residents highlighted in an informal discussion with the author,[176] the campaign had so far been well received and had a positive impact on reducing youth-led interface violence during the summer marching season. As an illustration, the poster for the 2009 'Keep Safe this Summer' campaign is shown below.

---

[176] This view was expressed by two members of NBIMG and two local residents – a Catholic from Ardoyne and a Protestant from Crumlin – in an informal talk with the author in the context of the poster launch for the 'Keep Safe this Summer' campaign at the NIFRS Westland Fire Station on 17 June 2009.

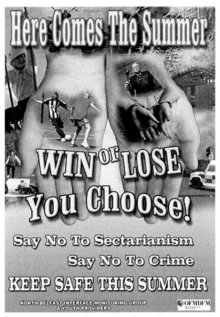

Plate 9. North Belfast Interface Campaign Poster 2009,
designed by young people living in interface areas (CCRF 2009)

Another example of successful cross-community cooperation was provided by Sam Cochrane, a Loyalist ex-combatant working for the North Belfast Community Development and Transition Group (NBCDTG) on interface issues in the Loyalist Tigers Bay and Mountcollyer areas. He recounted the wave of violent attacks by young people connected to Loyalist paramilitaries that had occurred the previous year in a fringe area of Duncairn Gardens close to an interface with the Republican New Lodge ward. The attacks were a particular cause for concern not only for the residents of the area, but also for the local businesses of the nearby Yorkgate Shopping Centre who felt at risk of closure. This posed the threat of significant job losses in an area that was already plagued by chronic unemployment. Hence, Loyalist community workers from NBCDTG were approached to get involved to stop the violence. Given the gravity of the situation, they got in touch with Republican community workers in the New Lodge to contrive ways and means of jointly tackling the issue. The approach included regular meetings with local business owners, residents and politicians from both sides and the involvement of the police. As Cochrane pointed out, they succeeded in their efforts and successfully put an end to the violence:

> "We sat down and said there should be no blame game because it's not the two communities; it's just anti-social behaviour that is involved in these sectarian attacks. And we met on a weekly basis and we met with the landlords of Yorkgate and with all the local businesses … that were under threat of closure because of the rioting. Businesses were saying, 'We're going to have to close Yorkgate and move on to somewhere else.' So, with the jobs and all put on the line we said we'd get rid of the blame game and we'll get down to the nitty gritty. We'll get the PSNI in. We all sit down around the table as a partnership, and we'll find out where the issues are. And I have to say, we meet once a month now, and the interface violence and the anti-social behaviour around Brougham Street, Queens Street and Duncairn Gardens over the last seven to eight months has been zero." (Cochrane, interview)

Not without pride of their accomplishment, he also mentioned that in the meantime the shopping centre has expanded and 200 new jobs have been created for local residents. This positive experience of joint crisis management spurred both sides to continue and strengthen cooperation in dealing with violent disorder in contentious interface areas. As Cochrane remarked, their joint intervention during the next incident of youth-led interface violence proved equally successful. He hailed the police for their supportive role. Instead of being subjected to internal punishments by Loyalist paramilitaries the offenders were now dealt with by the formal justice system. In his view, this experience of collaboration improved the reputation of the police among both communities and likewise initiated a process of gradual confidence-building with Sinn Féin.

> "We used that as a flagship and we … carried the same thing through there on Limestone Road. The PSNI had a big part to play in this. They helped us along with it. We held them to account and they showed what they were able to do. Rather than the punishment beatings it went through the courts. It did play a big part, but it was building the trust up with Sinn Féin. A Loyalist community and a Nationalist community never ever sat down around the table to discuss the issues on interfaces and I think we're unique and … no matter what the problems that come along here we're still able to sit down and discuss them, sorting out issues on parades or anything." (Cochrane, interview)

Thus, what can be deduced from the foregoing is that Republican and Loyalist ex-combatants have played a considerable role in peacebuilding work on the ground both within and between Catholic and Protestant working-class communities. Among those interviewed, several have become involved in networking activities across the interfaces in North and North-West Belfast.

As Winston Irvine stressed the significance of former paramilitary fighters in establishing dialogue and relationships between the two communities:

"I think that it is important to point out that those who are presently involved in the post-conflict reconstruction by and large had been those actors and players who were also involved at the very sharp end of the conflict. In terms of the efforts that have been made to date, dialogue has been going on for the best part of a decade, and relationships at an organisational and also at a personal level have been built. There are communication networks across most interfaces now through Belfast and further afield. They basically act as an early warning system, which allows community activists on both sides to basically deal with situations that unfold along and across those interfaces." (Irvine, interview)

In general, Malachy Mulgrew, a former Republican paramilitary and interface worker in North Belfast, shared this view. However, he also pointed to the different status of Republican and Loyalist ex-prisoners within their own communities. According to him, while former Republican inmates have been well received, their Loyalist counterparts have received a bad reputation:

"In our community ex-prisoners are seen as being very supportive of the community. The community supported them and when they came out of jail the community even looked to them for direction. On the Protestant/Unionist/Loyalist side ex-prisoners are looked at as dirt. The politicians put them down. Everybody in their community puts them down." (Mulgrew, interview)

This was confirmed by Neil Jarman. In his opinion, the reason for the negative image of Loyalist ex-prisoners in the Unionist community was partly because paramilitaries ranked bottom in terms of the reputation of organisations combating the IRA. Unlike their Catholic counterparts, working-class Protestants had more options available to become involved in the armed conflict. Hence, joining the UVF or UDA was seen as the least reputable alternative within Unionism.

"I don't think the prisoners had the same status within the Unionist community, generally. …Whereas within Republicanism, within the Nationalist community, the ex-prisoners had a higher status. And I think it partly comes down to … if you were a working-class Catholic and you wanted to fight the British, the obvious way was to join the IRA. But if you were a working-class Protestant and you wanted to fight the IRA, there were a number of opportunities. You could join the British Army, you could join the police, you could join the UDR, or you could join the paramilitaries. But joining the paramilitaries was the last option. It was for the people who were not capable of joining the British Army, or the police, or the UDR. So it was seen a bit less as a kind of a respectful habit within Unionism. I think it was always seen more as being a bunch of thugs." (Jarman, interview)

The positive contribution of ex-combatants to local peacebuilding was also confirmed by respondents who had never been involved in any paramilitary activity. Jackie Redpath, for instance, who has been engaged in community development work in the Shankill since the early 1970s, highlighted their efforts to tackle sectarian interface violence:

> "Ironically, the people some of whom who have been most involved in the war of the Troubles, who have been in the paramilitaries, are some of the people who are most trying to deal with these issues of sectarianism." (Redpath, interview)

There were others like Michael Hall and Derek Poole, both long-time peace activists with a profound expertise in interface and community relations issues, who held a more differentiated view concerning the role of ex-combatants. Likewise, they both acknowledged the great commitment of some to building community relations in interface areas. They, however, also emphasised the presence of spoilers among the Loyalist and Republican paramilitaries striving to disrupt rapprochement and thus maintain the status quo of community division and segregation (Hall, interview; Poole, interview). As Poole put it:

> "There would be ex-combatants who would be the best community workers in the area. Some of the paramilitaries both Republican and Loyalist are out there with a big vision and work hard, day and night, to build relationships across the divides. But there would be other paramilitary leaders who have a vested interest in keeping the situation segregated." (Poole, interview)

CURRENT ISSUES OF CONTENTION AND DEBATE

As described above, there have been considerable successes of cross-community cooperation and signs of improvement across Belfast's interface areas in the post-Agreement period. Yet, several key issues still remain unresolved. To date, cross-community work, by and large, has not extended beyond dealing with local tensions and violence around the interfaces. In this regard, the capacity to defuse interface conflict has been enhanced through increased networking and coordination between the various stakeholders involved. There is one notable exception, which is Suffolk and Lenadoon in Outer West Belfast, where cooperation between Protestant and Catholic community groups has not only led to a significant drop in violence but also to considerable economic regeneration of the interface area. Intercommunal tensions, however, continue to flare up along the interface during the parades season and other contentious events.

With regard to the situation in North Belfast, Rab McCallum expressed the view that large-scale rioting between Catholics and Protestants has more or less ceased (McCallum, interview). Yet, this has to be seen as a snapshot, capturing the level of violence at that juncture. Referring to more recent developments, Neil Jarman pointed out that serious intercommunal rioting around contentious parades has continued in the Ardoyne area. Furthermore, severe disturbances occurred across North Belfast's interfaces during the flags dispute. Gradually, this turned into a localised conflict, when Loyalists set up a permanent protest camp in Twaddell Avenue at the interface with Ardoyne. They joined forces with the Orangemen, who at the same time were holding protest marches in the area every night to protest against the ban of an Orange Order parade marching along the Ardoyne interface. According to Jarman, an increasing number of Catholic/Nationalist/Republican residents in the Greater Ardoyne area have taken a more aggressive stance towards the Loyalist flag protest and local Orange Order parades. These are mainly people who have become disaffected with the mainstream Republicanism of Sinn Féin and have aligned with a more radical residents' group called the Greater Ardoyne Residents Collective (GARC). Notably, the local flag protest has also mobilised a considerable amount of middle-aged women on both sides. Yet, then again, this was not that surprising, considering that there "was often a fair number of women involved when parades were stopped by the police." (Jarman, interview 2) In effect, as Jarman stressed, the sustained Loyalist protest has not only led to heightened intercommunal tensions in the area, but has also involved a substantial amount of public money for local policing: "It requires a daily police operation, which is costing a fair amount of money. … I would say it's costing around 40,000 to 50,000 pounds Sterling a day to police the ongoing protest in Ardoyne." (Jarman, interview 2)

Jim Auld pointed to the volatile and explosive situation in working-class communities in North and West Belfast, where minor issues of contention, such as a children's scuffle in the street, could escalate into broader violent unrest. According to him, this was because the underlying causes of conflict had not been resolved and, as a legacy of the past, many people in the communities were still used, able and ready to resort to violent means. In his words:

"So the causes are still there and they are underlying. But that has caused under the surface there to be just a fairness that's just slightly under control, but the least amount of aggravation can cause it to explode. Ardoyne was one example of it, but on a personal basis the simplest thing in the street can cause people to be in conflict. It can be over kids fighting in the street, playing ball and falling out. It can be over any sort of minor dispute, but this very quickly erupts then into a violent confrontation between adults within a family. And the extended family is very quickly brought into that conflict, and they bring support of numbers and violence to the situation. … And that's the danger, because there are people here who are even more willing to engage in violence based on their personal history, based on … their ability to engage in physical violence and using weapons. Because there are so many people here who can make a gun. There are so many people here who can make a bomb. There are so many people here who suffer from post-traumatic stress. There are so many people here who feel the need to be willing, to be seen, to be engaged in violence, as a first resort to try and protect their family." (Auld, interview)

As indicated by several respondents engaged in community and interface work, the nature and patterns of interface violence have changed over the past couple of years. In particular, the involvement of young people in stirring up interface tension and participating in violence and anti-social behaviour has become an increasing cause of concern. As McCallum explained:

"We have violence now that is more at the level of anti-social behaviour and young people involved in interface violence. Sectarianism is a contributing factor. It's not the sort of major factor, excitement of the chase on those things is the main factor for that, and sometimes sectarianism can be used as an excuse for that." (McCallum, interview)

In a similar vein, Shane Whelehan, the director of Ardoyne Youth Providers Forum who grew up in a Catholic village near Newry, stressed the significance of youth-led interface violence in the wider Ardoyne area. In his view, the excitement in taking part in rioting, joyriding and other anti-social activities certainly plays a role. Nevertheless, the specific social environment laden with memories of the Troubles in which young people grow up is likewise a contributing factor. As he remarked: "We are here in a Republican area where a lot of their peers and family and everyone else say that they have been affected by and involved in the Troubles." (Whelehan, interview) Another reason is the precarious socio-economic situation of the area with a considerable number of young people facing poverty and unemployment. As a consequence, under-age drinking and medication and drug abuse have become more prevalent and the number of suicides, especially among young men, has increased (Whelehan, interview). Furthermore, he pointed to rivalries between local youth from Ardoyne and the Bone, which stem from long-standing tensions between these neighbouring Catholic/Nationalist/Republican communities. This was confirmed by Verena McCaughan,[177] a local resident and youth worker at Ardoyne Youth Providers Forum. Accord-

---

[177] The name of the interview respondent has been anonymised upon request.

ing to her, there is usually no contact between young people from the two neighbourhoods:

"They don't mix. The children in the Bone would not … come down here and go to youth clubs and socialise with kids from here. They would get actually beat up, because they come from the Bone and this is Ardoyne. And although there is the same type of religion and all the rest of it, it was always like that." (McCaughan, interview)

Like in the Greater Ardoyne area, anti-social behaviour of young people has also become a growing concern across the Suffolk/Lenadoon interface. As Maria Bannon pointed out, "in Lenadoon it is very bad with anti-social behaviour, and there have been people just beyond the interface who would have their houses surrounded at night by young thugs drinking and all the rest of it." (Bannon, interview) According to Margaret Valente, the situation is mirrored in the New Lodge area: "Anti-social behaviour is a big theme. In the last few weeks there have been young burglars who broke into local people's homes and shops. People were getting serious beatings on the street, for no reason." (Valente, interview)

This ties in with the view shared by several respondents that there is a growing sense of alienation, disaffection and disillusionment among youth living in deprived working-class areas. Michael Hall, for instance, noted that "the larger body of young people that take part in any of the interface troubles are just bored, alienated and sort of aimless. And of course, they also think it is a good excitement." (Hall, interview) His opinion was echoed by Jackie Redpath, who referred in particular to the situation in the Greater Shankill area. He also added that the changing nature of the conflict has provided a fertile ground for recreational rioting of young people:

"When you had a war on and gunmen on the street you did not riot because you would have been just shot dead. ... Now that the guns are put away it is perfectly safe to riot. Ironically, you can go and riot almost for fun. Now that does not mean it's not serious. I think one of the problems in these communities that are intensely deprived is that young people do this for kicks, but also because they don't place any great value on themselves. Because their lives are pretty valueless to them they see others' lives as valueless. So all the things that go to build values in your life – your knowledge, your learning, your job, your friendships, your social interactions, your ability to deal with difference and diversity and embrace it rather than reject it – all those things are foreign concepts. So one of the words that has been used for them is alienation." (Redpath, interview)

Hall pointed to another worrying development. According to the initial findings of one of his recent pamphlet projects on the work of Republican and

Loyalist ex-combatants with youth, young people in disadvantaged areas have become more attracted to paramilitary activity. As he explained the reasons behind this development:

"UDA leaders and UPRG leaders were hearing from young people in Protestant areas a sense of 'our aim in life is to be the next generation of Loyalist prisoners'. And they were saying 'we have got peace, but here are the young people thinking that they've missed something.' They were looking at the paramilitaries and saying 'they've got kudos. They've got status. They're well looked up to. Some of them got big cars. Maybe that's the road to follow.' When the Loyalists mentioned this to their Republican associates, at first the Republicans said, 'No, we don't find that in our area.' But then, when the two soldiers were shot dead and the policeman was shot dead earlier this year, suddenly the Republicans were saying 'Yes we are hearing that. We are hearing young people saying that the war is not over, and you can picture that we'll take up with it.' So, it's a mixture of the old national question, and the old religious/cultural/national identity issues still being there, still being unresolved, but linking in with a disaffected and alienated youth population. So, in many ways it's the lack of a peace dividend for young people. It's proving every day to be dangerous in terms of taking them along the road which links in with traditional political violence." (Hall, interview)[178 179]

Some respondents involved in local community work reported an increase in activity of dissident Republican paramilitary groups within Catholic working-class communities, especially around interfaces in the Ardoyne and New Lodge areas but also in other parts of North and West Belfast. Although still operating at a relatively low level, these groups drew increasing support from young people. Regarding the situation in the New Lodge, Margaret Valente shared Hall's view that the perceived absence of a peace dividend among local youth has made them more susceptible to paramilitary influence.

"I can see why young people want to join the dissidents: because they did not see any improvement in the area. I think that young people just need a purpose in life. They need to belong to something. So they join a gang. … My son he's 21, and he

---

[178] UPRG stands for Ulster Political Research Group, which acts mainly as a political advisory body for the UDA. See also Footnote 76, p. 85.

[179] The incidents mentioned by Hall refer to two assaults committed by dissident Republican paramilitary groups. On 7 March 2009, two off-duty British soldiers were shot dead by members of the Real IRA outside a former British Army site in Antrim town. The shootings were the first British Army fatalities in Northern Ireland since 1997. Two days later, a PSNI police officer was killed in a gun attack by members of the Continuity IRA in Craigavon. This was the first incident of a Northern Irish police officer being killed by paramilitaries since 1998. The attacks marked an apex of violence by dissident Republican paramilitaries since the start of their campaign in the aftermath of the Agreement (Belfast Telegraph 2009a, Horgan & Morrison 2011: 643, Irish Times 2009).

and his friends, they were talking about the dissidents. His friends were saying that they want to join the dissident IRA and get a gun and shoot them – the PSNI, and Loyalists and the UDA. The war is not over. And they were really adamant about doing it." (Valente, interview)

Syd Trotter, a former Loyalist paramilitary and community relations worker in Tigers Bay, held a similar view. Moreover, he expressed the belief that on both sides dissident groups would not disappear, "because they are working for their own agendas" (Trotter, interview). In doing so, they engaged in drug-dealing, armed robberies, racketeering and other criminal activities. Regarding young people's motivation for joining a dissident group he remarked:

> "The problem is, in my view, that for young people to go to such an organisation it is not because they're politically motivated or they have any great aspirations in terms of an Ireland united or whatever. In my view it is the action, the physical action. They are adrenalin junkies. They may come from areas that are considered as socially and economically deprived. So in one sense, as we have in Liverpool, London and various parts of England, gangs and subcultures, so we have here in terms of dissidents. It is the feeling of belonging somewhere, the power it gives over others. If you don't succeed in the real world then you create a fantasy world on your own." (Trotter, interview)

Such views were confirmed by Brendan Murtagh and Neil Jarman, both experts in research on issues related to community relations and interface violence. They also pointed out that the dissident paramilitaries have gained momentum mainly due to growing support among disaffected and alienated local youth. According to Murtagh, this is a specific problem in Ardoyne, where many young people have not seen any tangible benefits from the peace process (Murtagh, interview). As regards more recent developments, Jarman noted that Republican and Loyalist dissident groups have become more active in stirring up trouble in North Belfast's interface areas, thus retarding and slowing down the process of local peacebuilding (Jarman, interview 2).

Notably, there was a divergence of views between respondents with Republican backgrounds and those with Loyalist ones about the role of sectarianism in the intercommunal conflict. Whereas Republican interviewees attributed sectarianism mainly to Protestant/Unionist/Loyalist communities, Loyalist respondents regarded it as a phenomenon equally present within both communities. Winston Irvine, for instance, expressed the view that by employing the term 'recreational rioting' Republicans try to conceal the existence of sectarianism within their communities. After all, sectarian attitudes persisted in both communities, and the intergenerational transmission of these attitudes within the family was an important factor contributing to youth violence. However, according to him, rather than young people being the main perpetrators of interface violence, "the reality is that adults and mainstream Republicans have been heavily involved in both inciting and carrying out that [sectarian] violence." (Irvine, interview) Republican respondents, by contrast, stressed that sectarianism on their side applied mainly to a small group of dissidents. In pursuit of their aim of reigniting armed conflict in Northern Ireland, these dissidents used sectarianism to manipulate young people into causing interface trouble. As Umberto Scappaticci, a former Republican combatant and youth and community worker in outer West Belfast, put it:

> "A lot of young people are being wound up by more sinister elements within our Nationalist community. That probably is the same within the Loyalist community. And it all boils down to people who disagree with the peace process. And they believe that by heightening sectarian trouble they would bring the peace process down." (Scappaticci, interview)

As regards the situation in the New Lodge, Margaret Valente likewise expressed the view that "here it is not so much about sectarianism. The main problem is criminality more than 'we are protecting our areas from the Protestants'." (Valente, interview) Dympna McGlade was confident that the dissidents would not gain a foothold in working-class communities on both sides. In her opinion, this was because the communities had a strong tradition of "'we don't give up our own'" (McGlade, interview), which ensued from their close-knit, extended family structure. Consequently, they did their utmost to protect young people from the influence of thugs who were regarded as outcasts threatening local peace and security.

Regarding sectarianism in Protestant/Unionist/Loyalist communities, some Republican respondents stressed the intransigence of sections of Loyalism and the Orange Order and their insistence on maintaining divisive cultural practices, such as contentious parades. As Michael George, a colleague of Scappaticci, remarked, "The Orange Order is very much opposed to doing any deals that they see as giving away any of their territory or any other things that they have built up over the years." (George, interview) Maybe somewhat exaggerated, but quite typical of the view shared by other Republican respondents, he noted that there were

> "a lot of hard-core Orange Order members and die-hard Unionists who don't want to give an inch. Most contentious marches serve that 'no-surrender' mentality: 'we'll guard what's ours. A compromise is as good as selling out. ...We march here because it's a Queen's highway. We have always done that, and it's our tradition.'" (George, interview)

What he indicated was the perception of the parades as an exhibition of sectarian triumphalism over the Catholic/Nationalist/Republican community. This was shared by Jim Auld, the director of the Republican Community Restorative Justice Ireland (CRJI) scheme. He stressed that only six of the over 3,000 annual parades were castigated by Catholics/Nationalists/Republicans, because the parades march through their residential areas. Referring to the insistence of the Orange Order on sticking to the route of those contentious parades, he drew an acute comparison between the Order and the Ku-Klux Clan:

> "Within the Nationalist community people are of a mind not to feel that they should have to put up with people trying to show their superiority. I think that the argument is, and the darkest similarity that I would be putting is: Would it be accepted for the Ku-Klux Clan to march through Harlem or Brixton, or any other area that is pre-dominantly black or Asian in whatever city in the world. Is that acceptable behaviour? Would that be considered a cultural thing to do?" (Auld, interview)

Eamonn Deane, the director of the Holywell Trust, a Derry/Londonderry-based peacebuilding charity, joined the chorus of critical voices. He showed his outright incomprehension for the Protestant/Unionist/Loyalist marching tradition, which was tantamount to a demonstration of their atavistic, supremacist and contemptuous attitudes towards Catholics/Nationalists/Republicans. In his opinion, this was clearly evidenced by the fact that the 12th of July Orange celebrations of Protestant victory over Catholics over four hundred years previously had been imposed upon them as a public holiday.

> "I would not want to march near people's houses and people's neighbourhoods, who do not want me there. I mean, what kind of culture is this? How can this be one person's culture and civilisation? This is atavistic. I don't understand, for example, how we as a society can still stay with the nonsense that each year the Twelfth of July is a public holiday. And the day after is also a public holiday. So our whole society is geared towards the needs of Orangemen marching. And what are they celebrating? They are celebrating the victory of the Battle of the Boyne. They are celebrating the victory of their closing the gates of Derry. They are celebrating Protestant supremacy. And we are all expected to turn and say this is a shared festival fun? This is absolute, total nonsense." (Deane, interview)

Lee Morgan held a more moderate, but essentially similar view. He doubted that parading was solely a cultural tradition. Instead, he suspected that it also served to demonstrate Protestant ascendancy over Catholics. As he remarked:

"I am not against parading per se and what is in their culture, if that is what they want to do. Although sometimes I doubt that that is what it is about. I feel that sometimes it is about passing our homes and waving a flag and saying something insulting like 'we still rule'." (Morgan, interview)

These perceptions were in stark contrast to the way some respondents from a Protestant/Unionist/Loyalist background viewed the Orange Order and the marching tradition. Mervyn Gibson, a senior Orangeman himself, offered a telling counter-perspective. As he stated, the parades were solely an expression of Protestant/Unionist/Loyalist culture and heritage and thus had nothing to do with triumphalism and sectarianism. After all, the 12th of July was a celebration of what he called the 'Protestant revolution' that spread democracy throughout Europe.

"An overwhelming majority of the Unionist Protestant community, of the wider Orange family, say they want to celebrate. And it is as much a cultural celebration today as it was back then. It is not a triumph. I do not go out and think I want to have my wee triumph over Roman Catholics. I have an ex-army member of the Army Council of the IRA sitting as Deputy Prime Minister of Northern Ireland. Sorry, is this the sort of triumph that we have? This is what we have. I go and celebrate the Protestant revolution, which I believe brought democracy throughout Europe, which was a major factor for building modern Europe. That is really what the Battle of the Boyne and all was about." (Gibson, interview)

Moreover, he accused Republicans of being intolerant towards Protestant/Unionist/Loyalist values and traditions. This was reflected, for example, in their opposition to parades that included bands affiliated to the UDA and the UVF. Whereas Republicans deem those bands inappropriate, he regards them as part of his culture. He went further, asserting that "in many ways Republicans want to fight a new war against our culture, to try to take away all that is British and meaningful to us." (Gibson, interview) By contrast, Protestants/Unionists/Loyalists have proved their tolerance towards Republicans. This was reflected in their readiness to accept the fact that former IRA members sit in the Government of Northern Ireland and also that the GAA hold their Gaelic football and hurling games in Protestant towns. Likewise, on the issue of contentious parades, he opposed the view held by Republicans. Instead, he emphasised that most of those parades took place in shared community spaces and that Republicans used false allegations to make further encroachments and assaults on the Protestant/Unionist/Loyalist community. In his words:

"There is not the same respect towards Protestants, and people say we want to march through Republican areas. I do not know of many parades that march through Republican areas. We go along and parade along the sides of it, but those are shared spaces. We are driving down those roads every day, Protestants and Roman Catholics. You know, it is they and those tactics that are making further territorial claims and further fighting our society." (Gibson, interview)

In a similar vein, Syd Trotter, himself also a member of the Orange Order, stressed the intolerance and disrespect of Republicans. Referring to the then recent 'Tour of the North', he refuted claims by Ardoyne residents of being offended by the parade. After all, the parade did not pass any residents' houses but just strode along the shops on the edges of the estate.

"Let's look at the Ardoyne shops now. There are no Nationalist houses facing that road, only those shops. The houses were behind the shops the streets down. So why would they want to protest? I mean, it would be different if they were passing the front doors, but they are not! This is a road of shops. The Ardoyne, the houses are on the back. Why would they say that they are offended?" (Trotter, interview)

William Moore, general secretary of the Apprentice Boys of Derry, shared this perception that Protestant/Unionist/Loyalist culture was under threat. In his account of the situation in Derry/Londonderry, he pointed to a general sense of alienation and exclusion within the local Protestant community. This was mainly due to their experience as a minority that has felt increasingly marginalised by the Catholic/Nationalist/Republican majority.[180] In particular, he referred to the vulnerable position of the Apprentice Boys in the city. As he pointed out, the ongoing attacks on their Memorial Hall were perceived as being part of a wider campaign to expel them from the centre of the city:

"The problem is that our hall is still constantly under attack. If you go out to the site there you'll see the recent attacks from the last couple of nights where there have been paint bombs and petrol bombs thrown at the hall. So our people still feel under attack. We still feel that we're not wanted in the city. We still feel that

---

[180] According to the 2011 Census, the city of Derry/Londonderry has a population of around 108,000, of which 74.8% are of Catholic and 22.3% are of Protestant backgrounds. Throughout the Troubles, the Protestant community experienced a substantial demographic decline, reflected in an ageing population and an overall loss of one-third of their population between the censuses of 1971 and 1991. This negative trend seems to have halted since the early 2000s. The majority – around two-thirds – of the city's population live in the Cityside on the west bank of the River Foyle. The remainder lives in the Waterside on the east bank of the river. The Cityside is overwhelmingly Catholic, whereas the population of the Waterside is almost evenly split between the two communities. However, as the figures from the 2011 Census show, Catholics now constitute also a majority, albeit only a slight one, in the Waterside area of the city (Moore et al 1995, Mullan 2013, NINIS 2013a, NISRA 2012, Shirlow et al 2005: 20-31).

there's a concerted effort to remove us from the city centre here." (Moore, interview)

Three issues that were seen as closely related to the issue of sectarianism figured prominently among the respondents, namely fear, territoriality and housing. Respondents from both communities agreed on the important role of these issues in exacerbating sectarian tensions and interface violence. Moreover, these issues all contributed to reinforcing community divisions. As indicated earlier, the fear of being attacked by the 'other' side is still present in Catholic and Protestant working-class communities, particularly in North, North-West, Outer West and Inner East Belfast. This fear has expressed itself in two ways: on the one hand, as a feeling of being at risk of physical harm and, on the other hand, as a perceived threat to the cultural identity of the community. The first kind of fear in particular has led to the avoidance of certain areas and thus to restricted mobility in getting around. Lee Morgan, for instance, who lives in an interface area in Ardoyne, explained that never in his life did he go to Glenbryn, nor did he ever walk down Twaddell Avenue – both Loyalist neighbourhoods in the immediate vicinity, only a few hundred metres away from his home.

"I just could not walk there because … there would be people that would not be alright about it. They would say 'that Sinn Féin man, he is in the dialogue group. Let's beat him up, or let's do this to him or stab him or whatever.' But also there would be a tension of somebody not even knowing me who would say 'ah, you are a Catholic from Ardoyne, because I've seen you walking from there.'" (Morgan, interview)

Likewise, Margaret Valente expressed the view that it was still too dangerous to walk in certain areas of North Belfast, especially at night. In particular, she referred to the interface area of Duncairn Gardens, which is close to her home in the New Lodge: "Duncairn Gardens at night is dead man's land. It is not safe to walk down Duncairn Gardens at night. I live in this area and even I would be afraid of walking about here at night." (Valente, interview) In her opinion, the feeling of insecurity was so deeply ingrained in people's psyches that it would prevent them from crossing interfaces even if the barriers were removed.

"You can take down those walls. You can take down anything. But you can't take down the walls in people's heads. No, you can't take down that feeling of 'I'm not safe, I won't cross there'. It's a psychological issue." (Valente, interview)

According to Chris Odley,[181] a Loyalist ex-combatant and local interface worker, the situation was similar in the Lower Shankill. On a guided tour through the Protestant interface areas bordering the Lower Falls and the New Lodge, he emphasised that many local residents were afraid of getting assaulted by Catholics from the other side of the interfaces. He pointed to the six-metre high open mesh fence at Denmark Street separating a Protestant/Loyalist neighbourhood from a Catholic/Republican one in the New Lodge (see Plate 10 below). There is a considerable buffer zone between the two sides. This buffer zone consists of an arterial road running between the Catholic houses and the interface fence and a green space with a walkway in-between separating the Protestant houses from the fence. According to Odley, the Protestants living there do not dare to use the walkway. This was due to the fact that, despite the distance, stones and all kinds of other objects have frequently been thrown at them over the fence. However, local young people from the Protestant community had also launched such attacks on Catholics living on the other side of the interface. As a countermeasure, he asked the city council for trees and hedges to be planted along the fence. As he proudly noted, this initiative has helped significantly to reduce the number of incidents (Odley, interview).

Plate 10. Denmark Street – Westlink Interface and Buffer Zone, seen from Lower Shankill (Photos taken by the author, 15/07/2009)

As Odley explained, there is another important impact of this sense of fear. This is the perceived need for greater protection against the 'other' community, which has become physically manifest in the installation of more interface barriers in the area since the peace agreement. Moreover, he warned that the

---

[181] The name of the interview respondent has been anonymised upon request.

removal of the barriers would be disastrous and would reignite armed conflict: "There is no peace wall here, as you can see, and these houses are still getting attacked. If they are tearing down the 'peace walls', there will be warfare again, open warfare." (Odley, interview) Michael Doherty, a peace activist involved in interface and community relations projects, mainly in the Derry/Londonderry area, was similarly pessimistic. He referred to the city's interfaces, particularly to the 'peace wall' between the Catholic/Republican Bishop Street and the Protestant/Loyalist Fountain Estate (see Plate 11 below),[182] and stressed the dearth of cooperation between community workers from both sides. In his view,

> "It is a sad reflection on our society that we actually have these interfaces. When we should be talking about taking these walls down, we have not even been going to think about how we should take them down. Because we are still afraid of a new war. And why community workers on the sites of our interfaces are not cooperating with one another? Because of the lack of trust they have an issue." (Doherty, interview)

Plate 11. Bishop Street – Fountain Interface in Derry/Londonderry, view on the Fountain estate, seen from Bishop Street (Photos taken by the author, 16/07/2009)

Unlike Odley, other respondents did not see these dramatic consequences, but likewise shared the view that the main purpose of the walls was to provide security for local residents. As Mervyn Gibson remarked, "Those 'peace

---

[182] The inscriptions on the two murals on the photo to the right read: "Londonderry west bank Loyalists still under siege no surrender" (left mural) and "British Ulster Alliance" (right mural). The photo also shows that the kerbstones, signposts and lamp-posts are painted in the colours of the British union jack. This is still a common practice by hard-line Loyalists to emphasise the Britishness of their neighbourhoods. It can also be seen in Loyalist working-class areas of Belfast, such as in Tigers Bay, the Shankill, Mount Vernon, and Cluan Place (cf. Craith 2002: 174-175, Morris 2015).

walls' are really security, comfort blankets for those who live in those areas, and when those people feel safe, the walls will come down." (Gibson, interview) However, aside from the safety issue, social and economic factors also played an important role in removing the walls. This view is exemplified by Malachy Mulgrew in the context of North Belfast. He thought substantial efforts would be required to build good relationships between interface communities and to improve their economic living conditions.

> "For me, you're never going to take down the barriers unless it's in the context of regenerating the interface. It's also social and economic regeneration, it's not just physical. There is a massive programme of work that needs to be done out there." (Mulgrew, interview)

In this respect, Derek Poole pointed out that it was essential to focus first on capacity-building within the interface communities on each side separately.

> "The first thing we need is to go back to the agenda of how do we create secure, cohesive communities of well-being – because if that's not created then those walls are not coming down, because the communities will not allow them to come down. They will not feel themselves strong enough, mature enough and capable enough to manage the emotion and the new relationships that would need to be built, when those walls come down." (Poole, interview)

According to him, this lack of community safety and cohesion can be attributed mainly to the legacy of hurt and trauma caused by the Troubles. Hence, the 'peace walls' were regarded by many even "as a gift, because it's the first bit of security and peace and quiet they've had living in North Belfast." (Poole, interview) Thus, although aware of the disruptive character of the interface barriers, many local residents had become accustomed to them. In fact, the walls had become indispensable elements of their daily lives. As illustrations of this phenomenon, Poole drew instructive comparisons with the Berlin Wall and the 'elephant in the room' metaphor. In his view, the prevalence of the 'peace walls' in North Belfast could be described as "the most abnormal thing in the world ... but within no time at all the abnormal becomes normal and you can't imagine living without it." (Poole, interview)

An elephant was employed in a metaphorical sense also by Rab McCallum, albeit in a different, but related context. He referred to the 'pink elephant syndrome' to illustrate the impossibility of discussing issues regarded as contentious among Protestant and Catholic working-class communities: "everybody talks about everything, but does not say anything that is contentious, because we cannot talk about those things." (McCallum, interview)

This view was mirrored by other respondents like Michael Doherty. As he expressed: "We have learned the use of ambiguity. We have learned how to avoid dealing with the major issues, and one of the main is sectarianism." (Doherty, interview) Moreover, according to McCallum, the avoidance of contentious topics not only applied to sectarianism and to cultural and political issues, but also extended to socio-economic issues like housing, education and employment. In the flashpoint interface areas of North Belfast, this basically included all matters going beyond addressing the issue of interface violence. Indeed, some of the people living in these areas were not even willing to engage in any discussions with their neighbours across the interface. In McCallum's view, the main reason for this was a sense of fear of the 'other' side that is still widespread among adjacent interface communities, especially in North Belfast with its patchwork geography of division.

> "The people, who have the most fear of each other, have been the people, who live geographically adjacent to each other. And they are the hardest people to engage with in terms of sitting down and talking." (McCallum, interview)

Hence, for example, the Protestant residents of Glenbryn by no means approached their Catholic neighbours in Ardoyne to discuss issues of common concern. As he stressed, this was the case despite the common issues faced by both communities.

> "The problems are the same: low educational attainment, high unemployment, crime, anti-social behaviour, drugs, poor healthcare. All the issues that are social issues in Glenbryn are exactly the same social issues that we are facing in Ardoyne 200 yards across away." (McCallum, interview)

As the foregoing has suggested, this fear of the 'other' side among interface communities is rooted in the legacy of the conflict. This view is similarly echoed by Tony Gallagher, professor of education at Queen's University Belfast with a research focus on the role of education in improving community relations. In his view, the relationship between the two communities has been shaped by fear caused by decades of violent conflict. Consequently, for many people living in conflict-ridden areas, avoiding contact with their neighbours from the 'other' community has become an entrenched habit.

> "In a situation where we have a history of conflict and continuing tensions people are used not to engage with one another, because it seems risky or dangerous. You've come out of a period when for thirty years at least relationships between the two communities have been largely influenced by a relationship of fear. In that situation, the safe default condition is just to stay with your own community. ... People are not prepared to take the risks of reaching out." (Gallagher, interview)

Nevertheless, this is not to say that people from Protestant and Catholic interface neighbourhoods did not meet at all. According to McCallum, there was informal interaction between residents from Ardoyne and Glenbryn, which until then, however, had been confined mainly to casual encounters during shopping and other routine activities. As an example, he mentioned a weekly car boot sale at the Ardoyne side of the interface that enjoyed popularity among both local Catholics and Protestants. Yet, at the same time he voiced his concern that in Ardoyne there were still "some young people who never knowingly sat down and had a conversation with someone who is a Protestant. And I dare say that is similar in Protestant communities." (McCallum, interview) In general, however, McCallum was confident that contacts between Catholic and Protestant working-class communities would increase. His optimism was shared by other respondents. In Mervyn Gibson's view, for instance, a new generation of young Catholics and Protestants has emerged who avail themselves of increased opportunities to meet and socialise with one another. Moreover, as he explained, "the older generation still have many friends across the divide that meet downtown for shopping or something." (Gibson, interview) Hence, he warned against exaggerating the significance of segregation.

It was widely acknowledged among respondents that to a large extent the Protestant and Catholic interface communities and the wider working-class communities in which they are embedded share the same problems and needs. Winston Irvine, for example, articulated the view that "there is certainly more that unites us than divides us. I think that there is a whole range of social issues that affect working-class communities from whatever persuasion in the same way." (Irvine, interview) Regarding the prospects for cross-community cooperation on these common social issues, he sounded cautiously optimistic. However, such cooperation was impossible without first overcoming the obstacles posed by sectarianism and cultural intolerance.

> "I think cooperation will grow around those social needs. But I think the barrier to that reconstruction … will be the issue of sectarianism, and that will be the issue of differing cultural identities. Until the two main communities in Northern Ireland can start to respect, tolerate and understand that there are different traditions within the whole country, until that time we will only be perpetuating the crisis management process that we are involved in currently." (Irvine, interview)

There was also widespread agreement among respondents across the board that Catholic and Protestant working-class communities, particularly those living in interface areas, suffer from similarly high socio-economic deprivation. Indeed, as Brendan Murtagh, a social geographer focussing on the spatial dimension of conflict in the city, indicated, interface areas are the most multiply deprived areas in Northern Ireland.

> "There is a lot of evidence that interface areas are the poorest, and they are getting even poorer. They are much more likely to have higher rates of educational failure. People who are leaving school cannot read or write. Even when there were massive jobs created here for a short period, they were not getting them." (Murtagh, interview)

In his opinion, the reasons for their inability to utilise these new employment opportunities were what "in planning terms is called the spatial mismatch and the skills mismatch." (Murtagh, interview) This means that, on the one hand, the new jobs are not created in interface areas, and, on the other hand, they require a level of skills that people living in these areas do not have. What further exacerbates the problem, especially in North Belfast's interface areas, is the restricted mobility of local residents as a result of the many 'peace walls' and poor public transport links. Thus, even if they met the skills requirements, it would be an arduous journey for them to get to the areas where these jobs are located, such as in the recently developed business and commercial parks in Titanic Quarter close to the city centre. Seen from a wider perspective, the working-class communities of North, West and Inner East Belfast have been affected by a massive lack of private investment. According to Malachy Mulgrew, this was above all due to the ongoing inter-communal violence in the flashpoint interface areas, for "people will not come in and spend money in a warzone." (Mulgrew, interview) As a consequence, the communities are excluded from the economic growth that has taken place in other parts of the city, mainly around the centre, in South Belfast and in suburban areas. As Murtagh pointed out, to some extent they have also deliberately cut themselves off from this "well-connected geography of hope, investment and opportunity". (Murtagh, interview) The reason is that they prefer to pursue their local regeneration projects in accordance with their cultural values and without external interference.

In his view, this uneven spatial economic development in Belfast, a phenomenon which, as also mentioned earlier, he called the "twin speed city" (Murtagh, interview),[183] has had another detrimental impact on Catholic and Protestant working-class communities. Due to the economic upswing during

---

[183] See also the section on 'The Local Communities', p. 148.

the peace process, there has been a considerable number of people from working-class areas who have managed to climb the social ladder. However, those now belonging to the middle classes have left their communities and have moved to new houses in more affluent neighbourhoods. As Murtagh explained, this has aggravated poverty and socio-economic deprivation in working-class communities and has widened the gap between rich and poor across both communities. Thus, the rich-poor divide in society was more important now than the ethno-national divide between the two communities.

"The new formed Catholic middle class and the Protestant middle class have increasingly differentiated themselves by tenure. They've found a way into home ownership. They've found a way into these sites in suburban spaces. What's been left behind is a residualised social housing sector. I mean, this is the point by these neighbourhoods. The level of disadvantage shared by Catholics and Protestants in the Lower Falls and the Lower Shankill – which is the most deprived, the Lower Falls or the Lower Shankill? There is nothing between them. They are both miserable. It is not so much the Green-Orange divide, but increasingly materially, it is now the rich-poor divide, and the rich have segregated themselves off spatially and created these spaces. The cleavage between rich and poor is much more significant than the difference between Orange and Green, between Protestants and Catholics." (Murtagh, interview)

Murtagh also referred to another striking trend that is closely related to the spatial segregation of the wealthier social strata. According to him, there is an "increasingly disconnected middle class" (Murtagh, interview) which has become indifferent towards segregation, poverty, violence and all the other issues affecting working-class communities on both sides of Belfast's interfaces.

Derek Poole had a similar view on the consequences of this development for working-class communities. Yet, rather than looking at the widening gap between the rich and the poor from a society-wide perspective he considered it more important to focus on the increasing class divide within both communities. In particular, the question would arise as to why the Catholic and Protestant working-class communities in Belfast are still plagued by the legacy of the conflict, whilst their middle- and upper-class counterparts have moved on and benefited from the socio-economic and cultural post-conflict development in the city.

"There is intra-community division that goes to the heart of an issue that has to be taken seriously in Northern Ireland, and that is that this conflict is not just rooted in ideological difference, in historical sectarianism. There is an enormous class dimension to this conflict. The class issue has often been underplayed and not explored thoroughly enough in terms of its contribution to not only the Troubles, but its contribution to why those at the forefront of the conflict, mainly working-class communities, are still struggling with this legacy while everyone seeks to move on to a bright new world, a cosmopolitan city and lattes, outside cafes and European identity and culture and whatever all that stuff means." (Poole, interview)

Similarly, regarding the situation in North Belfast, several respondents involved in local community work stressed the growing significance of class divisions and the inequality between rich and poor. Seán Brennan, for instance, pointed to the stark contrast in living conditions between working-class and upper-class people from both communities, which is clearly visible and palpable in certain residential areas in the outskirts of North Belfast, where the poor live in close proximity to the rich.

"So, what we have is an underclass where the people who suffered most from the conflict are still suffering on both sides from high rates of unemployment, poor health, poverty, drugs misuse, alcoholism, teenage pregnancy – all the determinants of a sick society are in these communities. But right beside them are some of the most sought-after residential properties on the island of Ireland. So, you have people earning 80,000 pounds living next to people who are earning 1,000 pounds on benefits. So again it is going back into that whole kind of this conflictual situation of the have and the have-nots." (Brennan, interview)

In this respect, there was mention of further adverse effects of class divisions and inequalities on working-class communities, affecting both their development and the relations between them. According to Jackie Redpath, the exodus of the new middle class from Republican/Nationalist and Loyalist working-class areas has led to a further hardening in positions on both sides.

"What happens is that people who can move out and leave the poorest here. So Catholics that begin to get better off will move out of hard-core Republican/Nationalist areas and leave them even more hard-core. And this is similarly the case in Loyalist communities." (Redpath, interview)

By contrast, Margaret Valentee expressed concern about the growing number of better-educated Catholics leaving the New Lodge area, which has caused a brain drain in the community. As she remarked: "You can see more people who are getting education, who are going to university and getting their degrees and they are moving out. And they are the people we want to stay." (Valente, interview)

So far, the similarities in the socio-economic situation of the working-class communities on both sides have been discussed. There are, however, also salient differences that have been highlighted by respondents across the board. In particular, both sides shared the view that there is a considerable lack of community development in Protestant/Unionist/Loyalist working-class areas. This is exemplified by Derek Poole, who stressed the poor community infrastructure of Loyalist communities, characterised by low social cohesion and a weak sense of neighbourhood and solidarity.

> "One of the great difficulties for the working-class Loyalist communities is what we call weak infrastructure. They tend to be very fractured communities. There's not much social cohesion in many of these communities, that once had a very strong sense of neighbourhood; but since certainly the last decade that sense of solidarity and neighbourliness appears to have fractured considerably." (Poole, interview)

The fragmentation of Protestant working-class communities in North and North-West Belfast began with the advent of the Troubles. Since then, the numbers of Protestants have steadily declined. As John Loughran stated, "In North Belfast, the Protestant population has declined by 30,000 in 30 years. If you look at the 2001 Census and contrast that to the 1971 Census the numbers have left. So, there is a real sense of loss in population." (Loughran, interview) Furthermore, there has been an exodus of the younger generation, which has led to the ageing population in Protestant working-class communities. At the same time, a reverse development has taken place in Catholic working-class communities, whose population is young and growing. According to Seán Brennan, these demographic shifts have become spatially manifest in Protestant/Loyalist and Catholic/Republican interface areas of North and North-West Belfast. As can be clearly seen at many interfaces, there is considerable open space on the Protestant side, whereas the houses on the Catholic side extend right up to the boundary line.

> "You see that in the interfaces, and especially in these marginalised and disadvantaged Loyalist communities, there is an ageing Protestant population on one side, and on the other side there is a young and vibrant Catholic population. If you look at the interfaces, the Catholic houses are filled up right up to the wall, and on the Protestant side there is a gap." (Brennan, interview)

In this regard, Redpath provided insight into the specific situation in the Greater Shankill area. Following on his earlier comments,[184] he explained that the community has undergone a very substantial population decline, partly caused by the Troubles. Yet, the main reason was the process of local redevelopment that was launched by government authorities in the late 1960s. As he pointed out, apart from an ageing population, the Shankill has been affected by enormous educational deficits:

---

[184] See in this section, pp. 167-168.

"In the mid-1960s, the population of the Shankill was 76,000 people. It is now 22,000 people. That was partly the Troubles, but mainly redevelopment that caused that big shift in population. Those left behind tend to be disproportionately elderly. That is a big issue. And the other big issue in the Shankill are the levels of educational underachievement, which are dreadful. And even compared to similar Catholic communities the levels of educational underachievement here in the Shankill are worse than in West Belfast." (Redpath, interview)

In his view, the educational shortcomings were mainly because the community had no tradition of appreciating education. Indeed, historically, people from the Shankill did not need educational qualifications to find employment, because, as Protestants, they automatically had access to jobs and apprenticeships in the traditional industries and trades. Moreover, jobs in these sectors were often passed on within families, through kinship or other beneficial personal connections. In the wake of Belfast's industrial decline, however, these privileges vanished, and the Shankill community was left with no educational resources to fall back on in order to find alternative employment opportunities (Redpath, interview).

Poor education and high unemployment were generally regarded as the major problems affecting Loyalist working-class communities. Tom Winstone, for instance, the director of Northern Ireland Alternatives (NIA), a Loyalist community-based restorative justice scheme, pointed to the difficulty of breaking the generational cycle of educational underachievement. According to him, many young people in Loyalist working-class areas "are still of the mind-set that education isn't for them, simply because some mothers and fathers haven't got the educational attainment to help their children themselves." (Winstone, interview) Regarding the situation in Tigers Bay, Sam Cochrane, a local interface worker, underscored the high level of unemployment, particularly among young people. He went on to emphasise the huge educational deficits in the area: "there was a survey done, and only 4.5 % of the children that left school last year in Tigers Bay left with qualifications. They reckon about 16% of the kids in Tigers Bay can't read or write." (Cochrane, interview)[185]

There was considerable congruence in the perceptions of respondents from Protestant/Loyalist and Catholic/Republican backgrounds concerning the issues and state of community development on the respective other side. Re-

---

[185] However, these figures were not verifiable, as the survey to which they refer could not be found despite extensive online research.

spondents agreed that both communities have evolved in opposite directions. As Billy Hutchinson, a Loyalist ex-combatant, community worker and leading member of the PUP, put it bluntly: "you can see the trends, Catholics were on the up and Protestants were on the down." (Hutchinson, interview) This was confirmed by his former paramilitary associate Syd Trotter, who held the opinion that "the whole dynamics of change have served the Nationalist-Republican community better." (Trotter, interview) In Hutchinson's view, whilst Protestant working-class communities were ageing and dwindling both in terms of numbers and skills, "the opposite was happening on the Catholic side, where you had a young, vibrant community, big families, and high levels of or high value in education." (Hutchinson, interview) The consequence was a rapidly growing Catholic middle class, which, he thought, evoked the feeling among working-class Protestants that "they have got everything and we have got nothing." (Hutchinson, interview) This, in turn, reinforced Protestants' siege mentality and need for physical segregation from their Catholic neighbours.

Lee Morgan, by contrast, provided a somewhat different perspective from a Catholic/Republican point of view on the situation in Protestant/Loyalist working-class communities. He acknowledged that the loss of employment privileges has exacerbated unemployment and poverty in Protestant/Loyalist areas. Yet, this has also created a sense of deprivation among them which is shared by Catholic/Republican working-class communities and hence, as he suggested, should be jointly addressed.

> "I think people now in the Loyalist areas are hit worse than they were before, because that tradition of just walking into a job is over now. And they know now how it feels to be long-time unemployed and to be on benefits. And I think that is a commonality that we should be looking into." (Morgan, interview)

Margaret Valente held a similar view. In addition, she pointed out that Catholic communities were far more advanced in community development than Protestant ones: "Unemployment is really high now in the Protestant community and they don't have the same community infrastructure as we have, because we have been working at it longer." (Valente, interview) As she explained, Catholic working-class communities have developed a strong tradition of community education and capacity-building. This was out of necessity, for unlike their Protestant counterparts, they never received support from the state. Moreover, she criticised Protestants for their inertia in seizing the funding opportunities available and developing their communities on their own.

> "Since we could never rely on the government for anything, we started a commu-
> nity development process and education in our areas. That was locally, in local
> houses or local churches. … The community was good in local fund-raising for our
> projects and programmes, and local people were doing that for a long, long time.
> When the ceasefires came about, the Protestant community started fund-raising.
> They were far behind us. So they have been brought up to levels. And they are still
> saying 'we should get better infrastructure in our areas', the same infrastructure
> that we have. But we cannot do it for them. They have to do it by themselves."
> (Valente, interview)

According to Umberto Scappaticci, the situation was similar in West Belfast. Loyalist working-class communities lagged behind in terms of community development. In his opinion, the main reason for this was that, until recently, many local people in Loyalist areas were enmeshed in paramilitary
drug racketeering, whilst Republicans kept the focus on improving the infrastructure and capacities of their communities. Yet, as he noted, there has been
a change in Loyalist attitudes, thus leading to an increase in inter-community
contacts. This proved to be beneficial to them, because they are thus able to
gain from Republican experiences in community development (Scappaticci,
interview).

Last but not least, a key issue in working-class communities remains to be
addressed, and this concerns housing. In the interviews, it became apparent
that housing was a particular bone of contention between respondents from
Catholic/Nationalist/Republican   and   Protestant/Unionist/Loyalist   backgrounds. Despite their profound disagreement, there was, however, consensus
in one respect, namely that the issue of housing is inextricably linked to the
equally contentious issue of territoriality. On the Protestant side, a typical
view was expressed by Mervyn Gibson. He was strongly opposed to an expansion of Catholic housing into Loyalist areas, because this would mean a
double assault on the Unionist community. Given the lack of tolerance by
Nationalists/Republicans for Unionist culture, a new interface would be inevitable. For the Unionist community, this would entail both a loss of territory
and a loss of the opportunity to express its cultural traditions and beliefs. Consequently, in his opinion, establishing a mixed housing environment would
only be possible, if Nationalists/Republicans proved their unconditional acceptance and proper respect for the culture and identity of the Unionist community.

> "If Roman Catholic housing is extended into Loyalist areas, what is going to be af-
> fected? Our traditions, our parades, our flag flying: things that we see as traditional
> parts of our celebrating of who we are and what we are. Because there is no tolera-

tion within Nationalism for those things. Not none, but there is little toleration. So … if those characteristic boundaries change, then there is an encroachment on the Unionist community. It can no longer celebrate its culture along that new interface. Because it's going to create a new interface. It's not going to be a mixed housing estate at this stage in the game. And this is the difficulty: until there is proper respect by Republicans for Unionist culture and acceptance of who we are and what we want to celebrate, and unless they stop trying to police our culture and stop trying to tell us what our culture should be, I think you are going to get that territoriality issue." (Gibson, interview)

Following a similar rationale, Winston Irvine also emphasised the territorial dimension of the housing issue. He disputed that Nationalist/Republican communities were in greater need of housing than Loyalist ones. Instead, he asserted, the ulterior motive behind their housing demands was to expel the Protestant/Loyalist residents from the area, if necessary by force.

"The issue of housing is a contentious one. I don't buy into the position that there is a greater need for housing within Nationalist/Republican areas than there would be in Loyalist areas. I think the contention around the issue of housing is linked directly to territoriality. I mean, I can take you to an entire Protestant community, which had to move out because of Republican violence and intimidation. And this is not a biased opinion that I hold. I can show you factually exactly what I mean and what I'm talking about. The issue of housing is a very sensitive one due to the cleansing almost of Protestants from certain areas in Belfast." (Irvine, interview)

Concerning the issue of mixed housing, respondents from a Protestant/ Loyalist working-class background were more reluctant to live in a neighbourhood with Catholics. Syd Trotter, for instance, had major reservations, because this would restrict his freedom of cultural expression and, vice versa, also that of the Catholic neighbours.

"If you would ask me, and this might surprise you, 'wouldn't you like to live beside Roman Catholics?' my answer would be: I wouldn't know, but I would have major concerns. I express my culture every year when I put my flag out. And I wouldn't want them to tell me when I can put it up or down. Likewise, they wouldn't like me to tell them when they can put their flag up and take it down, when they have their celebrations. …I'm happy where I live. My housing estate is hundred percent Protestant." (Trotter, interview)

On the Catholic/Republican side, a typical point of view was presented by Margaret Valente. According to her, the increase in local population has created an urgent need for housing in the Catholic working-class communities of North Belfast. There is a lack of residential space in Catholic areas. By contrast, such space lies empty in Protestant working-class areas due to local population loss. However, as she remarked, Catholics cannot move into these areas, because Protestants fiercely oppose sharing their neighbourhood with them. Moreover, she shared Gibson's view that at that stage the allocation of houses in Protestant areas to Catholics would create a new interface. This, she stressed, would be in nobody's interest.

> "The big issue that is at stake is housing. In North Belfast, the Catholic community has a younger population and it is a bigger population. In the Protestant community, the population is older and it's dwindling. There are a lot of young people who just moved out. But they are saying housing is a no-go. They don't want new houses to be built that would create a shared space, because they just don't want Catholics living in their area. … And I can see that if Catholics get the houses it will create a new interface. Which nobody wants, it's not the solution." (Valente, interview)

Likewise, Lee Morgan pointed to the huge demand for social housing in Catholic working-class areas of North Belfast, especially in Ardoyne, the New Lodge and Cliftonville, which by far exceeded the social housing need in neighbouring Protestant areas. Nevertheless, in his view, Catholic and Protestant working-class communities also shared a commonality in that they suffered equally from poor housing conditions.

> "I still think, and it is still fairly prevalent, the biggest waiting list for social housing in North Belfast is in areas like Ardoyne, the New Lodge and Cliftonville, and the waiting lists are maybe half that in all Protestant working-class areas like the Shankill Road. But there is a similarity in the fact that working-class people generally were given poor housing over the years or put on the back banner." (Morgan, interview)

The gravity of the housing issue in North Belfast was also stressed by John Loughran. In his opinion, the housing dispute was fundamental proof of the deep-rootedness and intractability of the wider encompassing conflict between the two communities.

> "For me the housing issue is the touchstone issue that our conflict is as yet not resolved. So, with all the disaffection, all the yearnings and needs, all the hopes and aspirations are contested in that issue, because it has been reduced to a sectarian issue rather than an issue around the right to housing." (Loughran, interview)

The situation between Suffolk and Lenadoon was a remarkable exception to the general lack of understanding and intransigence on housing between the communities. As Maria Bannon reported, the Protestant community of Suffolk was worried that Catholics from Lenadoon would lay territorial claims to their estate. Yet, as a result of the dialogue on contentious issues, their concerns were dispelled, and both communities agreed that Catholics would only move in with the consent of the Protestant residents.

"People in Suffolk had felt that people in Lenadoon because of the density of population and the green spaces in Suffolk were looking to take their land to build housing on it, and, in a shot, they would be over. And they were very surprised when people from Lenadoon said, 'You know we would not want that without your agreement. We would not want to just parachute in and disrupt your community. We would only ever do that if you were agreeable to let us come and do that. You know, that was on your terms.' So even that statement was shocking for people from Suffolk, who always had the perception that people from Lenadoon just want to come and steal their land, or whatever. But again, I think it is because we are so far down the dialogue process that those conversations … could even take place, and that the source of the people here saying them is held as trustworthy from the people hearing the message." (Bannon, interview)

So far, however, the residents of Suffolk have remained opposed to building mixed housing on the green spaces of their estate. According to Bannon, there is still a sense of insecurity in the local Protestant community due to its small size and enclave nature. Hence, the Protestant residents feel that the green spaces are needed as a safety buffer to protect them from Catholic incursions. (Bannon, interview)

In a similar vein to respondents from both sides, experts on community relations expressed the view that the controversy over housing boiled down to the issue of territory. As Neil Jarman aptly summed up the crux of the matter:

"There is a lot of available housing stock within Protestant areas. But you can't mix the two, because it is not just about housing, it is about control of territory. And therefore you can't put Catholics in Protestant housing, because the whole nature of the territory would change, and it would change from Protestant to Catholic." (Jarman, interview)

It seems that with the row over Brexit and the Irish border this issue of territory might boil up again. There are signs of growing uncertainty and concern among interface residents that community relations could deteriorate and the 'peace walls' could endure, with those already dismantled being re-erected and new ones being built. Thus, Rab McCallum of NBIN, who is involved in the 'peace walls' removal process, recently described the concern among interface residents and community workers in North Belfast in a newspaper interview as follows:

"There is that uncertainty [around Brexit], and though it isn't something people talk about all the time, it does seem to be seen through identity more than economics. It just raises the question, are we going to take a step backwards rather than a step forwards? It has in some ways sectarianised things again. People are worried about it economically, but also politically. It creates an unease." (McCallum, cited in Savage 2018)

RECAP: COMMUNITY ISSUES AND RELATIONS ON THE GROUND

The many diverse views expressed by people from different socio-economic, ethnic and cultural backgrounds, generations and gender demonstrate that similarities exist despite all the discrepancies. Many respondents from Catholic and Protestant backgrounds vividly recalled their experiences during the Troubles. As indicated by those who grew up in pre-conflict Northern Ireland in the 1950s and 1960s, the patterns of segregation between Protestant/Unionist/Loyalist and Catholic/Nationalist/Republican working-class communities were already in place long before the outbreak of the Troubles. Within both communities, ethno-national sentiments and sectarian prejudices were deeply rooted, dating back to the long-standing divide between them. Children growing up in such an environment learned and often adopted the sectarian preconceptions of the community, which prevented them from developing positive attitudes towards their neighbours from the 'other' side. Overall, inter-community contact was very limited at that time, and when it occurred, it was fraught with tension and violence. Concerning the internal fabric of the communities, there was a strong sense of social cohesion and group affiliation. One contributing factor to their close-knit character was the dire socio-economic situation, whilst another was the growing fear and sense of being threatened by the 'other' community.

With the outbreak of the Troubles, the living conditions of Catholic and Protestant working-class communities deteriorated dramatically together with the relations between them. The escalating violence loomed large in the memories of many respondents from both sides. Some became victims themselves of the forced evictions that took place on a tremendous scale in Catholic and Protestant working-class areas in Belfast and, to a lesser extent, also in Derry/Londonderry. These population movements reinforced the segregation between and homogenisation of the communities. The ongoing violence and militarisation in working-class areas of North and West Belfast during the early years of the Troubles fuelled feelings of fear and insecurity among local residents. Catholics/Nationalists/Republicans, particularly in the Ardoyne and New Lodge areas, felt under occupation due to the strong presence of the British Army and state security forces and the heightened level of Loyalist paramilitary activity. By contrast, the siege mentality of being under constant attack by militant Republicans became entrenched in Protestant/Unionist/Loyalist working-class areas such as the Greater Shankill, Tigers Bay and

Suffolk. In response, there was an increased need for protection and defence against aggression from the 'other' side. In part, this purpose was served by the numerous 'peace walls' and security barriers that were erected by the British Army in interface areas between Catholic and Protestant neighbourhoods. Alongside the psychological obstacles caused by fear and insecurity, these interface barriers severely restricted people's mobility in the city. In the absence of trusted security forces, the task of providing order and protection in Catholic and Protestant working-class areas was increasingly assumed by Republican and Loyalist paramilitary groups. Yet, their role of informal community policing also drew local criticism for their use of excessive modes of punishment.

The Troubles had a decisive impact on the life trajectories of many respondents across the communal divide. They all encountered the violence of the conflict during their youth or early adulthood, either through personal threat, personal loss, or by witnessing violent incidents. This caused them to make life-changing decisions at a young age, which dispatched them in opposite directions. While some chose to become involved in the armed conflict, others, though to a lesser extent, decided to dedicate themselves to community work and peacebuilding. The common denominator of most of those joining Republican or Loyalist paramilitary forces was their experience of growing up in highly segregated and deprived working-class areas that were marked by an atmosphere of sectarianism and political radicalisation. All of them lacked positive contact with people from the 'other' community. Indeed, such contact occurred for the first time during their imprisonment, during which they engaged in discussions with their paramilitary adversaries. These discussions led to more tolerance and respect for the 'other' side's perspective, and, moreover, promoted mutual understanding of common working-class issues. While in prison, they went through a personal transformation, which made them abandon their militancy and, upon release, become involved in community development and interface work, many also on a cross-community basis. However, notwithstanding their support for the peace process, they did not feel repentant about their past misdeeds and remained staunch in their political beliefs and affiliations.

By contrast, the respondents who decided to become community workers and peace activists during the early Troubles had more diverse backgrounds. Those on the Catholic side had quite an unusual upbringing, given the tense circumstances of the time. Although growing up in a traditional setting with Irish family values and Republican socialist beliefs, they were raised in an anti-sectarian manner and learned to display tolerance and respect for Protestants. In their youth, they were introduced to the Civil Rights Movement, which left an indelible impression on them. The peaceful forms of protest for equal rights and for better living conditions of the Catholic working-class were particularly appealing. Those on the Protestant side had a more typical childhood. They were brought up in traditional Protestant families with quite strong religious beliefs. Like their Catholic counterparts, they grew up in segregated neighbourhoods, but they had a greater lack of contact to the 'other' side. Similarly, the deteriorating living conditions in the 1960s were a matter of serious concern to them. As indicated in the responses, both sides perceived the Troubles as a sea change causing tremendous damage to the community fabric and to community relations. Thus, they were united in their response to act. Others were driven by a similar motivation. At first, the community groups that emerged in the early days of the conflict were primarily concerned with taking care of their own communities. This was mainly because of the increasing absence of state provision of vital services to working-class communities, especially in Catholic areas. The necessity of self-help generated a spirit of grassroots activism within working-class communities that gradually evolved into efforts of cross-community collaboration on dealing with violence and other joint non-contentious issues in several interface areas across Belfast.

In this respect, a prime example of successful cooperation is the experience made by the comparatively large Catholic/Nationalist/Republican community of Lenadoon and the small Protestant/Unionist/Loyalist community of Suffolk in Outer West Belfast. It shows how community groups from both sides have succeeded in setting aside divisions and joining forces in the Suffolk-Lenadoon Interface Group (SLIG). As a result, they have managed substantially to reduce intercommunal violence and regenerate the interface area economically. Moreover, they have also made some progress in tackling the issue of divisive cultural practices, particularly regarding the Loyalist parading and bonfire tradition. This has been possible because of several factors: firstly, the commitment, persistence and courage of grassroots community and peace activists on both sides to engage in convincing local residents of the benefits of cooperation; secondly, the common recognition of the necessity to work together on resolving interface issues of mutual concern; thirdly, the agreement to cooperate in SLIG on a strictly equal basis, irrespective of the great disparity in community size; fourthly, the establishment of participatory modes of decision-making, aiming at involving all sections of both communities; and fifthly, the development of a community-sensitive approach to tackling issues regarded as contentious by local residents. In addition, cooperation was facilitated by the involvement of a cross-community worker from outside the area, which mitigated tensions and enmities between the communities. Nevertheless, although many of SLIG's projects have come to fruition, several outstanding issues have so far proven to be too controversial to be addressed.

In the working-class areas of North and North-West Belfast more obstacles had to be mastered before cross-community cooperation became possible. When the first initiatives emerged during the peace process in the mid-1990s, community relations were characterised by deep-seated divisions and antagonisms caused by local internecine strife during the Troubles. These were manifested in a profound lack of mutual understanding and inherent distrust, suspicion, insecurity and fear vis-à-vis the 'other' side of the communal divide. The situation was complicated by the fragmented nature of space, resembling a patchwork quilt of small Catholic/Nationalist/Republican and Protestant/Unionist/Loyalist working-class neighbourhoods segregated by numerous interface barriers. In the early days of collaboration, the community workers and groups were faced with fierce sectarian interface violence unleashed first by the Drumcree parades dispute and then by the Holy Cross conflict. These incidents provided them with the motivation to increase cross-community efforts to respond effectively to sectarian tensions and violence in contentious interface areas. Eventually, they have managed to cope with this task, not least due to three contributory factors: firstly, the mobile phone networks connecting community workers across interfaces that have gradually expanded into more comprehensive interface networks, like the North Belfast Interface Network (NBIN); secondly, the commitment and engagement of many former Republican and Loyalist combatants in cross-community interface work; and, thirdly, the collaboration with local residents' groups, especially on parading issues. In general, despite the success of cooperation in terms of containing interface violence, intercommunal tensions have continued to mount around local Orange Order parades and other contentious incidents, such as the Loyalist flags protest in the Ardoyne area. What is more, attempts to tackle other issues impairing community life and relations have thus far failed to generate tangible benefits.

This leads to the questions: What issues still affect the living conditions in both Catholic/Nationalist/Republican and Protestant/Unionist/Loyalist working-class communities? What themes continue to constitute bones of contention, thus perpetuating the divide between them, and are there any signs of improvement in their relationship?

To expand on the first question: As could be gathered from the responses, the disadvantaged socio-economic position of the Catholic working class was already entrenched in the decade preceding the Troubles. At the onset of the armed conflict, Catholic working-class areas became more isolated and had to draw on their own scarce resources owing to the lack of support from the state. The situation became particularly critical in Ardoyne and the New Lodge, which suffered from an acute shortage of affordable homes, poor housing conditions and widespread unemployment. Local respondents expressed their perception of being discriminated in housing and employment. They attributed their disadvantaged employment position in part to Protestant prejudices about Catholics having deficient work ethics. In Protestant working-class communities socio-economic deprivation was also on the rise at the time. The industrial decline in the city was felt more acutely by them, as they had enjoyed prior privileged access to jobs in the traditional industries and trades. In particular, the Greater Shankill experienced a steep increase in local unemployment. Moreover, community life was disrupted by the urban redevelopment of the area, which, along with the Troubles, caused a profound demographic shift in the local population. What has been left is a dwindling and ageing community with major shortcomings in educational attainment. To go further, this trend has also been true of other Protestant working-class areas in North Belfast and in Derry/Londonderry. On the Catholic side, the opposite has taken place. As a result, Catholic working-class communities have a younger and growing population and show better educational performance.

The disparate development of the communities has also been reflected in their social fabric in other ways, which fits in with the second related question concerning the state of community relations and divisions. Specifically in North and North-West Belfast, Protestant/Unionist/Loyalist working-class communities have become increasingly fractured and disconnected, whereas their Catholic/Nationalist/Republican counterparts still evince a relatively strong cohesion with a far more advanced stage of community development. On the Protestant side, this has created a sense of loss and retreat, contributing to their siege mentality. In this respect, the perception was expressed that all the economic gains of the peace process accrued to the Catholic side. Catholics, by contrast, have experienced a sense of expansion and have become more self-assured and assertive in articulating their demands and perspectives. Some have maintained that the weak infrastructure and bleak living conditions of Protestant working-class communities were not least the results of their failure to seize the opportunities given to them.

Accordingly, positions have hardened, and there is reluctance to compromise on issues of crucial interest to both sides. This can be seen most clearly in two areas, namely in the Protestant/Unionist/Loyalist parading tradition and in the Catholic/Nationalist/Republican demands for housing, which are focussed mainly on the interface areas between the communities. As shown in the responses, both have been identified as the major sources of intercommunal discord as well as the main triggers of interface violence. The communities living along the flashpoint interfaces in North and North-West Belfast have borne the brunt of the conflicts over contentious parades and housing. There was a wide gulf in views on these issues between respondents from Protestant/Unionist/Loyalist and Catholic/Nationalist/Republican ones. Regarding parading, Unionists/Loyalists accused Nationalists/Republicans of being intolerant and disrespectful towards their culture and of obstructing their freedom to march along the interfaces, which they regarded as shared community spaces. In a similar vein, it was claimed that the Catholic demands for housing in adjoining Protestant neighbourhoods were a cultural assault and ultimately intended to expel them from the area. Conversely, Nationalists/Republicans reproached Unionists/Loyalists and especially the Orange Order for their intransigence in insisting on provocative marching routes, which demonstrated their sectarian, triumphalist and supremacist attitudes. Likewise, Catholics castigated the fierce opposition of Protestant residents towards mixed housing development on their estates as an indication of their hostility and antagonism. Thus, both conflicts essentially boil down to the issues of territoriality and insecurity, which in turn reinforce the need for protection in the form of interface barrier construction.

Notwithstanding the necessity of the 'peace walls' for providing security, their damaging impact on the communities has also been emphasised by respondents across the board. On the physical level, the walls obstruct contact between neighbours on both sides of the interface. This impedes the development of meaningful social interactions that would help to reduce intercommunal fear and prejudice. More recently, the walls have become a magnet for local disenfranchised working-class youth who have become increasingly involved in rioting and anti-social behaviour at the interfaces. Their sense of alienation and disaffection about the lack of a peace dividend has been exploited by dissident paramilitary groups for the latter's ends of stirring up violence and destabilising the peace process.

Despite the polarisation in views and attitudes, both sides acknowledged facing similar socio-economic issues and levels of deprivation. Moreover, they shared their concern about the increasing class inequalities and the gap between the rich and the poor that cut across the communal divide. Specifically, the trend of an increasing number of middle-class people to segregate themselves both spatially and emotionally from the working-class had detrimental effects on working-class communities. In particular, this had led to a brain drain and has contributed to a growing radicalisation with hardliners gaining momentum in the Loyalist and Republican neighbourhoods of North and North-West Belfast. As a corollary, criminal activity of paramilitaries has been on the rise in the area. Moreover, the interface communities and the wider working-class communities in which they live have become increasingly disconnected from the economic development of the city. Yet again, this was compounded by the numerous 'peace walls', which severely restricted the mobility of local residents, thus physically severing them from the city's employment centres. A further aggravating circumstance was the discouragement of private investment and business set-ups. This lack of economic activity, in turn, reinforces the cycle of interface violence. As a consequence of all these adverse developments, working-class communities, especially those in flashpoint interface areas, have experienced a downward spiral of socio-economic disadvantage, marginalisation, exclusion and violence.

Ultimately, there was consensus among respondents that the dilemma remains as to how to remove the 'peace walls'. In light of the current uncertainty and fear caused by Brexit and the Irish border issue this has become an even more daunting challenge. Three enabling conditions were identified: establishing the requisite intercommunal trust and security, facilitating capacity-building within the communities, and promoting economic regeneration of the interfaces. Given the depth of the divide, both sides were unanimous concerning the magnitude of the tasks to be faced. As already indicated, these tasks do not only pertain to socio-economic and cultural issues, but likewise concern political matters, such as community relations policies and political representation of working-class interests. After all, community divisions have also manifested in the political sphere, most notably through opposing political ideologies of Nationalism/Republicanism and Unionism/Loyalism. How these and other relevant issues have affected the living conditions of working-class communities and the relations between them will be examined in the following section, again mainly from the perspective of the interview respondents.

COMMUNITIES, POLITICS AND POWER RELATIONS: DIVISIVE AND INTEGRATIVE FORCES

The findings so far might suggest that the divide between Catholic and Protestant working-class communities is so deep that it causes, as Shirlow puts it, "a desire to remain uncontaminated by the presence of the ethno-sectarian 'other'." (Shirlow 2006: 226). This quote refers to the rather bizarre fact that there is a wall to keep the two communities divided even after death. The wall is located underground within Belfast City Cemetery to segregate the Catholic from the Protestant deceased.[186] Shirlow further backs up his claim by pointing to the more recent sectarian strife over the demarcation of Protestant and Catholic graves at Carnmoney Cemetery on the periphery of North Belfast (Shirlow 2006: 226; cf. McKay 2006, Vincent 2009).

Yet, notwithstanding the intensity of intercommunal tensions and divisions, there are also signs of rapprochement. The previous section showed that there is a convergence in the problems arising from socio-economic deprivation and interface violence, problems to be faced by Protestant and Catholic working-class communities alike, albeit to different degrees. Despite the awareness among respondents from both sides as to the nature of the problems, there was, however, profound disagreement concerning the means to be employed to tackle them. As has become apparent, this discord applies, above all, to the issues of Catholic/Nationalist/Republican housing demands and the Protestant/Unionist/Loyalist parading tradition. Both issues have been major causes of sectarian tensions and violence, casting dark shadows over community relations and severely impeding cooperation on matters of mutual interest. This has been especially true in the flashpoint interface areas of North and

---

[186] The underground wall, which is almost three metres high, running for a considerable distance, has been in place since the opening of Belfast City Cemetery in 1869. The separation of the Catholic and Protestant sections of the cemetery was established not least on the request of the Catholic Church, due to their specific notion of consecrated ground. It proved, however, unnecessary, since Catholics were not buried in the cemetery until a century later, and even then their graves were placed in different locations. Instead, Catholics have usually been buried in Milltown Cemetery, which is located in nearby Andersonstown, West Belfast (Di Cintio 2013: 270, Hartley 2010 & 2014).

North-West Belfast, where, essentially, cross-community cooperation has so far been limited to local conflict containment.

On the whole, the antagonism between the communities has obviously much to do with feelings of fear, insecurity and hostility that still shape their attitudes towards one another. However, as the preceding already indicates, there is also a significant political dimension. In this respect, several themes were briefly mentioned by respondents, touching on matters of the political representation of working-class interests, their perceptions and attitudes towards political actors, the peace agreement and policy-making on socio-economic and community relations issues, their involvement in the political process as well as their national and political affiliations, ideologies and aspirations. These matters will be focused on in the following analysis and elucidated against the backdrop of their influence on Catholic and Protestant working-class communities. As with the previous analysis, a bottom-up perspective will be used, exploring the themes and issues as seen and perceived by interview respondents. Likewise, empirical studies and theoretical approaches will be consulted for additional information and for the interpretation of the interview results. Finally, again, the cross-cutting theme is the issue of community relations, expressed in the overall guiding question of the analysis: How are the rifts between the communities manifested in the political domain?

Some explanatory remarks would seem appropriate to facilitate understanding of the specific course and content of the enquiry. Concerning the theme of political representation, a question of particular interest is whether and to what extent the respondents felt that working-class interests were represented by the political parties. Moreover, were any politicians mentioned, and if so, in what context? Arguably, Gramci's approach to hegemony, as discussed in the chapter on theory,[187] proves useful and insightful in analysing this issue. It should be noted, however, that his theory will be used in an eclectic manner, always bearing in mind not to distort its original meaning. Specifically, Antonio Gramsci's idea of 'organic intellectuals' will be borrowed for the purpose of interpreting and evaluating certain results. Above all, it will reveal whether any politicians were singled out who might be regarded as 'organic intellectuals' in a Gramscian sense. In essence, this means shaping

---

[187] See also the section in Chapter 2 on 'Hegemonic Relations of Power and Governance', pp. 49-54.

the opinions and attitudes of local working-class people in such a way to help push for the effective political representation of their interests across the ethno-national community divide. By extension, this could ultimately also herald a change in political power structure. It will, conversely, also shed light on the issue as to whether political actors were identified who obstructed the emergence of cross-community working-class politics. If so, what was their perceived motivation? To what extent were they driven by the ulterior motives of retaining power? In Gramscian terminology, such actors might be termed 'reactionary forces'. Another issue also requires further explanation, i.e. the use of political actors in the context of this analysis. Given the highly politicised atmosphere prevailing throughout the conflict, a broad spectrum of political actors may fall into this category. In particular, they include the Northern Irish political parties, the British Government and the British Army, the Irish Government, the paramilitary groups and the statutory agencies that provide vital services to local communities in Northern Ireland, such as the Housing Executive (NIHE) and the police (RUC, later PSNI).

POLITICAL PERCEPTIONS, ATTITUDES AND IDEOLOGIES

To start with, let us look back and summarise in a nutshell what the respondents already mentioned about their perceptions of the roles and involvement of political actors in the conflict and peace process. In their recollections the paramilitary groups featured prominently. Aside from condemnations and reproaches levelled at the respective other paramilitaries for their callous violence during the Troubles, criticism was also uttered of their brutal punishment regime within the communities. There were also others, however, who appreciated the paramilitaries for performing security and policing tasks in working-class areas. Respondents from both sides adopted a critical stance towards the British state. More severe censure came, of course, from the Catholic side, and, within it, from Republican respondents especially. They accused not only the state of partisanship and discrimination but, beyond that, its security forces of excessive violence against their community. The British Army and the British Government, for instance, were reproached for complicity in the fatal shootings on Bloody Sunday. In a similar vein, the RUC was castigated for the brutality of their police operations during the civil rights marches. Protestant and, in particular, Loyalist respondents, although generally justifying the state's actions during the Troubles, also criticised the security forces, yet for different reasons. In the main, their criticism centred on the deficiencies of the RUC and the British Army in providing policing and security to Protestant/Unionist/Loyalist working-class communities. A shift in perception occurred during the peace process and especially in the aftermath of the Good Friday/Belfast Agreement, when cross-community work gained momentum. The role of the paramilitaries was then perceived with ambivalence. On the one hand, the commitment of ex-combatants to local peacebuilding at contentious interfaces was commonly acknowledged, particularly in North and North-West Belfast. Yet, on the other hand, severe criticism was directed against dissident paramilitary factions for attempting to disrupt the peace process, above all by inciting local youth to interface violence. Similarly, the performance of the police, who underwent extensive reform also involving a name change to PSNI, was viewed equivocally. Whilst some respondents involved in interface work mentioned their positive experiences of collaboration with the PSNI, dissenting voices were also raised, pointing to the role of the police in contributing towards heightened intercommunal tension. On the whole, there were signs that many of the traditional antagonistic images of political actors still persisted, but there were also indications of emergent reconciliation.

Up to now, this has only been a jigsaw overview. A more detailed analysis is to follow, which will focus not only on the respondents' perceptions of the part and performance of political actors, but also on their attitudes towards political aspects of the Troubles, the peace process, the Agreement and subsequent governance arrangements and policies. Moreover, this will also touch on the question as to how their perceptions were influenced by nationalist political ideologies.

As to how the British Army was perceived by Catholic/Nationalist/Republican working-class communities in the Troubles, a revealing detail was provided by Dympna McGlade. In recalling her childhood in the Bone, she pointed out that the arrival of the Army was initially welcomed in the community because they expected protection. Yet, her Republican family was an exception, as she was told by her father to meet the soldiers with a cautious and detached attitude, aware that the Army was not an ally of Catholics. For, despite all outward friendliness, she suspected and indeed suggested that the British Army was taking sides in the conflict.

"On a personal level, my father had given to me his political understanding. When the British Army arrived, the advice he gave to me as a girl: He said, 'Look, the British Army is here. They are not your friend. But just ignore them completely. Don't shout at them, or don't smile at them, just ignore them. Pretend they are not here.' He had been involved for a long time, and he had seen many things, and he said, 'You know, people will welcome them, but it will be a myth. But it won't be long before there's a fallout.' So, you just keep yourself removed from it. Which for me, it was very difficult. We were different, because people wouldn't have been as politically astute. They were so glad for protection. We were five small streets that had been under siege for a long time. I remember being under the table and gun battles going on outside. And people being evacuated out to … a big community centre where old people and young families went up to stay there for safety, like refugees almost, you know. … So people in the area were glad. My father said, 'Step back and realise that as a Republican you recognise them as the enemy state, the occupation forces.' So I did that. And kids were all down chatting to them. And they were giving them a chewing gum. They had an English accent, some of them were black. So it was a big intrigue. But I was on the outside, because my father gave me advice not to get involved in this." (McGlade, interview)

Eamonn Deane, who grew up in the Bogside area in the 1950s and 1960s, confirmed that vulnerable Catholic/Nationalist/Republican communities welcomed the arrival of the British troops. In his opinion, they thought that by deploying soldiers, the British Government for the first time was assuming responsibility for local affairs and protecting them against attacks by the RUC and B-Specials. Until then, Northern Ireland had been treated as a British colony, left to its own devices and ruled by a small Unionist elite.

"The people in what became known as 'Free Derry' and the people in West Belfast welcomed the British Army, because, to them, for the first time, since the beginning of the state the British Government was actually paying attention to what was happening here, and taking responsibility for what was happening here, rather than leave it in the hands of an elite group of Unionists. So this is classic colonialism." (Deane, interview)[188]

The Catholic perception of the British Army changed quickly. As Séan Brennan pointed out, the Army played a significant role in the enforced popu-

---

[188] 'Free Derry', which took its name from a sign painted on a wall saying, "You are now entering Free Derry", was a self-proclaimed autonomous Catholic/Nationalist/Republican area in Derry/Londonderry, including the Bogside and surrounding neighbourhoods. It emerged in January 1969, when local residents and community activists began to build barricades to prevent the RUC and other state security forces from entering. 'Free Derry' was the first 'no-go' area, with others being subsequently established in Catholic/Nationalist/Republican areas in Belfast. In particular, it had its own local police that worked independently of Republican paramilitaries. At the end of July 1972, British troops equipped with armoured vehicles and bulldozers dismantled the barricades and occupied the area. This was part of the so-called 'Operation Motorman', which aimed to recapture the 'no-go' areas in Northern Ireland. With around 12,000 troops it proved to be the biggest British military operation since the Suez crisis of 1956 (Monaghan 2002: 6, O'Dochartaigh 1997).

lation movements of Catholics and Protestants during the early Troubles. Their military tactics operated in tandem with British government policy in that both were aimed at segregating the communities so as to control the Catholic ones. This was particularly true of Catholic working-class areas in North Belfast. As he explained,

"At that stage, we had all been kind of crawled into specific geographical areas. And that was a strategic programme by the British Army to get Catholics into areas and Protestants into areas. The British Government did not want mixed communities. They did not want good relations at that time. ... Especially in North Belfast, what the British Army did not want was Catholic housing estates at the back of them. So, in many regards British government policy and British Army tactics were responsible for the migration of Catholics from places like Rathcoole." (Brennan, interview)[189]

Concerning the reasons for the outbreak of the Troubles, some respondents from a Protestant/Unionist/Loyalist background expressed the view that they were sparked off by militant Republicans taking over the Civil Rights Movement to incite people from the Catholic/Nationalist community to street violence. This then turned the Troubles into a conflict over essentially constitutional aspirations, thus reinforcing the national divide between the communities. As William Moore remarked:

"There was the growth of the Civil Rights Movement. The belief among working-class Protestants was that the Civil Rights Movement was fanned or created, or whatever word you want to use, by militant Republicans. And that the IRA was probably behind them, forcing Nationalists and Catholics into street violence. So that it would upset the union between Northern Ireland and Great Britain. So it became something of Republicans wanting a United Ireland and Unionists wanting to remain part of Great Britain." (Moore, interview)

The perspective given by some respondents from the Catholic/Nationalist/Republican side was the opposite. Deane utterly rejected the allegation that the Civil Rights Movement had been hijacked by militant Republicans. On the contrary, in his view, the upsurge of Republicanism was the result of the repressive response of the state and of Loyalism to the Civil Rights Move-

---

[189] Rathcoole is a housing estate in Newtownabbey, in northern suburban Belfast. It was built in the early 1950s to provide housing for Catholics and Protestants who were displaced due to the demolition and redevelopment of working-class neighbourhoods in the inner-city areas of Belfast. As a consequence, it became the largest housing estate in Northern Ireland. The intimidation of Catholics in the early years of the Troubles led to their exodus, which turned Rathcoole into a segregated Protestant working-class estate and Loyalist stronghold (Darby & Morris 1974: 34-38, Fleming 2015).

ment's demands for equal rights and for equality of esteem. After all, the legitimacy of what he called the 'statelet' of Northern Ireland had always depended on the presence of Republicanism.

> "That's just straightforward nonsense. It was the reaction of the state and of Loyalism that created Republicanism. The state, I mean this 'statelet' of Northern Ireland has always needed Republicanism to justify its own existence. So, you know, the two things breed one after the other. In 1968, the Civil Rights Movement was an attempt to try to cut across that seemingly endless circle. It failed not because of the thinking, or the will or the energy behind the people involved in the Civil Rights Movement, but because of the nature of decision-making processes on this small island. It was not only for equal rights, but for equality of esteem, I suppose, more than anything else." (Deane, interview)

Thus, in his opinion, the Troubles had ultimately been triggered off by the British Government authorising the police to use excessive force to quell the peaceful civil rights march of October 1968. In his words: "It came by because of the reaction of the state, particularly the Home Secretary at that time, who was called Bill Craig. He ordered the police to baton people off the streets. It was a non-violent demonstration." (Deane, interview)

McGlade, in turn, pointed out that the Civil Rights Campaign was far from being Catholic and Republican mass movement. While not denying the involvement of militant Republicans, she likewise stressed that this was only a small group that was not welcome even in their own communities. Indeed, political apathy was widespread in her neighbourhood, with most people anxious to keep out of the conflict. This was shown when only little protest erupted in response to the arrest of her father after raising the Irish tricolour on the commemoration of the 1916 Easter Rising.

> "It was a minority of people leading up to the civil rights campaign. It was a small minority involved in the Republican movement who were quite ostracised within their own communities, in the Catholic community as well. You know, my father was arrested on many occasions. We put out the tricolour and the black flag to commemorate the 1916 Uprising. But there were very few people, and my father was arrested for that. They kept him overnight, to take the flags down. Four people of our street came out to protest, but no one else did… Most people were apolitical, wanting just to keep their heads down and stay out of it." (McGlade, interview)

Moreover, she adopted a critical stance towards leading Republican figures at that time, who, as she saw it, showed sympathies for the British cause. Not without irony, she referred to the split within the movement, where those Republicans chose the route of armed struggle and ostracised her family for their involvement in political Republicanism.

"And in particular, I have to say some of the key Republicans, and what did they say? Long-term or life-long Republicans would have been at that stage the most pro-British almost. I don't name them. Not like Gerry Adams, the families like that had been long-time involved. But others would have been actually anti-Republican. I remember when these people became involved in violence and our family, who were life-long Republicans, became involved in the political end of it, we were ostracised by them." (McGlade, interview)

She also emphasised that the power struggles between militant and political Republicans were fought with extreme brutality. These so-called 'pogroms' fractured many families in the community. It was sad for her to see that her own family got caught up in ideological infighting and eventually split up over differences concerning the legitimate means to use – and this despite the shared experience of internment.

"And there was a pogrom. That's another interesting thing: Feuds are between Loyalists. When there are feuds between Republicans, they are called pogroms. I never understood this. But there had been very violent and vicious pogroms between Republicans because of this division of the political route or the armed route. It has always been a big fracture. My own family fractured completely between my mother and my sister, and my father and his brother, completely, for life. My father's brother, be my uncle, he went Provisional. My father and him had been interned together for all those years, pre this current conflict. And they break away. It's very sad to see. And my mother and her sister, who had also been interned, went the armed route. And many families were like that. Very sad. When the Irish fight, they fight with themselves, and not with anyone else." (McGlade, interview)

As with Republicans, there were also violent power struggles within militant Loyalism. Winston Irvine depicted the public image of Loyalist feuds as pernicious in comparison with the more vicious nature of infighting between the Republican paramilitary groups of the Provisional IRA and the INLA. In his view, one of the driving forces behind Loyalist feuding was their perceived lack of political representation and attention. Furthermore, although not denying the presence of spoilers within Loyalist paramilitary organisations, he suspected a plot by external actors aimed at destroying them by means of manipulation.

"I think it is important to point out that internal feuds have broken out both within Republican and Loyalist communities over the course of the years, and some of the bloodiest feuds that we have seen played out were between the Provisional IRA and the INLA. But just to come back to the point on the conflict, the internal conflict between the armed Loyalist groups: I think, to be candid about it, there were a lot of people within Loyalist paramilitary organisations who were not receiving enough political representation and they needed to give themselves a voice. And I think that, like all organisations and all bodies, you have good and bad people right across the board. And for Loyalism, external actors, if you like, were in my opinion manipulating those armed organisations by way of distracting them, and trying to turn the organisations into what would be an implosion." (Irvine, interview)

In a similar vein to other Loyalist ex-combatants, he pointed out that notwithstanding the frequent occurrence of feuds between the UDA and UVF, "there was obviously a lot of cooperation between the two organisations." (Irvine, interview) In part, this was because of coordinating the considerable overlap in the security and defence tasks they performed in Loyalist working-class areas during the Troubles. Whereas the UVF was a centrally led paramilitary organisation operating country-wide, the UDA was a vigilante group mainly concerned with local ad-hoc security and defence measures. Irvine was also eager to affirm that no serious incidents have occurred since the Loyalist feuds in 2000, with the exception of the infighting with LVF rebels. According to him, "presently the relationship between those two organisations could not be stronger." (Irvine, interview) This opinion was, however, contested by Sam Cochrane, who accused the UVF of being heavily involved in brutal punishment beatings of very young people and other crime. By contrast, he stressed that the UDA, with which he was affiliated, were not engaged in crime, but former members abused its name in pursuit of their sinister activities (Cochrane, interview). Yet McGlade's account cast the UDA in a different light. She pointed out that

"In areas where the UDA are there, it's a more terrorised community. They have a stronger hold. …If you felt abandoned before, you are a hundred time more isolated. I say it with one word: Rathcoole. There are drugs, and all the rest of it. And people do not have a voice." (McGlade, interview)

Adding to the dissent, Tom Winstone painted a different picture of the UVF. A former member himself, he stressed that the UVF supported his efforts during the peace process to develop an alternative to its punishment regime within Loyalist communities. This was not least because, in general, paramilitaries were pressurised by their community to act in their interests.

"And in fairness, when I approached them to try to come up with an alternative they were very, very supportive. Because I think it exasperated them that in a lot of people's eyes paramilitaries were just, I suppose, running around in the communities trying to use their power to engage with young people in a negative way. But I think the opposite was true. They were put under extreme pressure from the communities to be doing things on their behalf because the peace abrogated their responsibility." (Winstone, interview)

Respondents from both sides provided a different rationale for the causes and the logic of Republican and Loyalist paramilitary violence, with many engaging in a mutual blame game. Building on his previous argument, Eamonn Deane claimed that the Republican armed campaign was the reaction to the violence emanating from the institutions of the state. This ultimately served the state as a pretext and justification for its aggression against the Catholic community.

> "The violence came first of all from the institutional violence of the state. And then people responded to that. And they responded in a predictable way, and in a way which gave the state great solace and comfort, which was through Republican paramilitary violence. This is exactly what the state wanted, and the state was then able to say, 'I told you so. It is all a Republican plot.'" (Deane, interview)

Furthermore, Republican ex-combatants accused Loyalist paramilitaries of having launched an indiscriminate murder campaign against Catholic civilians. Conversely, they stressed that Republican paramilitaries were simply waging a liberation struggle against the British state. As Umberto Scappaticci put it bluntly,

> "When we talk about Republican paramilitaries: our war was with the British and never ever with the Protestant communities. Whereas all the Protestant paramilitaries, all their role was just to kill Catholics." (Scappaticci, interview)

This perspective was countered by respondents with a Protestant/Unionist/Loyalist background, such as Mervyn Gibson. In his view, the Loyalist violence was always merely a response to incidents caused by Republican paramilitaries, who had, after all, sparked off the Troubles in the first place. Moreover, there were profound differences in strategy and orientation between the two sides. The IRA eventually abandoned their sectarian campaign, adopting the tactical approach of using violence to achieve political ends. This approach, which was pursued in tandem with Sinn Féin, became known as the so-called 'Armalite and the ballot box' strategy.[190] Conversely, the Loyalist paramilitary groups, who were less structured and organised, maintained their strategy of trying to incite fear and terror in the Nationalist com-

---

[190] The phrase was coined by Danny Morrison, a former IRA combatant and Sinn Féin politician. In his speech at the Sinn Féin *Ard Fheis* (annual party convention) in 1981 he called for a change in the party's constitution. In essence, this marked a shift in Republican strategy towards a coordinated approach between the IRA's paramilitary campaign and Sinn Féin's political activity, with the latter also beginning to contest elections (cf. Coogan 2002: 272, O'Brien 1993: 127).

munity, so as to pit them against the IRA and thus put an end to Republican violence.

> "The Loyalist violence has always traditionally been in Northern Ireland a reactionary violence. It was never proactive. Some would claim that it was Loyalists who started with 1966. Loyalists were just reacting to the 50th anniversary of the risings [Easter Rising]. So, Loyalist violence has always been reactive, and it has been more indiscriminate by and large, not solely. The IRA were pretty sectarian and indiscriminate during the 1970s and early 1980s, and indeed right up and particularly in some areas in Tyrone and North Belfast. But the Loyalist paramilitaries' reaction was simply to try and reign fear and deter the whole Nationalist community, so as they would turn against the IRA and try to stop the violence. Once Republican violence stopped, Loyalist violence was always going to stop. But sometimes they would not have been as well-organised, as well-planned as the mainstream Republicanism of the IRA. And they in the end were probably – in the pure terms of terrorism, they sought to strike terror into the Nationalist community, where the IRA violence in the end became very politically focused and tactical." (Gibson, interview)

Billy Hutchinson provided a slightly dissenting opinion on the reasons for the re-emergence of militant Loyalism in the mid-1960s. He believed that the UVF had been re-formed, not only in anticipation of the 50th anniversary of the Easter Rising and, concomitantly, the anticipation of Republican paramilitary violence, but also as a result of internal Unionist wrangling. In particular, the attempts of the then Prime Minister Terence O'Neill to introduce liberal reforms and to improve relations with the Irish Republic caused a revolt within the Ulster Unionist Party (UUP). Consequently, the dominant conservative faction used the paramilitary force of the UVF to thwart O'Neill's policies, which eventually eliminated the liberal wing as a political influence in the UUP. As Hutchinson pointed out,

> "What the government did, the Unionist party, people within it used paramilitary force to actually try to prevent O'Neill from doing what he was doing. And I suppose in many ways what they tried to do is … to scare people. And I think some of the things went wrong in a sense that people ended up being murdered, and that's probably not what they wanted. … What I'm saying is that yes, liberalism was here. But it was quickly put down by acts of violence that had come from the Unionist community. That was the reason why the UVF was re-founded in 1966, to challenge the 50th anniversary of the Easter Rising. But not only was it there to challenge that. It was also there as a reminder for O'Neill and others who wanted to do deals with Dublin." (Hutchinson, interview)

The campaign of the IRA and Sinn Féin during the Troubles was seen as very effective in political terms. According to respondents from both backgrounds, they enjoyed considerable support in the Catholic/Nationalist/

Republican community, particularly among the working class, which afford-
ed them political leverage for the peace process. A main reason for this was
that they became an effective grassroots organisation taking care of everyday
local needs and concerns, whilst concurrently campaigning for a united Ireland (Gibson, interview; Mulgrew, interview). The British state also contributed to the resurgence of the IRA. Mervyn Gibson, for instance, conceded
that mistakes had been made in government policies to combat the Republican armed struggle, which caused an influx of recruits to the IRA.

> "There were mistakes made: internment, while it is a good tool in the army of the
> state it was not effective against the IRA, because the intelligence was out of date,
> and so it turned a lot of people on. Major incidents were the hunger strikes, which
> would have driven people to become more militant. There was a sense – rightly,
> wrongly – of injustices of the past." (Gibson, interview)

This view was somewhat mirrored by Eamonn Deane, albeit he argued vehemently that it was the state's disregard for the legitimate claims of disadvantaged Catholics and its excessive use of coercion that led to the growth of
the IRA.

> "It grew organically. You know, it wasn't something that happened that there were
> all this slumbering Republicans, who were one night awakened. And they sprang
> from their beds, fully armed, ready to go. This is something which grew organical-
> ly through a multitude of mistakes by the British in terms of dealing with the right-
> ful claims of people in areas of deprivation, and their heavy-handedness in dealing
> with protest." (Deane, interview)

By contrast, the campaign of the Loyalist paramilitary groups of the UVF
and UDA never resulted in tangible community support for their political
goals and agendas. This was because their relationship with the Protestant/
Unionist community was characterised by tacit approval and benign neglect,
especially on the part of the middle classes. Gibson, for instance, noted that

> "Loyalist paramilitaries did not enjoy that widespread support. There would have
> been considerable support in the early 1970s, when they became defensive organi-
> sations and emerged as street-defence organisations. Most of the Unionist popula-
> tion would not have supported them actively from about the mid-1980s. Now,
> there would have been a known approval by the middle classes of what they were
> doing. ... There would have been another troop of our boys doing what they have
> to do. But this would not have been acknowledged or manifested itself in the polit-
> ical votes or political support." (Gibson, interview)

This relationship found a similar expression in the political arena. As Irvine
pointed out, close links between Loyalist paramilitary leaders and senior Unionist politicians had existed throughout the Troubles. However, the coopera-

tion took place behind closed doors and was publicly denied by the politicians.

"There has always been a relationship between the Loyalist armed groups' leadership and Unionist leadership within the political organisations. That has always been the case, and it is an open secret that people such as David Ervine and Gusty Spence were involved quite closely with the political leaders of their generation. So, that relation has always existed, albeit in a very private and non-visible way. Publicly, Unionism denied that relationship and denied that there was cooperation at a whole range of levels between those two protagonists." (Irvine, interview)[191]

The issue now arises as to how the role of the police in the Troubles was perceived by the respondents from both sides and if and to what extent that has changed during the peace process and in the aftermath of the Agreement. From what has been said previously, it will come as no surprise that their views diverged significantly and that Catholic/Nationalist/Republican respondents had a very adverse picture of the RUC. Lee Morgan's perspective was indicative of how biased the RUC was generally perceived as being in Catholic working-class areas.

"That just was a Unionist police force for a Unionist community. And basically, it was a military force, and their whole being was to deal with the Republicans, and particularly armed Republicans. So, it was not a proper police force. I never had any respect for the police, myself personally." (Morgan, interview)

In illustration, he presented a personal anecdote about the RUC's violent conduct at the funeral of an IRA volunteer who had been a family member.

"But him and my sister, let me put it this way, they were sort of pushed out of the city by the RUC. His father was an IRA volunteer, and the RUC wanted to take over the funeral. He made the stand that if they did not get enough room to respectfully put his father to rest they would bring the body back into the house. So it was like a three or four-day standoff between the RUC and the people in Ardoyne. It started maybe with a 200 at the funeral. Then, the next day it grew to 400. The next day it grew to nearly a thousand, and it was like a battle, a pitched battle with the RUC. At that stage they had given him enough space. The guy got his ... tricolour on his coffin and whatever paraphernalia and they were to say that you are not allowed to do this. That is the sort of people you have to deal with, you know." (Morgan, interview)

Aside from such special operations, the RUC generally stayed away from Catholic/Nationalist/Republican working-class areas. According to Jim Auld,

---

[191] Gusty Spence and David Ervine were both leading figures in the UVF and the PUP, in which they advocated a political, class-based approach for Loyalism (cf. Garland 2001, Sinnerton 2003).

the absence of community policing caused considerable dissatisfaction among local residents, heightening their distrust of the RUC. This even went to the extent that serious crimes were not reported to the police at all. The situation was different in Protestant/Unionist/Loyalist communities, because, after all, they regarded the RUC as their own police service. He also mentioned the unease with the police present in Protestant working-class areas, a view that was confirmed by other Loyalist respondents. As he explained,

"There was a lack, a total lack of policing going on in the areas, and a very serious level of frustration about what was happening in the areas. And yet, people from those areas would not come forward to the police. Even though there were very, very serious crimes. This was on the Nationalist side. For the Unionist communities, it was different, because the police were there. It was their police service. So they could feel comfortable about going to them. Even though there was a degree of reluctance in some of those, particularly in working-class communities. There is always a reluctance to come forward, but in serious crime they would have went to their own police service." (Auld, interview)

Furthermore, there were claims from several respondents with Nationalist/Republican backgrounds that the RUC used brutal interrogation techniques against paramilitary suspects, detaining them without informing family members about their whereabouts. A further reproach was that the RUC employed anti-insurgency tactics by using local petty criminals as informants about IRA activities. In Auld's view, this also served the purpose of destabilising the community by sowing doubts and suspicion. As he pointed out,

"Low-level criminals were being encouraged by the police to engage in that activity and also in watching individuals within the community that they came from with the understanding that they wouldn't be charged. And at the same time they were spending small amounts of money to watch individuals. And the term here was 'ten pound touts'. So, as an anti-insurgency tactic, they were using people and creating the conditions that people would object to what was going on in the areas." (Auld, interview)

The RUC was likewise accused of siding with Loyalist paramilitaries and supporting them in their assaults on Catholics/Nationalists/Republicans. This was utterly rejected by Mervyn Gibson, who had been a police officer himself during the Troubles. Although conceding that unfortunate assaults had been committed, he insisted there was no institutional collusion between the RUC and Loyalist paramilitaries.

"In the situations that emerged in the 1970s and 1980s there were things done that everyone regretted. But the thing I will say: there was no institutional collusion. The organisation did not collude with Loyalist paramilitaries to attack Republicans. That is not to say that there were no policemen that helped Loyalists as individuals.

In the same way that there were individual policemen that helped Republican organisations. So there was no institutional collusion, there was no 'shoot-to-kill' policy in the police." (Gibson, interview)

Moreover, he affirmed that by and large the RUC did not apply excessive force against Catholic civilians and that their detainment practices involved no systematic use of torture. Yet, this was not to say that no innocent people were shot by the police, even if only accidentally. Indeed, in Gibson's view, these rumours were to be attributed to the IRA's highly effective propaganda machine. (Gibson, interview)

As regards the post-Agreement situation, there was still a lot of suspicion about the police in both Catholic and Protestant communities. However, at the same time, the responses of both sides indicated that there were tentative signs of improvement in the relationship to the police. Likewise, respondents stressed the need for a proper local police service, not least due to an upsurge in crime and anti-social behaviour affecting all working-class areas. Yet, they also pointed to many shortcomings in terms of community policing. With reference to the police reform from RUC to PSNI, Morgan expressed doubts as to whether this had led to a genuine shift in police attitudes towards the equal treatment of Catholics. In particular, he shared his sentiment "that just sometimes there are still some people in the PSNI feeling that they are in the old system." (Morgan, interview) Nevertheless, he definitely preferred the new local policing system to the former paramilitary practice of dispensing instant and often brutal informal justice through so-called 'kangaroo courts'[192], with the RUC turning a blind eye to this. Like Morgan, Margaret Valente remained wary of the police. This was due to the violent legacy of the RUC, whom she held responsible for colluding with Loyalists and enabling them to kill young people in the New Lodge.

> "I still would not trust the police. I would go to them or call them when my house was broken into or something happened. But I would not trust them because of the past and the collusion they were involved in and lots of murders in this area. They allowed the Loyalist community to come in and kill young people, young men, and let them out again." (Valente, interview)

---

[192] Throughout the Troubles, these self-appointed tribunals were a common practice among both Republican and Loyalist paramilitaries, primarily to punish drug trafficking, petty crime and anti-social behaviour in their communities (Human Rights Watch (Helsinki) & Hall 1997: 125; Monaghan & Knox 2002; Morrison 2019; Silke 1999).

Morgan raised a further issue that also appeared in the narratives of other Republican respondents. Although policing was now accepted by mainstream Republicans, their values and aspirations were not equally accepted by the new police regime.

> "I often had this ... discussion with people. I can say that I am a Republican, and I am a non-violent Republican, and I want to be in the PSNI. If I walk into the recruiting station and I openly say that I am a Republican and I am looking forward to the day that a united Ireland comes about, does the PSNI gonna embrace me? Or are they gonna say 'hold on a minute. We're still aligned to the British law. We're still aligned to the Queen'? See, in the past the police stations here had pictures of the Queen. So this is not what you call a neutral environment. And in my eyes, we Republicans have accepted policing, and I still wonder 'has policing moved on enough to accept Republicanism?'" (Morgan, interview)

In a similar vein, Winston Irvine stressed that policing in Loyalist working-class areas was still fraught with tension, although this was improving. In part, this was because the police force was traditionally perceived as belonging to the Unionist establishment.

> "I think there are tensions that still exist around policing and how working-class communities are policed. The PSNI struggles to deal with the issue of policing working-class communities and that can be a source of conflict in itself. But I think relationships are improving. Historically, there have always been problems with working-class people and those police forces, which are part of the establishment." (Irvine, interview)

Another major issue concerned the composition of the police force. On the Catholic side, the efforts to recruit more police officers from their community were met with scepticism. Thus, despite the 50/50 PSNI recruitment policy for both communities, it was doubted that this would attract a substantial number of working-class Catholics to join the police. This was attributed not only to general suspicion of the police, but also to threats and intimidation from local people associated with dissident groups. Morgan remarked on the situation in Ardoyne:

> "Let me put it this way: there would be little or virtually no recruitment into the PSNI from Ardoyne – and that is a community of 7,000 people. That is my belief. I don't know whether this is true or not. If it was not true, if somebody did get recruited into the PSNI, first of all, it could not be repeated; and second of all, they probably would have to move, because there are still groups within Ardoyne and other areas too that are aligned to dissident groups, and they would take it badly. There is no doubt about it. They would be probably threatening their family or they would maybe attempt to assassinate the person themselves." (Morgan, interview)

According to Valente, Catholic residents in the New Lodge had similar concerns about joining the police. In addition, dissident Republicans also obstructed community groups' efforts to cooperate with the police by issuing death threats.

> "There are people who do not like the police. We just started to work with the PSNI. But we did not survey, we just asked people if they would want community representatives to work with the police. And they want the police in the area because of the anti-social behaviour. So we tried to work with the police. And then we got a death threat. All community workers trying to work with the police got a death threat by the Real IRA." (Valente, interview)

In West Belfast, the situation was slightly different. Jim Auld, the director of CRJI, pointed out that there was a considerable increase in Catholic applicants to the PSNI. However, that did not include many Nationalists, not to mention Republicans. So, CRJI advanced a proposal for so-called 'lateral entry' of Republicans at senior police officer level, which met with considerable interest on the part of the police and of Republicans. Furthermore, as another means to create favourable conditions for cooperation between the community and the police, CRJI made the proposal to create a 'Justice House' in Nationalist areas. As Auld explained, this would host all stakeholders involved in dealing with local offences, including the PSNI and other statutory agencies, such as probation services, youth justice and social services, as well as community groups and CRJI. The purpose would be to settle minor criminal cases in an extra-judiciary procedure (Auld, interview).[193]

Another question related to the fact that the police were not locally embedded. As was mentioned by respondents from Catholic and Protestant working-class backgrounds, the police force operating in the area did not originate from the communities. This led to a dearth of understanding of local needs and concerns, thus contributing to the poor image of the police and their lack of acceptance by the communities. As a further consequence, the collaboration between the communities and the PSNI was not without complications. This dilemma was illustrated by Sam Cochrane, who highlighted the difficulties in working with the police on interface matters in the Tigers Bay area.

---

[193] Yet, only little progress has been made so far on the implementation of these proposals. 'Lateral entry' has been included as a general recommendation in the recent PSNI workforce plan (PSNI 2015: 72). The 'Justice House' proposal has been further developed into a joint community project intended to locate the house in an interface area between the two communities. However, this has not yet left the planning stage (Chapman et al. 2017: 164-165, Rooney & Swaine 2012: 527).

"We have direct links to certain policemen that are willing to carry it through. Some policemen aren't willing to work with ex-paramilitaries. What we need to do is sit down with the area commander and say 'Look, if we want this to work, we need the policemen to want to work with the paramilitaries'. We don't want police that are going to come out in the cars, don't even get out of the car because they don't have the time for you. They just want to do their job and don't recognise the work that we do. Policing has changed. It's community-based policing now. If we're having problems in Tigers Bay, I'd like to lift the phone, speak to someone that I know and can trust and who'll respond properly, not come two or three days later. And we have had these issues in the past when certain policemen had no time for the ex-paramilitaries because of their past in the Troubles. Policing has moved on. The police need us as much as we need them, and the policing partnership has played a big part in it" (Cochrane, interview)

The problems were confirmed by Auld. Yet, he also pointed out that the cooperation with the PSNI, especially on youth issues, was beginning to bear fruit. Notably, the police were initially similarly wary of the community, but after their suspicions had been dispelled, they began to develop a better understanding of local affairs.

"Clearly, there's a lot more engagement with the police, and we are engaging much more as an organisation with the police. Not only in individual cases, but between the police as an organisation and us as people who represent the majority of youth within the Nationalist community. And I think that has been a very steep learning curve for the PSNI, who initially were very suspicious. They were wary of what our motivation was, and we have been expressing concern about their lack of engagement and understanding about the community that they are supposed to be policing, and the damage that that lack of understanding does to their credibility and to their ability to police that community. Because all that happens is that they parachute in for a period of time, where they engage in paramilitary policing, and then are driven away to the sanctuary of their own homes. But they never engage with the community on a personal level. They don't know the nuances of the community. They don't know what is acceptable and non-acceptable to that community, and therefore they are imposing their values on this community. So that without any knowledge of it they will come in, they concentrate on the things that concern them rather than what concerns the community." (Auld, interview)

Referring to the situation in Suffolk and Lenadoon, Maria Bannon, the operations manager of SLIG, pointed to the incapacity of the police to deal with smaller interface incidents. So, in order to prevent violence from escalating, SLIG took the initiative by creating a task force of community workers to perform policing duties in the interface area by themselves (Bannon, interview).

Finally, the following quote by Dympna McGlade indicates another fundamental issue, which may help to explain why suspicion of the police was still rife among Catholic/Nationalist/Republican and Protestant/Unionist/ Loyalist working-class communities. In her view, it was hardly surprising that the communities found it difficult to trust the police. During the Troubles, local policing duties were performed by the respective paramilitaries, who, upon achieving power in individual instances, passed the buck back to the communities themselves, claiming it had been the task of the communities in the first place. They condoned misconduct on the part of the communities, asserting this had resulted from failed government policies. This implied that the communities, who had previously been instructed not to engage with the police, were now called upon to do the exact opposite. As McGlade explained,

> "On both the Loyalist side and the Nationalist side people said to those communities whilst they were there and not in power, 'you're not responsible here. It's the government who is responsible. It's their problem. It's their fault. You are not responsible. You are a community. We'll do the policing for you. We'll stand up for your rights. No matter what you do. We'll protect you.' They suddenly go into power … and they are now turning on the communities and saying, 'it's your fault'. … And people don't understand process on the ground. People who have been told not to engage with the police for many years are suddenly told they must. That's very dangerous, very dangerous." (McGlade, interview)

Coming now to the issue of the respondents' perceptions of and attitudes towards the peace process, the main questions are: What were the key events and who were the key protagonists determining the peace process? How did they perceive these actors and events? Moreover, was the community sector involved in the process, and if so how?

Duncan Morrow, chief executive officer of the Community Relations Council (CRC) provided an expert's perspective on the salient stages and the inherent rationale of the political talks and negotiations leading up to the Good Friday/Belfast Agreement. In his view, the Anglo-Irish Agreement of 1985 between the British and Irish governments was precedent-setting. The treaty not only predetermined the institutional and constitutional framework, but likewise shaped the relations between the later ruling parties of Sinn Féin and the Democratic Unionist Party (DUP). As he clearly expressed:

> "The Anglo-Irish Agreement is the foundational framework of everything that we are doing now. I mean it is the critical issue …, because essentially the radicals were defeated by the British and Irish state cooperating together." (Morrow, interview)

Subsequently, central events were the Hume-Adams talks, the Brooke-Mayhew talks, the Downing Street Declaration and, following the Agreement, the St. Andrews Agreement. According to Morrow, the talks between SDLP party leader John Hume and Sinn Féin president Gerry Adams served essentially as a vehicle for getting the IRA on board the peace process. Likewise, an initiative, named after the Northern Ireland Secretaries of State Peter Brooke and Sir Patrick Mayhew, was launched by the British and Irish governments to restart devolution and to bring the Unionist parties to the negotiating table.[194] Using this stratagem, the British and Irish governments forced the more radical nationalist parties on both sides, i.e. Sinn Féin and the DUP, to acquiesce in power-sharing. And not only that, the conditions for such shared, devolved governance were imposed by the two governments. In Morrows' words:

> "The reality is they had to adopt the policies of the Anglo-Irish Agreement, which is cooperation and sharing in Northern Ireland, cross-border relations and the recognition of the special status of a zone like this. And the only alternative to that is that it is administered in that form from London and Dublin. But those are your choices. There is absolutely no military political majority for a pure ethnic solution here." (Morrow, interview)

In his opinion, the Anglo-Irish Agreement also reframed the intricate question of national self-determination in Northern Ireland, because the constitutional shift implied that it was not so much a matter of British/Unionist or Irish national identity, but rather an issue of recognition. As Morrow explained by referring to Austria's republican system enshrined in the constitution:

> "The Anglo-Irish Agreement set the frame. The key issue was the shift, partly because we are not a republic. You do not see this. We do not have a constitution. But essentially we got a 'zweite Republik', we had an 'erste Republik' Northern Ireland, and the moment is the Anglo-Irish Agreement, because the 'erste' had Northern Ireland simply as a devolved part of the United Kingdom. The 'zweite' had it as a part of the United Kingdom, but part of international relations between Britain and Ireland, in which sharing was an integral model. Majoritarianism was defeated, on both sides actually; so that the issue of national self-determination in Northern Ireland was shifted from neither Irish nor Unionist but to being a question of recognition. And in these kinds of circumstances, you have to compromise self-determination because of its effects on others." (Morrow, interview)

Thus, the core issue was how to induce the antagonists to participate in the peace process. Indeed, this proved to be even more difficult than anticipated,

---

[194] For further information on the Hume-Adams talks and the Brooke-Mayhew talks, see in Chapter 3 the section on 'Community and Power Relations: A Historical Perspective', Footnote 70, p. 80.

since the DUP adopted an obstructive attitude towards the peace negotiations. Yet, although disapproving of the Agreement, the party appointed their ministers and participated in government. The consequence of all this was that all sides had to make substantial concessions, which ultimately diluted the provisions of the peace agreement and of subsequent governance arrangements. As Morrow pointed out, "the issue was: how do you get antagonists to buy into this? How do you get them to see this as their best option? ... And even where we are now, it is hedged around with huge ambivalence, huge ambivalence." (Morrow, interview)

This ties in with Michael Doherty's view on the Agreement. In his eyes, the peace agreement was the outcome of a deliberate intent to deceive the people, an act he referred to as the 'power of ambiguity'.

> "The ... thing that we have learned is the 'power of ambiguity': when you deliberately write up a document to be misleading. And the clever way that the Good Friday Agreement of 1998 was written was a legacy to ambiguity, because people interpreted it differently. And that was deliberate." (Doherty, interview)

In a similar vein, Winston Irvine regarded the Agreement as the result of what he termed 'constructive ambiguity'. In essence, this meant that the text of the treaty was drafted in such a way that left it open to interpretation, thus making it fit the needs of each side.

> "A phrase that always sticks in my mind was the phrase 'constructive ambiguity', which basically means that a deal was produced, and basically depending on what community you came from, you basically looked at the Agreement in a particular way, which was meeting your needs at a particular time." (Irvine, interview)

This sense of ambiguity was generally shared by respondents from both sides. A vehement controversy arose regarding the assets and liabilities accorded by the Agreement to both sides. The only thing that they could agree on was that the Catholic/Nationalist/Republican community benefitted more from the Agreement. Let us look now in more detail at the different stances and interpretations. As to the reasons for Protestant/Unionist/Loyalist discontent with the Agreement, it was pointed out that major concessions had to be made to Republicans for them to renounce paramilitary violence. In Irvine's view, this included the sacrifice of the RUC, the dismantling of the security apparatus and the early release of Republican paramilitary prisoners. This created the impression "that the governments of both Britain and Ireland were basically willing to move backwards to a peace with the Republican movement." (Irvine, interview) As was widely agreed by Protestant/Unionist/Loyalist respondents, Republicans were less accommodating in return, and, moreover, failed to comply with their commitments, especially on decommissioning of the IRA's weaponry.[195] This raised suspicion about their commitment to the peace process. For Mervyn Gibson, for instance, who, as mentioned earlier, had adopted an anti-Agreement stance, the peace process posed a twofold dilemma: firstly, to overcome his serious doubts that Republicans were committed to peace and, secondly, to accept Republicans in government who, he suspected, had been involved in past evils against the Protestant/ Unionist community.

> "I think there was a real lack of belief that they were engaged in the peace process. I have to say, from my personal perspective. But then I realised they were serious about it. ... As key factors, there were talks with the government. There were short ceasefires to prove to the Americans that they could control the organisation and stop the violence if they so wished. Politically, you have seen how they begun to become more astute and active. The bombings became even more tactical. And it probably took me a while, more as an individual, to accept that they were committed to peace, that it was not just another tactic to achieve something and then go back to the violence. So that lack of trust for me, and I speak as an individual and as a police officer, that lack of trust I find hardly overcome. But when they said the war was over, I accepted that and believed they were serious, that it was not a tactic. ... But it is difficult to know there are people in government at high places who applauded and in some cases actually murdered friends, colleagues, Protestants because they were Protestants, Unionists because they were Unionists and security forces because they wore the Queen's badge, the Queen's crown in the uniform. But that is something I have to come to terms with as an individual. They have commanded it and I have to accept that. It does not mean that everything in the garden is going to be rosy." (Gibson, interview)

By contrast, Derek Poole offered an illuminating alternative perspective. Republicans had to make more significant concessions to be allowed to enter government, including the sacrifice of the Irish Republic's constitutional claim to Northern Ireland in particular. Unionists, in turn, achieved more substantial gains. Most notably, the Agreement consolidated the union with Great Britain. Nevertheless, whilst Republicans managed to turn that into a success and sell it to their community, Unionists failed to do so, claiming that they had lost everything.

---

[195] On 28 July 2005, the Provisional IRA publicly announced that they had finally disposed of their arms. This was confirmed by the IICD on 26 September 2005. Notably, it was not until the end of 2009 and the beginning of 2010 that the UVF, UDA and RHC on the Loyalist side and the Official IRA and INLA on the Republican side followed suit. See also Footnote 81, pp. 87-88.

"In the Good Friday Agreement, any objective political analysis of its content could not but conclude that Republicanism had to make massive compromises and that the Republican movement had to sacrifice everything from Articles 2 and 3 in the Irish Constitution to actually openly participating in British structures of government. Now those are quite unimaginable compromises within Republicanism. But what's the perception in Republican rank and file? The perception is that Republicans got the best deal … and so the night that the Agreement was signed, Sinn Féin Republicanism ordered a big celebration on the streets of Belfast. But … it meant that no-one read the small print. And it looked like a Republican victory, but in fact, at a constitutional level, Republicanism had to surrender every key tenet to get a place in the government of Northern Ireland. So there's the perception. The difference was Republicanism managed that perception brilliantly. Now, what is the opposite to that? The opposite to it was that Protestant Unionism and Loyalism actually got the union with Great Britain consolidated. The Good Friday Agreement and all the structures of power were absolutely tempered by the fact that under no circumstances could the majority of people in Northern Ireland ever be pushed into a united Ireland. That was possible only through democratic means and a political process. But, what was the perception among Loyalists and Unionists? That they lost everything. So the perception became everything, a civil servant told me. He said 'Republicanism turned a political defeat into victory, and Protestant Unionism turned a political victory into defeat'." (Poole, interview)

This was countered by other Protestant/Unionist/Loyalist respondents, who did not regard the Agreement as a major concession by Republicans. Billy Hutchinson, for instance, expressed the view that the Republic of Ireland had never had the intention to enforce its irredentist claim to the territory of Northern Ireland.

"In 1994, whenever the ceasefires were called, there was a notion around that the Irish Republic had the Articles 2 and 3 and wanted to take over the country, and all that stuff. You know, it was there. It was in writing. It was a Republican ideal. But there was no government in Dublin who has backed that up or ever wanted to enforce it. They didn't want half a million Protestants in some form of a united Ireland and become the opposite of the IRA. You know, pick up the problems that the Brits had, only this time it's gonna be Prods bombing Dublin. … Ideologically, I think that Republican politics in the Republic had moved way beyond all of that." (Hutchinson, interview)

Despite all the affirmations, however, there was a considerable sense of uncertainty among Unionists about the constitutional status of Northern Ireland, which the Agreement made contingent on the consent of the majority of the population. This was reflected in the numerous arguments they advanced in favour of the union with Great Britain, and which they sometimes advocated with great vehemence and with the sincerity of their convictions. As Irvine, for instance, argued, the actual constitutional status of Northern Ireland was safeguarded by the world recession, which was mastered much better by the UK than by the Republic of Ireland. This would cast serious doubt on the economic viability of a united Ireland (Irvine, interview). In Syd Trotter's opinion, Sinn Féin had abandoned their united Ireland aspirations, because, by participating in Northern Irish institutions, they had now become part of the British establishment. Hence, he predicted that Sinn Féin would soon slip into a political crisis (Trotter, interview). Another view advanced was that Republicans had not renounced their aspirations to a united Ireland. However, it was an erroneous assumption that all Catholics shared this ambition. On the part of Republican respondents, the belief was expressed that Irish unity constituted the best option for all people in Northern Ireland and that in the long run Unionists would join the cause. This was exemplified by Michael George, who also indicated the temporary nature of Northern Irish institutions.

"We do need a localised parliament here for the Six Counties. It needs to function to work things on the ground for the people within here. And long-term, you would hope from our perspective that it starts making sense to Unionism that having structures across Ireland is far more feasible. And it makes economic sense. What's the point in being linked to London, where the only link is through air, when you have a network within Ireland of hospitals, transport, education? I think over the next ten, fifteen years Unionism will start thinking that a united Ireland is far more feasible for all the people living in Ireland." (George, interview)

Yet, this view was utterly rejected by Irvine. His prediction of what would happen in the event of a united Ireland came tantamount to a warning that this would result in a mass uprising on the part of the Protestant/Unionist/Loyalist community.

"I think, in circumstances whereby the constitution would change altogether, there would be an enormous conflict. People have sacrificed a lot over the course of many generations to ensure that Northern Ireland does remain a part of the United Kingdom. I think if you were to alienate a million or so Protestants, it would be a bit like telling a state in America that it would not be any longer American, but Mexican. How would you feel?" (Irvine, interview)

Notwithstanding this rift, the legitimacy of the constitutional aspirations of both sides was generally acknowledged, as long as these were pursued through peaceful and democratic means. However, there was criticism by some Republican respondents about Unionist intransigence in this respect. Rab McCallum, for instance, denounced Unionists' steadfast refusal to engage in political dialogue with Republicans on constitutional issues, most notably on the political status of Northern Ireland.

"I don't agree with what our future is yet, but I do agree that we are allowed to have different ideas about how it should be. And that we work towards that in a non-destructive or non-threatening way through dialogue. Sinn Féin and I are for a united Ireland, because that should be seen as a legitimate aspiration as long as it is pursued in a peaceful political way through dialogue. Unfortunately, talk of a united Ireland or any other type of relation constitutionally is seen as a bogey monster we cannot talk about that yet." (McCallum, interview)

By contrast, Lee Morgan was more optimistic that the Protestant community might be convinced through preaceful dialogue that a united Ireland would be the better alternative. After all, Protestants did not enjoy the same status as the British, since, for instance, the latter derided them as 'Paddies'.

"I still got an aspiration for a united Ireland. I am not embarrassed to say that. You know, it is something that I still want. And I want it really badly, but I just want it in a different way now. And … I do not believe that we can bomb or shoot a million Protestants into a united Ireland. We can't. But maybe we can convince them. We can talk to them. Or over a period of time they can see that the British connection is not that big a deal. These people, when they go on holiday there they are called 'Paddies'." (Morgan, interview)

He went on to explain that his aspiration implied, in essence, a radical change in the way socio-economic and political relations were structured, not only in Northern Ireland, but also in the Republic.

"My aspiration to have a united Ireland is if that happens, we can affect change overall. And I am not just talking we have a united Ireland and do away the border… That is not what it's about. It's about affecting change through unity. And there is no way we contend just signing up to what is going on in the Republic at the moment. ... It is an emotional thing, a united Ireland, but it has not so much to do with I want the economy or I want the way they treat people. I want to change that and I want to change the way it goes here, too. We have not got it right here, because we are on a long journey, and that journey includes having a united Ireland. …I am not aspiring to live under Fianna Fáil or Fine Gael, you know what I mean?" (Morgan, interview)

A further point noted by respondents from both communities deserves attention. The Agreement had a detrimental impact on the UUP and the SDLP. As Mervyn Gibson, for instance, remarked, the fact that they were the main signatory parties on both sides cost them considerable support from their constituencies and also initiated a process of fragmentation, particularly within the UUP.

"Because the two parties signed the Agreement, I think it lost them the base of support. You know, the DUP grew out of so many people that said no to the Good Friday Agreement and went to the DUP. And equally the same with the SDLP: so many people voting for them went to Sinn Féin. The two parties signing the

Agreement sacrificed their parties in it. That was definitely the case with the Ulster Unionist Party. I do not think they have recovered from it yet with the loss of so many members and key figures and support, financially and otherwise. It is now a party with so many different views in it. It is quite difficult to see where they stand." (Gibson, interview)

Like the Agreement, its successor arrangement in the St Andrews Agreement was viewed very differently by respondents from both sides.[196] Gibson was in favour of it, and, as a consequence, he revised his anti-Agreement stance; once again concessions had been made to Unionism and Loyalism, and more time had also elapsed for Republicans to prove their commitment to peace (Gibson, interview). By contrast, Doherty held the view that the agreement was mainly due to the DUP's delaying tactics and efforts to undo the provisions of the Good Friday Agreement and strike a more favourable deal."So it took nine years to renegotiate an Agreement that had been agreed in 1998." (Doherty, interview)[197]

This now poses the question as to how the key protagonists in the political peace process and its implementation were perceived by the respondents. In Jackie Redpath's opinion, the Republican and Unionist parties displayed merely a lukewarm commitment to the peace process and also showed considerable reluctance to govern for the benefit of disadvantaged communities. As a result, there was an inherent instability in both the peace process and the power-sharing arrangements. However, even if there had been a full-hearted commitment by the two camps, it would have taken a long time to improve the living conditions of those deprived communities. As he explained,

"The problem is that, even though we have had ceasefires here since 1994, the paramilitary ceasefires more or less, even though we have had a peace process so-called, even though we have now a local devolved government with Unionists and Republicans sharing power, it has been a very difficult process establishing all of that. It has never been full-hearted. It has never been stable. And it has never man-

---

[196] The 'St Andrews Agreement' was the outcome of multi-party talks from 11 to 13 October 2006 between the British and Irish governments and the main political parties in Northern Ireland, including the DUP and Sinn Féin. As main results, it led to the reinstatement of power-sharing institutions and to Sinn Féin's declaration of support for the PSNI. See also the discussion in 'Post-Conflict Reconstruction in the Aftermath of the Agreement' in the section on 'Community and Power Relations' of Chapter 3, p. 88.

[197] What he was referring to was the time span between the signing of the Belfast/Good Friday Agreement on 10 April 1998 and the date when the St Andrews Agreement was ratified, which was at the first convention of the newly formed Northern Ireland Assembly on 8 May 2007.

aged, and actually it has never had the chance to translate itself onto the ground in a transformative way. It has not transformed these communities. And I would argue that part of that would be an unrealistic expectation in that even if there was full-hearted engagement at government level between Republicans and Unionists, and even if there was full-hearted will to do something about transforming these communities that are so deprived, that will take a long time." (Redpath, interview)

Likewise, many other respondents from both sides articulated their discontent with the government performance of the DUP and Sinn Féin. In general, both leading parties were criticised for acting in fundamental opposition to each other, reluctant to reach consensus on important policy issues. At the same time, it was appreciated, albeit mainly by respondents from a Catholic/ Nationalist background and by experts, that a power-sharing government was in place at least. This ambivalence was illustrated by Eamonn Deane, who blamed the parties for failing to set their divisions aside and begin forging a shared identity and vision for society.

"You have to be almost schizophrenic to deal with it. Because, at one level, you think it's natural that this is good. Let's hope it works, and let's not do anything which would damage it. That's that level. And the second level is: you know, people haven't really come to terms with one another and really begun to share power in a sense of creating a new vision, a shared vision, and a shared identity here." (Deane, interview)

Duncan Morrow showed himself to be similarly dissatisfied with the political system. Yet, in his view, it was inevitable to have the two radical parties in government, because that provided a necessary learning experience that would help eventually to resolve community divisions.

"They are, in my view, a totally hopeless government. The present institutions, awful, it is really unbearable. But, on the other hand, it is probably something we have to go through, because the alternative is this democratic deficit in which we never learn the issues. I suppose that is the price I am willing to pay, continue to be willing to pay." (Morrow, interview)

Margaret Valente criticised the government along similar lines. Moreover, she disapproved of the absence of any opposition, the lack of decision-making power and the fact that many former paramilitaries had assumed leading political positions. Nevertheless, she appreciated the fact that Catholics were now represented equally in government.

"The government of the two parties are just too opposed to each other. There is no opposition. I don't like that. ... They do not have much power. All I can see is that there are a lot of ex-paramilitaries who now are political leaders. A lot of people we were so frightened of when they were in their twenties and thirties. It was so scaring. And now they are political leaders. Yet, I 'm glad that there is now power-sharing, that it is half and half Catholics and Protestants. So we are represented in the government." (Valente, interview)

Likewise, Tony Gallagher expressed his unease with the political situation. In particular, he described the lack of government cohesion and the avoidance of decision-making on controversial matters.

"I am unhappy about the way some aspects of the political system are operating, because I think it is solidifying difference. The Assembly isn't working terribly well. The coalition isn't working as a coalition. They are avoiding making really difficult decisions. They haven't yet learned the need to make tough choices and to compromise on things. So politics is still a bit dysfunctional." (Gallagher, interview)

From a Republican perspective, Malachy Mulgrew cast serious doubt on whether power-sharing between Sinn Féin and the DUP could function at all. In his view, they were too fundamentally divided over national and constitutional aspirations. He also stressed that Sinn Fein's vision of equality and sharing encompassed all people on the island of Ireland, as opposed to the DUP's agenda.

"Sinn Fein is about an Ireland of equals so therefore ... it's about equality and sharing. Within the DUP it's not the case. And I suppose the biggest problem, as I've said before, is you have in Stormont an Assembly that is made up of two opposing parties and you can't have one agenda. You can't have one vision. There are two different visions. One is a united Ireland and the other is consolidating the union with Britain. There are two opposing visions." (Mulgrew, interview)

In Dympna McGlade's view, the government failed to learn from the legacies of the Troubles. Moreover, instead of identifying the crucial issues and developing problem-solving strategies, the DUP and Sinn Féin were preoccupied with establishing a political structure that allowed them to concentrate power in their hands.

"The government do not acknowledge the legacies of the past. You know, they kind of said: 'Here we are. We have the Assembly. We all talked to each other. What more can you ask for?' That's nonsense. ... It's not about that. It's just about saying, 'We had a conflict. This is how it impacted on the society. This is what we need to do to get out of it. And here is what's going to happen in the future in terms of a growing multicultural society, and some of the issues that come up with it that are negative, and the great opportunities that come with it that are extremely positive.' But they won't, they shy away: 'No, no, we manage.' And what happens then is they say: 'We have a great peace process here. It's great. And look, we're reforming policing. We're all talking to each other.' What they have is a political structure. It's not even a political process anymore. It's a political structure, which is controlled by the two lead parties." (McGlade, interview)

Explaining the government's reluctance to come up with anything, she provided an informative personal view. Firstly, the DUP and Sinn Féin were most fundamentally opposed of all the parties in their views and ideologies. Secondly, they had no government experience. Thirdly, there was a highly undemocratic system with ultimate decision-making power in the hands of the two leading parties, causing tensions both within and between them. Fourthly, addressing contentious issues had largely still been avoided. These points had to be addressed in order to show 'yes we can'.

> "I think, first of all, we've just been coming out of conflict. You have two parties, where the two main protagonists are against each other. Of all the parties they were the two who had the most difficulties with each other. ... Firstly, they have no experience in government, of how to behave as a government. They have never been in government before. That's a problem in itself. Secondly, it's a very undemocratic system. We have two main parties who make all the decisions and have the final say mainly to the exclusion of all others. So it causes a lot of angst within and between the parties. Thirdly, a lot of things are not on the table, because it's a difficult process, and … it's a fragile process. And it will continue to be so for some time. So, therefore, I think very difficult, contentious issues are put on the back banner and been avoided. Because it's back to the situation where people may feel that they will be held accountable and responsible for very serious and difficult legacies. And I think they need to move on from that and address them. … You're never going to satisfy anybody from announcing who's done what. But what you have to say is 'yes, it happened'." (McGlade, interview)

This was closely related to the reproach that the DUP and Sinn Féin were merely concerned about retaining their power base, thus engaging in sectarian politics. Derek Poole, for instance, stressed that both parties were reluctant to make concessions to the other side so as to ensure the support of their respective constituencies.

> "I think the government, everyone from the national government to the local councillors, are only concerned about their own constituency or their voting base, and therefore they cannot be seen on occasions to be giving an overall piece of support in a way that is going to give something to the other side." (Poole, interview)

In a similar vein, John Loughran criticised the sectarian nature of the politics of the DUP and Sinn Féin, which went at the expense of addressing real political issues. However, he welcomed the symbolic value of the two then party leaders demonstrating in public that they were working in tandem.

> "I don't see any sense of collective responsibility. One of the things that are important to me is at the strategic level. It's the symbolic import of Martin McGuinness and Peter Robinson working together. I like that. I feel good about that. … But when you see the latent sectarian politics coming to the fore, I have a serious problem with that. For me, that raises questions about how we do public admin-

istration, public service delivery in a contested society? We need to look at that."
(Loughran, interview)

Moreover, there was another source of division, which was pointed out by
Chris O'Halloran. The two parties differed significantly in their general policy orientation. As he concisely remarked, "There is a right versus left divide
between the two ruling parties. The DUP government programme is based on
economics. Sinn Féin's programme focusses more on social issues."
(O'Halloran, interview)

There was a controversy between respondents from both sides regarding
the issue as to who was more to blame for the government's failure. On the
Catholic side, particularly from Republicans, criticism was levelled at the
Unionists' obstruction policy. Doherty, for instance, pointed out that in the
Assembly the Unionist parties impeded all the initiatives deriving from the
Republican side.

> "The language even of the parties at Stormont showed very clearly that Unionism
> is still hell-bent on blocking anything to do with Sinn Féin, even though at that lev-
> el they seem to be in dialogue. But at the lower level, they are giving all the com-
> munity a bad message by showing the sectarian divisions." (Doherty, interview)

As regards the political attitudes of the two parties in power towards their
communities, Republicans held the view that Sinn Féin and the Nationalist/
Republican movement were empowering their community, whereas the DUP
were aiming at controlling their community by keeping them in fear of the
'other' side, due to their vested power interests. This was expressed by
Mulgrew, who emphasised that

> "The Nationalist community or the Republican community over the last forty or
> fifty years have been about empowering their people. ... It's about telling people
> 'you have rights'. It's about telling people, 'you have the ability to do these things.
> You don't have to wait for someone to do it for you.' The Protestant community to
> a large extent, by parties like the DUP, actively do the opposite. They tell their
> people not to think, because the day their people start thinking is the day they'll
> start worrying. They want their people to stay down there and let them do all the
> thinking for them, because that is control, because they have a vested interest in
> staying in power." (Mulgrew, interview)

This ties in with Brennan's criticism of the DUP's sectarian strategies to
retain power. In his view, the DUP was mainly concerned with securing their
electoral power base through false claims, like the ethnic cleansing of
Protestants, and manipulative practices, such as gerrymandering of voting
districts for electoral gains.

"Rather than saying 'yes, the policy that we enacted in our political leadership has failed', you can see this in Torrens, people from the DUP are saying 'Protestants have been ethnically cleansed'. So they will put that down to ethnic cleansing, which is not true. But rather than to admit that they failed, they will enrage people with this 'oh it's ethnic cleansing'. And it's the policies that a lot of Unionist governments implemented in the past. Those kind of logical discourses get lost in the territorial and sectarian struggle for dominance." (Brennan, interview)[198]

On the other hand, he was also sceptical of Sinn Féin, whom he regarded as being preoccupied with electoral victory over the DUP and with maintaining sectarian tensions over contentious parades. He remarked on the latter: "All those Loyalist parades, it's in Sinn Féin's interest to keep the sectarian pot boiling." (Brennan, interview)

In the Loyalist camp, it was striking that the mainstream Unionist parties of the DUP and the UUP generally had a poor image among respondents with Loyalist backgrounds. This applied especially to the DUP. Nigel Gardiner, for instance, accused Ian Paisley and the DUP of vacillation and hypocrisy in proclaiming 'no surrender to the IRA' for forty years and then entering into power-sharing with Sinn Féin (Gardiner, interview). In a similar vein, Syd Trotter criticised them for having performed a total volte-face in their attitude towards Republicanism. Referring to the split within the DUP, he expressed the view that the Traditional Unionist Voice (TUV) party was necessary to provide an alternative for an alienated Unionist electorate. Yet, he regarded it as more important for the Protestant/Unionist/Loyalist community to find common ground in standing up for their fundamental interests and concerns. In his words:

"I think in all honesty it's important it is there. Because for many, many years the DUP, you know, the party of Ian Paisley, came off with the speech "not an inch, never, never, never", and turned a full circle. So it takes the traditional Unionists to challenge them for those people that are, or do feel, disenfranchised by this whole process. But I think it has more to do with the Protestant/Unionist/Loyalist community rather than the fight Unionism versus Republicanism. We have to as a

---

[198] Torrens is a working-class housing estate in North Belfast where there have been repeated serious inter-community clashes during the peace process and after the Agreement. The place became infamous for the serious violent unrest in the week before and during the 12th of July Orange Order parades of 1996 (McLaughlin et al 1997: 27-42). The previously mixed housing estate became almost exclusively Catholic after the exodus of Protestant residents in 2004, who fled their homes for fear of sectarian violence (BBC News 2004). In response to the gradual decay of the estate the Department for Social Development (DSD) launched a redevelopment scheme in 2009 envisaging the construction of 166 family houses (Belfast Telegraph 2009b).

Protestant/Unionist/Loyalist community come together and say where do we now sit, where do we now stand and how do we feel about how it is now. And we have to consider several issues that have to be raised in terms of security, economic, social and cultural issues." (Trotter, interview)

In the context of the involvement of community groups and activists in the peace process, it was emphasised by respondents involved at that time that the peace process was actually a two-tier project consisting of the community peace process and the political one. Regarding the latter, Irvine highlighted the significance of secret communication networks that were established between the IRA and the British Government, on the one hand, and the UVF and the UDA, on the other.

"Beside the peace process there was a separate political process, which stands in its own right. There were various backchannel communications set up during the late 1980s and early 1990s, both between the Republican armed group, the Provisional IRA, and the British Government, and also between armed Loyalist groups, namely the UVF and the UDA. And again, they were communication networks, which were designed to begin the process of building peace." (Irvine, interview)

In this political peacebuilding process, community and peace activists also played an important role in paving the way and forming relationships between main actors. Derek Poole explained their involvement in establishing secret talks:

"And all peace-making in physical conflict situation involves secret negotiations behind the scenes, which makes the moment of a peace process: when it comes, it makes it possible. Anywhere in the world where I've heard that the arms have gone silent and a peace process has started, I know that probably for ten or even fifteen years before that peace agreement, someone was doing work somewhere to make that happen. It just doesn't fall out of the heavens, it didn't come from nowhere - someone made it happen. And so a lot of us would have been active in that kind of work, in preparing the ground and building relationships between key protagonists. People who would leave secret meetings and be on the media on Monday, swearing to the whole world that under no circumstances would they ever be talking to that person, but we had them talking to each other over that weekend." (Poole, interview)

This was confirmed by Chris O'Halloran, who noted, "The politicians didn't deliver the peace here. It was the communities who started and pushed politicians to start to talk to each other." (O'Halloran, interview) Hall went even further and stated that it was grassroots activism that initiated the peace process even at the time that the Troubles started. This they did without receiving any support from the state.

"You have to bear in mind when you're looking at it from a point of view of conflict and conflict resolution and conflict management is that to me there is a divide
between the peace process and the political process. When the Troubles started, the
peace process also started. Because right from the very beginning, right from when
the very first stone was thrown, there were individuals in both communities trying
to put a stop to it. They weren't helped by the government, they weren't helped by
the security forces; in fact they were handled. The security forces at one time
wanted everybody in Orange and Green areas so they knew where they were pa-
trolling. … So the peace process wasn't started by Gerry Adams and John Hume at
a certain date. It wasn't started by Tony Blair and Bertie Ahern. It was started by
the ordinary people as a community process. And it went up and down." (Hall,
interview)

However, there was a tense relationship between the two processes. Indeed, according to Hall, "the political process always had the power to undermine the community peace process." (Hall, interview) This was because
the political parties, especially on the Unionist side, were anxious not to lose
control of the overall peace process and thus aimed at keeping the communities at bay. As he described,

"I just wanted to make clear that to me the peace process and the political process
are not the same thing. At times, they have come close. One of the problems in
fact, whenever ceasefires were declared, the community I suppose from a bit of
exhaustion did step back a bit, and the politics came into the scenes. You know the
all-party talks at Stormont, all their push for the Good Friday Agreement. They became the dominant circus in town. So, I suppose ordinary people said: 'Look,
we're tired of the work we're doing. Let them get on with it.' But some of the politicians, particularly Unionist politicians, were saying to community groups: 'Oh,
leave politics to us. You go back to your wee community work. This is our job.'
(Hall, interview)

Moreover, as he went on, local politicians were also quite envious of the
good contacts that community groups had built up to the British Government
over the years of the Troubles, during direct rule.

"So, the politicians kept the community at a distance. I think some of the local politicians were quite jealous that during the direct rule community groups had access
to the British Government, sometimes even when the politicians didn't. You know,
if an issue was important, a delegation could go and see the Secretary of State, and
see civil servants. And I think the politicians didn't really like that. And I think they
would like to see the community group sector back in a subservient role. That's just
one reflection on the importance I feel between the peace process and the political
process." (Hall, interview)

WORKING-CLASS REPRESENTATION AND BREAD-AND-BUTTER POLITICS

So much on the respondents' perceptions of the political actors and their involvement in the peace process: but what about the issue as to how the Catholic and Protestant working classes were represented on the political level? This leads to the following specific questions. To what extent have the socio-economic issues of the working-class communities been dealt with? How far have their concerns and interests been taken into consideration?

To start with, let us look at the issue of working-class representation from a Protestant/Unionist/Loyalist perspective. Respondents with a Loyalist background were unanimous that the Protestant/Loyalist working class had always lacked political representation by the Unionist establishment. In this regard, a detailed historical account was provided by Billy Hutchinson. Building on his earlier remarks about the internal Unionist opposition to liberal reform attempts, he stressed that the UUP's majoritarian rule from 1921 to 1969 was not based on the equal political representation of Protestants. In particular, the interests of working-class Protestants were neglected. In his view, two reasons were responsible: firstly, the UUP was dominated by conservative elements who favoured policies for the Protestant middle and upper classes; and secondly, the Northern Ireland Labour Party (NILP), which traditionally drew considerable support from working-class Protestants, was part of the suppressed opposition and thus had only little political leverage. In effect, there were political divisions among working-class Protestants both in the neighbourhood and at the workplace. What is more, the ruling Unionists were anxious to ensure the support of the Protestant working-class. So, they fostered the fear that Catholics would first oust them from their jobs and then drive them into a united Ireland. As Hutchinson explained,

> "What we need to be clear about here is that a Unionist Government, you know from 1921 to 1973 or whatever, it obviously changed in the 1960s, because the British Government intervened after 1969. Prior to 1969, what we had was a strong Unionist majority. The opposition in Stormont only ever got one bill through and that was the Wild Birds Act. The second thing to remember is that it was built upon the slogan 'a Protestant state for Protestant people' and all that sort of stuff. The difficulty … and the irony was that the Labour party that was in opposition mainly got its votes from working-class Protestants. And it was very strong at places like the Woodvale, which is the top of the Shankill. It was very strong in the Oldpark, which is on the edge of the Shankill. So what I'm saying is, you had these paradoxes, people working in the shipyard and other places who were all Unionists and they were very strong Labour supporters, and they lived in these small enclaves. …

At the same time, you had the rest of the area around them, who were very Union-ist, thought Unionist, didn't care what the consequences were, because they were very conservative in their views. And their view was, and this was sold to them, that if they didn't go and work for a cheap wage, maybe then a Catholic would get the job and when the Catholics got the jobs, what would they do? Take over the state. So, there was confusion around. And people were chewed, and that was the difficulty. So, from that point of view, people believed that they lived in 'a Protestant state for a Protestant people'." (Hutchinson, interview)[199]

He went on to argue that up to the 1994 paramilitary ceasefires state rule had essentially been based on a politics of fear. In his view, this was a fairly common feature of governance in countries across the globe. However, what made Northern Ireland special was that, instead of being focused on socio-economic issues, the sense of fear centred on the idea of loss of culture and political identity. By extension, this fear had very practical implications in that it instilled in people the spectre of persecution.

"And here politics has been built on fear. And the fear has always been about what you gonna lose rather than what you can actually gain. I think politics is like that all over the world. But the difference between here and other countries is that there the fear is based around taxation, economic policies, educational policies, whereas here the fear is based around what a culture, a religion, or a political philosophy can lose. And all of those things then mean that the things that you gonna lose are things that are most dear to you in terms of the whole notion of your political iden-tity, the notion of your culture, whatever that is. I suppose … that people would ac-tually persecute you and … so there is that fear. And that fear was around probably up until 1994. And then some of those fears started subsiding for lots of people, but not for everybody." (Hutchinson, interview)

As he noted, the fear gradually receded for many people after 1994. How-ever, those at the lower end of society were, as always, excluded. Their anxie-ties were further fuelled and exploited for political ends.

"The difficulty is that in this society people have always, I suppose, in many ways played the lowest common denominator, and that is the people who are socially disadvantaged and excluded. And I think that they are the people who most likely will react in a violent way, because there is no other way of reacting. … And the people who want to manipulate them will sort of play those fears up." (Hutchinson, interview)

---

[199] The quote, which reads correctly 'A Protestant Government for a Protestant People', stems from Sir James Craig, then Prime Minister of Northern Ireland, 21 November 1934. Reported in: Parliamentary Debates, Northern Ireland House of Commons, Vol. XVII, Cols. 72-73 (Melaugh 2016c).

With reference to the post-Agreement situation, Nigel Gardiner accused the Unionist politicians of having failed to represent Loyalist working-class communities. In his opinion, this was clearly shown in their empty rhetoric and in their attempts to stir up fear with messages like "your heritage, your culture, your identity will be taken away from you." (Gardiner, interview) Likewise, Winston Irvine expressed the view that there had been a long historical tradition of political neglect of the Protestant working class by the Unionist and the British governments.

"I think that there is generally accepted that working-class Protestants ... were neglected by the political administrations. There was a sense that those communities were to be getting the worst, that they were to be left to their own devices. What we saw was a manifestation of that policy. And I have to say the main Unionist parties could not with any credibility claim to represent the working-class Protestant people - certainly not within Belfast." (Irvine, interview)

The British Government was criticised for having neglected the needs and interests of Loyalist working-class communities. Indeed, the perception was that the government's socio-economic policies in the 1970s and 1980s often had detrimental impacts on Loyalist communities. This was exemplified by Jackie Redpath, who described in more detail the redevelopment of the Shankill at that time, which, in his view, exacerbated socio-economic deprivation and likewise undermined the cohesion and fabric within the community.

"Going back to the 1970s and 1980s, it was wholesale clearance and destruction and redevelopment of areas like this. And really, what they had picked up on as a government was just import from the rest of the United Kingdom and from other cities across Europe, which was, you moved bulldozers in, you swept away the slums, and you replaced them with building tower blocks with flats; you know, a whole process of planning. And it was so different to the way people's lives were lived. And they destroyed the whole way of life. ... I mean, there were individual government ministers who had an interest, or who were quite progressive, or whatever, but they were very few. You know, the overall impact of policy was destructive. It was not until the very late 1980s and the early 1990s that the government realised that there was a connection between the fact that the areas of worst violence in Belfast, for example, were also the areas of greatest deprivation." (Redpath, interview)

As he explained, the British Government changed its policy in the late 1980s and early 1990s, shifting the focus to improving the living conditions of the most deprived areas as a means of combatting violence. In his opinion, this was triggered off by an upsurge of IRA violence in West Belfast, which was on the brink of getting out of control. Thus, he noted that

"The British Government had to intervene. So, they set up another policy called 'Targeting Social Need', which for the first time began to make the link between levels of deprivation and disadvantage and levels of violence. So, from that time there had been various initiatives by the British Government under direct rule to do things in relation to disadvantage and in relation to deprivation." (Redpath, interview)

He was, however, sceptical of the outcome of this so-called 'Targeting Social Need' policy. This was because the measure was not tailored to specific local conditions, but instead adopted a catch-all approach, treating all communities across Northern Ireland the same way. Moreover, this complicated, and, as he stressed, in many cases thwarted the implementation of local initiatives, which was particularly true of the efforts made by his organisation, the Greater Shankill Partnership, to tackle the issues of local regeneration and educational underachievement. Nevertheless, he welcomed the fact that indicators had been developed to assess the real levels of community deprivation and need. In addition, the local government agencies that had been set up, such as the Belfast Action Team initially and then the Belfast Regeneration Office, also met with his approval. Substantial government funding was made available too. (Redpath, interview)

There was also the perception that the British Government favoured Catholic/Nationalist/Republican communities in its efforts to improve the living conditions of disadvantaged communities. As a result, deprivation in Loyalist working-class communities was worse than in Catholic ones. In Mervyn Gibson's view, the reason for the government's focus on Catholic working-class areas was that it was part of the government's strategy to get the Republicans on board the political peace process. The issue of deprivation in Loyalist working-class areas was side-lined as a consequence. This was exacerbated by the fact that there were no local leaders who might have claimed the available funds due to the fragmentation and poor infrastructure in the communities. However, he also noted that there were some people, primarily with a Loyalist paramilitary background, who were active in grass-roots politics.

"The government as part of their campaign in the late 1980s to engage with Republicanism it was so through third-party organisations to improve their living conditions and housing, which needed to be done. So, I have no difficulty with that. But in many ways Loyalism then was left behind. I think the peace dividend bypassed a lot of Loyalist areas. Now I am speaking as someone who got involved in getting several millions for various Loyalist estates. I am not saying we missed it altogether, but there were a lot of Loyalists who did not know how to claim it for Loyalist areas. We did not have the same infrastructure within our community. We did not have the same community cohesion. ... So, there was no leader to begin to claim this money, and begin to do that traditional work within Loyalist communities. And there is no rule without exception to all of this. There were other individuals who emerged. So, there is a few amongst certain elements within Loyalism. They are distant from the middle class and the parties." (Gibson, interview)

This was confirmed by Duncan Morrow, who stressed that Republican communities benefitted most from British government funding. In his opinion, this made them also heavily dependent on the public sector.

"Here is a paradox: the key funder, the key money source for community development and all of these posts at local level to keep life going was the British Government, and the biggest beneficiaries were the Republican areas. So, the British Government effectively paid Republicans to be social workers. And that was the interface often with civil servants. The result economically has been an extreme dependence on the public sector." (Morrow, interview)

It was generally agreed among Loyalist respondents that working-class politicians were needed to challenge the existing political system. However, these local politicians were not rewarded by their communities in terms of electoral votes. As Redpath pointed out, the problem was the voting behaviour of the Protestant/Unionist/Loyalist community, which was based on fear and mistrust, as opposed to being forward-looking. (Redpath, interview) In a similar vein, Syd Trotter blamed it on people's electoral attitudes. However, he held both communities responsible for following traditional loyalty patterns of voting either mainstream Unionist or Republican/Nationalist parties, thus preventing the emergence of an effective working-class politics. To counteract this, a grassroots empowerment strategy for the community would be what is needed. Notably, he regarded also the Alliance Party (APNI) and the Green Party as having a long-standing record as advocates of bread-and-butter-politics.

"Of course, there are. Since thirty years. Let's be honest for a moment. Let's look at the Green party. Let's look at the Alliance party. They want to fight in the elections with what we call the bread and butter issues, social and economic issues, whereas the Unionist parties and the Nationalist parties fight on the Orange and Green card. And then the Republican Nationalists said: who could be 'greener' than the other? And then the Loyalist said: Who is the 'orangest' of us all? You know, that's the truth. And yes, they have stuff like 'what we're going to do for you' in terms of socio-economic relations. But by and large, the people, the mass from both communities, put the Orange or Green card into that box. And they have played that role out in terms of politicians and they have won on that. They have harvested that. And I suppose now it's how do we redefine ourselves, educate ourselves, as a community." (Trotter, interview)

There was a further major reason for the lack of local support for Loyalist politicians. In the Protestant working-class, there is no tradition of voting for political parties associated with Loyalist paramilitary groups. Indeed, there is only one Loyalist political party remaining, i.e. the PUP, which maintains close links to the UVF. Irvine, a former UVF combatant himself, dealt with this issue in greater depth, seeing the salient causes in the law-abiding character of the Protestant/Unionist/Loyalist community and in their contempt for the sacrifices made by the Loyalist paramilitaries in championing their cause. Yet, as he remarked with a reproachful undertone, this was not unique to Northern Ireland, because throughout the world the underprivileged have always been singled out and exploited for the purposes of the elites, particularly on the frontline.

> "I think that's a big question. And the answer to that is that the Unionist community by and large are a law-abiding community. Their natural home is for law and order, the police and the security forces, and whoever to be acting on their behalf. But at the same time in ghettos, and I suppose this is in ghettos all over the world, they tend to be the last people that anybody pays any interest to. And, therefore, if there are wars to be fought – and no matter where those wars may be, whether it's during the wars in Europe over the First and Second World Wars – it's young men, usually from working-class areas that are put to the front and fight the wars. And no-one is speaking on their behalf. And the politicians from whatever quarter they may come act on that and pray on that, and young soldiers are cannon fodder. When we were in prison and looked around the faces, it's the same young people that were going to war then during the First and Second World Wars. It's the same people from the same areas. It's the same background. It's just that this time we chose to fight, I suppose, a paramilitary war rather than a military war, simply because of the nature of the war that we were involved in." (Irvine, interview)

Echoing these words, Derek Poole, a long-standing peace activist with a Protestant background, articulated the view that Loyalists were frequently exploited by the Unionist establishment to carry out the dirty work during the Troubles and even on other occasions. Yet, they became aware of this only quite recently, and shortly after they had reached political maturity, they lost some of their most visionary political leaders.

> "They are very happy to use Loyalists as the strong arm of Unionism when needed, and Loyalists played into that game many, many times. Loyalist leaders only came lately to the realisation that they were often being used by respectable Unionism to do the dirty work of Protestant Unionism throughout this conflict and at other occasions. I think Loyalists came to political maturity and awareness late, but the problem was that three or four leading Loyalists with that kind of vision and perception and realisation died, all over the last two or three years." (Poole, interview)

This awareness was reflected in Irvine's remarks. He found it somewhat of a travesty that with the DUP and Sinn Féin the two most extreme parties in the conflict were in a power-sharing coalition. He lambasted the DUP for its hypocrisy. First, they denounced individual UVF members as traitors for engaging in talks with Republicans, and then they did the very opposite when they entered into coalition with Sinn Féin. In his opinion, this has encouraged some people to become politically active and espouse their own interests themselves instead of allowing themselves to be represented by the mainstream Unionist parties.

> "I think politicians have a lot to answer for. I think now it's a bit ironic that it's Sinn Féin and the DUP, two of the most extreme parties throughout the conflict, who are now sitting down in government, talking to each other, when those ideas were put forward by others a long time ago. But the DUP, for one, castigated those of us who were willing to sit down and speak with the enemy as traitors, and now they are doing exactly the same thing. And I think some people are more politically aware now to espouse their interests themselves as opposed to letting the DUP or UUP speak on their behalf. Unfortunately there are not enough of us." (Irvine, interview)

His former paramilitary associate, Tom Winstone, chimed into the chorus of criticism. He thought the main reason why the Loyalist paramilitaries, unlike their Republican counterparts, did not succeed in translating their military force into a substantial political clout was that the established Unionist parties exerted control over Loyalist communities by appealing to emotions. Likewise, he reproached the Loyalists for having abandoned the paramilitaries once they did not need them anymore.

> "The difficulty, I suppose, for Loyalism is that the military might that they had at one time wasn't able to be turned into a political force. Only Sinn Féin were able to turn their military operation into a political operation and get the support from the communities from which they came. Unfortunately, that did not happen within Loyalist communities, simply because there were mainstream political parties established within Unionism, and unfortunately they bred on the communities, I believe, and whipped up emotions within communities. And I'm not saying that myself or people like me were led by the nose by politicians. But they surely encouraged us to become actively involved in violence, and when we'd done that they abrogated their responsibilities and they didn't want to have anything to do with us." (Winstone, interview)

Finally, Poole outlined the poor situation and low political status of the Loyalist community in a rather drastic way. In his view, the common perception among Loyalists was that they were to blame for all the Troubles. In particular, there was a deep sense of having been abandoned by the wider Protestant community and by Unionist politicians in particular.

> "You might argue that the Loyalist community is the scapegoated community of the whole Troubles, that in one sense the unspoken interpretation of the conflict is that if Republicans started off as the bad boys then Loyalism became the really bad boys. And it was Loyalist violence and Loyalist intransigence, Loyalist unwillingness to disarm etc. that in fact perpetuated the Troubles over the last ten years. And I think that is a position held as much by middle-class Protestants who have disowned Loyalism and have very little time for it. I think the scapegoating of all things sectarian from the Protestant side through Loyalism is as strong as the rejection of Loyalism by radical Republicans. So, I think, Loyalist communities woke up some time between the Good Friday Agreement and today and realised, 'We are being dumped on by everything and everyone. We have no longer any value to the state. We are no longer an important community to our politicians, and we appear to be just crisis-managed in terms of the social infrastructures of our areas'." (Poole, interview)

In many ways, the Catholic/Nationalist/Republican perspective was the opposite. As some local respondents pointed out, the grassroots political approach of Sinn Féin was generally welcomed among Catholic working-class communities. This affirmation also materialised in substantial electoral support. This was illustrated by Lee Morgan, who appreciated the commitment of local party members in taking care of the concerns of residents in the Ardoyne community. As examples, he mentioned their involvement with the police and the Housing Executive on behalf of the locals. He also conceded that there was some discontent, which pointed to the possibility of corruption of the party. Yet, this could equally be attributed to a more widespread sense of political alienation.

> "Sinn Féin councillors and Sinn Féin activists are constantly working on behalf of the community. Some people within the community are a wee bit negative at the moment. But I think that has more to do with general disenfranchisement about politics all around. People are a wee bit annoyed about the expenses scandal, you know, and they feel it. They are wondering if anybody in Sinn Féin is parking a few quid. It's a strange thing that it is the only party that takes an industrial wage and the rest of the money goes into the party. But yet, you would have people that would doubt that here. I would not be one of them. I personally believe that they do a good job. I had dealings with them on many occasions. You know, you can come to them, and they come to see you in the evening even. It is not a nine-to-five job for these people, and they do get harassed to a certain degree by anti-social elements, because they attempt to improve the community." (Morgan, interview)

By contrast, as some respondents remarked, the SDLP had a lower reputation among Catholic working-class communities, as they were also less prevalent there as in middle- and upper-class neighbourhoods.

Morgan raised another issue in that he speculated as to why there had never been a common trade union representation of the Catholic and Protestant working classes, which would have been logical given the similar situation of socio-economic deprivation.

"One would imagine over the years when ... there are more similarities in terms of poverty, in terms of living standards, whatever, that you have a common problem, that there is a common trade and labour movement emerging. Yet the only joint strike I think was in the 1930s one time." (Morgan, interview)[200]

Poole also emphasised the similarities between the Loyalist and Republican working-class communities in terms of their living conditions and overall socio-economic impoverishment. Yet, there was a major difference concerning their political self-image. Whilst the outcome of the Agreement has perpetuated and even consolidated the siege mentality among Loyalists, it has given a substantial boost to the national self-esteem of Republicans.

"I would say that certainly the Protestant Loyalist working-class communities have come out of all this severely beleaguered and demoralized. I would say that was one of the overall failings, and also in terms of economics, considerably deprived in education, jobs, housing and so on. I think a similar argument could be made in Republicanism by deprivation. The only difference that might be is that Republicanism feels more confident about what it has come out with from the Good Friday Agreement, which ... is quite ironic. I think Republicanism feels quite buoyant about success and the dealing of a real sense of Irish Catholic Republicanism in the city of Belfast in parts of North Belfast." (Poole, interview)

In a similar fashion to the Catholic and Protestant working classes, there was, in Brendan Murtagh's view, considerable political alienation of the middle-class. This was because the political discourse promoted by the DUP and Sinn Féin imbued driven by rival nationalist agendas had nothing to offer them. Moreover, there was no really attractive alternative, as the middle-ground parties lacked both political leverage and a clear agenda. As a consequence, middle-class abstention from voting has been on the increase.

"And people who didn't vote I would imagine, and there is some research to back this up, are middle class. They don't need to vote. They are not interested. They are

---

[200] The event he referred to was the so-called 'Outdoor Relief Workers' Strike' in 1932. For more information see the discussion in the section of Chapter 3 on 'Community Inequalities, Class and Ethno-National Divisions', pp. 105-106.

disengaged. They are like what was called here in the 1970s the 'coasters', describing a middle class who just coasted along, had plenty of cash, privatised their lifestyles and did not need to worry about any of the sort-of formal political nonsense. And when you see a politics run by Sinn Féin and the DUP, why would you vote? What's in it for you? How are you really going to engage in that discourse in any meaningful way? The cross-cutting parties tend to be fairly weak or don't have a very clear agenda around policy or politics that you could sign up to. And some of the other fringe parties are really fringe. The Greens are marginal up to the point where they wouldn't get one MLA. So, what are you buying into in those sorts of circumstances?" (Murtagh, interview)

From what has been seen so far, there were many factors that prevented working-class interests and needs from being represented politically. However, grassroots political initiatives were also taken, but they met with a lack of support on the part of both the communities and the government. Were working-class politicians mentioned who had a positive image in one or the other community, or even had the standing to cut across the communal divide? If so, was anybody considered as having the potential not only to shape local opinions, but also to advocate and implement them in the political arena?

There were, indeed, several politicians who were mentioned by both sides, but one had a positive image within the Protestant/Unionist/Loyalist and the Catholic/Nationalist/Republican working-class community, namely David Ervine. Coming from a Loyalist working-class background, Ervine was a former UVF combatant and from 2002 to 2007 the party leader of the PUP (cf. Sinnerton 2003). Yet, as was commonly regretted, he died less than 54 years old in 2007. Nevertheless, the reasons given by respondents will provide a general notion of the traits that were considered important for a good working-class leader. The following interview quotes may serve to substantiate his standing as a grassroots political leader who was in the position not only to perceive the vital interests and needs of working-class people and forge them into political demands, but also to convey to his supporters the feeling that they were being taken seriously. To start with the Loyalist perspective, his eloquence and format as a political leader were lauded by Tom Winstone, who, at the same time, also pointed to the backing Ervine received from his party.

"David was the first of the PUP, but he wasn't a one-man band. There were other people behind him. He was very eloquent in what he was able to do. Unfortunately, he died too young. But David Ervine was the leader that Unionism, in my belief, was craving for, for a long time. He was able to speak with soldiers, but he was able to speak with prime ministers and world leaders as well." (Winstone, interview)

Winston Irvine, in turn, highlighted Ervine's passion about working-class issues and his conciliatory approach to politics, which side-lined religious and national differences.

> "David Ervine was passionate about working-class issues. Religion and nationality did not feature very highly in terms of David Ervine's work, and that is where he got a great deal of respect from, because he was seen very much as someone who was interested in social issues." (Irvine, interview)

Mervyn Gibson, coming from a Unionist background, acknowledged Ervine's dedication to the interests of Loyalist working-class communities.

> "David Ervine's phrase I always say, 'I never met a man who did not vote for David Ervine, but I did not meet a whole lot of Protestants who did sometimes'. You know he had an appeal. … And that is why I liked David Ervine, and I think in his working class thing he was brilliant in many things." (Gibson, interview)

Likewise, Ervine earned a lot of credibility and respect from respondents with a Catholic/Republican working-class background. Lee Morgan, for instance, appreciated his potential to build bridges between the communities and his socialist background.

> "There is some sort of connection there that could be made better, and particularly guys in the past like David Ervine, I have utmost respect for him. Although he was an ex-UVF man but he had this socialist background." (Morgan, interview)

Margaret Valente, in turn, hailed him for his sincerity and courage to rectify false Unionist claims about Catholics.

> "I found David Ervine was really, really brilliant. He said a lot about the perceptions that they [Unionists] had about the Catholic community. He said that they were better off and he told them that they were saying lies." (Valente, interview)

Besides, other leading figures in the PUP like Billy Mitchell and Dawn Purvis were also mentioned in an appreciative sense, though only in individual instances. The same applied to the Sinn Féin politicians Carál Ní Chuilín and Conor Maskey, as well as to Alban Maginness from the SDLP.

As to the socio-economic policies of the then existing power-sharing government, respondents from both sides were unanimous in their critique. Building up on his earlier argument, Jackie Redpath elaborated on the reasons for the government's failure to improve the living conditions of deprived working-class communities. In his view, the parties in government were preoccupied with keeping an eye on one other and, moreover, targeted their policies to the benefit of the wealthier sections in society. As he remarked,

> "Part of the problem is that there has not been a will or a focus on doing it, because people at government, at political level have been so out to see what the others are doing and so unwilling to join together attacking these things properly. That means

that the benefits of peace have not been translated on the ground. And until the recent world-economic recession … the benefits of peace were more readily available to people who are really well-off, or rich or wealthy." (Redpath, interview)

In a similar vein, John Loughran criticised the government's failure to deliver a peace dividend in deprived working-class areas:

"The government here has failed to tackle the inequality and deprivation for twenty years. If you look at the NISRA website, unemployment is now worse. Deprivation is worse. There is something wrong. So while we are having all these high-level political documents, the implementation plan falls down big time." (Loughran, interview)

Housing policy proved to be a particular source of discontent among the Catholic/Nationalist/Republican working-class communities. Jim Auld, for instance, accused NIHE of allocating public housing on a sectarian basis.

"The housing issue hasn't been addressed at all. There is a new housing authority now called the Housing Executive that engages in sectarian politics on housing, because it does not house people in terms of need, but by the sectarian make-up of the areas were they have housing stock." (Auld, interview)

In his view, the sectarian nature of the state's housing policy was clearly apparent in West Belfast. He pointed to NIHE's reluctance to accommodate the enormous housing need of Catholics. This was despite the fact that there was empty public housing stock in the Protestant Suffolk estate. Furthermore, according to him, this also demonstrated that Catholics were not treated equally in government policy and decision-making.

"So you know, in West Belfast the housing need is much greater than anywhere else. There's a massive waiting list for accommodation, all sorts of accommodation. … Yet, in the small Suffolk estate up the road in West Belfast, that is a Protestant estate in the middle of Andersonstown … the difficulty with it is that the Suffolk community will engage with Lenadoon on a range of issues where they can work jointly on. But they will not talk to Lenadoon about housing stock or the availability of housing stock in the area. So, in West Belfast you have the biggest housing waiting list in the North of Ireland, and yet you have empty public housing in that estate where Nationalists can't move into or can't be accommodated because they are Nationalists. And that, for me, is the state engaging in sectarianism. Because they will not confront that sectarianism itself. You know, they won't face down that the whole sectarianism is within that estate, because they don't want to create a conflict. But sometimes conflict is unavoidable." (Auld, interview)

However, as Duncan Morrow pointed out, the issue of public housing allocation posed a conundrum to the DUP. How could they accommodate the much bigger housing need of Catholics and sell this to their Protestant constituency? Thus, he explained:

"The question is the delivery of something like housing on the basis of equal citizenship and equal rights without simply reproducing segregation again is an extremely complicated one because the demand and the need is not equal. There is a bigger need on the Catholic side than there is on the Protestant side, much bigger. So that is the question: How does the DUP in government deliver more to Catholics than it does to its own supporters? How does it do that, in practical terms? And then go back to its electorate and say this was a success." (Morrow, interview)

This again indicated the salience of the constitutional divide, which, in Chris O'Halloran's view, prevented the emergence of a grassroots movement to challenge the existing political situation:

"The difficulty here is that up to now there has not been a grassroots movement. The movement has foundered on the rocks of the constitutional position. The disillusionment of people with the government is not enough." (O'Halloran, interview)

POLICIES ON COMMUNITY RELATIONS AND DEVELOPMENT

A lot has been mentioned already regarding the respondents' overall discontent with the role and performance of the political protagonists, with the lack of working-class representation and with shortcomings in socioeconomic policies. A key question, however, remains: How were the policies of the British and Northern Irish governments on community relations and development perceived by respondents? More specifically, regarding the policies' impact on Catholic and Protestant working-class communities: how satisfied were they with policy effectiveness? What were the reasons, if any, for policy failure?

As a starting point, let us look at the evolution of community relations policies. It was already mentioned that in the 1980s a shift occurred in the state's policy orientation towards targeting the needs of deprived working-class communities. Thus, the British Government began to make more substantial funds available to promote community development. As Hall explained earlier, government funding was done initially through tailored community employment schemes, involving intermediary agencies such as the churches.[201] Soon afterwards, private funders from Europe and America followed suit, specifically placing the focus on peace. Gradually, this also led to a corresponding adjustment of government policy that placed more emphasis on the

---

[201] See also the discussion on the development of 'Early Grassroots Activism and Cross-Community Interface Work' in the section of Chapter 4 on 'Community Issues and Relations', p. 187.

issue of community relations. However, in Hall's view, there were always worries among certain sections of the political elites that the funding of community development would promote reconciliation. As to the reasons why, he remarked:

"The suspicion about peace money was always that it had only to do with reconciliation. And the worry within many people was that reconciliation meant that you had to deal out or give up your own ideas, aspirations, identity." (Hall, interview)

Despite this shift in policy orientation, though, the state proved ill-equipped to deal with large-scale intercommunal violence. Chris O'Halloran, the director of BIP, provided insight into the way local authorities responded to the major disturbances that erupted in North Belfast in 1996 as a consequence of the Drumcree dispute.[202] He was involved in local crisis management activities at that time, especially in trying to help the many families who had been made homeless because of the riots. In the following he described vividly the local authorities' failure to provide them emergency aid, such as shelter, food or other vital assistance. In his opinion, the main reason behind was that the state had no mechanisms developed that were adapted to the specific circumstances of the Troubles. This had been intentional, because the state wanted to give the impression that the situation in Belfast was no different to that of any other place in the UK.

"I remember 1996. It was a very, very bad year. It was extremely violent. We were getting reports of people who were being made homeless, people who were burnt out of their houses, with their children, with nothing but their cloths on their back. I remember trying to enquire about 'whose job is it to push the big red button that says something like emergency, emergency?' I was given this person's name and his phone number. He was a very senior person within the social services here. And I phoned his number on a Saturday, on a bank holiday. And he was surprised to hear that there had been something like 42 families displaced, because he was only aware of something like 14. Actually, within days there were way over 100 homeless families. But the point was: he was only aware of 14. And it was his job to push the big red button that would have alerted all the emergency services. You know, 'how can we help? Do you need furniture, money, food? And none of that was happening, because nobody had pushed the big red button. And the reason was because he was only aware of 14, which is quite a small number, when there were actually 42. But the reason there were only 14 was that people wouldn't go to social services. If you're a family that's just been burnt out, you don't want to go to social services with your children. Because people would be afraid that their chil-

---

[202] For more information on these incidents, see the section in this chapter on 'The Local Communities', pp. 141-142.

dren would be taken away from them, that the children would be put into care and the families would be split up. So, basically the state had no mechanism for supporting the people who had been victims of large-scale civil disturbance. And part of the reason for that, that my experience makes me believe anyway, is that the way that the Northern Ireland statutory agency structure has survived throughout the Troubles here is essentially to pretend as if there were no Troubles. You know, as if Belfast is the same as Nottingham, is the same as Leeds, is the same as any other city. And the way that services are delivered here should be exactly the same as in any other city. Until very recently there have been no special policies, no procedures, no account essentially taken of the impact of the Troubles here, except by those agencies who are responsible for emergency services: the police and the ambulance service etc." (O'Halloran, interview)

He went on to point out that many state authorities still operated on this premise, thus delivering services according to the same principles as other British cities. This could be seen, for instance, in the inability of the Belfast Education and Library Board (BELB) to provide services tailored to the special needs of young people exposed to interface violence. As he explained,

"The BELB, the Belfast Education and Library Board responsible for youth services, sees its role as providing youth services for young people. It doesn't see its role as alleviating conflict. It doesn't see its role as protecting children from violence. You know what I mean? It sees its role as offering the same services as every youth service would offer in Nottingham, in Leeds. ... But what we need here is something different. So, what we end up with is a whole bunch of statutory agencies essentially acting as if there is no conflict here, except for those few that have to act as if there is a conflict here. And then we find that there are people who are naturally performing between those cracks. In the mid-1990s those were the homeless, who were made homeless through violence. Right up to now it's children and young people who have no resources, or very few resources expended on them." (O'Halloran, interview)

As has been said, the community and voluntary sector made a substantial contribution to the political peace process by facilitating talks between key protagonists. As Seán Brennan noted, the community and peace activists were also instrumental in motivating people to vote in favour of the Agreement. However, its involvement was not reflected by inclusion in the Agreement due to fierce opposition on the part of Sinn Féin and the DUP. Among the main parties, the SDLP was the driving force behind the community agenda. The UUP was reluctant, but given the inevitability they grudgingly acquiesced to the agenda. Yet, in outcome, the sector was professionalised and placed under control of formal community organisations.

"The emergence of the peace process in 1994 then created the context in which a lot of groups were able to work more collaboratively. And I suppose the combination of that piece of work, which became known as the third sector, was demonstrated in the 'Yes campaign' in 1998, when it was the community and voluntary sector that drove people to actually vote yes. You have to know, Sinn Féin was opposed to all this. The DUP was opposed to all this. So it was the SDLP and the UUP. The SDLP worked to the fore. The UUP was reluctant but knew that it was coming anyway and was sort of moving towards that resolution. In the process, what has happened is that a lot of the community and voluntary organisations that were active during the war have now been superseded by formal competence taking over community organisations and taking control of it." (Brennan, interview)

Moreover, he criticised that Sinn Féin created residents' groups to oppose Orange Order parades in order to keep people in Republican communities occupied and distract them from the more extensive peace process.

"You can see that through a lot of the parade disputes that Gerry Adams is on record of saying that they purposively went in and created a lot of residents' groups and used community actions as a means of opposing Orange parades. Really, that had to do with motivating his people, keeping his people active, while they we're doing the larger peace process." (Brennan, interview)

This was confirmed by Winston Irvine, who, furthermore, accused Sinn Féin of using the parading issue as a pretext to launch an assault on the cultural essence of Protestant/Unionist/Loyalist communities.

"I think the whole issue of parades and protests for that matter has been agitated certainly over the course of ten years or more by Sinn Féin. Gerry Adams publicly declared that Republican resident groups did not happen by accident. In other words, the Provisional IRA engineered pressure groups to basically oppose and dismantle expressions of Orange culture. So we are dealing with the hangover of the conflict." (Irvine, interview)

At the same time, he noted that Loyalist paramilitaries also kept their communities remote from the negotiations that were taking place between and within their leadership circles. It was not until the final stage of the peace process that the local level was consulted.

"Negotiations at the local level did not transpire until the late 1990s and they are the years that I name. Prior to that, the negotiations would have been at the highest level within organisations and armed groups. But the local negotiations and local communication networks were not established that laid peace." (Irvine, interview)

On the initiative of the middle-ground parties of the NIWC and the APNI, the Agreement also provided for a so-called 'Civic Forum for Northern Ireland'. However, instead of being an effective representative body for those involved in community relations and development, it proved to be a toothless tiger. After all, it turned out to be a short-lived consultative body that was created under the Agreement in 2000 and disbanded in 2002.[203] Duncan Morrow described the deficiencies of the Forum in a rather drastic way:

> "It was totally chaotic. One, because it did not get into proper institutional shape. They said there should be a Civic Forum, but they did not say what it was. So, some people would argue it was set up to fail. What it became was just a joke. It was like people fighting each other with no protocols, with no clear understanding of their relationship with the wider Assembly." (Morrow, interview)

As he argued, the reason for the Civic Forum's failure was rooted in the traditional lack of the political representation of community interests and needs. Under direct rule, the British administration in Northern Ireland had no local party structure and operated through a pragmatic cooperation with the public sector, the civil service and the community field. Thus, as he explained, "the issue of the constitution was separated out. That was dealt with by the political parties. Everything else was dealt with not by politicians at all, but by an interface between the administration and interests." (Morrow, interview) Moreover, this also implied that the political parties had no expertise in dealing with essential community issues. Those who had the expertise were actually in the civil service and the community sector. Thus, the political parties also lacked policy-making capacity in the areas of community development and community relations. What is more, there was unease and opposition among the political parties about collaborating with the Civic Forum and accounting for their activities. In the following Morrow explained the problem in more detail:

> "So you have actually when you try to go back to politics a really difficult situation, which is that the political parties actually do not exist and never existed to articulate the broad range of community needs that is required for government, so health and education and all these things they are actually responsible for. The people who have expertise in those areas … are actually in the civil service and the community sector. The Civic Forum in some ways was regarded as a bad arrival by the political parties. You know, the connectedness of the Civic Forum to the political parties was a very contested one. And so one of the things that has been happening is a readjustment of authority between those different interests." (Morrow, interview)

---

[203] The Civic Forum was suspended along with the Northern Ireland Assembly in October 2002. Although desires have been expressed by the DUP and Sinn Féin on several occasions, the Forum has not been reinstated up to now. Actually, there were plans underway to replace it with a small civil advisory panel (Bell 2004, Nolan & Wilson 2015). However, in response to ongoing government impasse, more voices have recently called for the establishment of a fully-fledged civic consultative body (cf.O'Doherty 2018, Spencer & Hudson 2018).

There was a more fundamental issue contributing to the neglect of the communities on the part of the political parties. This was to be found in both the logic of the peace process and the nature of the Agreement. As stated earlier, the ultimate aim of the British and Irish governments behind the peace process was to improve relations between themselves. They sought to resolve their problems by establishing an institutional framework of devolved power-sharing between the two antagonistic political camps, enabling a fair shared future for both communities. Yet, as Morrow pointed out, there was always the risk that only one of the two communities would emerge victorious from the peace process. Hence, the pivotal and likewise highly delicate task was to promote the political centre, and, at the same time, to keep the radical elements on board. It was hoped that this would lead to the marginalisation of the radical fringe, and thus facilitate the formation and stable working of a centre-led, power-sharing government. Morrow depicted the quandary as follows:

> "We are in a huge dilemma here, enormously complicated. I do not know whether there is a pure resolution of this. Anyway, there is a way looking at it that way. And I would argue something else here … that the reality is that both Sinn Féin and the DUP had to change their substantive positions, in relation to one another, but also in relation to any serious political strategy. And at their arrival at power the key question was the price. Now there were always two options: how does an inter-community future win over a single community victory? How does that work? And part of this answer, one of the answers back in 1998 was that the centre would form and essentially marginalise the radical edge." (Morrow, interview)

Initially, when the Agreement was signed, it seemed that the British and Irish governments had succeeded in their endeavour. The peace treaty provided for power-sharing institutions, which were to be headed by the largest parties on both sides, at the time the UUP and the SDLP.[204] Yet, there were two major shortcomings inherent in the Agreement. First, the preoccupation with the institutional framework went at the expense of setting guidelines for policy-making in a binding manner, especially in areas directly affecting the communities, i.e. socio-economic development and community relations. Secondly, the UUP-SDLP government proved unstable and inefficient, not least because they could not achieve progress on the most contentious issues of the Agreement, most notably on Loyalist and Republican paramilitary de-

---

[204] For more information, see the section in Chapter 3 on 'Community and Power Relations: A Historical Perspective', p. 83.

commissioning and on police reform. A main cause was obstruction on the part of the DUP and Sinn Féin. As a consequence, after a lengthy period of British direct rule, a shift in power took place in 2005 towards the DUP and Sinn Féin. As Morrow concluded,

> "So, the story if you like from a military-strategic point of view was that actually we had to have this run by the radicals. Paradoxically, now we have the inter-community institutional framework run by the ethnic separatists."

This power switch towards the radical end of the political spectrum aggravated the situation in terms of community policy. In the aftermath of the Agreement, a political initiative began slowly to take shape to develop an overall community relations strategy. As Brendan Murtagh explained, these first attempts, which were made by direct rule ministers from the Northern Ireland Office (NIO), were based on three pillars: first, the strategic framework document called 'A Shared Future' (cf. OFMDFM 2005); second, a Regional Development Strategy (RDS) (cf. DRD 2012); and, third, the so-called 'Community Cohesion Strategy' of the Housing Executive (cf. NIHE 2017). Originally, the overall strategy consisted of a specific focus on interface communities. Specifically, the aim was to improve local living conditions through measures, such as economic regeneration investment, and to develop good relations through measures like mixed housing schemes. Yet, as Murtagh remarked critically, the process of implementing this strategy was stalled, as soon as Sinn Féin and the DUP entered into power-sharing government. Consequently, the 'A Shared Future' document was abandoned and replaced by the two parties' new strategy, entitled 'Community, Sharing and Integration' (CSI) (cf. OFMDFM 2010). Likewise, the priority on interface community was deleted from the RDS. There was no progress either on NIHE's strategy in terms of an impact on interface areas, especially in North Belfast, because the issue of segregation was not considered. In Murtagh's view, the government's failure essentially emanated from the two parties' vested interest in gaining political advantage from a sectarian discourse that kept their constituencies segregated.

> "So, what you've seen now with this shift into devolution: a political discourse established around, for many of us, just fairly undisguised sectarianism, or at least segregation. And the belief in segregation has a real political capital: keep your electorate frightened, dysfunctional, and in resource competition over land and property." (Murtagh, interview)

In the context of the transition from 'A Shared Future' to 'Cohesion, Sharing, Integration', Drew Haire, a long-standing civil servant close to retirement and at the time the head of the Community Relations Unit (CRU) of the OFMDFM, provided insight into the government's difficulties in delivering a community relations strategy. As he explained, the overarching aim to which the two ruling parties committed themselves in the Programme for Government was "to build a peaceful, fair and prosperous society in Northern Ireland with respect for the rule of law." (Haire, interview) Yet, there was a major difference in their high-level strategic priorities. Whilst the salient issue for Sinn Féin was equality, the DUP placed special emphasis on peace and prosperity and respect for the rule of law. Moreover, as was agreed, all policies had to be demonstrably based on the cross-cutting approach of building a shared and better future for the whole of society. Both parties also publicly affirmed their commitment to retaining the key priorities of 'A Shared Future' and including them in the envisaged new CSI-programme. According to Haire,

> "Ministers are not saying and have not said that they are dispensing with these objectives. All they are saying is that they are looking to build on the achievements that these have – the achievements that are taking place on a progressive basis." (Haire, interview)

Furthermore, he outlined the vision behind community relations policy and the reasons for the prolonged delay and difficulties in devising a new strategy:

> "So the visions statement ... that is in 'A Shared Future' ... is about the establishment over time of a normal society, where individuals are considered as equals, differences are resolved through dialogue, people are treated impartially, a society where there is equity, respect for diversity and recognition of interdependence. We are not going to go away from that as a vision. It is simply putting a document together which teases this out in a way that our first minister and deputy first minister can stand together and say 'here is our document'. (Haire, interview)

He viewed the causes for this in the difficulty of striking a balance between promoting equality and good relations. This apparent ambiguity is to be found in Section 75 of the Northern Ireland Act 1998 (cf. ECNI 2010).[205]

> "The Section 75.1 is about giving regard to the equality issue on the equality grounds of nine different areas, and Section 75.2 is about giving due regard to the promotion of good relations. And what we are trying to sort bottom out is in a good relations policy how do we square that, so that those who regard equality as, I

---

[205] The Northern Ireland Act of 1998 is the legal basis for the implementation of the Good Friday/Belfast Agreement. Therein, Section 75 provides the legal framework for both the equality agenda and community relations policy (cf. UK National Archives 2019). See also the section in Chapter 3 on 'Community Inequalities, Class and Ethno-National Divisions', p. 106.

suppose, prime importance do not feel that the promotion of good relations between people is at the expense of equality. But that, on the other hand, it is saying
you cannot achieve equality: equality is best achieved in association with good relations." (Haire, interview)

A key question was whether the government's strategy on community relations would ensure the provision of coherent and consistent funding. In his
response, Haire pointed to the scarcity of government funds, and although
there was a modest increase "from 21 to 28 million pounds over a three-year
period," community groups were not to expect too much from the CSI-
programme. Moreover, in the context of the global economic crisis, he also
indicated the highly competitive nature of acquiring adequate funding for
community relations projects and activities of community groups. Even
though there was substantial international 'peace money' coming from the EU
and US at that time under the International Fund for Ireland (IFI) programme,
he warned that this would soon come to an end, i.e. by 2014. Hence, he called
on the government and the communities to place their focus on cooperation
instead of competition and self-interest (Haire, interview).

A further major issue concerned the fundamental disagreement between
the parties over Northern Ireland's constitutional status. Haire was convinced
that the DUP and Sinn Féin would not surrender their ultimate political aspirations, because, after all, these were deeply ingrained in their fabric. Yet, at
the same time, he firmly believed in their commitment to promoting good
relations between the communities. The crux was to find the right balance
and to contrive a policy that would respect the right to different opinions and
traditions and to resolve potential controversies through dialogue, not violence.

"This document has to take into consideration, if you like, these different political
agendas. The main thing is … the two main parties, which are in government here,
will not change their ultimate political objectives: the retention of the union or the
reunification of the island of Ireland. You know, that is within the DNA of both
parties in government here. But whilst not compromising on those two goals they
are very clear in their commitment to bringing and building relationships between
communities which hold those different points of view. But it is about getting to
the point of saying, 'I respect your right to hold a different point of view to me'.
And it goes back to the statement in 'A Shared Future', where differences are resolved through dialogue in the public sphere and not through reverting to violence.
And the way, in which ministers here go about their business, they will have their
differences on occasions about things which are from different political parties.
And that is politics. But I see them working in many ways together, which is giving this sort of political leadership to demonstrate that it is possible for people
holding different perspectives to work together. And I am not trying to pile the sky,

that everything is sweetness and light. It is hard. But it is work in progress." (Haire, interview)

However, his view was contradicted by Duncan Morrow, who painted a bleak picture of the policy-making performance of the two leading parties. He expressed his conviction that both the DUP and Sinn Féin were neither able nor willing to devise and implement a coherent and effective community relations policy. Instead, their prime interest was to overcome and defeat the other side.

> "At the moment, to be honest with you, there is an enormous problem in government, which is that they cannot agree on the frame in which that is done. And that policy is called, was called 'A Shared Future', and now it is CSI 'Cohesion, Sharing and Integration', but the bottom line is the symbolic issue they cannot agree on it. In practice there will not be anything any way. The policy that they come up with will be very weak, because they are not committed to it. They do not know how to promote a sharing. They actually want to promote victory. These parties actually exist who want to promote victory over each other." (Morrow, interview)

In Haire's opinion, the major policy challenge was to link strategy and implementation. He explained the issue with the example of housing. This posed the question of how to translate research findings into concrete policies, such as the support of a substantial majority of people for living in shared housing. However, he thought, progress has already been made, and specific programmes have been set up, for instance, the NIHE's 'Shared Neighbourhood Programme' that works in cooperation with local people. Yet, he also called on the government to commit to implementing relevant policies that would alleviate the dearth of shared housing stock.

> "I do not disagree that having an agreed strategic policy document would certainly be a very helpful thing. That is what I have been working on for the last two years. But I would say to you, in my opinion, while it would be very helpful, in itself it will not provide the solutions to all the things you were talking about. It simply sets a strategic context, and almost all there is the symbolism. … We still have a way to travel. So the point about the pressures for housing in particular areas, how communities can live together, you know we have surveys and reports produced where the majority of people – I think it is 80% of the people or more who say that they like to live in shared neighbourhoods. … I also think if that is the aspiration of the population, then government policy should be doing what it can to achieve that. But it is one thing people being asked that in a survey, and it is another thing to say we are going to change the way housing is allocated. I am not saying I do not believe that it is never going to happen, but there are hard challenges still to be faced up to. But there are programmes beginning to take place – for example, the Housing Executive has a programme which is called the 'Shared Neighbourhood Programme'." (Haire, interview)

Apparently, the parties' commitment continued to be absent. Indeed, the CSI strategy did not progress beyond the consultation stage. Eventually, in May 2013, the DUP and Sinn Féin issued their new community relations strategy entitled 'Together: Building a United Community', which essentially built upon the core pillars of 'A Shared Future' (OFMDFM 2013; cf. Knox 2011, Todd & Ruane 2010). In a follow-up interview, Neil Jarman worded his scepticism about the commitment of the two lead parties to community relations. In fact, they would lack the motivation to advance a broader peace-building agenda. Moreover, he went on to point out that the announcement of the new strategy was made without the knowledge of the other members of government from the UUP and SDLP, thus casting doubt on the formal status of the policy. In particular, he viewed it as a major problem that there was a substantial drop in peace and reconciliation funding, a circumstance that has exerted considerable pressure on the community sector.

> "Yes, it's been published. I think there is some announced earlier this week linked, working on youth policy and engaging with young people. There is some small work going on still. But a lot of the peace moneys are coming to an end. A lot of the big funders for peacebuilding work and work around 'A Shared Future' have come to an end. There's a bit of a gap in the funding at the moment. And because the government is so divided, things do happen, but not on some of the more crucial issues. And when they issued that document follow-up to 'A Shared Future', it was just a document from the First Minister and Deputy First Minister. The rest of the Executive have not even seen it when it was issued. And it's a bit uncertain as to what the status of the document is, whether it's formal policy. It's not executive policy, I think, at this stage, because it hasn't been adopted by the Executive. But it's departmental within the First Minister's and the Deputy First Minister's office. It's seen as being, I suppose, a start, but nobody is really convinced by it. I don't think so. There's not a great deal of support for it. And a lot of the community-based organisations are under pressure financially, and not thriving. ...To me, it doesn't feel that there is any great move to and impetus behind a wider peacebuilding agenda at the moment in Northern Ireland. It's been on hold now for a good few years." (Jarman, interview 2)

Apparently, his skepticism has proved true. As Jarman confirmed in two follow-up interviews, conducted in March 2017 and June 2019, no significant progress has been made on the implementation of the new strategic framework. In fact, since the collapse of the power-sharing institutions, policy-making has come to a complete standstill (Jarman, interview 3 & 4). Moreover, most recently, he stressed another development which has been detrimental to the implementation of community relations on the ground. In recent years, the mandate of the Community Relations Council (CRC) has been severely curtailed. It used to act as a coordination hub and think tank for the community groups, but now it has become merely a funding agency. As a result, the groups lack network capacity and, with even less funding available, some of them have already disbanded.

> "What has happened in recent years is that the Community Relations Council that was involved in a lot of the community relations work had its remit altered. So it does not have a policy remit anymore. It does not really have a role in coordinating and stimulating discussion within the community and voluntary sector. Instead it has really just become a funding body. So the groups on the ground have no real strong networks developed anymore. There are a lot of groups that have even closed. And a lot of the work in terms of the networking activities is no longer being done, because a lot has been done through the CRC and groups don't have the money to do it themselves. There is a lot less money in peacebuilding work now." (Jarman, interview 4)

Besides the growing scarcity of funds, the question arises as to whether the 'peace money' available was effectively employed to improve local community conditions and relations. According to Derek Poole, this was not the case with regard to the situation in interface communities in North Belfast. Although substantial subsidies were provided at that time, this neither translated into significant improvements in living conditions, nor did it resolve the 'peace wall' problem.

> "The evidence appears to be suggesting that with the millions and millions that have been spent in places like North Belfast the outcome is extremely little. There is no evidence of those hundreds of millions resulting in a transformed infrastructure, in terms of housing, jobs, new buildings, inward investment, and there's no evidence that those hundreds of millions have translated into addressing the interfaces. Or at least, it has helped ease the tensions of the interfaces, but to suggest that it has resolved the phenomenon of the interfaces would be utterly untrue." (Poole, interview)

This impression of the ineffectiveness of local community relations work was confirmed by Shane Whelehan. As he pointed out, the economic and social situation of young people in Ardoyne had remained the same, despite extensive funding.

> "It has not changed by the peace dividend. There has been a lot of money coming from Europe and overseas. And North Belfast in particular benefits from urban peace money for defined areas. But, you know, you can throw money at a problem, sometimes it won't stick." (Whelehan, interview)

As Haire indicated above, the equality agenda was a core element of the community package provided for in the Agreement. During the peace negotiations, the British and Irish governments and most Northern Irish parties, except the mainstream Unionists, placed a special emphasis on the inclusion of equality and the equal treatment of both communities.[206] This led to the adoption of a substantive equality agenda, consisting of a comprehensive set of equal rights and equal opportunities as well as the principle of 'parity of esteem', which provides for full expression of the communities' identities. In practice, this means that the political rights of both communities receive equal recognition, and that these rights can be exercised in political institutions (cf. Hayes & McAllister 1999: 41-43, McCrudden 1999: 103-108).[207]

However, some respondents highlighted problems associated with the impact of the equality agenda on community relations work. As Maria Bannon pointed out, "Section 75 does not take into account the reality of equity, and it does not take into account the equality of outcome. It is more so upfront equality." (Bannon, interview) In her opinion, policies considering the good relations element of Section 75 of the Northern Ireland Act had also created problems on the ground. The transport policy of the Belfast Education and Library Board (BELB), for instance, entitles pupils of primary school age to free transport, if they have to travel within three miles radius to get to their school. Yet, as she stressed, there was no special provision for interface areas. Therefore, given the patchwork of interfaces that pupils have to cross, especially in North and West Belfast, the practice of this policy has actually reinforced the "likelihood for sectarianism through attacks, because the safety issue has not been addressed." (Bannon, interview) Poole likewise held a critical view of the unnecessary complexities and rigour in the legal provi-

---

[206] The political parties promoting the equality agenda were: on the part of Nationalists and Republicans the SDLP and Sinn Féin, the Loyalist parties of the PUP and UDP, as well as the middle-ground parties of the NIWC and APNI. On the Unionist side, the UUP was rather indifferent to the equality issue, and thus did not play an active role in the negotiations. The DUP did not participate in the multi-party talks leading to the Agreement, due to its anti-Agreement stance (McCrudden 1999: 104).

[207] Article 75 of the Northern Ireland Act 1998 Section 1 obliges public authorities "to have due regard to the need to promote equality of opportunity" (ECNI 2010: 74) for all persons irrespective of religion, race, political or sexual orientation, marital and family status, age, sex or disability. Section 2 refers to community relations and commits public authorities to "have regard to the desirability of promoting good relations between persons of different religious belief, political opinion or racial group." (ECNI 2010: 74) Furthermore, the Act also established the Equality Commission for Northern Ireland (ECNI). The ECNI is a statutory, independent public body to monitor the effectiveness of public authorities in meeting their obligations of promoting equality of opportunity and good relations, inter alia, between the Catholic and Protestant communities (cf. ECNI 2010: 76-81, UK National Archives 2019).

sions for equality and equal rights. Moreover, the equality agenda was still fraught with elements mirroring the sectarian nature of community relations. All this could actually hamper the rapprochement and reconciliation process between the communities, especially in working-class interface areas. As he explained in greater detail,

"On a legislative level, Northern Ireland is absolutely thick with rights and equality legislation, we're probably monitored like no other country in Europe, in terms of making sure that everyone has the right to their rights under the law which are complicated in the extreme: the right to housing or to jobs, the right to your culture, the right to your language, the right to scrutinise the police, the right to education, the right to be able to protest against marches. We've actually created a culture in which at a legal level everything is in place, except the generosity of heart that's needed to make all those things function. So we have legally all of these rights, but emotionally and morally we have not negotiated a space with each other in which we can share these benefits mutually. So we've created an equality culture around a host of agendas, but it's equality for us, it's still a sectarianised equality agenda: 'Yes, we want the houses, we want the jobs, we want the education, and so on, but it's for our people'. So these very fractured and polarised societies and communities have now got a new arsenal to fight with, the rights culture, the arsenal of rights. But rather than helping to oil community cohesion and community relations, it might actually be contributing to more alienation and to more competitiveness." (Poole, interview)

In practical terms, several issues were raised concerning housing policies. Dympna McGlade, the programme director for community policy and development at CRC, pointed out that, due to the demographic shift in favour of Catholics, things had changed and they could not be regarded as a minority anyway. Given the segregated space bounded by interfaces, especially in North Belfast, this poses major challenges to housing policy, i.e. to the building and allocation of houses. Specifically, the fear and apprehension in Protestant/Unionist/Loyalist working-class communities about attacks from Catholics/Nationalists/Republicans has to be taken seriously. Thus, she explained,

"There is a growing Nationalist community over the years, and hence it can no longer be regarded realistically as a minority, now at 46 or 47%. You know it's hardly a minority in any country, I would think. And that's a growing number. So, there is a big housing issue. You have a growing Nationalist community and a shrinking Protestant/Unionist/Loyalist community, which is posing a problem again, because segregation has led to many interfaces between the communities, and fear and apprehension. And, in particular, within the Protestant/Unionist/Loyalist community whether it is perceived or real, it does not really matter. There is a view that their tradition has been trampled on and they are being squeezed out.

That must be addressed. Those fears must be genuinely listened to and considered." (McGlade, interview)

Jarman pointed to another major difficulty, which was rooted in the parties' electoral politics, based on a sectarian headcount. Building on his previous argument about the significance of the territorial issue in housing allocation, he expressed the belief that "if you would put more Catholics in [Protestant housing] and the population becomes more Catholic it will also change the voting dynamics." (Jarman, interview)[208] In a similar vein, Brendan Murtagh, referring to the style of policy-making of the DUP and Sinn Féin, expressed the view that the parties had manipulated the housing issue to their own ends of retaining power.

"They heat up the housing issue in particular: the Catholics are coming for your land … and Sinn Féin constantly brushing up on the housing issue, certainly in North Belfast: 'we want your houses, we want your land.' So it has sectarianised the housing issue in a way that you're not going to get shared space or desegregated interfaces. … So you just basically replaced one form of religious segregation with a new form of elite-social segregation." (Murtagh, interview)

Furthermore, as he went on, the interfacing issue in North Belfast was also used by Loyalist paramilitaries of the UDA in a similarly manipulative to ensure control on the ground.

"It can be seen how interfacing has been politicised especially by the UDA in North Belfast. That sort of extant paramilitary force that's there. … They are manipulating territory and they are manipulating the territorial issue. In some ways like Sinn Féin is manipulating the housing issue." (Murtagh, interview)

The perception of the local respondents on both sides was by and large negative concerning the impact of community relations policy on working-class communities. In the context of the housing dispute in North Belfast, Margaret Valente criticised Unionist parties for manipulating Protestant working-class communities by stirring sectarian hostilities towards Catholics.

"I mean they had a job, but they still lived in the same housing, in the same squat that we lived in. They had an issue with education. Their kids did not get educated… but they did not say that because their politicians told them 'you are better off than they are. They want your jobs. They want your houses. Don't let them have them.' (Valente, interview)

---

[208] See also his remark in the discussion on 'Current Issues of Contention and Debate' in the section of this chapter on 'Community Issues and Relations', p. 233.

A further bone of contention was parading. Winston Irvine, for instance, accused the political establishment of having ignored the issue of sectarianism, which was most clearly shown in violence during such parades.

"Let me just say, conflict in Northern Ireland has neither been transformed nor resolved – it has been managed. And the issue of sectarianism has not been even properly addressed. I believe the political classes of the administration in the Assembly have ignored the issue of sectarianism. I think the parades have been a catalyst for that sectarian violence to basically show itself." (Irvine, interview)

Going even further, Dympna McGlade held the view[209] that the conflict concerning parading had been deliberately sparked by the leading parties in the quest for power. In particular, she held Sinn Féin and the DUP to account for not providing sufficient police personnel to prevent violence from escalating around the 'Tour of the North' Orange Order parades. She described vividly that she herself witnessed how the police withdrew from a crowd of young rioters, which could easily have been kept under control. And then the Sinn Féin's spokesperson for Policing and Justice claimed that the riot could not be handled. As to the motivation behind this, she suspected a stratagem to strike a favourable financial deal with the British Government for the devolution of policing.

"They are still playing political games in terms of the final cutting of the apron strings from the British Government. I think there is evidence for that over the past three major rioting in Ardoyne, and the stewarding of the parades. I witnessed the 'Tour of the North' and thought that was the worst stewarding I'd ever seen in my life by people who had been at it three years. They drew back from a crowd of kids … I could have gone over and nearly controlled them myself with the help of water troopers. I wondered, what's this all about? Why would you reduce the number of police officers if there's such a violent conflict on the streets? That was deliberate. Then, Gerry Kelly was on television, and maybe I'm over resenting, saying 'Oh we cannot steward this'. And at the same time he's negotiating with Gordon Brown a financial package for devolution of policing and justice. It's a stratagem for a financial package for policing. We're not getting the same financial package if we're a normalised society with just ordinary crime. … They are not difficult riots. They are serious, but they are rowdy youngsters, who with a better work and a better direction could be very easily been brought into and make them feel that they are part of a society and part of a community. And you quell that if you'd put the effort in. No effort deliberately was put in, nor has been." (McGlade, interview)

---

[209] Notably, as she pointed out, the following reflects her personal opinion and by no means expresses the view of CRC.

As Malachy Mulgrew critically remarked, the government's community relations policy also failed to take the spatial peculiarities of Belfast into account. In particular, he pointed to North Belfast, which, unlike the other homogenous parts of the city, was fractured into a patchwork of Protestant/ Unionist/Loyalist and Catholic/Nationalist/Republican working-class communities. As a consequence, there was no common vision on the development of the area. This was demonstrated especially in their discord in the North Belfast Partnership (NBP) Board, which was made up of community, political and business representatives, in dealing with local community development and relations issues. Both sides could not agree on how to tackle local community needs, above all interface issues. As an example, he quoted the use of an abandoned army base located at an interface and still vacant after some years.

> "If you go to West Belfast, it's mostly Nationalist/Republican. If you go to East Belfast, it's mostly Loyalist or Unionist or Protestant. If you go to North Belfast, it's split down the middle, it's all different parts. And it's a very important thing, because at least in other parts of Belfast, you have what is known as a Partnership Board: people come together from the political level, from the community and from business, and they'd have a look at the needs of the area. Now, for a board like that to succeed they need to have a vision, a mission statement. In North Belfast, you have two. There's a split down the middle, because the group in the room want two different things. And it's very hard then to promote North Belfast when we don't even have one vision of what we want for North Belfast. A prime example is … there's a barrack site. It's an army base that's been vacated some years ago. It's now off the Clifton road, it's a 26-acre site … and it should be a real key to unlock North Belfast. Whatever goes in there, it should be for both communities and it should be 21st century. Whatever goes in there, we can't even agree about this either. It sits on an interface." (Mulgrew, interview)

Some further striking examples may demonstrate the shortcomings and failures in policy-making on issues pertinent to community relations and development, specifically in interface neighbourhoods. The first one concerns the closure of Suffolk Primary School in 2009, situated adjacent to the interface with Catholic Lenadoon. As mentioned earlier,[210] it was a major blow to SLIG's cross-community development work when the primary school for Protestant children and, concomitantly, the mixed nursery had to shut down following a government decision. The school's application for integrated

---

[210] See the discussion on 'The Suffolk-Lenadoon Interface Group' in the section in this chapter on 'Community Issues and Relations', p. 197.

status was supported by both communities, yet the Sinn Féin Minister of Education rejected it, stating there would not be enough future pupils to sustain the school. Notably, the school met all the other eight criteria that were required. Moreover, as Maria Bannon pointed out, this also thwarted SLIG's plan to open an integrated day care centre on the site, thus offering educational facilities to Protestants and Catholics from infancy to the end of elementary school. As a consequence, there was the serious risk then that this could have reversed the progress that had been made in building bridges between Suffolk and Lenadoon. Furthermore, the ministers' erroneous decision might also discourage other interface communities from taking the risk of reaching out to the 'other' side. In the following, Bannon provides detailed insight into the events leading to the closure of the school and also makes no secret of her disappointment with the minister's decision:

"In Suffolk, there is a primary school, and it is only for Protestant children. It is a Protestant primary school. Well, they would say no, but it is a state primary school. Underneath that at the same site was a nursery, which was a mixed nursery, and it was full for the capacity, you know Catholics and Protestants. So we had considered that we open Sparkles Day Care, which is an integrated day care. What would happen is it takes from age nought upwards, that children likely that are integrated there would be able to progress to the nursery school and then progress into integrated education. At the time, in the Protestant primary school the numbers were falling. It was led by Suffolk Community Forum and supported by us and SLIG. We had spent eighteen months working with both communities in getting support for an integrated educational system on that site. And that would be taking a risk, because, you know, it is a Protestant housing estate, but there was full support for it. Politicians supported it. West Belfast Partnership supported it. Lenadoon community forum supported it. Everyone supported it. And we put in an application to the Department of Education, and that was passed up then to the minister, Caitríona Ruane. And at that time we had said to her 'look we do not want permanent status for integrated education. If you would allow us two to three years, we will show you that this is possible and that we can do it.' And there were basically nine criteria, and one of the criteria was numbers. So we had said at that time, 'if you would base it on current numbers, we might as well go home. We will fail, because you are basing it on the current Protestant numbers, at the current Protestant school, which were falling. But if you would base it on the potential numbers from all of the support that we have?' And parents at the school were interviewed, and they said yes, if it would become integrated they would like to sit on the board, and make up an integrated board. There were other integrated schools that said yes, we will help you, because we are full. But in the end, she did not take the risk and decided to close the school down. … So that was in May, it was last year and Caitríona Ruane announced her formal decision last month. She is the education minister here, and she is Sinn Féin. That sends out a very stark message to other interface communities, that, if you take the risk, you will not be supported. So what is the point? So a lot of the statutory bodies that we work with were very, very concerned, because Suffolk not only is an area of deprivation, so that people could not send their children to a school on the doorstep. They would have to travel to go to another school, and those parents who could not afford that they were likely to move. And that had started to happen. Parents were requesting through the Housing Association if they could be moved to another area closer to a school." (Bannon, interview)

As discussed earlier,[211] SLIG managed to take effective steps to counteract the threat of a Protestant exodus from the Suffolk estate. Notably, as Jean Brown, the chairwoman of Suffolk Community Forum (SCF) pointed out, the Nationalist and Republican parties of the SDLP and Sinn Féin were very supportive after the closure of the school, whereas the Unionist parties of the DUP and UUP neglected them as they had always done.

"All of the Nationalist parties gave us their support and none of the Unionist parties. They are not really interested in us, you know. I mean I did a radio interview, when the school closed. And one of the things that I said very unapologetically was that if they asked Protestants to move out of Suffolk, then the lights of the DUP and the official Unionists will all be on the media, you know, complaining about it. But actually, they should be doing something to support us now, and they are not." (Brown, interview)

Nevertheless, the aftermath of the incident left scars in the Suffolk community. Brown, who dedicated more than thirty years of her life to local peacebuilding and reconciliation, could not conceal her profound disappointment. As she stated in a newspaper interview a few years later:

"We fought hard to save our local primary school and make it integrated, but it was demolished. That was so very disappointing. … Children should be mixing with those from outside their community from a very young age." (Brown, cited in Belfast Telegraph 2015)

Likewise, Chris O'Halloran, who had been involved in SLIG's projects since its foundation, expressed his discontent over the minister's decision. As he stressed, the main reason for the rejection was the fact that the viability of the Suffolk school was assessed according to the normal criteria applied to all parts of the UK.

"I would argue that the reason that Suffolk primary school got the decision that it got was that the viability of Suffolk Primary School was assessed on the same criteria that any primary school would be assessed, whether it was in Nottingham or Leeds or anywhere else: what's the number of children that attend the school? And on that criterion it made sense to close the school. The whole other argument about

---

[211] See p. 197.

the viability of the integrated school is the social desirability of an integrated school in that interface context. It wasn't part of their thinking at all, because they treat the Suffolk Primary School as they would treat a primary school in Nottingham or Leeds." (O'Halloran, interview)

He suspected that the reason for the decision was simply that she had no other choice, because the legal framework of policy-making did not permit anything else. Hence, an effective government strategy on community relations is needed to prevent such blatant mistakes.

"But the Minister of Education has 50 pieces of paper a day to decide. I was really disappointed when I heard that that decision had been made. But I just don't know if it would have been possible for Caitríona Ruane to make a different decision, without having some kind of basis to make it on: a legal framework, you know. …That's where government policy lags behind the progress we've made on the ground. That's why people are waiting for CSI, Cohesion, Sharing and Integration, to come out. …While it isn't there, decisions like Suffolk Primary School will just continue. If that document was there, then you would have a case to say to the minister, 'I think we should keep this school open, because it's in line with your strategy.' But while there is no strategy, then the Department of Education will close it, because that's in line with their strategy. Because their strategy is only about the numbers that attend the school permanently. So that's why the strategy is important." (O'Halloran, interview)

Michael Hall, who has also played a role in SLIG's cross-community work, joined the chorus of critical voices. In his view, there was a deeper problem behind these erroneous decisions, i.e. they actually institutionalised sectarianism. In illustration, he presented a witty anecdote about his experience with the Education Board in the early period of the Troubles, when he organised activities with Catholic and Protestant children.

"The tragedy is that the school in Suffolk has been closed, so I mean, unless there is a solution found to that, Suffolk is going to get smaller and smaller. … The irony about it, I mean, at the beginning of the Troubles, I used to have organised children's activities. And at that time you were able to get money for children's activities from the Education Board. They actually payed for youth clubs, I'm not sure if they do that at the moment, because of the lack of money they pulled back from a lot of money. But we were able to get money for bus trips and other things. But there had to be a 60:40 percentage, and either way. And I remember joking with some of the children. We would organise groups, and they didn't fit into the 60:40. But we just pretended that they did. … There was no likelihood that any of the Department of Education people would arrive and get onto the minibus. We just joked with the children and I said, 'Sean, if anybody asks you're Billy today.' You know, we just sort of dealt with it. Those criteria were institutionalising sectarianism. I understand that there is no point in giving money for cross-community projects, if it's only a token thing. But at the same time, by insisting on it you institutionalise it. You make it a big important issue." (Hall, interview)

The issue of 'peace walls' proved another major area of policy failure. Hall illustrated this with the case of the building of a new 'peace wall' on the property of Hazelwood Integrated College.[212] He castigated the political parties for having ignored the incident. What is more, they failed to provide general guidelines on interface problems, but instead their activities centred on publicly condemning incidents and calling for peace. Ultimately, in his view, they had no interest in dealing with issues of reconciliation and conflict transformation.

> I think to me as a tragedy, … our future has been handed over to these people. … And it was ironic that in the same week that the Assembly was been set up a new peace line was built on the property of the school. You know? But did any of the Assembly people come up? Did any of them come up to give advice? No, that's still, people are still being left with their problems. And interface problems are not being given guidance by anybody at Stormont. And then again at Stormont, ministers would come out and condemn things and appeal for peace. But there is no ministry of reconciliation. There's no ministry of conflict transformation. They are almost hoping that it just sort of goes away. It's just business as usual, except for that there are different worlds. (Hall, interview)

Dympna McGlade struck a similar chord, expressing her dismay at the interface construction. Like Hall, she gave the political establishment a poor rating. Yet, she also pointed out that the Catholic and Protestant communities affected actually wanted the 'peace wall' to be built, as a result of previous violent incidents.

> "I think that shocked everyone. I mean we are eleven years down the process of the Good Friday Agreement and up goes a fence at an integrated primary school. I think that reflects a very poor start for a peace process. And the communities are adamant that it needs to be there. First of all, because there had been very serious attacks that could have caused injury or death or loss of property. And that's fine. But they also recognised that it's a symptom of fractured relationships." (McGlade, interview)

There was severe criticism of the government's failure to meet the demands of interface communities to remove local 'peace walls'. But censure came only from the Catholic/Nationalist/Republican camp and from experts. Protestant/Unionist/Loyalist respondents did not mention the issue. O'Halloran, for instance, explained that

---

[212] The interface, a five-metre high mesh fence, was set up in 2007 (cf. BIP 2011: 108). For more information on the Hazelwood Integrated College see the section in this chapter on 'The Local Communities', Footnote 149, p. 143.

"There are people in different parts of the city trying to get interface walls and fences away. And they are finding that government won't take them away. Even when there is local agreement, they won't take them away. That's just ridiculous. That's a scandal. (O'Halloran, interview)

According to him, the reason given by the government was that they had no funds available to eliminate the walls (O'Halloran, interview). McGlade, in turn, criticised the absence of coordination between the departments in charge of community relations, and also their inflexibility to adapt to the specific circumstances of local interface communities. As a consequence, this led to erroneous decisions on the issue of tearing down local 'peace wall'. In illustration, she outlined a telling incident that had occurred in Ardoyne. The local community was prepared to take the risk and open the interface gates at Flax Street, which had been closed for decades. Yet, for safety reasons they demanded traffic-calming measures. Their request was, however, rejected by the Road Service on the grounds that there had been no accidents and no traffic, and therefore it did not meet their criteria of a certain threshold level of road incidents.

"What we have then are individual departments who work as individuals. You have to go to each department. ...They don't interlink in terms of community relations. If you take, for example, Flax Street: the community were interested in opening the gates at Flax Street. They had been closed for many, many years, thirty years probably. At Flax Street, a community has been built up. The mill has been transformed into apartments, and there's been no housing. So, there is now a community where it was there like before. So, the community said, 'oh, we don't mind the gates to be opened, but we don't want lots of traffic'. And they went to the road service and said, 'we'd like traffic common measures to enable us to open these gates. If it works, we take the gates away'. So that would be one interface down. The road service officer came back and said, 'we don't know the amount of traffic in the area'. There was none. 'We looked at the number of accidents'. This is how they engage when you want traffic common measures. 'There were no accidents', the road service officer said. But the gates have been closed. So there was no traffic. We explained that to them: 'You can't manage the traffic, because there is none. What we want to do will cause traffic.' And they said, 'We can't. There are criteria for this'. The point I'm making is that they have a road service. We don't have a peace plan. They are not flexible enough to take on board that this could be part of a peace plan that normalises that part of Belfast. That's just incredible." (McGlade, interview)

A similar case was described by O'Halloran, who also reported, and in almost the same diction as McGlade, about the Flax Street incident. It was about a community in a different part of Belfast, who wanted to get their interface removed so as to allow a faster route to school for their children.

However, their request for a footpath was turned down by the Department of the Environment (DOE) for financial reasons.

> "Another situation in a different part of Belfast is where similarly they wanted to open a gate. And it'll allow children a faster route to school. But to open the gate would allow traffic on the road. The parents don't want their kids to go down the road unless there's a footpath in the road. There is no footpath in the road. They don't want the kids walking down a road with no footpath. It's dangerous. And the DOE are saying, 'Oh no, we can't afford to make a footpath.' 'Well, ok, then don't open the gate'." (O'Halloran, interview)

McGlade presented another incident, which occurred in South West Belfast, where the elevation of a bridge led to the creation of a new interface barrier. This demonstrated once more the unwillingness of the Road Service to consider local needs in its decisions. Indeed, as McGlade noted, it did not view itself as being responsible for community relations.

> "Likewise, there is the bridge at Roden Street, where there had been an interface. And when they built the motorway, they built the fancy bridge. The Roden Street had been an interface area, but roughly foliage. To accommodate the bridge and the motorway, they took away the foliage. They built the bridge higher and they created a new interface. … So, there was an interface and they took it away and created a new interface. And with one of them I'd spoken he said, 'We don't do community relations'. (McGlade, interview)

As for the pledge by the DUP and Sinn Féin to remove all 'peace walls' by 2023, there was apparently profound scepticism from all sides and also resistance from local communities. Many experts, such as Neil Jarman and Joe O'Donnell, the new director of BIP, shared the view that the large majority of interface barriers would remain in place beyond the projected date. As O'Donnell remarked in an online media interview:

> "I do not see the wall that runs between the Shankill and Falls being removed in six years. … I don't think it is particularly important if we miss the target date of 2023. I'm not sure now in 2017 that anyone considers that we are going to hit that target." (O'Donnell, cited in Campbell 2017)

The doubts were shared by community workers on both sides of the Suffolk/Lenadoon interface. According to Roisin Erskine of SCF, the prospects were slim that the barriers surrounding the Protestant/Unionist/Loyalist Suffolk estate could be removed within that short timeframe. This was mainly due to deep-seated fear and insecurity in the community, which is why residents were reluctant to even talk about removing the barriers. On the Catholic/Nationalist/Republican side, Renee Crawford of LCF was of the same opinion, adding that it would take much longer to bring down the walls – if that ever succeeds. As she pointed out,

"There was a feeling of fear – particularly if you lived in the smaller community that someone would come in and say 'Right, in 2023 all of this is gone'. This is what people have grown up with. This is their protection. It took generations to create them and I believe that it is going to take generations to turn that around. Some people will never want the walls to go. Some might if they felt safe and secure – some sort of environmental enhancement to it and that is legitimate. But to say that by 2023 they would all be gone? No." (Crawford, cit. Campbell 2018)

In addition, she expressed concern about the tightening of funding for interface work, mainly due to the collapse of power-sharing. In her opinion, this would only complicate efforts to remove the 'peace walls':

"To hear that groups like SLIG are losing funding because of the current situation – if you lose the infrastructure that we have created between the two communities, what happens then?" (Crawford, cited in Campbell 2018)

In conclusion, like many respondents earlier, McGlade emphasised how important a governmental strategy for community relations would be for peacebuilding on the ground: "Whilst no strategy for community relations is in place, there is no peace process. …We don't have a policy." (McGlade, interview) In fact, as Jarman pointed out recently, there is a community relations policy, but it is hardly in place and largely dysfunctional, because it lacks the commitment and leadership of the two main Unionist and Nationalist parties. In his view, this is why community politics has failed so far to move beyond the containment of violence to addressing the structural causes of inequality and sectarianism. Thus, as he concluded,

"Although there is a policy, the T:BUC [Together: Building a United Community] policy, there is no real strong sense of political leadership and direction. In my view, the two main parties, the DUP and Sinn Féin, are fairly happy with the situation on the ground. It's what Galtung called a 'negative peace'. There is an effective absence of violence. But it has not moved beyond that to address the structural inequalities and structural underpinnings of sectarianism. So there is no move to address differences in segregation in education. There is very little impact on segregation in housing. There is very limited work done in terms of removing interface barriers." (Jarman, interview 4)

PRECIS: COMMUNITIES, POLITICS AND POWER RELATIONS

To start with most trivial finding it is worth saying that none of the respondents remained unaffected by politics. The highly politicised atmosphere in Northern Ireland was reflected in widespread political awareness. What can be gathered from their perceptions is that respondents were unanimously critical of the role and performance of political protagonists. As was to be expected, those with a Catholic/Nationalist/Republican background had a poor view of both the British state and the Unionist parties, those endorsing a Republican ideology with the most hostile stance. The same applied to their view on the Loyalist paramilitaries. Likewise, it is hardly surprising that those with a Protestant/Unionist/Loyalist background had an adverse picture of the Nationalist and especially of the Republican movement. This was most pronounced among Loyalists. However, it is indeed a surprise that Loyalist respondents had a similarly negative attitude towards the Unionist and British establishment. The contents of their criticism were in many ways similar, although there were substantial differences.

There were profound discrepancies in respondents' views of the conflict. The role of the state security forces in the Troubles was a major source of controversy. As local respondents with Catholic/Nationalist/Republican backgrounds pointed out, the British Army's arrival was initially welcomed by Catholic working-class communities. However, this reception changed quickly, and the Army was soon regarded as operating in tandem with the British Government, both aiming at controlling Catholic working-class communities by means of segregating them from their Protestant counterparts. This consolidated their hostile image of the state, which they accused, apart from discrimination, of exerting excessive violence against Catholics.

Here, criticism centred on the role of the police. There were claims that the RUC used brutal interrogation techniques against paramilitary suspects, detaining them without informing family members about their whereabouts. A further reproach was that the RUC employed anti-insurgency tactics by using local petty criminals as informants. The RUC was also accused of siding with Loyalist paramilitaries and supporting them in their aggression against Catholics/Nationalists/Republicans. Aside from special operations, the RUC generally stayed away from Catholic working-class areas. Yet, the absence of community policing caused considerable dissatisfaction among local residents, heightening their distrust of the RUC. As a consequence, serious crimes were not reported to the police, which meant that law and order were solely in the hands of the Republican paramilitaries. By contrast, Protestant respondents generally justified the government's actions and the violence of the security forces during the Troubles. However, they also criticised the security forces for having failed to provide effective policing and security to Protestant/Unionist/Loyalist working-class communities. As has been noted, there was unease with the police in Protestant working-class areas. Yet, this did not keep people from reporting to the police, because, after all, it was their police force. Accusations by the Catholic/Nationalist/Republican side were vehemently rejected. This view stated there was neither institutional collusion between the RUC and Loyalist paramilitaries, nor was excessive force applied against Catholics. Likewise, no torture was involved in police detainment practices.

As part of the Agreement, the police underwent extensive reform, also involving a name change from RUC to PSNI. In the post-Agreement situation, there was, however, still considerable suspicion about the police in both Catholic and Protestant working-class neighbourhoods. Nevertheless, at the same time the responses of both sides indicated that there were tentative signs of improvement in the relationship to the police. Likewise, respondents stressed the need for a proper local police service, not least due to an upsurge in crime and anti-social behaviour in all working-class areas. Simultaneously, they also pointed to many shortcomings in community policing, which was more frequent on the part of local Catholic/Republican respondents. They expressed doubts as to whether the police reform had led to the equal treatment of Catholics. Moreover, it was claimed that the values and aspirations of Republicans were not fully accepted, despite their recognition of the PSNI. Another major issue concerned the composition of the police force. The efforts to recruit more police officers from the Catholic community were met with scepticism. In particular, it was doubted that the 50/50 PSNI recruitment policy for both communities would induce a substantial number of working-class Catholics to join the police. This was also due to threats and intimidation from dissident groups. Another question related to the fact that the police were not locally embedded. As respondents from both camps mentioned, the police force operating in the area did not originate from the communities themselves. This led to a lack of understanding of local needs and concerns, thus contributing to the poor image of the police and their lack of acceptance by the communities. As a further consequence, the collaboration between the communities and the PSNI, especially on interface issues, was not without friction. However, signs could also be glimpsed that the police were beginning to develop a better understanding of local affairs.

Moreover, respondents from both sides disagreed on the causes of the Troubles and the logic of the violence. Nationalists/Republicans claimed that the IRA's armed campaign had been triggered off by the violence of the state, and, by extension, of the Loyalist paramilitaries. Indeed, the Republican respondents regarded the conflict as a liberation struggle against British rule. Unionists/Loyalists maintained the exact opposite. Ostensibly, the starting point was actually the Civil Rights Campaign, which was exploited by the IRA to launch their offensive on the state. Thus, the violence of the state and Loyalist paramilitaries was nothing but a legitimate response. This view was also contested. Accordingly, the UVF's paramilitary force served not only to prevent the resurgence of the IRA, but was also used by the dominant conservative faction within the UUP to thwart liberal reform in the mid-1960s. Furthermore, both sides blamed the paramilitaries of the other side for having committed atrocities during the Troubles. A general consensus, however, prevailed that the IRA's campaign was much more effective in achieving political ends than the Loyalist counter-strategy. In particular, this was because the IRA became an effective grassroots organisation taking care of everyday local needs and concerns, whilst concurrently campaigning for a united Ireland. Loyalist paramilitaries, by contrast, were regarded as having failed to turn their military clout into a political force. In the main, this was because of their lack of support within the Protestant/Unionist community, especially among the middle classes, who treated them with a mixture of tacit approval and benign neglect. This relationship was mirrored in the political arena. There were, however, close links between Loyalist paramilitary leaders and senior Unionist politicians throughout the Troubles. Yet, this cooperation took place behind closed doors and was publicly denied by politicians.

There was a broad consensus that working-class interests were neglected or even suppressed during Unionist and British rule. This had a long tradition in the Unionist approach to government, indeed dating back to the inception of Northern Ireland. As their rule was based on a discriminating view of the sole representation of Protestants, it merely goes without saying that Catholics were generally disadvantaged in the socio-economic and political arenas. However, as Loyalists commonly lamented, the Protestant/Loyalist working class had also always lacked political representation by the Unionist establishment. Indeed, the UUP's government policy during its majoritarian government from 1921 to 1969 favoured the Protestant middle and upper classes.

Moreover, the Protestant/Loyalist working class was divided into Unionist and Labour party supporters. Yet, as part of the opposition, the NILP had only little political leverage. What is more, the ruling Unionists were always anxious to ensure the support of the Protestant working-class, especially to safeguard the union with Great Britain. To this aim, they employed a policy of fear-raising, based on the idea of loss of culture and political identity. In particular, they stirred up anxieties among the Protestant working-class that Catholics would not only take over their jobs, but also coerce them into a united Ireland. The British Government was charged with having neglected the needs and interests of Loyalist working-class neighbourhoods. Indeed, it was seen that the government's socio-economic policies in the 1970s and 1980s had often had detrimental impacts on their living conditions. The government changed its policy in the late 1980s and early 1990s, shifting the focus to targeting the needs of the socio-economically most deprived areas as a means of combatting violence. It did not do so, however, of its own accord, but only in response to a massive upsurge of IRA activity in West Belfast. But government policy was accused of ignoring specific local conditions, thus compounding the implementation of community development initiatives. Republican working-class communities benefitted most from British government funding. This was part of the government's strategy to get the Nationalist/Republican movement on board the political peace process. As a consequence of this government policy, deprivation in Loyalist working-class communities became worse than in Catholic ones. It also reinforced the sense of discrimination and exclusion among Loyalist working-class communities.

Loyalist respondents were unanimous that working-class politicians were needed to challenge the political system. There were some people, primarily with a Loyalist paramilitary background, who were active in grassroots politics. However, these local politicians were not rewarded by their communities in terms of electoral votes. One major cause was their electoral behaviour, which was based on traditional patterns of voting for the mainstream Unionist parties, out of loyalty and mistrust and fear of the 'other' side. Another reason was that working-class Protestants had no tradition of voting for political parties associated with Loyalist paramilitary groups. Loyalist ex-combatants attributed this to the law-abiding nature of Protestants and their contempt for the paramilitaries' efforts to defend the state and the sacrifices made for the community during the Troubles. Above all, however, the established Unionist parties exerted control over Loyalist working-class communities by fostering anxieties and exploiting them for political ends. Yet, Loyalists became aware of this only quite recently, and once they had achieved political maturity, they lost some of their most visionary political leaders. This awareness was reflected in their severe criticism of the DUP and its hypocrisy in entering into a power-sharing coalition with Sinn Féin, whilst earlier having denounced UVF members as traitors for engaging in talks with Republicans. The Catholic/Nationalist/Republican perspective was quite the opposite. The grassroots political approach of Sinn Féin was generally welcomed among Catholic working-class communities, and materialised in substantial electoral support. Yet, there was also dissatisfaction with the representation of their interests by Sinn Féin on the government level. By contrast, the SDLP had a lower reputation among Catholic working-class communities, as they were also less prevalent there than in middle and upper-class districts. In a similar fashion to the Protestant and Catholic working classes, there was considerable political alienation among the middle classes, which led to higher abstention from voting because the political discourse advocated by the DUP and Sinn Féin had nothing to offer them.

Both sides acknowledged that the living conditions and overall socioeconomic impoverishment of Catholic and Protestant working-class communities was similar. But there was never common union representation for the Catholic and Protestant working classes, which respondents would have welcomed. And, needless to say, there was no notable joint representation on the party plane. Given the grassroots political activities, the question arises as to what is the likelihood that such an effective representation might emerge? Was any politician considered as having the potential to influence the opinions and attitudes of local working-class people to urge the effective political representation of their interests across the ethno-national divide? Furthermore, this might ultimately be a preliminary to initiating change in political power structures. Such a person might then be regarded as an 'organic intellectual' in a Gramscian sense. Conversely, the question arises as to whether specific actors were identified who were seen as obstructing such an implementation, thus classifying as 'reactionary forces'. Indeed, one politician was identified by both sides as having a positive image within both working-class communities. This was the late David Ervine, the former leader of the PUP and an ex-UVF combatant. In a number of respects, he fitted the picture of an 'organic intellectual': First, he came from a working-class background himself. Secondly, he was well-respected by both sides for both perceiving and advocating local working-class interests. However, he and the PUP did not manage to attract sufficient electoral support to give their political demands leverage, largely for the reasons mentioned: the traditional voting patterns along ethno-national lines of working-class Protestants and Catholics and the general reluctance among the Protestant working class to vote for parties associated with Loyalist paramilitaries.

Both sides commented negatively on the role and performance of the key protagonists in the political peace process and its implementation Many respondents articulated their discontent with the DUP and Sinn Féin both regarding their commitment to the peace process and their performance in government. As a result, there was an inherent instability in both the peace process and the power-sharing arrangements. In general, both leading parties were criticised for acting in fundamental opposition to each other, reluctant to reach consensus on key policy issues. In fact, the impression dominated that they actually avoided decision-making on controversial matters. This lay in their fundamental dissent over national and constitutional aspirations. They had failed to learn from the legacies of the Troubles. Instead, they were preoccupied with establishing a political structure allowing them to concentrate power in their own hands. The DUP and Sinn Féin were viewed as merely being concerned about retaining their power base and engaging in sectarian politics. They were reluctant to make concessions to the other side to ensure the support of their respective constituencies. Moreover, the two parties differed significantly in their general policy orientation, with the DUP focussing on economics and Sinn Féin more on social issues. There was also some censure that the existing power-sharing arrangements excluded any opposition. Despite all the criticism, however, it was appreciated, that a power-sharing government was at least in place, albeit mainly by respondents from a Catholic/Nationalist background and by experts.

There was disagreement between respondents from both sides regarding the issue as to who was more to blame for the government's failure. On the Catholic side, particularly from Republicans, criticism was levelled at the Unionists' obstructionist policy. As far as the political attitudes of the two parties in power towards their communities were concerned, Sinn Féin and the Nationalist/Republican movement were empowering their community, whereas the DUP were aiming at controlling their community by keeping them in fear of the 'other' side, due to their vested power interests. In pursuing their sectarian strategy, the DUP were mainly concerned with securing their electoral power base through false claims, like that of the ethnic cleansing of Protestants, and manipulative practices, such as gerrymandering of voting districts for electoral gains. In the Loyalist camp, it was striking that the mainstream Unionist parties of the DUP and the UUP generally had a poor image among respondents with Loyalist backgrounds. This applied especially to the DUP, which was accused of vacillation and hypocrisy in having proclaimed 'no surrender to the IRA' for forty years and then entering into power-sharing with Sinn Féin.

From an expert's perspective, the Anglo-Irish Agreement of 1985 between the British and Irish governments was both groundbreaking and precedent-setting. The treaty not only laid down the institutional and constitutional framework, but likewise shaped the relations between the later ruling parties of Sinn Féin and the DUP. Moreover, the Anglo-Irish Agreement also re-framed the intricate question of national self-determination in Northern Ireland, because the constitutional shift implied that it was not so much a matter of British/Unionist or Irish national identity, but rather an issue of recognition. The core concern for the British and Irish governments was how to in-duce the antagonists to participate in the peace process. The ultimate conse-quence of this political tug-of-war was that all sides had to make substantial concessions, in the end diluting the provisions of the peace agreement and of subsequent governance arrangements. This sense of ambiguity, which was understood as a deliberate intention to deceive the people or accommodate to the needs of both sides was generally shared by respondents. Vehement dis-cord arose regarding the assets and liabilities accorded by the Agreement to both sides. The only thing that they could agree on was that the Catholic/ Nationalist/Republican community benefitted more from the Agreement. Otherwise, they held divergent stances and interpretations. As to the reasons for Protestant/Unionist/Loyalist discontent with the Agreement, it was point-ed out that major concessions had had to be made to Republicans for them to renounce paramilitary violence. This included, above all, sacrificing the RUC, early releasing Republican paramilitary prisoners and accepting former Re-publican combatants in government, who, it was suspected, had been in-volved in past evils against the Protestant/Unionist community. By and large, they did not regard the Agreement as a major concession by Republicans. Despite all the affirmations, however, there was a considerable sense of un-certainty among Unionists about the constitutional status of Northern Ireland, which the Agreement made contingent on the consent of the majority of the population. The legitimacy of the constitutional aspirations of both sides was generally acknowledged, as long as these were pursued through peaceful and democratic means. However, there was criticism by some Republican respondents about Unionist intransigence in engaging in political dialogue with Republicans on constitutional issues. Many were, however, convinced that the Protestant community would eventually come to the insight that a united Ireland might be the better and more livable alternative.

In the context of community groups' and activists' involvement in the peace process, it was emphasised by respondents involved at that time that the peace process was actually a two-tier project, consisting of the community peace process and the political one. In the political peace process, community and peace activists as well as paramilitary groups played an important role: the latter through secret communication networks between the IRA and the British Government and between the UVF and the UDA, the former in facilitating relationships between main political actors and in inducing people to vote in favour of the Agreement. However, there was a tense relationship between the two processes. The political parties took a poor view of community involvement because they were anxious not to lose control of the overall peace process and thus sought to keep the communities at a distance. This became manifest also in the area of community development funding. In particular, there were worries among certain sections of the political elites that the funding of community development would promote reconciliation. Thus, the community and voluntary sector's contribution to the peace process was not provided for in the Agreement due to fierce opposition on the part of Sinn Féin and the DUP. The only main party that substantially supported the community agenda was the SDLP. On the initiative of the middle-ground parties of the NIWC and the APNI, the Agreement also envisaged a Civic Forum of Northern Ireland. However, instead of being an effective representative body for those involved in community relations and development, it proved to be an ineffective short-lived consultative body that was disbanded after only two years in operation. From an experts' point of view, its failure was rooted in the traditional lack of political representation for community interests and needs. Under direct rule, the British administration in Northern Ireland had no local party structure and operated through a pragmatic cooperation with the public sector, the civil service and the community field. This implied that the political parties had no expertise in dealing with issues of community development and relations and thus lacked policy-making capacity. Moreover, the parties were also reluctant to collaborate with the community representatives of the Civic Forum and take responsibility for their activities.

It was, however, not just a question that Catholic and Protestant working-class communities had no political representative body, the state also proved ill-equipped to deal with large-scale intercommunal violence. The main reason for this was that the state had no mechanisms that were adapted to the specific circumstances of the Troubles. This had been intentional, because the state wanted to give the impression that the situation in Belfast was no different to that of any other place in the UK. Many state authorities still operated according to this premise, which, for instance, was shown in the inability to provide services appropriate to the special needs of young people exposed to interface violence.

There was a more fundamental issue contributing to the neglect of the communities on the part of the political parties. This was to be found in both the logic of the peace process and the nature of the Agreement. The ultimate aim of the British and Irish governments behind the peace process was to improve relations between themselves. They sought to resolve their problems by establishing an institutional framework of devolved power-sharing between the two antagonistic political camps, enabling a fair and shared future for both communities. In their eyes, this could only be achieved by promoting the political centre, and, at the same time, keeping the radical elements on board, who were ultimately aiming at winning over the 'other' side. It was hoped that this would lead to the marginalisation of the radical fringe, and thus facilitate the formation and stable working of a centre-led, power-sharing government. Initially, it seemed as if the plan of the two governments were succeeding. Yet, the power-sharing government led by the more moderate parties on both sides, the UUP and the SDLP, proved inherently unstable and inefficient, mainly due to obstruction on the part of the DUP and Sinn Féin on resolving the crucial contentious issues of paramilitary decommissioning and police reform. As a consequence, there was a growing polarisation, which had a detrimental impact on the UUP and the SDLP. The fact that they were the main signatory parties to the Agreement on both sides cost them considerable support from their constituencies and also initiated a process of fragmentation, particularly within the UUP.

The shift in power towards the DUP and Sinn Féin aggravated the situation in terms of community policy. As was criticised by respondents across the board, there is reluctance and inability by the two parties to come up with an effective community relations strategy. In the aftermath of the Agreement, a political initiative was launched under direct rule to develop an overall community relations strategy called 'A Shared Future'. Yet, the process of implementing this strategy was stalled, as soon as Sinn Féin and the DUP entered into power-sharing government. Consequently, the 'A Shared Future' document was shelved and replaced by the two parties' new strategy, entitled 'Community, Sharing and Integration', which was again abandoned and replaced by a new and currently in-effect strategy called 'Together: Building a United Community', essentially building on the core pillars of 'A Shared Future'. To date, no significant progress has been made on the implementation of the new strategic framework. There was a major difference between the two parties regarding their high-level strategic priorities. Whilst the salient issue for Sinn Féin was equality, the DUP placed special emphasis on peace and prosperity and respect for the rule of law. Moreover, there was a cross-cutting approach of building a shared and better future for the whole of society, on which all policies had to be demonstrably based. The major obstacle was to strike a balance between promoting equality and good relations, an apparent ambiguity to be found in the legal basis for the implementation of the Agreement.

The major policy challenge was to link strategy and implementation. Thus, the crux was to find the right balance and to contrive a policy that would respect the right to different opinions and traditions and to resolve potential controversies through dialogue, not violence. A key question was whether the government's strategy on community relations would provide coherent and consistent funding. However, the funds promised by the government came to modest sums. Moreover, the scarcity of funding resources was exacerbated by the global economic crisis, exerting strong competitive pressure on community groups to obtain adequate funding for their community relations activities and projects.The 'peace money' available was also not effectively employed to improve community conditions and relations on the ground, as it neither translated into significant improvements in living conditions, nor did it resolve the 'peace wall' problem. Indeed, recent years have actually witnessed a substantial drop in peace and reconciliation funding.

Respondents across the board criticised the DUP and Sinn Féin-led government for its failure to deliver a community relations strategy. Its absence created huge problems for community relations work. The perception of the local respondents on both sides was by and large negative concerning the impact of community relations policy on working-class communities. In practical terms, several issues were raised about housing policies. Given the segregated space bounded by interfaces, the demographic shift in favour of Catholics, especially in North Belfast, poses major challenges for housing policy, i.e. the construction and allocation of houses. The DUP and Sinn Féin manipulated the housing issue to their own ends of retaining power. In particular, the DUP was accused of manipulating Protestant working-class communities by conjuring the spectre of fear and thus stirring sectarian hostilities towards Catholics. A related difficulty was rooted in the parties' sectarian headcount politics. Thus, the allocation of housing in Protestant areas to Catholics would mean a shift in voting dynamics and increase the electoral power base of the Republican and Nationalist movement. Another issue was parading, which had been ignored and sometimes even exploited by the leading parties in a quest for power. The government's community relations policy also failed to take the spatial peculiarities of Belfast into account, in particular North Belfast's patchwork of Protestant/Unionist/Loyalist and Catholic/Nationalist/Republican working-class neighbourhoods. As a consequence, there was no common vision on the development of the area, and thus the two sides could not agree on how to tackle local community needs, above all interface issues.

Problems were associated with the impact of the equality agenda on community-relations work. The equality agenda was a core element of the community package provided for in the Agreement. The unnecessary complexities in the legal provisions for equality and equal rights were criticised. Moreover, the equality agenda was still fraught with elements mirroring the sectarian nature of community relations. It also did not take the specific needs and circumstances of interface areas into account, heightening the threat of violence. The field of education proved equally problematic, especially in interface areas, as, for instance, the closure of the primary school in Suffolk showed. The school's application for integrated status was supported by both communities of Protestant Suffolk and Catholic Lenadoon, yet the Sinn Féin Minister of Education rejected it, stating there would not be enough future pupils to sustain the school. Notably, the school met all the other eight criteria that were required. The criteria applied to all parts of the UK, as Northern Ireland was not regarded as a special case.

Finally, the issue of 'peace walls' proved to be another major area of policy failure. A new 'peace wall' was built, for instance, on the property of Hazelwood Integrated College. The political parties ignored the incident. What is more, in an act of hypocrisy they failed to provide general guidelines on interface problems, but instead focused their activities on publicly condemning incidents and calling for peace. There was severe criticism of the government's failure to meet the demands of interface communities to remove local 'peace walls'. Notably, censure came only from the Catholic/Nationalist/Republican side and from experts. Protestant/Unionist/Loyalist respondents did not mention the issue at all. Points of criticism were: the absence of coordination between the departments in charge of community relations and their inflexibility in adapting to the specific circumstances of local interface communities as well as the lack of funds available to eliminate the walls. Respondents were unanimous that an effective government strategy on community relations is needed to prevent such obvious blunders. For the time being, however, given the continuing absence of a power-sharing government in Northern Ireland, such a strategy does not appear to be in sight. Actually, there is the concern that Brexit and the Irish border issue adds another sectarian strut to community politics. Moreover, as was also suspected, the two leading parties of the DUP and Sinn Féin had no real intention of advancing community relations, since it would serve their interest in power to maintain the status quo.

Thus, the 'current' situation presents the following picture. As responses suggest, the political camps on both sides sought to exert power and control over their respective clientele. Above all, the two leading political parties of Sinn Féin and the DUP were most harshly criticised for having manipulated vital community issues to their own ends of retaining power. Moreover, their failure to deliver effective policies on community development and community relations was ultimately the result of their opposing political aspirations for the constitutional future of Northern Ireland. This similarly prevented the initiation of effective joint class policies. Apparently, they can be termed 'reactionary forces', to use Antonio Gramsci's diction. By contrast, there are no indications of an 'organic intellectual' who can effectively represent the interests of both working classes on the political plane. Instead of taking the socio-economic concerns of working-class people seriously, especially those in interface communities, the two parties pursued a political agenda reinforcing sectarian division. They did so, on the one hand, by stirring fear, resentment and rivalries among their electorate and, on the other hand, by promoting exclusivist politics. Yet, on the part of the communities, there was a major difference in terms of their political self-image. Whilst the outcome of the Agreement has perpetuated and even consolidated the siege mentality and sense of loss among Loyalists, it has given substantial stimulus and confidence to Republicans.

5 CONCLUSION
"AND THE WALLS REMAIN THE SAME?"

"Plus ça change, plus c'est la même chose." (Karr 1849)[213]

This French epigram, meaning "the more it changes, the more it is the same thing", may provide a vague indication of continuing situation of simmering local intergroup conflict in Northern Ireland. Seen from a particular outcome-oriented perspective, it connects to the afore-mentioned common belief in the immutability of certain social, economic and political circumstances and conditions.[214] Since the cessation of armed conflict in 1994, a great deal of dynamism has evolved in terms of peacebuilding activities both at community and political levels. Yet, as this study has demonstrated, seen from the perspective of the Protestant and Catholic working-class communities, the outcome has been modest to date. In a basic sense, the status can be summarised in a single word: ambiguity. Ambiguity implies lack of clarity, potentially causing insecurity and a lack of understanding, and may at times even aggravate existing intercommunal tensions. At the same time, however, ambiguity also hints at a plethora of options that might lead to improvement or progress in community relations.

In many ways, ambiguity pervades Northern Ireland's political landscape. The term, or its synonym 'ambivalence', was used by respondents across the board in their assessment of the Good Friday/Belfast Agreement and its impact on Catholic and Protestant working-class communities. Indeed, the peace treaty is rife with ambiguous provisions, thus causing divergent interpretations on both sides. Above all, this applies to the specific constitutional formula, which makes the political status of Northern Ireland contingent on the majority consent of the population. On the one hand, the large scope for interpretation has given rise to false hopes and expectations for a local peace dividend, and, on the other, it has reinforced the long-standing winner/loser dichotomy, especially between Nationalist/Republican and Unionist/Loyalist aspirations. Similarly, the implementation of the Agreement has been fraught

---

[213] This epigram (cited in Knowles 1999: 426) is from Jean-Baptiste Alphonse Karr, a French novelist, critic and journalist. It first appeared in the January 1849 issue of his monthly satirical journal *Les Guêpes* ("The Wasps").

[214] See also the opening paragraph in the section on "The Perennial Problem of Intergroup Conflict" of Chapter 2, p. 34.

with ambivalence. Whereas cross-community power-sharing institutions have been set up that enjoy endorsement by the majority in both communities, they have, however, so far proven largely dysfunctional and prone to policy failure. Although publicly affirming their commitment to community relations, the two leading parties of the DUP and Sinn Féin have continuously omitted to deliver a strategy. As a consequence, erroneous decisions have been made that have thwarted the implementation of peacebuilding projects across the divide. Moreover, the communities have been left with no guidance, let alone concrete assistance, on how to deal with interface issues. This situation is compounded by the government's inability to respond effectively to large-scale intercommunal riots at parades and other contentious incidents and to meet local needs concerning the 'peace walls'. Ambiguity also characterises the perceptions and attitudes of the working-class communities towards their political leaders. There is widespread discontent with their performance and a sentiment that working-class interests are not being adequately represented. Yet, the working classes keep following traditional loyalty patterns of voting for either mainstream Unionist or Republican/Nationalist parties. Even if there were politicians to represent their interests and command their respect, they would still deny them political support.

On the ground, ambiguity has permeated relations both between and within Catholic and Protestant working-class communities. They share a sense of socio-economic disadvantage and common interface issues. Indeed, the interface communities are the most multiply deprived areas in Northern Ireland. Notwithstanding the awareness of common interests, however, cross-community cooperation has hardly extended beyond defusing interface tensions and violence. And even there, both sides often engage in a blame game as to who is to be held responsible for the violence. This is particularly true in the flashpoint areas of North and North-West Belfast. Beyond that, there is an avoidance culture, which is manifested in evading discussion on contentious issues, such as housing, education and employment, not to mention cultural and political issues. What is more, people living in interface communities, especially those in flashpoint areas, show a general tendency to avoid contact with their neighbours from the 'other' side, mainly out of feelings of fear, insecurity and hostility.

An ambivalent relationship can likewise be seen between the working-class communities and their former paramilitary combatants. This applies especially to Loyalist ex-combatants, who have generally experienced much less appreciation for their efforts on the part of their communities during the

Troubles than their Republican counterparts in the Catholic communities. Moreover, on both sides, friction is growing with dissident factions attracting increasing support from within the communities, especially from local youth. In a similar vein, the communities' attitudes towards cross-community workers are shaped by ambivalence. Despite the general acknowledgement of their efforts to contain interface tensions, there is some resistance to activities aiming at interface regeneration and reconciliation with the 'other' side. A further area of ambiguity concerns the relationship between working-class people and their middle-class counterparts, especially those who have ascended the social ladder, left the communities and moved to more prosperous areas elsewhere. On the one hand, the working class tend to bond with the middle class as part of the wider community; on the other, they feel left behind, believing that this new middle class has benefitted from the peace dividend, whilst they have not. In this respect, a more profound ambivalence has arisen in Loyalist working-class communities. There is a general sense of feeling disrespected and abandoned by the wider Protestant community and by the Unionist political establishment. At the same time, however, they share a strong sense of common belonging and continue to champion the Unionist cause. Finally, one more aspect of ambiguity arises, which can be viewed as the outcome of all the others. This is on the personal plane and affects the dichotomy in which many working-class people and, above all, those living in interface neighbourhoods find themselves. On the one hand, they affirm peaceful co-existence towards a shared future within the given polity of Northern Ireland, and do not want the Troubles to return. But on the other, they engage in sectarian cultural practices and territorial struggles, embracing exclusivist Nationalist or Unionist aspirations that would undermine or maintain this polity respectively.

Where does this ambiguity come from? What are the underlying causes for the ongoing divide between both the communities and their political camps? Are there signs for more clarity, rapprochement and reconciliation between the two sides? Three key analytical dimensions may help to shed light here: conflicting ethno-national identities, socio-economic class inequalities and the hegemonic power interests of the political elites. As indicated in the analysis, these three dimensions, in particular, correlate to one another in a specific way and have formed into patterns over the course of time. A Gramscian perspective may help to comprehend this development. Several catchwords that featured prominently in the respondents' narratives may also be revealing in this respect. These included: 'benign neglect', 'tacit approval', 'siege mentality', and 'triumphalism'.

Let us return to the inception of Northern Ireland and explore in fast motion the political power relations between Unionists/Loyalists and Nationalists/Republicans as well as the relations between the Catholic and Protestant communities. At the time of state formation, both relationships were profoundly permeated by ambiguity. The state of Northern Ireland emerged from an internecine nationalist civil war over power, in which the Unionists/Loyalists emerged victorious. In effect, the British Government handed over substantial governing authority for Northern Irish affairs to the Unionist elite, which had already dominated the political and socio-economic sphere for more than two centuries. Subsequently, British policy towards Northern Ireland was characterised by benign neglect and non-interference. The Irish Republic, for its part was mostly concerned with internal affairs and by and large did not involve itself either. However, in their mission to establish hegemonic power over the state and ensure Protestant supremacy, the Unionist elite was confronted with a two-fold dilemma: how to appease the restless Catholic minority within the state and how to combat the Nationalist/ Republican threat both within Northern Ireland and across the border from the Irish state? To solve these vexing questions, they set up a one-party regime that excluded Nationalists/Republicans from power and pursued policies of the political and socio-economic disenfranchisement and discrimination of Catholics. They endeavoured to secure their rule by the means of coercion and armed force. Those who bore the brunt were the Catholic/ Nationalist/Republican working-class communities. This reinforced their sense of alienation and of being under the occupation of a foreign power. This sentiment was augmented by a sense of abandonment, as their hopes that their Irish Nationalist/Republican fellows across the border would help liberate them proved to be in vain. However, there was also ambivalence in their relationship to the Unionist regime. They could not just simply abstain from the state, because they were ultimately dependent on its service provision.

By contrast, the Protestant, and mainly Loyalist working class, was in a much better socio-economic position, though also in an ambivalent dependency on the state. The Unionist elite ruled with calculated benevolence and ensured that their basic needs were supplied, especially in terms of employment and public housing. But they were excluded from power, which was vested exclusively in the hands of conservative middle and upper classes. This clientele system represented one pillar of Unionist hegemony over the

Loyalist working class, whilst the other was a strategy of promoting fear that the Catholics/Nationalists/Republicans would usurp the state. Both means ensured that its working class toed the line. This politics of fear contributed to a widespread 'siege mentality' among the Protestant/Loyalist working class. A consequence of the overriding concern with the national question resulted in no effective working-class politics being able to develop. The relations between the working-class communities were also shaped by ambiguity. There was a profound lack of contact due to high residential segregation, especially so in interface areas. And when such contact occurred, it was fraught with sectarian tensions and violence. This created ambiguity on both sides. On the one hand, it served their need for protection, yet on the other, it increased the lack of understanding, thus consolidating community divisions. Beyond that, it also prevented the development of of a shared sense of deprivation and of cross-community class consciousness and representation.

In the 1960s, power structures and relations between the communities began to change radically. There was ambivalence within the Unionist party as to whether to accommodate or to suppress the growing Catholic demands for equal rights. The conservatives emerged from the ensuing internal power struggles victorious, yet the resulting violent clashes fuelled the concurrent resurgence of Republican paramilitaries and their employment as a counter-hegemonic force. At the outbreak of the Troubles, the British Government assumed authority over the state. From then until the mid-1980s, the scene was dominated by armed power struggles between Republicans, on the one hand, and the British/Unionist security forces and Loyalist paramilitaries, on the other. This deepened the ambivalence between the working-class communities. Whereas the erection of interface barriers served the heightened need for protection against attacks from the 'other' side, these 'peace walls' further intensified reciprocal hostile images and incomprehension. Ambiguity also grew between the Protestant/Loyalist working-class community and the Unionist elite. The immense Republican paramilitary threat to both them and the very existence of the state heightened their loyalty to the Unionist establishment. At the same time, there was a mounting sense of loss and discontent with the Unionist elite, as the latter could no longer guarantee their privileges. They had a similarly ambivalent relationship to the British Government. On the one hand, they had a strong feeling of loyalty. By contrast, however, they also had a highly negative stance towards certain government policies, such as the government urban redevelopment policy, which was viewed as having a profoundly negative impact on socio-economic development and as under-mining the cohesion and fabric of the community.

Finally, one crucial element still remains open in this historical outline of 'conflict ambiguity', so to say. The Anglo-Irish Agreement of 1985 led to a further radical shift in the relations between the communities and between the political elites. With this agreement, the British and Irish governments essentially redefined the overall framework. So, both governments departed from their previous stance of treating Northern Ireland as 'a place apart'. It was their over-riding concern to improve Anglo-Irish relations by means of the peace treaty between the conflicting parties in Northern Ireland. But, on both sides, this led to a growth in the ambiguities, as was pointed out in the previous discussion. But there was, above all, ambiguity in the governments' main strategy to bring about a stable peace agreement based on inclusive power-sharing, equality and good community relations. How could the key Unionist and Nationalist antagonists be kept on board the peace process without undermining the moderate political centre? After all, a strong, centre-led government was essential to ensure a win-win situation instead of the victory of one community over the other. Yet, as the shift in power towards the two radical parties of the DUP and Sinn Féin has shown, the strategy did not bear fruit.

What has been said up to now should show the complexity and inter-relatedness of ambiguity in its adverse form in the relations between all sides involved in the Northern Ireland conflict and its transformation process. The negative side of this ambivalence has prevented substantial improvement in the relations between the communities and between the political camps so far. However, are there any projects that point in an optimistic direction and give cause for hope that the age-old conflict can be resolved?

Even at the beginning of the Troubles, there was grassroots activism in the communities that initially focused on community development, but soon turned into joint peacebuilding efforts. A particular aim was to reduce tensions and violence at the interfaces between deprived working-class communities. These efforts were, however, thwarted and suppressed both by stakeholders on the political level and paramilitaries so as not to lose control of power in the conflict. Their main objective of both sides was to vanquish the 'other' one and achieve hegemony in the state. Only when it became clear to both sides that the opponent could not be overcome by military means did they gradually become more conciliatory towards the community sector. But only the peace process led to a shift in focus on community development.

Yet, so far the key political protagonists still continue to engage in power struggles and thus see cross-community work largely as limited to the prevention of violence.

A unique example can be cited demonstrating that commitment, courage and the willingness to set divisions aside can extend beyond the containment of violence and bear fruit, leading to peacebuilding and cross-community cooperation, especially in interface areas. This is the experience of the working-class communities of Protestant/Unionist/Loyalist Suffolk and Catholic/Nationalist/Republican Lenadoon, where economic regeneration of their interface area was initiated in times of large-scale sectarian strife. However, despite all the progress made, their efforts to expand cooperation have so far been stalled for the same perennial reasons: housing and territoriality disputes between the communities. Moreover, there is a further major stumbling block, which has clearly been shown in their integrated school project for the benefit of both communities. This was also thwarted, but this time by sectarianism on the part of policy-makers and the Northern Ireland Government.

Hence, this leads to the major quandary: How can essentially adverse ambiguous relations be developed into lucid and commonly agreed upon strategies to solve community issues of common interest and concern?

The prospects for that seem rather remote at this juncture, because, all this having been said, the core issues between the Catholic/Nationalist/Republican and Protestant/Unionist/Loyalist working-class communities have not been resolved. In fact, the relations between them have remained fraught with ambiguity, insecurity and tensions. Much boils down to the Good Friday/Belfast Agreement, both in terms of its cross-community principles and its governance architecture. In essence, the Agreement is the outcome of an elite bargain with little involvement of civil society. It thus bears the hallmark of the Unionist and Nationalist political parties and the British and Irish governments and has been largely shaped by their interests. Consequently, particular emphasis was placed on making arrangements for internal power-sharing and community relations within the wider framework of Anglo-Irish and all-Ireland relations. Both areas, however, have proved to be detrimental to the relations between Protestant and Catholic working-class communities, especially those living close to interfaces.

After all, the modus operandi of power-sharing governance, based on consociational principles, has solidified the two ethno-national blocs in Northern Ireland. It has not, however, succeeded in stabilising the balance of power between the Unionist and Nationalist political camps. Instead, it has provided them a stage to engage in their power struggles. It has also led to increasing political polarisation with a shift in power from the moderate to the more radical Unionist and Nationalist parties and a maginalisation of the middle-ground. Indeed, the power-sharing institutions have proved to be largely dysfunctional and unstable, as their repeated suspensions and recent collapse have shown. In particular, the DUP and Sinn Féin as the two leading parties have lacked the drive to create a roadmap for peacebuilding and to move it forward.This is specifically evidenced by their failure to deliver an effective community relations strategy and policy. Hence, the community groups on both sides are left without the leadership and guidance that they urgently need for their cross-community peacebuilding and interface work. Instead of seeking to improve local community relations beyond the containment of violence, the two main Unionist and Nationalist parties are apparently content with the current situation of sectarian division in working-class interface areas in Belfast and also in Derry/Londonderry and Portadown. For this ensures to keep their ethno-national constituencies in line and thus serves their primary interest in power and hegemony. After all, the collapse of power-sharing more than two and a half years ago indicates not only that there is not enough basis for cooperation between the two sides; it also suggests a lack of joint commitment to govern for all and strive to transform Northern Ireland from what has often been termed 'a place apart' (cf. Cash 2009: 237, McGarry 2001: 1, Murphy 1979) into a stable, peaceful and inclusive society – a society that has overcome sectarian divisions, and where the Agreement's principle of equality has been fully translated into practice.

What has been said so far also points to a larger, general problem inherent in consociational power-sharing as a means of peacebuilding and conflict transformation in deeply divided societies. In fact, consociational governance arrangements, such as those in Bosnia and Herzegovina, Kosovo, South Africa, East Timor, Lebanon and Northern Ireland, have proved successful in significantly reducing and containing intercommunal violence on the ground. However, they have failed so far to transform the root causes of conflict and thus to create the conditions for a shared 'culture of peace'. Instead, the elitist nature of concociational arrangements all too often reinforces ethno-national antagonisms and encourages hegemonic power struggles, thus hampering policies aimed at improving community relations and building peace on the ground. In short, to employ Galtung's terminology, although in many cases consociationalism has enabled a state of 'negative peace' it has so far fallen short of achieving a 'positive peace'.

Finally, a major problem pertains to the Agreement's principle of 'parity of esteem'. As a core element for promoting relationships between the two main traditions in Northern Ireland, it demands equal recognition of British and Irish identity. Therefore, in practice, people in Northern Ireland have the right to choose British or Irish citizenship, or both. Likewise, it entitles Unionists/Loyalists to aspire to remain part of the UK and Nationalists/Republicans to aspire to a united Ireland. In essence, however, this means that the polity of Northern Ireland is conditional on a majority community and that it can change. Given the strong national sentiments among working-class Protestants and Catholics, this ambiguity of the constitutional status poses a threat to their identity and thus to the fragile state of community relations. In particular, the possibility of a hard Brexit and its seemingly inevitable hard Irish border has brought the status question to the fore again, thus boosting hopes among Nationalists/Republicans and reinforcing worries among Unionists/Loyalists. Consequently, the issue of working-class representation has receded even further into the background. Moreover, there is growing concern among residents in Protestant and Catholic working-class interface areas that the 'peace walls' will remain and that even new ones might emerge. This keeps them apart and may even drive them further away.

So, in the light of the uncertainty and lack of clarity prevailing in Northern Ireland at this juncture, any attempt to predict the future development of local community relations and the peacebuilding process will remain mere speculation. For the time being, hope seems to rest mainly on the commitment and efforts on the part of community groups and grassroots activists to seek new opportunities for positive change – for a change that will finally break down the barriers in place on the ground and in people's minds.

BIBLIOGRAPHY

ACP Ardoyne Commemoration Project (2002). *Ardoyne: The Untold Truth*. Belfast: Beyond the Pale.

Adamson, W L (2002) "Towards the Prison Notebooks: the Evolution of Gramsci's Thinking on Political Organization 1918 – 1926." In: Martin, J (Ed.) *Antonio Gramsci: Critical Assessments of Leading Political Philosophers. Volume 1: Intellectual and Political Context*. London: Routledge, pp. 296-319.

Adshead, M & Tonge, J (2009) *Politics in Ireland: Convergence and Divergence in a Two-Polity Island*. Basingstoke: Palgrave.

Allen, N (2019) "Theresa May resigns as British prime minister – here's where it all went wrong." *The Conversation*. 24 May 2019. www.theconversation.com/theresa-may-resigns-as-british-prime-minister-heres-where-it-all-went-wrong-117763. [Accessed 27 July 2019]

Almond, G, Powell, G B, & Mundt, R (1996) *Comparative Politics: a Theoretical Framework*. New York, NY: HarperCollins.

Andersen, A (2002) *Transforming Ethnic Nationalism - the Politics of Ethno-Nationalistic Sentiments in Kosovo*. Oslo: University of Oslo.

Anderson, B (1991) *Imagined Communities: Reflections on the Origin and Spread of Nationalism*. Rev. Ed. London: Verso.

Anderson, C (2004) *The Billy Boy: The Life and Death of LVF Leader Billy Wright*. Edinburgh: Mainstream Publications.

Anderson, J & Shuttleworth, I (1998) "Sectarian Demography, Territoriality and Political Development in Northern Ireland." *Political Geography* 17 (2): 187-208.

Anheier, H K, Gerhards, J & Romo, F P (1995) "Forms of Capital and Social Structure in Cultural Fields: Examining Bourdieu's Social Topography." *American Journal of Sociology* 100 (4): 859-903.

APNI Alliance Party of Northern Ireland (2019) "Brexit". *APNI*. www.allianceparty.org/brexit. [Accessed 09/08/2019]

Archibugi, D (2003) "A Critical Analysis of the Self-determination of Peoples: A Cosmopolitan Perspective." *Constellations* 10 (4): 488-505.

ARK Access Research Knowledge NILT Northern Ireland Life and Times Survey

(1998) NILT 1998 data – zip format. *ARK – Access Research Knowledge Northern Ireland*. www.ark.ac.uk/nilt/1998/NILT98W2.ZIP. [Retrieved 30/03/2019]

(2000) NILT 2000 data – zip format. *ARK – Access Research Knowledge Northern Ireland*. www.ark.ac.uk/nilt/2000/NILT001.ZIP. [Retrieved 30/03/2019]

(2003) NILT 2003 data – zip format. *ARK – Access Research Knowledge Northern Ireland*. www.ark.ac.uk/nilt/2003/NILT031.zip. [Retrieved 30/03/2019]

(2008) NILT 2008 data – zip format. *ARK – Access Research Knowledge Northern Ireland*. www.ark.ac.uk/nilt/2008/nilt08w1.zip. [Retrieved 20/07/2019]

(2018) "If there was a referendum tomorrow about whether Northern Ireland should leave the UK and unite with the Republic of Ireland, how do you think you would vote?" NILT 2017. *ARK – Access Research Knowledge Northern Ireland*. Last updated: 11 June 2018. www.ark.ac.uk/nilt/2017/Political_Attitudes/BORDPOLL.html. [Accessed 12/08/2019]

Armstrong, K & Holton, K (2019) "Northern Ireland to face job losses and road blockages in no-deal Brexit: leaked government report." *Belfast Telegraph*. 18 August 2019. www.belfasttelegraph.co.uk/news/northern-ireland/northern-ireland-to-face-job-losses-

and-road-blockages-in-nodeal-brexit-leaked-government-report-38413174.html.
[Accessed 18/08/2019]

Armstrong, R (2014) "The War and the Three Kings." In Jackson, A (Ed.) *The Oxford Handbook of Modern Irish History*. Oxford: Oxford University Press., pp. 375-397.

Arthur, P (1994) *Government and Politics of Northern Ireland*. 2nd ed. London: Longman.

Aughey, A (1996) "Direct Rule", in Aughey, A & Morrow, D (Eds.) *Northern Ireland Politics*. London: Longman, pp. 85-93.

Aughey, A (2005) *The Politics of Northern Ireland: Beyond the Belfast Agreement*. London & New York, NY: Routledge.

Badke, W B (2004) *Research Strategies: Finding Your Way through the Information Fog*. Lincoln, NE: iUniverse, Inc

Baker, J, Lynch, K, Cantillon, S & Walsh, J (2004) *Equality: From Theory to Action*. Basingstoke & New York, NY: Palgrave Macmillan.

Bähr, H & Treib, O (2007) "Sectorialised Policy-Making in the EU: Modes of Governance in Social and Environmental Policy." *NewGov Policy Brief* No 07. Florence: European University Institute (EUI).

Bakke, K M & Wibbels, E (2006) "Diversity, Disparity and Civil Conflict in Federal States." *World Politics* 59: 1-50.

Bardon, J (1996) "Loyal tributes to culture under siege." *The Irish Times*. 27 April 1996. www.irishtimes.com/culture/loyal-tributes-to-culture-under-siege-1.43613.
[Accessed 01/08/2019]

Bardon, J (2001) *A History of Ulster*. Belfast: The Blackstaff Press.

Barlovac, B (2013) "Kosovo and Serbia Reach Historic Deal in Brussels." *Balkan Insight*, 19 April 2013. www.balkaninsight.com/en/article/kosovo-and-serbia-may-seal-eu-deal
[Accessed 01/08/2019]

Barma, N H (2006) "Democracy through Transitional Governance in Cambodia, East Timor and Afghanistan." *International Journal on Multicultural Societies* (IJMS) 8 (2): 127-161.

Barnes, L P (2005) "Was the Northern Ireland Conflict Religious?" *Journal of Contemporary Religion* 20 (1): 55-69.

Barritt, D & Carter, C (1972) *The Northern Ireland Problem: A Study in Group Relations*. 2nd ed. London: Oxford University Press.

Barth, F (1969) "Introduction." In: Barth, F (Ed.) *Ethnic Groups and Boundaries: The Social Organization of Culture Difference*. Boston, MA: Little, Brown & Company, pp. 9-38.

Bartlett, T (2010) *Ireland: A History*. Cambridge: Cambridge University Press.

Barton, B (1996) *A Pocket History of Ulster*. Dublin: The O'Brien Press.

Barton, B (2003) "Northern Ireland 1920–25," in Hill, J R (Ed.) *A New History of Ireland: Ireland, 1921–84*. New York, NY: Oxford University Press, pp. 161-198.

Barton, B & Foy, M (1999) *The Easter Rising*. Stroud: Sutton.

Bates, T R (1975) "Gramsci and the Theory of Hegemony." *Journal of the History of Ideas* 36 (2): 351-366.

Bauböck, R (2004) "Federal Arrangements and Minority Self-Government." *EIF-Working Paper* No. 02. Austrian Academy of Sciences, September 2004.

Bauer, M W, Gaskell G & Allum N C (2000) "Quality, Quantity and Knowledge Interests: Avoiding Confusions." In: Bauer M W & Gaskell G (Eds.) *Qualitative Researching with Text, Image and Sound: A Practical Handbook*. London: Sage Publications, pp. 3-17.

Bauer, O (2000) *The Question of Nationalities and Social Democracy*. English Translation by Joseph O'Donnell. Foreword by Heinz Fischer. Edited by Ephraim Nimni. Minneapolis: University of Minneapolis.

BBC British Broadcasting Corporation
(2000) "Bloody Sunday Inquiry, Chronology: the Widgery report." *BBC News.* 24 March 2000. news.bbc.co.uk/2/hi/in_depth/northern_ireland/2000/bloody_sunday _inquiry/665100.stm. [Accessed 01/08/2019]

(2001a) "Children injured in bus attack." *BBC News.* 28 September 2001. news. bbc.co.uk/2/hi/uk_news/northern_ireland/1568666.stm. [Accessed 01/08/2019]

(2001b) "'Head to head: Ardoyne school dispute." *BBC News.* 4 September 2001. news.bbc.co.uk/2/hi/uk_news/northern_ireland/1524510.stm. [Accessed 01/08/2019]

(2001c) "Officers hurt in school protest blast." *BBC News.* 5 September 2001. news. bbc.co.uk/2/hi/uk_news/northern_ireland/1526032.stm. [Accessed 01/08/2019]

(2002) "Rioting follows NI school dispute." *BBC News.* 9 January 2002. news. bbc.co.uk/2/hi/uk_news/northern_ireland/1751257.stm. [Accessed 01/08/2019]

(2004) "Tears flow as families flee." *BBC News*, 26 August 2004. news.bbc. co.uk/2/hi/uk_news/northern_ireland/3602290.stm. [Accessed 01/08/2019]

(2006) "Loyalist group ousts its chairman." *BBC News.* 3 April 2006. news.bbc. co.uk/2/hi/uk_news/northern_ireland/4874308.stm. [Accessed 01/08/2019]

(2007) "'Chuckle brothers' enjoy 100 days". *BBC News.* 15 August 2007. news. bbc.co.uk/2/hi/uk_news/northern_ireland/6948406.stm. [Accessed 13/07/2019]

(2009a) "Forty years of peace lines." *BBC News.* 1 July 2009. news.bbc.co.uk/ 2/hi/uk_news/northern_ireland/8121228.stm. [Accessed 01/08/2019]

(2009b) "Loyalist groups 'destroy weapons'." *BBC News.* 18 June 2009. news.bbc. co.uk/2/hi/uk_news/8106907.stm. [Accessed 01/08/2019]

(2010a) "David Ford secures justice job." *BBC News.* 12 April 2010. news.bbc. co.uk/2/hi/8615741.stm. [Accessed 01/08/2019]

(2010b) "Northern Ireland crisis talks adjourn in early hours." *BBC News.* 26 January 2010. news.bbc.co.uk/2/hi/uk_news/northern_ireland/8479889.stm. [Accessed 01/08/ 2019]

(2010c) "Policeman shot dead in Northern Ireland." *BBC News.* 10 March 2010. news. bbc.co.uk/2/hi/uk_news/northern_ireland/7933990.stm. [Accessed 01/08/2019]

(2010d) "'Real IRA was behind army attack." *BBC News.* 8 March 2010. news. bbc.co.uk/2/hi/uk_news/northern_ireland/7930995.stm. [Accessed 01/08/2019]

(2010e) "Special Reports 2010: Bloody Sunday." *BBC News.* 17 June 2010. news.bbc. co.uk/2/hi/in_depth/northern_ireland/2010/bloody_sunday. [Accessed 01/08/2019]

(2014) "Former first minister and DUP leader Ian Paisley has died." *BBC News.* 12 September 2014. www.bbc.com/news/uk-northern-ireland-29177705. [Accessed 31/07/ 2019]

(2016a) "Ardoyne peace wall: Martin McGuinness hails replacement as 'sign of progress'". *BBC News.* 11 August 2016. www.bbc.com/news/uk-northern-ireland-37046677. [Accessed 23/08/2019]

(2016b) "EU referendum: Northern Ireland votes to Remain." *BBC News.* 24 June 2016. www.bbc.com/news/uk-northern-ireland-36614443. [Accessed 21/07/ 2019]

(2016c) "Twaddell: Agreement reached over long-running parade dispute." *BBC News.* 24 September 2016. www.bbc.com/news/uk-northern-ireland-37458065. [Accessed 01/ 08/2019]

(2018a) "'Hooded Men' appeal rejected by European court." *BBC News.* 11 September 2018. www.bbc.com/news/uk-northern-ireland-45483381. [Accessed 06/08/2019]

(2018b) "Mary Lou McDonald replaces Gerry Adams as Sinn Féin leader." *BBC News*. 10 February 2018. www.bbc.com/news/uk-northern-ireland-43012340. [Accessed 05/08/2019]

(2019a) "Ciaran McKeown: A driving force behind the Peace People." *BBC News*. 2 September 2019. www.bbc.com/news/uk-northern-ireland-49553203. [Accessed 25/09/2019]

(2019b) "Supreme Court: Suspending Parliament was unlawful, judges rule." BBC News, 24 September 2019. www.bbc.com/news/uk-politics-49810261. [Accessed 25/09/2019]

(2019c) "Trump: US and UK working on 'very substantial' trade deal." *BBC News*. 27 July 2019. www.bbc.com/news/uk-politics-49135045. [Accessed 02/08/2019]

Beatty, R (2004) "Northern Ireland Multiple Deprivation Measure 2001 – A User's Guide." *NISRA Occasional Paper* 20. Belfast: NISRA.

Belfast Telegraph

(2009a) "Dissident Real IRA claims responsibility for army barracks attack." *Belfast Telegraph*. 8 March 2009. www.belfasttelegraph.co.uk/news/dissident-real-ira-claims-responsibility-for-army-barracks-attack-28470436.html. [Accessed 27/07/2017]

(2009b) "New homes for Torrens." *Belfast Telegraph*. 28 July 2009. www.belfasttelegraph.co.uk/news/northern-ireland/new-homes-for-torrens-28488544.html. [Accessed 01/08/2019]

(2010a) "Agreement at Hillsborough Castle, 5 February 2010." *Belfast Telegraph*. www.belfasttelegraph.co.uk/news/politics/the-hillsborough-castle-agreement-14668977.html. [Accessed 01/08/2019]

(2010b) "Alliance leader Ford is new Justice Minister." *Belfast Telegraph*. 12 April 2010. www.belfasttelegraph.co.uk/news/politics/northern-irelands-justice-minister-takes-back-powers-14763809.html. [Accessed 01/08/2019]

(2010c) "Tensions flare over Orange Order parades as panel ends work." *Belfast Telegraph*. 22 February 2010. www.belfasttelegraph.co.uk/news/local-national/tensions-flare-over-orange-order-parades-as-panel-ends-work-14693637.html. [Accessed 01/08/2019]

(2015) "In an inspirational story of friendship across the divide, how Jean and Renee worked tirelessly to unite their two communities." *Belfast Telegraph*. 9 July 2015. www.belfasttelegraph.co.uk/life/features/in-an-inspirational-story-of-friendship-across-the-divide-how-jean-and-renee-worked-tirelessly-to-unite-their-two-communities-31362725.html. [Accessed 01/08/2019]

(2017a) "How Martin McGuinness and Ian Paisley forged an unlikely friendship". *Belfast Telegraph*. 21 March 2017. www.belfasttelegraph.co.uk/news/ northern-ireland/how-martin-mcguinness-and-ian-paisley-forged-an-unlikely-friendship-35550640.html. [Accessed 13/07/2019]

(2017b) "Brexit: Northern Ireland will leave on same terms as rest of UK, insists DUP chief Foster." *Belfast Telegraph*. 21 November 2017. www.belfasttelegraph.co.uk/news/ brexit/brexit-northern-ireland-will-leave-on-same-terms-as-rest-of-uk-insists-dup-chief-foster-36339677.html. [Accessed 06/08/2019]

(2018) "Survey reveals 65% in Northern Ireland would now vote Remain - and 60% think united Ireland more likely after Brexit." *Belfast Telegraph*. 10 December 2018. www.belfasttelegraph.co.uk/news/brexit/survey-reveals-65-in-northern-ireland-would-now-vote-remain-and-60-think-united-ireland-more-likely-after-brexit-37609187.html. [Accessed 13/08/2019]

(2019a) "Brexit helps us recruit more supporters, says New IRA." *Belfast Telegraph*. 28 April 2019. www.belfasttelegraph.co.uk/news/northern-ireland/brexit-helps-us-recruit-more-supporters-says-new-ira-38057597.html. [Accessed 20/08/2019]

(2019b) "Brexit live: Boris Johnson speech – 'We will, under no circumstances, have checks near border in Ireland'." *Belfast Telegraph*. 2 October 2019. www.belfasttelegraph.co.uk/news/northern-ireland/brexit-live-boris-johnson-speech-we-will-under-no-circumstances-have-checks-near-border-in-ireland-38555263.html. [Accessed 02/10/2019]

(2019c) "'It cannot work' – Nigel Dodds shoots down Boris Johnson's plan to break Brexit deadlock." *Belfast Telegraph*. 12 October 2019. www.belfasttelegraph.co.uk/news/brexit/it-cannot-work-nigel-dodds-shoots-down-boris-johnsons-plan-to-break-brexit-deadlock-38588000.html. [Accessed 13/10/2019]

Belfrage, S (1987) *The Crack: A Belfast Year*. London: Grafton Books.

Bell, C & McVeigh, R (2014) *A Fresh Start for Equality? The Equality Impacts of the Stormont House Agreement on the 'Two Main Communities' – An Action Research Intervention*. Belfast: Equality Coalition.

Bell, J (2007) *Parades and Protests: An Annotated Bibliography*. Belfast: Institute for Conflict Research (ICR).

Bell, J (2017) "Prison chief rejects report Magilligan to close and jail jobs to be axed." *Belfast Telegraph*. 1 June 2017. www.belfasttelegraph.co.uk/news/northern-ireland/prison-chief-rejects-report-magilligan-to-close-and-jail-jobs-to-be-axed-35778162.html. [Accessed 22/07/2017]

Bell, J (2019) "Journalist Lyra McKee murdered during Derry rioting - police treating death as terrorist incident." *Belfast Telegraph*. 19 April 2019. www.belfast telegraph.co.uk/news/northern-ireland/journalist-lyra-mckee-murdered-during-derry-rioting-police-treating-death-as-terrorist-incident-38031128.html. [Accessed 14/07/2019]

Bell, J B (1997) *The Secret Army: The IRA*. Revised 3rd ed. New Brunswick, NJ & London: Transaction Publishers.

Bell, V (2004) "In Pursuit of Civic Participation: The Early Experiences of the Northern Ireland Civic Forum, 2000–2002." *Political Studies* 52 (3): 565-584.

Benz, A (2004) "Governance—Modebegriff oder nützliches sozialwissenschaftliches Konzept?." In Benz, A & Dose, N (Eds.) *Governance—Regieren in komplexen Regelsystemen*. Wiesbaden: VS Verlag für Sozialwissenschaften, pp. 11-28.

Berberoglu, B (2004) *Nationalism and Ethnic Conflict: Class, State, and Nation in the Age of Globalization*. Oxford: Rowman & Littlefield.

Beresford, D (1994) *Ten Men Dead: The Story of the 1981 Irish Hunger Strike*. 7th imp. London: HarperCollins.

Berg, B L (2012) *Qualitative Research Methods for the Social Sciences*. 8th ed. Boston, MA: Allyn and Bacon.

Berghof Foundation (Ed.) *Berghof Glossary on Conflict Transformation: 20 Notions for Theory and Practice*. Berlin: Berghof Foundation.

Bernard, H R (2000) *Social Research Methods: Qualitative and Quantitative Approaches*. Thousand Oaks, CA: Sage Publications.

Bevir, M (2007) "Governance." In: Bevir, M (Ed.) *Encyclopedia of Governance*. Thousand Oaks, CA: Sage Publications, pp. 364-378.

Bew, P & Gordon G (1999) *Northern Ireland: A Chronology of the Troubles 1968-1999*. Dublin: Gill & Macmillan.

Bew, P, Gibbon, P & Patterson, H (1979) *The State in Northern Ireland – Politics and Government*. Manchester: Manchester University Press.

Bew, P & Norton, C (1979) "The Unionist State and the Outdoor Relief Riots of 1932." *Economic and Social Review* 10 (3): 255-265.

Bieber, F (2005) *Post-War Bosnia: Ethnicity, Inequality and Public Sector Governance.* Basingstoke: Macmillan.

Bingham, J, Prince, R & Harding, T (2010) "Bloody Sunday Inquiry: Cameron apologises as Saville says shootings 'unjustified'." *The Telegraph.* 15 June 2010. www.telegraph.co.uk/news/uknews/northernireland/7829208/Bloody-Sunday-Inquiry-Cameron-apologises-as-Saville-says-shootings-unjustified.html. [Accessed 01/08/2019]

BIP Belfast Interface Project

(1999) *Inner East Outer West: Addressing Conflict in Two Interface Areas.* Belfast: BIP. www.belfastinterfaceproject.org/sites/default/files/publications/Inner East - Outer West.pdf. [Accessed 01/08/2019]

(2011) *Belfast Interfaces: Security Barriers and Defensive Use of Space.* Belfast: BIP. www.belfastinterfaceproject.org/sites/default/files/publications/Belfast interfaces.pdf. [Accessed 01/08/2019]

(2013a) "BIP History." *BIP.* www.belfastinterfaceproject.org/bip-history. [Accessed 01/08/2019]

(2013b) "Map – Cluster 9: Crumlin Road-Ardoyne-Glenbryn." Interfaces Map and Database. *BIP.* www.belfastinterfaceproject.org/map/cluster-9-crumlin-road-ardoyne-glenbryn?type[]=interface. [Accessed 01/08/2019]

(2017) *Interface Barriers, Peacelines and Defensive Architecture.* Belfast: BIP. www.belfastinterfaceproject.org/sites/default/files/publications/Interfaces PDF.pdf. [Accessed 23/08/2019]

Black, R (2018) "Changing attitudes over Belfast peace walls threatened by Stormont deadlock." *Belfast Telegraph.* 23 May 2018. www.belfasttelegraph.co.uk/news/northern-ireland/changing-attitudes-over-belfast-peace-walls-threatened-by-stormont-deadlock-36935976.html. [Accessed 02/08/2019]

Blake, J S (2019) Contentious Rituals: Parading the Nation in Northern Ireland. New York, NY: Oxford University Press.

Blanchard, J (2019) "Inside Westminster: Who's who in Team Boris." *Politico.* 25 July 2019. www.politico.eu/article/boris-johnson-new-cabinet-whos-in/. [Accessed 27/07/2019]

Boal, F W (1969) "Territoriality on the Shankill-Falls divide, Belfast." *Irish Geography* 6 (1): 30-50.

Boal, F W (1981) "Residential Segregation and Mixing in a Situation of Ethnic and National Conflict: Belfast." In: Compton, P A (Ed.) *The Contemporary Population of Northern Ireland and Population-related Issues.* Belfast: Institute of Irish Studies, Queen's University Belfast.

Boal, F W (2002) "Belfast: Walls within." *Political Geography* 21: 687-694.

Boal, F W & Murray, R C (1977) "A City in Conflict." *Geographical Magazine* 49: 364-371.

Borooah, V K, McKee, P M, Heaton, N & Collins, G (1995) "Inequality, segregation and poor performance: the education system in Northern Ireland." *Educational Review* 69 (3): 41-56.

Bourdieu, P (1984) *Distinction: A Social Critique of the Judgement of Taste.* Translated by R Nice. Cambridge, MA: Harvard University Press.

Bourke, J (2005) *Fear: A Cultural History.* London: Virago.

Bowman, T (2007) *Carson's Army: The Ulster Volunteer Force, 1910-1922.* Manchester: Manchester University Press.

Boyce, D G (1996) *The Irish Question and British Politics, 1868 – 1996.* London: Macmillan.

Boyce, G (1991) "Northern Ireland: A Place Apart?" In: Hughes, E (Ed.) *Culture and Politics in Northern Ireland, 1960-1990.* Buckingham & Bristol, PA: Open University Press, pp. 13-26.

Bradley, J (1996) *Exploring Long-Term Economic and Social Consequences of Peace and Reconciliation in the Island of Ireland.* Dublin: Forum for Peace and Reconciliation.

Brady, H E, Collier D & Seawright J (2004) "Refocusing the Discussion of Methodology." In: Brady, H E & Collier D (Eds.) *Rethinking Social Inquiry: Diverse Tools, Shared Standards.* Oxford: Rowman & Littlefield, pp. 15-31.

Brand, U (2007) "Die Internationalisierung des Staates als Rekonstitution von Hegemonie. Zur staatstheoretischen Erweiterung Gramscis." In: Buckel, S & Fischer-Lescano A (Eds.) *Hegemonie gepanzert mit Zwang. Zivilgesellschaft und Politik im Staatsverständnis Antonio Gramscis.* Baden-Baden: Nomos, pp. 161-181.

Brannen, J (1988) "Research Note: the Study of Sensitive Subjects." *The Sociological Review* 36 (3): 552-563.

Breen, R (2000) "Class Inequality and Social Mobility in Northern Ireland, 1973 – 1996." *American Sociological Review*, 65 (3): 392-406.

Breen, R & Hayes, B (1997) "Religious Mobility and Party Support in Northern Ireland." *European Sociological Review* 13 (3): 225-239.

Breen, S (2019a) "Rivals slam DUP support for Boris Johnson's unlawful Westminster proroguing." *Belfast Telegraph.* 25 September 2019. www.belfasttelegraph.co.uk/news/northern-ireland/rivals-slam-dup-support-for-boris-johnsons-unlawful-westminster-proroguing-38531983.html. [Accessed 25/09/2019]

Breen, S (2019b) "Varadkar: I oppose border poll in wake of a no-deal Brexit." *Belast Telegraph.* 7 August 2019. www.belfasttelegraph.co.uk/news/varadkar-i-oppose-border-poll-in-wake-of-a-nodeal-brexit-38381324.html. [Accessed 08/08/2019]

Brewer, J D (1992) "Sectarianism and Racism, and their Parallels and Differences." *Ethnic and Racial Studies* 15 (3): 352-64.

Brewer, J D & Higgins, G I (1998) *Anti-Catholicism in Northern Ireland, 1600-1998.* Basingstoke: Macmillan.

Brown, D (1970) *Bury My Heart at Wounded Knee: An Indian History of the American West.* New York, NY: Holt, Rinehart & Winston.

Brubaker, R (1996) *Nationalism Reframed: Nationhood and the National Question in the New Europe.* Cambridge: Cambridge University Press.

Brubaker, R (2002) "Ethnicity without Groups." *Archives Européènnes de Sociologie* 43 (2): 163-89.

Bruce, S (1992) *The Red Hand: Protestant Paramilitaries in Northern Ireland.* New York, NY: Oxford University Press.

Bruce, S (1994) *The Edge of the Union: The Ulster Loyalist Political Vision.* New York, NY: Oxford University Press.

Bruce, S (2004) "Turf war and peace: Loyalist paramilitaries since 1994." *Terrorism and Political Violence* 16 (3): 501-521.

Bryan, D (2000) *Orange Parades: the Politics of Ritual, Tradition and Control.* London: Pluto Press.

Buchanan, A (1991) *Secession: The Legitimacy of Political Divorce From Fort Sumter to Lithuania and Quebec.* Boulder, CO: Westview Press.

Burnham, P, Gilland, K, Grant, W & Layton-Henry, Z (2004) *Research Methods in Politics.* Basingstoke: Palgrave.

Burns, S, Leitch, R & Hughes, J (2015) *Education Inequalities in Northern Ireland: Final report to the Equality Commission for Northern Ireland*. March 2015. Belfast: ECNI. www.equalityni.org/ECNI/media/ECNI/Publications/Delivering Equality/EducationInequality-FullReportQUB.pdf. [Accessed 01/08/2019]

Burton, F (1978) *The Politics of Legitimacy: Struggles in a Belfast Community*. London: Routledge.

Byrne, D (2005) *Social Exclusion*. 2nd ed. Maidenhead: McGraw-Hill Education.

Byrne, J, Gormley Heenan, C, Robinson, G (2012) *Attitudes to Peace Walls. Research Report to Office of First Minister and Deputy First Minister*. University of Ulster, June 2012. Belfast: OFMDFM. www.executiveoffice-ni.gov.uk/publications/attitudes-peace-walls-research-report-office-first-minister-and-deputy-first-minister [Accessed [Accessed 01/08/2019]

Byrne, J, Gormley Heenan, C, Morrow, D, Sturgeon, B (2015) *Public Attitudes to Peace Walls. Survey Results*. Ulster University, December 2015. Belfast: Department for Justice. socsci.ulster.ac.uk/pws.pdf [Accessed 01/08/2019]

Byrne, J, Hansson, U & Bell, J (2006) *Shared Living: Mixed residential communities in Northern Ireland*. Belfast: Institute for Conflict Research (ICR).

Byrne, S (2001) "Consociational and Civic Society Approaches to Peacebuilding in Northern Ireland." *Journal of Peace Research* 38 (3): 327-352.

Byrne, S & Carter, N (2002) "Social Cubism: Six Social Forces of Ethnopolitical Conflict in Northern Ireland and Québec." *ILSA Journal of International & Comparative Law* 8: 741-769.

Cable, R (2012) "Fighting to stay British: The strange history of the Ulster Covenant." *BBC News*. 27 September 2012. www.bbc.com/news/uk-northern-ireland-politics-19718680. [Accessed 01/08/2019]

CAIN Conflict Archive on the Internet
ARK Access Research Knowledge, Northern Ireland Social and Political Archive (2011) "Visualising the Conflict, Geographic Informations Systems (GIS) Maps: Ward Boundaries – Belfast." *CAIN Web Service*. www.cain.ulst.ac.uk/victims/gis/gismaps.html#outline. [Accessed 01/08/2019]

Lynn, B (2016) "Dissident Republican Groupings, and a Chronology of Dissident Republican Activity, 1994-2011." *CAIN Web Service*. www.cain.ulst.ac.uk/issues/violence/chrondissidents.htm. [Accessed 01/08/2019]

Lynn, B (2019a) "A Chronology of Key Events in Irish History 1169 to 1799." With additional text by M. Melaugh *CAIN Web Service*. www.cain.ulster.ac.uk/othelem/chron/ch1169-1799.htm. [Accessed 30/09/2019].

Lynn, B (2019b) "A Chronology of Key Events in Irish History 1169 to 1799." *CAIN Web Service*. www.cain.ulster.ac.uk/othelem/chron/ch1800-1967.htm. [Accessed 30/09/2019].

McKenna, F (2016a) "Parades and Marches - Chronology 2: Historical Dates and Events." *CAIN Web Service*. www.cain.ulst.ac.uk/issues/parade/chpa2.htm. [Accessed 01/08/2019]

McKenna, F (2016b) "The Sunningdale Agreement – December 1973: Tripartite agreement on the Council of Ireland – the Communiqué issued following the Sunningdale Conference." British Government, Irish Government, and the Northern Ireland Executive designate. *CAIN Web Service*. www.cain.ulst.ac.uk/events/sunningdale/agreement.htm. [Accessed 01/08/2019]

McKenna, F & Melaugh, M (2016) "Parades and Marches - Developments at Drumcree, 1995-2000." *CAIN Web Service*. www.cain.ulst.ac.uk/issues/parade/

develop.htm. [Accessed 01/08/2019]

Melaugh, M (2005) "Irish Republican Army (IRA) Statement on the Ending of the Armed Campaign (28 July 2005)." Text: Irish Republican Army (IRA). *CAIN Web Service.* www.cain.ulst.ac.uk/othelem/organ/ira/ira280705.htm. [Accessed 01/08/2019]

Melaugh, M (2007) "Assembly Election (NI), Wednesday 7 March 2007." *CAIN Web Service.* www.cain.ulst.ac.uk/issues/politics/election/2007nia/ra2007.htm. [Accessed 01/08/2019]

Melaugh, M (2009), "Statement by the Ulster Volunteer Force (UVF), 27 June 2009." Text: Ulster Volunteer Force (UVF). *CAIN Web Service.* www.cain.ulst.ac.uk/othelem/organ/uvf/uvf270609.htm. [Accessed 01/08/2019]

Melaugh, M (2013) "Note on the protests related to the Union Flag at Belfast City Hall, December 2012 - January 2013." *CAIN Web Service.* www.cain.ulster.ac.uk/issues/identity/flag-2012.htm. [Accessed 01/08/2019]

Melaugh, M (2016a) "Abstracts on Organisations." Additional Material: B Lynn & F McKenna. *CAIN Web Service.* www.cain.ulst.ac.uk/othelem/organ/. [Accessed 01/08/2019]

Melaugh, M (2016b) "Belfast Religious Breakdown." *CAIN Web Service.* www.cain.ulst.ac.uk/images/maps/belfast_religion.gif. [Accessed 01/08/2019]

Melaugh, M (2016c) "Discrimination – Quotations." *CAIN Web Service.* www.cain.ulst.ac.uk/issues/discrimination/quotes.htm. [Accessed 01/08/2019]

Melaugh, M (2016d) "Distribution of Catholics, at ward level, across Northern Ireland (2001)." *CAIN Web Service.* www.cain.ulst.ac.uk/images/maps/belfast_religion.gif; www.cain.ulst.ac.uk/images/maps/2001religionwardsni1.jpg. [Accessed 01/08/2019]

Melaugh, M (2016e) "Portadown Garvaghy Area, Drumcree Orange Parade 1996." *CAIN Web Service.* www.cain.ulst.ac.uk/images/maps/drumcree_parade.gif. [Accessed 01/08/2019]

Melaugh, M (2016f) "Violence – Information on Deaths during the Conflict." *CAIN Web Service.* www.cain.ulst.ac.uk/issues/violence/deaths.htm. [Accessed 01/08/2019]

Melaugh, M (2019a) "A Chronology of the Conflict - 1968 to the Present." *CAIN Web Service.* www.cain.ulster.ac.uk/othelem/chron.htm. [Accessed 30/09/2019].

Melaugh, M (2019b) "Draft List of Deaths Related to the Conflict from 2002 to April 2019." CAIN Web Service. www.cain.ulster.ac.uk/issues/violence/deathsfrom2002draft.htm. [Accessed 30/09/2019]

Melaugh M & Lynn, B (2017) "A Glossary of Terms Related to the Conflict." Last update: March 2017. *CAIN Web Service.* www.cain.ulst.ac.uk/othelem/glossary.htm. [Accessed 01/08/2019]

Melaugh M & Lynn, B (2019) "Devolved Government in Northern Ireland - The Civic Forum." *CAIN Web Service.* www.cain.ulster.ac.uk/issues/politics/civicforum/. [Accessed 01/08/2019]

Mullan, C (2016) "Joint Declaration on Peace: The Downing Street Declaration, Wednesday 15 December 1993." Text: British and Irish Governments. *CAIN Web Service.* www.cain.ulst.ac.uk/events/peace/docs/dsd151293.htm. [Accessed 01/08/2019]

Calame, J & Charlesworth, E (2009) *Divided Cities: Belfast, Beirut, Jerusalem, Mostar, and Nicosia.* Philadelphia, PE: University of Pennsylvania Press.

Cammaerts, B (2007) "Jamming the Political: Beyond Counter-Hegemonic Practices." *Continuum* 21 (1): 71-90.

Campbell, B (2008) *Agreement! The State, Conflict and Change in Northern Ireland.* London: Lawrence & Wishart.

Campbell, C (2017) "Flaws exposed in plan to remove Northern Ireland's peace walls." *The Detail.* 22 May 2017. www.thedetail.tv/articles/government-revise-down-interface-removal-target. [Accessed 02/08/2019]

Campbell, G (2000) "The Peace Process and the Protestants." In: Murray, D (Ed.) *Protestant Perceptions of the Peace Process in Northern Ireland.* Limerick: Centre for Peace and Development Studies, pp. 137-154.

Campbell, J (2019) "Brexit: What is the Irish border backstop?" *BBC News.* 1 August 2019. www.bbc.com/news/uk-northern-ireland-politics-44615404. [Accessed 08/08/2019]

Campbell, N (2013) "On the Peace Line: The Experience of an Integrated School." In: McGlynn, C, Zembylas, M & Bekerman, Z (Eds.) *Integrated Education in Conflicted Societies.* New York, NY: Palgrave, pp. 45-57.

Canning, M (2009) "Anarchy in Ardoyne... now it's death threats." 17 July 2009. *Belfast Telegraph.* www.belfasttelegraph.co.uk/news/anarchy-in-ardoyne-now-its-death-threats-28487892.html. [Accessed 01/08/2019]

Capener, D (2017) "Belfast's housing policy still reflects religious and economic division." *The Guardian.* 3 October 2017. www.theguardian.com/housing-network/2017/oct/03/northern-ireland-shared-communities-economic-inequality-religion-neighbourhood. [Accessed 01/08/2019]

Carr, H (2019) "Sky Data poll: Irish overwhelmingly back government's pressure on back-stop." *Sky News.* 8 February 2019. news.sky.com/story/sky-data-poll-irish-overwhel mingly-back-governments-pressure-on-backstop-11629673. [Accessed 13/08/2019]

Carroll, R (2019) "Northern Ireland's Alliance leader gets anti-Brexit boost in EU elections." *The Guardian.* 27 May 2019. www.theguardian.com/uk-news/2019/may/27 /northern-ireland-alliance-leader-naomi-long-gets-push-in-eu-elections-from-anti-brexit-stance. [Accessed 06/08/2019]

Cash, J (2009) "Squaring Some Vicious Circles: Transforming the Political in Northern Ireland." In: Taylor, R (Ed.) *Consociational Theory: McGarry and O'Leary and the Northern Ireland Conflict.* New York, NY: Routledge, pp. 236-252.

Castle, S (2019) "Boris Johnson's 'Explosive' Move to Get His Way on Brexit: Suspend Parliament." *The New York Times.* 28 August 2019. www.nytimes.com/2019/08/28/world/europe/boris-johnson-brexit-parliament.html. [Accessed 28/08/2019]

CCRF Cliftonville Community Regeneration Forum (2009) "Community Relations." www.ccrf.org.uk/Cliftonville_Community_Regeneration_Forum/Good_Relations.html. [Accessed 01/08/2019]

CCRU Central Community Relations Unit (1995) "The Shankill: A Minority Experience by Jackie Redpath, Greater Shankill Development Agency." Report, Fifth Public Discussion, The Shankill and the Falls: The Minority Experiences of Two Communities in West Belfast. Central Library, June 1, 1995. *CAIN Web Service.* www.cain.ulster. ac.uk/ccru/research/temple/discus5.htm. [Accessed 01/08/2019]

CDC Community Development Centre (2000) Community Development Centre Annual Review, 1998-1999. *CAIN Web Service.* www.cain.ulst.ac.uk/cdc/review/review9899 .htm. [Accessed 01/08/2019]

Chapman, T, Campbell, H, Wilson, D & McCready, P (2017) "Working across frontiers: Community based restorative justice in Northern Ireland." In: Vanfraechem, I & Aertsen, I (Eds.) *Action Research in Criminal Justice: Restorative justice approaches in intercultural settings.* New York, NY: Routledge, pp. 141-168.

Chenoweth, E & Stephan, M J (2011) *Why Civil Resistance Works: The Strategic Logic of Nonviolent Conflict*. New York, NY: Columbia University Press.

Clark, G (2014) *Everyday Violence in the Irish Civil War*. Cambridge: Cambridge UP.

Clark, H (2000) *Civil Resistance in Kosovo*. London: Pluto Press.

Clarke, A (2001) "The Colonisation of Ulster and the Rebellion of 1641: 1603-60." In: Moody, T W & Martin, F X (Eds.) *The Course of Irish History*. Blackrock: Mercier Press, pp. 189-203.

Clarke, S, Mac Guill, A, Conlon, A M & Dickson, C (2017) "Northern Ireland assembly election: final results." *The Guardian*. 3 March 2017. www.theguardian.com/uk-news/ng-interactive/2017/mar/03/northern-ireland-assembly-election-latest-results. [Accessed 02/08/2019]

Clubb, G (2013) "Causes of the Northern Ireland Flag Dispute." *Open Democracy UK*. 4 February 2013. www.opendemocracy.net/ourkingdom/gordon-clubb/causes-of-northern-ireland-flag-dispute. [Accessed 01/08/2019]

Coakley, J (Ed.) (2003) *The Territorial Management of Ethnic Conflict*. 2nd ed. London: Frank Cass.

Cochrane, F, Duffy, R & Selby, J (Eds.) *Global Governance, Conflict and Resistance*. London: Palgrave.

Coleman, M (2014) *The Irish Revolution, 1916-1923*. Oxon & New York, NY: Routledge.

Combs, B H (2013) *From Selma to Montgomery: The Long March to Freedom*. Oxon & New York, NY: Routledge.

Collins, P, Moore, R & Smyth, M (1996) *Life in Two Enclave Areas in Northern Ireland*: A Field Survey in Derry Londonderry after the Ceasefires. Derry/Londonderry: Templegrove Action Research Limited.

Connolly, S (Ed.) (1998) *The Oxford Companion to Irish History*. Oxford: Oxford University Press.

Connor, F (2002) *A Shared Childhood: The Story of the Integrated Schools in Northern Ireland*. Belfast: Blackstaff Press.

Connor, W (1994) *Ethnonationalism: the Quest for Understanding*. Princeton, NJ: Princeton University Press.

Conversi, D (1995) "Reassessing Current Theories of Nationalism: Nationalism as Boundary Maintenance and Creation." *Nationalism & Ethnic Politics* 1 (1): 73-85.

Coogan, T P (1993) *The IRA*. 11th ed. London: Harper Collins.

Coogan, T P (1996) *Michael Collins: the Man Who Made Ireland*. Boulder, CO: Roberts Rinehart.

Coogan, T P (2002) *The Troubles: Ireland's Ordeal, 1966-1996 and the Search for Peace*. New York, NY: Palgrave.

Coogan, T P & Morrison G (1998) *The Irish Civil War*. London: Seven Dials.

Cordell, K & Wolff, S (2009) *Ethnic Conflict: Causes, Consequences and Responses*. Cambridge & Malden, MA: Polity.

Cormack, B, & Osborne, B (1987) "Fair Shares, Fair Employment: Northern Ireland Today." *Studies: An Irish Quarterly Review* 76 (303): 273-285.

Cormack, B & Osborne, B (1995) "Education in Northern Ireland: The Struggle for Equality." In: Clancy, P, Drudy, S, Lynch K & O'Dowd, L (Eds.) *Irish Society: Sociological Perspectives*. Dublin: Institute of Public Administration, pp. 495-528.

Cormack, R & Osborne, R (1983) *Religion, Education and Employment: Aspects of Equal Opportunity in Northern Ireland*. Belfast: Appletree Press.

Coulter, C (1999) *Contemporary Northern Irish Society: An Introduction*. London: Pluto Press.

Coulter, C (2019) "Northern Ireland's elusive peace dividend: Neoliberalism, austerity and the politics of class." *Capital & Class* 43 (1): 123-138.

Cowan, R (2002) "Violence erupts in Belfast. Holy Cross school dispute reignites tensions and brings nationalist and loyalist mobs on to the streets." *The Guardian*. 10 January 2002. www.theguardian.com/uk/2002/jan/10/northernireland.rosiecowan. [01/08/2019]

Cox, K, Low, M & Robinson, J (Eds.) (2008) *The Sage Handbook of Political Geography*. London: Sage.

Cox, R W (1983) "Gramsci, Hegemony and International Relations: an Essay in Method." *Millennium* 12 (2): 162-175.

Craith, M N (2002) *Plural Identities – Singular Narratives: The Case of Northern Ireland*. New York & Oxford: Berghahn Books.

Cramer, C (2005) *Inequality and Conflict: A Review of an Age-Old Concern*. Geneva: United Nations Research Institute for Social Development (UNRISD).

Crawford, C (2003) *Inside the UDA: Volunteers and Violence*. Foreword by Marie Smyth. London & Dublin: Pluto Press.

CRC Community Relations Council (2008) *Towards Sustainable Security: Interface Barriers and the Legacy of Segregation in Belfast*. Belfast: CRC.

CRC Community Relations Council (2009) *CRC News*, Issue 52, June 2009. Belfast: CRC.

Crehan, K (2002) *Gramsci, Culture and Anthropology*. London: Pluto Press.

Cronin, M (2001) *A History of Ireland*. New York, NY: Palgrave.

Crush, J & Frayne, B (2010) "Surviving on the Move." In: Crush, J & Frayne, B (Eds.) *Surviving on the Move: Migration, Poverty and Development in Southern Africa*. Cape Town: Idasa & Development Bank of Southern Africa (DBSA), pp. 1-24.

CSJ Campaign for Social Justice (1969) *Northern Ireland: The Plain Truth*. Dungannon: The Campaign for Social Justice.

Cunningham, K G & Weidmann, N B (2010) "Shared Space: Ethnic Groups, State Accommodation, and Localised Conflict." *International Studies Quarterly* 54: 1035-1054.

Cunningham, N (2013) "'The Doctrine of Vicarious Punishment': Space, Religion and the Belfast Troubles of 1920-22." *Journal of Historical Geography* 40: 52-66.

Cunningham, N & Gregory, I (2014) "Hard to Miss, Easy to Blame? Peacelines, Interfaces and Political Deaths in Belfast during the Troubles." *Political Geography* 40: 64-78.

Curran, E (2014) "We're marching towards another summer of parades chaos: yet another July of foreboding is staring Northern Ireland in the face. *Belfast Telegraph*. 16 June 2014. www.belfasttelegraph.co.uk/opinion/columnists/were-marching-towards-another-summer-of-parades-chaos-yet-another-July-of-foreboding-is-staring-northern-ireland-in-the-face-30355647.html. [Accessed 01/08/2019]

Darby, J (1976) *Northern Ireland. The Background of the Conflict*. Dublin: Gill & Macmillan.

Darby, J (1985) "Controls of Conflict." *L'Irlande Politique et Sociale (Ireland, Politics and Society)* 1 (1): 77-89.

Darby, J (1986) *Intimidation and the Control of Conflict in Northern Ireland*. Dublin: Gill & Macmillan.

Darby, J (1995) "Conflict in Northern Ireland: A Background Essay." In: Dunn, S. (Ed.) *Facets of the Conflict in Northern Ireland*. Basingstoke: Macmillan, pp. 15-23.

Darby, J (2001) *The Effects of Violence on Peace Processes*. Washington, DC: United States Institute of Peace (USIP) Press.

Darby, J & Morris, G (1974) *Intimidation in Housing*. Belfast: Northern Ireland Community Relations Commission.

Davies, C A (2008) *Reflexive Ethnography. A Guide for Researching Selves and Others.* 2nd ed. New York, NY: Routledge.

Davis, H (2004) *Understanding Stuart Hall.* London: Sage Publications.

Della Porta, D (2008) "Comparative analysis: case-oriented versus variable-oriented research." In: Della Porta, D & Keating, M (Eds.) *Approaches and Methodologies in the Social Sciences: A Pluralist Perspective.* Cambridge: Cambridge University Press, pp. 198-222.

Deltapoll (2018) "Northern Ireland Poll". *Deltapoll.* 3 September 2018. www.deltapoll.co.uk/polls/ni-ofoc-bfb. [Accessed 12/08/2019]

Devenport, M (2013) "Northern Ireland peace walls should 'come down by 2022'." *BBC News.* 24 January 2013. www.bbc.com/news/uk-northern-ireland-21187673. [Accessed 02/08/2019]

Devenport, M (2018) "Fewer NI people feel British than other UK regions – survey." *BBC News.* 8 June 2018. www.bbc.com/news/uk-northern-ireland-44398502. [Accessed 12/08/2019]

Devlin, B (1969) *The Price of My Soul.* London: Pan Books.

Devlin, P (1981) *Yes, We Have No Bananas: Outdoor Relief in Belfast, 1920-39.* Belfast: Blackstaff Press.

DfC Department for Communities Northern Ireland (2016) *Lenadoon & Glencolin Action Plan, September/October 2016: Building Successful Communities.* Belfast: Housing Investment. www.communities-ni.gov.uk/sites/default/files/publications/communities/lenadoon-glencolin-action-plan.PDF. [Accessed 01/08/2019]

Di Cintio, M (2013) *Walls: Travels Along the Barricades.* Berkeley, CA: Soft Skull Press.

Dickson, A (2018) "Northern Ireland's other unionists." *Politico.* 23 November 2018. www.politico.eu/article/northern-ireland-brexit-other-unionists-uup-dup/. [Accessed 14/08/2019]

Dickson-Swift, V, James, E L, Kippen, S & Liamputtong, P (2007) "Doing Sensitive Research: What Challenges do Qualitative Researchers Face?" *Qualitative Research* 7 (3): 327-353.

Díez Medrano J (1995) *Class, Politics and Nationalism in the Basque Country.* Ithaca, NY: Cornell University Press.

Dignan, T (2003) *Low Income Households in Northern Ireland 1990-2002.* Office of the First Minister and Deputy First Minister (OFMDFM), Research Branch. Belfast: Northern Ireland Statistics & Research Agency (NISRA).

Dignan, T & McLaughlin, E (2002) *New TSN Research: Poverty in Northern Ireland*, Belfast: OFMDFM.

Dillon, M (1999) *The Dirty War: Covert Strategies and Tactics Used in Political Conflicts.* New York, NY: Routledge.

Dingley, J (2009) "The Cook Report and Perceptions of Loyalists in Northern Ireland: Lessons for Counterterrorism." In: Forest, J (Ed.) *Influence Warfare: How Terrorists and Governments Fight to Shape Perceptions in a War of Ideas.* Westport, CT & London: Praeger Security International, pp. 275-290.

Dixon, P (2001) *Northern Ireland: The Politics of War and Peace.* New York, NY: Palgrave.

DRD Department for Regional Planning (2012) *Regional Development Strategy (RDS) 2035: Building a Better Future.* Belfast: DRD. www.planningni.gov.uk/index/policy/rds2035.pdf. [Accessed 01/08/2019]

Doherty, P & Poole, M A (1995) *Ethnic Residential Segregation in Belfast.* University of Ulster: Coleraine.

Dolci, D (1970) *The Man Who Plays Alone* [Chi gioca solo (1966)]. Translated by Antonia Cowan. Garden City, NY: Doubleday.

Dooley, B (1998) *Black and Green: The Fight for Civil Rights in Northern Ireland & Black America*. London: Pluto Press.

Doyle, J, & Connolly, E (2019) "The Effects of Brexit on the Good Friday Agreement and the Northern Ireland Peace Process." In: Baciu, C A & Doyle, J (Eds.) *Peace, Security and Defence Cooperation in Post-Brexit Europe: Risks and Opportunities*. Cham: Springer, pp. 79-95.

Doyle, M (2010) *Fighting like the Devil for the Sake of God: Protestants, Catholics and the Origins of Violence in Victorian Belfast*. Manchester: Manchester University Press.

Duckitt, J (2003) "Prejudice and Intergroup Hostility." In: Sears, D O, Huddy, L & Jervis R (Eds.) *Oxford Handbook of Political Psychology*. New York, NY: Oxford University Press, pp. 559-600.

Duffy, M & Evans, G (1996) "Building Bridges? The Political Implications of Electoral Integration for Northern Ireland." *British Journal of Political Science* 26 (1): 123-140.

Duffy, M & Evans, G (1997) "Class, community polarisation and politics." In Dowds, L, Devine, P & Breen, R (Eds.) *Social Attitudes in Northern Ireland: The Sixth Report*. Belfast: Appletree Press, pp. 102-137.

Dujzings, G (2000) *Religion and the Politics of Identity in Kosovo*. New York, NY: Columbia University Press.

Dunn, S & Dawson, H (2000) *An Alphabetical Listing of Word, Name, and Place in Northern Ireland and the Living Language of Conflict*. Lewiston, NY: Edwin Mellen Press.

Eastwood, C (2016) "Eastwood proposes legal recognition of Ireland's unique position in EU." *SDLP*. 17 October 2016. www.sdlp.ie/news/2016/eastwood-proposes-legal-recognition-of-irelands-unique-position-in-eu/. [Accessed 09/08/2019]

EC European Commission
(2001) "Étymologie du terme "gouvernance"." *EC*. ec.europa.eu/governance/docs/doc5_fr.pdf. [Accessed 09/08/2018]
(2018) "Draft Agreement on the withdrawal of the United Kingdom of Great Britain and Northern Ireland from the European Union and the European Atomic Energy Community, as agreed at negotiators' level on 14 November 2018." TF50 (2018) 55 – Commission to EU. *EC Task Force for the Preparation and Conduct of the Negotiations with the United Kingdom under Article 50 TEU*. ec.europa.eu/commission/files/draft-agreement-withdrawal-united-kingdom-great-britain-and-northern-ireland-european-union-and-european-atomic-energy-community-agreed-negotiators-level-14-november-2018_en. [Accessed 09/08/2018]

ECDL European Commission for Democracy through Law (2002) "The Protection of National Minorities by their Kin-State." *Collection Science and Technique of Democracy*, No. 32. Strasbourg: Council of Europe Publishing.

ECNI Equality Commission for Northern Ireland
(2019) *Section 75 duties for Public Authorities*. ECNI. www.equalityni.org/S75duties. [Accessed 01/09/2019]
(2010) *Section 75 of the Northern Ireland Act 1998. A Guide for Public Authorities*. March 2010. Belfast: ECNI.

ECUK Electoral Commission of the UK (2016) "EU referendum results." 8 July 2016. www.electoralcommission.org.uk/find-information-by-subject/elections-and-referendums/past-elections-and-referendums/eu-referendum/electorate-and-count-information. [Accessed 17/07/2019]

Edwards, A (2009) *A History of the Northern Ireland Labour Party: Democratic Socialism and Sectarianism*. Manchester: Manchester University Press.

Edwards, A (2010) "The Progressive Unionist Party of Northern Ireland: A Left-Wing Voice in an Ethnically Divided Society." *British Journal of Politics and International Relations* 12 (4): 590-614.

Elazar, D J (1985) "Federalism and Consociational Regimes." *Publius* 15 (2): 17-34.

Eller, J D (1999) *From Culture to Ethnicity to Conflict: An Anthropological Perspective on Ethnic Conflict*. Ann Arbor, MI: University of Michigan Press.

Elliott, M (2007) "Religion and Identity in Northern Ireland." In: Elliott, M (Ed.) *The Long Road to Peace in Northern Ireland*. Revised 2nd ed. Liverpool: Liverpool University Press, pp. 175-191.

Elliott, M (2013) "The Role of Civil Society in Conflict Resolution: The Opsahl Commission in Northern Ireland, 1992–93." *New Hibernia Review / Iris Éireannach Nua* 17 (2): 86-102.

Elsie, R (2011) *Historical Dictionary of Kosovo*. 2nd ed. Lanham, MD: The Scarecrow Press.

Elster, J (1985) *Making Sense of Marx. Studies in Marxism and Social Theory*. Cambridge: Cambridge University Press.

Emerson, R M, Fretz, R I, & Shaw, L L (2011) *Writing Ethnographic Fieldnote*s. 2nd ed. Chicago, IL: University of Chicago Press.

English, R (2005) *Armed Struggle: the History of the IRA*. Oxford: Oxford University Press.

Ercikan, K & Roth, W-M (2006) "What Good is Polarizing Research into Qualitative and Quantitative?" *Educational Researcher* 35 (5): 14-23.

EU European Union
(2012) "Consolidated version of the Treaty on European Union." OJ C 326, 26.10.2012, pp. 13–45. *EUR-Lex*. eur-lex.europa.eu/eli/treaty/teu_2012/oj. [Accessed 30/08/2019].
(2019) "Brexit". *EU Newsroom* Highlights, Special Coverage. www.europa.eu/news room/highlights/special-coverage/brexit_en. [Accessed 26/08/2019]

Evans, J & Tonge, J (2009) "Social Class and Party Choice in Northern Ireland's Ethnic Blocs." *West European Politics* 32 (5): 1012-1030.

Eversley, D (1989) Religion and Employment in Northern Ireland. London: Sage.

Fay, M-T, Morrissey, M & Smyth, M (1999) *Northern Ireland's Troubles*: The Human Costs. London: Pluto Press.

FEC Fair Employment Commission for Northern Ireland (1995) *Religion and Community Background in Northern Ireland: Population and Workforce*. Belfast: FEC.

Fenton, S (2018) *The Good Friday Agreement*. London: Biteback Publishing.

Fenton, S & May, S (2002) "Ethnicity, Nation and 'Race': Connections and Disjunctures." In: Fenton, S & May, S (Eds.) *Ethnonational Identities*. Basingstoke: Palgrave, p. 1-20.

Ferguson, A (2015) "Council votes to rename Londonderry as Derry."24 July 2015. *The Irish Times*. www.irishtimes.com/news/politics/council-votes-to-rename-londonderry-as-derry-1.2296065. [Accessed 01/08/2019]

Ferguson, A (2017) "Ulster says no, maybe and yes to Irish passports." *The Irish Times*. 21 October 2017. www.irishtimes.com/news/ireland/irish-news/ulster-says-no-maybe-and-yes-to-irish-passports-1.3263466. [Accessed 14/08/2019]

Ferriter, D (2019) *The Border. The Legacy of a Century of Anglo-Irish Politics*. London: Profile Books.

Fields, R M (1980) *Northern Ireland: Society Under Siege*. New Brunswick, NJ & London: Transaction Publishers.

Filestead, W J (1979) "Qualitative Methods: a Needed Perspective in Evaluation Research." In: Cook, T D & Reichardt, C S (Eds.) *Qualitative and Quantitative Methods in Evaluation Research.* Beverly Hills, CA: Sage Publications, pp. 33-48.

Finlay, A (2001) "Defeatism and Northern Protestant 'Identity'." *The Global Review of Ethnopolitics,* 1 (2): 3-20.

Fisher, R J (1990) *The Social Psychology of Intergroup and International Conflict Resolution.* New. York: Springer.

Fisher, R J (2001) *Cyprus: The Failure of Mediation and the Escalation of an Identity-Based Conflict to an Adversarial Impasse.* Journal of Peace Research 38 (3): 307-326.

Fisher, R J (2006) "Intergroup Conflict." In: Deutsch, M, Coleman, P T & Marcus, E C (Eds.) *The Handbook of Conflict Resolution.* 2nd ed. San Francisco, CA: Jossey-Bass, pp. 176-197.

Fitzduff, M C (1988) *Community Conflict Skills: A Handbook for Anti-Sectarian Work.* Belfast: CRC.

Fitzduff, M C (2002) *Beyond Violence - Conflict Resolution Processes in Northern Ireland.* New York, NY: Brookings Institute/United Nations University Press.

Fitzduff, M C (2003) "Interviewed by Julian Portilla." *Beyond Intractability.* www.beyond intractability.org/audiodisplay/fitzduff-m. [Accessed 01/08/2019]

Fleming, J (2015) "Fury at claim 90% of Rathcoole estate residents linked to loyalist paramilitaries." 1 October 2015. *Belfast Telegraph.* www.belfasttelegraph.co.uk/news/northern-ireland/fury-at-claim-90-of-rathcoole-estate-residents-linked-to-loyalist-paramilitaries-31572354.html. [Accessed 01/08/2019]

Follis, B A (1995) *A State Under Siege: the Establishment of Northern Ireland, 1920 – 1925.* Oxford: Clarendon Press.

Fontana, A & Frey, J (1994) "Interviewing: the Art of Science." In: Denzin, N K (Ed.) *The SAGE Handbook of Qualitative Research.* Thousand Oaks, CA: Sage Publications, pp. 361-376.

Forsyth, D R (2010) *Group Dynamics.* 5th ed. Belmont, CA: Wadsworth, Cengage.

Foster, J W (1988) "Who Are the Irish?" *An Irish Quarterly Review* 77 (308): 403-416.

Foster, P (2000) "Inside story of the Maze, a jail like no other." 28 July 2000. *The Telegraph.* www.telegraph.co.uk/news/uknews/1350686/Inside-story-of-the-Maze-a-jail-like-no-other.html. [Accessed 01/08/2019]

Foster, R F (Ed.) *The Oxford Illustrated History of Ireland.* New York, NY: Oxford UP.

Fowler, H W, Fowler F G & Sykes, J B (Eds.) *The Concise Oxford Dictionary of Current English.* 8th ed. Oxford: Clarendon Press.

Foy, H (2010) "Bloody Sunday: Saville report vs. Widgery report." *The Guardian.* 15 June 2010. www.theguardian.com/uk/2010/jun/15/bloody-sunday-saville-report-widgery. [Accessed 01/08/2019]

Fox, A (Ed.) *Plato and the Christians.* London: SCM Press.

Frampton, M (2012) "Dissident Irish Republican Violence: A Resurgent Threat?" *The Political Quarterly* 83 (2): 227-237.

Fraser, N (1997) *Justice Interruptus: Critical Reflections on the 'Postsocialist' Condition.* New York, NY: Routledge.

Fraser, N (2000) "Rethinking Recognition." *New Left Review* 3, May/June 2000: 107-120.

Gailey, A & Adams, G (1977) "The Bonfire in North Irish Tradition." *Folklore* 88 (1): 3-38.

Gallaher, C (2007) *After the Peace: Loyalist Paramilitaries in Post-accord Northern Ireland.* Ithaca, NY: Cornell University.

Gallagher, A M (1989a) *Majority Minority Review 1: Education and Religion in Northern Ireland.* Centre for the Study of Conflict, University of Ulster.

Gallagher, A M (1989b) "Social Identity and the Northern Ireland Conflict." *Human Relations* 42 (10): 917-935.

Gallagher, A M (1991) *Majority Minority Review 2: Employment, Unemployment and Religion in Northern Ireland*. Coleraine: Centre for the Study of Conflict, University of Ulster.

Gallagher, P (2015) "How Britain's treatment of 'The Hooded Men' during the Troubles became the benchmark for US 'torture' in the Middle East." *The Independent*. 20 February 2015. www.independent.co.uk/news/uk/home-news/how-britains-treatment-of-the-hooded-men-during-the-troubles-became-the-benchmark-for-us-torture-in-10060242.html. [Accessed 01/08/2019]

Galtung, J (1969) "Violence, Peace, and Peace Research." *Journal of Peace Research* 6 (3): 167-191.

Galtung, J (1990) "Cultural Violence." *Journal of Peace Research* 27 (3): 291-305.

Galtung, J (2007 "Peace by Peaceful Conflict Transformation – the TRANSCEND Approach." In: Webel, C & Galtung, J (Eds.) *Handbook of Peace and Conflict Studies*. New York, NY: Routledge, pp. 14-32.

Galtung, J & Fischer, D (2013) *Johan Galtung: Pioneer of Peace Research*. New York, NY: Springer.

Ganiel, G (2003) "The Politics of Religious Dissent in Northern Ireland." *IBIS working paper* no. 32. Belfast: Institute for British-Irish Studies, University College Dublin (UCD). www.ucd.ie/ibis/filestore/wp2003/32_gan.pdf. [Accessed 01/08/2019]

Ganiel, G (2008) *Evangelicalism and Conflict in Northern Ireland*. New York, NY: Springer.

Gans, C (2003) *The Limits of Nationalism*. Cambridge: Cambridge University Press.

Garland, R (2001) *Gusty Spence*. Belfast: Blackstaff Press.

Garry, J (2016) *Consociation and Voting in Northern Ireland: Party Competition and Electoral Behavior*. Philadelphia: University of Pennsylvania Press.

Garry, J, McNicholl, K, O'Leary, B & Pow, J (2018) *Northern Ireland and the UK's Exit from the EU. What do people think?* The UK in a Changing World, Report May 2018. Belfast: Queen's University Belfast & Economic & Social Research Council.

Garry, J, O'Leary, B & Coakley, J (2017) "How Northern Ireland voted in the EU referendum – and what it means for border talks." The Conversation.27 April 2017. www.theconversation.com/how-northern-ireland-voted-in-the-eu-referendum- and-what-it-means-for-border-talks-76677. [Accessed 19/07/2019]

Garvaghy Residents (1999) *Garvaghy: A Community Under Siege*. Belfast: Beyond the Pale.

Garvin, T (1982) "Defenders, Ribbonmen and Others: Underground Political Networks in Pre-Famine Ireland." *Past & Present* 96: 133-155.

Gaskell, G (2000) "Individual and Group Interviewing." In: Bauer, M W & Gaskell, G (Eds.) *Qualitative Researching with Text, Image and Sound: A Practical Handbook*. London: Sage Publications, pp. 38-56.

Geoghan, P (2014) "Divided Cities, Space & Territory: Belfast, Skopje & Mitrovica." 3 November 2014. *The University of Edinburgh: The New Metropolitan – new cultures of urban citizenship*. www.newmetropolitan.hss.ed.ac.uk/2014/11/03/divided-cities-space-and-territory-belfast-skopje-and-mitrovica/ [Accessed 01/08/2019]

Geoghegan, P (2017) "Who are the Democratic Unionists and what do they want?" *Politico*. 9 June 2017. www.politico.eu/article/hung-parliament-who-are-the-democratic-unionists-and-what-do-they-want-uk-elections/. [Accessed 06/08/2019]

Gellner, E (1998) *Nationalism*. London: Phoenix.

Gellner, E (2006) *Nations and Nationalism*. 2nd ed. Oxford: Blackwell Publishers.

Gerring, J (2007) *Case Study Research: Principles and Practices*. Boston, MA: Boston University Press.

Giddens, A (2009) *Sociology*. 6th ed. Revised and updated with P W Sutton. Cambridge: Polity Press.

Gill, S (2009) "Pessimism of the Intelligence, Optimism of the Will: Reflection on Political Agency in the Age of Empire." In: Francese, J (Ed.) *Perspectives on Gramsci: Politics, Culture and Social Theory*. New York, NY: Routledge, pp. 97-109.

Gillespie, G (2017) *Historical Dictionary of the Northern Ireland Conflict*. 2nd ed. Lanham, MA: Rowman & Littlefield.

Goemans, H E (2006) "Bounded Communities: Territoriality, Territorial Attachment, and Conflict." In: Kahler, M & Walter, B F (Eds.) *Territoriality and Conflict in an Era of Globalization*. Cambridge: Cambridge University Press, pp. 25-61.

Gormally, B, McEvoy, K & Wall, D (1993) "Criminal Justice in a Divided Society: Northern Ireland Prisons." *Crime and Justice* 17: 51-135.

Gormley-Heenan, C, Byrne J & Robinson G (2013) "The Berlin walls of Belfast." *British Politics* 8: 357-382.

Graham, B & Nash, C (2006) "A Shared Future: Territoriality, Pluralism and Public Policy in Northern Ireland." *Political Geography*, 25(3): 253-278.

Graham, B & Shirlow, P (1998) "An Elusive Agenda: the Development of a Middle Ground in Northern Ireland." *Area* 30 (3): 245-254.

Gramsci, A (1971) *Selections from the Prison Notebooks of Antonio Gramsci*. Edited and Translated by Q Hoare & G N Smith. London: Lawrence & Wishart & New York, NY: International Publishers.

Gramsci, A (1994) *Pre-Prison Writings*. Edited by R Bellamy. Translated by V Cox. New York, NY: Cambridge University Press.

Gramsci, A (2000) *The Antonio Gramsci Reader. Selected Writings 1916 – 1935*. Edited by D Forgacs. New York, NY: New York University Press..

Green, A (2007) *Selling the Race: Culture, Community and Black Chicago, 1940-1955*. Chicago, IL: University of Chicago Press.

Green, E R R (2001) "The Great Famine 1845-50." In: Moody, T W & Martin, F X (Eds.) *The Course of Irish History*. Blackrock: Mercier Press, pp. 263-274.

Grix, J (2010) *The Foundations of Research*. 2nd ed. Basingstoke & New York, NY: Palgrave Macmillan.

Gudgin, G (1999) "The Northern Ireland Labour Market." *Proceedings of the British Academy* 98: 251-284.

Guelke, A (2013) *Politics in Deeply Divided Societies*. Cambridge: Polity Press.

Gurr, T R (1970) *Why Men Rebel*. Princeton, NJ: Princeton University Press.

Hachey, T E (1996) "The Northern Specter, 1920-1988: A Continuing Crisis in the Conflict of Cultures." In: Hachey, T E, Hernon J M & McCaffrey L J (Eds.) *The Irish Experience: A Concise History*. Revised Ed. New York, NY: Sharpe, pp. 214-234.

Hadden, P (1994) *Beyond the Troubles? Northern Ireland's Past and Future: A Socialist Analysis*. Belfast: Herald Books.

Hall, M (Ed.) (2003) "Beginning a debate. An exploration by Ardoyne community activists." *Island Pamphlets* 56. Newtownabbey: Island Publications.

Hall, M (Ed.) (2007a) "Building bridges at the grassroots: The experience of the Suffolk-Lenadoon Interface Group." *Island Pamphlets* 81. Newtownabbey: Island Publications.

Hall, M (Ed.) (2007b) "Loyalism in Transition (3): Is there a shared Ulster heritage?" *Island Pamphlets* 83. Newtownabbey: Island Publications. Belfast: Island Publications/ Farset Community Think Tanks Project.

Hall, M (Ed.) (2008) "Suffolk-Lenadoon Reminiscences." *Island Pamphlets* 91. New-townabbey: Island Publications.

Hall, M (2016) "Farset Community Think Tanks Project (Island Publications). Last update 14 April 2016. *CAIN Web Service.* www.cain.ulst.ac.uk/islandpublications/index.html. [Accessed 01/08/2019]

Hall, R C (2002) *The Balkan Wars 1912-1913: Prelude to the First World War.* London & New York, NY: Routledge.

Hancock, L. E. (2013) "Zones of Peace", in Mac Ginty, R (Ed.) *Routledge Handbook of Peacebuilding.* London & New York, NY: Routledge, pp. 237-248.

Hanley, B & Millar, S (2009) *The Lost Revolution: The Story of the Official IRA and the Workers' Party.* London: Penguin Books.

Hansson, U (2005) *Troubled Youth? Young People, Violence and Disorder in Northern Ireland.* Belfast: Institute for Conflict Research (ICR).

Harff, B & Gurr T (2004) *Ethnic Conflict in World Politics.* 2nd ed. Boulder, CO: Westview Press.

Hartley, T (2010) *Written in Stone: The History of Belfast City Cemetery.* Belfast: Brehon Press.

Hartley, T (2014) "Milltown Cemetery: Graveyard tells the complex story of Belfast." *Belfast Telegraph*, 5 August 2014. www.belfasttelegraph.co.uk/opinion/columnists/milltown-cemetery-graveyard-tells-the-complex-story-of-belfast-30482330.html. [Accessed 14/09/2017]

Hartmann, E, Kunze C & Brand, U (Ed.) (2009) *Globalisierung, Macht und Hegemonie.* Münster: Westfälisches Dampfboot.

Hayes, B C & McAllister I (1995) "Social Class, Class Awareness and Political Beliefs in Northern Ireland and the Republic of Ireland." *Economic and Social Review* 26 (4): 349-368.

Hayes, B & McAllister, I (1999) "Ethnonationalism, Public Opinion and The Good Friday Agreement." In: Ruane, J & Todd, J (Eds.) *After the Good Friday Agreement: Analysing Political Change in Northern Ireland.* Dublin: University College Dublin Press, pp. 30-48.

Hayes, B & McAllister, I (2001) "Who Voted for Peace? Public Support for the 1998 Northern Ireland Agreement." *Irish Political Studies* 16 (1): 73-93

Hayes, B & McAllister, I (2005) "Public Support for Political Violence and Paramilitarism in Northern Ireland and the Republic of Ireland." *Terrorism and Political Violence* 17: 599-617.

Hayes, B, McAllister, I & Dowds, L (2007) "Integrated Education, Intergroup Relations, and Political Identities in Northern Ireland." *Social Problems* 54 (4): 454-482.

Hayes, M (2005) "Left without a political voice, loyalists go for confrontation." *Irish Independent*, Dublin, 13 September 2005, p.7.

Heatley, C (2004) Interface: Flashpoints in Northern Ireland. Belfast: Lagan Books. *CAIN Web Service.* www.cain.ulst.ac.uk/issues/interface/docs/heatley04.htm. [Accessed 01/08/2019]

Heatley, F (1974) "The Early Marches." *Fortnight* 81: 9-11.

Heclo, H (1972) "Review Article: Policy Analysis." *British Journal of Political Science* 2 (1): 83-108.

Heenan, D & Birrell, D (2010) *Social Work in Northern Ireland: Conflict and Change.* Bristol: The Policy Press.

Helle, A. (1998) "Shifting Loyalties: Protestant Working-Class Politics in Ulster." In: Pasture, P. & Verberckmoes, J. (Eds.) *Working-Class Internationalism and the Appeal of National Identity: Historical Debates and Current Perspectives*. Oxford and New York, NY: Berg, pp. 173-202.

Hennessey, T (1997) *A History of Northern Ireland: 1920 – 1996*. Dublin: Gill & Mac Millan.

Hennessey, T (2001) *The Northern Ireland Peace Process: Ending the Troubles?* New York, NY: Palgrave.

Hepburn, A C (1990) "The Belfast Riots of 1935." *Social History* 15 (1): 75-96.

Hepburn, A C (1996) *A Past Apart: Studies in the History of Catholic Belfast, 1850-1950*. Belfast: Ulster Historical Foundation.

Hepburn, A C (2004) *Contested Cities in the Modern West*. Basingstoke & New York, NY: Palgrave Macmillan.

Herron T & Lynch J (2007) *After Bloody Sunday: Ethics, Representation, Justice*. Cork: Cork University Press.

Hewitt, J J (2008) "Trends in Global Conflict, 1946-2005." In: Hewitt, J J, Wilkenfeld, J & Gurr T R (Eds.) *Peace and Conflict 2008*. Boulder, CO: Paradigm Publishers, pp. 5-20.

Higgins, G I & Brewer, J D (2004) "The Roots of Sectarianism in Northern Ireland." In: Hargie, O & Dickson, D (Eds.) *Researching the Troubles: Social Science Perspectives on the Northern Ireland Conflict*. Edinburgh: Mainstream Publishing, pp. 107-122.

HIIK Heidelberg Institute for International Conflict Research (2019) *Conflict Barometer 2018*. Heidelberg: HIIK. www.hiik.de/conflict-barometer/current-version/?lang=en. [Accessed 01/08/2019]

Hillyard, P, Kelly, G, McLaughlin, E, Patsios, D & Tomlinson, M (2003) *Bare Necessities: Poverty and Social Exclusion in Northern Ireland. Key Findings. Democratic Dialogue, Report No. 16*. Belfast: Democratic Dialogue.

Hillyard, P, Rollston, B & Tomlinson, M (2005) *Poverty and Conflict in Northern Ireland: An International Perspective*. Dublin: Combat Poverty Agency.

Hindess, B (1996) *Discourses of Power. From Hobbes to Foucault*. Oxford: Blackwell.

Hirst, C (2005) "Politics, Sectarianism and the Working Class in Nineteenth-Century Belfast." In: Drisceoil, D Ó, & Lane, F (Eds.) *Politics and the Irish Working Class, 1830–1945*. Basingstoke: Palgrave, pp. 62-86.

Hobsbawm, E J (1992) *Nations and Nationalism since 1780: Programme, Myth, Reality*. 2nd ed. Cambridge: Cambridge University Press.

Hobsbawm, E J (2012) "Ethnicity and Nationalism in Europe Today." In: Balakrishnan, G (Ed.) *Mapping the Nation*. With an Introduction by Benedict Anderson. London: Verso, pp. 255-266.

Hollander, J A (2004) "The social context of focus groups." *Journal of Contemporary Ethnography* 33 (5): 602-637.

Holton, J R (1998) *Globalization and the Nation-State*. Basingstoke: Macmillan.

Horgan, J & Morrison, J F (2011) "Here to Stay? The Rising Threat of Violent Dissident Republicanism in Northern Ireland." *Terrorism and Political Violence* 23 (4): 642-669.

Horowitz, D (2000) *Ethnic Groups in Conflict*. 2nd ed. Berkeley & Los Angeles, CA: University of California Press.

Horowitz, D (2002) "Explaining the Northern Ireland Agreement: The Sources of an Unlikely Constitutional Consensus." *British Journal of Political Science* 32: 193-220.

Howard, M C & King, J E (1988) *The Political Economy of Marx*. 2nd ed. New York, NY: New York University Press.

Human Rights Watch (Helsinki) & Hall, J (1997) *To Serve Without Favor: Policing, Human Rights, and Accountability in Northern Ireland*. New York, NY: Human Rights Watch.

ICG International Crisis Group
  (2005) "Bridging Kosovo's Mitrovica Divide." *Europe Report* N°165. 13 September 2005. *ICG*. www.crisisgroup.org/europe-central-asia/balkans/kosovo/bridging-koso vos-mitrovica-divide. [Accessed 01/08/2019]
  (2012) "Setting Kosovo Free: Remaining Challenges." *Europe Report* N°218. 10 September 2012. *ICG*. www.crisisgroup.org/europe-central-asia/balkans/kosovo/setting-kosovo-free-remaining-challenges. [Accessed 01/08/2019]
  (2019) "Crisis Watch, June 2019." *ICG*. www.crisisgroup.org/crisiswatch/june-2019. [Accessed 01/08/2019]
IICD Independent International Commission on Decommissioning
  (2005) Report of the Independent International Commission on Decommissioning, 26 September 2005. Belfast: *IICD*. www.cain.ulst.ac.uk/events/peace/decom mission/iicd260905.pdf. [Accessed 01/08/2019]
  (2009) Report of the Independent International Commission on Decommissioning, 4 September 2009. Belfast: *IICD*. www.cain.ulst.ac.uk/events/peace/decom mission/iicd040909.pdf. [Accessed 01/08/2019]
  (2010a) "Statement on INLA Decommissioning, 8 February 2010." Belfast: *IICD*. www.cain.ulst.ac.uk/events/peace/decommission/iicd080210inla.pdf. [Accessed 01/08/2019]
  (2010b) "Statement on OIRA Decommissioning, 8 February 2010." Belfast: *IICD*. www.cain.ulst.ac.uk/events/peace/decommission/iicd080210oira.pdf. [Accessed 01/08/2019]
  (2010c) "Statement on UDA Decommissioning, 6 January 2010." Belfast: *IICD*. www./cain.ulst.ac.uk/events/peace/decommission/iicd060110.pdf. [Accessed 01/08/2019]
  (2011) Final Report of the Independent International Commission on Decommissioning, 4 July 2011. Belfast: *IICD*. www.cain.ulst.ac.uk/events/peace/decom mission/iicd040711.pdf. [Accessed 01/08/2019]
IEP Institute for Economics and Peace (2017) Global Peace Index. *IEP Report* 48, June 2017. visionofhumanity.org/app/uploads/2017/06/GPI17-Report.pdf. [Accessed 01/08/2019]
Independent Commission on the Future for Housing in Northern Ireland (2010) *Report of the Independent Commission on the Future for Housing in Northern Ireland*. Belfast: Chartered Institute of Housing. www.cih.org/resources/PDF/NI policy docs/Housing Commission Report.pdf [Accessed 01/08/2019]
Irish Times (2009) "Shootings were attempt at mass murder, says PSNI." *The Irish Times*. 8 March 2009. www.irishtimes.com/news/shootings-were-attempt-at-mass-murder-says-psni-1.837232. [Accessed 27/07/2017]
Irwin, C J (2002) *The People's Peace Process in Northern Ireland*. Basingstoke & New York, NY: Palgrave.
Jackson, M W (1979) "The Least Advantaged Class in Rawls's Theory." *Canadian Journal of Political Science / Revue Canadienne de Science Politique* 12 (4): 727-746.
Jacoby, T (2008) *Understanding Conflict and Violence: Theoretical and Interdisciplinary Approaches*. London & New York, NY: Routledge.
Jarman, N (1999) *Drawing Back from the Edge: Community Based Response to Violence in North Belfast*. Belfast: Community Development Centre.
Jarman, N (2002) *Managing Disorder: Responding to Interface Violence in North Belfast*. Belfast: OFMDFM Research Branch.

Jarman, N (2004) *Demography, Development and Disorder: Changing Patterns of Interface Areas*. Belfast: Institute for Conflict Research (ICR).

Jarman, N (2005a) "Changing Places, Moving Boundaries: The Development of New Interface Areas." *Shared Space: A research journal on peace, conflict and community relations in Northern Ireland* 1: 9-19.

Jarman, N (2005b) *No Longer A Problem? Sectarian Violence in Northern Ireland*. Belfast: ICR.

Jarman, N (2005c) *Mapping Interface Barriers. BIP Interface Mapping Project*. Belfast: Belfast Interface Project. www.cain.ulst.ac.uk/issues/segregat/docs/jarman0805.pdf. [Accessed 01/08/2019]

Jarman, N (2006) *Working at the Interface: Good Practice in Reducing Tension and Violence*. Belfast: ICR.

Jarman, N (2019) "A Bitter Peace: Flag Protests, the Politics of No and Culture Wars." In: Armstrong C, Herbert D, Mustad, J E (Eds). (2019) *The Legacy of the Good Friday Agreement*. Cham: Palgrave Macmillan, pp. 109-132.

Jarman, N & O'Halloran, C (2001) "Recreational Rioting: Young People, Interface Areas and Violence." *Child Care in Practice* 7 (1): 2-16.

Jarman, N, Rallings, M-K & Bell, J (2009) *Local Accommodation: Effective Practice in Responding to Disputes over Parades*. Belfast: ICR.

Jarstad, A (2007) "To Share or to Divide? Negotiating the Future of Kosovo." *Civil Wars* 9 (3): 227-242.

Jenkins, R (1984) "Understanding Northern Ireland." *Sociology* 18 (2): 253-264.

Jenkins, R (1997) *Rethinking Ethnicity: Arguments and Explorations*. London: Sage.

Jenkins, R (2008) *Social Identity*. 3rd ed. London & New York, NY: Routledge.

Jess, M (2012) *The Orange Order*. Dublin: The O'Brien Press.

Jesse, N G & Williams, K P (2005) *Identity and Institutions: Conflict Resolution in Divided Societies*. Albany, NY: State University of New York Press.

Johnson, P (2005) *Ireland: A Concise History from the Twelfth Century to the Present Day*. Chicago, IL: Chicago Review Press.

Johnston, W (2001) "Portadown Garvaghy Area." *Ireland Story: History and Maps*. www.wesleyjohnston.com/users/ireland/maps/drumcree_parade.gif. [15/06/2019]

Jones, E (1956) "The Distribution and Segregation of Roman Catholics in Belfast." *Sociological Review* 4: 167-89.

Jones, E (1960) *A Social Geography of Belfast*. London: Oxford University Press.

Jones, S (2006). *Antonio Gramsci. Routledge Critical Thinkers*. London & New York, NY: Taylor & Francis.

Jordan, A & Schout, A (2006) *The Coordination of the European Union: Exploring the Capacities of Networked Governance*. Oxford: Oxford University Press.

Jordan, R L (2013) *The Second Coming of Paisley: Militant Fundamentalism and Ulster Politics*. New York, NY: Syracuse University Press.

Judah, T (2008) *Kosovo: What Everyone Needs to Know*. Oxford & New York, NY: Oxford University Press.

Kahler, M (2006) "Territoriality and Conflict in an Era of Globalization." In: Kahler, M & Walter, B F (Eds.) *Territoriality and Conflict in an Era of Globalization*. Cambridge: Cambridge University Press, pp. 1-24.

Karr, J-P A (1849) *Les Guêpes*, January 1849 (6th series, 1859).

KAS/ASK Kosovo Agency of Statistics (2013) "Kosovo in Figures 2012". *Statistical Office of Kosovo*. May 2013. ask.rks-gov.net/media/2153/kosovo-in-figures-2012.pdf. [Accessed 01/08/2019]

Katz, D (1965) "Nationalism and Strategies of International Conflict Resolution." In: Kelman, H C (Ed.) *International Behavior: A Social Psychological Analysis*. New York, NY: Holt, Rinehart & Winston, pp. 356-390.

Kaufmann, E P (2007) *The Orange Order: a Contemporary Northern Irish History*. Oxford: Oxford University Press.

Keating, M (2001a) *Plurinational Democracy: Stateless Nations in a Post-Sovereignty Era*. Oxford & New York, NY: Oxford University Press.

Keating, M (2001b) "Northern Ireland and the Basque Country." In: McGarry, J (Ed.) *Northern Ireland and the Divided World. The Northern Ireland Conflict and the Good Friday Agreement in Comparative Perspective*. Oxford: Oxford University Press, pp. 181-208.

Kearney, R (1997) *Postnationalist Ireland: Politics, Culture, Philosophy*. London: Routledge.

Kearney, V (2012) "Magilligan Prison to close in six years time." *BBC News*. 23 April 2012. www.bbc.com/news/uk-northern-ireland-17818240. [Accessed 01/08/2019]

Kegley, C W (2008) *World Politics: Trend and Transformation*. 12th ed. Belmont, CA: Cengage Learning.

Kennedy-Pipe, C (1997) *The Origins of the Present Troubles in Northern Ireland*. New York, NY: Longman.

Kenny, M (2004) *The Politics of Identity: Liberal Political Theory and the Dilemmas of Difference*. Cambridge & Malden, MA: Polity Press.

Kerr, M (2005) *Imposing Power-Sharing: Conflict and Coexistence in Northern Ireland and Lebanon*. Dublin: Irish Academic Press.

Kevlihan, R (2013) *Aid, Insurgencies and Conflict Transformation: When Greed is Good*. Oxon & New York, NY: Routledge.

Khazanov, A (2005) "Ethnic and National Conflicts in the Age of Globalisation: Withering Away, Persisting, or Domesticated?" *Totalitarian Movements & Political Religions* 6 (2): 271-286.

Kilbane, P (1995) "Partners in Health?" In: Democratic Dialogue (Ed.) *Social Exclusion, Social Inclusion. Democratic Dialogue, Report No. 2*. Belfast: Democratic Dialogue, pp. 65-67.

Kilpatrick, C (2014) "I'll keep meeting terrorists: Orange chaplain Mervyn Gibson defends engaging with loyalist paramilitaries." *Belfast Telegraph*. 22 September 2014. www.belfasttelegraph.co.uk/news/northern-ireland/ill-keep-meeting-terrorists-orange-chaplain-mervyn-gibson-defends-engaging-with-loyalist-paramilitaries-30604711.html. [Accessed 01/08/2019]

Kilpatrick, C (2015) "Orange Order's Mervyn Gibson debates parades with old republican adversary on Falls Road." *Belfast Live*. 31 July 2015. www.belfastlive.co.uk/news/belfast-news/orange-orders-mervyn-gibson-debates-9770241. [Accessed 01/08/2019]

King, G, Keohane, R & Verba, S (1994) *Designing Social Inquiry: Scientific Inference in Qualitative Research*. Princeton, NJ: Princeton University Press.

King Jr, M L K (1965/2019) "Address at the Conclusion of the Selma to Montgomery." March. 25 March 1965. *The Martin Luther King, Jr. Research and Education Institute*. Text and audio available at: kinginstitute.stanford.edu/king-papers/documents/address-conclusion-selma-montgomery-march. [Accessed 01/09/2019]

Kinealy, C (2002) *The Great Irish Famine: Impact, Ideology and Rebellion*. Basingstoke: Palgrave.

Kissane, B (2007) *The Politics of the Irish Civil War*. Oxford: Oxford University Press.

Knowles, E M (Ed.) (1999) *The Oxford Dictionary of Quotations*. 3rd ed. ed. Oxford & New York, NY: Oxford University Press

Knox, C (2013) "From the Margins to the Mainstream: Community Restorative Justice in Northern Ireland." *Journal of Peacebuilding & Development* 8 (2): 57-72.

Knox, C & Monaghan, R (2002) *Informal Justice in Divided Societies: Northern Ireland and South Africa*. Basingstoke & New York, NY: Palgrave.

Kramer, H & Džihić, V (2006) *Die Kosovo-Bilanz. Scheitert die internationale Gemeinschaft?* 2nd ed. Wien: LIT Verlag.

Kvale, S (2007) *Doing Interviews*. London & Thousand Oaks, CA: Sage Publications.

Kymlicka, W (1995) *Multicultural Citizenship*. Oxford: Oxford University Press.

Kymlicka, W (1996) "Social Unity in a Liberal State." *Social Philosophy and Policy* 13 (1): 105-136.

Kymlicka, W (2005) "Identity Politics in Multination States." In: Venice Commission (Ed.) *State Consolidation and National identity. Collection Science and Technique of Democracy*, No. 38. Strasbourg: Council of Europe, pp. 45-77.

LaMarche, G (2012) "Funding an Unfinished Revolution." In: Worden, M (Ed.) *The Unfinished Revolution: Voices from the Global Fight for Women's Rights*. Bristol: Policy Press, pp. 307-316.

Landy, M (1986) "Culture and Politics in the Work of Antonio Gramsci." *Boundary 2*, 14 (3): 49-70.

LCF Lenadoon Community Forum (2003) *The Development of Lenadoon Area and the Community Forum 1992–2002*. Belfast: Lenadoon Community Forum.

Leahy (2019) "Irish Times poll: Northern Ireland voters do not want DUP-Tory Brexit." *The Irish Times*. 7 March 2019. www.irishtimes.com/news/politics/irish-times-poll-northern-ireland-voters-do-not-want-dup-tory-brexit-1.3818264. [Accessed 01/08/2019]

Lederach, J P (1997) *Building Peace: Sustainable Reconciliation in Divided Societies*. Washington, DC: United States Institute of Peace.

Lee, R M (1993) *Doing Research on Sensitive Topics*. London: Sage Publications.

Legg, G (2016) "Redeveloping the Long Kesh/Maze prison: profiting from the hunger strikes?" *The Irish Times*. 5 May 2016. www.irishtimes.com/culture/books/redeveloping-the-long-kesh-maze-prison-profiting-from-the-hunger-strikes-1.2636134. [Accessed 01/08/2019]

Lehane, M (2019) "New Brexit proposals do not meet backstop objectives - Taoiseach." *RTÉ*. 2 October 2019. www.rte.ie/news/brexit/2019/1002/1079600-customs-reaction/ [Accessed 03/10/2019]

Lennon, B (2004) *Peace Comes Dropping Slow: Dialogue and Conflict Management in Northern Ireland*. Belfast: Community Dialogue.

Leonard, M (2010) "What's Recreational about 'Recreational Rioting'? Children on the Streets in Belfast." *Children & Society* 24 (1): 38-49.

Levy, J S (2007) "International Sources of Interstate and Intrastate War." In: Crocker, C A, Hampson F O & Aall, P (Eds.) *Leashing the Dogs of War: Conflict Management in a Divided World*. Washington, DC: United States Institute of Peace, pp. 17-38.

Levy, J T (2000) *The Multiculturalism of Fear*. New York, NY: Oxford University Press.

Lijphart, A (1977) *Democracy in Plural Societies: A Comparative Exploration*. New Haven & London: Yale University Press.

Lijphart, A (1984) *Democracies: Patterns of Majoritarian and Consensus Government in Twenty-One Countries*. New Haven: Yale University Press.

Lijphart, A (2002) "The Wave of Power-Sharing Democracy." In: Reynolds, A (Ed.) *Architecture of Democracy: Constitutional Design, Conflict Management, and Democracy.* Oxford: Oxford University Press, pp. 37-54.

LT LucidTalk

(2017) "NI Post Elections Poll (June 2017) – Report." *LucidTalk*. 12 July, 2017. www.lucidtalk.co.uk/single-post/2017/07/12/NI-Post-Elections-Poll-June-2017---Report. [Accessed 18/08/2019]

(2018) "LT NI Opinion Panel 'Tracker' Poll – Winter 2018." *LucidTalk*. 7 December 2018. www.lucidtalk.co.uk/single-post/2018/12/07/LT-NI-Tracker-Poll--Winter-2018. [Accessed 11/08/2019]

(2019) "LT NI European Election 'Tracker' Poll – May 2019." *LucidTalk*. 14 May 2019. www.lucidtalk.co.uk/single-post/2019/05/14/LT-NI-European-Election-'Tracker'-Poll---May-2019. [Accessed 19/08/2019]

Lueger, M (2001) *Auf den Spuren der sozialen Welt: Methodologie und Organisierung interpretativer Sozialforschung.* Frankfurt am Main & Wien: Lang.

Lukács, G (1972) *History and Class Consciousness: Studies in Marxist Dialectics.* Cambridge: The MIT Press.

Lukes, S (2005) *Power: A Radical View.* 2nd ed. Basingstoke: Palgrave.

Lynch, J (1998) *A Tale of Three Cities: Comparative Studies in Working-Class Life.* Consultant Editor: Jo Campling. Basingstoke: Macmillan Press.

Lynch, P & Hopkins, S (2001) "The British-Irish Council: Structure, Programme and Prospects." *Irish Studies in International Affairs* 12: 133-150

Lynn, B (1997) *Holding the Ground: The Nationalist Party in Northern Ireland, 1945-72.* Aldershot: Ashgate.

Mac Ginty, R (2010) "No War, no Peace: Why so Many Peace Processes Fail to Deliver Peace." *International Politics* 47 (2): 145-162.

Mac Ginty, R & Darby, J (2002) *Guns and Government: The Management of the Northern Ireland Peace Process.* Basingstoke & New York, NY: Palgrave.

Madden, A (2010) "Call to tackle Northern Ireland segregation with mixed housing estates." *Belfast Telegraph*. 28 May 2010. www.belfasttelegraph.co.uk/news/call-to-tackle-northern-ireland-segregation-with-mixed-housing-estates-28538497.html. [Accessed 01/08/2019]

Madden, A (2019) "Calls for border poll 'breach' Good Friday Agreement and we're not 'molly coddled,' says DUP after Johnson meeting." *Belfast Telegraph*. 31 July 2019. www.belfasttelegraph.co.uk/news/northern-ireland/calls-for-border-poll-breach-good-friday-agreement-and-were-not-molly-coddled-says-dup-after-johnson-meeting-38362772.html. [Accessed 11/08/2019]

Maguire, A (2013) "Beacons to be used as eco-friendly alternative to Eleventh Night bonfires in Northern Ireland." *Belfast Telegraph*. 10 July 2013. www.belfasttelegraph.co.uk/news/northern-ireland/beacons-to-be-used-as-ecofriendly-alternative-to-eleventh-night-bonfires-in-northern-ireland-29408182.html. [Accessed 01/08/2019]

Maguire, M C (1999) *The Vision of Peace: Faith and Hope in Northern Ireland.* Edited by J. Dear. Foreword by the Dalai Lama and by Archbishop Desmond Tutu. Eugene, OR: Wipf and Stock Publishers.

Maguire, P (2017) "Hard border 'would be target for violence'." *The Times*. 8 December 2017. www.thetimes.co.uk/article/hard-border-would-be-target-for-violence-zkt0frr5n. [Accessed 20/08/2019]

Malcolm, N (2002) *Kosovo: A Short History.* Ed. with a new preface. Basingstoke & Oxford: Pan Books.

Mangione, J G (1972) *The World Around Danilo Dolci*. New York, NY: Harper & Row.

Manheim, J B & Rich, R C (1995) *Empirical Political Analysis: Research Methods in Political Science*. 6th ed. White Plains, NY: Longman.

Mansvelt Beck J (2005) *Territory and Terror: Conflicting Nationalisms in the Basque Country*. London & New York, NY: Routledge.

Mansvelt Beck J (2008) "The Basque Power-sharing Experience: from a Destructive to a Constructive Conflict?" *Nations and Nationalism* 14 (1): 61-83.

Margalit, A & Raz, J (1990) "National Self-Determination." *The Journal of Philosophy* 87 (9): 439-461.

Marsh, S (2019) "Hard Brexit would be 'detrimental' to peace process, says PSNI chief." *The Guardian*. 13 July 2019. www.theguardian.com/uk-news/2019/jul/13/psni-chief-constable-says-hard-brexit-would-be-absolutely-detrimental. [Accessed 20/08/2019]

Martin, F X (2001) "The Normans: Arrival and Settlement: 1169- c.1300." In: Moody, T W & Martin, F X (Eds.) *The Course of Irish History*. Blackrock: Mercier Press, pp. 106-119.

Marx, K (1977). *Capital, Volume 1*. Translated by B Fowkes. New York, NY: Vintage Books.

Maruna, S (2002) *Making Good: How Ex-Convicts Reform and Rebuild Their Lives*. Washington, DC: American Psychological Association.

Mason, R & Elgot, J (2019) "Boris Johnson calls for EU 'common sense' over Brexit backstop." *The Guardian*. 8 August 2019. www.theguardian.com/politics/2019/aug/08/no-10-refuses-to-rule-out-election-shortly-after-31-october-brexit. [Accessed 09/08/2019]

Matthews, N (2012) "The Northern Ireland Assembly Election 2011." *Irish Political Studies* 27 (2: Data Yearbook): 341-358.

May, T (2011) *Social Research: Issues, Methods and Research*. 4th Ed. Maidenhead: McGraw Hill Education.

Mayring, P (2000) "Qualitative Content Analysis." *Forum Qualitative Social Research* 1 (2) June 2000.

Mayring, P (2003) *Qualitative Inhaltsanalyse: Grundlagen und Techniken*. 8th ed. Weinheim & Basel: Beltz Verlag.

Maza, C (2018) "Northern Ireland Breaks Record for Longest Time Without a Government, Sparking Protests." *Newsweek*. 29 August 2018. www.newsweek.com/northern-ireland-breaks-record-longest-time-without-government-sparking-1095600. [Accessed 11/08/2019]

McAleese, D (2005) "Loyalist jailed for Harryville horror. I'm still living in fear says Catholic victim." *Belfast Telegraph*. 17 September 2005. www.belfasttelegraph.co.uk/imported/loyalist-jailed-for-harryville-horror-28228327.html. [Accessed 01/08/2019]

McAleese, D (2011) "Marchers and police clash at Tour of the North parade in Belfast." *Belfast Telegraph*. 20 June 2011. www.belfasttelegraph.co.uk/news/northern-ireland/marchers-and-police-clash-at-tour-of-north-parade-in-belfast-28628688.html. [Accessed 01/08/2019]

McCann, E (1995) "Managing Sectarianism." *New Statesman and Society* 8 (367): 20-22.

McCann, E (2016) "People Before Profit fights for those left behind by Stormont – Eamonn McCann." *The Irish News*. 3 May 2016. www.irishnews.com/news/2016/05/03/news/people-before-profit-fights-for-those-left-behind-by-stormont-eamonn-mccann-506028. [Accessed 23/08/2019]

McCaffrey, R (2013) "The Civic Forum." *Northern Ireland Assembly: Research and Information Service Research Paper* 109/13. 30 August 2013. Belfast: Northern Ireland Assembly.

McCartney, D (2001) "From Parnell to Pearse 1891-1921." In: Moody, T W & Martin, F X (Eds.) *The Course of Irish History*. Blackrock: Mercier Press, pp. 294-312.

McCleery, M (2015) *Operation Demetrius and its Aftermath: A New History of the Use of Internment without Trial in Northern Ireland, 1971–75*. Manchester: Manchester University Press.

McCord, J A, McCord, M J, Davis, P T, Haran, M E & MacIntyre, S (2017) "The Political Cost? Religious Segregation, Peace Walls, and House Prices." *Peace and Conflict Studies* 24 (2): 1-37.

McCormack, J (2019) "Brexit talks: What does the DUP want?" *BBC News*. 17 January 2019. www.bbc.com/news/uk-northern-ireland-46903876. [Accessed 05/08/2019]

McCreary, A (2014) "Ian Paisley death: From firebrand to First Minister ...the remarkable journey of a true political colossus." *Belfast Telegraph*. 13 September 2014. www.belfasttelegraph.co.uk/news/northern-ireland/ian-paisley-death-from-firebrand-to-first-minister-the-remarkable-journey-of-a-true-political-colossus-30583383.html. [Accessed 31/07/2019]

McCrone, D & Kiely, R (2000) "Nationalism and Citizenship." *Sociology* 34 (1): 19-34.

McCrudden, C (1999) "Equality and the Good Friday Agreement." In: Ruane, J & Todd, J (Eds.) *After the Good Friday Agreement: Analysing Political Change in Northern Ireland*. Dublin: University College Dublin Press, pp. 96-121.

McCulloch, A (2014) *Power-Sharing and Political Stability in Deeply Divided Societies*. London & New York, NY: Routledge.

McCurry, C (2016) "Former Maze prison site new home for Northern Ireland's first air ambulance base." *Belfast Telegraph*. 17 November 2016. www.belfasttelegraph.co.uk/news/northern-ireland/former-maze-prison-site-new-home-for-northern-irelands-first-air-ambulance-base-35222196.html. [Accessed 01/08/2019]

McDonald, H (2005) "Gun attack escalates loyalist feud." *The Guardian*. 30 January 2005. www.theguardian.com/uk/2005/jan/30/northernireland.northernireland. [Accessed 01/08/2019]

McDonald, H (2009) "We've lost control of Ardoyne, IRA warns." *The Guardian*. 5 April 2009. www.theguardian.com/politics/2009/apr/05/ira-ardoyne-republican-belfast. [Accessed 01/08/2019]

McDonald, H (2010) "Northern Ireland appoints first justice minister for 38 years." *The Guardian*. 13 April 2010. www.guardian.co.uk/uk/2010/apr/13/northern-ireland-justice-minister. [Accessed 01/08/2019]

McDonald, H (2012) "Belfast city hall attacked by loyalist demonstrators over union flag vote." *The Guardian*. 3 December 2012. www.theguardian.com/uk/2012/dec/03/belfast-city-hall-flag-protest. [Accessed 14/07/2019]

McDonald, H (2013a) "Belfast: house and cars damaged in sectarian attack." *The Guardian*. 27 July 2013. www.theguardian.com/uk-news/2013/jul/27/belfast-ringford-park-stones-attack. [Accessed 01/08/2019]

McDonald, H (2013b) "Belfast: 'It's not just the flag. They want to take everything British away'." *The Guardian*. 12 January 2013. www.theguardian.com/uk/2013/jan/13/belfast-protest-flag-young-loyalists. [Accessed 01/08/2019]

McDonald, H (2013c) "Maze prison redevelopment gets green light." *The Guardian*. 18 April 2013. www.theguardian.com/uk/2013/apr/18/maze-prison-redevelopment -green-light. [Accessed 01/08/2019]

McDonald, H (2017) "Belfast 'peace wall' between communities felled after 30 years." *The Guardian*. 20 September 2017. www.theguardian.com/uk-news/2017/sep/20/belfast-peace-wall-between-communities-felled-after-30-years. [Accessed 23/08/2019]

McDonald, H & Cusack, J (2008) *UVF – The Endgame*. Dublin: Poolbeg Books.

McDonald, H & Holland, J (2010) *I.N.L.A – Deadly Divisions*. Dublin: Poolbeg Books.

McDowell, R B (2001) "The Protestant Nation 1775-1800." In: Moody, T W & Martin, F X (Eds.) *The Course of Irish History*. Blackrock: Mercier Press, pp. 190-203.

McEvoy, D (2014) *The Little Green Book of Irish Wisdom*. New York, NY: Skyhorse Publishing.

McEvoy, J (2008) *The Politics of Northern Ireland*. Edinburgh: Edinburgh University Press.

McEwen, A (1999) *Public Policy in a Divided Society: Schooling, Culture, and Identity in Northern Ireland*. Aldershot: Ashgate.

McGarry, F (2010) *The Rising: Ireland, Easter 1916*. New York, NY: Oxford University Press.

McGarry, J (2001) "Introduction: The Comparable Northern Ireland." In: McGarry J (Ed.) (2001) *The Comparable Northern Ireland: The Northern Ireland Conflict and the Good Friday Agreement in Comparative Perspective*. New York, NY: Oxford University Press, pp. 1-33.

McGarry, J & O'Leary, B (1995) *Explaining Northern Ireland: Broken Images*. Oxford: Blackwell Publishers.

McGarry, J & O'Leary, B (2004) *The Northern Ireland Conflict: Consociational Engagements*. Oxford: Oxford University Press.

McGarry, J, Keating, M & Moore, M (2006) "Introduction: European Integration and the Nationalities Question." In: McGarry, J & Keating, M (Eds.) *European Integration and the Nationalities Question*. New York, NY: Routledge, pp. 1-20.

McGovern, E (2019) "Brexit: Threats from paramilitaries aren't basis for decisions, says Donaldson." *Belfast Telegraph*. 13 October 2019. www.belfasttelegraph.co.uk/news/northern-ireland/brexit-threats-from-paramilitaries-arent-basis-for-decisions-says-donaldson-38589452.html. [Accessed 13/10/2019]

McGrattan, C (2010) "Explaining Northern Ireland? The limitations of the ethnic conflict model." *National Identities* 12 (2): 181-197.

McGregor, P & McKee, P (1995) "A Widening Gap." In: Democratic Dialogue (Ed.) *Social Exclusion, Social Inclusion. Democratic Dialogue, Report No. 2*. Belfast: Democratic Dialogue, pp. 39-44.

McHardy, A (2017) "Martin McGuinness obituary." 21 March 2017. *The Guardian*. www.theguardian.com/uk-news/2017/mar/21/martin-mcguinness-obituary. [Accessed 01/08/2019]

McKay, S (2006) "North's divisions follow victims to their graves." *The Irish Times*, 14 September 2006. www.irishtimes.com/opinion/north-s-divisions-follow-victims-to-their-graves-1.1002563. [Accessed 01/08/2019]

McKenny, K (2008) "The Restoration Land Settlement in Ireland: A Statistical Interpretation." In: Dennehy, C A (Ed.) *Restoration Ireland: Always Settling and Never Settled*. Aldershot: Ashgate.

McKittrick, D (1996) *The Nervous Peace*. Belfast: Blackstaff Press.

McKittrick, D (1996) "Paramilitaries tell 'King Rat': Leave Ulster or die." *The Independent*. 28 August 1996. www.independent.co.uk/news/paramilitaries-tell-king-rat-leave-ulster-or-die-1311914.html. [Accessed 01/08/2019]

McKittrick, D & McVea, D (2002) *Making Sense of the Troubles: The Story of the Conflict in Northern Ireland*. Chicago, IL: New Amsterdam Books.

McLaughlin, E, Law, J, Morrow, D & Jarman, N (1997) *On the Edge: Community Perspectives on Civil Disturbances in North Belfast June-Sept 1996*. Edited by N Jarman. Belfast: North Belfast Community Development Centre.

McLoughlin, P J (2009) "The SDLP and the Europeanization of the Northern Ireland Problem." *Irish Political Studies* 24 (4): 603-619.

McNally, M (2007) *Easter Rising 1916: Birth of the Irish Republic*. Illustrated by Peter Dennis. Botley & New York, NY: Osprey.

Meehan, E (2000 "Bringing in Europe: The Peace Process and the Europeanisation of the Irish Question." *Irish Studies in International Affairs* 11: 179-191.

Melaugh, M (1994) *Majority Minority Review 3: Housing and Religion in Northern Ireland*. Coleraine, University of Ulster, 1994.

Melaugh, M (1995) "Majority-Minority Differentials: Unemployment, Housing and Health." In: Dunn, S. (Ed.) *Facets of the Conflict in Northern Ireland*. Basingstoke: Macmillan, pp. 131-148.

Mertus, J A (1999) *Kosovo: How Myths and Truths Started a War*. Berkeley & Los Angeles, CA: University of California Press.

Mészáros, I & Bottomore T (Eds.) (1971) *Aspects of History and Class Consciousness. Essays by Tom Bottomore*. London: Routledge & Kegan.

Miller, D (1995) *On Nationality*. Oxford: Clarendon Press.

Miller, G & Dingwall, R (Eds.) (1997) *Context and Method in Qualitative Research*. London: Sage Publications.

Minahan, J (2002) *Encyclopedia of the Stateless Nations: Ethnic and National Groups Around the World. 4 Volumes, A-Z*. Westport, CT & London: Greenwood Press.

Mitchell, A (2011) *Lost in Transformation: Violent Peace and Peaceful Conflict in Northern Ireland*. Basingstoke: Palgrave.

Mitchell, C (2006) *Religion, Identity and Politics in Northern Ireland: Boundaries of Belonging and Belief*. Aldershot & Burlington, VT: Ashgate.

Mitchell, P, Evans, G & O'Leary, B (2005) "Party Competition and Public Opinion at the Northern Ireland Assembly Elections 2003." *ARK Research Update* 36. www.ark.ac.uk/publications/updates/update36.pdf. [Accessed 01/08/2019]

Mitchell, S (2017) *Struggle Or Starve: Working-class Unity in Belfast's 1932 Outdoor Relief Riots*. Chicago, IL: Haymarket Books.

Mohdin, A (2019) "Timeline of Northern Ireland's power-sharing crisis." *The Guardian*. 26 April 2019. www.theguardian.com/politics/2019/apr/26/northern-ireland-power-sharing-stormont-crisis-timeline. [Accessed 01/08/2019]

Mohdin, A, Wolfe-Robinson, M & Kalukembi, M (2019) 'Stop the coup': Protests across UK over Johnson's suspension of parliament." *The Guardian*. 28 August 2019. www.theguardian.com/politics/2019/aug/28/protests-sparked-by-boris-john sons-plan-to-suspend-parliament. [Accessed 29/08/2019]

Monaghan, R (2002) "The Return of "Captain Moonlight": Informal Justice in Northern Ireland." *Studies in Conflict & Terrorism*, 25 (1): 41-56.

Monaghan, R (2004) "'An Imperfect Peace': Paramilitary 'Punishments' in Northern Ireland." *Terrorism and Political Violence* 16 (3): 439-461.

Monaghan, R & Shirlow, P (2011) "Forward to the Past? Loyalist Paramilitarism in Northern Ireland Since 1994." *Studies in Conflict & Terrorism* 34 (8): 649-665.

Moody, T W (2001) "Fenianism, Home Rule and the Land War." In: Moody, T W & Martin, F X (Eds.) *The Course of Irish History*. Blackrock: Mercier Press, pp. 228-244.

Moore, A (2019) "Border community 'concerned' as customs cars arrive amid Brexit row." Belfast Telegraph. *1 October 2019*. www.belfasttelegraph.co.uk/news/northern-ireland/border-community-concerned-as-customs-cars-arrive-amid-brexit-row-38552725.html. [Accessed 02/10/2019]

Moore, R, Smyth, M & Collins, P (1995) Aspects of Sectarian Division in Derry Londonderry - Third public discussion: The Changing Population Balance and Protestant Drift. Central Library, 13 April 1995. *CAIN Web Service*. cain.ulst.ac.uk/issues/segregat/temple/discus3.htm. [Accessed 01/08/2019]

Morgan, V, Smyth, M, Robinson, G & Fraser, G (1996) *Mixed Marriages in Northern Ireland*. University of Ulster: Coleraine.

Moriarty, G (2019) "Gerry Adams says Government has a duty to plan for Irish unity." *The Irish Times*. 7 June 2019. www.irishtimes.com/news/ireland/irish-news/gerry-adams-says-government-has-a-duty-to-plan-for-irish-unity-1.3918300. [Accessed 01/08/2019]

Moriarty, G & McGarry, P (2015) "Orange Order parades: Missiles hurled as PSNI block march." *The Irish Times*. 13 July 2015. www.irishtimes.com/news/politics/orange-order-parades-missiles-hurled-as-psni-block-march-1.2283794. [Accessed 01/08/2019]

Morris, A (2015a) "Loyalists paint road markings red, white and blue." *The Irish News*. 17 June 2015. www.irishnews.com/news/2015/06/17/news/loyalists-paint-road-markings-red-white-and-blue-137675/. [Accessed 01/08/2019]

Morris, A (2015b) "New group is latest in line of attempted loyalist unity projects." *The Irish News*. 14 October 2015. www.irishnews.com/news/2015/10/14/news/group-latest-in-line-of-loyalist-unity-projects-293166/. [Accessed 01/08/2019]

Morris, A (2016) "Over 90% of social housing in NI still segregated." *The Irish News*. 20 February 2016. www.irishnews.com/news/2016/02/20/news/over-90-of-social-housing-in-ni-still-segregated-423726/. [Accessed 01/08/2019]

Morrison, J F & Horgan, J (2016) "Reloading the Armalite? Victims and Targets of Violent Dissident Irish Republicanism, 2007–2015." *Terrorism and Political Violence* 28 (3): 576-597.

Morrison, J F (2019) "The Provisional Irish Republican Army." In: Silke, A (Ed.) *Routledge Handbook of Terrorism and Counterterrorism*. Oxon & New York, NY: Routledge, pp. 341-350.

Morrow, D (2000) "Nothing to Fear but …? Unionists and the Northern Ireland Peace Process." In Murray, D (Ed.) *Protestant Perceptions of the Peace Process in Northern Ireland*. Limerick: Centre for Peace and Development Studies, pp. 10-35.

Mortimore, R (2019) "One in three Britons would mind if Northern Ireland voted to leave the UK, poll finds." *Ipsos MORI*. 3 April 2019. www.ipsos.com/ipsos-mori/en-uk/one-three-britons-would-mind-if-northern-ireland-voted-leave-uk-poll-finds. [Accessed 01/08/2019]

Morton, A D (2007) *Unravelling Gramsci: Hegemony and Passive Revolution in the Global Political Economy*. London: Pluto Press.

Moxon-Browne, E (1991) "National Identity in Northern Ireland." In: Stringer, P & Robinson, G (Eds.) *Social Attitudes in Northern Ireland: The First Report*. Belfast: Blackstaff Press, pp. 23-30.

Mulholland, M (2002) *The Longest War: Northern Ireland's Troubled History*. Oxford & New York, NY: Oxford University Press.

Mullan, K (2013) "Catholics outnumber Protestants on both banks of the Foyle." *Londonderry Sentinel*. 31 January 2013. www.londonderrysentinel.co.uk/news/catholics-outnumber-protestants-on-both-banks-of-the-foyle-1-4737478. [Accessed 01/08/2019]

Murphy, D (1979) *A Place Apart*. London: Penguin Books.

Murray, D (1985) *Worlds Apart: Segregated Schools in Northern Ireland*. Belfast, Appletree.

Murray, W & agencies (2019) "Brexit: Lords agree to push through bill preventing no deal by end of Friday." *The Guardian.* 5 September 2019. www.theguardian.com/politics/2019/sep/05/brexit-lords-agree-to-push-through-bill-preventing-no-deal-by-end-of-friday. [Accessed 05/09/2019]

Murtagh, B (1996) "On Derry's Walls: Segregation and Space in Northern Ireland." *Administration* 44 (1): 30-47.

Murtagh, B (2002) *The Politics of Territory: Policy and Segregation in Northern Ireland.* Basingstoke: Palgrave.

Murtagh, B (2008) "New Spaces and Old in 'Post-Conflict' Belfast. *Divided Cities/Contested States Working Paper* No. 5. www.conflictincities.org/PDFs/Working Paper5_10.9.08.pdf. [Accessed 01/08/2019]

Newbery, S (2009) "Intelligence and Controversial British Interrogation Techniques: the Northern Ireland Case, 1971–2." *Irish Studies in International Affairs* 20: 103-119.

NIA Northern Ireland Assembly

(2012a) *Constituency Profile Belfast North – Dec*ember *2012.* www.niassembly.gov.uk/globalassets/Documents/RaISe/Constituency-Profiles/2012/belfast_north.pdf.   [Accessed 01/08/2019]

(2012b) *Constituency Profile Belfast West – December 2012.* www.niassembly.gov.uk/globalassets/Documents/RaISe/Constituency-Profiles/2012/belfast_west.pdf. [Accessed 01/08/2019]

NICRA Northern Ireland Civil Rights Association (1978) *"We Shall Overcome"...: The History of the Struggle for Civil Rights in Northern Ireland 1968-1978.* Belfast: NICRA.

NIE Northern Ireland Executive / The Executive Office

(2015) *A Fresh Start: The Stormont Agreement and Implementation Plan.* 17 November 2015. Belfast: NIE & NIO. www.northernireland.gov.uk/publications/fresh-start-stormont-agreement-and-implementation-plan. [Accessed 20/08/2019]

(2017) *Labour Force Survey Religion Report 2015. Annual update - January 2019.* Belfast: National Statistics & NISRA. www.executiveoffice-ni.gov.uk/publications/labour-force-survey-religion-report-2015. [Accessed 20/08/2019]

(2019a) *Labour Force Survey Religion Report 2017. Annual update - January 2019.* Belfast: National Statistics & NISRA. www.executiveoffice-ni.gov.uk/publications/labour-force-survey-religion-report-2017. [Accessed 20/08/2019]

(2019b) *Together: Building a United Community Strategy (T:BUC) Annual Update 2018/19.* 23 August 2019. Belfast: NIE. www.executiveoffice-ni.gov.uk/publications/together-building-united-community-strategy-tbuc-annual-update-201819.   [Accessed 05/09/2019]

NIHE Northern Ireland Housing Executive (2017) "Community cohesion - building good relations through housing". *NIHE.* www.nihe.gov.uk/index/community/community_cohesion.htm. [Accessed 01/08/2019]

NINIS Northern Ireland Neighbourhood Information Service (provided by NISRA)

(2001) "Census 2001. Table KS07b : Community Background (administrative geographies)." *NINIS.* www.ninis2.nisra.gov.uk. [Retrieved 21/02/2019]

(2013a) "Census 2011. Table KS212NI : Religion or Religion Brought Up In (administrative geographies)". *NINIS.* www.ninis2.nisra.gov.uk. [Retrieved 21/02/2019]

(2013b) "Census 2011. Table KS501NI : Qualifications and Students (administrative geographies)." *NINIS.* www.ninis2.nisra.gov.uk. [Retrieved 21/02/2019]

(2013c) "Census 2011. Table KS601NI : Economic Activity (administrative geographies)." *NINIS.* www.ninis2.nisra.gov.uk. [Retrieved 21/02/2019]

(2016a) "Electoral Ward information for Ardoyne, Glencolin, Ladybrook, Poleglass, Shankill." Profile last updated August 2016. *NINIS*. www.ninis2.nisra.gov.uk. [Retrieved 18/03/2019]

(2016b) "Neighbourhood Renewal Area Information for Greater Shankill." *NINIS*. www.ninis2.nisra.gov.uk. [Retrieved 18/03/2019]

NIO Northern Ireland Office

(1985) Anglo-Irish Agreement 1985: Agreement between the Government of the United Kingdom of Great Britain and Northern Ireland and the Government of the Republic of Ireland. Hillsborough, 15 November 1985. Belfast: NIO.

(1998) The Agreement: Agreement reached in the Multi-Party Negotiations. Belfast: NIO.

(2006) *Agreement at St Andrews, 13 October 2006.* Belfast: NIO. www.nio.gov.uk/ st_andrews_agreement.pdf. [Accessed 01/08/2019]

(2010) *Agreement at Hillsborough Castle, 5 February 2010.* Belfast: NIO. www.gov. uk/government/publications/hillsborough-castle-agreement. [Accessed 01/08/2019]

NISRA Northern Ireland Statistical Research Agency

(2001a) *A Profile of Protestants and Roman Catholics in the Northern Ireland Labour Force. Source Book.* 1st Edition, March 2001. NISRA Monitor 2/01. Belfast: NISRA. www.equality.nisra.gov.uk/Labour Force Religion Source Book.pdf. [Accessed 01/08/2019]

(2001b) *Measures of Deprivation in Northern Ireland.* Report by the Social Disadvantage Research Centre, University of Oxford. June 2001. Belfast: NISRA.

(2001c) "Northern Ireland Ward Level Data and LGD Level Summaries – spreadsheet (*Multiple Deprivation Measure scores)." *NISRA.* www.nisra.gov.uk/deprivation/ nimdm_2001.htm. [Retrieved 22/02/ 2019]

(2005a) *Northern Ireland Multiple Deprivation Measure 2005.* May 2005. Belfast: NISRA.

(2005b) "MD 2005 Super Output Area Level (spreadsheet)." *NISRA.* www.nisra.gov. uk/deprivation/nimdm_2005.htm. [Retrieved 22/02/2019]

(2010a) *Northern Ireland Multiple Deprivation Measure 2010.* Belfast: NISRA.

(2010b) "NIMDM Electoral Ward (spreadsheet)." *NISRA.* www.nisra.gov.uk/ deprivation/nimdm_2010.htm. [Retrieved 22/02/2019]

(2012) "Census 2011: Key Statistics for Northern Ireland, Statistics Bulletin 11 December 2012." *NISRA.* www.nisra.gov.uk/Census/key_stats_bulletin_2011.pdf. [Accessed 01/08/2019]

(2013a) "2011 Census: Key Statistics for Wards and Small Areas for Northern Ireland. 30 January 2013." *NISRA.* www.nisra.gov.uk/publications/2011-census-key-statistics-wards-and-small-areas-northern-ireland. [Accessed 01/08/2019]

(2013b) "Census 2011: Detailed Characteristics for Northern Ireland on Health, Religion and National Identity. Statistics Press Notice, 16 May 2013." *NISRA.* www.nisra. gov.uk/Census/detailedcharacteristics_press_release_2011.pdf. [Accessed 01/08/2019]

(2019) "2021 Census." *NISRA.* www.nisra.gov.uk/statistics/census/2021-census. [Accessed 07/07/2019]

Niens, U, Cairns, E & Hewstone, M (2003) "Contact and Conflict in Northern Ireland." In: Hargie, O & Dickson, D (Eds.) *Researching the Troubles: Social Science Perspectives on the Northern Ireland Conflict.* London, UK: Mainstream, pp. 123-39.

Nimni, E. (1991) *Marxism and Nationalism: Theoretical Origins of a Political Crisis.* London: Pluto Press.

Nolan, P (2013) *Northern Ireland Peace Monitoring Report: Number Two*. Belfast: Community Relations Council (CRC). www.community relations.org.uk/sites/crc/files/media-files/NIPMR2.pdf [Accessed 01/08/2019]

Nolan, P (2014) *Northern Ireland Peace Monitoring Report: Number Three*. Belfast: Community Relations Council (CRC). www.community-relations.org.uk/sites/crc/files/media-files/Peace-Monitoring-Report-2014.pdf. [Accessed 01/08/2019]

Nolan, P (2018) "The Cruel Peace: Killings in Northern Ireland since the Good Friday Agreement." *The Detail TV*. 23 April 2018. www.thedetail.tv/articles/the-cruel-peace-killings-in-northern-ireland-since-the-good-friday-agreement. [Accessed 01/08/2019]

Nolan, P, Bryan, D, Dwyer, C, Hayward, K, Radford, K & Shirlow, P (2014) *The Flag Dispute: Anatomy of a Protest*. Belfast: Queen's University Belfast.

Nolan, P & Wilson, R (2015) *Dialogue and Engagement: Lessons from the Northern Ireland Civic Forum*. December 2015. Belfast: Joseph Rowntree Charitable Trust. www.cain.ulst.ac.uk/othelem/organ/jrct/Nolan_Wilson_2015_JRCT.pdf. [Accessed 30/07//2019]

Norris, P (2008) *Driving Democracy: Do Power-Sharing Institutions Work?* Cambridge: Cambridge University Press.

Norton, C (1998) "Trade Unions in a Divided Society: The Case of Northern Ireland." In: Pasture, P & Verberckmoes, J (Eds.) *Working-Class Internationalism and the Appeal of National Identity: Historical Debates and Current Perspectives*. Oxford & New York, NY: Berg, pp. 151-172.

Novy, A (2002) "Die Methodologie interpretativer Sozialforschung." *SRE - Discussion Papers* Nr. 2002/01. Institut für Wirtschaftsgeographie, Abt. Stadt- und Regionalentwicklung. Wien: Wirtschaftsuniversität.

O'Brien, B (1993) *The Long War: The IRA & Sinn Féin – from Armed Struggle to Peace Talks*. Dublin: The O'Brien Press.

O'Carroll, S (2019a) "Boris Johnson yet to make a phone call to Irish PM Leo Varadkar." *The Guardian*. 27 July 2019. www.theguardian.com/politics/2019/jul/27/boris-johnson-yet-to-make-a-phone-call-to-irish-pm-leo-varadkar. [Accessed 08/08/2018]

O'Carroll, S (2019b) "Sharp rise in Britons making applications for Irish passports." *The Guardian*. 16 July 2019. www.theguardian.com/world/2019/jul/16/first-time-applications-irish-passports-up-sharply-since-2015-brexit. [Accessed 01/08/2019]

O'Connell, H (2019) "Johnson and Varadkar 'close to hammering out Brexit deal' with border in Irish Sea." *Belfast Telegraph*. 11 October 2019. www.belfasttelegraph.co.uk/news/northern-ireland/johnson-and-varadkar-close-to-hammering-out-brexit-deal-with-border-in-irish-sea-38583269.html. [Accessed 13/10/2019]

O'Connor, E (2014) "Labour and Left Politics." In: Aughey, A & Morrow, D (Eds.) *Northern Ireland Politics*. London & New York, NY: Routledge, pp. 48-55.

O'Dochartaigh, N (1997) *From Civil Rights to Armalites: Derry and the Birth of the Irish Troubles*. Cork: Cork University Press.

O'Doherty, M (2018) "The Civic Forum promised to replace impassioned debate with informed discussion ... is that why the big parties let it wither and die?" *Belfast Telegraph*. 6 September 2018. www.belfasttelegraph.co.uk/opinion/news-analysis/malachi-odoherty-the-civic-forum-promised-to-replace-impassioned-debate-with-informed-discussion-is-that-why-the-big-parties-let-it-wither-and-die-37287636.html. [Accessed 04/06/2019]

O'Dowd, L, Robson, B & Tomlinson, M (1980) *Northern Ireland: Between the Civil Rights and Civil War*. London: CSE Books.

O'Driscoll, S (2017) "UUP ends anti-Brexit stance and sides with DUP to oppose Sinn Fein." *Belfast Telegraph*. 11 May 2017. www.belfasttelegraph.co.uk/news/general-election-2017/uup-ends-antibrexit-stance-and-sides-with-dup-to-oppose-sinn-fein-35702386.html. [Accessed 01/08/2019]

O'Duffy, B & O'Leary, B (1990) "Appendix 3: Violence in Northern Ireland, 1969-June 1989." In McGarry, J & O'Leary, B (Eds.) *The Future of Northern Ireland*. Oxford: Oxford University Press.

O'Hara, V (2013) "Terrified family is forced to flee after sectarian attack." *Belfast Telegraph*. 19 August 2013. www.belfasttelegraph.co.uk/news/northern-ireland/terrified-family-is-forced-to-flee-after-sectarian-attack-29508890.html. [Accessed 01/08/2019]

O'Leary, B (1999) "The Nature of the Agreement." *Fordham Journal of International Law* 22 (4): 1628-1667.

O'Leary, B (2001) "The elements of right-sizing and right-peopling the state," in O'Leary, B, Lustick, I, & Callaghy, T M (Eds.) *Right-Sizing the State: the Politics of Moving Borders*. Oxford: Oxford University Press, pp.15-73.

O'Leary, B (2019) *A Treatise on Northern Ireland, Volume III: Consociation and Confederation. From Antagonism to Accommodation*. Oxford: Oxford Universiy Press.

O'Leary, B & McGarry, J (1993) *The Politics of Antagonism: Understanding Northern Ireland*. London: Athlone Press.

O'Leary, J (2016). "The Interface: Peace Walls, Belfast, Northern Ireland." *Spaces of Conflict*, Autumn/Winter: 137-144.

O'Loughlin, J & Hendrix, C (2019) "Will climate change lead to more world conflict?" *The Washington Post*. 11 July 2019. www.washingtonpost.com/politics/2019/07/11/how-does-climate-change-impact-conflict-world/ [Accessed 22/07/2019]

O'Malley, P (1990) *Biting at the Grave: The Irish Hunger Strikes and the Politics of Despair*. Boston, MA: Beacon Press.

O'Malley, P (1994) "Northern Ireland: A Manageable Conflict?" *The Irish Review* 15: 14-39.

O'Malley, E & Walsh, D (2013) "Religion and Democratization in Northern Ireland: Is Religion actually Ethnicity in Disguise?" *Democratization* 20 (5): 939-958.

Ó Scannáil, M (2019) "'Regardless of Brexit, there will be a unity referendum'- Mary Lou McDonald calls for a vote on Irish unity." *Irish Independent*. 2 February *2019.* www.independent.ie/irish-news/news/regardless-of-brexit-there-will-be-a-unity-referendum-mary-lou-mcdonald-calls-for-a-vote-on-irish-unity-37776122.html. [Accessed 01/08/2019]

OFMDFM Office of the First Minister and Deputy First Minister
    (2005) *A Shared Future - Improving Relations in Northern Ireland: Policy and Strategic Framework for Good Relations in Northern Ireland*. 21 March 2005. Belfast: CRU, OFMDFM. www.niacro.co.uk/sites/default/files/publications/A Shared Future-OFMDFM-Mar 202005.pdf. [Accessed 05/08/2019]
    (2010) *Programme for Cohesion, Sharing and Integration: Consultation Document*. 27 July 2010. Belfast: OFMDFM. cain.ulst.ac.uk/issues/politics/ofmdfm/ofmdfm_270710_sharing.pdf. [Accessed 05/08/2019]
    (2013) *Together: Building a United Community*. 23 May 2013. Belfast: OFMDFM. www.executiveoffice-ni.gov.uk/publications/together-building-united-community-strategy. [Accessed 05/08/2019]

Opsahl, T, O'Malley, P, Elliott, M, Lister, R, Gallagher, E., Faulkner, E. & Gallagher, E. (1993) *A Citizens' Inquiry: The Opsahl Report on Northern Ireland*. Edited by Andy Pollak. Dublin: Lilliput Press.

Osborne, R D & Cormack R J (1986) "Unemployment and Religion in Northern Ireland." *The Economic and Social Review* 17 (3): 215-225.

Osborne, R D & Murray, R C (1978) *Educational Qualifications and Religious Affiliations in Northern Ireland.* Belfast, Fair Employment Agency.

Page, C (2011) "NI internment remembered 40 years on. 9 August 2011." *BBC News.* www.bbc.com/news/uk-northern-ireland-14458270. [Accessed 01/08/2019]

Parker, G & Boland, V (2019) "Johnson government refuses to exclude direct rule over Northern Ireland." *Financial Times.* 29 July 2019. www.ft.com/content/ 3f6f0cf4-b1d6-11e9-8cb2-799a3a8cf37b. [Accessed 15/08/2019]

Parkin, F (2006) "Marxism and Class Theory: A Bourgeois Critique." In: Levine, R F (Ed.) *Social Class and Stratification: Classic Statements and Theoretical Debates.* 2nd ed. Lanham, MA: Rowman & Littlefield, pp. 121-142.

Parkinson, A F (2004) *Belfast's Unholy War: The Troubles of the 1920s.* Dublin: Four Courts Press.

Payne, S (2019) "Boris Johnson admits quick US trade deal will be a challenge." *Financial Times.* 25 August 2019. www.ft.com/content/2de04bdc-c726-11e9-a1f4-3669401ba76f. [Accessed 25/08/2019]

PBP People Before Profit (2019) "Our Vision." *PBP.* www.pbp.ie/ourvision. [Accessed 23/08/2019]

PCNI Parades Commission for Northern Ireland (2010) *Annual Report and Financial Statements for the Year ended 31st March 2009.* London: The Stationery Office.

Pearse, P ([1916] 1975). *The Easter Proclamation of the Irish Republic, 1916.* Dublin: Dolmen Press.

Peers, S (2019) "The debate over the Benn bill is plagued by a fundamental misunderstanding". Prospect. 4 September. 2019. www.prospectmagazine.co.uk/politics/the-debate-over-the-benn-bill-is-plagued-by-a-fundamental-misunderstanding [05/09/2019]

Peleg, I (2007) *Democratizing the Hegemonic State: Political Transformation in the Age of Identity.* New York, NY: Cambridge University Press.

Petroska-Beska, V & Najcevska, M (2004) *Macedonia: Understanding History, Preventing Future Conflict.* USIP Special Report 115, February 2004. Washington, DC: United States Institute of Peace.. www-preview.usip.org/sites/default/files/sr115.pdf. [Accessed 01/08/2019]

Pinckney, J (2018) *When Civil Resistance Succeeds: Building Democracy After Popular Nonviolent Uprisings.* ICNC Monograph Series. Washington, DC: International Center on Nonviolent Conflict Press.

Pinos, J C (2016) "Mitrovica: A City (Re)Shaped by Division." In: Ó Ciardha, É & Vojvoda, G (Eds.) *Politics of Identity in Post-Conflict States: The Bosnian and Irish Experience.* Oxon & New York, NY: Routledge, pp. 128-142.

Polanyi, K ([1944] 2001) *The Great Transformation. The Political Origins of Our Time.* Foreword by Joseph S. Stiglitz. Boston, MC: Beacon Press.

Pollak, A (2001) "Cross-Border Bodies and the North-South Relationship – Implementing Strand Two." *IBIS working paper no. 12*, pp. 10-19.

Poole, M (1971) "Riot displacement in 1969." *Fortnight* 22: 9-11.

Potter, J (2001) *A Testimony to Courage: The History of the Ulster Defence Regiment 1969-1992.* Barnsley: Leo Cooper – Pen & Sword Books.

Poulsen M, Johnston R & Forrest J (2001) "Intraurban Ethnic Enclaves: Introducing a Knowledge-based Classification Method." *Environment and Planning* 33 (11): 2071-2082.

Prelec, M (2017) "New Balkan Turbulence Challenges Europe." Commentary, Europe & Central Asia. 28 April 2017. *ICG*. www.crisisgroup.org/europe-central-asia/balkans/macedonia/new-balkan-turbulence-challenges-europe. [Accessed 01/08/2019]

Preiss, B & Brunner, C (2013) "Setting the Scene: On the Crisis of Democracy and the Potential for Civil Protest and Resistance." In: Preiss, B & Brunner, C (Eds.) *Democracy in Crisis: The Dynamics of Civil Protest and Civil Resistance*. Peace Report 2012. Vienna/Berlin: LIT, pp. 9-32.

Preiss, H (2003) *Economic, Social, and Political Justice and Stability for Northern Ireland? Examining the Good Friday Agreement from the Perspective of John Rawls's Social Contract Theory*. Master thesis. 17 July 2003. Vienna: University of Economics and Business & Stadtschlaining: Peace Library.

Pringle, P & Jacobsen, P (2000) *Those Are Real Bullets. Bloody Sunday, Derry, 1972*. New York, NY: Grove Press.

Proctor, K (2019) "What does the Letwin amendment mean for Brexit timetable?" *The Guardian*. 19 October 2019. www.theguardian.com/politics/2019/oct/19/what-does-the-letwin-amendment-mean-for-brexit-timetable-boris-johnson. [Accessed 20/10/2019]

PSNI Police Service of Northern Ireland (2015) *The Workforce Plan: Equality Impact Assessment*. Belfast: PSNI.

Pullan, W & Baillie, B (Eds.) (2013) *Locating Urban Conflicts: Ethnicity, Nationalism and the Everyday*. Basingstoke & New York, NY: Palgrave Macmillan.

PUP Progressive Unionist Party (2019) "About the Progressive Unionist Party." *PUP*. www.pupni.com/#about-us. [Accessed 23/08/2019]

Purdie, B (1990) *Politics in the Streets: The Origins of the Civil Rights Movement in Northern Ireland*. Belfast: Blackstaff Press.

Purdy, M (2014) "Catholics now outnumber Protestants in Belfast." 3 April 2014. *BBC News*. www.bbc.com/news/uk-northern-ireland-26875363. [Accessed 01/08/2019]

Putnam, R D (2000) *Bowling Alone: The Collapse and Revival of American Community*. New York, NY: Simon & Schuster.

Ramsbotham, O, Woodhouse, T & Miall, H (2012) *Contemporary Conflict Resolution: The Prevention, Management and Transformation of Deadly Conflicts*. 3rd ed. Oxford: Polity Press.

Ranelagh, J O (1999) *A Short History of Ireland*. Cambridge: Cambridge University Press.

Rawls, J (1971) *A Theory of Justice*. New York, NY: Oxford University Press.

Rawls, J (1993) *Political Liberalism*. New York, NY: Columbia University Press.

Reka, A (2008) "The Ohrid Agreement: The Travails of Inter-ethnic Relations in Macedonia." *Human Rights Review* 2008 (9): 55-69.

Renan, E (1992) "What is a Nation?" Text of a conference delivered at the Sorbonne on March 11th 1882, in Renan, E (1992) *Qu'est-ce qu'une nation?* Translated by E Rundell. Paris: Presses-Pocket.

Renan, E (1996) "What is a Nation?" In: Eley, G & Suny, R (Ed.) *Becoming National: A Reader*. New York, NY and Oxford: Oxford University Press, 1996, pp. 41-55.

Rhodes, R A W (1996) "The New Governance: Governing without Government." *Political Studies* 44 (4): 652-667.

Richmond, O (1999) "The Cyprus Conflict, Changing Norms of International Society, and Regional Disjunctures." *Cambridge Review of International Affairs* 13 (1): 239-253.

Ridenour, C S & Newman, I (2008) *Mixed Methods Research: Exploring the Interactive Continuum*. Carbondale, IL: Southern Illinois University Press.

Ritchie, J, Spencer, L, Bryman, A & Burgess R G (1994) *Analysing Qualitative Data*. London: Routledge.

Robin, C (2004) *Fear: The History of a Political Idea*. Oxford: Oxford University Press.

Roeder, P G (2007) *Where Nation-States Come From: Institutional Change in the Age of Nationalism*. Princeton, NJ: Princeton University Press.

Rooney, E & Swaine, A (2012) "The 'Long Grass' of Agreements: Promise, Theory and Practice." *International Criminal Law Review* 12 (3): 519-548.

Rose, P (2000) *How the Troubles Came to Northern Ireland*. Basingstoke & New York, NY: Palgrave.

Rose, R (1971) *Governing Without Consensus: An Irish Perspective*. London: Faber & Faber.

Rose, R (1976) *Northern Ireland: A Time of Choice*. London & Basingstoke: Macmillan Press.

Rowan, B (2000) "History of the loyalist feud." *BBC News*. 23 August 2000. news.bbc. co.uk/2/hi/uk_news/northern_ireland/892131.stm. [Accessed 01/08/2019]

Rowan, B (2009) "Dissident killings drove us to brink of war, says loyalist." *Belfast Telegraph*. 3 July 2009. www.belfasttelegraph.co.uk/news/local-national/dissident-killings-drove-us-to-brink-of-war-says-loyalist-14381929.html. [Accessed 01/08/2019]

Rowthorn, B & Wayne, N (1988) *Northern Ireland: The Political Economy of Conflict*. Cambridge: Polity Press.

RTÉ Radio Telefis Éireann
"The Taoiseach on the Situation in the North 1969." Speech by Jack Lynch on 13 August 1969. *RTÉ*. Archives. Text and audio available at: www.rte.ie/archives/exhibitions/1042-northern-ireland-1969/1048-august-1969/320416-broadcast-by-an-taoiseach/. [Accessed 01/09/2019]
"PSNI says Twelfth parades pass off peacefully across NI." *RTÉ*. 12 July 2017. www.rte.ie/news/2017/0712/889567-orange-order/. [Accessed 02/08/2019]
"Thousands march in NI to mark Twelfth of July." *RTÉ*. 12 July 2019. www.rte.ie/news/ireland/2019/0712/1061633-12-July-northern-ireland/. [Accessed 02/08/2019]

Ruane, J & Todd, J (1996) *The Dynamics of Conflict in Northern Ireland*. Cambridge: Cambridge University Press.

Ruane, J & Todd, J (1999) "The Belfast Agreement: context, content, consequences." In: Ruane, J & Todd. J (Eds.) *After the Good Friday Agreement: Analysing Political Change in Northern Ireland*. Dublin: University College Dublin Press, pp. 1-29.

Rudolph, J R Jnr (Ed.) *Encyclopedia of Modern Ethnic Conflicts*. Westport, CT & London: Greenwood Press.

Runciman, W G (1966) *Relative Deprivation and Social Justice: a Study of Attitudes to Social Inequality in Twentieth Century Britain*. London: Routledge & Kegan Paul.

Russell, R (2013) "Census 2011: Key Statistics at Northern Ireland and LGD level." *Northern Ireland Assembly: Research and Information Service Research Paper*. 20 May 2013. Belfast: Northern Ireland Assembly.

Russell, R (2017) "Election Report: Northern Ireland Assembly Election, 2 March 2017." *Northern Ireland Assembly: Research and Information Service Research Paper* 22/17. 8 March 2017. Belfast: Northern Ireland Assembly.

Ruxton, D (2017) "10 years on: The ceremony that 'marked the end of the Troubles'." 8 March 2017. *The Irish Times*. www.irishtimes.com/news/ireland/irish-news/10-years-on-the-ceremony-that-marked-the-end-of-the-troubles-1.3075304. [Accessed 01/08/2019]

Ryan, D (2019) "Stanford-led study investigates how much climate change affects the risk of armed conflict." *Stanford News*. 12 June 2019. news.stanford.edu/2019/06/12/climate-change-cause-armed-conflict/ [Accessed 22/07/2019]

Ryder, C (2000) *Inside the Maze: The Untold Story of the Northern Ireland Prison Service*. London: Methuen.

Sassen, S (2005) "When National Territory is Home to the Global: Old Borders to Novel Borderings." *New Political Economy* 10: 4, 523-541.

Savage, M (2018) "In Belfast fear is growing that the hated barriers will go up again." *The Guardian*. 6 May 2018. www.theguardian.com/global/2018/may/06/no-one-wants-border-ireland-belfast-barriers-stay-up. [Accessed 02/08/2019]

Savage, M & McDonald, H (2017) "Theresa May's plan to govern with DUP support thrown into confusion." *The Guardian*. 11 June 2017. www.theguardian.com/politics/2017/jun/10/theresa-may-dup-deal-snag-tory-rebellion. [Accessed 01/08/2019]

Schreier, M (2012) *Qualitative Content Analysis in Practice*. London: Sage Publications.

Scott, J (2001) *Power: Key Concepts*. Cambridge: Polity Press.

Seaver, B M (2000) "The Regional Sources of Power-Sharing Failure: The Case of Lebanon." *Political Science Quarterly* 115 (2): 247-271.

Sekaran, U (1992) *Research Methods for Business: A Skill-Building Approach*. 2nd ed. New York, NY: Wiley & Sons.

Shapiro, I (2005) "Theories of Change." January 2005. *Beyond Intractability*. www.beyondintractability.org/essay/theories_of_change/. [Accessed 01/08/2019]

Shaw, G B (1946) *Plays Pleasant: Arms and the Man. Candida, The Man of Destiny, You Never Can Tell*. London: Penguin Books.

Sheehan, M & Tomlinson, M (1999) *The Unequal Unemployed: Discrimination, Unemployment and State Policy in Northern Ireland*. Aldershot: Ashgate.

Shirlow, P (2003) "'Who Fears to Speak': Fear, Mobility, and Ethno-sectarianism in the Two 'Ardoynes'." *The Global Review of Ethnopolitics* 3 (1): 76-91.

Shirlow, P (2006) "Segregation, Ethno-Sectarianism and the 'New' Belfast. In: Cox, M, Guelke, A & Stephen, F (Eds.) *A Farewell to Arms? Beyond the Good Friday Agreement*. 2nd ed. Manchester: Manchester University Press, pp. 226-237.

Shirlow, P & Coulter, C (2007) "Enduring Problems: The Belfast Agreement and a Disagreed Belfast." In: Elliott, M (Ed.) *The Long Road to Peace in Northern Ireland*. Revised 2nd ed. Liverpool: Liverpool University Press, pp. 207-220.

Shirlow, P & Murtagh, B (2004) "Capacity-building, Representation and Intracommunity Conflict." *Urban Studies* 41 (1): 57-70.

Shirlow, P & Murtagh, B (2006) *Belfast: Segregation, Violence and the City*. London: Pluto Press.

Shirlow, P, Graham, B, McMullan, A, Murtagh, B, Robinson, G & Southern, N (2005) *Population Change and Social Inclusion Study Derry/Londonderry*. Coleraine: University of Ulster.

Shklar, J (1998) "The Liberalism of Fear", in: Hoffmann, S (Ed.) *Judith N. Shklar: Political Thought and Political Thinkers*. Chicago, IL: University of Chicago Press.

Shuttleworth, I G & Lloyd, C D (2008) *Mapping Segregation on Belfast NIHE Estates*. Belfast: NIHE. www.nihe.gov.uk/mapping_segregation_final_report.pdf.

Sidanius, J & Pratto, F (1999) *Social Dominance: An Intergroup Theory of Social Hierarchy and Oppression*. Cambridge: Cambridge University Press.

Siddique, H & Phipps, C (2019) "Brexit: 'I will not negotiate a delay with the EU,' Boris Johnson tells MPs after vote defeat – as it happened." *The Guardian*. 19 October 2019. www.theguardian.com/politics/live/2019/oct/19/brexit-mps-vote-boris-johnson-deal-super-saturday-erg-tory-rebels-labour-live-news. [Accessed 20/10/2019]

Silke, A (1999) "Ragged Justice: Loyalist Vigilantism in Northern Ireland." *Terrorism and Political Violence* 11 (3): 1-31.

Silke, A (2000) "The Impact of Paramilitary Vigilantism on Victims and Communities in Northern Ireland." *The International Journal of Human Rights* 4 (1): 1-24.

Simpson, M (2009) "Turning hotspot into friendly fire." *BBC News.* 10 July 2009. news. bbc.co.uk/2/hi/uk_news/northern_ireland/8145554.stm. [Accessed 01/08/2019]

Simpson, M (2010) "New era for policing and justice in Northern Ireland." *BBC News.* 12 April 2010. news.bbc.co.uk/2/hi/uk_news/northern_ireland/8613253.stm. [Accessed 01/08/2019]

Sinn Féin (2019) "Brexit." *Sinn Féin.* www.sinnfein.ie/brexit. [Accessed 06/08/2019]

Sinnerton, H (2003) *David Ervine: Uncharted Waters.* Revised Ed. Dublin: O'Brien Press.

Sisk, T D (1996) *Power Sharing and International Mediation in Ethnic Conflicts.* Washington, DC: United States Institute of Peace (USIP) Press.

SLIG Suffolk Lenadoon Interface Group
(2008a) "About Us." "Introduction" & "History". *SLIG.* www.slig.co.uk/site/about-us/introduction and www.slig.co.uk/site/about-us/history. [Accessed 01/06/2019]
(2008b) "The Interface and Beyond 2008 – 2013." September 2008. *SLIG.* www.slig. co.uk/slig.pdf. [Accessed 12/06/2019]

Smismans, S (2008) "New Modes of Governance and the Participatory Myth." *West European Politics* 31 (5): 874-895.

Smith, A D (1986) *The Ethnic Origins of Nationalism.* Oxford: Blackwell Publishers.

Smith, A D (2004) "Dating the Nation." In: Conversi, D (Ed.) *Ethnonationalism in the Contemporary World: Walker Connor and the Study of Nationalism.* London & New York, NY: Routledge, pp. 53-71.

Smith, D J and Chambers, G (1991) *Inequality in Northern Ireland.* Oxford: Clarendon Press.

Smith, J (2002) "Unionists demand exclusion of Sinn Fein from Assembly." *The Independent.* 7 October 2002. www.independent.co.uk/news/uk/home-news/unionists-demand-exclusion-of-sinn-fein-from-assembly-139431.html. [Accessed 01/08/2019]

Smith, J (2014) *Making the Peace in Ireland.* London & New York, NY: Routledge.

Smithey, L A (2011) *Unionists, Loyalists, and Conflict Transformation in Northern Ireland.* Oxford & New York, NY: Oxford University Press.

Smyth, M (2001) "Introduction." In: Smyth, M & Robinson, G (Eds.) *Researching Violently Divided Societies: Ethical and Methodological Issues.* London: Pluto Press, pp. 1-11.

Smyth, M (2006) "Lost Lives: Victims and the Construction of 'Victimhood' in Northern Ireland." In: Cox, M, Guelke, A & Stephen, F (Eds.) *A Farewell to Arms? Beyond the Good Friday Agreement.* 2nd ed. Manchester: Manchester University Press, pp. 6-23.

Southern, N (2011) "Loyalism: Political Violence and Decommissioning." In: McAuley, J W & Spencer, G (Eds.) *Ulster Loyalism after the Good Friday Agreement: History, Identity and Change.* Basingstoke: Palgrave, pp. 199-213.

Sparrow, A (2019a) "Theresa May resignation: Tories to choose new prime minister by July – as it happened." *The Guardian.* 24 May 2019. www.theguardian.com/politics/live/2019/may/24/theresa-may-resignation-uk-prime-minister-politics-brexit-live-news. [Accessed 27/07/2019]

Sparrow, A (2019b) "Boris Johnson wraps up Northern Ireland talks with no sign of progress on reviving power-sharing - as it happened." *The Guardian.* 1 August 2019. www.theguardian.com/politics/live/2019/jul/31/boris-johnson-holds-talks-in-belfast-as-sinn-fein-says-border-poll-must-follow-no-deal-brexit-live-news. [Accessed 11/08/2019]

Spencer, G (2012) *Protestant Identity and Peace in Northern Ireland.* Basingstoke: Palgrave.

Spencer G & Hudson, C (2018) "Politics in Northern Ireland are sclerotic... a civic forum could hold the answer, but it must be more than just a glorified talking shop." *Belfast Telegraph*. 22 October 2018. www.belfasttelegraph.co.uk/opinion/news-analysis/poli tics-in-northern-ireland-are-sclerotic-a-civic-forum-could-hold-the-answer-but-it-must-be-more-than-just-a-glorified-talking-shop-37442902.html. [Accessed 04/06/2019]

Spruyt, H (1994). "Institutional Selection in International Relations: State Anarchy as Order." *International Organization* 98 (4): 527-557.

SRPP Stewartstown Road Regeneration Project (2001) "Aerial photograph." *SRPP*. www.stewartstownroad.org/location.html. [Accessed 21/03/2019]

Staunton, E (2001) *The Nationalists of Northern Ireland, 1918-1973*. Dublin: The Columba Press.

Stewart, H & Boffey, D (2019) "EU ready to grant Brexit extension in build-up to key summit." *The Guardian*. 13 October 2019. www.theguardian.com/politics/2019/oct/13/eu-ready-to-grant-brexit-extension-as-johnson-prepares-for-key-summit. [Accessed 13/10/2019]

Strating, R (2015) *Social Democracy in East Timor*. London & New York, NY: Routledge.

Sutton, M (Ed.) (1994) *An Index of Deaths from the Conflict in Ireland 1969 – 1993: Bear in Mind these Dead* ...Belfast: Beyond the Pale Publications.

Sutton, M (2016a) "An Index of Deaths from the Conflict in Ireland 1969 – 2001: Cross-tabulations." *CAIN Web Service*. www.cain.ulst.ac.uk/sutton/crosstabs.html. [Retrieved 10/02/2019]

Sutton, M (2016b) "An Index of Deaths from the Conflict in Ireland 1969 – 2001: Geographical Location of the Death." *CAIN Web Service*. www.cain.ulst.ac.uk/sutton/tables/Location.html. [Retrieved 08/02/2019]

Tamir, Y (1995) *Liberal Nationalism*. Princeton, NJ: Princeton University Press.

Taylor, C (1994) *Multiculturalism: Examining the Politics of Recognition*. Edited and Introduced by Amy Gutmann. Princeton, NJ: Princeton University Press.

Taylor, G R (2005) "Introduction and Overview of the Research Process." In: Taylor, G R (Ed.) *Integrating Quantitative and Qualitative Methods in Research*. Lanham, MD: University Press of America, pp. 1-11.

Taylor, P (2014) *Loyalists*. London: A&C Black.

Teague, P (Ed.) (1993) *The Economy of Northern Ireland: Perspectives for Structural Change*. London: Lawrence & Wishart.

Tempest, M (2002) "Fourth suspension for Stormont." *The Guardian*. 14 October 2002. www.guardian.co.uk/Northern_Ireland/Story/0,2763,811537,00.html. [Accessed 01/08/2019]

The Guardian (2018) "Orange Order parades take place amid violence in Northern Ireland." *The Guardian*. 12 July 2018. www.theguardian.com/uk-news/2018/jul/12/northern-ireland-orange-order-parades-12-July-amid-violence-belfast-derry. [Accessed 02/08/2019]

The Independent (2010) "Car bombing heightens fears of escalation in dissident violence." *The Independent*. 5 October 2010. www.independent.co.uk/news/uk/crime/dissident-republicans-blamed-after-car-bomb-blast-2097970.html. [Accessed 01/08/2019]

Thomas, D & Noble, J (2019) "Boris Johnson becomes new UK prime minister – as it happened." *Financial Times*. 24 July 2019. www.ft.com/content/c4e08973-9974-3adf-b57b-cc42f939d029. [Accessed 27/09/2019]

Thompson, P (Director) (1973) A Place Called Ardoyne. Documentary film. United States: Blackstone Edge Studios. *IMDB International Movie Database*.

www.imdb.com/title/tt1617621. Excerpts uploaded by Blackstone Edge on 17 March 2008. *YouTube*. www.youtube.com/watch?v=rhR1w6Iz3_Y. [Accessed 23/03/2019]

Thompson, S (2002) "Parity of Esteem and the Politics of Recognition." *Contemporary Political Theory* 1 (2): 203-220.

Tierney, S (2000) "Introduction." In: Tierney, S (Ed.) *Accommodating National Identity: New Approaches in International and Domestic Law*. The Hague: Kluwer Law International, pp. 1-12.

Todd, J & Ruane, J (2010) *From 'A Shared Future' to 'Cohesion, Sharing and Integration'. An Analysis of Northern Ireland's Policy Framework*. Dublin: Institute for British Irish Studies, UCD, for the Joseph Rowntree Charitable Trust.

Todosijević, B (2001) "Macro-Political Means of Ethnic Conflict Management in Southeast Europe: A Critical Examination." *Southeast European Politics* 2 (2): 77-93.

Tonge, J (2000) "From Sunningdale to the Good Friday Agreement: Creating Devolved Government in Northern Ireland." *Contemporary British History* 14 (3): 39-60.

Tonge, J (2006) *Northern Ireland: Conflict and Change*. Cambridge: Polity Press.

Tonge, J (2014) "A Campaign Without End? 'Dissident' Republican Violence in Northern Ireland." *Political Insight*, April 2014: 14-17.

Topping, J & Byrne, J (2012) "Paramilitary punishments in Belfast: policing beneath the peace." *Behavioral Sciences of Terrorism and Political Aggression* 4 (1): 41-59.

Torfing, J (2007) "Introduction: Democratic Network Governance." In Sørensen, E & Torfing, J (Eds.) *Democratic Network Governance in Europe*. Basingstoke: Palgrave, pp. 1-22.

Townshend, C (2013) *The Republic: The Fight for Irish Independence, 1918–1923*. London: Penguin Books.

Treib, O, Bähr, H, & Falkner, G (2007) "Modes of Governance: Towards a Conceptual Clarification." *Journal of European Public Policy*, 14 (1): 1-20.

Tully, J (2001) "Introduction." In: Gagnon, A-G & Tully, J (Eds.) *Multinational Democracies*. Cambridge: Cambridge University Press, pp. 1-33.

UK DCMS Department for Digital, Culture, Media & Sport (2013) "Designated days for Union Flag flying." 27 February 2013. *UK Government*. www.gov.uk/guidance/ designated-days-for-union-flag-flying. [Accessed 14/07/2019]

UK National Archives (2019) *Northern Ireland Act 1998 c. 47, Part VII, Equality of opportunity, Section 75*. http://www.legislation.gov.uk/ukpga/1998/47/section/75. [Accessed 11/10/2019]

UN United Nations

(1945) *United Nations Charter, Chapter 11: Declaration Regarding Non-Self-Governing Territories*. San Francisco, 26 June, 1945. UN Documents. www.un-documents.net/ch-11.htm. [Accessed 24/04/2019]

(1960) *Declaration on the Granting of Independence to Colonial Countries and Peoples. Adopted by General Assembly resolution 1514 (XV)* of 14 December 1960. Department of Public Information. www.un.org/Depts/dpi/decolonization/declaration.htm. [Accessed 24/04/2019]

(2003a) *Declaration on the Inadmissibility of Intervention and Interference in the Internal Affairs of States*. United Nations, General Assembly. 9 December 1981, A/RES/36/103. UN Documents. www.un.org/documents/ga/res/36/a36r103.htm. [Accessed 24/04/2019]

(2003b) *Prevention of Armed Conflict*. Resolution adopted by the General Assembly. 3 July 2003, A/RES/57/337. UN Documents. www.un-documents.net/a57r337.htm. [Accessed 01/08/2019]

(2017) *Member States. United Nations*. www.un.org/en/member-states/ [Accessed 01/08/2019]

US DOS United States of America, Department of State (2017). "Independent States in the World." *Fact Sheet, Bureau of Intelligence and Research*, Washington, DC, 20 January 2017. www.state.gov/s/inr/rls/4250.htm. [Accessed 22/04/2017]

UUP Ulster Unionist Party (2016) "A Vision for Northern Ireland outside the EU." *UUP*. September 2016. www.uup.org/assets/policies/a vision for ni outside the eu.pdf. [Accessed 01/08/2019]

Verme, P. (2004) *Multidimensional Poverty and Social Cohesion in Kosovo. Background paper for the Kosovo Poverty Assessment: Promoting Opportunity, Security and Participation for All*. World Bank Report No. 32378 XK. Washington, DC: World Bank.

Vincent, F (2009) *Everybody Got a Hug that Morning ... From Desecration to Reconciliation*. July 2009. Belfast: Institute for Conflict Research.

Walker, P & Elgot, J (2019) "Sinn Féin: vote on Irish reunification must follow no-deal Brexit." *The Guardian*. 31 July 2019. www.theguardian.com/uk-news/2019/jul/31/sinn-fein-border-poll-ireland-unity-must-follow-no-deal-brexit. [Accessed 05/08/2019]

Walker, S (2019) "Colum Eastwood: 'Brexit can still be stopped'." *BBC News*. 8 May 2019. www.bbc.com/news/uk-northern-ireland-48206796. [Accessed 06/08/2019]

Wall, M (2001) "The Age of the Penal Laws." In Moody, T W & Martin, F X (Eds.) *The Course of Irish History*. Blackrock: Mercier Press, 217-231.

Warren, C A B & Karner T X (2005) *Discovering Qualitative Methods: Field Research, Interviews, and Analysis*. Los Angeles: Roxbury Publishing.

Watkins, C (1975) "Language and its History." In: Haugen, E & Bloomfield, M (1975) *Language as a Human Problem*. Guildford: Lutterworth Press, pp. 85-97.

Weaver, M & Rawlinson, K (2019) "Lyra McKee: New IRA says its activists killed journalist." *The Guardian*. 23 April 2019. www.theguardian.com/uk-news/2019/apr/22/lyra-mckee-friends-stage-protest-derry-offices-saoradh. [Accessed 01/08/2019]

Weber, M (1991a) "Class, Status, Party." In: Gerth, H H & Mills, C W (Eds.) *From Max Weber: Essays in Sociology*. New Ed. Abingdon: Routledge, pp. 180-191.

Weber, M (1991b) "Politics as a Vocation." In Gerth, H H & Mills, C W (Eds.) *From Max Weber: Essays in Sociology*. New Ed. Abingdon: Routledge, pp. 77-128.

Weber, M (1997) "What is an Ethnic Group?", in Guibernau, M & Rex, J (Eds.) *The Ethnicity Reader: Nationalism, Multiculturalism and Migration*. Cambridge: Polity Press, pp. 17-26.

Wengraf, T (2001) *Qualitative Research Interviewing: Biographic, Narrative and Semi-Structured Methods*. Thousand Oaks, CA: Sage Publications.

Werrell, C E & Femia, F (2018) "Climate change raises conflict concerns." *UNESCO Courier* 2018-2. United Nations Educational, Scientific and Cultural Organization. en.unesco.org/courier/2018-2/climate-change-raises-conflict-concerns. [Accessed 22/07/2019]

White, R W (1993) *Provisional Irish Republicans: An Oral and Interpretive History*. Westport, CT & London: Greenwood Press.

Whyte, J (1983) "How much discrimination was there under the unionist regime, 1921-68?." In Gallagher, T. & O'Connell, J (Eds.) *Contemporary Irish Studies*. Manchester: Manchester University Press, pp. 1-35.

Whyte, J (1990) *Interpreting Northern Ireland*. Foreword by Garret FitzGerald. Oxford: Oxford University Press.

Whyte, J H (2001a) "The Age of Daniel O'Connel." In Moody, T W & Martin, F X (Eds.) *The Course of Irish History*. Blackrock: Mercier Press, pp. 248-262.

Whyte, J H (2001b) "Ireland: 1966-82." In Moody, T W & Martin, F X (Eds.) *The Course of Irish History*. Blackrock: Mercier Press, pp. 299-316.

Whyte, N (1998) "The 1996 Forum Elections and the Peace Process." Last updated 7 May 2003 by Tineke Vaes. *ARK – Access Research Knowledge Northern Ireland*. www.ark. ac.uk/elections/ff96.htm. [Accessed 02/08/2019]

Whyte, N (2002) "Northern Ireland Assembly Elections 1998." Last modified 14 October 2002. *ARK – Access Research Knowledge Northern Ireland*. www.ark.ac.uk/ elections/fa98.htm. [Accessed 02/08/2019]

Whyte, N (2004) "Northern Ireland Assembly Elections 2003." Last modified 6 January 2004. *ARK – Access Research Knowledge Northern Ireland*. www.ark.ac.uk/elections/ fa03.htm. [Accessed 05/04/2017]

Whyte, N (2013) "Election results in Northern Ireland since 1973." Last modified 26 May 2013. *ARK – Access Research Knowledge Northern Ireland*. www.ark.ac.uk/elections/ gallsum.htm. [Accessed 05/04/2017]

Whyte, N (2017) "Northern Ireland Assembly Elections 2017." 2 March 2017. Last updated by Conal Kelly, 25 May 2017. *ARK – Access Research Knowledge Northern Ireland*. www.ark.ac.uk/elections/fa17.htm. [Accessed 02/08/2019]

Wickersham, J M (1994) *Hegemony and Greek Historians*. London: Rowman & Littlefield.

Widgery, J P W B (1972) *Report of the Tribunal Appointed to Inquire Into the Events on Sunday, 30th January 1972, which Led to Loss of Life in Connection with the Procession in Londonderry on that Day*. 18 April 1972. London: Her Majesty's Stationary Office (HMSO). www.cain.ulst.ac.uk/hmso/widgery.htm. [Accessed 01/08/2019]

Wilford, R (2008) "Northern Ireland: St Andrews – the long Good Friday Agreement." In Bradbury, J (Ed.) *Devolution, Regionalism and Regional Development: The UK Experience*. Abingdon: Routledge, pp. 67-93.

Williamson, C (2016) "Jamie Bryson calls for an end to all loyalist flag protests." *Belfast Telegraph*. 22 January 2016. www.belfasttelegraph.co.uk/news/northern-ireland/jamie-bryson-calls-for-end-to-all-loyalist-flag-protests-34387769.html. [Accessed 01/08/2019]

Willis, P & Trondman, M (2000) "Manifesto for Ethnography." *Ethnography* 1 (1): 5-16

Wilson, S (2017) "No special EU status for N.I. says Wilson." *DUP*. 1 February 2017. www.mydup.com/news/article/no-special-eu-status-for-n.i.-says-wilson. [Accessed 06/08/2019]

Wolff, S (2003) "Introduction: From Sunningdale to Belfast, 1973–98." In: Neuheiser, J & Wolff, S (Eds.) *Peace at Last? The Impact of the Good Friday Agreement on Northern Ireland*. New York & Oxford: Berghahn Books, pp. 1-24.

Wolff, S & Rodt, A P (2013) "Self-Determination after Kosovo." *Europe-Asia Studies* 65 (5): 799-822.

Wolff, S & Weller, M (2005) "Self-Determination and Autonomy." In: Wolff, S & Weller, M (Eds.) *Autonomy, Self-Governance and Conflict Resolution: Innovative Approaches to Institutional Design in Divided Societies*. Oxon & New York, NY: Routledge, pp. 1-25.

Wood, I S (2006) *Crimes of Loyalty: A History of the UDA*. Edinburgh: Edinburgh University Press.

World Bank, Poverty Reduction and Economic Management Unit Europe and Central Asia Region (2005) *Kosovo Poverty Assessment: Promoting Opportunity, Security and Participation for All*. World Bank Report No. 32378 XK. Washington, DC: World Bank.

Worth, O (2009) "Beyond World Order and Transnational Classes: the (Re)Application of Gramsci in Global Politics." In McNally, M & Schwarzmantel, J (Eds.) *Gramsci and Global Politics: Hegemony and Resistance*. London & New York, NY: Routledge.

Wright, E O (Ed.) (2005) *Approaches to Class Analysis*. Cambridge, MC: Cambridge University Press.

Young, D (2019) "DUP and SF clash over Johnson's claim Brexit backstop a threat to peace." *Belfast Telegraph*. 21 August 2019. www.belfasttelegraph.co.uk/news/brexit/dup-and-sf-clash-over-johnsons-claim-brexit-backstop-a-threat-to-peace-38421518.html. [Acccsscd 24/08/2019]

Young, I M (1990) *Justice and the Politics of Difference*. Princeton, NJ: Princeton University Press.

Young, I M (2000) *Inclusion and Democracy*. New York, NY: Oxford University Press.

INTERVIEWS

Auld, Jim. Community Restorative Justice Ireland (CRJI), Director. *Personal Interview*. Belfast, 17 July 2009.

Bannon, Maria. Suffolk Lenadon Interface Group (SLIG), Operation Manager. *Personal Interview*. Belfast, 2 July 2009.

Brennan, Seán. Intercomm Belfast, Development Officer. *Personal Interview*. Belfast, 24 June 2009.

Brown, Jean. Suffolk Community Forum, Community Development Worker & Chair Management Committee SLIG. *Personal Interview*. Belfast, 2 July 2009.

Burgess, Norman. Interface Community Worker. *Personal Interview*. Belfast, 8 July 2009.

Cochrane, Sam. North Belfast Community Development and Transition Group (NBCDTG), Community and Interface Worker. *Personal Interview*. Belfast, 22 June 2009.

Deane, Eamonn. Holywell Trust, Director, *Personal Interview*. Derry/Londonderry, 16 June 2009.

Doherty, Michael. Peace & Reconciliation Group (PRG), Director. *Personal Interview*. Derry/Londonderry, 1 July 2009.

Gallagher, Tony. Queen's University Belfast, School of Education, Professor. *Personal Interview*. Belfast, 3 July 2009.

Gardiner, Nigel. Ex Prisoner's Interpretative Centre (EPIC), Project Manager. *Personal Interview*. Derry/Londonderry, 16 July 2009.

George, Michael. Colin Neighbourhood Partnership, Community Safety Development Officer. *Personal Interview*. Belfast, 20 July 2009.

Gibson, Mervin, Westbourne Presbyterian Community Church, Reverend and Minister. *Personal Interview*. Belfast, 29 June 2009.

Hall, Michael. Island Pamphlets, Publisher and Author. *Personal Interview*. Newtownabbey, 21 July 2009.

Haire, Drew. Community Relations Unit, Good Relations and Reconciliation Division, Office of the First Minister and Deputy First Minister (OFMDFM), Head. *Personal Interview*.Belfast, 10 July 2009.

Hutchinson, Billy. Mount Vernon Community Development Forum, Co-ordinator and Community Development Worker and Progressive Unionist Party (PUP) Member. *Personal Interview*. Belfast, 21 July 2009.

Irvine, Winston. North & West Belfast Parades and Cultural Forum, Community Development Interface Worker. *Personal Interview*. Belfast, 23 June 2009.

Jarman, Neil. Institute for Conflict Research (ICR), Director. *Personal Interview* 1. Belfast, 21 July 2009; *Skype Interview* 2. 13 February 2014; *Skype Interview* 3. 28 March 2017; *Personal Interview* 4. Vienna, 8 July 2019.

Loughran, John. Intercomm Belfast, Developing Leadership Initiative Project Manager. *Personal Interview*. Belfast, 24 June 2009.

MacNiallais, Donncha. An Gaeláras, Irish Language Programme Manager. *Personal Interview*. Derry/Londonderry, 1 July 2009.

McCallum, Rab. North Belfast Interface Network (NBIN), Coordinator. *Personal Interview*. Belfast, 11 June 2009.

McCaughan, Verena. Ardoyne Youth Providers Forum, Youth Worker, *Personal Interview*. Belfast, 8 July 2009.

McGlade, Dympna. Community Relations Council (CRC), Programme Director 'Policy and Development'. *Personal Interview*. Belfast, 17 July 2009.

McKendrick, Dennis. SLIG, Advocacy Team Leader Suffolk. *Personal Interview/ Guided Tour*. Belfast, 9 July 2009.

Moore, William. Apprentice Boys of Derry, General Secretary. *Personal Interview*. Derry/Londonderry, 16 July 2009.

Morgan, Lee. Ardoyne resident. *Personal Interview*. Belfast, 16 June 2009.

Morrow, Duncan. Community Relations Council (CRC), Chief Executive Officer. *Personal Interview*. Belfast, 3 July 2009.

Mulgrew, Malachy. NBIN – Cliftonville Regeneration Forum, Community Development Interface Worker. *Personal Interview*. Belfast, 22 June 2009.

Murtagh, Brendan. Queen's University Belfast, School of Environmental Planning, Reader. *Personal Interview*. Belfast, 30 June 2009.

O'Halloran, Chris. Belfast Interface Project (BIP), Director. *Personal Interview*. Belfast, 17 July 2009.

Poole, Derek. LINC Resource Centre, Director. *Personal Interview*. Belfast, 23 June 2009.

Ramsey, George. Northern Ireland Fire & Rescue Service (NIFRS), Watch Commander 'Community Development', *Personal Interview*. Belfast, 25 June 2009.

Redpath, Jackie. Greater Shankill Partnership, Executive Director. *Personal Interview*. Belfast, 17 July 2009.

Scappaticci, Umberto. Colin Neighbourhood Partnership, Youth and Education Community Officer. *Personal Interview*. Belfast, 20 July 2009.

Trotter, Syd. LINC Resource Centre, Community Relations Co-ordinator. *Personal Interview*. Belfast, 26 June 2009.

Valente, Margaret. Star Neighbourhood Centre, Community and Youth Worker. *Personal Interview*. Belfast, 17 June 2009.

Whelehan, Shane. Ardoyne Youth Providers Forum, Director. *Personal Interview*. Belfast, 8 July 2009.

Winstone, Tom. Northern Ireland Alternatives (NIA), Director. *Personal Interview*. Belfast, 8 July 2009.

APPENDIX

CHRONOLOGY OF KEY EVENTS IN NORTHERN IRISH HISTORY

In the compilation of this comprehensive, yet not exhaustive chronology, a number of sources have been consulted for reference purposes. In particular, these include: Bew & Gillespie 1999, Gillespie 2017, Lynn 2019a & 2019b), Melaugh 2019a &,2019b, Sutton 1994 and Whyte 2013. In addition, the chronolgy draws on various news articles from Belfast Telegraph, the Guardian, the Irish Times and BBC News, and on online material from organisations and actors mentioned in the text.

1170 – English invasion of Ireland under Strongbow and his Norman troops.

1175 *(1 May 1170)* Arrival of Richard 'Strongbow' de Clare in Co. Wexford. Strongbow became King of Leinster

(Oct 1171) Arrival of Henry II, King of England, in Ireland

(6 Oct 1175) Treaty of Windsor between Henry II and Ruaidrí Ua Conchobair, High King of Ireland.

1264 *(18 Jun)* First Irish Parliament meeting in Castledermot, Co. Kildare.

1460 *(21 Jul)* Declaration of Independence by the Irish Parliament in Drogheda.

1607 'The Flight of the Earls': Hugh O'Neill, Earl of Tyrone, and Rory, son of Hugh O'Donnell, Earl of Tyrconnell, left Ireland and went into exile.

1641–1642 Irish Rebellion of dispossessed Irish Catholics against British Protestant settlers, which was finally crushed in 1649.

1641–1652 'The Eleven Year Wars': Irish Confederate Wars (1641–1649) and Cromwellian War (1649–1653).

1652 Cromwellian Plantation: Irish land confiscation by the English Crown, under the leadership of Oliver Cromwell.

1689 *(18 Apr–1 Aug)* Siege of Derry: Protestants loyal to King William III of Orange resisted besieging Irish Catholic forces of King James II .

1690 *(1 Jul)* Battle of the Boyne: victory of William III over James II.

1691 *(12 Jul)* Battle of Aughrim: final defeat of James II.

1695 First 'Penal Laws' were passed against Catholics in Ireland (the last 'Penal Laws' were repealed 1829).

1791 Society of the United Irishmen was founded in Belfast.

1795 Orange Order, officially named Loyal Orange Institution, was formed in County Armagh.

1798 United Irishmen Rebellion, led by Theobald Wolfe Tone, suppressed by British Crown forces.

1800   Act of Union was passed by the British and Irish Parliaments.

1801   *(1 Jan)* United Kingdom of Great Britain and Ireland was established, Irish Parliament abolished and Ireland placed under British direct rule.

1823   Catholic Association, campaigning for Catholic emancipation, was founded by Daniel O'Connell.

1829   Violent sectarian unrest in Belfast and in counties Armagh and Tyrone due to the ban of 12th of July Orange Order parades.

1830   Repeal Association, an Irish mass political movement campaigning for Irish home rule, was formed by Daniel O'Connell. It dissolved in 1848.

1845–   Great Famine in Ireland: over 1 million deaths and more than 1 million
1849   emigrations

1849   Battle of Dolly's Brae: armed clashes in Co. Down, between Catholic 'Ribbonmen' and Protestant 'Orangemen'.

1857   10 days of severe sectarian riots in Belfast around 12th of July parades.

1858   Irish Republican Brotherhood (IRB), originally unnamed, was founded in Dublin by James Stephens.

Fenian Brotherhood was established in the US, precursor to Clan na Gael, a sister organisation to the IRB, founded in 1867.

1874   Irish Parliamentary Party (IPP), aiming for Irish legislative independence and land reform, was formed by Isaac Butt. In 1880 Charles Stewart Parnell became elected party leader, dismissed in 1890. IPP dissolved 1922.

1879   Irish National Land League, a political organisation seeking redress for poor Irish tenant farmers, was founded by Charles Stewart Parnell.

1879–   Irish Land War: series of violent clashes between Irish tenants and
1882   landowners,

1885   Gaelic Athletic Association (GAA) founded in Thurles, Co. Tipperary.

1886   *(Jun)* First Irish Home Rule Bill defeated in House of Commons,

(Jun–Sep) '1886 Belfast riots' between Catholics and Protestants.

1893   Second Irish Home Rule Bill was rejected in the House of Lords.

1903   Land Purchase Act (Wyndham Act) providing Irish tenant farmers with more rights, was passed by the British Parliament.

1905   *(3 Mar)* Ulster Unionist Council (UUC), an umbrella for opposition to Irish home rule, formed in Belfast. Edward Carson became UUC leader in 1910.

(28 Nov) Sinn Féin was founded under the leadership of Arthur Griffith.

1912   *(11 Apr)* Third Irish Home Rule Bill ('Government of Ireland Bill'), introduced by British Government led by PM Herbert Henry Asquith.

(28 Sep) Ulster Covenant ('Ulster Solemn League and Covenant') was signed by almost 500,000 people to resist home rule for Ireland.

1913   *(Jan)* Ulster Volunteer Force (UVF) was formed by Northern Irish Unionists.

(Nov) Irish Citizen Army and Irish (National) Volunteers were founded by Irish Nationalists.

1914   *(Apr)* Provisional Unionist Government led by Edward Carson first met in Belfast.

1914 *(28 Jul) – 1918 (11 Nov)* First World War.

1916   *(24–29 Apr)* Easter Rising in Dublin, by Irish Republican forces to establish an independent Irish Republic. The Rising was suppressed by the British Army, 16 rebel leaders were executed, including Patrick Pearse, James Connolly, Tom Clarke and Joseph Plunkett.

(Jul) Battle of the Somme: 36th (Ulster) Division lost 5,500 men.

1918   *(14 Dec)* Sinn Féin, led by Éamon de Valera, won a majority of Irish parliamentary seats in the UK general election.

1919   *(21 Jan)* First *Dáil Éireann* (Irish Parliament) met in Dublin.It recognised the Irish Republican Army (IRA) as its legitimate army.

1919–   *(21 Jan)* Anglo-Irish War (Irish War of Independence):
1921   *(11 Jul)* guerillla war between the IRA and British forces.

1920   *(Jul)* Anti-Catholic 'pogroms', initiated by Edward Carson in Belfast and Derry/Londonderry, driving thousands of Catholics from their work.

(Oct) Ulster Special Constabulary (USC), or 'B-Specials', was established as a semi-military auxiliary police force.

1921   *(3 May)* Government of Ireland Act 1920 became effective, providing for the partition of Ireland into Northern and Southern Ireland.

(24 May) First Northern Ireland general election: 40 seats for Ulster Unionist Party (UUP) and 6 each for Sinn Féin and the Northern Ireland Nationalist Party (NINP).

(7 Jun) First Northern Ireland Parliament opened at Stormont, Belfast by King George V; James Craig became the first Prime Minister.

(6 Dec) Anglo-Irish Treaty ('The Treaty') signed in London between UK Government, led by PM David Lloyd George, and Irish Republic representatives, including Michael Collins and Arthur Griffith.

1922   *(Jan)* Irish Parliament voted o accept the Anglo-Irish Treaty.

(7 Apr) Civil Authorities (Special Powers) Act was introduced in NI.

(1 Jun) Royal Ulster Constabulary (RUC) was founded, replacing the RIC as the police force in Northern Ireland.

1922–   *(28 Jun)* Irish Civil War, between pro-Treaty forces, led
1923   *(24 May)* by Collins and Griffith, and anti-Treaty forces, led by de Valera and Cathal Brugha, resulting in the victory of the pro-Treaty forces.

(12 Aug) Griffith died.

(22 Aug) Collins was killed.

(6 Dec) Irish Free State (*Saorstát Éireann*) came into being.

(7 Dec) Northern Ireland opted out of the Irish Free State.

1924   Northern Ireland Labour Party (NILP) was formed.

1925   The Irish Boundary Commission's report was shelved by the Irish and Northern Irish governments, no changes were made to the Irish border.

1926   *(6 May)* Emergency Powers Act was introduced in Northern Ireland.

1931   *(17 Oct)* IRA was declared an illegal organisation in the Irish Free State.

(11 Dec) Statute of Westminster, passed in the UK Parliament, established the Irish Free State's legislative independence from the UK.

1932   *(16 Feb)* General election in the Irish Free State, with de Valera forming the first Fianna Fáil government in the *Dáil*.

(3–14 Oct) Outdoor Relief Workers Strike in Belfast, organised by Jack Beattie, Harry Midgley, Tommy Geehan and Betty Sinclair (RWG)

Wild Bird Act was passed in Northern Ireland, the only Nationalist initiative ever enacted into law until 1998.

1933   Special Powers Act in Northern Ireland was made permanent.

1937   *(29 Dec)* Irish Constitution (*Bunreacht na hÉireann*) became effective, with a constitutional claim (articles 2 & 3) on Northern Ireland.

1939 (1 Sep) –1945 (2 Sep) Second World War

Irish Free State declared its neutrality as a 'non-belligerent' state.

1939–   IRA bombing and sabotage campaign ('S-Plan') against the UK's civil,
1940   economic and military infrastructure.

1940   IRA hunger strike in Mountjoy prison, Dublin: two of the seven IRA men died after 51 and 54 days.

1941   *(Apr–May)* 'Belfast Blitz': 4 German Air raids on strategic targets in Belfast.

(Aug) (accidental) German bombing of Dublin.

1943   *(1 May)* Basil Brooke became Prime Minister of Northern Ireland, succeeding John Miller Andrews.

1945   *(14 Nov)* Anti-Partition League (APL) was established by NPNI members in Dungannon, Co Tyrone.

1947   *(27 Mar)* Education Act was introduced by the Northern Ireland Parliament, providing for compulsory education for all children up to the age of 15 and for increased funding for the Voluntary (Catholic) schools.

1949   *(18 Apr)* Republic of Ireland ('*Poblacht na hÉireann*') came into being and left the Commonwealth, thus becoming fully independent.

Ireland Act 1949 guaranteed Northern Ireland's position within the UK.

1954   *(6 Apr)* Flags and Emblems (Display) Act introduced in Northern Ireland, used exclusively against flying the Irish 'Tricolour' flag.

1955   *(14 Dec)* Republic of Ireland joined the UN.

1956–   *(11 Dec)* IRA 'Border Campaign'. Internment was introduced in
1962   *(26 Feb)* Northern Ireland and the Republic of Ireland.

1959   *(Jun)* Seán Lemass was elected as *Taoiseach* (Irish Prime Minister), and de Valera became President of Ireland.

1963   *(25 Mar)* Terence O'Neill became Prime Minister of Northern Ireland.

       (Jun) US President John F. Kennedy visited the Republic of Ireland.

1964   *(17 Jan)* Campaign for Social Justice (CSJ) was inaugurated in Dungannon by Patricia and Conn McCluskey.

       (28 Sep) 'Tricolour Riots' in West Belfast, triggered by the RUC's forceful seizure of the 'Tricolour' from Republican Party offices.

1965   *(14 Jan)* Lemass met O'Neill in Belfast, which was the first official meeting of an Irish and Northern Irish PM since the partition of Ireland. In February, O'Neill paid a reciprocal visit to Dublin.

1966   *(24 Apr)* Severe rioting in Belfast, due to Loyalist counter-protests against Catholic/Nationalist/Republican Easter Rising commemorations.

       (May) Modern version of the UVF emerged under Gusty Spence, which subsequently carried out several bomb attacks and shootings of Catholics.

       (28 Jun) The Government of Northern Ireland declared the UVF illegal.

       (10 Nov) Jack Lynch became Irish *Taoiseach*.

1967   *(9 Apr)* Northern Ireland Civil Rights Association (NICRA) was officially established in Belfast. Betty Sinclair became the first chairperson.

       (Nov) Derry Housing Action Committee (DHAC) was formed.

1968   *(24 Aug)* First civil rights march in Northern Ireland, held by NICRA, CSJ and others, from Coalisland to Dungannon against anti-Catholic housing discrimination. The march proceeded without incident.

       (5 Oct) Second civil rights march by DHAC and NICRA in Derry/ Londonderry was stopped by the RUC, leading to two days of serious rioting between Catholic residents and the RUC.

       (9 Oct) People's Democracy (PD) was formed by QUB students, including Bernadette Devlin, Eamon McCann and Michael Farrell.

       (9 Oct) Derry Citizen's Action Committee (DCAC) was formed.

       (15 Oct) NPNI withdrew as 'official' parliamentary opposition.

       (30 Oct) Irish *Taoiseach* Lynch met with British PM Harold Wilson in London, calling to end partition to resolve unrest in NI.

       (4 Nov) Talks between O'Neill and Wilson in London: Wilson stated there would be no change in Northern Ireland's constitutional status without popular consent.

       (22 Nov) O'Neill announced a reforms package that granted political and economic concessions to Catholics.

(30 Nov) RUC stopped a NICRA march in Armagh, because of Loyalist counter-protest led by Ian Paisley and Ronald Bunting (both imprisoned in March 1969 for unlawful assembly and released after 2 months under an amnesty).

1969 *(1–4 Jan)* A four-day march held by PD members from Belfast to Derry/Londonderry was attacked by Loyalists, leading to serious riots.

(15 Jan) Cameroon Inquiry into the riots in Derry/Londonderry and elsewhere was set up; its report was published on 12 September.

(Jan 1969) 'Free Derry' emerged as the first Catholic/Nationalist/Republican 'no-go' area' in Northern Ireland.

(Mar–Apr) Loyalists planted a series of bombs as part of a campaign to destabilise O'Neill and stop the reforms.

(17 Apr) Bernadette Devlin was elected on a Unity ticket (a pact of Nationalists, Republicans and Socialists) to British Parliament, aged 21.

(28 Apr) O'Neill resigned as PM of Northern Ireland, due to lack of party support, and was succeeded by James Chichester-Clark.

(12 Jul) Serious rioting in Derry/Londonderry, Belfast and Dungiven surrounding 12th of July Orange Order parades. Beginning of forced population movements in Belfast (lasting until 1973)

(5 Aug) First Loyalist bomb in the Republic of Ireland planted by the UVF, damaging the RTÉ headquarters in Donnybrook.

(12–14 Aug) Battle of the Bogside: serious rioting in Derry/London-derry, which spread across Northern Ireland.

(13 Aug) Lynch announced on TV to set up 'field hospitals' in border areas and stated that "the Irish government can no longer stand by and see innocent people injured and perhaps worse." (RTÉ [1969] 2019)

(14 Aug) British Army troops were deployed in Derry/Londonderry at Northern Irish Government request and British Government permission.

(14 Aug) John Gallagher, a Catholic civilian, was shot dead by the B-Specials' during riots in Armagh, making him the first 'official' victim of 'the Troubles' (according to RUC records).

(14–15 Aug) Vicious sectarian riots in Belfast, in which 7 people were killed, including a young Catholic boy who was shot by the RUC.

(15 Aug) British troops arrived in West Belfast.

(19 Aug) British and Northern Irish governments issued a Communiqué and Declaration, affirming Northern Ireland's status within the UK.

(9 Sep) Chichester-Clark announced the building of 'peace lines' by the British Army between Catholic and Protestant areas in Belfast; first 'peace wall' between Falls and Shankill was completed on 10 September.

(10 Oct) Hunt report was published, recommending the disarmament of the RUC and disbandment of the USC/B-Specials.

(11 Oct) First RUC officer killed, by Loyalists in Shankill riots.

1970   *(11 Jan)* Provisional IRA split from the (Official) IRA.

(26 Mar) Police Act (Northern Ireland) 1970 became effective, providing for the RUC's disarmament and the establishment of a police reserve force and the Police Authority of Northern Ireland (PANI).

(1 Apr) Ulster Defence Regiment (UDR) replaced the USC.

(16 Apr) Paisley won a seat in Northern Irish Parliament in a by-election.

(21 Apr) Alliance Party of Northern Ireland (APNI) was formed.

(26 Apr) Devlin was arrested and sentenced to 6 months in jail for riotous behaviour during Battle of the Bogside (released after 4 months).

(28 Jun) Around 500 Catholic shipyard workers in Belfast were driven out of their workplace by Protestant employers.

(2 Jul) Criminal Justice (Temporary Provisions) Act NI came into force, providing for 6 months compulsory imprisonment for rioting.

(3–4 Jul) Falls Road Curfew: British Army raided houses for IRA members and arms and imposed a 36 hours military curfew in the area; 4 people were killed by the Army during gun battles with the IRA

(2 Aug) British Army started using rubber bullets for riot control.

(21 Aug) Social Democratic and Labour Party (SDLP) was founded, with Gerry Fitt being the first leader and John Hume the deputy leader.

(12 Nov) Northern Ireland Housing Executive (NIHE) was set up.

(16 Nov) IRA killed two men for being involved in anti-social behaviour, which was their first punishment killing.

1971   *(6 Feb)* First British soldier killed in the 'Troubles', shot by the IRA.

(16 Mar) Chichester-Clark resigned as Northern Ireland's PM on in protest to 'insufficient' British security measures in Northern Ireland. He was succeeded by Brian Faulkner.

(8 Jul) 2 Catholic civilians killed by a British soldier. No official inquiry was announced, leading to the SDLP's withdrawal from NI Parliament.

(9 Aug) Internment was reintroduced by the British Government, upon Northern Ireland Government request. It lasted until 5 December 1975, with 1,874 Catholic/Republican and 107 Protestants/Loyalist detainees.

(10 Aug) Worst violence since August 1969 led to forced evictions of some 7,000 people throughout Northern Ireland, most of them Catholics.

(15 Aug) SDLP launched civil disobedience campaign in protest against internment; followed by major workers strike in Derry/Londonderry and withdrawal of many non-Unionist district councillors.

(Sep) Ulster Defence Association (UDA) was formed. The name Ulster Freedom Fighters (UFF) was often used as a cover name.

(27–28 Sep) Tripartite talks in Englang between the PMs of Northern Ireland, Britain and the Republic of Ireland.

(30 Sep) Democratic Unionist Party (DUP) founded by Paisley.

(16 Nov) Compton report rejected claims of systematic brutality and torture by the security forces against those interned without trial. The Irish Republic announced to take the allegations to the ECtHR.

1972   *(18 Jan)* PM Faulkner banned all parades and marches until end of year.

(22 Jan) An anti-internment march at Magilligan Strand, Co. Derry was attacked by the British Army.

(30 Jan) 'Bloody Sunday': 13 civilians were shot dead and 13 more injured by British Army paratroopers during a NICRA anti-internment march in Derry/Londonderry. The soldiers claimed that they responded to a sustained gunfire attack, yet this is seriously disputed.

(1 Feb) Widgery Tribunal was set up to inquire into the events of Bloody Sunday. Its report, published on 18 April, confirmed the British Army's official position.

(2 Feb) British Embassy in Dublin was burnt down by protesters.

(9 Feb) William Craig founded 'Ulster Vanguard' as a right-wing Unionist umbrella movement.

(22 Feb) Official IRA planted a bomb at the Parachute Regiment headquarters in Aldershot, killing 7 people.

(20 Mar) IRA car bomb in inner West Belfast killed 6 people.

(24 Mar) Northern Ireland Parliament was suspended and British Direct Rule imposed.

(26 Mar) William Whitelaw was appointed as first Secretary of State for Northern Ireland, and Northern Ireland Office (NIO) was established.

(29 May) Official IRA ceasefire, ending their armed campaign.

(20 Jun) Secret meeting between IRA and British officials close to the Derry/Donegal border, upon initiative by Hume and Devlin (SDLP).

(26 Jun–9 Jul) Truce between the IRA and British Army.

(7 Jul) Secret talks between British Govvernment and IRA delegation with Gerry Adams and Martin McGuinness in London.

(21 Jul) 'Bloody Friday': 22 IRA bombs killed 9 and injured 130 people in Belfast.

(31 Jul) 'Operation Motorman': 12,000 British Army troops were deployed to dismantle 'no-go' areas. A Catholic teenager and an IRA member were shot during the operation in Derry.

(31 Jul) 'Claudy Bombings': IRA car bombs in Claudy, Co. Derry, killed 5 Catholic and 4 Protestant civilians.

(22 Aug) 'Newry Customs Office Bomb' planted by the IRA in Newry, Co. Down killed 6 civilians and 3 IRA members.

(31 Oct) UFF car bomb killed two Catholic children.

(1 Dec) Two car bombs in Dublin city centre killed 2 and injured 127 people. No one claimed responsibility for the attack.

(31 Dec) McGuinness was arrested in the Irish Republic (and released from prison after 6 months).

1973   *(1 Jan)* The UK and the Irish Republic joined the EU (then EEC).

(7 Feb) Unionist Loyalist Council (ULC) led by Craig organised a general strike, aimed at regaining Protestant control over security and other NI affairs. The strike was accompanied by heavy violence.

(1 Mar) Liam Cosgrave succeeded Lynch as Irish *Taoiseach*, leading a Fine Gael/Labour coalition government.

(8 Mar) Border Poll: a referendum on the maintenance of the union with Great Britain was held in NI, which was boycotted by Nationalists. With 57% turnout, 98% of those who took part were in favour of the UK.

(8 Mar) Two IRA car bombs in London injured over 200 people.

(20 Mar) A government White Paper on 'Northern Ireland Constitutional Proposals' was published, suggesting a devolved power-sharing assembly in Northern Ireland and a Council of Ireland.

(12 Jun) IRA car bomb in Coleraine killed 6 Protestant civilians.

(26 Jun) Paddy Wilson, SDLP MP, and his secretary killed by the UFF.

(28 Jun) Northern Ireland Assembly Election: The parties supporting the White Paper gained 52 seats, those against it 26 seats.

(31 Jul) First meeting of the new Northern Ireland Assembly.

(21 Nov) Agreement on a power-sharing Northern Ireland Executive was reached, consisting of 11 members (6 UUP, 4 SDLP, 1 APNI).

(5 Dec) Craig, Paisley and others formed the United Ulster Unionist Council (UUUC) to bring down the Executive.

(9 Dec) Sunningdale Agreement was reached between the PM of the UK, Irish *Taoiseach* and Northern Ireland Executive.

(10 Dec) Ulster Army Council (UAC) was set up as an umbrella group by the UDA and UVF to resist the proposed Council of Ireland.

1974   Community Development Centre (CDC) was formed as an independent NGO It was to serve as the main support agency for the local community sector.

(1 Jan) New Northern Ireland Executive, headed by Faulkner, officially took office. Security and certain economic powers remained with the British Government.

(4 Jan) UUC voted by a majority against the Council of Ireland. Consequently, Faulkner resigned as UUP leader.

(4 Feb) 'M62 Coach Bomb' by the IRA, planted on a coach bus carrying British soldiers and their families, killing 12 people.

(17 Feb) British Army killed 3 UDA members in East Belfast riots.

(28 Feb) UK general election: A UUUC coalition of anti-Sunningdale Unionists gained 11 of the 12 Northern Ireland seats.

(2 May) UVF bomb on Ormeau Road, Belfast, killed 6 and injured 18 Catholic civilians.

(14–28 May) Ulster Workers Council (UWC) Strike aimed to bring down the Sunningdale Agreement. The strike gained increasing workers' support, causing disruptions in electricity, transport, water, food supply etc.

(17 May) Dublin and Monaghan Bombings: 4 Loyalist car bombs killed 33 and injured over 250 civilians, the largest death toll in a single day of the Troubles. No one was ever arrested or convicted of the crime.

(28 May) Northern Ireland Executive collapsed, when Faulkner and his Unionist colleagues resigned. The Assembly was suspended and British direct rule imposed.

(3 Jun) IRA prisoner Michael Gaughan died in Parkhurst Prison, England, after 64 days of hunger strike.

(5 Oct) Guildford Bombs: IRA bombs in two pubs in Guildford, England killed 5 and injured 54 people. The 'Guildford Four', 4 young Irish people, were wrongly convicted to life imprisonment in October 1975; they were released on appeal after 15 years. Likewise, the 'Maguire Seven', 7 members of the Maguire family were wrongly sentenced to long imprisonment on 3 March 1976; they were released on appeal after 15 years.

(21 Nov) Birmingham Pub Bombs: bombs in two Birmingham pubs, attributed to the IRA, killed 21 and injured 182 civilians. The 'Birmingham Six', all Irish men, were wrongly found guilty and sentenced to life imprisonment in August 1975; they were freed on appeal after 16 years.

(5 Dec) Prevention of Terrorism (Temporary Provision) Bill was introduced by the British Government and extended to Northern Ireland.

(8 Dec) Irish National Liberation Army (INLA) was founded.

1975   *(10 Feb–23 Jan 1976)* IRA truce, broken several times.

(12 Apr) Loyalist paramilitaries killed 6 Catholic civilians in East Belfast.

(1 May) Elections for the Northern Ireland Constitutional Convention (NICC): attempt to find an agreed political settlement to the conflict (based on an NIO White Paper of July 1974). NICC collapsed on 4 March 1976.

(17 Jul) IRA bomb in Co. Armagh killed 4 British soldiers.

(31 Jul) 'Miami Showband Massacre' by the UVF killed 3 band members and 2 UVF members.

(13 Aug) IRA attack in a Shankill bar killed 5 and injured 40 people.

(1 Sep) Gun attack by Republican paramilitaries on an Orange Hall in Co. Armagh killed 5 and injured 7 Protestant civilians.

(2 Oct) UVF attacks across Northern Ireland killed 12 people. Subsequently, UVF was declared an illegal ('proscribed') organisation.

(19 Dec) Red Hand Commando (RHC) killed 5 Catholic civilians.

1976   *(5 Jan)* Kingsmills Killings: Republican Action Force (RAF) killed 10 Protestant civilians in an attack on their bus in Co. Armargh.

(12 Feb) IRA prisoner Frank Stagg died in Wakefield Prison, England, after 61 days of hunger strike.

(1 Mar) Special category status for paramilitary prisoners ended.

(25 Mar) 'Police Primacy' ('Ulsterisation'): Northern Ireland Secretary of State Merlyn Rees announced that the RUC were to take over the leading role in security from the British Army.

(2 Jul) Loyalist paramilitary attack on a pub in Co. Antrim killed 6 civilians (5 Protestants and 1 Catholic).

(21 Jul) Christopher Ewart-Biggs, British Ambassador to Ireland, was killed in his car by an IRA landmine attack.

(10 Aug) 3 Catholic children were accidentally killed in West Belfast, when an IRA member was shot dead in a car by the British Army. Consequently, the 'Peace People', formed by Mairead Corrigan Maguire, Betty Williams and Ciaran McKeown, organised peace rallies throughout Northern Ireland, in the Irish Republic and in England.

(14 Sep) Blanket protest of IRA and INLA prisoners began in the Maze. The protest lasted until October 1981.

(1 Dec) Fair Employment (Northern Ireland) Act became effective.

1977   *(11 Mar)* 26 UVF members were sentenced in a Belfast court to a total of 700 years imprisonment.

(3–13 May) United Unionist Action Council (UUAC) Strike, led by Paisley; 3 people killed, 41 RUC officers injured, many people charged.

(5 Jul) Lynch became again Taoiseach, succeeding Cosgrave.

(27 Jul) Feud between Provisional and Official IRA, 4 people killed.

(5 Oct) Seamus Costello, Irish Republican Socialist Party (IRSP) and INLA leader, was shot dead in Dublin. No one claimed responsibility.

(10 Oct) Williams and Corrigan Maguire, co-founders of the Peace People, were awarded the 1976 Nobel Peace Prize.

1978   *(17 Feb)* La Mon Restaurant Bombing: IRA planted a bomb in a hotel near Belfast, killing 12 and injuring 23 Protestant civilians.

(25 Feb) Gerry Adams was charged with IRA membership and released in September due to insufficient evidence, as a court decided.

(1 Jun) David Cook (APNI) first non-Unionist Lord Mayor of Belfast.

(21 Jun) Undercover British Army members killed 3 IRA members and a Protestant civilian passing by.

(27 Aug) Civil rights march from Coalisland to Dungannon, in commemoration of the first march 10 years ago, attended by 10,000 people.

1979   *(20 Feb)* The 'Shankill butchers', a group of 11 Loyalists, were convicted to 12 life sentences for 112 offences, including 19 murders.

(3 May) UK general election: Conservative Party won and Margaret Thatcher became British Prime Minister.

(7 Jun) First European Parliament elections: Paisley, Hume and John Taylor (UUP) were elected.

(27 Aug) Louis Mountbatten, a cousin of the Queen, and three other people were killed by an IRA bomb near Sligo in the Irish Republic.

(27 Aug) Warrenpoint Attack: 18 British soldiers were killed in an IRA bomb attack in Warrenpoint, Co. Down.

(7 Sep) James Molyneaux became UUP leader.

(29 Sep) Pope John Paul II visited the Irish Republic and called for peace in Northern Ireland. The IRA rejected his call.

(28 Nov) John Hume became SDLP leader, succeeding Gerry Fitt.

(7 Dec) Charles Haughey succeeded Lynch as Irish *Taoiseach*.

(16 Dec) IRA killed 5 British soldiers and a former UDR member.

1980   *(7 Jan–24 Mar)* Atkins talks: called by NI Secretary of State Humphrey Atkins to discuss potential political settlements, with DUP, SDLP and APNI; UUP did not participate; no consensus was achieved.

(27 Oct–18 Dec) Hunger strike by 7 Republican prisoners in protest of the ending of political prisoner status. Thatcher stated that there would be no government concessions to the hunger strikers.

(8 Dec) Thatcher met Haughey in Dublin, together with senior officials – the first visit by a British PM since partition in 1921.

1981   *(16 Jan)* Bernadette McAliskey (formerly Devlin) and her husband were shot and seriously wounded in their home. UDA was suspected to have perpetrated the gun attack.

(1 Mar–3 Oct) Irish Hunger Strike in the Maze, started and led by Bobby Sands, then IRA leader. In total 23 Republican prisoners went on hunger strike, 10 died, including Sands (on 5 May).

(5 Apr) Northern Ireland Census boycott in many Republican areas

(9 Apr) Sands was elected as a member of the British Parliament.

(5 May) Sands died after 66 days on hunger strike. Around 100,000 people attended his funeral in West Belfast on 7 May.

(2 Jun) Ulster Democratic Party (UDP) was formed by UDA members.

(30 Jun) Garret FitzGerald replaced Haughey as Irish *Taoiseach*.

(1 Sep) Lagan College opened as NI's first integrated secondary school.

(6 Oct) Improvements in prison policy were announced.

(31 Oct) 'Armalite and the ballot box' speech by Danny Morrison at Sinn Féin's *Ard Fheis* (annual party conference) in Dublin.

(14 Nov) Robert Bradford, a Methodist reverend and Unionist MP, was fatally shot by the IRA in West Belfast.

1982   *(20 Jul)* Hyde Park and Regent's Park Bombs: two IRA bombs killed 11 British soldiers, causing a public outrage in Britain.

(23 Jul) Northern Ireland Act 1982 provided for the establishment of an Assembly, as proposed earlier in a government White Paper.

(20 Oct) Northern Ireland Assembly elections: UUP 26, DUP 21, SDLP 14, APNI 10 and Sinn Féin 5 seats, SDLP and SF refused to take their seats.

(Nov–Dec) 3 IRA and 2 INLA members, all unarmed, were killed by undercover RUC units, which gave rise to Republican claims of a 'shoot to kill' policy by security forces.

(6 Dec) Droppin Well Bomb: INLA bomb in a bar in Co. Derry killed 11 British soldiers and 6 civilians.

1983   *(5 Jan)* INLA was declared illegal in the Irish Republic.

(11 Mar) New Ireland Forum was set up by the Irish Government to discuss political alternatives for a peaceful 'new Ireland'. The participants were Fianna Fáil, Fine Gael, Labour and SDLP, the Unionist parties refused. Its report (May 1984) suggested 3 options: a united Ireland, British-Irish joint authority and a (con)federation.

(11 Apr) First 'supergrass' trial in Belfast: 14 UVF members were imprisoned for in total 200 years.

(9 Jun) Gerry Adams (Sinn Féin) was elected to the British Parliament.

(13 Jul) IRA land mine killed 4 UDR soldiers in Co. Tyrone.

(5 Aug) 'Supergrass' trial in Belfast: 22 IRA members were jailed for a total of more than 4,000 years.

(25 Sep) Mass escape of 38 IRA members from Maze prison.

(13 Nov) Adams was elected President of Sinn Féin.

1984   *(24 Jan)* Londonderry District Council changed its name by NIO permission to Derry District Council.

(14 Mar) Adams was shot and wounded by the UFF in Belfast.

(12 Oct) Brighton Bombing: IRA bomb attack on the Grand Hotel in Brighton, attempted to assassinate Thatcher. 5 people were killed.

(19 Nov) Anglo-Irish summit meeting between Thatcher and FitzGerald:Thatcher rejected the New Ireland Forum's proposals.

1985   *(28 Feb)* IRA mortar attack killed 9 and injured 30 RUC officers.

(15 Nov) Anglo-Irish Agreement (AAI) between British and Irish Governments.

(16 Nov) NIAssembly voted for calling a referendum on the AAI.

(23 Nov) Unionist anti-AAI rally with over 100,000 people at Belfast City Hall.

(17 Dec) All Unionist MPs resigned in protest against the AAI.

1986   *(3 Mar)* Unionist 'Day of Action': widespread general strike in NI in support of Unionist demands for suspending the AAI; Loyalist riots.

(24 Mar) Thatcher rejected demands for the suspension of the AAI.

(23 Jun) NI Assembly was officially dissolved.

(18 Sep) International Fund for Ireland (IFI) was set up by the British and Irish governments to support economic development in Northern Ireland and the Irish border region.

1987   Central Community Relations Unit (CCRU) was set up to advise the NI Secretary of State on all aspects of community relations.

(12 Feb) A DUP-UUP petition with 400,000 signatures against the AAI was handed into the Queen's residence at Buckingham Palace.

(8 May) Loughgall Killings: British soldiers of the Special Air Service (SAS) killed 8 IRA members and one civilian.

(15 Sep) NIO issued fair employment guidelines.

(8 Nov) Enniskillen Bombing: IRA bomb during the Remembrance Day ceremony in Enniskillen killed 11 and injured 63 people.

1988   (11 Jan–30 Aug) Hume-Adams talks

(6 Mar) Gibraltar Killings: undercover SAS soldiers killed 3 underarmed IRA members in Gibraltar.

(16 Mar) Milltown Cemetery Killings: 3 people were killed and 50 injured by UDA gunman Michael Stone during the funeral of the 3 IRA members shot dead in Gibraltar.

(25 May) British Government issued a White Paper on fair employment.

(15 Jun) IRA bomb in Lisburn killed 6 British Army soldiers.

(20 Aug) IRA bomb in Ballygawley killed 8 British Army soldiers.

(19 Oct) British Government.introduced broadcasting restrictions on organisations proscribed in Northern Ireland (ban was lifted 1994).

1989   *(12 Feb)* Patrick Finucane, a Catholic solicitor from Belfast who had represented several Republicans, was killed by the UDA. There were claims of collution between the security forces and Loyalist paramilitaries. After three police inquires, it was concluded in 2003 that there had been collusion in the killing of Finucane.

(22 Sep) IRA bomb in England killed 10 musicians of the Royal Marines staff band.

1990   *(Jan)* Community Relations Council was formed to promote community relations between Catholics and Protestants and recognition of cultural diversity.

(17 May) Stevens Report found evidence for collusion between the security forces and Loyalist paramilitaries, albeit limited to a few cases only.

(20 Jul) IRA bomb at London Stock Exchange caused massive damage.

(30 Sep) British Army paratroopers fatally shot two Catholic teenagers, who were 'joy riding' in a stolen car.

(24 Oct) 'Proxy Bomb' attacks by the IRA at British Army checkpoints killed 6 soldiers and a civilian.

(9 Nov) NI Secretary of State Peter Brooke stated in a major speech in London that Britain had no 'selfish or strategic interest' in Northern Ireland and would accept a united Ireland by popular consent.

(9 Nov) Mary Robinson was elected as Irish President.

(22 Nov) Thatcher resigned as PM and Conservative Party leader and was succeeded by John Major.

1991   *(29 Apri–4 Jul)* Combined Loyalist Military Command (CLMC) ceasefire.

(16 Jun–3 Jul) 'Brooke/Mayhew' talks began: First round of talks between UUP, DUP, SDLP and APNI on Northern Ireland's future, chaired by Brooke.

(2 Nov) IRA bomb at the military wing of Musgrave hospital in Belfast killed two British soldiers.

(9 Nov) Loyalist bomb killed two Catholics in their home in Co. Antrim.

(24 Nov) A bomb planted by Republican prisoners inside Crumlin Road Prison in Belfast killed 2 Loyalist prisoners.

(19 Dec) Initiative '92 was launched. Subsequently, the 'Opsahl Commission', chaired by Prof. Torke Opsahl, collected the the views on the Troubles of some 3,000 Northern Irish citizens (published in the Opsahl report 1993) and made proposals for the political party talks.

1992   *(17 Jan)* Teebane Bombing: IRA bomb killed 8 Protestant civilians in a minibus in Co. Tyrone.

(6 Feb) Albert Reynolds was elected as *Irish Taoiseach*.

(16 Feb) British undercover soldiers killed 4 IRA members in near Coalisland, Co. Tyrone.

(10 Apr) Baltic Exchange Bombing: IRA bomb in central London killed 3 people.

(11 Apr) Patrick Mayhew replaced Brooke as NI Secretary of State.

(10 Aug) The UDA was proscribed by Mayhew.

(10 Nov) Unionist parties withdrew from the political talks, now chaired by Mayhew, thus bringing the talks temporarily to an end.

1993   *(20 Mar)* 2 IRA bombs killed 2 young boys in Warrington, England.

(25 Mar) UFF shot dead 4 Catholics in Castlerock, Co. Derry.

(24 Apr) IRA bomb killed 1 and injured 30 people at Bishopsgate, London.

(23 Oct) Shankill Road Bombing by the IRA killed 9 Protestant civilians and one IRA member and injured 57 people.

(30 Oct) UFF killed 6 Catholics and a Protestant in Greysteel, Co. Derry.

(28 Nov) Secret talks between British Government and Republicans.

(15 Dec) Downing Street Declaration ('Joint Declaration on Peace') by British PM Major and Irish Taoiseach Reynolds.

1994   *(Mar)* 3 mortar attacks by the IRA on Heathrow Airport, London.

(24 Apr) IRA fatally shot 2 Protestant civilians in Co. Derry.

(17–18 May) UVF attacks in Tigers Bay, Belfast and Armagh killed 4 Catholic civilians.

(16 Jun) INLA shot dead 3 UVF members in Shankill, Belfast.

(18 Jun) UVF killed 6 and injured 5 Catholic civilians in a bar in Loughinisland, Co. Down.

(31 Aug) IRA announced a complete cessation of military operations.

(13 Oct) CLMC announced a Loyalist ceasefire.

(15 Dec) John Bruton replaced Reynolds as Irish *Taoiseach*.

1995   Belfast Interface Project (BIP) was founded in 1995 to promote community relations and development in Belfast's interface areas.

(3 Jan) Senator George Mitchell was appointed by US President Bill Clinton as US Special Envoy for Northern Ireland.

(22 Feb) British Prime Minister Major and Irish *Taoiseach* Bruton launched the Framwork Documents for agreement and for accountable government in Northern Ireland.

(9–11 Jul) Drumcree parade stand-off between Oranger Order and Gravaghy Road Residents in Portadown, Co. Armagh.

(18 Jul) Secret meeting between the British Government and Sinn Féin.

(8 Sep) David Trimble was elected as UUP leader.

(28 Nov) Joint Communiqué by the British and Irish governments, outlining a twin-track peace process (decommissing and all-party negotiations taking place in parallel).

(30 Nov–1 Dec) Clinton visited Northern Ireland for the first time.

1996   *(24 Jan)* Report of the International Body on Arms Decommissioning (Mitchell Report).

(Mar) Suffolk Lenadoon Interface Group (SLIG was formed by Catholic and Protestant community activists in West Belfast.

(30 May) Elections to Northern Ireland Forum and all-party negotiations.

(10 Jun) Multi-party peace talks in Stormont began, chaired by Mitchell.

(7–11 Jul) Drumcree parade stand-off with widespread sectarian riots across Northern Ireland.

(13 Jul) Car bomb by the Continuity IRA (CIRA) injured 17 people in Enniskillen, Co. Fermanagh.

(7 Oct) 2 IRA bombs in the British Army Headquarters in Lisburn, Co. Antrim, killed one soldier and injured a further 30 people.

1997   Suffolk Lenadoon Interface Group (SLIG) was formed by members of Suffolk Community Forum (SCF) and Lenadoon Community Forum (LCF).

(12 Feb) IRA killed a British soldier at Army checkpoint in Co. Armagh.

(27 Apr) Loyalists fatally injured a Catholic civilian in Portadown.

(2 May) Tony Blair replaced Major as British Prime Minister.

(3 May) Marjorie "Mo" Mowlam was appointed as NI Secretary of State.

(2 Jun) Alban Maginness (SDLP) was elected as the first Nationalist Lord Mayor of Belfast.

(16 Jun) IRA killed 2 RUC officers in Lurgan, Co. Armagh.

(26 Jun) Bertie Ahern was elected as Irish *Taoiseach*.

(27 Jun) Parades Commission for Northern Ireland (PCNI) was formed.

(6–9 Jul) Drumcree parade stand-off, with widespread sectarian riots across Northern Ireland.

(20 Jul) IRA renewed ceasefire.

(26 Aug) Agreement between the British and Irish governments on setting up of the International Commission on Decommissioning (IICD).

(29 Aug) Mowlam announced that Sinn Féin were allowed to enter the multi-party peace talks. Subsequently, SF signed a pledge to abide by the Mitchell principles on decommissioning.

(7 Oct) Multi-party talks on substantive issues began.

(11 Dec) Meeting between Blair and Adams and SF delegates in London.

(27 Dec) INLA members killed Billy Wright, Loyalist Volunteer Force (LVF) leader, in Maze prison.

1998   *(18 Jan)* LVF fatally shot a Catholic man in Maghera, Co. Derry.

(19 Jan) INLA killed Jim Guiney, UDA commander, in West Belfast.

(19–23 Jan) Loyalist paramilitaries killed 4 Catholic civilians in Belfast.

(23 Jan) UFF renewed ceasefire.

(26 Jan) Multi-party talks moved to Lancaster House, London.

(16 Feb) Multi-party talks switched venue to Dublin castle.

(20 Feb) Sinn Féin was expelled from the multi-party talks, due to suspected IRA involvement in killings. SF re-entered the talks on 23 March.

(3 Mar) Loyalist paramilitaries killed a Catholic and a Protestant civilian in a bar in Poyntzpass, Co. Armagh.

(17 Mar) First St. Patrick's Day parade in Belfast passed without incident.

(25 Mar) Final round of Stormont talks: Mitchell set a two weeks deadline for the parties to reach an agreement.

(10 Apr) Peace 'Agreement Reached in the Multi-Party Negotiations' (Belfast/Good Friday Agreement), signed by the British and Irish governments and the Northern Irish political parties (UUP, PUP, UDP SDLP, SF, APNI, NIWC and Labour), except DUP and UKUPwho opposed the Agreement.

(21 Apr) LVF shot dead a Catholic civilian in Portadown.

(8 May) Real IRA (RIRA) renounced ceasefire.

(15 May) LVF announced ceasefire.

(22 May) Referendum on the Agreement in Northern Ireland (71.1% Yes) and in the Republic of Ireland (94.4% Yes).

(25 Jun) Northern Ireland Assembly elections: UUP 28, SDLP 24, DUP 20, SF 18, APNI 6, UKUP 5, PUP 2, NIWC 2.

(1 Jul) First Meeting of 'Shadow' Northern Ireland Assembly (as powers were not yet devolved): David Trimble (UUP) was elected 'First Minister Designate' and Seamus Mallon (SDLP) 'Deputy First Minister Designate'.

(5-17 Jul) Drumcree parade stand-off, causing widespread sectarian violence across Northern Ireland.

(12 Jul) Loyalist petrol bomb killed 3 Catholic boys in Co. Antrim.

(15 Aug) Omagh Bomb by RIRA killed 29 and injured hundreds of people.

(22 Aug) INLA declared ceasefire.

(3 Sep) British Parliament passed new anti-terrorism legislation.

(7 Sep) RIRA announced ceasefire.

(10 Sep) First meeting between Adams and Trimble (first meeting between Sinn Féin and a Unionist leader since partition in 1921).

(11 Sep) First paramilitary prisoner released under the Agreement's terms.

(31 Oct) Deadline for formation of the Northern Ireland Executive (NIE) and North-South bodies was missed, mainly due to disagreements of Unionists and Nationalists on decommissioning.

(19 Nov) Northern Ireland Act 1998 providing for the implementation of the Agreement became effective.

(10 Dec) Hume and Trimble were awared the Nobel Peace Prize 1998.

(18 Dec) Agreement on government department and North-South bodies.

1999   *(8 Mar)* British and Irish governments signed 4 international treaties providing the legal framework for North-South and East-West institutions.

(1 Mar) Northern Ireland Human Rights Commission (NIHRC) was established under the terms of the Agreement and the Northern Ireland Act 1998.

(15 Mar) Car bomb by Red Hand Defenders (RHD) killed Rosemary Nelson, a human rights solicitor, in Lurgan, Co. Armagh.

(29 Mar–1 Apr) Multi-party talks on decommissioning at Hillsborough Castle. Hillsborough Declaration set out framework for forming the NIE.

(5 Jun) Loyalist pipe-bomb attack killed a woman in Portadown.

(4–10 Jul) Drumcree stand-off, with sectarian riots across NI.

(30 Jul) IRA fatally shot a young Catholic man in West Belfast.

(6 Sep–18 Nov) Mitchell Review of the Agreement.

(9 Sep) Patten Report of the Independent Commission on Policing in Northern Ireland.

(1 Oct) Equality Commission for Northern Ireland (ECNI) became operational under the terms of the Agreement and Northern Ireland Act 1998.

(11 Oct) Peter Mandelson replaced Mowlam as NI Secretary of State.

(29 Nov) Northern Ireland Executive (NIE) was appointed.

(2 Dec) Powers were devolved to the Northern Ireland Assembly (NIA), thus ending 25 years of British direct rule.

(13 Dec) First meeting of North-South Ministerial Council (NSMC) in Armagh.

(17 Dec) First meeting of British-Irish Council (BIC) in London.

2000 *(11 Feb)* NI Assembly and Executive were suspended and direct rule reinstalled, as there was no progress on IRA decommissioning.

(30 May) British Government restored devolution to NIA and NIE.

(26 Jun) IRA arms inspections began.

(2–3 Jul) Drumcree violence due to the ban of the Orange Order parade.

(28 Jul) Last of in total 428 paramilitary prisoners were released.

(21 Aug–15 Dec) Loyalist paramilitary feud between UDA and UVF, resulting in 7 deaths and many injuries.

2001 *(Jan-Feb)* Over 40 Loyalist pipe-bomb attacks on Catholic civilians caused several injuries and evacuations of homes.

(24 Jan) John Reid replaced Mandelson as NI Secretary of State.

(Mar-May) 3 bomb explosions in London; Real IRA was suspected to be responsible for the attacks.

(31 Mar) Loyalists mortally injured a Protestant man in Co. Antrim.

(19 Jun–11 Jan 2002) Holy Cross dispute: sustained Loyalist attacks on Catholic children and parents and blockades of Catholic Holy Cross Girls' Primary School in the Ardoyne, North Belfast.

(1 Jul) Trimble resigned as First Minister and called on Blair for suspension of the Northern Ireland Assembly, which was rejected.

(4 Jul) UDA fatally shot a young Catholic man in Co. Antrim.

(8 Jul) Drumcree Orange Order parade passed without incidence.

(11-12 Jul) Serious violence in Belfast around the 12th of July parades.

(29 Jul) UDA killed a young Protestant man in Co. Antrim.

(1 Aug) Implementation plan for the Agreement was published by the British and Irish governments.

(14 Aug) IRA renounced their decommissioning proposals submitted to IICD.

(17 Aug) Policing implementation plan (revised Patten report) published.

(Aug-Sep) Series of paramilitary punishment attacks caused serious injuries to more than 10 civilians.

(28 Sep) RHD fatally shot a Catholic journalist at his home in Lurgan.

(28 Sep) Sectarian attack on a school bus carrying pupils from Hazelwood Integrated College in North Belfast injured 7 children.

(9 Oct) Northern Ireland Civic Forum was set up as a consultative body under the terms of the Agreement. It was dissolved on 14 October 2002 with the suspension of devolution.

(18 Oct) UUP and DUP ministers resigned from the NI Executive.

(21–23 Oct) Sectarian riots in several interface areas of North Belfast.

(23 Oct) IRA resumed decommissioning after being asked by Adams.

(4 Nov) New Police Service of Northern Ireland (PSNI) replaced RUC.

(6 Nov) Trimble and Mark Durkan (SDLP) were elected by the Assembly as First and Deputy First Minister.

(11 Nov) Durkan succeeded Hume as SDLP leader.

(28 Nov) Ulster Political Research Group (UPRG) was set up as a political advisory body of the UDA, and the UDP dissolved.

2002   North Belfast Interface Network (NBIN) was set up by community groups in North Belfast as resource to deal with interface community relations and issues.

(12 Jan) UDA killed a Catholic postman in Rathcoole, Newtownabbey.

(18 Jan) Anti-sectarian rallies across Northern Ireland in protest against Loyalist paramilitary death threats and calling for an end of all paramilitary activities were attended by over 25,000 people.

(22 Feb) Series of Loyalist pipe-bomb attacks in Co. Derry.

(23 Mar) Sectarian riots in North Belfast, injuring several police officers and civilians.

(8 Apr) IRA decommissioned a second batch of weapons.

(5–6 May) Severe riots in North Belfast, sparked by the Scottish soccer cup final Glasgow Rangers vs. Celtic Glasgow (3:2). 31 police officers and 10 civilians were injured.

(31 May–7 Jun) Heavy sectarian violence and paramilitary gun battles in Short Strand, East Belfast.

(2 Jun) 3 people injured by IRA and UVF gunmen in East Belfast clashes.

(3 Jun) Sectarian riots along the Irish border, injuring 5 people.

(7 Jul) Drumcree: sectarian violence during Orange Order Parade.

(17 Jul) IRA issued first apology to the families of the civilians killed during their armed campaign in the Troubles.

(21 Jul) RHC killed a young Catholic man during riots in North Belfast.

(25 Sep) UDA expelled their West Belfast leader Johnny Adair because of his links with the LVF.

(4 Oct) Police raid of Sinn Féin offices at Stormont in investigation into Republican intelligence gathering ('Stormontgate affair').

(14 Oct) Suspension of devolution in NI and reinstatement of direct rule.

(24 Oct) Paul Murphy succeeded Reid as NI Secretary of State.

2003   *(1 Feb)* 2 UDA members were killed in an internal feud with Adair supporters.

(22 Feb) UDA declared a 12-month ceasefire.

(1 May) British and Irish governments issued a blueprint setting out the final issues of the Agreement, including decommissioning.

(13 Jul) Drumcree parade passed off peacefully.

(18 Jul) Orange Order made a formal proposal to Garvaghy residents aimed at ending the Drumcree dispute. They suggested holding a final annual parade along Garvaghy Road, after which all future marches were subject to the residents' approval.

(17 Aug) RIRA fatally shot a Catholic civilian in West Belfast.

(21 Oct) IRA decommissioned a third batch of arms.

(8 Nov) UVF killed a Protestant civilian in Ballyclare, Co. Antrim.

(26 Nov) Northern Ireland Assembly elections: DUP (30 seats) and Sinn Féin (24 seats) became the largest Unionist and Nationalist parties.

(18 Dec) 3 UUP Assembly members resigned from the party.

2004   *(7 Jan)* British and Irish governments established the Independent Monitoring Commission (IMC) to report on paramilitary activities, security measures and claims of violations of the Agreement's code of conduct by Assembly members.

(3 Feb) Review of the Agreement.

(24 Mar) UVF shot dead a Protestant civilian in Newtownards, Co. Down.

(16-18 Sep) Multi-party talks at Leeds Castle ended without result.

(17 Nov) British and Irish governments presented a set of proposals to the DUP and Sinn Féin, which failed to break the political deadlock.

(21 Dec) Northern Bank robbery in central Belfast. £26.5 million were stolen. PSNI stated on 7 January that the IRA carried out the robbery.

2005   *(18 Jan)* IRA rejected any involvement in the Northern Bank robbery.

(30 Jan) IRA (allegedly) killed a Catholic civilian in central Belfast.

(10 Feb) IMC report stated that senior Sinn Féin members authorised the Northern Bank robbery.

(12 Mar) Orange Order formally severed its links with the UUP.

(21 Mar) 'A Shared Future – Policy and Strategic Framework for Good Relations in Northern Ireland' was published by the NIO.

(5 May) UK general election: DUP 9 seats, SF 5, SDLP 3 and UUP 1.

(7 May) Peter Hain replaced Murphy as NI Secretary of State.

(24 Jun) Reg Empey succeeded Trimble as UUP leader.

(11 Jul) UVF fatally shot a young Catholic man in North Belfast.

(12–13 Jul) Severe riots in Ardoyne around 12th of July parades, injuring 80 PSNI officers and 7 civilians.

(28 Jul) IRA announced the end of their armed campaign.

(10–12 Sep) Serious rioting in the Springfield Road area of West Belfast and in Co. Antrim due to the re-routing of the Whiterock Orange Order parade.

(26 Sep) IICD stated it believed the IRA had decommissioned all arms.

(Oct) People Before Profit (PBP) was formed as a socialist polical party active in the Irish Republic and Northern Ireland.

2006   *(25 Feb)* Republican protest against a proposed Unionist rally in Dublin led to the arrest of 40 people.

(4 Apr) Denis Donaldson, who was exposed as having spied on Republicans for the government ('Stormontgate'), was found fatally shot in Co. Donegal. RIRA later claimed responsibility for his killing.

(11 May) NIWC announced their disbandment.

(15 May) Parties met at Stormont but failed to reach Agreement on forming a new Northern Ireland Executive.

(11–13 Oct) St Andrews Agreement between the British and Irish governments and NI political parties on the terms for devolution.

2007   *(8 Jan)* PUP leader David Ervine died of a stroke.

(28 Jan) Sinn Féin voted to support the PSNI.

(7 Mar) Northern Ireland Assembly Election: DUP 36, SF 28, UUP 18, SDLP 16, APNI 7 seats.

(26 Mar) Paisley and Adams met for direct talks for the first time.

(8 May) Power was devolved to the Assembly and Executive and Ian Paisley (DUP) and Martin McGuinness (Sinn Féin) were elected First Minister and Deputy First Minister.

(27 Jun) Gordon Brown became British PM, succeeding Blair.

(1 Aug) Violent clashes between PSNI officers and Loyalists in Bangor, Co. Down, following police searches.

(3 Aug) Sectarian riots in North Belfast with police being attacked.

(7 Aug) PSNI found large amount of homemade explosives of dissident Republicans.

2008   *(1 May)* Commission for Victims and Survivors in Northern Ireland (CVSNI) was established.

(7 May) Brian Cowen succeeded Ahern as Irish *Taoiseach*.

(5 Jun) Paisley resigned as NI First Minister and DUP leader and was succeeded by Peter Robinson.

(16 Aug) CIRA grenade attack injured 3 PSNI officers in Co. Fermanagh.

2009   *(7 Mar)* Massereene Barracks killing: RIRA shot dead 2 off-duty British soldiers in Antrim town.

(9 Mar) CIRA fatally shot a PSNI officer in Craigavon, Co. Armagh.

(27 Jun) UVF and RHC declared they had decommissioned their arms.

(1 Dec) Bill on Devolution and Policing was passed in the NI Assembly.

2010   *(6 Jan)* UDA announced it had decommissioned its weapons.

(5 Feb) DUP and SF agreement over policing and justice devolution.

(8 Feb) Official IRA and INLA declaration of final decommissioning.

(9 Feb) IICD finished its work.

(24 Feb) RIRA shot dead a Catholic civilian in Derry/Londonderry.

(12 Apr) Devolution of policing and justice powers to the NI Assembly. APNI leader David Ford was appointed as Minister of Justice.

(11 May) David Cameron succeeded Brown as British Prime Minister.

(27 Jun) Robinson and McGuinness issued the 'Programme for Cohesion, Sharing and Integration' (CSI), setting out the government's intended community relations strategy (subject to consultation).

(11–15 Jul) Severe sectarian riots in Belfast, Derry/Londonderry and Co. Armagh, injuring 83 PSNI officers and many civilians.

2011   *(25 Jan)* Adams (SF) was elected as a member of the Irish Parliament.

(9 Mar) Enda Kenny was elected as Irish *Taoiseach*.

(2 Apr) Car bomb by dissident Republicans killed a PSNI officer outside his home in Omagh, Co. Tyrone,

(5 May) Northern Ireland Assembly Elections confirmed the DUP and Sinn Féin as the largest parties.

(20–23 Jun) Sectarian riots in Short Strand, East Belfast.

(9–15 Jul) Riots in Loyalist areas across NI, sparked by the PSNI removal of Loyalist flags ouside a Catholic church in Ballyclare, Co. Antrim.

2012   *(12 Jul)* Sectarian riots in North Belfast around the 12th of July Parades, injuring up to 20 PSNI officers.

(26 Jul) RIRA announced it was linking with other dissident Republican groups and they intended to come together under the banner of a 'new IRA'.

(Aug–Sep) Series of riots in North Belfast; some 60 PSNI officers injured.

(1 Nov) RIRA shot dead a prison officer near Craigavon, Co. Armagh.

(3 Dec) Belfast City Hall flag protests against the city council's decision to limit the days of flying the UK flag from the city hall.

2013   Flag protests and rioting continued throughout 2013.

(30 Mar) CIRA fatally shot a Catholic civilian in West Belfast.

(23 May) Robinson and MacGuinness published the government's new intended community relations strategy, called 'Together: Building a United Community' (T:BUC). In it DUP and SF announced the commitment to remove all 'peace walls' until 2023.

(12–17 Jul) Widespread riots in Belfast and across Northern Ireland after the PSNI prevented an Orange Order parade from passing an interface area to Ardoyne. Around 70 police officers were injured.

(Jul) In response to the ban of the parade, Loyalists set up a protest camp at Twaddell Avenue close to Ardoyne interface. Protest ended in September 2016, after an agreement between local Orange Order and Catholic residents group.

(9 Aug) Sectarian riots during a dissident Republican march through Belfast city centre.

(17 Sep–31 Dec) 'Haass talks': interparty talks on flags, parades and dealing with the past, chaired by US-diplomat Richard Haass, ended without agreement.

2014   *(Jan)* DUP and UUP rejected the Haass proposals, Sinn Féin backed them.

(12 Sep) Ian Paisley died after a prolonged severe illness.

(23 Dec) Stormont House Agreement: British and Irish governments and main Northern Irish parties agreed on issues related to dealing with the past, fiscal policies, welfare reform, devolution reform and the Irish language.

2015   *(12–15 Jul)* Sectarian riots in North Belfast and other areas of the city.

(12 Aug) An ex-IRA member was shot dead in Short Strand, Belfast. PSNI held the IRA responsible; the IRA denied involvement in the killing. This caused a serious government crisis between DUP and Sinn Féin.

(10 Sep) Robinson resigned as NI First Minister and called on the British Government to suspend devolution. PM Cameron rejected and Arlene Foster replaced Robinson as First Minister.

(20 Oct) Robinson reassumed office.

(17 Nov) 'A Fresh Start: the Stormont Agreement and Implementation Plan' was published, which was the result of a 10-weeks talks series between UK and Irish governments and NI Executive. It included the UK government's pledge of additional £500 million financial support for 'peace walls' removal.

(17 Dec) Foster was elected as UUP leader.

2016   *(17 Jan)* Foster was elected as NI First Minister.

(4 Mar) RIRA carbomb fatally wounded a prison officer in East Belfast.

(5 May) Northern Ireland Assembly elections: DUP 38, SF 29, UUP 16, SDLP 14, APNI 8, Green 2, PBP 2, TUV 1.

(23 Jun) Brexit referendum: 51.9% in the UK voted in favour of leaving the EU. 55.8% in Northern Ireland voted to remain in the EU.

(15 Jul) Theresa May succeeded Cameron as British Prime Minister.

(11 Aug) An 8ft/2.5m-high brick 'peace wall' in an interface area close to Holy Cross Church, Ardoyne, was removed after having been in place for 30 years.

2017   *(9 Jan)* Power-sharing Executive collapsed, due to a political row between Sinn Féin and DUP over suspected mismanagement of public funds, the Irish language and same-sex marriages. McGuinness resigned as Deputy First Minister, forcing Foster to also step down as First Minister.

(2 Mar) Northern Ireland Assembly Elections: DUP and Sinn Féin confirmed as the largest parties, yet DUP (28) only 1 seat ahead of SF (27). For the first time Unionist parties lost their parliamentary majority in Northern Ireland.

(21 Mar) Martin McGuinness died of ill health.

(29 Mar) UK government invoked Article 50 of Treaty on European Union, triggering a two-year process of for the UK's EU withdrawal. Subsequently, Brexit talks between the UK Government and the EU began.

(Apr-Nov) Talks between DUP and SF on the restoration of a power-sharing government failed to reach agreement, despite 6 deadline extensions by NI Secretary of State James Brokenshire.

(8 Jun) UK general elections: PM May's Conservative party lost its parliamentary majority.

(26 Jun) 'Confidence and Supply Agreement' between Conservative Party and DUP: DUP supports May's minority government in exchange for financial aid for Northern Ireland and assurance of Conservatives' commitment to the union and the Belfast/Good Friday Agreement.

(14 Nov) EU and British Government published a draft Withdrawal Agreement, including an Irish backstop to ensure open Irish border after Brexit. This was met with fierce opposition from the DUP and Loyalists.

2018   *(8 Jan)* Karen Bradley replaced Brokenshire as NI Secretary of State.

(10 Feb) Gerry Adams resigned and Mary Lou McDonald was elected as new Sinn Féin president and Michelle O'Neill as new vice-president. McDonald pledged to secure and win a referendum on a united Ireland ('border poll').

(2 Apr) Riots during an illegal dissident Republican Easter Rising commemoration parade in Creggan area of Derry/Londonderry. PSNI was attacked with petrol bombs and missiles and 5 men were arrested.

(14 Jun) Leo Varadkar succeeded Kenny as Irish *Taoiseach*.

(11-12 Jul) Sectarian violence around 12th of July parades in Belfast and Derry/Londonderry; vecicles set on fire and petrol bomb attacks on police.

(20 Sep) A 10ft/3m-high 'peace wall' in Springfield Road/Avenue interface area was removed after its construction 30 years ago.

2019   *(11 Apr)* EU and British Prime Minister May agreed to extend the Brexit deadline to 31 October 2019 so to avoid a no-deal UK withdrawal.

(19 Apr) Lyra McKee, an investigative journalist, was shot dead by dissident Republicans of the 'New IRA' during riots in Derry/Londonderry.

(7 May) Talks between main Northern Irish parties to restore power-sharing began in Stormont, on initiative of the British and Irish governments. Talks collapsed without a deal in early July.

(24 Jul) Theresa May resigned as British Prime Minister, after several unsuccessful attempts to win a majority in Parliament for her Brexit proposals. She was succeeded by Boris Johnson, who favours a no-deal Brexit.

(31 Jul) Meeting between Johnson and main Northern Irish parties in Belfast failed to break the impasse on power-sharing.

(Aug) Opposition group against Johnson's hard Brexit policy formed in British Parliament.

(28 Aug) Johnson asked Queen Elizabeth II to suspend the Parliament between 12 September and 14 October. The Queen approved.

(9 Sep) PSNI found a bomb after police searches in the Creggan area of Derry/Londonderry and was attacked with petrol bombs and stones. PSNI held 'New IRA' responsible for attempting to murder police officers.

(10 Sep) British Parliament was prorogued, causing fierce protest among the opposition and public demonstrations across the UK.

(24 Sep) UK Supreme Court ruled upon appeal that Johnson's suspension of British Parliament was unlawful and void. Parliament reconvened next day.

(1 Oct) Irish customs cars arrived at Dundalk, Co. Louth, close to the Irish border, causing concerns among border communities about the setup of border checks in the event of a hard Brexit (cf. Moore 2019).

(11 Oct) Johnson and Varadkar reached a general agreement on a 'pared down' free trade agreement which would effectively create an Irish Sea border and preserve the open Irish land border. DUP announced its opposition.

(13 Oct) EC President Jean-Claude Juncker announced the EU's readiness to negotiate and if necessary to grant a Brexit extension on the UK's request.

(13 Oct) Loyalist paramilitary organisations declared they would resort to civil disobedience if Northern Ireland's status within the UK is diluted post-Brexit.

(17 Oct) At the European Council summit EU leaders endorsed Johnson's Brexit proposal, which would keep Northern Ireland in the UK's custom union but also aligned with some EU customs regulations – initially for 4 years with an extension conditional on majority approval by the NI Assembly.

(19 Oct) In an extraordinary sitting the British Parliament withheld approval for Johnson's proposal until the Withdrawal Act Implementation Bill is passed.

(19 Oct) In fulfilment of his legal obligation, Johnson requested an extension from the EU, but also confirmed his commitment to Brexit on 31 October.

MAPS OF NORTHERN IRELAND

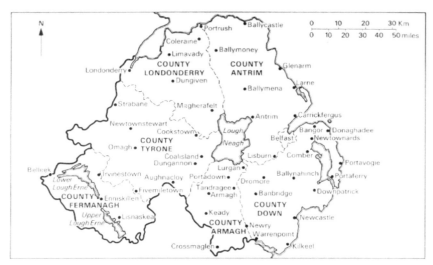

Figure 8. Northern Ireland – The Six Counties, Outline Map (Arthur 1994: 16)

Figure 9. Ireland - The 32 Counties,
Outline Map (Arthur 1994: viii)

Distribution of Catholic population in Northern Ireland, by Electoral Wards
(as defined by Community Background (Table KS07b), Census 2001)

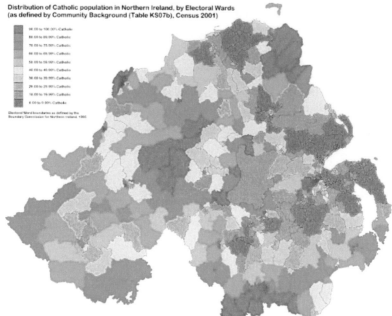

Figure 10. Distribution of Catholics and Protestants in Northern Ireland, 2001
(Melaugh 2016d)

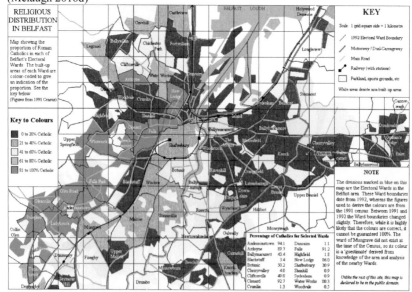

Figure 11. Distribution of Catholics and Protestants in Belfast, 1991 (Melaugh 2016b)

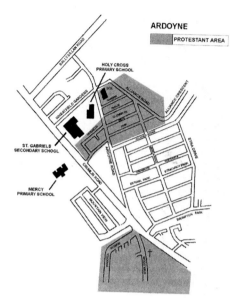

Figure 12. Holy Cross School Dispute,
Outline Map (Heatley 2004)

The yellow line along the red roads is the proposed route of the
Portadown Loyal Orange Lodge 1 Drumcree Parade on July 5. The green
area is the predominantly Catholic area. The black bar marks where the
parade is banned. The small 'S' shows where the front line of the 1996
standoff between Orangemen and the police was.
Unlike the rest of this site, this map is declared to be in the public domain.

Figure 13. Drumcree Parade and the
Garvaghy Road, Portadown, 1996,
Outline Map (Johnston 2001)

PHOTO GALLERY: LIFE AROUND THE INTERFACE

The following photos were all taken by the author. Dates are indicated in parentheses.

MURALS

Plate 12. Republican Murals in North and West Belfast (10/06 – 16/07/2009)

Plate 13. Loyalist Murals in West and East Belfast (10/06 – 16/07/2009)

Plate 14. Republican Murals in the Bogside, Derry/Londonderry (01/07 & 16/07/2009)

Plate 15. Loyalist Murals in the Waterside, Derry/Londonderry (01/07 & 16/07/2009)

Plate 16. Anti-Sectarian Murals in Belfast and Derry/Londonderry (10/06 – 16/07/2009)

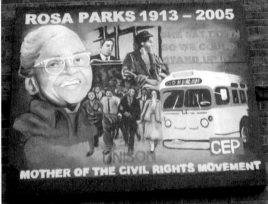

PARADES AND BONFIRES

Plate 17.Tour of the North, Orange Order Parade, North Belfast (27/06 /2009)

Plate 18. Whiterock Orange Order Parade, the Shankill (27/06 /2009)

Plate 19. 12th of July, Orange Order Parade and its Aftermath, Belfast City Centre (12/07/2009)

Plate 20. Bonfire Preparations, East Belfast (11/07/2009)

Plate 21. Bonfire Preparations, Suffolk (09/07/2009)

Plate 22.Beacon (Safer Bonfire), the Shankill (09/07/2009)

MEMORIAL GARDENS

Plate 23. Loyalist Memorial Gardens (27/06 & 11/07/2009)

Plate 24. Republican Memorial Gardens (02/07 & 09/07/2009)

PLACES AND SITES

Plate 25. Ardoyne Area, view from Glenbryne (left, 1st row), Holy Cross church and Ardoyne (right, 1st row) fenced house in Ardoyne (left, 2nd row), Ardoyne Youth Club (right, 2nd row) (10/06 – 16/07/2009)

Plate 26. The New Lodge (17/06/2009)

Plate 27.The Shankill (22/06 &15/07/2009)

Plate 28. Mount Vernon (13/06/2009)

Plate 29. Cluan Place (11/07/2009)

Plate 30. Suffolk (09/07/2009)

Plate 31. Lenadoon (09/07/2009)

Plate 32. Drumcree and Garvaghy Road Area, road to Drumcree church (left, 1st row), Orange Order base at Drumcree church (right, 1st row) Garvaghy Road residential area (left, 2nd row), Garvaghy interface, view from Loyalist Portadown area (right, 2nd row) (14/07/2009)

Plate 33. Beacon of Hope and Titanic Quarter, Belfast City Centre (11/06/2009)

Plate 34.Stormont, Parliament Building (10/07/2009)

Plate 35.David Ervine Memorial, East Belfast (11/07/2009)

'PEACE WALLS'

Plate 36. New Lodge/Duncairn Gardens Interface (10/06/2009)

Plate 37. Interfaces in North, West and East Belfast (10/06 – 16/07/2009)

INDEX OF PERSONS

This index presents a list of personal names that appear in the book. All persons mentioned in the text, footnotes and chronology are included, with the exception of the authors and interview respondents cited.

Bruno Schoch; Andreas Heinemann-Grüder; Corinna Hauswedell; Jochen Hippler; Margret Johannsen (Eds.)
Peace Report 2017
A Selection of Texts. Peace Research Institute Frankfurt, Member of Leibniz Association – Bonn International Center for Conversion – Protestant Institute for Interdisciplinary Research (Heidelberg) – Institute for Development and Peace (Duisburg) – Institute for Peace Research and Security Policy at the University of Hamburg
Bd. 29, 2017, 108 S., 29,90 €, br., ISBN 978-3-643-90932-9
Reihe: Internationale Politik / International Politics

Margret Johannsen; Bruno Schoch; Max M. Mutschler; Corinna Hauswedell; Jochen Hippler (Eds.)
Peace Report 2016
A Selection of Texts. Institute for Peace Research and Security Policy at the University of Hamburg – Peace Research Institute Frankfurt – Bonn International Center for Conversion – Protestant Institute for Interdisciplinary Research (Heidelberg) – Institute for Development and Peace (Duisburg)
Bd. 26, 2016, 112 S., 12,90 €, br., ISBN 978-3-643-90794-3
Reihe: Internationale Politik / International Politics

Blanka Bellak; Jaba Devdariani; Benedikt Harzl; Lara Spieker (Eds.)
Governance during Conflict
Selected Cases in Europe and beyond
Bd. 70, 2017, 272 S., 9,80 €, br., ISBN 978-3-643-90905-3
Reihe: Dialog

Bert Preiss; Claudia Brunner (Eds.)
Democracy in Crisis
The Dynamics of Civil Protest and Civil Resistance
The *Peace Report 2012* – an annual edited volume in the Austrian Study Center for Peace and Conflict Resolution (ASPR) publication series *"Dialog: Beiträge zur Friedensforschung (Dialogue: Contributions to Peace Research)"* at LIT Verlag – addresses urgent issues surrounding the current crisis of democracy and the potential consequences and possibilities for civic protest and civic resistance. This 26th edition has two novelties: For the first time it is published in English and edited by the ASPR in cooperation with the partner institutions of the recently formed Conflict Peace and Democracy Cluster (CPDC) – the Centre for Peace Research and Peace Education at the Alps-Adriatic University of Klagenfurt/Celovec, the Institute of Conflict Research Vienna and the Democracy Centre Vienna.
Bd. 64, 2013, 456 S., 29,80 €, br., ISBN 978-3-643-90359-4
Reihe: Dialog

Österreichisches Studienzentrum für Frieden und Konfliktlösung (Hg.)
Die State-of-Peace-Konferenz
Ein Rückblick auf 25 Jahre österreichische Friedens- und Konfliktforschung. Friedensbericht 2011. Projektleitung: Bert Preiss, Ronald H. Tuschl
25 Jahre österreichische Friedens- und Konfliktforschung, 25 Jahre friedenspolitisches Engagement und gesammeltes Erfahrungspotential, das über all diese Jahre nicht weniger als 360 engagierte Beiträge von 200 Autorinnen und Autoren hervorbrachte – das ist Grund genug für einen Rückblick auf eine wissenschaftlich erfolg- und ertragreiche Zeit, eine Zeit des politischen Umbruchs, eine Zeit der friedenspolitischen Wende, eine Zeit internationaler Konflikte und zugleich vermehrter Erprobung neuer Formen der Friedensstiftung.
Dieser in Kooperation mit der European Peace University entstandene Band stellt eine Anthologie ausgewählter Beiträge der am Friedenszentrum Burg Schlaining in den vergangenen 25 Jahren stattfindenden State-of-Peace-Konferenzen dar.
Bd. 62, 2012, 464 S., 9,80 €, br., ISBN 978-3-643-50363-3
Reihe: Dialog

LIT Verlag Berlin – Münster – Wien – Zürich – London
Auslieferung Deutschland / Österreich / Schweiz: siehe Impressumsseite